D1201934

Components of
MACMILLAN
ENGLISH
THINKING
AND WRITING
PROCESSES

Pupil's Edition

Teacher's Edition with Teacher's Manual

Teacher's Resource Book, which includes the following:

  Teacher's Professional Resources

  Overhead Transparencies

  Study and Composition Blackline Masters

  Practice Blackline Masters (also available in consumable format)

  Practice Teacher's Edition

  Test Blackline Masters (also available in consumable format)

  Test Teacher's Edition

PWR: Macmillan English Composition Software

Macmillan English Test Generator

Authors and Advisors

ELIZABETH ACKLEY
English Teacher
Indian Hill High School
Cincinnati, Ohio

PAULA A. CALABRESE
Assistant Principal
Ingomar Middle School
North Allegheny School District
Pittsburgh, Pennsylvania

SANDRA A. CAVENDER
English Teacher
Nathan Hale High School
West Allis, Wisconsin

SYLVIA COLLINS-KIMBELL
Supervisor of Language Arts
Hillsborough County Schools
Tampa, Florida

SONYA POHLMAN
English Teacher
Rangeview High School
Aurora, Colorado

JUDI PURVIS
Secondary Language Arts Appraiser
Carrollton–Farmers Branch School District
Texas

ROBERT RANTA
English Department Head
Lacey Township High School
Lanoka Harbor, New Jersey

MARJORY CARTER WILLIS
English Teacher
Midlothian High School
Midlothian, Virginia

FOR "THINKING ABOUT THINKING"

SHARON FLITTERMAN-KING
Faculty Associate
Bard Institute for Writing and Thinking
Annandale-on-Hudson, New York

DAVID C. KING
Educational Writer
Director, Curriculum Design
for Tomorrow's World, Inc.

The Publisher would also like to thank the following educators for their contribution to the TEACHER'S PROFESSIONAL RESOURCES, *which accompanies* MACMILLAN ENGLISH:

EMILY BUTLER
Vanguard High School
Marion County, Florida

KAROL CAMP
Dixie Hollins High School
St. Petersburg, Florida

DELANIE B. FANT
Robert E. Lee Senior High School
Jacksonville, Florida

BRIAN ROWLAND
Western High School
Broward County, Florida

BARBARA S. WILSON
Lake Gibson Senior High School
Lakeland, Florida

Special Consultants

FRANKLIN E. HOROWITZ
Adjunct Assistant Professor of Education
Teacher's College, Columbia University
New York, New York

ROY PETER CLARK
Associate Director
The Poynter Institute for Media Studies
St. Petersburg, Florida

Contributing Writers

Harrison B. Bell, Robert A. Bell, Sally R. Bell, Larry and Susan Berliner, Sheila C. Crowell, Richard Foerster, Eleanor Franklin, Carol Goldman, Joan C. Gregory, Florence W. Harris, Paula R. Hartz, Barbara Klinger, Ellen D. Kolba, Christopher T. McMillan, William Maxey III, Cynthia Miller, Carroll Moulton, Eileen Hillary Oshinsky, Milton Polsky, John David Richardson, Derrick Tseng, Gail Schiller Tuchman, Sidney Zimmerman

MACMILLAN ENGLISH

THINKING AND WRITING PROCESSES

 **Glencoe McGraw-Hill**

New York, New York   Columbus, Ohio   Woodland Hills, California   Peoria, Illinois

Copyright © 1988 by Scribner Laidlaw.
All rights reserved. Except as permitted under the United States Copyright Act, no part of this publication may be reproduced or distributed in any form or by any means, or stored in a database or retrieval system, without prior written permission of the publisher.

Send all inquiries to:

Glencoe/McGraw-Hill
8787 Orion Place
Columbus, OH 43240

Pupil's Edition ISBN 0-02-242540-3
Teacher's Edition ISBN 0-02-242580-2

8 9 10 11 12   026   04 03

Acknowledgments

Grateful acknowledgment is given authors, publishers, and agents for permission to reprint the following copyrighted material. In the case of any omissions, the Publisher will be pleased to make suitable acknowledgments in future editions.

AMHERST COLLEGE
"A Friendly Letter" from *Letter of Emily Dickinson.* Copyright 1951, published by World Publishing Co. Reprinted by permission of the Trustees of Amherst College.

MADELEINE BLAIS
Interview © 1987 by Madeleine Blais. All rights reserved.

BRANDT AND BRANDT LITERARY AGENTS
Excerpts from "Sharing" by Leslie Norris. Copyright © 1977 by Brandt & Brandt Literary Agents and used with their permission.

CARCANET PRESS LIMITED
"Winter Trees" by William Carlos Williams from *Collected Poems,* 1938. Reprinted by permission of Carcanet Press Limited.

CARCANET PRESS, NEW YORK
Excert from "Barbarian in the Garden" by Zbigniew Herbert. Copyright 1962, 1985. Reprinted by permission of the publisher.

E. P. DUTTON
Excerpt from *Shakespeare of London* by Marchette Chute. Copyright 1949 by E. P. Dutton, renewed 1977 by Marchette Chute.
Excerpt from *The Journals of Denton Welch* by Denton Welch, edited by Michael De-la-Noy. Text copyright 1952, 1973, 1984 by University of Texas.
Both reprinted by permission of the publisher, E. P. Dutton, a division of NAL Penguin Inc.

EDUCATIONAL TESTING SERVICE
Sample questions are from *1979 PSAT/NMSQT Student Bulletin* and *Taking the SAT: A Guide to the Scholastic Aptitude Test* and the *Test of Standard Written English.* Reprinted by permission of the College Board and of Educational Testing Service, copyright owner of the sample questions.

HARPER & ROW, PUBLISHERS, INC.
"A Letter Home" is from pages 202–203 from *Letters of E. B. White* collected and edited by Dorothy Lobrano Guth. Copyright © 1976 by E. B. White.
"Through the Tunnel" from *The Habit of Loving* by Doris Lessing (Thomas Y. Crowell). Copyright © 1955 by Doris Lessing.
Both reprinted by permission of Harper & Row, Publishers, Inc.

HENRY HOLT AND COMPANY, INC.
Excerpt from "The Mistress of Complication" by Julian Symons in *Agatha Christie: First Lady of Crime* edited by H. R. Keating. Copyright © 1977. Published by Henry Holt and Company, Inc., and used with their permission.

HOUGHTON MIFFLIN COMPANY
Excerpt from *India* (Revised Edition) by Hyman Kublin. Copyright © 1973 by Houghton Mifflin Company. Used by permission.

ALFRED A. KNOPF, INC.
Excerpt for "Her First Ball" from *The Short Stories of Katherine Mansfield.* Copyright 1922, 1950. Reprinted by permission of Alfred A. Knopf, Inc.

MCINTOSH & OTIS, INC.
"Through the Tunnel" from *The Habit of Loving* by Doris Lessing (Thomas Y. Crowell). Copyright © 1955 by Doris Lessing. By permission of McIntosh & Otis, Inc.

NASSP
Material excerpted from *HM Study Skills Program, Level II.* Copyright © 1979 by NASSP, 1904 Association Drive, Reston, Va. 22091. All rights reserved. Selections reprinted by permission of the publisher.

NEW DIRECTIONS
"Winter Trees" from *Collected Poems Volume I: 1909–1939* by William Carlos Williams. Copyright 1938 by New Directions Publishing Corporation. Reprinted by permission of the publisher.

THE NEW YORK TIMES
"The Airport World" by William Safire, November 20, 1978. Copyright © 1978 by The New York Times Company. Reprinted by permission.

W. W. NORTON & CO.
"Personal Insight: Writing Poetry" from *Journal of Solitude* by May Sarton. Copyright © 1973 by May Sarton. Reprinted by permission of the publisher.

OREGON HISTORICAL SOCIETY
Excerpt from "Diary of an Oregon Pioneer of 1853" by Amelia Stuart Knight in *Transactions of the Oregon Pioneer Association, Fifty-Sixth Annual Reunion, 1928*. Reprinted by permission of the Oregon Historical Society.

OXFORD UNIVERSITY PRESS
Excerpts from *The Notebooks and Papers of Gerard Manley Hopkins*. Copyright 1937. Published by Oxford University Press and reprinted with their permission.

SOUVENIR PRESS OF LONDON
Excerpt from *Shakespeare of London* by Marchette Chute. Copyright 1949 by E. P. Dutton, renewed 1977 by Marchette Chute. Reprinted by permission of the publisher.

TIME
Excerpt from "Essa v. Beulah." Copyright 1967 Time Inc. All rights reserved. Reprinted by permission from *Time*.

UNIVERSITY OF CHICAGO PRESS
"A Letter of Condolence" from *Letters from Africa: 1914–1931* by Isak Dinesen. Copyright © 1981. Published by the University of Chicago Press and reprinted with their permission.

U.S. NEWS & WORLD REPORT
Chart on "Living Standards" from the February 4, 1985, issue. Copyright 1985 *U.S. News & World Report. Reprinted by permission.*

VIKING PENGUIN INC.
Excerpt from "Clever Animals" from *Late Night Thoughts on Listening to Mahler's Ninth Symphony* by Lewis Thomas. Copyright © 1982 by Lewis Thomas.
Excerpt from "First Lesson" from *Letter from a Distant Land* by Philip Booth. Copyright © 1946 by Philip Booth.
"The Open Window" from *The Complete Short Stories of Saki* by Saki (H. H. Munro). Copyright 1930, renewed 1958 by the Viking Press, Inc. All reprinted by permission of Viking Penguin Inc.

GEORGE WEIDENFELD & NICOLSON LTD.
Excerpt from *Letters from Africa: 1914–1931* ("A Letter of Condolence") by Isak Dinesen. Copyright © 1981. Reprinted by permission of the publisher.

BOOK DESIGN AND PRODUCTION: Textart Inc.
COVER DESIGN: Textart Inc.
TECHNICAL ART: Network Graphics

Photo Credits

© Beth Bergman: p 464. THE BETTMANN ARCHIVE, INC.: pp 451, 511, 550, 615. © Walter Chandoha p 435. CONTACT STOCK IMAGES/WOODFIN CAMP: © Alon Reininger 1984 p 113. CULVER PICTURES, INC.: pp 235, 424, 446, 469, 492, 536, 587; © Barbara Morgan p 422. DE WYS, INC.: © Richard Laird p 416; © Richard Walters p 62. EKM-NEPENTHE: © Cathy Cheney p 652. FOCUS WEST: © William Hart p 598. © Jerry Jacka p 672. © Ken Karp, pp 683, 697. MONKMEYER PRESS: © Paul Conklin pp 82, 219; © Mimi Forsyth pp 413; © Michael Kagan p 479; © Ray Solomon p 429. NASA: p 24. NYPL PICTURE COLLECTION: p 40. ODYSSEY PRODUCTIONS: © Robert Frerck p 394. PHOTO RESEARCHERS, INC.: © Stephen Dalton p 171; © George Gerster p 87; © 1986 Robert Houser p 292; © L&D Klein 1978 p 540; © Omikron p 66; © Barbara Riis p 49; © Bruce Roberts p 336; © Leonard Lee Rue p 664; © Bernard G. Silberstein p 123; © Joe Van Wormer p 145. PHOTOTÈQUE: p 576. THE PICTURE CUBE: © Peter Baylies p 533; © Denley Karlson p 515; © Jaye R. Phillips 1982 p 459; © Sarah Putnam p 212; © Frank Siteman pp 198, 288. © Frank Siteman 1985 p 644. STOCK, BOSTON: © George Bellerose p 100; © Owen Franken p 634; © Michael Hayman p 299; © Jerry Howard p 528; © Ira Kirschenbaum p 391; © Peter Menzel pp 177, 606; © Christopher Morrow p 37; © Joseph P. Schuyler p 544; © Peter Vandermark p 343; © Cary Wolinsky p 325. © Martha Swope, p 156. TAURUS PHOTOS: © Laima Druskis p 18. UPI/BETTMANN NEWSPHOTOS: p 505, 657. © Ulrike Welsch 1981 pp 72, 410. WOODFIN CAMP & ASSOCIATES: © 1981 Gerald Davis p 257; © Sepp Seitz 1984 p 399.

Unit Opener Credits
ART RESOURCE: David Smith, *Raven IV* (iron, 1957) Hirshhorn Museum & Sculpture Garden, Smithsonian Institution, Joseph Martin/Scala pp 230–231. EKM-NEPENTHE: © Richard Reinhold pp 602–603. THE IMAGE BANK: © Steve Dunwell 1984 pp 2–3. PHOTO RESEARCHERS, INC.: © Georg Gerster 1975 pp 284-285. STOCK, BOSTON: © Jeff Albertson pp 386–387; © Ellis Herwig pp 494–495; © Jean-Claude Lejeune pp 140–141; © Nicholas Sapieha 1973 pp 680–681; © Ulrike Welsch pp 94–95T. © Ulrike Welsch pp 560–561.

Art Credits
MICHAEL ADAMS—54, 105
STEPHEN MARCHESI—Chapter Opener 94–95, 16, 151, 163, 320
DONNA RUFF—33, 98, 126, 501, 521, 527, 535, 546, 553, 641, 691
SAMANTHA SMITH—75, 187, 253, 287, 348, 404, 485, 568, 669
EVA BURG VAGRETI—192, 216, 245, 444, 573, 611, 648, 687

Part Opener Credits
ART RESOURCE: Anderson, Rome p 1. STOCK, BOSTON: © Cary Wolinsky p 385. WOODFIN CAMP & ASSOCIATES/Contact: © Alon Reininger 1981 p 605.

Writer's Sourcebook Credits
BRUCE COLEMAN, INC.: © Dr. E. R. Degginger FPSA. pp 363TL, 363BL. COLUMBIA PICTURES CORPORATION: p 381. © DR. E. R. DEGGINGER FPSA: pp 370T and BR, 371TL and TR. EARTH SCENES: © Stouffer Enterprises p 364BL. LIBRARY OF CONGRESS: p 358T, Walker Evans. MAGNUM PHOTOS: © Paul Fusco pp 365TL, 379BR. THE METROPOLITAN MUSEUM OF ART: p 359TL, Gaya y Lucientes, Francisco de (1746–1828), Don Manuel Osorio Manrique de Zuniga (born 1784); oil on canvas, H. 50 in. W. 40 in. (127 × 101.6 cm.); signed (on card in bird's beak): Dn Franco Goya; The Metropolitan Museum of Art, The Jules Bache Collection, 1949; (49.7.41). MONKMEYER PRESS PHOTO: © George Zimbel p 380T. MUSEUM OF FINE ARTS, BOSTON: p 355TL (detail), p 356T, 41.631 LONG BRANCH, NEW JERSEY, Winslow Homer, American, 1836–1910; oil on canvas, 16 × 21¾ in. (40.6 × 55.2 cm.), signed and dated 1868; Charles Henry Hayden Fund; p 362 BL, 47.1185 SKATING, Thomas Birch, American, 1779–1851; oil on canvas; 20 × 30 in; M. and M. Karolik Collection. NASA PHOTO: p 383B. NEBRASKA STATE HISTORICAL SOCIETY: p 359B, A547–7P He Dog (Sunka Bloka) a subchief, Cut Meat District, 1900 (John A. Anderson Collection, #918) PHOTO RESEARCHERS, INC.: Mary Evans Picture Library 367B; © Douglas Faulkner p 365B; © Jerry L. Ferrara pp 354T, 382B, and T; © Todd Gipstein p 354TR; © Richard Hutchings p 380B; © Susan McCartney 366B; © Peter Miller p 364; © Robert Perron p 383TL; © Bruce Roberts pp 372Bl, BR, 373T; © Harry Rodgers p 376T; © Wasyl Sskidzinsky p 373B; © L. West. RAINBOW: p 361 CL and BL. © Camilla Smith. KAY REESE &. ASSOCIATES: © Claude Huber p 356B. COURTESY VICTORIA AND ALBERT MUSEUM: p 367B. © WAYNE SOURCE: p 358B. WHITNEY MUSEUM OF AMERICAN ART: p 362TL, John Sloan, BACKYARDS, GREENWICH VILLAGE, 1914; oil, 26 × 32 inches; collection of Whitney Museum of American Art; purchase, Acq#36.153. WOODFIN CAMP & ASSOCIATES: © David Burnett/Contact pp 360TL and TR, 360BL and BR; © George Fischer/Visum p 354BR; © Robert Frerck p 355B; © Michael Heron p 357B; William Hubbell p 357T.

Illustration Credits
BOB JACKSON: pp 362BR, 366T, 368–369T, 369B.

Contents

UNIT I
The Paragraph and the Writing Process

THINKING ABOUT THINKING:
Demonstrating Flexibility   3

UNIT II
The Development of a Personal Writing Style

UNIT III
The Modes of Writing

UNIT IV
The Essay and the Research Report

THINKING ABOUT THINKING:
Distinguishing Fact from Opinion   231

UNIT V
Writing Across the Curriculum

THINKING ABOUT THINKING:
Recognizing Relationships   285

WRITER'S SOURCEBOOK   353

PART 2 Grammar, Usage, and Mechanics 385

UNIT VI
Grammar

THINKING ABOUT THINKING:
Classifying Information   387

UNIT VII
Usage

THINKING ABOUT THINKING:
Recognizing Appropriateness   495

UNIT VIII
Mechanics

PART *3* *Skills and Resources*   601

UNIT IX
Skills

THINKING ABOUT THINKING:
Making Associations   603

UNIT X
Resources

THINKING ABOUT THINKING:
Asking Questions   681

Special Features

Student Writers

Many models of student writing appear in this textbook. In the "Writers on Writing" feature, models and commentaries by the following student writers appear on the pages indicated.

Professional Writers

Excerpts from the work of many writers appear in this textbook. Here is a list of some of the writers included.

The "Writer's Sourcebook" contains the following literary selections:

Thinking Skills

Thinking About Thinking

When you write, you think. At each stage of the writing process, you use a variety of thinking skills to come up with new ideas and make decisions about how to express those ideas. You will discover, as you progress through this textbook, how applying certain thinking skills can help you become a better writer.

Each unit in *Macmillan English* opens with a special feature called "Thinking About Thinking." This feature defines one particular thinking skill that is part of a larger thinking process. Each skill is one you will find useful as you engage in the activity of that unit.

"Thinking About Thinking" helps you to become aware of what you do when you think. Each feature asks you to think in a certain way about a photograph. By becoming more aware of the way you think, you can gain greater mastery of the thinking skills you use as you write.

Here, in everyday language, are descriptions of the thinking skills you will apply at the start of each unit in this book.

UNIT I   THE PARAGRAPH AND THE WRITING PROCESS

THINKING PROCESS   *Invention*

THINKING SKILL   **Demonstrating Flexibility**

Demonstrating flexibility means being able to change direction as you write and to consider new possibilities. This skill helps you to be truly inventive and to avoid locking yourself into the first idea or word that comes to mind.

UNIT IX	SKILLS
THINKING PROCESS	*Problem Solving*
THINKING SKILL	**Making Associations**

Here you create your own connections. This skill helps you to solve a variety of language problems by coming up with solutions that are especially meaningful to you.

UNIT X	RESOURCES
THINKING PROCESS	*Problem Solving*
THINKING SKILL	**Asking Questions**

This skill involves recognizing what you do not know and asking about it. It is a skill that helps you to identify new directions for writing, using the known to inquire into the unknown.

SPEAKING OF ENGLISH

A winner of the Pulitzer Prize, MADELEINE BLAIS *writes feature stories for the* Miami Herald's Tropic *magazine. Earlier, she wrote for the* Trenton Times *and the* Boston Globe. *She was featured in the PBS documentary series entitled* Writers Writing *and is one of twenty-four journalists profiled in Barbara Belford's* Brilliant Bylines: A Biographical Anthology of Notable Newspaperwomen in America. *Ms. Blais wrote the following answers in response to questions by an editor from Scribner Educational Publishers.*

Editor: When did you first realize you were interested in newspapers?

Blais: Picture a child in the third grade in a small and unsung town in Massachusetts. It is time for a civics lesson and Mrs. McGrath is trying to instruct us in the value of reading the newspaper daily.

"How many students," she asks, "read the paper?"

All hands are raised.

"What part?"

"The comics," comes the answer in a chorus.

"What else?"

"Sports," answer a few of the boys.

"That is it?"

My hand alone remains in the air. I wave it with a wild force. The teacher urges me with her gaze to explain. I start spouting headlines: FOOD POISONING FELLS DOZENS, BLOCK PARTY ENDS IN MELEE

"That," said Mrs. McGrath, holding her hand as if to stop traffic, "is enough, I think."

ESTRANGED WIFE STRIKES HUBBY IN LAUNDERETTE

"Enough, I say, enough." Mrs. McGrath had covered her ears with her hands and appeared to be cowering against the blackboard.

To me there was always something

beckoning about newspapers, something special and palpably different about the language in papers: where else do you find melees on a routine basis?

Editor: When did you decide you wanted to become a writer?

Blais: This is a common question to which I have a simple answer: All along.

Writers are always writing. When you read, you are writing. When you look with any intensity at any spectacle or event or human exchange, you are writing. Drown yourself in good talk; that is writing too.

Cultivate what George Orwell called the "lonely child's habit of reading incessantly"—not only books but also newspapers, and even the back of cereal boxes. Don't, when you are reading, describe this activity to anyone as "doing nothing." If, as often happens, some rude person interrupts, ask him to apologize for disturbing you while you are in the presence of great thinking.

Editor: What else would you like to say directly to a teen-age writer?

Blais: Many people are going to say to you that at your age you have nothing to say; nothing important has happened in *your* life. In fact, almost three quarters of everything important has already happened to you. The problem is you lack "perspective," a fancy word for "objectivity," which is yet another fancy word for, well, "vision." Vision seems to amount to a certain common sense that writers finally develop about what to put in and what to leave out and how to cut to the energy and how to write to the best moment and somehow get to the point where the reader thinks you have read his mind.

Editor: What was your first writing effort?

Blais: Well, I guess we should once again trip back in time: Mrs. O'Connor's fifth grade. The assignment was a fictionalized biography of the Wright Brothers. I imagined two boys, just a tad older than their ten-year-old sister, who, obsessed as always with locomotion, decide to go sledding of a winter's afternoon on a sloping hill (which bore a remarkable resemblance to a hill near my very own

house) during which time they bumped their heads on a big tree and lost all ability to invent, and so it was up to their sister to come up with the airplane idea. The fires of feminism burned at an early age.

After that, I read and read and read and read and diagrammed a few sentences here and there and wrote now and then and tried to get a new vocabulary word every day and read and read and read, and then when I got to high school, I thought nothing was quite as romantic as the writing of poetry. My favorite gambit was to use the words *bittersweet* and *honeysuckle* because to me there could be no other words quite so heartbreaking and evocative. Also I used ellipsis, those dot-dot-dot formations favored by young poets to indicate…ineffability.

Editor: Were you always a "good" writer?

Blais: At the point in my literary career just described, it can be said that I lacked all promise, and I pass that on to young writers as a way of encouraging them not to abandon their hope of becoming a writer if right now they are capable only of finding words like *seat* and *meat* to rhyme with bitter "you-know-what."

Editor: How did you prepare yourself to be a newspaper writer?

Blais: It was in college that a chance visit to the offices of the campus weekly revived my old interest in the news, and I did volunteer work on the paper for four years. I went to journalism school for a year after that, and when it was finally time to get my first job, I found that I qualified for the broken fire-hydrant beat by day and at night I got to go to meetings of town fathers, dyspeptic men who pondered municipal bonds and kept themselves together body and soul through the endless consumption of breath mints and digestive aids. Where was the food poisoning, the melees?

It took a while.

Editor: How and where did you find your own niche in journalism?

Blais: What I found finally is that the mayor of the town is far less interesting (to me) than the people he or she governs, and so I look for the news in the lives of people not normally in the news. I think I learned this lesson on a paper in New Jersey when as a society writer I was asked to cover an ethnic debutante ball. What I found was a community of people for whom this annual event meant weeks of preparation, and while they made glittering decorations and delicious food, they also spoke of what was important to them—who had graduated, who had retired, the births and the deaths. Here was passion, here was story.

Editor: What was your breakthrough to the job you really wanted?

Blais: I took jobs I didn't want solely to get that dread word *experience,* so I could get jobs I did want. I freelanced. And I read. Through it all, I was able to keep sight of that one first love which made me want to write in the first place. And that's why I am repeating what I said in the beginning: read, look, and listen.

Editor: How do you get ideas for your feature stories?

Blais: Story ideas can come from anywhere. Something someone says at dinner could inspire a story, a letter from a reader asking you to write about something could prove to be a goad, an inch or

two of copy buried deep in the paper. In general, if you are a feature writer, you want to generate your own material so that "assignment," in the sense of something one is ordered to do, never occurs. The best stories often contain a generous measure of hidden autobiography. Over the years I often found myself drawn to profiles of excellent teachers, and I presume this reflects my gratitude to the excellent teachers in my own life. I like to spend as long as I can on anything I have to research, and then write.

Editor: How do you feel about rewriting and revising?

Blais: Norman Mailer once said, "Journalism is chores"; so is rewriting. Yet it is a tedium for which I have a surprising store of energy, and I suppose that is one mark of a writer.

One secret about writing: If you can't think of how to begin, try to think of how to end. I do that all the time and find it utterly liberating. Show your work mostly to yourself and sometimes to editors you can trust but not so often to anyone in your family, especially Aunt Tillie, who thinks everything you do is perfect no matter what, and never to the people you are writing about because they are least equipped to judge whether what you have done is good or not.

The blank page is always threatening. There are tons of words out there, capable of an infinity of combinations. The one thing you should know if you really decide to heed that most glorious, yet ornery, of callings and become a *Writer* with a capital *W* is this:

It's scary.

MACMILLAN ENGLISH

THINKING AND WRITING PROCESSES

Composition

A Latin inscription: written communication
in the ancient world

The Paragraph and the Writing Process

Thinking About Thinking: Demonstrating Flexibility

Each stage of the writing process—prewriting, writing, and revising—involves thinking. You think when you discover new ideas, when you express those ideas, and when you revise your expression. Prewriting is the stage that puts a special emphasis on coming up with ideas. This process is called invention, and you can master a variety of specific thinking skills to help you be inventive.

Defining the Skill

Inventive thinkers often demonstrate flexibility. **DEMONSTATING FLEXIBILITY** means being able to change, to take a different direction, to "bend in the wind" like a willow tree. A rigid thinker, one who is not flexible, is locked into one idea or one form. Such a thinker often fails to notice when something new or useful comes along.

Applying the Skill

To demonstrate how you can think flexibly about this photograph, write about it from at least three different points of view. First write for one minute as if you were near the writer, observing her as she writes. Then write for one minute as if you were the letter writer herself. Then write for one minute as if you were the person receiving her letter. What other ways of writing about the picture can you invent?

Introduction: Personal Writing

Unlike more formal kinds of writing, such as the research report, **personal writing** focuses on the writer's own thoughts, values, experiences, and feelings.

Personal writing may be in the form of a diary entry, a letter to a friend, an entry in a writer's journal, an autobiography or memoir, or a personal narrative or essay. What usually sets all personal writing apart is its conversational style and its first-person point of view.

Whether you are addressing yourself alone in a diary or the general public in a published memoir, your personal-writing style should have the same spontaneity and openness you display when speaking directly to a friend. Like a good conversation, personal writing can be one of life's great pleasures—a means of self-discovery and a chance to share your unique personality with others.

In this chapter you will examine the characteristics of several kinds of personal writing and will practice developing your skills in three specific areas:

>   personal letters
>   the writer's journal
>   autobiography or memoir

Personal Letters

The great eighteenth-century dictionary-maker Samuel Johnson thought that corresponding with a friend was a special pleasure because in such letters "doubt and distrust have no place, and everything is said as it is thought." Despite advanced telecommunications, writing personal letters remains an important—and inexpensive—way for people to communicate over long distances. Moreover, Dr. Johnson's observations are as true today as they were two hundred years ago. Unlike most other forms of writing, a personal letter that is open, honest, and spontaneous can strengthen the bonds between the writer and the recipient.

Here, for example, is a letter that essayist E. B. White sent from New York City in June 1940 to his young son back home. As you read, notice that White shares his experiences by describing the city to his son and in turn asks the boy to write about his experiences in Brooklin, Maine. Such give-and-take is an important characteristic of any good personal letter.

A LETTER HOME

The Grosvenor
35 Fifth Avenue
New York
Sunday

Dear Joe,

From my hotel window I can see the apartment building on Eighth Street where we used to live when you were a baby. I can also see the trees of Washington Square, and the backyards of the houses on Ninth Street with their little gardens of potted plants and trellises. The Sixth Avenue Elevated is gone, and New York looks very different on that account. People still like to come out in their sun-suits on Sunday morning and sun themselves in their roof gardens, and they still spend a good deal of time taking dogs out for a walk, not realizing how lucky they are that there are no porcupines. Everybody that I talk to is very gloomy about the war and about the defeat of France, but that is true everywhere today. In Radio City, where we used to skate, there is an open-air restaurant, with people sitting at little tables under big green umbrellas. The fountain is going and makes a great noise.

How has everything been going in Maine? I miss you a lot and wish I could be there right now, although my hay fever bothers me less in the city than in the country. Is Barney coming to cut the hay? I hope so. And did you get any Barred Rock chicks from Mr. Sylvester? Tell me all about these things, and whether you have caught any fish.

There is a church right opposite the hotel, and every afternoon the chimes ring at about five o'clock when people are coming home from work. It reminds me of being a student at Cornell, where the chimes in the library tower used to ring every afternoon toward the end of day. I suppose right now the bell in the church in Brooklin is ringing, too, five hundred miles from here.

Tell Mother that everything is going along all right, and that I'll try to get a good deal of work done in the next few days so that I'll be able to be back in Maine soon. I'm still hoping that you and I can take a little camping trip this summer, so you better keep your ax sharpened up and your boots oiled. I hope you'll help Mother as much as you can while I'm away. Give my love to her and to everybody, and write me if you get time.

Affectionately,

Dad

Another type of personal letter that can strengthen the emotional ties between two people is the **letter of condolence or sympathy.** The words *condolence* and *sympathy* both connote the idea of sharing another person's grief at losing a loved one. In the following example, author Isak Dinesen writes from Africa to her mother in Denmark, not only to express her grief at the news of her sister Ea's death but also to offer comfort.

A LETTER OF CONDOLENCE

My own beloved Mother,

Your telegram came today. It is almost impossible to write,—one is far too overwhelmed, but I do so want to feel as close to you all as possible; the distance that separates us seems so abysmal.

Dearest Mother, we have all lost so indescribably much; I cannot understand that we have been bereft of so much richness and beauty, so much warmth and love, and it is such infinite loss, such great emptiness that I am quite unable to comprehend it now; but above everything else I feel gratitude toward her. I feel that every single thing I come to think of is so sweet and like a blessing, and I think that everyone who came into contact with her felt that, no matter how slightly. I can't imagine anyone more deeply loved; I think everyone who knew her came to love her. . . .

Tommy [Dinesen's husband] is such a dear, I am so thankful that he is here, but when are we going to see all of you? Give our love to everyone, to poor Viggo, and to Elle. I am quite unable to write about what I am thinking; every moment more and more comes rushing into my mind. I think of Ea's singing, and I feel that there is something, something so glorious, so sweet and rich and loving shining over us all, that will always continue. Goodbye, dearest Mother, all, all my thoughts are with you.

Goodbye, dearest Mother

Your Tanne

Both White's and Dinesen's letters are **occasional letters**—that is, their writing was prompted by specific occasions: a trip away from home, a relative's death. In contrast, **friendly letters** are not usually prompted by occasions. Instead, they spring from a desire to keep in touch with distant friends or relatives. Friendly letters are usually long and freewheeling—full of recent news. As Samuel Johnson noted, in such letters "everything is said as it is thought." Good friendly letters, however, are not chaotic, but spontaneous. They reveal the writer's natural intelligence and spirit, concerns and aspirations—in short, the writer's unique personality.

Here, for example, is a friendly letter that the poet Emily Dickinson wrote when she was fourteen years old to her good friend Abiah Root, who had moved from Amherst to Springfield, Massachusetts, the year before. As you read, note the enthusiasm that colors everything that Dickinson writes.

A FRIENDLY LETTER

Amherst, May 7, 1845

Dear A.,

It seems almost an age since I have seen you, and it is indeed an age for friends to be separated. I was delighted to receive a paper from you, and I also was much pleased with the news it contained, especially that you are taking lessons on the "piny," as you always call it. But remember not to get on ahead of me. Father intends to have a piano very soon. How happy I shall be when I have one of my own!. . . Viny [Emily's sister] went to Boston this morning with father, to be gone a fortnight, and I am left alone in all my glory. I suppose she has got there before this time, and is probably staring with mouth and eyes wide open at the wonders of the city. I have been to walk tonight, and got some very choice wild flowers. I wish you had some of them. Viny and I both go to school this term. We have a very fine school. There are 63 scholars. I have four studies. They are Mental Philosophy, Geology, Latin, and Botany. How large they sound, don't they? I don't believe you have such big studies. . . . How do you enjoy your school this term? Are the teachers as pleasant as our old schoolteachers? I expect you have a great many prim, starched up young ladies there, who, I doubt not, are perfect models of propriety and good behavior. If they are, don't let your free spirit be chained by them. I don't know as there [are] any in school of this stamp. But there 'most always are a few, whom the teachers look up to and regard as their satellites. I am growing handsome very fast indeed! I expect I shall be the belle of Amherst when I reach my 17th year. I don't doubt that I shall have perfect crowds of admirers at that age. Then how I shall delight to make them await my bidding, and with what delight shall I witness their suspense while I make my final decision. But away with my nonsense. I have written one composition this term, and I need not assure you it was exceedingly edifying to myself as well as everybody else. Don't you want to see it? I really wish you could have a chance. We are obliged to write compositions once in a fortnight, and select a piece to read from some interesting book the week that we don't write compositions. . . . I had so many things to do for Viny, as she was going away, that very much against my wishes I deferred writing you until now, but forgive and forget, dear A., and I will promise to do better in future. Do write me soon, and let it be a long, long letter; and when you can't get time to write, send a paper, so as to let me know you think of me still, though we are separated by hill and stream. All the girls send much love to you. Don't forget to let me receive a letter from you soon. I can say no more now as my paper is all filled up.

Your affectionate friend,

Emily E. Dickinson

EXERCISE 1 **Thinking About a Letter Home.** Reread the letter from E. B. White to his son on page 5. Then write your answers to the following questions.

1. List five details that would help White's son visualize the city.
2. With what does White want his son to associate the church bells in Maine? Why might White want his son to make this association?
3. What does White say in the last paragraph that would especially make the boy look forward to his father's return?

EXERCISE 2 **Thinking About a Letter of Condolence.** Reread Isak Dinesen's letter to her mother on page 6. Then write your answers to the following questions.

1. What does Dinesen say troubles her about her sister's death?
2. What does Dinesen say are sources of comfort to her?
3. What are the three ways according to Dinesen that she and her family can feel close?

EXERCISE 3 **Thinking About a Friendly Letter.** Reread Emily Dickinson's letter beginning on page 6. Then write your answers to the following questions.

1. List five separate topics that Emily discusses in her letter.
2. Which topics can best be categorized as new?
3. Which topics can best be categorized as aspirations, or wishes for the future?
4. List five questions from the letter that Emily would probably expect Abiah to answer in her next letter.

EXERCISE 4 **Writing a Friendly Letter.** Imagine that you are Abiah Root and that you have received the letter on pages 6–7 from your friend Emily Dickinson. Write a friendly letter in response.

EXERCISE 5 **Writing a Personal Letter.** Plan to write one of the following kinds of personal letters:

a letter to a family member who is away from home

a letter of condolence to a friend who has recently lost a loved one

a friendly letter to a distant friend or relative

Spend a few moments before you write to jot down the topics that you want to discuss in your letter. As you write, remember to be sincere and considerate and to let your personality shine through.

A Writer's Journal

The words *journal* and *diary* are often interchangeable. Both are derived from the Latin word *dies* meaning "day," because both journals and diaries were originally day-by-day records of the writer's life. Today, however, the word *diary* often implies a private record not intended for publication. For example, the famous diary of Samuel Pepys, which gives us a lively picture of life in seventeenth-century England, was written in a personal shorthand that was not completely deciphered for over 150 years. On the other hand, *journal* implies a record intended to be shared. James Boswell's *Journal of a*

Tour to the Hebrides, which recounts the journey he and Samuel Johnson made to Scotland in 1773, was originally written to be circulated among friends and was published during the writer's lifetime.

The **writer's journal** is an informal written record, kept over an extended period of time, of the writer's experiences, thoughts, and feelings.

What distinguishes a writer's journal from other kinds of journals is its focus on writing. In addition to recording and reflecting on personal experiences, the author of a writer's journal can use it to practice writing in different styles and to store ideas for future writing. This last purpose—using the journal as a storehouse of ideas for future writing—makes the journal into something more than a personal chronicle; rather, the journal becomes a handy reference, a rich source of raw material to be refined later into finished pieces of writing.

Here are some entries that you may put in your writer's journal.

INCIDENTS

You may relate incidents or events that happen to you or that you observe, either commonplace or extraordinary. In the following entry, a young artist and writer observes a gun fortification during World War II.

18 May 1943

Today I am by the river below East Peckham. I'm writing letters, roasting in the sun, sweating, burning, turning red. The feathers of the grass tickle me and I am almost stupefied. Oh, how lovely it is. Bang in front is a concrete pillbox covered with nets, slowly being swallowed up by weeds. *They'll* win, every time.

—Denton Welch

DESCRIPTIONS

You may describe people, places, and things in precise and vivid word-pictures using sensory details. The young poet Gerard Manley Hopkins recorded the following description of a seascape in 1868.

Aug. 1.   Through Paris to Dieppe and by Newhaven home.

Day bright. Sea calm, with little walking wavelets edged with fine eyebrow crispings, and later nothing but a netting or chain-work on the surface, and even that went, so that the smoothness was marbly and perfect and, between the just-corded near sides of the waves rising like fishes' backs and breaking with darker blue the pale blue of the general field, in the very sleek hollows came out golden crumbs of reflections from the chalk cliffs.—Peach-colored sundown and above some simple gilded messes of cloud, which later became finer, smaller, and scattering all away.—Here the sunlight had been dim.

The fields are burnt white, the heat has gone on.

PERSONAL INSIGHTS

A writer's journal is also the perfect place to record any discovery that gives you a better understanding of yourself or the world. In the following entry, poet and novelist May Sarton combines deep introspection with vivid natural details to celebrate "a point of clarification" in her life.

October 9th

Has it really happened at last? I feel released from the rack, set free, in touch with the deep source that is only *good,* where poetry lives. We have waited long this year for the glory, but suddenly the big maple is all gold and the beeches yellow with a touch of green that makes the yellow even more intense. There are still nasturtiums to be picked, and now I must get seriously to work to get the remaining bulbs in.

It has been stupidly difficult to let go, but that is what has been needed. I had allowed myself to get overanxious, clutching at what seemed sure to pass, and clutching is the surest way to murder love, as if it were a kitten, not to be squeezed so hard, or a flower to fade in a tight hand. Letting go, I have come back yesterday and today to a sense of my life here in all its riches, depth, freedom for soul-making.

It's a real breakthrough. I have not written in sonnet form for a long time, but at every major crisis in my life when I reach a point of clarification, where pain is transcended by the quality of the experience itself, sonnets come. Whole lines run through my head and I cannot *stop* writing until whatever it is gets said.

Found three huge mushrooms when I went out before breakfast to fill the bird feeder. So far only jays come, but the word will get around.

—May Sarton, *Journal of a Solitude*

WORDPLAY

Evocative words, expressions, figures of speech, or quotations that delight you also belong in the safekeeping of your writer's journal. Gerard Manley Hopkins jotted down the following bits of wordplay in his journal of 1865.

Shapes of frozen snow-drifts. Parallel ribs. Delightful curves. Saddles, lips, leaves.

Whorlèd wave, whelkèd wave,—and drift.

Crocus candles yellow and white.

Notes for poetry. Feathery rows of young corn. Ruddy, furred and branchy tops of the elms backed by rolling cloud.

CHRONICLES

Records of journeys or of any other important events that extend over time can be kept in your writer's journal. A pioneer woman who chronicled her family's five-month journey by wagon train from Iowa to Oregon made the following journal entries.

Sunday, July 31st—Cool and pleasant, but very dusty. Came 12 miles and camped about one o'clock not very far from Boise River. We will stay here a day or two and rest and revive our cattle.

Monday, August 1st—Still in camp, have been washing all day, and all hands have had all the wild currants we could eat. They grow in great abundance along this River. There are three kinds, red, black, and yellow. This evening another of our best milk cows died. Cattle are dying off very fast all along this road. We are hardly ever out of sight of dead cattle on this side of Snake River. This cow was well and fat an hour before she died. Cut the second cheese today.

Tuesday, August 2nd—Traveled 12 miles today and have just camped about one-half mile from the river. Plenty of good grass.

Thursday, August 4th—We have just crossed Boise or Reed's River. It is deep fording, but, by raising the wagon beds about a foot, and being very careful, we are all landed safe and about to camp not far from the bank of the river. Have traveled 20 miles today. Have also seen a good many Indians and bought fish of them. They all seem peaceable and friendly.

Friday, August 5th—We have just bid the beautiful Boise River, with her green timber and rich currants, farewell, and are now on our way to the ferry on Snake River. Evening—Traveled 18 miles today and have just reached Fort Boise and camped. Our turn will come to cross some time tomorrow. There is one small ferry boat running here, owned by the Hudson's Bay Company. Have to pay three dollars a wagon. Our worst trouble at these large rivers is swimming the stock over. Often after swimming half way over the poor things will turn and come out again. At this place, however, there are Indians who swim the river from morning till night. There is many a drove of cattle that could not be got over without their help. By paying them a small sum, they will take a horse by the bridle or halter and swim over with him. The rest of the horses all follow, and by driving and hurrahing to the cattle they will almost always follow the horses, sometimes they fail and turn back.

—Amelia Stewart Knight

Other kinds of entries that you may put in your writer's journal are rough drafts of poems, stories, or essays; experiments with writing in different styles; praise or criticism of your writing; and pencil sketches to accompany entries.

Writer's Journals as Prewriting Aids

As a storehouse of raw material for future writing, your writer's journal is a good place to use prewriting techniques for generating ideas.

The greater the variety of entries that you make in your writer's journal, the more valuable it will become as a source of ideas for future writing. To see how a journal entry can be the basis for another piece of writing, compare the following two excerpts written by Washington Irving. The American author recorded this journal entry during a visit to England.

JOURNAL ENTRY

July 25, 1815

From the Birth place of Shakespeare I made a transfer to the grave. He lies buried in the chantry of the church, and never had poet a more enviable grave. Thus to come back and lay his dust at the place of his nativity—To be treasurd up in his native town & to be the theme & pride of his townsmen and then such a place of sepulture. The church is one of the most beautiful old county churches in England and its situation is almost unrivalled. It stands on the banks of the Avon. The river runs dimpling along at the end of the church yard and the elms which stand at the bottom of the burying ground droop their branches into the water—An avenue of limes whose branches are curiously interwoven so as to form an arch lead up to the church. The yard is green, the very tomb stones are half covered with moss—small birds were fluttering & chirping about every fissure of the old walls and rooks were sailing and cawing about the spire.

Now here is the material from the preceding journal entry as it was reworked later for Irving's famous *Sketch-Book*.

EXCERPT FROM PUBLISHED ESSAY

Notice that Irving deletes the journal's bare statement about the church ("and never had poet a more enviable grave") and replaces it with vivid details.

Notice that Irving improves his word choice. For example, he changes *dimpling* to *murmuring*.

Notice that the journal's errors in spelling (*Birth place* and grammar (*An avenue . . . lead*) are corrected in the published version.

From the birthplace of Shakespeare a few paces brought me to his grave. He lies buried in the chancel of the parish church, a large and venerable pile, mouldering with age, but richly ornamented. It stands on the banks of the Avon, on an embowered point, and separated by adjoining gardens from the suburbs of the town. Its situation is quiet and retired; the river runs murmuring at the foot of the church-yard, and the elms which grow upon its banks droop their branches into its clear bosom. An avenue of limes, the boughs of which are curiously interlaced, so as to form in summer an arched way of foliage, leads up from the gate of the yard to the church-porch. The graves are overgrown with grass; the gray tombstones, some of them nearly sunk into the earth, are half covered with moss, which has likewise tinted the reverend old building. Small birds have built their nests among the cornices and fissures of the walls, and keep up a continual flutter and chirping; and rooks are sailing and cawing about its lofty gray spire.
—Washington Irving, "Stratford-on-Avon"

Hints for Beginning a Writer's Journal

To help you form the habit of keeping a writer's journal, here are a few tips:

1. Find a sturdy notebook (not a loose-leaf binder) that will endure extended use. Use it only as a writer's journal.
2. Do not feel that you must write in your journal every day. However, keep your journal handy, and make an effort to establish a pattern for writing, such as every other day or once a week.
3. Feel free to use abbreviations or any kind of shorthand as long as you are able to read your submissions easily.
4. Periodically reread your entries—for pleasure, for discovering how you have changed over time, or for inspiration for other writing.
5. Read famous journals—by authors, explorers, scientists, musicians, travelers. Use your library, and ask your teacher and classmates for recommendations.

EXERCISE 6 **Beginning a Writer's Journal.** Over the next two weeks, write at least three entries in your writer's journal. Review the models on pages 9–12 for entry ideas.

Autobiography and Memoir

Auto- means "self."

An **autobiography,** therefore, is a self-written biography—in other words, the story of the writer's own life. A **memoir** is a kind of autobiography, but it usually covers a more limited part of the writer's life.

These kinds of personal writing differ from letter writing and journal writing in two important ways. First, unlike letters, diaries, and journals, which normally have limited audiences (a friend or the writer or a small group of special readers), autobiographies and memoirs are normally intended for larger audiences. Second, autobiographies and memoirs are less spontaneous and less informal than personal letters and journals; on the contrary, memoirs and autobiographies are carefully planned and carefully worked out.

Good autobiographies and memoirs share many of the characteristics of carefully crafted fiction. As an autobiographical writer, you select and order the events of your life so that they tell an interesting and true story. You are in a sense developing "plot," with conflict and suspense. Like any good storyteller, you will want to include vivid descriptions of the people and places—the "characters" and "settings"—that are important in the story of your life. The main "character," of course, is you. Finally, an autobiography or memoir should have a unifying purpose and not be merely a cut-and-dry assemblage of biographical data. For example, do you want to show how you became your school's star athlete? Or do you want to explain what makes your sense of humor as zany as it is? Whatever your purpose, keeping it clearly in mind will help you select and order the events of your life that you wish to present to your audience.

EXERCISE 7 **Writing a Memoir.** Plan to write about a person, place, or event that was important in making you the person you are today. Begin by stating in a sentence what your purpose will be in writing. Next, select significant details about your subject that will help you fulfill your purpose. Then order those details so that the story you tell will be interesting to your readers. When you have finished planning, write a draft of your memoir, revise it, and prepare a final copy for distribution to your classmates.

CHAPTER 1

The Steps of the Writing Process

Writing and rewriting are a constant search for what one is saying.
—*John Updike*

The **writing process** is the means by which you discover what you want to say and how you can best say it. In this process you constantly shuttle back and forth between your ideas and the world outside, translating your thoughts into language that others can understand. Writers use the writing process whether they are involved in personal writing (such as describing a childhood experience) or more formal kinds of writing (such as constructing a research paper).

When you write, you head for unknown territory. You cannot always predict where the writing process will lead you. Like the best writers, you may hit dead ends, change directions, and retrace your steps. Nevertheless, if you understand what happens during the writing process, you will never lose your bearings.

This chapter will provide you with an overview of the writing process, and the next three chapters will present in greater detail the three types of activities that make up the writing process:

> **prewriting**—generating ideas and preparing to write; writing notes and following your ideas; determining your audience and purpose.
>
> **writing a first draft**, or a **discovery draft**—getting your thoughts down on paper
>
> **revising**, or **postwriting**—questioning, rethinking, and editing your draft until it says what you want it to say; preparing a final copy, proofreading it, and "publishing" it so that you can present it to and share it with others

The following pages will show you how one writer used the writing process to write a paragraph. Of course, you can follow the steps of the writing process when you are working on longer pieces of writing as well. Please note that although prewriting, drafting, and revising are described in sequence here, you may actually alternate between one type of activity and another as you write. For example, in revising you may change only a single word but as a result suddenly discover a whole new line of thought to explore. At that point you may do some additional prewriting and expand or even refocus your draft. Always remember that a true picture of the writing process shows you the perpetual motion of your mind in search of what you really want to say.

Prewriting   *Writing a First Draft*   *Revising*

Prewriting

Prewriting supplies you with the raw material for writing. When you prewrite, you concentrate on a subject and write notes that help you gather, explore, and focus your ideas about that subject. You also prepare to write for a particular **audience**—the person or persons whom you expect to read your work—and for a particular **purpose**—the goal that you hope to reach through writing. You may want, for example, to inform, entertain, or persuade your intended audience. You may have in mind an even more specific purpose: You may want to share a discovery, express a regret, make your reader laugh *and* cry, or do any one of a thousand other things people do when they communicate with one another.

Prewriting will deepen your writing with specific, interesting information. On the other hand, writing that does not grow from prewriting is likely to be skimpy, repetitive, and rambling. For example, look at the following paragraph, written without prewriting:

> [1]I spend much of my spare time working with one type of art or another. [2]Art is very important to everyone. [3]I paint, I also sculpt and do some woodcarving. [4]Perhaps my favorite artistic activity is drawing, but I like painting, sculpting, and carving, too. [5]I have several favorite artists. [6]Even as a child I used to sketch when I watched television. [7]The television would play, and I would sketch. [8]Nowadays whenever I have spare time after school I turn happily to one kind of art project or another. [9]It would be wonderful if I could earn my living as an artist one day.

EXERCISE 1 **Thinking About Prewriting.** Reread the preceding paragraph, and write sentences that answer the following questions.

1. What different ideas about art are mentioned in this paragraph?
2. Sentences 1 and 8 express the same basic idea: They both say that the writer spends her spare time working with art. Find two other instances in which an idea stated in one sentence is repeated by another.

The writer of the paragraph about art sounds as if she really does not care very much about what she has to say. After she wrote her unsuccessful paragraph, she was asked to set it aside and list all the different topics, questions, and comments that interested her as she thought about art. You can see some of her prewriting notes on the following page.

FIRST SET OF PREWRITING NOTES

painting with a 3-year-old
realistic vs. primitive drawings of animals
my first oil painting (forgot turpentine!)
copying old masters--inhibiting or inspiring?
possible careers using art skills
how I discovered I could draw
how The Last Supper is being restored
which painter(s) do I admire most?
does an artist need to go to college?
doing a self-portrait--what I learned about my face

The writer then began to explore a few of the items on the list, experimenting with different writing ideas and making judgments about which seemed more interesting or more workable. She eliminated some writing ideas and began to refine some others:

SECOND SET OF PREWRITING NOTES

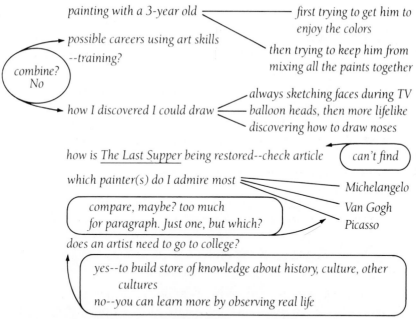

After she worked more with her notes, the writer began to think about choosing a single item to develop into a new paragraph. In making this choice she needed to consider her audience: Would her readers be fellow artists, for example, or people who know less about her subject than she does? She also needed to think about her purpose for writing: Did she want to entertain her audience with the story about the three-year-old, for example, or to inform readers of her own development as an artist? Remember that such decisions are never irreversible in the writing process; you can always change your mind and retrace your steps if a better idea occurs to you. Save your first draft until you are sure of your decisions.

EXERCISE 2   **Thinking About Prewriting.** Look back at the writer's two sets of prewriting notes on page 5, and write your answers to the following questions.

1. From the first set of notes, list the items that seem to be based on the writer's personal experiences.
2. Point out one item on the first list that would lend itself to humorous writing.
3. Find one item that would be of interest to specialists in the field of art.
4. Imagine that the writer is a friend of yours who has come to you for advice. From the second list pick out two items that you think are promising writing ideas, and explain why you think so.

Writing a First Draft

The **first draft** is your initial attempt to express your ideas in a series of related sentences. The first draft is truly a **discovery draft** because it enables you to discover exactly what you think about your subject at this point in the writing process and whether you have managed to say it yet. Usually your first draft will help you see just what you have left out.

Some people write a first draft quickly, without stopping. Others experiment with the draft as they go along, changing words and sentences many times. In any case, you should treat your first draft as a working paper, one that suggests, but may not exactly express, your ideas.

Take a look at the first draft that the writer produced after she reread her prewriting notes, chose a topic that truly interested her, and decided on a purpose and an audience. Notice that she made several changes in wording and raised a few questions for herself as she wrote this draft:

FIRST DRAFT

~~Drawing for me~~ My interest in drawing began with the face. From ~~childhood~~ the

button noses

age of four, I was drawing ~~round~~ balloon heads, round eyes, and U-shaped mouths.

I was fascinated with the ~~effort~~ attempt to ~~draw~~ record the ~~face~~ features of the

human face. as I grew older, I became more skilful (skillful?) The eyes ~~were~~ became

(lifelike?)

more ~~realistic~~ life-like, at least in shape. The mouth took on lips and shading. But

(created on paper)

the nose still stumped me. Then one day I finally ~~drew~~ a nose that seemed ~~realistic~~

(--hair, cheeks, chin--) (was the)

to have 3 dimensions. After that, everything came easily. That day I decided I

would be an artist. ~~Some day~~

EXERCISE 3 **Thinking About the First Draft.** Reread the draft, review the prewriting notes, and write your answers to the following questions.

1. Which item in her second prewriting list did the writer develop in this draft? Find two *new* details or ideas.
2. Point out one change in wording that the writer made as she wrote, and explain the effect of this change.
3. What do you think was the writer's purpose in writing this draft? Who do you think her audience was?

Revising

Revising means questioning your draft, testing it to see how close it comes to your intention. Sometimes you may find that you cannot improve your draft. More often, however, you will discover that you can.

You can revise on both a large scale and a small scale. On a large scale you may add a whole new portion to a draft; for example, you may realize that you have left out an important link in the development of an idea or that a point you thought was minor actually ties everything else together. On a small scale you may **edit** your draft; that is, you may change sentence structure and wording.

Before you are finished with your paper, you should check for grammar, usage, capitalization, punctuation, and spelling. When you are satisfied with your work, you may need to prepare a final copy of it. Remember to spend some time **proofreading** the final copy, checking again for any mistakes in spelling or punctuation.

On rereading her discovery draft the writer spotted several small-scale problems of grammar, punctuation, and spelling. More important, she also saw that she needed to make a large-scale change. From her final sentence she discovered that what she really wanted to communicate was the feel of her breakthrough—her discovery of how to draw a nose. She revised her paragraph to focus on that moment:

FINAL VERSION

[1]My interest in drawing began with the face. [2]At the age of four, I began drawing balloon heads with round eyes, button noses, and U-shaped mouths. [3]I grew more skillful over the years, but one part of the face always stumped me: the nose. [4]I could not re-create on paper a three-dimensional nose. [5]Then one day five years ago I tried using a line for one edge of the nose bone and a softer shadow for the other edge. [6]Cleaning a smudge, I happened to erase the area down the middle. [7]I saw that I had created a highlight that made the bone stand out sharply. [8]I had finally drawn my first recognizable, three-dimensional nose. [9]That was the day I day I decided to become an artist.

After you have completed these final steps in the writing process, you will be ready to present your work to an audience. If you have used the writing process to say something that you really wanted to say, you will know the special satisfaction that comes from finally getting the ideas and the words just the way you want them.

EXERCISE 4 **Thinking About Revision.** Compare this revision with the draft on page 19, and write your answers to the following questions.

1. Find three small-scale changes in the revision. Why do you think the writer made these changes?
2. What specifically has the writer of this passage done to emphasize her "breakthrough"?

Writer's Choice

In this chapter you have seen how one writer used the writing process to say what she wanted to say. Now it is your turn. Choose one of the following assignments, and apply the writing process to your own ideas.

Writer's Choice #1

ASSIGNMENT   To write a paragraph about a hobby

LENGTH   Six to eight sentences

AUDIENCE   A friend

PURPOSE   To relate one interesting or amusing experience

PREWRITING   Prewrite by deciding which hobby you want to write about. Jot down an interesting or amusing incident that you experienced in connection with this hobby.

WRITING   Begin by identifying your hobby. Then relate your experience in the order in which it happened. End by saying how it affected your feelings about your hobby.

REVISING   Reread your draft to make sure that your reader can understand what happened and why it is worth remembering.

Writer's Choice #2

ASSIGNMENT   To write about something that seems unfair

LENGTH   Your choice

AUDIENCE   Your choice

PURPOSE   To explain what happened and why it was unfair

PREWRITING: Think about an unfair incident that involved you or someone you know. Decide what made the incident unfair.

WRITING   Begin by explaining who was involved in the incident and the circumstances that led to it. Then relate the incident as it happened. Tell why it seemed unfair.

REVISING   Imagine that you are your audience. Ask yourself whether the incident as you related it truly seems unfair to an "outsider." If not, you may need to add more information.

Writer's Choice #3

ASSIGNMENT   To write a paragraph on any subject

LENGTH   Your choice

AUDIENCE   Your choice

PURPOSE   Your choice

OPTIONS   You might use the photographs in the Writer's Sourcebook on pages 354–357 for writing ideas.
Be sure to jot down some prewriting notes before you actually begin to write your first draft.

CHAPTER 2

Prewriting: Main Idea and Support

Write from abundance.

—Donald Murray

Prewriting • **Writing** • *Revising*

Most writers will tell you that the hardest part of writing is getting past the blank page. Robert Benchley, an American humorist, once tried to break this barrier by rolling a sheet of paper into his typewriter and typing the following:

The

He took a little break, hoping that newer, better words would spring miraculously into his mind and onto the page. As you might guess, he hoped in vain. No one—not even the best writer—can write successfully in a vacuum.

Instead, write from abundance. That is, get yourself past the blank page by prewriting.

Prewriting is that part of the writing process in which you find an appealing writing idea and prepare to write about that idea.

Prewriting is the most open, least judgmental stage of the writing process. When you prewrite, you experiment with all kinds of ideas. You do not care about logic, neatness, or correctness. You care only about finding something that you truly want to say. You let your ideas flower where they will, and you see how deep into your imagination their roots go. Most important of all, you develop a *commitment* to your ideas—an excitement that will carry over into your writing and make your reader want to read more.

Prewriting helps you to face down that blank page. With just a little effort you will fill your page with notes, comments, questions, and opinions about various subjects. If you keep going, you will wind up with a focused idea and material supporting that idea.

How do you get there? Prewriting simply follows your natural thought processes, which move in a kind of spiral. First you circle a large area, scanning many different writing ideas. Then you focus on a few ideas. Then you look at one idea in more and more specific terms. Finally you zero in on what you want to say.

This chapter will divide prewriting into the following steps:

generating ideas
exploring subjects
focusing on a topic
forming a main idea
developing the main idea

In this chapter you will follow the prewriting activities of several writers preparing to write paragraphs, and you will prewrite for a few paragraphs of your own. Of course, you can use these prewriting activities to prepare to write longer works as well—for instance, essays, research papers, and stories. No matter what you are writing, always write from *abundance*. Fill your prewriting notes with possibilities, ideas, and questions. Whether or not you use all your notes, every scrap of prewriting will add color, depth, and breadth to your writing. Remember: As soon as you start prewriting, you have beaten the blank page.

Prewriting

GENERATING IDEAS
EXPLORING SUBJECTS
FOCUSING ON A TOPIC
FORMING A MAIN IDEA
DEVELOPING THE MAIN IDEA

Generating Ideas

Always write about something that makes you want to grab your pen, pencil, typewriter, or word processor. Never settle for anything less than an idea that intrigues you.

Potential writing ideas lurk everywhere—in your childhood memories and current hobbies, in what you see on television and hear in the classroom. Whenever your imagination touches the world, you create a writing idea. Spur your imagination to generate writing ideas by using the following techniques: **freewriting**, **brainstorming**, and **charting**. In the next few pages, you will experiment with each of these techniques to find out which ones work best for you. They may also help you to invent your own methods for getting started. As you experiment, be aware that you can practice generating ideas in at least two different ways:

You can work by yourself in a personal journal, or notebook.

You can work with another person or several other people in a small group, or conference.

Freewriting

Freewriting is writing done continuously for a specified, very brief period of time.

When you freewrite, you begin to write at a signal and do not lift your pen from the paper until the time is up. Just as exercise loosens your muscles, freewriting limbers your writing and gets it flowing. You set your mind sprinting for a few minutes and record your thoughts and free associations without any concern for logic, grammar, or eloquence.

Even if you begin your freewriting with a kind of verbal doodling, you will usually come up with an idea before very long. Look, for instance, at the following example of freewriting; it rambles and contains errors, but note how many ideas and associations thread through it:

FREEWRITING SAMPLE:
A WRITER LOOKING FOR A SUBJECT   (IDEAS SHADED)

I have to write for five minutes without stopping. I have no idea what I will say but I just have to keep going. How long have I written so far. Not even one minute. Seems longer. Time is relative--if I was trying to catch a bus the time would have been up long ago but since I have to keep writing for five minutes--OK, now get serious, have I said anything worthwhile yet? How about relativity. Space travelers who go through millions of light years and don't grow older while everone else they know on earth has died. Something like that. What about those stars that are so far away that they actually exploded long ago but we still see them. How about the opposite--a planet somewhere that sees earth as it was hundreds of years ago--an earth where Shakespeare is still alive? That's someone I'd like to meet. How about time travel? What would that be like? Beam me up Scotty.

As this writer found, freewriting can give you a running start when you have been asked to come up with a subject of your own and do not know where to begin. This writer now has several possible ideas to write about: relativity, space travelers, exploded stars, the earth as it was long ago, Shakespeare, and time travel. Later on he will choose one of these ideas to develop into a paragraph.

You can also use freewriting to discover approaches to more definite writing assignments or to work around a stumbling block in the writing process. For example, a student assigned a paragraph about her career goals discovered several ideas about this subject during a few minutes of freewriting. Again, the freewriting contains ideas as well as errors.

FREEWRITING SAMPLE:
A WRITER WITH A GENERAL SUBJECT

Career goals--I wanted to be a veterinarian. I know why--because I have always loved helping sick animals. That's simple, now what am I going to say in a whole paragraph? This all seems cut and dried. Think about what I really like about taking care of animals. I love animals, I always have. It's also such a challenge, to find what is wrong with animals, more than "human" medicine would be for me, because animals can't say what they feel, but it's more than that. It's like getting as close as a human can to nature with a big N. Animals are the real thing, they can't fake anything or deceive you, they show you just what they feel. But I just said that they can't tell you what they feel--does that make any sense? I need to think about that one.

EXERCISE 1 **Generating Ideas in Freewriting.** Take another look at the sample of freewriting by the writer interested in veterinary medicine. On your paper identify one possible writing idea in her passage.

EXERCISE 2 **Freewriting in Pairs.** Join another writer in freewriting on a subject of interest to both of you. Agree on a time to start, begin writing, and do not stop writing until the time is up—say, five minutes later. After you have finished, read what you have written, and list all the possible writing ideas that you find. (Any scrap of an idea counts as long as you justify it as a possible starting point for a paragraph.) Compare the ideas you developed from prewriting with the ideas that your partner developed. Save your notes for a composition that you will write later on.

Brainstorming

Like freewriting, **brainstorming** can help you generate ideas through free association.

Brainstorming takes a different form from freewriting. When you brainstorm, you do not write a constant stream of words; rather, you jot down your thoughts in any order, pausing whenever you like and writing disconnected phrases if you choose.

Different people feel comfortable with different formats for brainstorming. Some writers prefer orderly lists like the one shown here. This list was created by the writer who did the freewriting up above on the general subject of veterinary medicine. She started with one of her original ideas and then jotted down a few more:

BRAINSTORMING SAMPLE: LIST FORMAT

1. *getting close to Nature with a big N--human patients can hide their feelings; animals can't.*
2. *What kinds of people become vets (instead of "people" physicians)?*
3. *books by James Herriot*
4. *different types of veterinary medicine*
5. *What animals do I especially like to work with? (I think large animals)*
6. *special problems with helping small animals, different from those with helping large animals*
7. *What special experiences have I had? giving first aid to my pets, helping the calf with toothache, assisting at the colt's birth*

Other writers like to brainstorm in a more open format, with circles and lines that show connections between ideas. This kind of brainstorming may be referred to as **clustering**. Look at the following example of open-form brainstorming, or clustering, which was created by the writer who did the freewriting on page 24. Here he brainstormed on the subject of *time*:

CLUSTERING

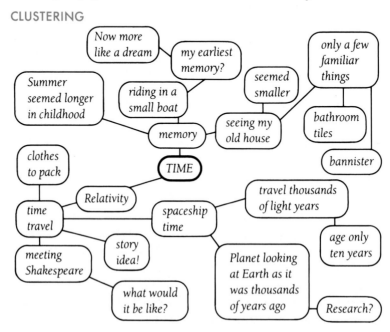

You can try freewriting first and then brainstorming, as these two writers did, but you have many other alternatives. You may find brainstorming more comfortable than freewriting, or you may find each one especially helpful for certain writing situations. You may brainstorm first and then freewrite on an idea that comes from your brainstorming. Experiment. Use what works best for you.

EXERCISE 3 **Brainstorming from a Photograph.** Choose a photograph from the Writer's Sourcebook (pages 353–383), and take ten minutes to brainstorm about it. Jot down in any format all the writing ideas that come to you. Be sure to indicate any connections between your writing ideas. Save your notes for a composition.

EXERCISE 4 **Generating Ideas by Brainstorming.** Choose one of the items listed here, or one idea that you came up with while you were freewriting for Exercise 2. Brainstorm for ten minutes on the idea, writing down any comments, issues, or questions that occur to you. Save your notes for a composition.

1. physical fitness
2. the environment
3. creativity
4. advertising slogans
5. social status
6. styles of comedy
7. television journalism
8. presidential politics
9. competitiveness versus cooperation
10. a bachelor's degree
11. today's heroes
12. differences between generations
13. the power of memory
14. city life versus suburban life
15. raising children
16. the twenty-first century
17. manned space travel
18. population control
19. foreign travel
20. professional sports

Charting

Charting helps you focus on specific life experiences in order to generate writing ideas.

Whenever you are asked to write on a subject of your choice, you can sort through your experiences for possible writing ideas by making the kind of chart that is on page 28. The left-hand column lists general areas of personal experience in which any writer might find writing ideas. The writer who completed this chart filled the middle column with specific examples of these experiences from her own life. Then in the right-hand column she noted writing ideas suggested by these instances.

SAMPLE CHART FOR GENERATING WRITING IDEAS

AREA OF EXPERIENCE	SPECIFIC INSTANCE	WRITING IDEA
Childhood Memories	• Halloween	• all-time best costume • history of Halloween
Family	• Aunt Marion • being the firstborn	• character sketch? • would I rather be the youngest?
Friends	• Andrea • John	• first impressions were deceiving! • character sketch?
Hobbies, Interests	• tennis • singing	• a psychological game • women's vs. men's tennis • barbershop harmony
Prized Possessions	• pine cone from Grandpop's childhood home always under the tree • faded jeans	• Christmas in 1910 and now • best way to fade jeans
Pet Peeves	• smoking in public places • biology class	• should it be banned? • other science electives should be available
Current Events	• election campaign	• political commercials • reforming the Electoral College
Interesting, Funny, or Infuriating Experiences	• planting tulip bulbs upside-down	• funny sketch?
Assigned Reading, Classwork	• history reading • Julius Caesar	• Roman Republic ends • compare play to real events
Leisure Reading, Newspapers, Magazines	• article on whales • Mary Renaults' The Nature of Alexander	• how whales raise their young • Alexander the Great--the greatest hero?
Television, Radio, Films, Records, Tapes	• Star Wars	• outgrowing Star Wars?? • funny ideas for sequels

EXERCISE 5 **Generating Ideas by Charting.** Create your own chart by drawing three columns like the preceding ones. In the left-hand column you can copy the entries used in the left-hand column in the model, or you can add or invent your own general entries. Fill the middle column in the chart with specific instances of your own. Then in the right-hand column list writing ideas suggested by these instances. Save your notes.

EXERCISE 6 **Compiling Your Writing Ideas.** Review the prewriting notes and writing ideas that you generated in Exercises 2–5 as you practiced freewriting, brainstorming, and charting. Evaluate your writing ideas, and star five that you think you may want to write about later.

Prewriting
GENERATING IDEAS
EXPLORING SUBJECTS
FOCUSING ON A TOPIC
FORMING A MAIN IDEA
DEVELOPING THE MAIN IDEA

Exploring Subjects

You have generated a number of possible writing ideas, some promising, some not so promising. However, you may not yet know exactly what you want to say. Now it is time to explore your most appealing writing ideas, or subjects, with the goal of focusing on a topic—the specific aspect of your subject about which you will write.

One of the best ways to explore a subject is to ask and answer specific questions about it. You may invent any questions of your own that seem appropriate to your subject. The following pages will give you an idea of the kinds of questions that you can use to explore a subject. Sometimes you might even try several different kinds of questions to explore a subject. Use these questions any way you like, but always adapt them to the subjects you have in mind.

Informational Questions

The most basic questions you can ask about any subject are those that reporters try to answer in writing their lead paragraphs for news stories: *Who? What? When? Where? How?* and *Why?* Reporters refer to these questions as the five *Ws* and *H.* Notice how on page 30 a writer adapted or expanded these questions to explore the subject of Alexander the Great, one of the subjects she had noted earlier in her "experience" chart.

INFORMATIONAL QUESTIONS TO EXPLORE A SUBJECT	SAMPLE ANSWERS
1. Who or what is my subject? *For human subjects:* What sort of person is my subject?	*Alexander the Great--brilliant general, king of Macedon, founder of a great empire. Imaginative, ambitious, brave; military genius. Thousands adored him. Physical beauty too--great charismatic eyes.*
2. What happened regarding my subject? What memorable incident(s) can I relate about my subject?	*Conquered most of the known world before he was 30. Combined Greek civilization with culture of East. When he was dying, his men asked when they should honor his memory; he said, "When you are happy." For centuries people remembered his golden funeral chariot.*
3. When did these events occur? In what way did my subject change over time?	*He lived 356-323 B.C., died at 32. Showed military gifts at 14; became a general by 20. Later adopted many Persian customs (Greeks of his time viewed Persians as barbarians).*
4. Where did all this happen?	*A. born in Macedon--mountainous, rough land north of Athens. His conquests spread from Egypt to India.*
5. How did it happen?	*He was fascinated with military history and learned strategy from it. He inspired his men by this fearlessness. They would follow him anywhere.*
6. Why did it happen?	*His father, Philip, was a great general--A. wanted to outdo him. A. also modeled himself on the Iliad's heroes.*
7. With whom or what can I compare my subject?	*Mythical heroes like King Arthur Great conquerors like Napoleon Young charismatic leaders like John F. Kennedy*

EXERCISE 7 **Exploring a Subject with Informational Questions.** Choose one subject that you starred in Exercise 6. Then adapt the informational questions from the preceding chart, and answer these questions. Save your notes.

Personal Questions

If you have had direct personal experience of your subject, you can explore it by asking questions like the ones presented here. The writer working with the subject of veterinary medicine used some of these questions to guide her thinking, as shown.

PERSONAL QUESTIONS TO EXPLORE A SUBJECT	SAMPLE ANSWERS
1. What are my own experiences of the subject?	*Many--most memorable: trying to give first aid to a parakeet; helping a calf with a toothache (my first success); assisting at a colt's birth.*
2. What sensations (sight, sound, smell, taste, touch) do I associate with the subject?	*Eyes of the calf in pain and the look of relief when I dripped oil of cloves on its gum; at the colt's birth--cold air, the smell of hay.*
3. What were my emotions during these experiences?	*When I helped the calf, I had a great sense of accomplishment. At the colt's birth I was scared and moved.*
4. What did I learn?	*That I had the ability to make animals trust me; that I would be happy helping animals the rest of my life.*
5. What problems did I have?	*It's always a little scary at first, when it's more difficult to get the animal to calm down and trust you. Also, I worry about pulling away from the human world!*

EXERCISE 8 **Exploring a Subject Through Personal Questions.** Choose one subject, either from the list you made in Exercise 6 or from the following list. Using a separate sheet of paper, explore the subject through personal questions. Save your notes.

1. a significant person from your childhood
2. from history or literature a person from whom you learned something
3. a possession that could symbolize your childhood
4. an item in contemporary life that you believe is vastly overrated
5. an item about which you have special and unusual knowledge
6. a place that has changed over time
7. a place that has always intrigued you
8. an experience in which you learned that your actions could make a difference or bring about some kind of change

Creative Questions

Sometimes you can find a specific writing topic by looking at a subject from an unconventional point of view. Here are some creative questions that you can ask about your subject. Notice how the writer who freewrote about time (page 24) used these questions to explore avenues to one subject he found—time travel.

CREATIVE QUESTIONS TO EXPLORE A SUBJECT	SAMPLE ANSWERS
1. What might be an unusual use for or way of looking at my subject? (For example, how might my grandfather, or an ancient Greek, or a Martian view it?)	• *Using time travel to rewrite history.* • *Think of time travel as a regular trip--get reservations, pack.* • *How would the ancient Greek view the time traveler? Time travelers would have to fit into any society of the past or future.*
2. What figures of speech involving my subject could I construct?	*Time travel--like ice skating on top of history (or is it like jumping off of a diving board into time?)*
3. What story, real or imagined, could revolve around my subject?	• *Getting destinations mixed up?* • *Also, look again at Mark Twain's Connecticut Yankee, who jumped from 19th C. America to King Arthur's Britain.*
4. How might my subject be represented in music or a painting?	*Music--bits from all periods, like spinning a radio dial.*
5. What might be funny about my subject?	*Maybe the idea of trying to pack for different eras--what the well-dressed time traveler must wear.*

EXERCISE 9 **Exploring a Subject Through Creative Questions.** Choose one of the subjects you listed in Exercise 6, or use the list below. Using a separate sheet of paper, explore the subject through creative questions. Review and respond to the questions in the chart above, and add some of your own creative questions if you wish. Save your notes.

1. food processors
2. newspapers
3. the Grand Canyon
4. automobiles
5. Mount Rushmore
6. standardized tests

Prewriting

GENERATING IDEAS

EXPLORING SUBJECTS

FOCUSING ON A TOPIC

FORMING A MAIN IDEA

DEVELOPING THE MAIN IDEA

Focusing on a Topic

Do you remember the prewriting spiral? You scan a broad subject area and gradually close in on a well-focused idea. You will be happy to know that you have already begun to close in on your well-focused idea, for exploring your most appealing subjects has helped you to isolate a few narrower topics within these subjects.

Now you are ready to focus on one of these topics and narrow its scope further so that you can write a paragraph about it. Keep in mind that a broad, aerial view of a topic will not show your readers anything new, since everyone sees the same hazy landscape from ten thousand feet. Try showing your readers the cracks on one blade of grass instead; they might see something they never saw before.

How do you choose a topic and then narrow it? Take a look at how one writer went about this task. Her original subject was Alexander the Great. On reviewing her exploring notes (page 30), she decided that she wanted to contrast Alexander with another great conqueror, Napoleon. She had moved from a broad subject to a narrower topic, but she realized that this topic needed to be still narrower. Then one dramatic difference between the two men struck her: Alexander died young, an undefeated conqueror, whereas Napoleon died in middle age, a defeated exile. By writing about each man's death, she saw that she could contrast the two conquerors in an interesting and yet focused way.

Here are two other examples in which writers began with broad subjects and narrowed them to topics that could be covered in a single paragraph. The techniques shown here are only two of the ones you might use.

TECHNIQUE	Use one incident to illustrate an idea.
BROAD SUBJECT	Veterinary medicine
NARROWER TOPIC	Getting close to nature by helping animals
STILL NARROWER	Helping a calf with a toothache
TECHNIQUE	Identify one problem, and solve it.
BROAD SUBJECT	Time travel
NARROWER TOPIC	Problems of time travel
STILL NARROWER	Clothes for the time traveler to wear

EXERCISE 10 **Narrowing Topics.** For each group of topics below, indicate in writing which one topic is the narrowest.

1. a. *Macbeth*—Shakespeare's greatest tragedy
   b. three hundred years of *Macbeth* productions
   c. an interpretation of Macbeth's "Tomorrow" speech

2. a. why the British lost the Revolutionary War
   b. the first hour of the Battle of Saratoga
   c. the military strategies of George Washington

3. a. air bags versus seat belts: pros and cons of each
   b. automobile safety
   c. how air bags work

4. a. why *Abbey Road* is the best album by the Beatles
   b. the Beatles' influence on popular music
   c. the evolution of the Beatles' music

EXERCISE 11 **Focusing on Your Topic.** Choose one of the subjects you explored in Exercises 7–9. Narrow it to a topic that you can cover in a paragraph. Save your written response.

Prewriting

| GENERATING IDEAS |
| EXPLORING SUBJECTS |
| FOCUSING ON A TOPIC |
| **FORMING A MAIN IDEA** |
| DEVELOPING THE MAIN IDEA |

Forming a Main Idea

Now that you have generated and explored several ideas and narrowed the scope of your topic, you are ready to form a **main idea** about your topic. You will give yourself more direction if you express that main idea in a complete sentence. However, before you can state your main idea, you must think about your **purpose**—the goal you hope to accomplish in writing—and your **audience**—the person or persons whom you expect to read your writing.

Thinking About Purpose

As you generated, explored, and narrowed ideas, you probably had some basis for making choices, some purpose at the back of your mind. Clarify that purpose by asking yourself the questions on the next page.

1. Why do I want to write about this particular topic?
2. Is my purpose to **inform** my readers of something or **explain** something to them?
3. Is my purpose to **persuade** them to change their minds about something or take some action?
4. Is my purpose to **amuse** or **entertain** them?
5. Is my purpose to **narrate** a story of some kind?
6. Is my purpose to **describe** something or someone?
7. Is my purpose some **combination** of these different goals? For example, do I want to entertain in order to persuade?
8. Do I have some other, more specific purpose in mind? For instance, do I want to narrate an incident in order to make my readers understand why I have made a particular decision?

The writer working on the topic of time travel found that he could pursue several alternative purposes, as shown here:

SUBJECT	NARROWED TOPIC	ALTERNATIVE PURPOSES
time travel	*clothes to wear for time travel*	• *to explain how one or two science-fiction writers have dressed their time travelers* • *to entertain readers with a light look at time-travel wardrobes* • *to describe a suit that would be appropriate for time travel*

EXERCISE 12 **Thinking About Purpose.** For each of the following topics, list two possible purposes that a writer could pursue.

1. learning how to use a computer
2. your first airplane ride
3. your favorite television program
4. the major types of students in your school
5. this week's clothing fad

Becoming Aware of an Audience

You always write for a particular audience—your intended reader or readers. You will eventually write for many different audiences: family, friends, business associates, government officials. In each case you will adjust what you say to suit your audience; for example, you will describe a business project one way in a letter to a friend and quite differently in an office memo.

The best writers develop a finely tuned awareness of their audience. They can anticipate how readers might react almost the way a speaker can sense the response of a live audience. The following questions will help you become more aware of your audience's identity, needs, and interests. Note the answers given by the writer treating the subject of veterinary medicine:

QUESTIONS ABOUT AUDIENCE	SAMPLE ANSWERS
1. Am I writing for the general public or for a special audience, such as a group of children or the readers of a professional journal?	*For a class assignment--so, a general audience. But it might be really interesting to write for an audience of children (I could add a note explaining).*
2. What in particular do I want to say to my audience?	*I'd want the children to see my experience with the calf as I did when I was 8--to understand how I felt when the calf trusted me. I'd want them to understand the joy I feel in working with animals.*
3. How much do my readers already know about my topic? What information will they need?	*Children wouldn't know anything technical, so I should just tell the story very simply.*
4. What areas of my topic are likely to interest them most?	• *how the calf looked* • *how I helped him* • *what he did* • *how I felt*
5. What ideas about my topic do they already have? What preconceptions and objections do I need to counteract?	*Probably none.*
6. What special techniques would help accomplish my purpose with this audience? For example, would humor be helpful?	*Tell the story moment by moment. No need for humor.*

EXERCISE 13 **Thinking About Audience.** For each of the topics below, identify in writing one appropriate audience.

1. special problems in using frogs' cells for research
2. how *not* to dissect a frog
3. a pollywog's diary
4. techniques for sautéing frogs' legs
5. the ancient Greek comic play *The Frogs*

Stating the Main Idea

Your work from this point on will be easier if you set down in a sentence your **main idea**—the thought that you plan to develop in your paragraph. Your main idea might be a statement of fact or an opinion; it might convey your impression of a scene or your insight about an experience. Written as a complete sentence, your main idea crystallizes your thinking on your topic. It will direct you when you write your paragraph.

Keep the following points in mind:

1. Your main idea should appeal to you and your audience.
2. Your main idea should make some point about your topic.
3. You should develop your main idea adequately in a paragraph.
4. Your purpose should be clear from your main idea.

In this chapter we have been following the prewriting progress of several writers. Take a look at the main ideas that emerged from their work:

ORIGINAL TOPIC	Alexander the Great
NARROWED TOPIC	Alexander's death and Napoleon's death
PURPOSE	To persuade
AUDIENCE	The general public
MAIN IDEA	Alexander the Great lived and died a legendary hero; Napoleon Bonaparte outlived his legend and then died in oblivion.
ORIGINAL TOPIC	Why I Want to Be a Veterinarian
NARROWED TOPIC	Helping a calf with a toothache
PURPOSE	To narrate
AUDIENCE	Children
MAIN IDEA	When I helped a calf through a toothache, I experienced a special closeness to nature—a closeness that "people doctors" never know.
ORIGINAL TOPIC	Time Travel
NARROWED TOPIC	Clothes for the time traveler
PURPOSE	To entertain
AUDIENCE	The general public
MAIN IDEA	Time travelers have a special problem: They need clothing that will be suitable for any period in history.

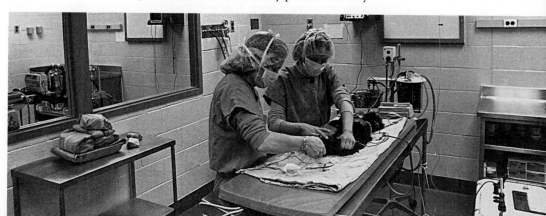

EXERCISE 14 **Reflecting Purpose and Audience in a Main Idea.** For each of the following topics, select one purpose and one audience. Then write a sentence that expresses a specific main idea about the topic. You may need to use various prewriting techniques to come up with your main idea. Be sure that your main idea reflects your choice of purpose and audience. In the example here the underlined words represent the purpose and audience chosen by one writer and the main idea written by that writer:

GENERAL TOPIC	The Super Bowl
PURPOSE	To persuade *or* to <u>narrate</u>
AUDIENCE	The President of the National Football League *or* a <u>high school football team</u>
MAIN IDEA	<u>Play by play, one of the most exciting Super Bowl games ever was the 1979 contest between the Dallas Cowboys and Pittsburgh Steelers.</u>
1. GENERAL TOPIC	My last summer [or part-time] job
PURPOSE	To entertain *or* to inform
AUDIENCE	The general public *or* a group of schoolchildren
2. GENERAL TOPIC	The films of Steven Spielberg [or those of another film-maker]
PURPOSE	To describe *or* to persuade
AUDIENCE	A group of film critics *or* a foreign exchange student

EXERCISE 15 **Forming Your Main Idea.** For the topic that you narrowed in Exercise 11 on page 34, list two possible purposes and two possible audiences. Then write two main ideas that you might develop in a paragraph.

Prewriting

GENERATING IDEAS

EXPLORING SUBJECTS

FOCUSING ON A TOPIC

FORMING A MAIN IDEA

DEVELOPING THE MAIN IDEA

Developing the Main Idea

The paragraph you will soon write will consist of more than a statement of your main idea: It will **develop** —express, prove, clarify, and expand upon—that main idea. You need to find *facts, details, examples, incidents,* and *reasons* that flesh out your main idea.

Your prewriting notes may already contain many of the items you need. In that case you may simply need to review your notes and choose relevant facts, details, examples, incidents, and reasons. On the other hand, you may need to add to your notes if they do not already contain many specific items supporting the main idea that you have formulated. You may even need to consult sources in order to check facts or find a few additional details.

Specific Support: Facts, Details, Examples, Incidents, Reasons

Specific support will ground your main idea in reality and will also give it the individual twist that only you can provide. When you review your prewriting notes searching for supporting items, you should look in particular for the following:

facts—objective statements that can be proved by experience, observation, or study

sensory details—concrete, specific features of an item or an experience

examples—particular cases or instances of a larger pattern

incidents—particular events

reasons—logical arguments used to support an opinion or interpretation

Here you see the support that one writer listed for her main idea of comparing the deaths of Alexander the Great and Napoleon. Note that she has used mostly facts to support her idea:

MAIN IDEA Alexander the Great lived and died a legendary hero; Napoleon Bonaparte outlived his legend and died forgotten.

SUPPORT Alexander died at thirty-two. [FACT]

Napoleon died at fifty-two. [FACT]

Alexander died at the height of his conquests. [REASON]

Napoleon died in defeat. [REASON]

Alexander died surrounded by adoring soldiers. [INCIDENT]

Alexander's last words, in response to his men, who asked when they should honor his memory: "When you are happy." [FACT]

Alexander's body was taken in a golden chariot to Alexandria, Egypt. [FACT]

Napoleon died alone, in exile, on the barren island of St. Helena, in the custody of a stern British governor. [INCIDENT]

Napoleon's last words: "I am dying before my time, murdered by the English oligarchy. . . ." [FACT]

EXERCISE 16 **Developing a Main Idea with Specific support.** Read the following notes on the subject of time travel. First identify in writing the *type* of support that each numbered item is: fact, sensory detail, example, incident, or reason. Then write two new items that you can add to support the main idea.

MAIN IDEA The time traveler has a special problem: He or she needs to wear clothing that will be suitable for any period in history.

SUPPORT

1. People in different times dressed very differently from the way we do.
2. Women in the Middle Ages wore elaborate headdresses and voluminous robes with many layers.
3. Men of ancient Greece wore short tunics.
4. Men in the eighteenth century wore knee breeches, elegant fitted tailcoats, and, often, wigs.
5. Contemporary clothes are more varied—in fact, might reflect past eras.
6. Clothes of poorer people tended to change less in earlier times; one solution might be to dress as a poor person.
7. Maybe an all-purpose garment could be designed—like a space suit.

EXERCISE 17 **Developing Your Main Idea with Specific Support.** For one of the main ideas that you formulated in Exercise 15, list at least five supporting items. Try to use as many different kinds of support—facts, incidents, sensory details, examples, and reasons—as you can.

Preparing to Write a First Draft

You may feel that *pre*writing is a strange term to apply to all the written work you have been doing in this chapter. Yet you should think of this work as your raw material for writing. You have generated writing ideas, explored them, narrowed them down to topics, formed main ideas, and found specific support to develop these main ideas. You should be ready now to shape that raw material into a first draft.

 Checklist for Prewriting

1. What writing ideas can I generate through such techniques as freewriting, brainstorming, and charting? Can I combine any of these techniques or alternate among them?
2. Would informational, personal, or creative questions or some combination of these kinds of questions work best to explore my subject? What topics within my subject can I identify by exploring it?
3. Which topic appeals to me most? How can I narrow that topic? Can I focus on one incident in a person's life, use one experience to illustrate something larger, or identify a problem in the subject and solve it? Would some other method work for narrowing my topic?
4. What is my purpose? Who is my audience? What main idea about my topic will accomplish my purpose and appeal to my audience?
5. What specific facts, sensory details, incidents, examples, and reasons can I use to develop my main idea?

The following three paragraphs grew from the prewriting work presented in earlier parts of this chapter. For each writer these various prewriting activities—generating ideas, exploring various subjects, narrowing a topic, and forming and developing a main idea—probably took no more than an hour or two. Having spent this time thinking about what they would say, the writers found themselves ready and eager to tackle their first drafts.

Notice how each paragraph draws on the abundance of the writer's prewriting notes. Notice also that each writer has not used every note that he or she has recorded, and that each added a few new thoughts in writing the draft.

CAREER GOALS: WHY I WANT TO BE A VETERINARIAN (FIRST DRAFT)

I think that veterinarians can feel a closeness to nature that doctors who treat humans can never know. I will never forget the first time I helped an animal in pain. I was only eight, but as soon as I saw the calf, I knew something was wrong. His eyes looked hot, and he jerked his head away when I touched his jaw. I wondered if he could be having a toothache. I had never realized that animals could get toothaches and other human problems. I ran to find the oil of cloves my grandmother used for my toothaches. I noticed that the calf's worst pain seemed to come in waves. So I waited as one of those passed, and then very carefully I brushed his mouth with the oil. I could smell the heavy, sharp odor of the cloves, mixed with the dried hay smell. Then the calf licked, and I somehow poured the whole bottle into his mouth. In a few minutes I could tell that the pain was going. His body relaxed and his eyes looked cooler and clearer. I stayed with my arms around him until he went to sleep. I matched my breathing to his heartbeat. He had never let me hold him for so long before.

WHEN IN ROME (FIRST DRAFT)

If time travel ever becomes possible, it will present tourists with many challenges. One of the more interesting problems will be what to wear. Time travelers will have to wear clothes that fit in with the styles of many periods in human history—especially those periods that made life difficult for nonconformists. Wary time travelers could buy out costume shops and build up wardrobes of clothes from all ages, heavy medieval gowns hanging side by side with Sumerian mantles and elegant eighteenth-century tailcoats. However, such clothes would probably not pack well, especially in eras before drycleaning, and at their best might not look very convincing next to the real thing. A better idea might be for social scientists to design one all-purpose garment suitable to most ages in history, just as physicians and engineers have designed suits for travel through space. A specially designed "time suit" would stand up to the wear and tear of time travel and still enable the time traveler to fit in anywhere—or rather, anytime.

ALEXANDER THE GREAT AND NAPOLEON (FIRST DRAFT)

Alexander the Great was only thirty-two years old when he died and at the height of his conquests. Napoleon Bonaparte was fifty-two, middle-aged, and defeated at last. He died in exile on the island of Saint Helena, a captive of his enemies, the English. Alexander died surrounded by his men. Thousands of rough Macedonian soldiers walked through his tent weeping openly to see their young general one last time. His men asked him when they should pay his memory honor, and he whispered, "When you are happy." His body was taken in a magnificent golden chariot to the city that still bears his name, Alexandria, where it was honored in a temple. Napoleon, on the other hand, died alone and was buried on Saint Helena under a tombstone with no name. He had complained in his will, "I am dying before my time, murdered by the English oligarchy." In one sense he was wrong: It was Alexander who died tragically before his time. Napoleon died, sadly, *after* his.

One by one, this chapter has given you practice in activities that prepare you to write. Now you can put all these skills together by doing one or more of the Writer's Choice assignments listed on the following pages. Please concentrate on prewriting, but, in addition, see how well you can channel your prewriting into a first draft and revision.

Writer's Choice

Writer's Choice #1

ASSIGNMENT In this chapter you have done many exercises to become acquainted with the elements of prewriting. To prepare this Writer's Choice, you will have to look back at your notes from various exercises in particular. The assignment is to write a paragraph using the main idea and the support that you listed in Exercises 15 and 17.

LENGTH Eight to ten sentences

AUDIENCE One of the audiences that you selected in Exercise 15

PURPOSE One of the purposes that you selected in Exercise 15

PREWRITING Review your prewriting notes from Exercises 6–9, 11, 15, and 17 in this chapter.

WRITING Make the statement of your main idea the first sentence of your paragraph. Then choose your strongest supporting items, and write sentences expressing each. Try to end your paragraph by making an interesting observation or drawing a conclusion.

REVISING Reread your paragraph to see if you have done justice to your writing idea and your prewriting efforts. If something in your notes would improve your paragraph, use it. Double-check grammar, spelling, capitalization, and punctuation.

Writer's Choice #2

ASSIGNMENT To write a character sketch of a person who stands out in a crowd

LENGTH Five to seven sentences

AUDIENCE A friend who does not know the person

PURPOSE To describe

PREWRITING First freewrite briefly about a few different people. Then choose the one who seems most interesting, and explore your subject using personal questions like those on page 31 or creative questions like those on page 32. Write down a main idea—your overall impression of this person—and list details that support this impression.

WRITING Begin by identifying your subject. Devote a few sentences to your subject's physical appearance. Then mention his or her main personality traits. End by giving your overall impression of the person. Be sure to stress the qualities—either physical or psychological—that make the person stand out.

REVISING Can you picture your subject from your description? If not, add the necessary details.

Writer's Choice #3

ASSIGNMENT To write letter about a local landmark or park that you think should be improved

LENGTH Ten sentences

AUDIENCE A member of your city council

PURPOSE To persuade

PREWRITING Decide on the place that you want improved. You might explore your subject with questions like the informational questions on page 30 or the personal questions on page 31. Then note the most important facts about the place, along with details about its present appearance. List at least two reasons why it needs special attention.

WRITING Begin by identifying the place. Then describe its current condition. Point out what the landmark adds to your community, and then give several reasons why you think it should be improved.

REVISING Make sure that your writing appeals to your audience.

Writer's Choice #4

ASSIGNMENT To write an account of a well-known historical event to which you have "time-traveled"

LENGTH Your choice

AUDIENCE Your choice

PURPOSE To narrate

OPTIONS You might brainstorm about a few historical events that you are currently studying in school.

You might combine a few informational, personal, and creative questions to explore your subject.

Decide on your audience, your purpose, and the main idea about your historical event.

Writer's Choice #5

ASSIGNMENT Your choice

LENGTH Your choice

AUDIENCE Your choice

PURPOSE Your choice

OPTIONS You might use one of the photographs in the Writer's Sourcebook on pages 353–357 as a source of ideas.

Use any technique to generate and explore ideas.

Be sure to decide on a purpose and audience and to develop one main idea.

Writers on Writing

An Eagle Scout, Eric White plans to major in history and study law. He wrote the following pieces as a student at Rangeview High School in Aurora, Colorado.

THE PRODUCT

Most people associate comic books with children and teenagers, but collecting comic books is a hobby that is becoming more and more popular among adults. Why? The chief reason for peaking adult interest in comic books is their rising value. Many comics from the 1950s and 1960s have appreciated a great deal. Three factors boost the value of a comic: the age of the book, the popularity of the characters in it, and the artist who created it. The challenge of finding a rare old comic book or of discovering a new one that may grow in worth over the years attracts many collectors.

In addition to their monetary value, comic books have an emotional appeal. Adults have discovered that comic books offer an escape from the real world. After a long day at work, a person can come home and tumble into the fantasy world of Spider-Man or Batman. So, collecting comic books adds to the possibility of future returns the thrill of instant psychological gratification.

THE PROCESS

This is Eric's own account of his prewriting process.

When I was first asked to write a paper and discuss my prewriting activities, I thought over a long list of topics. I considered writing about history but discovered that I would need much more space. Then I decided that if I wrote about one of my own hobbies, I could be sure of drafting a paper that had some good strong facts in it. I finally narrowed down my ideas to the topic of comic book collecting. I knew that I could write many things about this topic, so I began to taper it down. I made a list of what I knew about comic book collecting. One of my scribblings mentioned adults who collect comic books. Since I had noticed increasing adult interest in comics, I decided that this would be the focus of my paper. Then I made an outline and wrote my first draft. After two revisions I did a final draft, in which I just basically polished each sentence.

YOUR TURN   *Prewriting and Writing About a Hobby*

As Eric did, plan and write a paragraph or two about an interest of your own, using the prewriting activities you have practiced.

CHAPTER 3

Writing Paragraphs

Everybody my age had written a novel and I was still having difficulty writing a paragraph.

—Ernest Hemingway

Prewriting • *Writing* • *Revising*

Knowing how to create a good paragraph is one of the essential elements of the writer's craft. Suppose that the paragraphs were eliminated from a page you were reading. Would you still be able to read it? In the following passage the paragraphs have been run together. Where do you think each paragraph begins and ends?

1 No longer is an airport a place just outside of town to which travelers run
2 to catch a flight. We are in the era of the Airport World—an eerily quiet,
3 climate-controlled series of concrete caverns. Molded plastic chairs stare at
4 coin-operated television sets; doors careen open by themselves; escalators
5 never stop and conversations never start. Here at "Everywhere Interna-
6 tional," the human cargo numbly waits in line, looks for answers on too-
7 high screens, watches luggage disappear behind rubber-toothed curtains,
8 gets electronically frisked, is moving-sidewalked to buses or subways, is
9 directed by tape recordings to a telescoping sleeve, and finally is wedged
10 into a seat in a wide room which purports to be an airplane. But that is only
11 part of the experience of life at Everywhere International. Thanks to com-
12 puter-planned disconnecting flights, and to sales agents who demand the
13 passenger's presence at the airport long in advance of flight time, the
14 person inserting himself into the travel cocoon is encouraged to spend
15 enough time in the Airport World to browse in the gift shops, . . .peruse
16 the paperback racks, and enjoy an invigorating sauna and shoe shine in the
17 men's room. What's going on here? A bureaucrat's idea of the future is
18 going on, I submit, and submission is the name of the game. Most modern
19 airports are built by "authorities," quasi-governmental entities removed
20 from voter accountability. The guiding mission of the faceless authority is
21 supposed to be efficiency, but its passion is the expression of a social
22 manipulator's dream. This is no plea for the rinky-dink aerodrome, with
23 pilots in leather caps and goggles, without needed radar, meteorological
24 devices, and quick-opening air-sick bags. But I suggest that some urban
25 planners' idea of modernity is at least a generation behind the times.
26 Massive scale is now out; regimentation is out; while our dehumanizing
27 airport-builders have zigged, American society has zagged.

Whether you make three, four, or five paragraphs out of the preceding passage, you naturally group sentences together around a *main idea,* or *topic sentence,* and look for *development* of that sentence. You aim for *unity*—each sentence relating directly to the topic sentence. You look for *coherence*—sentences sticking together. You aim for clear *organization*—each sentence growing logically out of the preceding sentence. The author of this passage, journalist William Safire, began new paragraphs at lines 5, 10, 17, and 22.

A **paragraph** is a group of sentences that develops one main idea.

When you look at a page of a newspaper, a novel, or even a personal letter, you see immediately that the sentences are grouped into paragraphs. You assume that the paragraphs are separated from one another for good reasons, and you expect the paragraphs to make your reading easier. As the novelist Ernest Hemingway suggests in the quotation at the head of this chapter, a good writer knows that good paragraphs are fundamental.

This chapter is designed to make you even more alert to the qualities of good paragraphs and, of course, to help you write some good ones yourself. In this chapter you will be focusing on one stage of the writing process, but you will actually be producing complete paragraphs. These are the concerns that you will concentrate on at this stage of the writing process:

    topic sentences
    developing a topic sentence into a paragraph
    writing a unified paragraph
    writing a coherent paragraph
    organizing a paragraph

Writing Paragraphs

TOPIC SENTENCES
DEVELOPING A TOPIC SENTENCE INTO A PARAGRAPH
WRITING A UNIFIED PARAGRAPH
WRITING A COHERENT PARAGRAPH
ORGANIZING A PARAGRAPH

Topic Sentences

A **topic sentence** states the main idea of a paragraph and points the direction for the other sentences to follow.

For the reader a topic sentence makes the main idea immediately clear and the supporting sentences easier to follow. In other words, a topic sentence is actually a useful summary, or generalization. Consider the underlined topic sentence in the following example of a paragraph.

Many people shopping for a car base their decision primarily on style. Car customers readily admit that a worthwhile automobile must get good mileage. These same poeple also agree that safety and reliability are important considerations for any model they might purchase. Sales analyses reveal, however, that in fact the average car buyer weighs the looks of an automobile more than any other feature.

Not every paragraph needs a topic sentence. You probably noticed that the second and third paragraphs in the model on page 46 do not have topic sentences. In general, narrative paragraphs, those that tell a story, do not have a topic sentence. Expository paragraphs, those that inform, also may not have a topic sentence. The specifics of an expository paragraph may speak for themselves so clearly that they do not need a generalization to accompany them. Yet even though professional writers do not always use topic sentences, you should be aware of how helpful they are to readers.

Some topic sentences are definitely better than others; that is, they are clearer, more direct, and more useful for organizing the paragraph. For example, look again at the paragraph about cars, and compare the following two topic sentences:

TOPIC SENTENCE A   Many people shopping for a car base their decision primarily on style.
TOPIC SENTENCE B   Buying a car is hard.

Why is sentence A a better topic sentence? Consider the questions and the sample answers on the following checklist:

 Checklist for Evaluating Topic Sentences

1. What is the one main idea presented by the topic sentence?

Sentence A presents one main idea—the importance of style. Sentence B also presents one main idea—the difficulty of buying a car.

2. Is the topic sentence an over-generalization; that is, does it make a statement too broad to be really useful in understanding the paragraph?

Sentence A is a summary, or generalization, about the specific topic to be discussed in the paragraph. Sentence B, however, is an overstatement; it is much broader than necessary.

3. Do all of the other sentences in the paragraph take their direction and focus from the topic sentence?

Only sentence A, not sentence B, gives a strong direction to the specific content of the other sentences in the paragraph.

Variety of Topic Sentences

Like all sentences, topic sentences should be appropriate to audience and purpose. Most topic sentences are declarative, or statement, sentences. Some topic sentences, however, may take the form of questions.

A QUESTION AS THE TOPIC SENTENCE

Are you aware that to many car buyers style is more important than other factors? Car customers readily admit that a worthwhile automobile must get good mileage. These same people also agree that safety and reliability are important considerations for any model they might purchase. Sales analyses reveal, however, that, in fact, the average car buyer weighs the looks of an automobile more than any other feature.

Be aware, also, that a topic sentence can be two sentences long. It may be a question *and* an answer. Depending on your audience and your purpose, you may sometimes simply want to reword one sentence into two.

TWO-SENTENCE VERSION

Many people shopping for a car have a surprising criterion in mind. They look for style. Car customers readily admit that a worthwhile automobile must get good mileage. These same people also agree that safety and reliability are important considerations for any model they might purchase. However, sales analyses reveal that, in fact, the average car buyer weighs the looks of an automobile more than any other feature.

EXERCISE 1 **Writing a Variety of Topic Sentences.** Choose a topic of your own or one of the topics below, and write two different topic sentences for a paragraph—one statement and one question. Identify your purpose—such as to inform, persuade, entertain, narrate, or describe.

1. old movies   2. new fashions   3. voting   4. choosing a career

Placement of Topic Sentences

A topic sentence at or near the beginning of a paragraph immediately captures the reader's attention and alerts the reader to what is to come. When the topic sentence appears in the middle of a paragraph, it can unite the sentences that come before and after it. When placed at the end of a paragraph, it can summarize the specifics of the paragraph, serving as a clincher sentence to ensure that the reader has a firm grasp of your idea.

TOPIC SENTENCE IN THE MIDDLE

Car customers readily admit that a worthwhile automobile must get good mileage. These same people also agree that safety and reliability are important considerations for any model they might purchase. Many people shopping for a car nevertheless base their decision primarily on style. Sales analyses reveal that, in fact, the average car buyer weighs the looks of an automobile more than any other feature.

TOPIC SENTENCE AT THE END

Car customers readily admit that a worthwhile automobile must get good mileage. These same people also agree that safety and reliability are important considerations for any model they might purchase. Sales analyses reveal, however, that, in fact, the average car buyer weighs the looks of an automobile more than any other feature. In short, many people shopping for a car base their decision primarily on style.

EXERCISE 2 **Placing Topic Sentences.** Choose a paragraph from the passage about airports, on page 46. Indicate the topic sentence. Then move the topic sentence, rewording it if necessary, so that it appears in a different position—at the beginning, in the middle, or at the end. In a sentence or two describe the effect that the change has on the paragraph.

Writing Paragraphs

| TOPIC SENTENCES |
| DEVELOPING A TOPIC SENTENCE INTO A PARAGRAPH |
| WRITING A UNIFIED PARAGRAPH |
| WRITING A COHERENT PARAGRAPH |
| ORGANIZING A PARAGRAPH |

Developing a Topic Sentence into a Paragraph

Developing a topic sentence into a complete paragraph gives substance and fullness to your writing. One star on a team cannot win a championship without the support and participation of the other team members.

Developing means expressing more fully, proving, clarifying, and expanding upon your main idea, or generalization. In short, developing means supporting the generalization with specifics. Four of the most common kinds of support—or methods of development—for a topic sentence are (1) concrete details, (2) examples or incidents, (3) facts or statistics, and (4) reasons.

By prewriting one writer created a list of items about a summer vacation. Then, by placing the items into four smaller groups—one group for each kind of support—the writer was able to come up with four different main ideas about that vacation.

CONCRETE DETAILS

the fineness of the sand at Amagansett that summer
our clattering old jalopy
tire tracks in the sand
building sand castles
the extra-salty surf
no fog, no sunburn
pollution
sounds: squeaky sand, rolling waves, happy babies
local net fishing

MAIN IDEA The sand and surf were special that summer.

EXAMPLES OR INCIDENTS

the Fourth of July
the clambake
the spectacular burning of the *Vicki*
the Coast Guard in action
the marathon volleyball game
private fireworks on Bastille Day
fire at the Big House—almost a disaster

MAIN IDEA We saw spectacular fires that summer.

FACTS OR STATISTICS

the glorious summer weather—eighty degrees
the Weather Bureau report
the high price of gas that summer
ten percent fewer tourists than usual

MAIN IDEA The beach was different that summer.

REASONS

a great bunch of friends
memories of the beach at night
vacation reading

MAIN IDEA I would not hesitate to return to Amagansett.

After placing the support into the four different groups, the writer was able to compose four different paragraphs, each of which contains a strong *topic sentence* and a number of effective *supporting sentences*.

Development with Concrete Details

In the following model the writer used a strong topic sentence to state a main idea that encompasses several of the items on the prewriting list, particularly the items about sand and surf. The topic sentence is developed with concrete details to make us feel, see, hear, and even taste the beach that summer. Because we live in a physical world, we are all especially attracted to words that describe the feel, appearance, sound, smell, and taste of our world.

> The sand and surf at Amagansett that summer possessed a very special quality. The sand was finer than usual, or so it seemed, but was crisply punctuated more than ever by tire tracks from the haul seiners (net-fishing locals). The tracks were a series of small mounds that would crumble underfoot but squish delightfully as they fell between the toes. The fineness of the sand may have caused the surprising squeakiness that greeted each footstep and made each baby gurgle in delight. Even the surf itself seemed different—more friendly, more playful, and curiously more salty.

EXERCISE 3 **Developing a Topic Sentence with Concrete Details.** Write a paragraph using concrete details to develop the following topic sentence, or write on a topic of your own choosing. Be sure to read over and revise your paragraph after you have written it.

The weather last summer made our neighborhood seem like the landscape of some distant planet.

SUGGESTED DETAILS

SIGHT gray air, motionless clouds, shimmering heat, no people, withered grass

SOUND muffled noises, fire alarms, insects

SMELL air pollution; acrid, smoky, slight breezes

TOUCH hot air, perspiration, sunburn, dust

TASTE thirst, cool water, ice cream

Development with Examples or Incidents

In the following paragraph the writer selected from the prewriting list two incidents with something in common—fire. The incidents reveal the spectacular qualities of two fires. An example, incident, or anecdote can help a reader not only understand the main idea but *feel* it as well.

I will never forget the fires at Amagansett that summer. First, there was the offshore July Fourth bonfire, visible for miles to sun worshipers who lined the shore. What made this bonfire unusual was that its fuel was a fifty-five-foot pleasure craft named *Vicki*. Smoke had been noticed in the electrical wiring system, and eventually fire and spectacular explosions awed those on the beach until the Coast Guard used its firehoses to sink *Vicki*. Later that month—on Bastille Day—vacationers witnessed one more special event, the private fireworks at a celebrity's beach house. The fireworks were misdirected and came down on the house instead of in the dunes. Again public servants came to the rescue. This time the fire department hosed down the area, preventing a possible disaster.

EXERCISE 4 **Developing a Topic Sentence with Examples or Incidents.** Write a paragraph using examples or incidents to develop the following topic sentence, or develop a topic sentence of your own. Be sure to read over and revise your paragraph after you have written it. Remember that the sentences you use to develop your paragraph should take their direction and focus from the topic sentence.

Following the crowd creates many advantages [or disadvantages].

SUGGESTED EXAMPLES AND INCIDENTS
a time when a crowd gives a feeling of security
a time when we need the support of friends
an event that shows the practical results of teamwork
a crowd that robs a person of a sense of responsibility
a time when a crowd cannot break a routine

Development with Facts or Statistics

In the following paragraph the writer chose several specific facts and statistics from the prewriting list. A **fact** is a statement that has been proved by experience, observation, or study. **Statistics** are one particular kind of fact—precise numerical information. Here the writer uses facts and statistics to develop the main idea that special conditions made that summer seem different.

The beach at Amagansett seemed different that summer. Because gasoline prices had soared to well over a dollar, the summer community decreased a good ten percent. The high cost of transportation made the beach almost a private retreat. The beach also seemed different because of the clear air. The fog that most vacationers expect to battle every summer never materialized, being replaced by one glorious weekend after the next. The Weather Bureau report confirmed our feeling: Fewer storms occurred that summer, and the temperature was generally a comfortable eighty degrees.

EXERCISE 5 **Developing a Topic Sentence with Facts or Statistics.** Write a paragraph using facts or statistics to develop a topic sentence of your own or one of the following.

1. Nutrition in America is better than ever, or worse than ever.
2. Establishing a space station is a much more formidable task than is landing on the moon.
3. Americans are inventing more and more unusual uses for their increased leisure time.

Development with Reasons

In the following paragraph the writer developed the topic sentence with several reasons to support the main idea. Why would the writer return? The people, the memories, and the environment itself provide powerful reasons. By the end of the paragraph, the topic sentence has not merely been restated: It has been *developed*.

> I would not hesitate to return to Amagansett. The summer I spent there was definitely one of the most wonderful vacations I ever had. Why? The people, of course, are the number one reason. The friends I made that summer are still my closest ones. Other memories, too, draw me back: walking on the unusually fine sand, listening to the gulls, celebrating the Fourth of July, sitting on the beach at night. I even recall the books I read that summer and how much I enjoyed them. The place itself seemed to be a perfect spot not only for getting in touch with nature but also for letting my imagination fly.

EXERCISE 6 **Developing the Topic Sentence with Reasons.** Write a paragraph using reasons to develop the following topic sentence.

_____ is the one place on earth I would most like to visit.

You may want to consider some of the following reasons: what I would do there, what I would see there, memories I have of the place, why the place is different from all other places, the people who live there. Keep the details of your paragraph pointed toward your topic sentence. Be sure to reread and revise your paragraph after you have written it.

Writing a Concluding Sentence

A well-developed paragraph often needs more than a strong topic sentence and sufficient supporting sentences. To be truly effective, a paragraph often requires a good concluding sentence. A strong concluding sentence gives the reader a sense of finality. It can clinch an argument, restate the idea of the topic sentence, announce a conclusion or decision, give a personal opinion, or ask a question. The result for the reader is a satisfying feeling that a main idea has been expressed, supported, and given clear boundaries. The reader now moves on.

Notice the different kinds of concluding sentences that can be used with the paragraph about cars.

CLINCHING AN ARGUMENT

Many people shopping for a car base their decision primarily on style. Car customers readily admit that a worthwhile automobile must get good mileage. These same people also agree that safety and reliability are important considerations for any model they might purchase. <u>Sales analyses reveal, however, that, in fact, the average car buyer weighs the looks of an automobile more than any other feature.</u>

RESTATING THE TOPIC SENTENCE

Many people shopping for a car base their decision primarily on style. Car customers readily admit that a worthwhile automobile must get good mileage. These same people also agree that safety and reliability are important considerations for any model they might purchase. <u>These people, however, still put subjective looks before objective statistics.</u>

Here are a few other examples of how that paragraph could be concluded:

ANNOUNCING A CONCLUSION OR DECISION

. . . Considering sales analyses, however, car manufacturers realize there are advantages to promoting a car's looks.

GIVING A PERSONAL OPINION

. . . I know that for most of my friends, however, the sleekness of a car is the most important factor.

ASKING A QUESTION

. . . Are mileage, safety, and reliability the final determining factors, however?

EXERCISE 7 **Writing Closing Sentences.** The closing sentence has been deleted from the following paragraph. Indicate in writing which of the three sentences given after the model would make the best closing sentence, and give at least two clear reasons for your choice.

When, in the last act of *The Tempest,* Shakespeare's Miranda sees for the first time the group of men shipwrecked on her father's island, and exclaims: "O brave new world/That has such creatures in't," she speaks as sincerely and ingenuously as only a child can. But the phrase "brave new world" now carries negative connotations; Aldous Huxley's remarkably effective literary treatment of the world of the then-future—our present—has turned that phrase into a synonym for a mechanized, dehumanized universe. Today we find ourselves asking how long the world and the people who inhabit it can exist. If we don't blow ourselves to pieces in one last foolish display of fireworks, we may well achieve the same results by failing to recognize and cope successfully with our self-willed ecological crisis. We no longer hope for a return to paradise. . .

—Margaret Mead

CLOSING SENTENCE A But what kind of world are we willing to settle for?

CLOSING SENTENCE B We are willing to settle for survival in a reasonably healthy environment.

CLOSING SENTENCE C Our lowered expectations may make us more realistic than Miranda, but they may also make it more difficult to improve the world in which we live.

Writer's Choice

Writer's Choice #1

ASSIGNMENT   Write a topic sentence on a topic of your own choice or use one of the following topics. Use concrete details to develop the topic sentence into a paragraph.

the North Pole   an egg   a thunderstorm
an armadillo   a flower   a dancer

LENGTH   Five to seven sentences

AUDIENCE   Your class

PURPOSE   To describe

PREWRITING   List concrete details that apply to your topic, and group them according to the senses.

WRITING   Develop your topic sentence by writing at least one sentence using concrete details based on each of the senses. Write an effective concluding sentence that does one of the following: restates the topic sentence, clinches an argument, announces a conclusion or decision, gives a personal opinion, or asks a question.

REVISING   Make sure that each detail is clear, specific, and directly relevant to your topic. Make sure that each noun, verb, and adjective is the exact word you want.

Writer's Choice #2

ASSIGNMENT   Using examples, facts, or reasons, write one paragraph developing a topic sentence of your own or one of the following topic sentences:

Making decisions becomes more difficult as we age.
Making mistakes is an essential part of education.
Making movies is more complicated now than ever.

LENGTH   Your choice

AUDIENCE   Your choice

PURPOSE   To state and support your opinion

OPTIONS   Begin with a topic sentence that states your opinion directly. Decide which method of development you will use, and include only those sentences that use that method. Draw from experience, discussions, or reading.

Writer's Choice #3

ASSIGNMENT   Write one paragraph on a subject of your own choice, or choose one of the following subjects: *music, mammals, movies, minnows, Mayans, Manitoba*. Choose your own length and identify your audience and purpose.

Writing a Unified Paragraph

The composer Wolfgang Amadeus Mozart was said to be able to hear an entire symphony in his mind before he sat down to write it. His composition was unified before a note of it was put on paper. Most of us, however, need to work at creating unity.

A **unified paragraph** is a paragraph in which all the sentences belong together and develop one main idea.

After you have written a topic sentence, you continue the writing process by drafting additional sentences *directly related* to the topic sentence. Each sentence should be relevant to the main idea in the topic sentence.

Which of the following model paragraphs is unified?

PARAGRAPH A

In *The Revenge of the Pink Panther,* Peter Sellers stars once again as the expert in *gaffes,* Inspector Clouseau, whose armored ineptitude periodically drives Herbert Lom, as his boss, into mental institutions. The story is by Blake Edwards. He also directed the picture. The result is familiar and amusing.

—*The New Yorker*

PARAGRAPH B

You have to let Mel Brooks's comedy, *Young Frankenstein,* do everything for you, because that's the only way it works. Mary Shelley, who wrote the original story about Frankenstein, was married to the famous poet, Percy Bysshe Shelley. If you accept the silly, zizzy obviousness of the movie, it can make you laugh helplessly. Gene Wilder is the old Baron's scientist-grandson. Peter Boyle is the new Monster, and Madeline Kahn is the scientist's fiancee, who becomes the Monster's bride. The picture is in black and white, which holds it visually close to the film it takes off from. Black and white has generally not been used effectively since color was introduced in the earlier part of the century. It's Brooks's most sustained piece of moviemaking—the laughs never let up.

—*The New Yorker* (with underlined sentences added)

Paragraph B is not unified because the two underlined sentences do not relate directly to the main idea of the paragraph. They are interesting, and they may make excellent sentences in other paragraphs. Here, however, they draw the reader's attention away from the main idea—one director's achievement in a particular movie.

As you write, remember that unity is largely a matter of maintaining your concentration so that your readers will be able to do the same. Keep your sentences on track—the one track laid down by your topic sentence.

 Checklist for Writing a Unified Paragraph
1. How does each supporting sentence relate to the topic sentence?
2. If a sentence is not related to the topic sentence, should I delete it, revise the topic sentence, or save the sentence for another paragraph?

EXERCISE 8 **Writing a Unified Paragraph.** Write a unified paragraph on any topic you choose, or use one of the following topics.

1. communication among animals
2. different kinds of courage
3. trees in our area
4. the value of laughter
5. styles of singing
6. famous monuments

In your prewriting pay special attention to identifying those ideas directly related to your topic. When you revise, make sure each sentence is directly related to the main idea expressed in the topic sentence.

Writing Paragraphs
TOPIC SENTENCES
DEVELOPING A TOPIC SENTENCE INTO A PARAGRAPH
WRITING A UNIFIED PARAGRAPH
WRITING A COHERENT PARAGRAPH
ORGANIZING A PARAGRAPH

Writing a Coherent Paragraph

When you concentrate on writing a unified paragraph, you concern yourself with the relevance of each individual sentence. When you concentrate on writing a coherent paragraph, you concern yourself with the way each individual sentence is connected to the sentences around it.

A **coherent paragraph** is a paragraph in which the sentences are clearly and logically connected to one another.

Notice how in the following model Ernest Hemingway ties his individual sentences together. As the connecting lines and arrows indicate, he uses repeated words, pronoun references, and transitions to create a coherent paragraph.

It was wonderful to walk down the long flights of stairs knowing that I'd had good luck working. I always worked until I had something done and I always stopped when I knew what was going to happen next. That way I could be sure of going on the next day. But sometimes when I was starting a new story and I could not get it going, I would sit in front of the fire and squeeze the peel of the little oranges into the edge of the flame and watch the sputter of blue that they made. I would stand and look out over the roofs of Paris and think, "Do not worry. You have always written before and you will write now. All you have to do is write one true sentence. Write the truest sentence that you know." So finally I would write one true sentence, and then go on from there. It was easy then because there was always one true sentence that I knew or had seen or had heard someone say. If I started to write elaborately, or like someone introducing or present-ing something, I found that I could cut that scrollwork or ornament out and throw it away and start with the first true simple declarative sentence I had written. Up in that room I decided that I would write one story about each thing that I knew about. I was trying to do this all the time I was writing, and it was good and severe discipline.

—Ernest Hemingway, *A Moveable Feast*

By using the same word in two sentences, or by using words with the same meanings, you can forge strong connections between sentences.

Remember, however, that you must use repetition carefully. If you over-use it, your reader may become bored or consider your writing too simplis-tic. Use synonyms to introduce some variety while maintaining the con-nections between sentences.

Use pronouns to refer to a word, a group of words, or an idea that appears in a preceding sentence.

Up in that room I decided that I would write one story about each thing that I knew about I was trying to do this all the time I was writing, and it was good and severe discipline.

Transitional words create coherence by making the movement from one sentence to another clear, smooth, and easy to follow. Transitions help the reader follow your train of thought and show how you are progressing from one idea to the next. Here are some of the most familiar transitions:

TRANSITIONS THAT SHOW TIME

after	finally	immediately	meanwhile	soon
always	first	last	now	then
before	following	later	sometimes	until

TRANSITIONS THAT SHOW PLACE

above	beneath	horizontally	opposite	there
ahead	down	inside	outside	under
around	far	near	over	vertically
below	here	next to	parallel	within

TRANSITIONS THAT SHOW ORDER OF IMPORTANCE

at first	former	latter	second
first	last	primarily	secondarily

TRANSITIONS THAT SHOW CAUSE AND EFFECT

as a result	consequently	so	therefore
because	for that reason	so that	

TRANSITIONS THAT SHOW COMPARISON AND CONTRAST

but	in the same way	on the other hand	similarly
however	like	on the contrary	unlike

TRANSITIONS THAT SHOW EXAMPLES

for example	for instance	namely	that is

 Checklist for Writing a Coherent Paragraph

1. What can I do to connect all the sentences clearly and logically?
2. Which words can I repeat while still giving my sentences sufficient variety? What synonyms can I use?
3. Are all the pronouns absolutely clear?
4. What are the best possible transitions to use in order to tie the sentences together?

EXERCISE 9 **Identifying Kinds of Transitions.** Reread the paragraph by Ernest Hemingway on page 60. Identify each kind of transition the writer uses.

EXERCISE 10 **Using Transitions to Achieve Coherence.** Write a newspaper story consisting of three short coherent paragraphs. Use the items of information in the following prewriting list as the basis for your paragraphs. Use a total of at least six different transitions to achieve coherence. Be sure to reread and revise your paragraphs.

PREWRITING LIST

Joe Kittinger completed the first solo balloon flight across the Atlantic.

Joe landed on September 18, 1984.

Joe is an American.

The balloon was ten stories tall.

The balloon was silver and blue.

The balloon was named the *Rosie O'Grady.*

The balloon was filled with helium.

Joe took off from Caribou, Maine.

Joe planned to land in France.

Joe flew 3,535 miles.

Joe was in the air nearly eighty-four hours.

The balloon was blown off course.

Joe landed the balloon in northwest Italy.

Joe broke the record for solo balloon flight distance.

The previous record was 2,475 miles.

Ed Yost of South Dakota set the previous record.

Joe Kittinger broke his ankle.

Joe said the broken ankle was a small price to pay.

Joe said, "You just have to go for it. That's the American way."

Six other people have made the solo attempt.

Two died trying to solo across the Atlantic in a balloon.

—Information from *The New York Times*, September 19, 1984

EXERCISE 11 **Writing a Coherent Paragraph.** Write a coherent paragraph on a topic of your own choice, or choose one of the following topics.

1. how to break a routine
2. foolproof ways to study for tests
3. what makes a joke funny
4. my most embarrassing moment

In your paragraph use and identify at least one example of *repeated words or synonyms* and one example of *pronoun reference* and use at least two *transitions*. Reread and revise your paragraph.

Writing Paragraphs

TOPIC SENTENCES
DEVELOPING A TOPIC SENTENCE INTO A PARAGRAPH
WRITING A UNIFIED PARAGRAPH
WRITING A COHERENT PARAGRAPH
ORGANIZING A PARAGRAPH

Organizing a Paragraph

To produce a unified and coherent paragraph, you must make sure that all the sentences are related to the main idea and are connected to one another. To produce a well-organized paragraph, make sure that the sentences are presented according to a clear, logical plan of development.

A **well-organized paragraph** is one in which the sequence of sentences is logical and orderly.

The reader of such a paragraph can sense your thoughts flowing without interruption toward a clearly established goal. As a result, the reader develops confidence in you as a writer and as a thinker.

Which of the following two paragraphs is well organized?

PARAGRAPH A

Poets are often quite able to do rough work and to earn their living in ordinary ways. John Masefield was an able seaman. William Henry Davies was a cattleman and a tramp. Ralph Hodgson was a dog expert and boxing authority. Robert Frost worked in mills and farmed for years.

PARAGRAPH B

Farmers and millworkers are not always famous poets or literary lights. Robert Frost was all three at one time or another, however. Masefield, Davies, and Hodgson were not farmers or millworkers necessarily, but, at one time or another, they also did rough work or were interested in sports.

Why is Model A easier to follow than Model B? The sentences in Model B weave back and forth, never revealing a clear organization. Is the writer talking about farmers or millworkers or poets? The reader cannot tell.

Chronological Order

Chronological order is time order, the order in which we say events take place in the real world.

Ever since people began telling stories, chronological order has been the most satisfying way in which to relate an event, summarize an incident, or organize a narrative. The model on the next page uses chronological order.

At first I attacked the brontosaurus with all my strength. For a long time my efforts did not seem to make much difference to the brontosaurus. Finally the creature opened his jaws and was about to put an end to me. At that moment I realized I had to change my plan. I ran back toward the cliff and lured the huge monster after me. I placed myself in just the right spot. Then the brontosaurus charged. I stepped aside, and the creature toppled over the cliff.

EXERCISE 12 **Using Chronological Order.** Write a paragraph on a topic of your own choice, or use one of the following topics.

1. a football game
2. making a great hamburger
3. a hero's adventure
4. boarding an airplane
5. passing a bill in Congress
6. a day in the life of a _____

7. building a birdhouse
8. sailing a boat
9. a picnic
10. a school trip
11. climbing a mountain
12. making breakfast

Follow the prewriting, writing, and revising process, and use chronological order. Make sure that the order of events is clear.

Spatial Order

Spatial order is order in terms of space.

Spatial order has one basic rule: Always make sure your reader knows where you stand. Are you in one spot looking at something? Are you moving through or away from something? Let your reader know your *position* and your *direction,* as this writer does as she reveals the interior of a jeweled Easter egg:

> The first [Fabergé Easter egg] was made for Alexander III as an Easter gift for his wife, Maria Feodorovna, probably in 1886. It was a relatively simple white-enameled gold shell which opened to reveal a matte gold yolk containing a nest of gold straw. On the straw sat an enameled gold hen. When the beak of the hen is lifted, the body opens. Originally, hidden inside was a tiny replica of the Imperial crown which, itself, contained a ruby pendant. The crown and pendant have since disappeared. That magnificent gift began a fashion and tradition among the wealthy which lasted until the Russian revolution.
>
> —Erica Brown

The writer remains on the outside looking in. Yet she allows us to penetrate the egg. The shell opens to reveal the yolk; the yolk contains a nest; on the nest is a hen; inside the hen is a crown; within the crown is a ruby. The example on the next page shows the confusion that results from letting the paragraph fall into spatial *disorder.*

FAULTY MODEL

The egg consisted of an enameled gold hen on a bed of straw. There was a ruby pendant inside a replica of the Imperial crown. The bed of straw was contained in a matte gold yolk. A white-enameled gold shell surrounded the entire egg, and the Imperial crown was hidden inside the body of the hen.

EXERCISE 13   **Using Spatial Order.** Write a paragraph on a topic of your own choice, or use one of the following topics.

1. a baseball or football field
2. a piece of sculpture
3. the view from an airplane window
4. a farm
5. an automobile engine
6. an imaginary landscape

Follow the prewriting, writing, and revising process, and use spatial order to organize the paragraph. When you revise, make sure that your position and direction are clear.

Order of Importance

Paragraphs can be organized in order of *decreasing* importance and in order of *increasing* importance. Order of *decreasing* importance is useful if you want to capture your reader's attention immediately, as in the following model. The author begins with the information that should make the strongest impression. As you will notice, the paragraph moves from a statement about great works to a statement about good works to a statement about lesser works:

> There is no doubt that of all the works of John Keats, the odes—"On a Grecian Urn," "To a Nightingale," and "To Autumn"—are the greatest accomplishments of his brief career. They tower above his other lyrics, such as the sonnet "On First Looking into Chapman's Homer." His long narrative poems, like "The Eve of St. Agnes," are admired but do not have the power of the odes. His poetic drama *Otho the Great* finds its admirers mainly among scholars.

When you use order of *increasing* importance to organize a paragraph, you present ideas of greater and greater importance and save the most important idea for last:

> These days, some of the works of John Keats, like his poetic drama *Otho the Great,* are savored mainly by scholars. His long narrative poems, such as "The Eve of St. Agnes," have gained greater acceptance. And although his many fine lyrics, including "On Looking into Chapman's Homer," have maintained a high place in poetic history, the pinnacle of his achievement is the composition of the great odes—"On a Grecian Urn," "To a Nightingale," and "To Autumn."

EXERCISE 14 **Using Order of Importance.** Write a paragraph on a topic of your own choice, or use one of the following topics.

1. my priorities
2. dressing with style
3. what to do in case of fire
4. our national goals
5. what makes an educated person
6. the best programs on television

Follow the prewriting, writing, and revising process, and use order of importance to organize the paragraph. When you revise, make sure that the order of importance is clear.

Cause-and-Effect Order

When you organize a paragraph based on cause and effect, you want your reader to see that one event takes place *because* another event has taken place. This kind of paragraph is especially useful in writing on scientific or historical subjects, as in this passage about a hurricane.

> The low death toll was largely attributable to the technology of mid-century America. Thanks to a covey of "Hurricane Hunter" aircraft and a hat-box-shaped, 320-lb. weather satellite called Essa (for the Commerce Department's Environmental Science Services Administration), Beulah's every move was tracked and reported round the clock by radio, thus permitting more than 150,000 Texans to dodge the big storm's flailing fist. Watching from a polar orbit 865 miles above the earth, Essa's twin TV cameras gave the Texas Gulf Coast twelve days' advance warning on her course. In the Caribbean and Mexico, where Beulah rampaged for two weeks before striking Texas, the storm took about 40 lives—in part because of inadequate radio warning.
>
> —*Time*

Using Order Based on Cause and Effect. Write a paragraph on a topic of your own choice, or use one of the following topics.

1. motivations for learning
2. lack of oxygen
3. wealth
4. changes in fashions
5. love at first sight
6. poverty

Follow the prewriting, writing, and revising process, and use order based on cause and effect to organize the paragraph. When you revise, make sure that the relationship between the events is absolutely clear.

Comparison and Contrast

Comparison describes similarities; **contrast** describes differences.

By telling how something is similar to or different from something else, you can give a subject more precise definition and clearer boundaries.

> A match between tennis stars Jimmy Connors and John McEnroe often seems like a meeting of opposites. The two men have very different styles of play. Connors plays with intensity, visibly concentrating on every move, grunting at every serve. He pays close attention to correct form in order to get the greatest power out of every shot. He grips the racket with two hands for the highest possible combination of strength and control. McEnroe, on the other hand, seems to be almost casual as he hits blistering cross-court winners and perfect volleys. His form is not at all correct, yet his shots are amazingly powerful. Sometimes he even seems to hold the racket so loosely in one hand that it looks like he'll drop it. These surface characteristics of the two players, however, should not disguise the essential characteristic they have in common, the real reason that their matches are so electric: They both possess the passionate will to win.

Notice that the writer of this model first gives us *all* of the qualities of one player and then compares them with *all* of the qualities of the other player. In other words, the structure of the paragraph is *AAABBB*—where all the *As* are statements about Connors and all the *Bs* are statements about McEnroe.

EXERCISE 16 **Using Order Based on Comparison and Contrast.** Write a paragraph on a topic of your own choice, or use one of the following topics.

1. maturity and immaturity
2. stars and planets
3. towns and cities
4. pessimists and optimists
5. heroes and villains
6. two household items

Follow the prewriting, writing, and revising process, and use order based on comparison and contrast to organize your paragraph. When you revise, make sure that the specific points of comparison and contrast are clear.

Checklist for Organizing a Paragraph

1. Is the paragraph best organized in chronological order? If so, what is the sequence of events?
2. Is the paragraph best organized in spatial order? If so, how does the reader always know my position and direction?
3. Is the paragraph best organized in order of importance? If so, should the most important statement be placed first or last?
4. Is the paragraph best organized in cause-and-effect order? If so, what is the cause? What is the effect?
5. Is the paragraph best organized in comparison-and-contrast order? If so, are all the similarities and differences grouped together, or is a point-by-point comparison made clear to the reader?

Writer's Choice

Writer's Choice #1

ASSIGNMENT A paragraph of a friendly letter
LENGTH Six or seven sentences
AUDIENCE A close friend who has moved away
PURPOSE To relate an event that took place yesterday
PREWRITING Review the event in chronological order.
WRITING Begin by stating why your friend will be interested in reading about the event. Then describe what happened, using concrete details, examples, or facts. End by telling how the event would have been different if your friend had been there.
REVISING Make sure that you have used transitions.

Writer's Choice #2

ASSIGNMENT A paragraph applying for a job that you really want
LENGTH Six or seven sentences
AUDIENCE Your prospective employer
PURPOSE To persuade the employer to hire you
PREWRITING Decide on at least three reasons why you are qualified.
WRITING In your topic sentence identify the job and express your interest in it. Then write list your specific qualifications. End with a sentence telling why you are a good choice for the job.
REVISING Make sure that you sound businesslike.

Writer's Choice #3

ASSIGNMENT A paragraph for a social studies examination
LENGTH Your choice
AUDIENCE Your social studies instructor
PURPOSE To answer the question: Which event in the twentieth century has had the greatest impact on your life?
OPTIONS You may base your answer on an event depicted in the Writer's Sourcebook on pages 354–357.
You may want to use cause-and-effect order, chronological order, or order of importance.

Writer's Choice #4

ASSIGNMENT A paragraph of any kind
LENGTH Your choice
AUDIENCE Your choice
PURPOSE To describe what your life will be like in ten years
OPTION You might focus on your community or environment, or you might discuss your personal dreams and goals.

Writers on Writing

Born in Costa Rica, Mariano Fernández finds that his knowledge of Spanish helps him in speaking and writing English—and vice versa. He wrote the following paragraph and commentary as a student at Indian Hill High School in Cincinnati, Ohio.

THE PRODUCT

Pessimism plays an important role in the tone George Orwell creates in his novel *1984*. Winston, the main character, sees nothing as good; everything is described in negative terms. Even normally pleasant-sounding phrases are qualified to express an extremely pessimistic attitude, as in this example: "Outside, even through the shut window pane, the world looked cold. . . .Though the sun was shining and the sky a harsh blue, there seemed to be no color in anything except the posters. . . ." Orwell uses this tone for a purpose. He wishes the reader to associate this bleakness with societies like Oceania. Another example is the moment when Winston realizes that he will be killed: "Mrs. Parsons would be vaporized. Syme would be vaporized. Winston would be vaporized." Again, Orwell creates a pessimistic tone so that readers will be appalled by the society of *1984* and do more to prevent it.

THE PROCESS

When I start writing, I get a piece of paper and just jot down anything that pops into my head. If I think of something better, I add it. Once I run out of ideas, I do something else and return to writing later, or I try to arrange my ideas into some kind of order.

Usually by this time I have written a topic sentence. Next, I include more specific information. I might add examples to illustrate the point I am making. For instance, here I quoted from *1984*.

Once the paragraph starts taking form, I read it and change any words that do not say what I want them to say. I also change the topic sentence and the final sentence. The whole paragraph depends on the topic sentence. It cannot be too limited, and it should not be vague or confusing.

I go over a piece of writing several times before it sounds the way I want it to. I use a word processor so I can easily change any words I do not like.

YOUR TURN   *Writing a Paragraph*

Choose a writer you admire and write a paragraph about that writer's word choice. Take care with the topic sentence; as Mariano says, it should not be vague or too limited. Restate your main idea at the paragraph's end.

CHAPTER 4

Revising, Editing, and Proofreading

I have never thought of myself as a good writer. Anyone who wants reassurance of that should read one of my first drafts. But I'm one of the world's great rewriters.

—James Michener

Prewriting • *Writing* • *Revising*

A good writer rarely—perhaps never—gets it all right in the first draft. Good writing usually means good revising. Revising is "re-seeing." It is looking again at what you have done and seeing it as you have not seen it before. Revising is not simply one extra step tacked on at the end of the writing process: It is an essential part of that process.

Professional writers know that writing *is* revising. Do you think that great writing springs perfectly from the writer's mind? Think again. Think of the image that Maya Angelou, a contemporary writer, uses in discussing the writing process: "Putting down on paper what you have to say is an important part of writing, but the words and ideas have to be shaped and cleaned, cleaned as severely as a dog cleans a bone." Some writers have been known to go through dozens of drafts of a poem or story before deeming it ready for publication. Two or three drafts may be sufficient for you, but your first draft will nearly always need more work.

The purpose of this chapter is to provide you with practical methods to use during the stage of the writing process called revising. Some of these methods will be more useful to you than others, depending on the kind of writer you are. You must become your own critical reader and decide which methods will help you to improve each of the paragraphs you produce. Of course, the techniques of revising also apply to works of more than one paragraph. These activities will help you:

revising for purpose and audience
revising the topic sentence
revising support and development
revising for coherence
revising word choice
editing, **proofreading**, and **publishing**

Revising the Paragraph

Revising for Purpose and Audience

Never be afraid to make changes in your first draft when you discover that they are needed. Sometimes student writers do not want to "mess up" what they have written. After all, they reason, it looks so neat, why ruin its appearance? Remember, however, that at this stage in the writing process *what* you say is much more important than creating a paper with no cross-outs or erasures.

The purpose of your paragraph should be as clear to your reader as it is to you. Identify for yourself the purpose of the paragraph by filling in this sentence:

The purpose of this paragraph is to _____ [*inform, persuade, amuse, entertain, narrate, describe,* or *combine several purposes*].

Next read the paragraph from beginning to end. If the paragraph *as a whole* does not seem to accomplish its purpose, reread each sentence *individually* to identify which sentence does not fulfill your purpose.

Your success as a writer will always depend on knowing your audience and enabling them to understand or enjoy what you are saying. For example, if you are telling the tale of Goldilocks and the three bears to a kindergarten class, you would not tell them that the little girl arrived serendipitously at the sylvan abode of a family of Ursidae. If you did, you would definitely have lost sight of your audience!

Do not forget that your audience is composed of *people*, other human beings with ideas and emotions and cares just as deeply felt as yours are to you. So do not write *at* your audience; write *to* them.

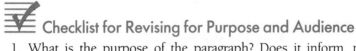 Checklist for Revising for Purpose and Audience

1. What is the purpose of the paragraph? Does it inform, persuade, amuse, entertain, narrate, describe, or combine several purposes?
2. Which sentence or sentences, if any, do not directly fulfill the purpose of the paragraph? What changes should be made to put every sentence on track?
3. Who is the audience for this paragraph? What changes should be made to make every sentence understandable or enjoyable?
4. What facts or details need to be added to help the audience understand me? If this is a specialized audience—people who share a particular body of knowledge—what can I assume they know?

EXERCISE 1   **Revising for Purpose and Audience.** Read the following paragraph, and then write answers to questions 1 through 4.

Almost everyone knows that a rabbit shouldn't be picked up by its ears, everyone, that is, except very young children who should probably only be allowed to pet the animal. Rabbits can be lifted by the skin of the back as long as one hand supports the body and the ears are kept close to the neck. This seems to keep their sense of balance intact and they are less inclined to kick, scratch, or bite. Some breeds are more nervous than others, but all are easily tamed, and the best approach with a new rabbit is a gradual one, restricted to petting or stroking at first and eventually expanded to lifting and carrying about.

—Emil P. Polensek and Barbara Burn

1. What do you think the purpose of this paragraph is? Does it inform, persuade, amuse, entertain, narrate, describe, or does it combine several purposes?
2. This paragraph is a final draft and was printed in a book called *A Practical Guide to Impractical Pets*. Assume that an earlier draft of the paragraph included a few sentences about the proper feeding of rabbits. Why would the authors have removed those sentences when they revised the paragraph?
3. Who is the audience for this paragraph? Is every sentence understandable or enjoyable by that particular audience?
4. Assume that in a first draft the authors had written the following sentence: "Beatrix Potter knew how to pick up Peter Rabbit when he wasn't hippity-hopping all over the place." Why would the authors have dropped that sentence during the process of revising the first draft of the paragraph?

Revising the Paragraph

REVISING FOR PURPOSE AND AUDIENCE
REVISING THE TOPIC SENTENCE
REVISING SUPPORT, DEVELOPMENT, AND ORGANIZATION
REVISING FOR COHERENCE
REVISING WORD CHOICE
EDITING, PROOFREADING, AND PUBLISHING

Revising the Topic Sentence

The **topic sentence** not only states the main idea of a paragraph; it also determines the scope and the direction of all the other sentences in the paragraph. Suppose you had to revise the topic sentence (the underlined sentence) of the following paragraph. How would you revise it so that it expresses the main idea clearly and succinctly?

> These days calendars do more than simply indicate the date. It is rare to find one that is nothing more than thirty-one numbered squares. People want different kinds of calendars. Calendars have pictures of trees, pets, musical instruments, seashells, cartoon characters, fine art, movie stars, foods, hair styles, skyscrapers, even pictures of old-fashioned calendars. Some calendars come complete with farm information, school information, famous birthdays, great days in history, and even a quotation for the day. This amazing variety seems to reflect more than personal tastes: It points to a universal desire to make the passing of time as delightful as possible.

To revise any topic sentence, first focus on the *main idea* of the paragraph. This topic sentence, People want different kinds of calendars, does not capture the main idea of the paragraph. You might revise the sentence this way, focusing on the main idea and then refining the focus:

People want different kinds of calendars.

↓

People want their calendars to say something.

↓

People want their calendars to say something about themselves.

↓

People want their calendars to say something about their interests, their hobbies, or their personal lives.

What does the final revised sentence do? It expresses the *main idea* with proper *scope* and adequate *direction*.

Is the *placement* of the topic sentence now correct? It works well, but you may want to try it in different places.

Checklist for Revising the Topic Sentence

1. If the topic sentence circles around the main idea without ever stating it directly, how can I revise it?
2. What noun or nouns would make the *subject* of the topic sentence more specific? What *verb* would express the action of the subject more accurately? What *adjective* or *adverb* would describe the main idea more precisely?
3. What is the scope of the topic sentence? Too large to be treated in one paragraph? Too specific to cover all that the paragraph needs to say?
4. Based on the topic sentence, what does the reader expect the rest of the paragraph to do?
5. How, if at all, would the topic sentence improve the paragraph if I moved it elsewhere in the paragraph?

EXERCISE 2 **Revising the Topic Sentence.** Read the following paragraphs, and revise the underlined topic sentence in each. Move the topic sentence within the paragraph if necessary.

PARAGRAPH A

<u>Seabirds include gulls.</u> Their graceful flight and shrill cries are easily recognized by many people. Gulls have trim gray-and-white bodies, long wings, and hooked bills. Their webbed feet enable them to swim as well as fly. Carnivorous birds, they feed primarily on marine life and insects. They inhabit coastal areas and many inland waters.

PARAGRAPH B

<u>People enjoy glass.</u> Historians believe that the first glass vessels and articles of adornment were produced about 1500 B.C. in Egypt. Early glass manufacture was slow and costly, and it required hard work. Glass blowing and glass pressing were unknown at that time, but glassmakers somehow learned to make beautiful colored glass jewelry as well as small jars and jugs. A short time later practical merchants realized that wines and oils could be preserved much better in glass containers than in clay ones.

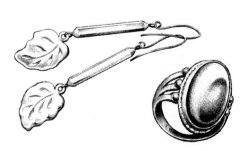

Revising the Topic Sentence 75

Writer's Choice

Writer's Choice #1

ASSIGNMENT Write a paragraph on a topic of your own choice, or choose one of the following topics:
the definition of justice
a cure for the common cold
what most people read

LENGTH Six sentences

AUDIENCE The editor-in-chief of your local newspaper

PURPOSE To inform

PREWRITING Brainstorm to provide yourself with several paths by which to approach your topic. You will have to narrow the suggested topics before you can begin to write.
Review your notes, and choose a main idea that would be appealing to an intelligent adult audience.

WRITING First write a topic sentence that expresses the main idea. Then write four sentences that support your main idea with concrete details, facts, or reasons. End with a sentence that would encourage the reader to read further.

REVISING Revise the paragraph. Use the checklists on pages 73 and 75 to examine the purpose, audience, and topic sentence.

Writer's Choice #2

ASSIGNMENT Write a paragraph on a topic of your own choice, or use one of the following topics:
different kinds of rocks
different kinds of rock music
why rocking chairs are comforting

LENGTH Your choice

AUDIENCE Your choice

PURPOSE Your choice

OPTIONS Determine your own prewriting strategy. As you revise, however, pay special attention to the purpose, audience, and topic sentence. Refer to the checklists on pages 73 and 75.

Writer's Choice #3

ASSIGNMENT Write a paragraph on any subject, choosing carefully the kind of support you use for your main idea. Determine and identify your own length, audience, and purpose. Make sure that your purpose, audience, and topic sentence are clear.

Revising the Paragraph

Revising Support, Development, and Organization

Supporting sentences form the body of a paragraph. They need to be strong and clear. As you revise, return to your prewriting notes to make sure that you have chosen the details, facts, examples, or reasons that best support the main idea. Keep your audience and purpose in mind, and ask yourself what supporting statements would have the greatest effect on that particular audience.

Development is largely a matter of fulfilling your reader's expectations. For example, if your topic sentence is *People print the craziest things on T-shirts these days,* your reader will expect you to give examples of the crazy things you have noticed. If your topic sentence is *Julius Caesar stands out as Shakespeare's most noble hero*, your reader will expect you to give reasons and examples to support your opinion. Make your development sufficient, neither skimpy nor overwhelming.

A common criticism of inexperienced writers is that their paragraphs "do not go anywhere." Such writers simply repeat the topic sentence or restate it in different words and assume that they are developing the main idea. As the following model shows, *repetition is not development:*

> *The training program for astronauts is definitely grueling.* Those fortunate enough to be admitted into the program in the first place face long months of technical education. *The candidates are put through an extremely difficult course.* The purpose is to prepare them for any emergency, to make them capable of responding instantly to any situation. They do, of course, have computers to back them up at all times. *Nevertheless, the trainees must complete a series of activities that is terribly demanding.*

Notice that the three italicized sentences say the same thing. Synonyms disguise the fact that the sentences provide no new information, reasons, or examples: *Astronauts, candidates,* and *trainees* are synonyms in this context, as are *training program, course,* and *series of activities.* Even the adjectives *difficult* and *demanding* add no meaning to *grueling.*

Make sure that the organization you have used for your paragraph is the best possible one. Consider other possibilities. For example, you may have used spatial order to describe a landscape, but perhaps order of importance would be more effective, especially if you want to focus the reader's attention on one aspect of the landscape.

If you decide to reorganize a paragraph, do not hesitate to *rewrite* the sentences in your first draft. Sometimes trying to rearrange sentences is more difficult than rewriting them. Moreover, the process of rewriting may generate some new approach or idea for your paragraph.

Checklist for Revising Support, Development, and Organization

1. Which details, facts, examples, or reasons form the strongest support for the main idea?
2. Which sentence or sentences, if any, merely repeat the main idea instead of developing it?
3. Why is the method of organization used in the paragraph the best possible one?

EXERCISE 3 **Revising Support, Development, and Organization.** Rewrite the following pargraph, revising for correct support, sufficient development, and logical organization. Feel free to rewrite, reword, rearrange, or replace any sentence to improve the paragraph.

An atom is the toughest thing in the world to crack. It is so tiny that it is more than a million times smaller than the thickness of one strand of human hair. In 1930 Ernest O. Lawrence developed a way to split the core of an atom. Atoms form the building blocks of the chemical elements. Lawrence split the atom by building a machine called a cyclotron. He fed electrical particles into this machine. The particles traveled quickly around in a circle. When they went almost as fast as the speed of light, they were shot through an opening against a metal plate and were thus ripped apart. The cyclotron is a type of particle accelerator that makes the particles travel in a circle. The development of this machine marked the beginning of the atomic age.

Writer's Choice

Writer's Choice #1

ASSIGNMENT Write a paragraph on a subject of your own choice, or use one of the following topic sentences:

America's most important natural resource is [coal, farmland, climate, business sense, imagination].

Few people recognize the difference between [skill and knowledge, beauty and charm, experience and wisdom].

More poets, painters, and sculptors deal with [love, death, war, change, beauty] than with any other subject.

LENGTH Six or seven sentences

AUDIENCE Your classmates

PURPOSE To introduce a well-known public figure who will speak to the class on the topic

PREWRITING Freewrite for at least five minutes.

WRITING Organize your paragraph according to comparison and contrast or order of importance. Include details, facts, examples, or reasons in your support.

REVISING Use the checklists on pages 73, 75, and 78.

Writer's Choice #2

ASSIGNMENT Write a paragraph on a topic of your own choice, or narrow down one of the following subjects to a topic that can be handled in one paragraph:

games   graffiti

gnus   galaxy

LENGTH Your choice

AUDIENCE Your choice

PURPOSE Your choice

OPTIONS Use the organization that seems appropriate to your topic—chronological order, spatial order, order of importance, cause and effect, or comparison and contrast. Revise your support and development according to the checklist on page 78.

Writer's Choice #3

ASSIGNMENT Write a paragraph on any topic you choose, using your choice of development. Determine and identify your own length, audience, and purpose. As you revise your support and development, use the checklist on page 78.

Revising for Coherence

A coherent paragraph is one in which the sentences are clearly and logically connected to one another. Once you have revised the support and development of a paragraph to guarantee unity and logical organization, you will find it easier to revise for coherence.

As you revise, see if repeating any words or using synonyms can improve the coherence of the paragraph. For example, study the following model, and notice how it was revised. In the revised version the repeated words tie the second sentence closely to the first sentence, giving an impression of one continuous thought:

> During the Renaissance an artist was not only a painter. Michelangelo, Raphael, and Leonardo were also sculptors and architects.

> During the Renaissance an artist was not only a painter. The Renaissance geniuses Michelangelo, Raphael, and Leonardo were not only painters but also sculptors and architects.

Using pronouns can help you achieve both coherence and conciseness. Make sure your reader always knows to what each pronoun refers.

> During the Renaissance, artists were not only painters. Michelangelo, Raphael, and Leonardo were also sculptors and architects.

> During the Renaissance, artists were not only painters. They were also sculptors and architects.

Transitions can improve sentences by tying them together. Writers use a variety of transitions to link sentences and improve coherence. Transitions not only help to present ideas clearly and logically; they also contribute to a smooth and flowing writing style. Writers use transitions that show time, place, examples, order of importance, cause and effect, and comparison and contrast. The following model shows the use of a transition.

> During the Renaissance an artist was not only a painter. Michelangelo, Raphael, and Leonardo were also sculptors and architects.

> During the Renaissance an artist was not only a painter. For example, Michelangelo, Raphael, and Leonardo were also sculptors and architects.

Checklist for Revising for Coherence

1. Which words can I repeat and still give my sentences sufficient variety? What synonyms can I use?
2. Which pronouns can I use to achieve coherence and conciseness? Are all the pronouns absolutely clear?
3. What kinds of transitions can I add to the paragraph: time or place transitions; transitions that show order of importance, cause and effect, or comparison and contrast; example transitions? Are these the best possible transitions to tie the sentences together?

EXERCISE 4 **Revising for Coherence.** Rewrite the following paragraph, revising for coherence by using *repeated words and synonyms, pronoun references,* and *transitions.*

Flying saucers, or unidentified flying objects (UFOs), pose one of the greatest mysteries of our time. Thousands of people say that they have seen flying saucers. For hundreds of years people have reported seeing mysterious objects in the sky. These mysterious objects have been spotted by radar, and these mysterious objects have been photographed. Some of these mysterious objects resemble an inverted saucer or a glowing tube. Scientists have provided logical explanations for many UFO reports. In many cases scientists have reported that UFOs are in fact meteors, rockets, stars, artificial satellites, or weather balloons. Atmospheric conditions may produce optical illusions that are described as UFOs. Scientists cannot explain all the UFO reports.

Revising the Paragraph

REVISING FOR PURPOSE AND AUDIENCE
REVISING THE TOPIC SENTENCE
REVISING SUPPORT, DEVELOPMENT, AND ORGANIZATION
REVISING FOR COHERENCE
REVISING WORD CHOICE
EDITING, PROOFREADING, AND PUBLISHING

Revising Word Choice

Word choice must be appropriate to the *audience,* to the *occasion,* and to the *subject.* If your words are inappropriate in any of these areas, they will jar the reader and defeat your *purpose.*

Think of your audience. Are the words appropriate to the identity and character of the audience? To an audience of computer programmers, for example, you can use words such as *bits* and *bytes.* On the other hand, to an

audience not well versed in computers you should use everyday words to express your meaning, or use computer terms only if you define them. Be sure that your audience shares the meanings you give to your words.

Think of the occasion. Are you writing a personal letter or a public address, a note or an essay? Are you using the words that are correct for the occasion? For example, *So what is this thing all about?* would not be appropriate as the opening of a final exam essay on *Julius Caesar.*

Think of the subject. Are you taking terms from one field and applying them to another field? For example, medical terminology is appropriate in talking about a delicate brain operation but is totally out of place in talking about tuning up your car.

These extreme examples indicate how jarring inappropriate words can be. In contrast, appropriate words will make your audience feel at ease and be more receptive to what you have to say. (You will study more about word choice, or diction, in Chapter 5.)

Once you decide on how formal or informal your words will be, you need to remain consistent. Your first sentences will give your reader a set of expectations, and failure to fulfill those expectations is unnecessarily jarring. Unless you are striving for a shocking or a humorous effect, avoid mixing formal and informal words. Notice the collision of different levels of diction in these sentences:

> For lunch today I ingested a whole mess of chili.
> This court hereby sentences the defendant to ten years in the slammer.

 ## Checklist for Revising Word Choice

1. Which words, if any, are not appropriate to the audience, to the occasion, to the subject? How should they be changed?
2. Which words or expressions, if any, are too formal or informal? How should they be changed?

EXERCISE 5 **Revising Word Choice.** Rewrite the following paragraph, paying special attention to word choice. Assume that your audience is the board of directors of a corporation and that your purpose is to convince them to make a donation to your organization. Decide how formal or informal your words need to be.

No bunch of people with the responsibility for giving out money to help worthwhile organizations can afford to decide these big-league things with their eyes closed. As the representative of the Newburgh Community Center, I can tell you that the folks I represent know how hard it is for you guys to decide who will be funded and who not. Another thing—we do not want to waste your time and good will by claiming that our center is better than the others that are fighting it out for your bucks. We do not intend to go that route. But we can tell you that a lot of people really get a kick out of our community center. That is the bottom line of our application, and that is what I want to rap to you about this afternoon.

Revising the Paragraph

REVISING FOR PURPOSE AND AUDIENCE
REVISING THE TOPIC SENTENCE
REVISING SUPPORT, DEVELOPMENT, AND ORGANIZATION
REVISING FOR COHERENCE
REVISING WORD CHOICE
EDITING, PROOFREADING, AND PUBLISHING

Editing, Proofreading, and Publishing

The final stage of revising involves polishing the grammar, usage, capitalization, punctuation, spelling, and physical appearance of your writing. This stage is not simply one extra, tacked-on procedure. It consists of the refinements that give your writing the clean and correct appearance that is so important as you reach the goal of the writing process—presenting your writing to readers. Thus, editing is an essential part of the writing process, just as revising is.

In general, **editing** means making changes in sentence structure and wording.

Use the following checklist to spot and correct possible errors in the drafts of your writing. The standard editing marks at the right of the chart provide a shorthand method of revising or commenting on any piece of writing. Chapter 6 of this book will provide much practice in sentence options, and Part Two offers detailed instruction in grammar, usage, capitalization, and punctuation.

CHECKLIST FOR EDITING

QUESTION	TYPICAL ERRORS	MARK
Does every verb agree with its subject?	Jennifer ~~don't~~ doesn't see the problem. Each of us need_s_ friends.	agree
Is every pronoun in the correct case?	They gave gifts to Bob and ~~I.~~ me Go with whoever you want.	case
Is every pronoun reference correct and clear?	The director ~~told~~ knew that the actor ~~that he~~ was going to be very busy. and told him so.	ref
Are all double negatives avoided?	Gandhi didn't like ~~no~~ any violence.	neg
Is each verb tense correct and consistent?	Linda use_d_ to live in Rhode Island, but now she lives in Texas.	tense
Are all comparisons properly expressed?	Heracles was supposedly the ~~most~~ strongest of all mortals.	adj
Are all clauses complete and properly joined?	King was A man who was born to lead.	frag
	Katherine Anne Porter grew up in the South, and she often writes about it.	run-on
Have all dangling or misplaced words been avoided?	When I stepped ~~Stepping~~ on the brake, the car stopped.	dangling
	Geraldine Ferraro spoke of responsibilities and rights. at the convention.	misplaced
Has all redundancy (unnecessary repetition) and wordiness been avoided?	The ~~proposed~~ plan laid out the ~~important~~ essentials and called for ~~mutual~~ cooperation.	redundancy

In general, **proofreading** means checking for errors in spelling, capitalization, and punctuation.

Use the following proofreading marks as you revise your own writing or comment on someone else's paper.

CHECKLIST FOR PROOFREADING

MEANING	EXAMPLE	MARK
punctuation	How many dairy farms are there.	*punct*
delete	this very up-to-date list	
insert	Edward Hopper painted many American scenes.	⌃
space	the great places I wanted to visit	#
close up	the places I wanted to visit	⌒
capital	Queen elizabeth I ruled until 1603.	≡
lower case	Queen Elizabeth I Ruled until 1603.	/
spelling	Who is the auther of *The Pearl*?	*sp*
transpose	The space probe millions cost.	∿
new paragraph	never again. The following day	¶
stet (let stand something marked for change)	Lionel Richie is a talented entertainer and composer.	. . . .

When you have completed your revisions and are ready to make a final copy, follow these rules of standard manuscript form. (Be sure to ask your teacher about any additional or different rules for your class.) Your work will then be ready for **publishing**—that is, any form of sharing your writing with an audience. You may, for example, send a letter to a newspaper.

GUIDELINES FOR MANUSCRIPT PREPARATION
1. Use standard-size paper ($8^1/_2$ by 11 inches) and blue or black ink or a black typewriter or word processor ribbon or cartridge.
2. If you are writing by hand, use only one side of each page. If you are typing, double space.

3. Maintain an even margin of $1^1/_2$ inches on the left and a margin of about 1 inch on the right.
4. Indent the first line of each paragraph five spaces.
5. If you are writing by hand, be sure that every word is legible—readable—so that your audience does not have to strain.

The following model paragraph demonstrates how editing and proofreading can apply the finishing touches to a piece of writing. The first version of the paragraph about shopping malls shows the correct editing and proofreading marks used by the writer to indicate a variety of revisions. Notice as you read the first version that the writer has corrected not only spelling errors, capitalization errors, and punctuation errors, but also wordiness, misplaced modifiers, verb tense, and other matters of usage.

PARAGRAPH WITH EDITING AND PROOFREADING MARKS

agree/sp	Shopping malls has become an enormusly popular feature of the
misplaced cap/lc	American cultural landscape. Early in the morning it is possible to
redundancy	go to a Mall and spend a whole entire day and night shopping,
wordy	eating, and being entertained. In fact some people might possibly
adj	say that they feel the most major attraction of the mall seems to be
tense sp	have been its completeness—great size coupled with great varietey,
stet	with everything in one place, like a self-contained world.
cap frag/lc	sometimes a mall even seems to have its own citizens. Colonies of
#	regulars who go to see and be seen. The world that created
ref	consumerism has finally come full circle: It has itself created a
	world.

FINAL REVISED PARAGRAPH

Shopping malls have become an enormously popular feature of the American cultural landscape. It is possible to go to a mall early in the morning and spend an entire day and night shopping, eating, and being entertained. In fact the major attraction of the mall seems to be its completeness—great size coupled with great variety, with everything in one place, like a self-contained world. Sometimes a mall even seems to have its own citizens, colonies of regulars who go to see and be seen. The world that created consumerism has finally come full circle: Consumerism has itself created a world.

Editing and Proofreading. Revise the following paragraphs, editing and proofreading to correct all errors.

PARAGRAPH A

In the dictionary it says that the word *be-bop* is an imitation of the sound made on a trumpet. Be-bop music are characterized by complex rhythms and experimental harmonies. A jazz movement that is associated with the great trumpet player Dizzy Gillespie. Born John Birks Gillespie, many people consider him the ambassador of jazz. Actually Charlie Parker and him invented be-bop music in the 1940s. Gillespie's musical improvisations are noted for their energy and wit. Many gillespie composition, including "Salt Peanuts" and "Billie's Bounce," are now considered jazz Standards. Gillespie has been called the world's greatest virtuoso trumpet, most jazz trumpet players are indebted to him. Some even consider him the world's most unique jazz soloeist. Indeed, Dizzy Gillespie's bulgeing cheeks and upturned trumpet has almost come to stand for and symbolize jazz.

PARAGRAPH B

Frank Lloyd Wright once said that there were not no better dwellings in the world than the seashell. A snail's home, Wright said, is both beautiful and also functional. In his view, "Nature only knows circular forms." He considered the spiral the most ideal shape of all in his later buildings. One of him most famous structures, New Yorks Guggenheim Museum, is shaped in the shape of a spiral. Many modern architects consider theirselves airs of Frank Lloyd Wright. Wright hisself never had such a high opinion of most other architects and called their high-rise buildings "glassified filing cabinets." Wright will have been more popular with the architectural estabishment if he would not have had such a sharp wit. Even so. Frank Lloyd Wright has been more influential than any twentieth-century architect. The beauty of his buildings is time less: Each was built for it's site, its purpose, and its inhabitance.

 General Checklist for Revising

PURPOSE AND AUDIENCE

1. Which sentence or sentences, if any, do not directly fulfill the purpose of the paragraph?
2. What changes should be made to make every sentence understandable or enjoyable?

TOPIC SENTENCE

3. If the topic sentence circles around the main idea without ever stating it directly, how can I revise the topic sentence?
4. What revision would improve the scope, the direction, or the placement of the topic sentence?

SUPPORT, DEVELOPMENT, AND ORGANIZATION

5. Which details, facts, examples, or reasons form the strongest support for my main idea? Which sentence or sentences, if any, merely repeat the main idea?
6. Why is the method of organization used in the paragraph the best possible one?

COHERENCE

7. Which words can I repeat and still give my sentences sufficient variety? What synonyms can I use?
8. Which pronouns can I use to achieve coherence and conciseness?
9. What kinds of transitions can I use?

WORD CHOICE

10. Which words, if any, are not appropriate to the audience, to the occasion, to the subject?
11. Which words or expressions, if any, are inconsistent with the others?

EDITING, PROOFREADING, AND PUBLISHING

12. Does every verb agree with its subject?
13. Is every pronoun in the correct case? Is every pronoun reference correct and clear?
14. Are all double negatives avoided?
15. Is each verb tense correct and consistent?
16. Are all comparisons properly expressed?
17. Are all clauses complete and properly joined?
18. Have all dangling or misplaced words been avoided?
19. Has all redundancy and wordiness been avoided?
20. Has all proofreading been done carefully?
21. Have the rules of manuscript preparation been followed?

Writer's Choice

Writer's Choice #1

ASSIGNMENT   Write a paragraph on a topic of your own choice, or use one of the following topics:
the most popular American pets
why I should be the first student on the space shuttle
enjoying the cycle of the seasons

LENGTH   Seven sentences

AUDIENCE   Students one hundred years from now

PURPOSE   To provide one paragraph to be added to a time capsule

PREWRITING   Freewrite for five minutes on your topic. Then review your writing, identify the main idea, and list supporting ideas.

WRITING   Write a clear topic sentence that states precisely your main idea. Then write five supporting sentences, using details, facts, statistics, examples, or reasons. End with a sentence that summarizes your position.

REVISING   Refer to the general checklist on page 88.

Writer's Choice #2

ASSIGNMENT   Write a paragraph on a topic of your own choice, or narrow down one of the following subjects:

money   responsibility
fashion   computers

LENGTH   Seven sentences

AUDIENCE   Viewers of the television show *American Youth*

PURPOSE   To present your generation's viewpoint

OPTIONS   Brainstorm for five minutes. Use examples and reasons for development, but also consider details and statistics. As you revise, refer to the checklist on page 88.

Writer's Choice #3

ASSIGNMENT   Write a paragraph on a topic of your own choice, or use one of the following topics, narrowing it as necessary:
sandwiches I have known and loved
the five best records ever made
an endangered species
Alternatively, you may find inspiration for a writing idea in the Writer's Sourcebook, pages 354–357.

OPTIONS   Determine your own length, audience, and purpose. Consider order of importance as your method of organization. Refer to the revising checklist on page 88.

Writers on Writing

Roselle Graskey wrote the following story opener and commentary as a student at Eastwood High School in El Paso, Texas. She plans to major in drama and writing at Trinity College in Ireland.

THE PRODUCT

Rachel and Arlene sat in the hallway at lunch. They munched content-edly on their sandwiches. Rachel's legs stretched out in front of her as she spoke of the math class she disliked so much. Arlene sat cross-legged on the floor, a clipboard in one hand and a pen in the other, scribbling on a sheet of white lined paper—undoubtedly another assignment that she would not complete. Rachel leaned back against the wall and watched as people passed by. She spoke in smooth, onrushing sentences.

THE PROCESS

My process of revision begins the moment I start thinking about a subject. If an idea or action conflicts with my general purpose, I alter it. For example, my story "Lunch Time" originally started out with four students in the hallway. I decided that two students would be more intimate, and so I made the change.

The first draft is the roughest—this is the draft in which I retain my best ideas and discard the weaker ones. After I write this draft, I reread and change the sentences that seem to take up space without adding anything important. I also add examples and details where needed. For example, the detail about Rachel speaking in "smooth, onrushing sentences" was a late addition to "Lunch Time."

Revising generally takes up more of my time than actually writing the first draft. The results, though, are well worth the time I spend hunched over my paper or wading through the mind of my latest character. Often I find myself wondering if a character wouldn't be better off doing some-thing else or saying another word. Sometimes sentences travel the length of a story trying to find a home. Revising can also be a springboard for another story or other form of writing. Sometimes I begin one story and end up writing two.

Revising becomes a habit once you start.

YOUR TURN *Revising a Paragraph*

As Roselle says, "Revising becomes a habit once you start." Choose a paragraph that you have already written, and revise it using the skills that you practiced in this chapter. Remember, never hesitate to make changes, even on a draft that already seems adequate.

CHAPTERS 2–4   THE PARAGRAPH AND THE WRITING PROCESS

CHAPTER 2   PREWRITING

Generating and Exploring Ideas [pages 23–33] Read the following brainstorm notes, and then answer the following questions.

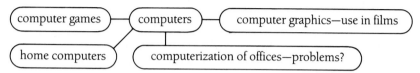

1. Which idea could be generated from these brainstorming notes?
   (a) how a computer works
   (b) new computer companies
   (c) computerizing our school's records
   (d) different computer languages
2. Which question(s) could be used to explore this idea?
   (a) What might be funny about it?   (c) Why did it happen?
   (b) What are my experiences of it?   (d) All of these

Topic, Purpose, and Audience [pages 33–34]   Write the letter of the item that correctly answers the question.

3. Which of the following topics is the most focused?
   (a) the brain (b) testing infants' IQs (c) infant intelligence
4. Which purpose would be more suited to this topic?
   (a) to inform (b) to move readers to act (c) to amuse
5. Which audience would probably be most interested in this topic?
   (a) teen-agers (b) high school teachers (c) child psychologists

Writing for Review   Plan to write a paragraph about something that intrigues you. Generate ideas through freewriting, and then explore your ideas with questions. Then list a purpose, audience, and main idea. Finally, express your main idea in a sentence. Hand in all your notes.

CHAPTER 3   WRITING PARAGRAPHS

Answer the questions based on the following paragraph.

¹Some great writers were also doctors and therefore had a special sensitivity to life. ²Chekhov, for example, was a doctor who wrote with realism and compassion, qualities of a fine writer and a fine doctor. ³Some doctors also became good musicians. ⁴Like Chekhov, Doctor William Carlos Williams used his experience to write about bringing new life into the world. ⁵Of course many writers were not sensitive simply because they were doctors. ⁶But a doctor's experience can result in putting life itself into literature.

Topic Sentences [pages 47–50]
1. Which sentence is the topic sentence of the paragraph?
   (a) sentence 1 (b) sentence 2 (c) sentence 5 (d) sentence 6

Developing a Topic Sentence [pages 50–56]
2. The topic sentence in this paragraph is developed with
   (a) details (b) examples (c) facts (d) reasons

Unity, Coherence, and Organization [pages 58–68]
3. Which sentence is not directly related to the topic sentence?
   (a) sentence 2 (b) sentence 3 (c) sentence 4 (d) sentence 6
4. Sentence 4 contains a transitional expression that shows
   (a) time (b) place (c) order of importance (d) comparison
5. The order used to organize the paragraph is
   (a) chronological (b) spatial (c) importance (d) cause and effect

Writing for Review   Write a paragraph based on the prewriting notes you made in the Writing for Review for Chapter 2. (You may have saved these notes, or your teacher may have returned them to you.)

CHAPTER 4   REVISING, EDITING, AND PROOFREADING
Read the following paragraph and answer the questions based on it.

   ¹Sarah Bernhardt was a popular star. ²She toured the world and acted in great plays. ³Bernhardt became immensely successful. ⁴She had her own place to perform plays and named it after herself. ⁵In this theater she even played, Shakespeare's Hamlet.

Revising the Topic Sentence [pages 74–75]
1. Which of the following sentences is the best revision of sentence 1?
   (a) French actress Sarah Bernhardt was a popular stage star.
   (b) Sarah Bernhardt was a popular and successful actress.
   (c) French actress Sarah Bernhardt was one of the most popular, successful, and versatile stage stars of all time.

Revising Support and Development [pages 77–78]
2. Which of the following revisions of sentence 2 would provide the best support and development of the topic sentence?
   (a) She toured the world, not using her real name—Henriette Bernard.
   (b) She toured the world in leading roles by Racine and Shakespeare.
   (c) She acted in great plays around the world.

Revising for Coherence [pages 80–81]
3. To which sentence would you add the transition word *eventually*?
   (a) sentence 1 (b) sentence 2 (c) sentence 4

Revising Word Choice [pages 81–83]

    4. Which of the following sentences is the best revision of sentence 4?

      (a) She had her own theater and named it after herself.

      (b) She founded her own theater and named it after herself.

      (c) She founded her own theater and named it after Sarah Bernhardt.

Editing and Proofreading [pages 83–87]

    5. Which of the following sentences is the correct revision of sentence 5?

      (a) In this theater she even played Shakespeare's Hamlet.

      (b) In this theater she even played Shakespeares Hamlet.

      (c) In this theater she even played, Shakespeare's Hamlet.

Writing for Review   Revise the paragraph you wrote in the Writing for Review for Chapter 3.

The Development of a Personal Writing Style

Thinking About Thinking: Making Choices According to Criteria

Styles are all around us—hairstyles, building styles, working styles. We praise an athlete's playing style; we enjoy an entertainer's singing style. Each style is the result of choices, many decisions that together form a style. Writing style develops in the same way. As a writer, you make decisions about which words to use as well as when and how and why you use them.

Defining the Skill

When you make a decision about what word or sentence structure works best in a particular situation, you are **MAKING CHOICES ACCORDING TO CRITERIA**. Criteria are standards or tests that you apply when you make a decision. For example, if one of your criteria is simplicity, you may say, "It's raining." However, if concreteness is more important to you, you may say, "The rain is coming down in sheets, and the streets are flooded."

Applying the Skill

Look at the photograph and the drawing. The person who took the photograph and the person who drew the picture each made choices according to criteria. Which one was more interested in details? Which one was more interested in an overall impression? What decisions were based on those criteria? What other criteria do you think were applied?

Thinking About Thinking 95

CHAPTER 5

Choosing Words

Ernest Hemingway: I rewrote the ending to Farewell to Arms, *the last page of it, thirty-nine times before I was satisfied.*
Interviewer: Was there some technical problem there? What was it that had you stumped?
Hemingway: Getting the words right.

—*quoted by Donald Murray in* A Writer Teaches Writing

Word choice is "getting the words right." Often referred to as diction, **word choice** means finding and using the word that fits your meaning and tone exactly. As Hemingway realized, a writer cannot go very far until the words are right.

Words are the writer's tool. Skillful writers are lifetime students of words. They are fascinated by words and their shades of meaning, knowing that a large vocabulary makes communication easier and more exact.

However, skillful writers are not content just with knowing the meanings of countless words. They also want to know how words are categorized and labeled and when it is appropriate to use a given word. For example, is the word *hairdo* slang? Would its use be appropriate in formal writing? When is it appropriate to use an idiom such as "go fly a kite"?

In this chapter you will practice the skills necessary for making informed choices about words:

> writing precisely
> writing concisely
> writing with figurative language

Your goal in this chapter is to recognize that word choice is a deliberate act. It is an act that you can control during prewriting, writing, and revising. Only you know what you want to say, and only you can choose the words that express your idea.

Writing Precisely

Connotation is the unspoken or unwritten meaning associated with a word beyond its exact, dictionary meaning, or its **denotation.**

Knowing the connotations and denotations of words will help you to express ideas with exactness. You can easily verify a word's denotation by looking up the word in a dictionary. However, you will usually not find the word's connotations there. No matter—you have already learned countless connotations from speaking and writing. Your intuitions, based on your study and use of the English language, help you to judge which word is right for a given situation. For instance, what connotations do you associate with the words *home* and *residence*? Which of the two words would you use to complete the following sentence? Why?

As we turned into the long, tree-lined drive, we saw the stately stone _____, which was recently designated a historic landmark.

The denotations of the words *home* and *residence* are the same; one can be used to define the other. The connotations of the two words are different, however, and the words cannot be used interchangeably without affecting the meaning. For example, *residence* brings to mind a dignified, formal structure that was built or occupied by an important person: "The prime minister returned to her residence after addressing Parliament." *Home* connotes comfort, warmth, and protection: "Be it ever so humble, there's no place like home." Imagine replacing *home* in that sentence with the word *residence*.

EXERCISE 1 **Determining Denotations and Connotations.** Using the dictionary, write the denotation of each of the following words. Then, based on your knowledge of English and your imagination and experiences, list at least three connotations you associate with each defined word.

SAMPLE Paris
DENOTATION Capital and largest city of France, in the north-central part of the country, on the Seine.
CONNOTATIONS City of Light; picturesque; sophisticated, romantic; timeless; stylish

1. automobile   3. cuisine   5. computer
2. football   4. Washington, D.C.

EXERCISE 2 **Selecting Words by Connotation.** The following quotations are by famous writers. Above each quotation are three words that may be used to complete the writer's thought; in fact, one of the three *is* the writer's precise word. Based on your knowledge of English and your intuitions, choose the word that best completes each quotation. Write one reason for each of your choices.

1. unchosen   unlucky   untimely
   Death lies upon her like an _____ frost
   Upon the sweetest flower of all the field.
                                        —William Shakespeare

2. good   legitimate   authorized
   The will of the people is the only _____ foundation of any government, and to protect its free expression should be our first object.

   —Thomas Jefferson

3. comfort   blessing   delight
   There is certain relief in change, even though it be from bad to worse; as I have found in traveling in a stagecoach, that it is often a _____ to shift one's position and be bruised in a new place.

   —Washington Irving

4. answer   reply   echo
   True ease in writing comes from art, not chance
   As those move easiest who have learned to dance.
   'Tis not enough no harshness gives offense,
   The sound must seem a [n] _____ to the sense.

   —Alexander Pope

5. thought   reaction   request
   When I come across a generalization or general statement in history unsupported by illustration I am instantly on my guard; my _____ is "Show me."

   —Barbara Tuchman

General and Specific Words

A **general** word is all-embracing, indefinite, and broad in scope, while a **specific** word is explicit, definite, and narrower in scope.

GENERAL	SPECIFIC	MORE SPECIFIC
entertainment	play	*Julius Caesar*
insect	butterfly	Eastern swallowtail
talk	confer	wrangle

Use as many specific words in your writing as possible. Specific words, since they are narrower in scope, are more informative than general words and help your readers to understand your meaning more exactly. Notice, for example, how much more you learn about Mary's mother's kitchen when the general word *gadgets* is replaced by specifics. Also notice how much more interesting the sentence becomes.

GENERAL Mary's mother's kitchen is filled with lots of gadgets.
SPECIFIC Mary's mother's kitchen is filled with the latest in food processors, toaster ovens, coffee grinders, pasta makers, and even an electric wok.

Ordering Words from General to Specific. Arrange in a written list the words in each item below, starting with the most general word and ending with the most specific.

1. song, soprano aria, music, "Vissi d'arte," aria
2. Cutlass, transportation, Oldsmobile, car
3. citrus, food, tangelo, fruit
4. baseball player, athlete, Mookie Wilson, Met, center fielder
5. dog, mammal, bull terrier, animal

Concrete and Abstract Words

Concrete words refer to a thing or a feature that you can see, touch, taste, smell, or hear. Words are **abstract** when they refer to ideas, qualities, and feelings.

CONCRETE movie, sandpaper, carrot, fragrant, noisy
ABSTRACT beauty, joy, freedom, fierce, impossible

Using concrete words will help you to convey your precise meaning to your reader. When you write about such abstract ideas as freedom or honor, use concrete words to make your ideas explicit. For example, the phrase "animal's loyalty" may be made more exact by adding details: "Many pet owners are rewarded by an animal's loyalty either at a time of danger, such as a fire, or on a simple day-to-day basis over many years." This sentence could be made even more explicit: "Not until our dog Fritz saved my brother Pete from a fire did I fully appreciate Fritz's loyalty."

To decide whether or not a sentence contains words that are concrete ask yourself *Who? What? When? Where? Why?* and *How?*—the *Five W*s and *H* that were introduced in Chapter 2. If the sentence can answer one or more of these questions precisely, it probably contains concrete words.

EXERCISE 4 **Recognizing Concrete and Abstract Words.** As you read the following passage, decide which of the underlined words and phrases are abstract and which are concrete. Then on a separate sheet of paper list the underlined words under the headings *abstract* and *concrete*, and indicate to which of the five senses each item on the concrete list refers. Some of the words may be put into more than one sensory category.

There are many ways to learn how to live dangerously. Men of the plains have had the experience in the trackless blizzards that sweep in from the north. Those who go out in boats from Gloucester have known it in another form. The mountains that traverse this country offer still a different way, and one that for many is the most exciting of all. The mountains can be reached in all seasons. They offer a fighting challenge to heart, soul, and mind, both in <u>summer</u> and in <u>winter</u>. If, throughout <u>time</u>, the youth of the nation accept the challenge the mountains offer, they will help keep alive in our <u>people</u> the <u>spirit</u> of <u>adventure</u>. That spirit is a measure of the <u>vitality</u> of both nations and men. The people who climb the <u>ridges</u> and sleep under the <u>stars</u> in the high mountain <u>meadows</u>, who enter the <u>forest</u> and scale the <u>peaks</u>, who explore <u>glaciers</u> and walk ridges buried deep in <u>snow</u>— these people will give their country some of the <u>indomitable</u> spirit of the mountains.

—William O. Douglas

Levels of Diction

The three levels of diction are informal, middle, and formal. Being aware of these levels will help you to choose the right words for your purpose and audience. Some purposes and audiences require serious treatment, whereas other purposes and audiences call for casual treatment. The lists below present examples of the three levels.

INFORMAL	MIDDLE	FORMAL
bread	money	capital
specs	glasses	spectacles
threads	clothes	attire

Informal diction includes words used in everyday conversations.

Informal diction is too casual for most essays written for school but is often perfect for dialogue in a narration. For example, a character in one of your stories may say, "Washing my threads was a real drag." However, you probably would not use this sentence as the topic sentence of a formal paragraph written for English class. If you are uncertain of whether or not a word is informal, check the dictionary. You may find the label *informal* or the labels for two other kinds of informal words—*colloquial* and *slang*.

Colloquial is a term that refers to everyday language used in conversation and in writing intended to have the same feeling as actual speech. Words such as *cute, exam,* and *sure* (for *certainly*) are typical colloquialisms.

Slang is a label given to extremely informal (or extremely colloquial) words or meanings. **Slang** is composed mostly of new words or unusual uses of existing words. In both writing and speech slang creates a noticeable effect, such as humor or exaggeration. *Cool, wheels, split,* and *vibes* are familiar slang words. Neither slang nor colloquialisms are considered "incorrect" or "bad" English. What was slang twenty years ago may have become quite respectable today. The words *hairdo, handout* and *shabby,* for example all began as slang and now belong to the category of middle diction.

Middle diction falls between informal and formal diction.

Middle diction represents the words most often used in newspaper and magazine writing and in television newscasts. Middle diction is the best choice for your writing, whether for school or in a letter to a newspaper. The words are familiar both to you and to your audience, and they will enable you to present your ideas straightforwardly and unpretentiously. For example, if you are writing an article for the school newspaper on clothes shopping, you may begin with this sentence: "While most students enjoy wearing new clothes, many find shopping for them an annoyance."

Formal diction is the language used in scholarly books and journals.

You are much more likely to read these words than hear them or speak them. If you use formal words without knowing their connotations and denotations, your writing will sound unnatural and forced. Avoiding formal diction unless it is appropriate to your subject and audience eliminates the danger of mixed diction, a condition that can confuse your readers. For example, if you are writing a serious article on shopping for clothes but mix formal, middle, and informal diction, your readers may find your article humorous: "While most students enjoy wearing new clothes, many find shopping for threads a vexation."

EXERCISE 5 | **Determining Level of Diction.** To which level of diction—informal, middle, or formal—does each of the following words belong? Make a heading for each level, and categorize the words. Use a dictionary if necessary. Provide a middle-level synonym for each word on your formal and informal lists.

For example, if the word *pal* appeared below, you would put it on the list headed *informal*, and you might note *friend* as a middle-level equivalent.

1. pageant
2. estuary
3. idea
4. guy
5. erudite

6. abrogate
7. nerd
8. inflation
9. well-heeled
10. go-getter

Idioms

An **idiom** is an expression that is unique to a particular language.

Derived from a Latin word meaning "peculiarity in language," an idiom cannot be translated word for word into another language because the literal meaning of its individual words is different from its overall meaning. For example, "Rita lost her temper" means that Rita became angry, not that she misplaced her anger.

Most idioms are listed under the main entry of their key word, after the basic list of meanings (see the sample dictionary entry in Chapter 33). For instance, the idiom "to keep one's own counsel" may be found under the main entry of its key word, *counsel*. According to the dictionary, it is a formal idiom that means "to keep one's thoughts and plans to oneself." Informal idioms are labeled *informal, colloquial,* or *slang*.

EXERCISE 6 **Finding Idioms.** Using a dictionary, find an idiom based on each of the key words listed below. Then write a sentence using the idiom.

SAMPLE   throw
        to throw out
        They threw out all his suggestions.

1. hand   3. back   5. easy
2. take   4. ground

Writing Concisely

Inflated diction is unnatural, pretentious, imprecise, and overly formal language.

Some writers use inflated diction because they think readers will be impressed by the weight of their words. Unfortunately, their readers are too busy translating the verbiage into plain English to be impressed. The best way to control inflated diction is to ask yourself two questions: How would I express this idea in speech? and Are my words specific and concrete enough to convey my meaning? Look, for example, at the sentence below. How might it be more simply stated?

> The primary hindrance to my participating in the activities of Saturday last was a slight indisposition on my part.

An alternative might be "I missed the game last Saturday because I had a cold." This second version uses precise words to tell exactly what happened and would sound natural in conversation. The first version, on the other hand, sounds unnatural and may actually confuse people.

Deflating Inflated Diction. Rewrite the following sentences using middle-level diction. Asking yourself these questions will help eliminate inflated diction: How would I express this idea in speech? Are the words specific and concrete enough to convey the meaning?

SAMPLE Elizabeth was beset by a multitude of pressing activities.
REWRITE Elizabeth was very busy.

1. Numerous concepts of information became apparent to me after having been present at the lecture.
2. Harry's predominant concern of the moment was to extricate himself from poverty by finding gainful employment.
3. Torrents of water descended from above.
4. The town's expansion in terms of population grew in the period of time following the turn of the century.
5. This critic's feelings in regard to foreign cinema can only be described as favorable.

Clichés

A **cliché** is an expression that has become trite through excessive use.

Clichés were once vital, effective expressions, but overuse has robbed them of their meaning and freshness. Although it may be appropriate to use a cliché in writing now and then, your writing will be livelier if you invent your own expressions and use straightforward language. Writing that is full of clichés sounds flat and unimaginative. Consider the following:

CLICHÉ Mary's mother made a cake that was lighter than air.
BETTER Mary's mother made a cake so light it almost floated off the plate.

CLICHÉ Martin was green with envy at his sister's success.
BETTER Martin was envious of his sister's success.

To decide whether or not an expression is a cliché, read the first few words of the expression and see if the last part automatically comes to mind. Try this approach with the following examples: *from the bottom. . ., as a rule of. . ., go in one ear. . . .*

EXERCISE 8 **Replacing a Cliché with a Specific Word.** Substitute one specific, carefully chosen word for each cliché below.

1. mass of humanity
2. abreast of the times
3. crack of dawn
4. last but not least
5. scratch the surface
6. few and far between
7. down to earth
8. burn the midnight oil
9. funny for words
10. a loss for words

EXERCISE 9 **Eliminating Clichés.** Rewrite the following sentences, substituting more original words for the cliches. Some sentences have more than one cliché.

1. Her grandmother is the very picture of health; she is a hale and hearty woman.
2. Robert realized his chances of winning the race were gone with the wind when he sprained his ankle.
3. Despite the difficulty of the assignment, Kate stuck to her guns and kept a stiff upper lip.
4. I'm sorry, but what you just told me went in one ear and out the other.
5. The extra rehearsals really paid off: The performance went like clockwork.

Jargon

Jargon is a specialized vocabulary of a group or profession.

Lawyers, doctors, computer programmers, mechanics, and other groups have their own jargon, or terminology. Jargon is appropriate and acceptable when used by a specialist writing or speaking to other specialists in the same field. It is inappropriate in school writing when ordinary words will convey meaning just as well. Taken out of its professional surroundings, jargon obscures the clarity of your writing. As with inflated diction, jargon must often be translated into plain English to be understood. Study the following examples:

> JARGON The council's decision on fall entertainment priorities was mandated: Due to poor cash flow, the dance was off, but the fund-raiser got the nod.
>
> BETTER Despite complaints from students, the council canceled the fall dance because of a lack of funds and approved the fund-raiser.
>
> JARGON Interfacing with consumers produced input on user-friendly features of the latest campaign.
>
> BETTER A survey showed which parts of the new advertisements consumers liked best.

EXERCISE 10 **Replacing Jargon.** Write an alternative word or phrase for each of the items listed below. Use the dictionary if necessary to determine the exact meaning of these words.

1. state of the art
2. expenditure
3. prognosis
4. upscale
5. time-frame

Writing with Figurative Language

A **figure of speech,** or **figurative languate,** is a word or phrase used in an imaginative, rather than a literal, sense. **Literal language** is language that means exactly what it says, word for word.

Figurative language is used to make writing more vivid and lively. The three figures of speech that you are most likely to use when you write are simile, metaphor, and personification.

A **simile** is a figure of speech that directly compares two seemingly unlike things, using a comparing word such as *like* or *as.*

The items compared in a simile are basically not alike, but they do share some characteristics. For example, when the English poet Alfred, Lord Tennyson writes that the eagle "watches from his mountain walls / And like a thunderbolt he falls," he is drawing on the sudden, swift power characteristic of both the eagle and thunder. Statements comparing items that are actually alike are not similes. For example, "My dog looks like a guard dog" is not a simile; "My dog looks like a bank guard on duty" is a simile.

A **metaphor** is a figure of speech that makes an implied comparison between two seemingly unlike things.

Unlike a simile, a metaphor does not use a comparing word:

SIMILE   My hand is like a starfish.
METAPHOR   My hand is a starfish.

Metaphors make writing lively and exciting by revealing surprising similarities in objects not normally considered alike. When they are unusual, metaphors can lend dramatic power to a piece of writing, as in the following example:

> She was very old and small and she walked slowly in the dark pine shadows, moving a little from side to side in her steps, with the balanced heaviness and lightness of a pendulum in a grandfather clock.
>
> —Eudora Welty

Personification is a figure of speech in which an animal, object, or idea is given human qualities.

Personification implies that a nonhuman thing has personality, intelligence, and emotion. For example, through personification a writer may say that the sky will glower and threaten rain one day and that the sun will reach out a warm caress the next. One should be careful not to overuse personification or to use it inappropriately.

EXERCISE 11   **Identifying Figurative Language.** Identify in writing the figurative language in each of the following sentences, and note whether each example is a simile, metaphor, or personification. Then write a sentence explaining why the figure is effective. Some of the sentences have more than one figure.

1. The trees began softly to sing a hymn of twilight.

—Stephen Crane

2. He gave her a look you could have poured on a waffle.

—Ring Lardner

3. This is a snail shell, round, full, and glossy as a horse chestnut.

—Anne Morrow Lindbergh

4. All about between the horizons, the carpet of land unrolled itself to infinity.

—Frank Norris

5. The storm howled and whined, driving the snow before it like giant breakers.

—O.E. Rølvagg

EXERCISE 12   **Writing Figurative Language.** Select five items from the following list. For each one, write a sentence that expresses an idea through figurative language. Write at least one example each of simile, metaphor, and personification. See, for example, the sentences in Exercise 11.

1. trees bending in the wind
2. a deserted building
3. the way an animal walks
4. music
5. cars in a traffic jam
6. a person's hand gestures
7. waking up in the morning
8. sore muscles
9. a landscape
10. shadows

 Checklist for Choosing Words

1. What are the denotations of my words? What are their connotations? Would other words be more precise?
2. Which of my general words can I replace with specific words?
3. Which of my abstract words can I replace with concrete words?
4. What level of diction have I used—informal, middle, or formal? Which, if any, of my words should be changed to make my word choice more consistent?
5. Which, if any, idioms, cliches, or instances of inflated diction or jargon should be replaced?
6. What similes, metaphors, and personification would improve my writing?

7. Have I avoided cliches, such as "blind as a bat," "fit as a fiddle," "mad as a hornet," and so on?

8. Have I avoided mixed metaphors, or inconsistent comparisons, such as, "The King's fiery temper was quenched by an avalanche of applause from his subjects."

9. Have I avoided far-fetched, elaborate figures of speech, such as, "The grazing cow gazed out across the pasture with a soulful, philosophic stare"?

10. In sum, how appropriate is my word choice for my purpose and audience?

Writer's Choice

Throughout this chapter you have concentrated on skills that help you make informed choices about words. To give yourself practice in applying what you have learned to writing compositions, try one or more of the following Writer's Choice assignments. Some are highly structured and give you specific ideas on how to proceed. In others you determine your own direction. Whichever assignment you choose, however, remember that the practice will be most valuable to you if you apply all the skills you have learned in this chapter.

Writer's Choice #1

ASSIGNMENT To write a paragraph about a violent storm

LENGTH Six or seven sentences

AUDIENCE A neighbor who was away when the storm occurred

PURPOSE To describe the storm, its noise, colors, smells, and so forth

PREWRITING Close your eyes, and run a movie of the storm in your mind. Using vivid, concrete words, list at least ten things that you see in the movie.

WRITING Begin by stating what kind of storm you are describing and when and where the storm takes place. Then in four or five sentences use precise, colorful words to explain how the storm looks to you. End with a statement about the way you reacted to the violence of the storm.

REVISING Make sure that you have used the exact words to convey your impression of the storm. Ask yourself the questions on the checklist on pages 106–107. Then edit and proofread your paragraph.

Writer's Choice #2

ASSIGNMENT To write a paragraph of advice that could be included in a letter

LENGTH Six to seven sentences

AUDIENCE Your older brother or sister, who is living away from home and thinking of buying a used car

PURPOSE To point out the connotations of the names of cars your brother or sister is considering

PREWRITING Assume that your brother or sister is thinking of buying a Duster, Dart, Mustang, or Pinto. Make a list of at least three connotations that you associate with each of the car names. Then decide which car name best suits the personality of your brother or sister.

WRITING   In your topic sentence tell why you are writing the letter. Then write four or five sentences to explain the connotations you link to the name of each car. End with a sentence in which you suggest which car your brother or sister should buy, and include the reason for your choice.

REVISING   Ask yourself the questions on the checklist on pages 106–107. Then edit and proofread your paragraph.

Writer's Choice #3

ASSIGNMENT   To revise a paragraph

LENGTH   Your choice

AUDIENCE   Your choice

PURPOSE   To rework a paragraph that you wrote for an earlier assignment. In your revision your goal is to include precise, concise, and vivid language.

OPTIONS   You may want to concentrate on using specific and concrete words to evoke an appropriate mood, or atmosphere.

You may want to introduce similes, metaphors, and personification to bring life to your paragraph.

You may find brainstorming and charting helpful techniques to use now even though you are in the revising stage. Remember: Writing is a process that involves moving back and forth from one stage to another.

Writer's Choice #4

ASSIGNMENT   To write a paragraph on any topic

LENGTH   Your choice

AUDIENCE   Your choice

PURPOSE   To describe exactly what you see

OPTIONS   You may base your description on a photograph in the Writer's Sourcebook, pages 354–357.

You may base your description on the view from the library window.

Remember to use prewriting techniques and then to revise your work—including editing and proofreading.

Writers On Writing

Born in Los Angeles, Peter Wilke spent his childhood in several cities. His plans include travel and a career in advertising or real estate development. He wrote the following paragraph and commentary as a student at Indian Hill High School in Cincinnati, Ohio.

THE PRODUCT

The timber crackled and popped as the fire licked the flame from it, and beyond the red ring of light a hoot owl hooted, answering the call of a wolf in the distance. Inside the warm, orangy circle little stirs, as we lean, or rather lie, on soft logs, eyes dozing, eyes staring at dancing flames mesmerizing the mind, stirring pleasant memories. We are drifting, slowly drifting, away from conscious thought, wrapped in dreams of yesterday. Then all are startled by four legs trotting, four leaves rustling, and light panting. "Oh, just the dog," who pushes through the perimeter of light, just to the outside, and lies down to sleep, back from the cold distance.

THE PROCESS

In this piece I wanted to convey the drowsy security that people feel around a campfire. I was also trying to capture an impression that most readers can relate to: the warm, secure campfire contrasted with the stark, bleak, potentially threatening world beyond. It was helpful to include concrete images to create this impression: the hoot owl, the wolf call, the red ring of light.

Word choice was important in getting this piece to where I was satisfied with it. The word "licked" instead of "burned" creates a finer image; "orangy" calls up a softer image than just "orange." "Startled" shakes the reader more than "awakened" would, and "the dog who pushes" through the light reinforces the idea of an inner sphere more than "the dog who walks" would. In any piece of writing, strong images and careful word choice are important factors in the feeling and impression that the writer wants to share.

YOUR TURN *Writing with Vivid Words*

As Peter Wilke did, write a paragraph using specific language and concrete images to describe a place or a moment that was special to you. Use vivid details that appeal to several senses.

CHAPTER 6

Combining and Varying Sentences

To shift the structure of a sentence alters the meaning of that sentence . . . [just as shifting] the position of a camera alters the meaning of the object photographed. . . . The arrangement of the words matters, and the arrangement you want can be found in the picture in your mind.

—Joan Didion

The way you arrange the words in your sentences can mean the difference between making your point and not making it. Read the following sentences, for instance. Do they hold your attention?

> The biology students walked down to the beach. They knelt around a large tide pool. They peered intently at the creatures inside. Sea anemones and starfish clung to the rocks. Tiny fish floated in the still water. Small crabs crept along the bottom. A student touched the water. The fish quickly darted behind the rocks. The crabs burrowed into the sand. They vanished.

Are you still awake? The choppy, monotonous, and boring sentences plod along, stamping out any spark of interest you might feel in the scene being described. Now see what happens when the writer pays some attention to sentence structure:

> The biology students walked down to the beach, knelt around a large tidal pool, and peered intently at the creatures inside. Clinging to the rocks of the pool were brightly colored starfish and sea anemones. Tiny fish floated in the still water, while small crabs crept along the bottom. A student touched the water. Quickly, the fish darted behind the rocks, as the crabs, burrowing into the sand, vanished.

Suddenly the picture snaps into focus. What happened? The words are almost exactly the same, but how they are arranged into sentences is different. The writer has combined some sentences, effectively balancing short ones against long ones, highlighting some ideas and playing down others. The sentences vary in their beginnings and in their structure. One sentence, "Clinging to the rocks of the pool were brightly colored starfish and sea anemones," inverts normal sentence order so that you will pause to see the creatures on the rocks. A short sentence, "A student touched the water," delicately signals a change in the action. The writing is lively, fluent, and unpredictable—and much more satisfying.

To help you write more satisfying sentences, this chapter will give you practice in the following skills:

> expanding sentences with words and phrases
> combining sentences through coordination
> combining sentences through subordination
> combining sentences through coordination and subordination
> combining sentences by using other structures
> writing concise sentences and paragraphs
> creating variety in sentences
> using parallelism for effect

Exercising these skills will give you scope and variety as a writer of sentences. You will find it easier to make words flow together gracefully and compellingly. Best of all, you will find that you are creating sentences worthy of the pictures in your mind as you transform your mental images into verbal images.

Expanding Sentences with Words and Phrases

When you read your first drafts, do your sentences sometimes seem short and choppy? One short sentence is fine, but a string of them can sound halting and awkward, not to mention vague. Expanding short sentences with details will make your writing smoother, clearer, and much more specific.

You can expand choppy sentences by adding words and phrases that tell more about the nouns and verbs.

> A kayak is a boat.
>
> A kayak is a **light, narrow** boat **with an enclosed deck.** [expanded with adjectives and a prepositional phrase that modify the noun *boat*]
>
> The kayakers paddled their boats.
>
> **Swiftly and easily** the kayakers paddled their boats **through the rapids.** [expanded with adverbs and a prepositional phrase that modify the verb *paddled*]

Where do you find information to add to sentences? You can generate additional details about a sentence by asking questions such as *how many? what kind? when? how?* and *where?*

Whenever you add information to a sentence, you need to decide where to place the additional words and phrases. Usually you will have some choices. Always try to place words and phrases near the terms they describe. When you want to emphasize a detail, place it at either the beginning or the end of the sentence.

Expanding Sentences by Adding Details. Rewrite each of the following sentences, adding words or phrases to each. The questions after each item suggest the kinds of details you can add.

SAMPLE Snow started to fall. (a) What kind of snow was it? (b) When did the snow start to fall?

REVISION *Around midnight a wet, heavy snow* started to fall.

REVISION *A wet, heavy snow* started to fall *around midnight.*

1. A car raced down the street. (a) What color was the car? (b) How did the car race?
2. The waitress brought the meal. (a) Of what did the meal consist? (b) Where did she bring the meal?
3. The members of the club voted. (a) When did they vote? (b) For whom or what did they vote?
4. The driver honked his horn. (a) Which driver honked? (b) At whom or what did the driver honk?
5. Jim worked in the darkroom. (a) When or how did Jim work? (b) On what did Jim work?

Combining Sentences Through Coordination

Almost as soon as you learned to speak, you began to coordinate your sentences. That is, you tied two or more sentences together with words such as *and, or, nor, but,* and *for*—words called coordinating conjunctions. Now you need to think about how your writing can take advantage of this coordination. Look, for instance, at the following two sentences:

Certain bacteria live harmlessly in the body. Others cause diseases.

The ideas in these two sentences are almost equally important and are so closely related that they could be combined in one sentence. You can show that they are related and equal by combining them with *but:*

Certain bacteria live harmlessly in the body, **but** others cause diseases.

If two sentences are closely related and almost equal in importance, stress their relatedness and equality by combining them through coordination.

You decide when to use coordination. Be selective: Joining idea after idea through coordination can turn your writing into an endless string pieced together. You also need to find the most appropriate word or phrase to signal the coordination. The following chart groups the most common coordinating words and phrases. The purpose of the coordination comes first, then the coordinating words, and finally the examples. Note the punctuation used with each example. For rules about punctuating coordinated sentences, see Chapter 27.

COORDINATION CHART

PURPOSE	COORDI-NATOR	EXAMPLE
To show an alternative	or, nor, otherwise	Follow the map, **or** you will lose your way. Follow the map; **otherwise** you will lose your way.
To signal an addition	and, also, furthermore, in addition, similarly	The new building will cover a whole block, **and** its plaza will be the largest in the area. The new building will cover a whole block; **also**, its plaza will be the largest in the area.
To show a reason	for	Long-distance trains move people comfortably, **for** they come equipped with sleeping and dining cars.
To signal contrast	but, yet, instead, nevertheless, still, however	Long-distance trains move people comfortably, **but** some travelers prefer to drive. Long-distance trains move people comfortably; **still**, some travelers prefer to drive.
To signal an example	for example, for instance	A bicycle is designed to suit its purpose; **for example**, a touring bicycle has a very strong frame.
To show a result	as a result, thus, so, therefore	Japanese passengers line up to ride subways; **as a result**, they board the trains in an orderly way.
To show balance	a semicolon	"Anchors Aweigh" is the Navy's marching song; blue and gold are its official colors.

Combining Sentences Through Coordination. Rewrite each of the following pairs of sentences as one sentence. Use a word or phrase that expresses the relationship shown in parentheses. Refer to the words and phrases on the preceding coordination chart. Notice that the sentences in each pair are closely related. Also notice that they are almost equal in importance.

SAMPLE   Marine training has always been rigorous. It has recently become more scientific. (contrast)

REVISION   Marine training has always been rigorous, *but it has recently become more scientific.*

1. A boomerang is curved in the middle. Its two ends are shaped like airplane wings. (addition)
2. A spinning boomerang creates differences in air pressure. These differences cause the boomerang to stay airborne. (balance)
3. A returning boomerang must be thrown carefully. It might injure the thrower or a bystander. (alternative)
4. The thrower releases the returning boomerang. It spins through the air in a curving path. (addition)
5. Throwing a boomerang is difficult. With practice it can be done with ease. (contrast)
6. A nonreturning boomerang can be thrown accurately at a target. It makes a good weapon. (result)
7. Australian aborigines use nonreturning boomerangs as weapons. The boomerang can strike a target with great force. (reason)
8. Boomerangs have many other uses. Aborigines decorate them for religious ceremonies. (example)

EXERCISE 3   **Combining Sentences Through Coordination.** Rewrite the following paragraph, combining sentences through coordination. You may combine any number of sentences; you may also leave some sentences as they are. The paragraph now contains thirteen sentences. Your version should contain between seven and nine.

Most oceangoing vessels rely on powerful engines. Sailboats use only the wind and the currents. Adventurous sailors embark on long ocean crossings in sailboats. Often these small craft lack sophisticated navigational equipment. The sailors must navigate by the sun. An ocean crossing takes many days. The sailors are rarely bored. Each day they plot their position. The boat might sail on the wrong course. Other chores keep the members of the crew busy. For example, they must constantly tend to the condition of the sails and rigging. These sailors attempt such journeys despite the dangers. The challenge of the open sea outweighs the dangers.

Combining Sentences Through Subordination

Although coordination is useful, coordinating too many ideas in a row can make your writing monotonous, as in this example:

> I threw the basketball, and it bounced off the backboard. It had done this sixty times before, but I still hoped for better luck. I was tired, yet I threw the ball one last time. It balanced on the edge of the hoop, and I held my breath. Then it dropped through, and I felt like a superstar.

Because this passage strings together five coordinated sentences, it clops along predictably, giving every idea equal emphasis. Now look at a revision of the passage. This version is livelier and more varied:

> I threw the basketball, which hit the backboard just as it had done sixty times before. Still, I hoped for better luck. I was tired, yet I threw the ball one last time. As it balanced on the edge of the hoop, I held my breath. When it dropped through, I felt like a superstar.

This passage uses some coordination, but it also highlights certain ideas and puts others in the background through a method known as *subordination. To subordinate* means "to place below another in rank or importance."

Subordinate a less important idea to a more important one.

The following pages will give you practice in using subordination.

Subordinating Information About Nouns

How would you combine these two sentences?

1. Edgar Allan Poe is an American writer.
2. Edgar Allan Poe surprises me.

You know that you can coordinate the two sentences, giving equal weight to each of them:

3. Edgar Allan Poe is an American writer, and he surprises me.

If, however, you wish to stress one statement and deemphasize the other, you can combine the two sentences in one of the following ways:

VERSION A Edgar Allan Poe, **who is an American writer**, surprises me. [Sentence I has been subordinated to an adjective clause that tells more about the noun *Edgar Allan Poe.*]

VERSION B Edgar Allan Poe, **who surprises me**, is an American writer. [Sentence 2 has been subordinated to an adjective clause that modifies *Edgar Allan Poe.*]

VERSION C Edgar Allan Poe is an American writer **who surprises me**. [Sentence 2 has been subordinated to an adjective clause that modifies *writer.*]

Version A subordinates the information about Poe's nationality. Versions B and C subordinate the information about Poe's effect on the reader. Notice that in all three versions the subordinated idea is introduced by the word *who*. In each case *who* replaces Edgar Allan Poe, a noun in the original sentence.

Subordinate information in one sentence to modify a noun or pronoun in another sentence by using the words *who, whom, whose, that, which, when,* and *where*.

The subordinated sentence that tells more about a noun is called a *relative clause,* or an *adjective clause.* The word that introduces the relative clause, or adjective clause, is called a *relative pronoun.*

Now notice that the relative clause in version A and the one in version B are separated from the rest of the sentence by commas. They are set off this way because neither is essential to the meaning of the rest of the sentence. These relative clauses merely give extra information about a noun that is already clear to us—Edgar Allan Poe. In version C, however, the relative clause is essential to the meaning of the sentence; that is, it limits or restricts the meaning of "American writer." You would not want to use commas and set off a clause that is essential to your meaning. You will find more information about essential and nonessential relative clauses in Chapters 20 and 27.

Here is a chart that illustrates the use of relative pronouns for subordinating information about nouns:

SUBORDINATING INFORMATION ABOUT NOUNS

ORIGINAL SENTENCES	COMBINED BY SUBORDINATION
Leonardo da Vinci was a genius. He sketched the first helicopter.	Leonardo da Vinci, **who** sketched the first helicopter, was a genius.
He is an inventor. I admire him.	He is an inventor **whom** I admire.
He is an artist. I have studied his paintings.	He is an artist **whose** paintings I have studied.
Leonardo sketched a helicopter. This helicopter is very different from modern ones.	Leonardo sketched a helicopter **that** is very different from modern ones.
I visited the city heliport. Tourists can take short flights there.	I visited the city heliport, **where** tourists can take short flights.
I remember a day last fall. I first saw the city from a helicopter.	I remember a day last fall **when** I first saw the city from a helicopter.

EXERCISE 4 **Subordinating Information About Nouns.** Rewrite each of the following pairs of short sentences as a single sentence with subordinated information about a noun. You may have several options.

SAMPLE   Henry Ford set up the first assembly line. He launched the Model T in 1909.

REVISION   Henry Ford, *who launched the Model T in 1909*, set up the first assembly line.

REVISION   Henry Ford, *who set up the first assembly line*, launched . . .

1. In 1892 a Connecticut dentist designed a squeezable tube. This tube could dispense toothpaste.
2. Edwin Land invented the Polaroid camera. He was inspired by his daughter.
3. Alexander Graham Bell wanted to be remembered for his services to the deaf. His invention of the telephone stunned the world.
4. King Gillette revolutionized shaving in the year 1895. He invented a safety razor then.
5. My grandfather patented seventy-three inventions. I never met him.
6. Benjamin Franklin designed a cast-iron fireplace. It was three times as effective as a traditional fireplace.
7. In 1922 two Englishmen entered a deserted tomb. There they found the mummy of Tutankhamen, or King Tut.
8. The first high school for girls was founded by Emma Willard. It opened in 1821.

Subordinating Information About Verbs

You can also subordinate information in one sentence to modify a verb in another sentence. That is, one sentence can be subordinated to tell *when, where, how, why, to what extent,* or *under what conditions* the action of the verb is performed.

How many different statements can you make by combining these two sentences?

I enjoyed myself. I went to the party.

Here are a few possibilities:

I enjoyed myself **before I went to the party.**
I enjoyed myself **because I went to the party.**
I enjoyed myself **although I went to the party.**

The important information in each sentence is *I enjoyed myself.* The less important, subordinated information in each sentence concerns *when, why,* or *under what conditions* I enjoyed myself. The subordinated information is presented in adverb clauses, which modify the verb *enjoyed.*

Subordinate one sentence to another in order to tell when, where, how, why, to what extent, and under what conditions the action of the other sentence was performed.

You have many options for writing sentences using this kind of subordination. First you can choose *which idea to subordinate:*

> Felice is happy. She is productive.
> Felice is happy **because she is productive.**
> Felice is productive **because she is happy.**

You can also try placing the subordinated information in *different positions.* Finally, you have the option of determining the *exact relationship* you want to show between the two ideas. The word you choose to introduce the subordinated idea will clarify that relationship. Note how the following sentences express different relationships:

> We dream **because** our brains produce impulses.
> We dream **when** our brains produce impulses.
> We dream **as long as** our brains produce impulses.

You will find more information about adverb clauses in Chapter 20. For information about punctuating adverb clauses, see Chapter 27. Here is a list of words that can introduce adverb clauses:

1. To introduce subordinate ideas that tell *when:*

after	before	when
as	since	whenever
as soon as	until	while

2. To introduce subordinate ideas that tell *where:*

where	wherever

3. To introduce subordinate ideas that tell *how:*

as	as if	as though

4. To introduce subordinate ideas that tell *why:*

as	in order that	so that
because	since	

5. To introduce subordinate ideas that tell *to what extent:*

as far as	as long as	than
as fast as		

6. To introduce subordinate ideas that state *conditions:*

although	whether (or not)	unless
so long as	inasmuch as	while
considering (that)	(even) if	

EXERCISE 5   **Subordinating Information About Verbs.** Rewrite each of the following pairs of sentences as a single sentence with a subordinate idea that tells more about its verb. You will have to choose between several alternative ways of rewriting each pair.

SAMPLE   Alexander the Great died young. He had conquered most of the world.

REVISION   Alexander the Great died young, *after he had conquered most of the world.*

REVISION   *Although he died young,* Alexander the Great had conquered most of the world.

1. The soldiers stood at attention. The general's motorcade passed.
2. The marathon runner sprinted across the finish line. She had fought muscle spasms in her final two miles.
3. Children now learn about computers very early in school. Children are more at ease with computers than their parents are.
4. Blake kidded Julie about her new hair style. She "accidentally" stepped on his new running shoes.
5. Bulbs survive the winter. They are planted six inches underground.
6. Clipper sailing ships became obsolete. The British developed the oceangoing steamship.
7. We camped last summer. We saw mosquitoes as large as houseflies everywhere.
8. Roger gave me his ticket. I could see the show.
9. Caitha practices the piano two hours every day. Sometimes she does not feel like practicing.
10. The presidential primary campaign should be shortened. Most voters are tired of the candidates by election time.

Creating Noun Substitutes

Combine the following two sentences so that you subordinate the underlined sentence:

You want the book. We will buy the book.

Here are a few possibilities:

VERSION A   We will buy the book **that you want.** [information subordinated to a relative, or adjective, clause to tell more about the noun *book*]

VERSION B   We will buy the book **if you want.** [information subordinated to adverb clause to modify the verb *buy*]

VERSION C   We will buy **whatever you want.** [information subordinated to a noun clause to replace the noun *book*]

You already know that you can insert one sentence into another in order to present more information about a *noun,* as in version A here. You also have the option of subordinating a sentence to tell more about a *verb,* as in version B. Now you will see how you can use a third subordination option: You can subordinate one sentence and use it *in place of a noun or a pronoun* in another sentence, as in version C. You can use this option whenever you want to state a fact or include a question within another sentence. You can place the subordinated sentence at the beginning or at the end of the other sentence.

In the first example below, one sentence is added to the beginning of the other to answer a question. In the second example one sentence is added to the end of the other to answer a question.

> Should the networks project early election returns? This question has become an issue in the 1980s.
>
> **Whether or not the networks should project early election returns** has become an issue in the 1980s.
>
> Is he going to college next year? He hasn't told me yet.
>
> He hasn't yet told me **whether he is going to college next year.**

When you want to state a fact or question within a sentence, subordinate the material to replace a noun or pronoun.

You can use the following words to subordinate a sentence that you are adding to another sentence in place of a noun or a pronoun. For more information about noun substitutes, see Chapter 20.

CREATING NOUN SUBSTITUTES

INTRODUCTORY WORD	ORIGINAL SENTENCES	COMBINED WITH SUBORDINATION
who, whoever, whom, whomever, whose	Who wrote this story? He or she has a wild imagination.	**Whoever wrote this story** has a wild imagination.
what, whatever	What did you see? Will you tell me?	Will you tell me **what you saw?**
which, whichever	Which restaurant have you chosen? You will enjoy it.	You will enjoy **whichever restaurant you have chosen.**
how, that, when, where, why, if, whether (or not)	He finished his paper by dinnertime. I was surprised.	I was surprised **that he finished his paper by dinnertime.**

Creating Noun Substitutes at the End of a Sentence.
Rewrite the following pairs of sentences so that one sentence is added to
the end of the other in order to state a fact or answer a question.

SAMPLE Aretha calls me "Roscoe." I do not know why.
REVISION I do not know *why Aretha calls me "Roscoe."*

SAMPLE Who designed this building? The guide does not know.
REVISION The guide does not know *who designed this building.*

1. Glenn bent this soda bottle. Only Glenn knows how.
2. Who wrote the book of love? No one knows.
3. This class will end in exactly two and one-half minutes. I predict it.
4. Whose woods are these? I do not know.

EXERCISE 7 **Creating Noun Substitutes at the Beginning of a Sentence.** Rewrite the following pairs of sentences so that one sentence is
added to the beginning of the other in order to state a fact or answer a
question.

SAMPLE We arrived late. This did not bother our hosts.
REVISION *That we arrived late* did not bother our hosts.

SAMPLE Who has the most points? That person wins the game.
REVISION *Whoever has the most points* wins the game.

1. What happened to Montezuma's millions? This is a mystery.
2. Should we take the car or not? This makes no difference to me.
3. The audience disliked the play. That must have discouraged the writer
   a great deal.
4. Where did she hide the gifts? It was no mystery to us.
5. Who ate the plastic cake? He or she must have been very hungry.

Combining Through Coordination and Subordination

Assume that you are writing a social studies paper and have decided to
combine all the following related statements into a single sentence:

1. In the 1800s cities often had several fire companies.
2. These companies competed against one another.
3. Rival fire fighters fought for water.
4. Fires blazed around them.

You plunge in and write the following:

In the 1800s cities often had several fire companies that competed against
one another; consequently, rival fire fighters often fought for water while
fires blazed around them.

By mixing coordination and subordination, your new sentence clarifies the relationships among all these ideas. You made statements 1 and 3 the major ideas in your sentence, coordinating them with a semicolon and the word *consequently*. With the word *that* you subordinated the information in statement 2 to tell more about the noun *fire companies*. Finally you subordinated statement 4 to modify the verb *fought*.

You can use both coordination and subordination to join two or more equally important ideas with ideas that are less important.

You will have to decide which ideas to highlight and which to subordinate. You will also decide on the order in which you will write your ideas and the words you will use to join them. Most important, as with every other structure you have practiced so far, you always have the option *not* to use both coordination and subordination in a single sentence. Lengthy sentences are effective when used sparingly.

EXERCISE 8 **Revising a Paragraph.** Rewrite the following paragraph, which consists of short sentences. Combine many of these sentences using a variety of the methods you have practiced so far: (1) coordination, (2) subordination, and (3) coordination and subordination within one sentence. Your revised paragraph should contain eight to twelve sentences.

Glaciers are one of nature's most effective carving tools. Glaciers are formed by the gradual accumulation of snow. A glacier creeps slowly across the terrain. It drags rock fragments along its base. These rock fragments grind and scrape the bedrock. The bedrock is beneath the glacier. In this way the glacier dramatically sculpts the landscape. Continental glaciers once covered much of North America. They gouged deep basins. The glaciers then receded. At this time many of these basins filled with water. They became lakes. Glaciers are still at work today. Alpine glaciers etch valleys. These valleys are long and narrow. They extend down the sides of mountains. Glaciers may work slowly. Over the eons they have shaped many spectacular landforms. We see these landforms today.

Combining by Using Other Structures

If coordination and subordination were your only options for tying ideas together in sentences, most writing would begin to sound a little on the heavy side. Now you will study other ways to combine sentences.

Combining with Appositives

When you want to identify or briefly describe a noun in a sentence, you do not always need to insert an entire statement into that sentence. Instead, you can often use a word or phrase that does the job more economically. Such a word or phrase is called an *appositive*. Look, for instance, at different ways of putting together these two pieces of information:

> People can ride hydrofoils across the English Channel. The English Channel is the body of water between England and France.

> VERSION A People can ride hydrofoils across the English Channel, **which is the body of water between England and France.**

> VERSION B People can ride hydrofoils across the English Channel, **the body of water between England and France.**

You might prefer version A if you are writing a paragraph and feel that you need a slightly longer sentence at that point. Also, since version A gives the identification more weight, you might use it if you suspect that your readers have never heard of the English Channel. Version B is more economical, lopping off the subject and verb and going right to the identification: "the body of water between England and France." This phrase is an example of an appositive. You might use version B if you are writing a paragraph and need a shorter sentence or if you think that your readers need only a brief reminder about the English Channel. You can read more about appositives in Chapter 19.

When one statement identifies or briefly describes a noun, you can shorten that statement, making it into an appositive.

Normally appositives follow the nouns they identify or describe. In some cases, however, you can place them at the beginning of a sentence for greater emphasis, as in version B:

> VERSION A Elizabeth Blackwell, **a determined woman,** was the first female physician in this country.

> VERSION B **A determined woman,** Elizabeth Blackwell was the first female physician in this country.

You can also rearrange the sentence to make another term the appositive, as in this example:

> VERSION C Elizabeth Blackwell, **the first female physician in this country,** was a determined woman.

Combining Sentences by Using Appositives. Rewrite each of the following pairs of sentences by using an appositive. In some cases you must decide which sentence to make the appositive and where to place it.

SAMPLE   Mike Nichols is a filmmaker. He began as a comedian.
REVISION   Mike Nichols, *a filmmaker*, began as a comedian.

1. Margaret Bourke-White worked for *Life* magazine. She was a news photographer.
2. Willa Cather was the author of *My Ántonia*. She was a Midwesterner.
3. Eleanor Roosevelt was a leader in her own right. She was the wife of a president.
4. Mary L. Stowe ran for vice president in 1872. She was Victoria Woodhulls's running mate.
5. Hatshepsut was an Egyptian pharaoh. She was a powerful woman.
6. Emily Dickinson was a brilliant poet. She was a recluse.
7. Indira Gandhi was the prime minister of India twice. She was the daughter of Prime Minister Nehru.
8. Mary Pickford was a star of silent films. She was a cofounder of United Artists.
9. Geraldine Ferraro was the daughter of Italian immigrants. She was the Democratic candidate for vice president in 1984.
10. Olympias was the queen of Macedon. Olympias was the mother of Alexander the Great.

Combining with Participles and Participial Phrases

How would you combine the following sentences to highlight the sense of action?

> The halfback sprinted down the field. He was dodging tacklers. He was splattered with mud.

Here is one possibility:

> The halfback, **who was dodging tacklers and splattered with mud,** sprinted down the field.

That sentence is an improvement, but it still does not create the sense of action that you want. Below are two other options. Notice that the versions have the same meaning but are arranged differently.

VERSION A   The halfback, **splattered with mud,** sprinted down the field **dodging tacklers.**
VERSION B   **Splattered with mud,** the halfback sprinted down the field **dodging tacklers.**

These concise sentences capture the action more vividly. They condense the statements about the halfback's appearance and movement into two participial phrases: "splattered with mud" and "dodging tacklers."

You can use participles and participial phrases to signal simultaneous action and clarify cause-and-effect relationships.

The following three sentences refer to actions that are taking place simultaneously—at the same time:

SIMULTANEOUS ACTION 1   The actress recited her lines.
SIMULTANEOUS ACTION 2   She paced.
SIMULTANEOUS ACTION 3   She gestured nervously.

Here they are combined to show the actions occurring at once:

VERSION A   **Gesturing nervously and pacing,** the actress recited her lines.
VERSION B   The actress paced, **reciting her lines and gesturing nervously.**

Notice how version A was formed by changing action 2 into the concise word *pacing* and action 3 into the phrase *gesturing nervously.* Similarly, version B was formed by converting action 1 into the phrase *reciting her lines* and action 3 into *gesturing nervously.* Whichever action you choose to leave in its original form will stand out as the main action.

The following two sentences express a cause and its effect:

CAUSE   Many students were concerned about the exam.
EFFECT   They spoke to their parents.

Here they are combined to show this relationship more clearly:

VERSION A   **Concerned about the exam,** many students spoke to their parents.
VERSION B   Many students, **concerned about the exam,** spoke to their parents.

In both cases the writer took care to put the phrase in a logical place. Look at what would have happened had the writer not been so careful:

Many students spoke to their parents, concerned about the exam.

The *parents* were not concerned about the exam; the students were!

Why use participles when other structures convey the same meaning? The point is that participles convey this meaning more concisely and more dynamically. For more information about participles and participial phrases, see Chapter 19.

EXERCISE 10   **Combining Sentences by Using Participles and Participial Phrases.** Rewrite each of the following groups of sentences, combining them by forming at least two participles or participial phrases.

SAMPLE The sailboats rounded the mark. They were heeled over. They cut through the waves.

REVISION *Heeled over and cutting through the waves,* the sailboats rounded the mark.

REVISION The sailboats were heeled over, *cutting through the waves and rounding the mark.*

1. He spent several hours in the garden. He pulled weeds. He spread fertilizer. He pruned branches.
2. The old car coughed and sputtered. It lurched down the street. It was spewing black smoke from its exhaust pipe.
3. The little girl was standing on tiptoe. She peered over the counter. She clutched a dollar bill tightly in her fist.
4. I was pressed for time. I rushed out of the house. I forgot my keys.
5. The telephone rang. It jarred him from sleep. It interrupted his dream.
6. The speed skater was sweeping into the turn. She moved into the lead. She was pumping her arms rhythmically.
7. The diver was concentrating intently. He was tucking his body into a tight ball. He executed a perfect one-and-a-half gainer.
8. At the starting line the runners warmed up for the race. They stretched their leg muscles. They jogged in place.
9. The hikers were huddled under a tree. They studied the map. They were trying to pinpoint their position.
10. James was convinced that he could find a better price. He spent two hours on the telephone. He called one store after another.

Writing Concisely

You can make your writing concise by removing unnecessary or repetitious language and by simplifying long structures.

1. Eliminate unnecessary words and phrases, including:

    phrases such as "I think" or "in my opinion." Your reader knows that your writing is your opinion.

    hedging words such as "probably" or "somewhat"

    redundant, or excess, words and phrases

    UNNECESSARY WORDS IN BLUE   In my opinion, a state-wide recycling program for everyone in the state should probably be instituted to replace the somewhat haphazard and random method now used as a means of collecting together all of the cans, bottles, newspapers, and other recyclable products.

    CONCISE REVISION   A state-wide recycling program should be instituted to replace the haphazard method now used to collect recyclable products.

2. Combine related sentences, subordinating or coordinating ideas.

CHOPPY   Boston has a subway system. It was the first in America. This system operates today. It transports Bostonians efficiently.

CONCISE   Boston's subway system, the first in America, still transports Bostonians efficiently.

3. Reduce clauses to words or phrases.

WORDY   Tom baited his hook, and Jeff baited his.
CONCISE   Tom and Jeff baited their hooks.

WORDY   Since the director was pleased with the band's performance, he dismissed practice early.
CONCISE   Pleased with the band's performance, the director dismissed practice early.

WORDY   My uncle was a man who was educated.
CONCISE   My uncle was an educated man.

4. Break up rambling sentences into shorter sentences:

RAMBLING   The audience filed slowly out of the theater, and some were still dabbing at their eyes with handkerchiefs, while others were talking quietly among themselves, and it was obvious that they had seen a sad movie.

CONCISE   The audience filed slowly out of the theater. Some were still dabbing at their eyes with handkerchiefs, while others talked quietly among themselves. Obviously, they had seen a sad movie.

EXERCISE 11   **Writing Concisely.** Rewrite the following paragraph to make the sentences more concise. In some cases you will need to remove repetitious language and simplify long structures; in other cases you will need to combine short sentences or break up a long one.

In my judgment the problem of nutrition still continues to remain a serious problem for many Americans in the United States even in spite of the plentiful abundance of food that is available to them. Malnutrition usually results from the lack of food, but even a sufficient amount of food may not have an adequate supply of nutrients, and this, too, can cause malnutrition. Scientists have discovered somewhere around fifty or sixty nutrients. They have classified these nutrients into about five groups.

Creating Variety in Sentences

You have practiced a number of options for combining sentences. Now you will see how to use these options in paragraphs to make your writing more interesting and effective.

Varying Sentence Length and Structure

Sentences are not soloists. They work together in groups. A series of similar-sounding sentences makes your writing sound unsophisticated. Worse, it makes your readers' eyes glaze over. Yet if you mix short, simple sentences with longer, more complicated sentences, your writing will sound lively and mature, and your readers will pay attention to it.

Vary the length and structure of your sentences.

The following suggestions will help you.

1. Find a sample of your own writing, and read it aloud, listening to your sentences. Are all the sentences the same length, or do they vary?
2. Use coordinated structures for a series of items or for balancing or contrasting ideas.
3. Subordinated structures not only sound more sophisticated but also are quite versatile: They offer many possibilities for arranging and emphasizing ideas.
4. Use participles and appositives as shorthand ways of expressing information. Participles also create a sense of dynamic action.
5. One short sentence following several longer ones will accent a point, indicate a change of thought, or clinch a paragraph.

Here is an example of a paragraph made up of sentences whose length and structure are varied.

> **Participle conveys simultaneity; then adverb clause subordinates an idea.**
>
> **Short sentence contrasts with long one using coordination and subordination.**
>
> **Appositives add variety, and short sentence clinches the passage.**

Sighing, she surveyed the long, dirty kitchen floor and then turned to her mop and pail. If she could only get her work done in time, she might have a chance. She sloshed some water on the kitchen floor and looked at her reflection, hoping to cheer herself up. Instead, her heart sank. She saw that her clothes were tattered, her hair was tangled, and, worst of all, she had just broken another nail. A night at the ball dancing with the prince seemed nothing more than a lovely, impossible dream, a storybook romance. Cinderella wept bitterly.

EXERCISE 12 **Varying Sentence Length and Structure.** Rewrite the following paragraph, combining sentences and rearranging the information within them to produce a variety of lengths and structures.

It was the spring of 1912. The *Titanic* embarked on its maiden voyage. The voyage was across the Atlantic Ocean to New York City. The *Titanic* was a British steamer. It measured 882.5 feet. Its gross tonnage was 46,329 tons. The *Titanic* was the largest ship in the world. Many experts considered it unsinkable. They were to be proved wrong. It was the night of April 14. The *Titanic* was sixteen hundred miles off the coast of New England. The crew of the *Titanic* spotted an iceberg. The iceberg was directly in the ship's path. The crew tried to turn the ship. They were too late. The *Titanic* hit the iceberg with great force. This tore a 300-foot hole in the ship's hull. The tragedy occurred in less than three hours. The massive, unsinkable *Titanic* sank.

Varying Sentence Beginnings

A sentence in English typically begins with its subject. You can give your sentences greater impact by beginning some of them differently. Because the beginning is a strong position, the information that you place there will receive greater emphasis.

Try to vary the beginnings of successive sentences.

Here are different ways to begin sentences:

1. You can begin a sentence with a single word that is set apart:

   Unfortunately, she had forgotten all about the witch.

2. You can begin a sentence with a phrase:

   With a videocassette recorder people can record their favorite television programs.

3. You can begin a sentence with a subordinated idea:

   Although porcelain appears to be very delicate, it is actually the hardest of ceramic products.

4. You can invert the order of a sentence from subject-verb-modifier to modifier-verb-subject:

   MODIFIER   VERB   SUBJECT
   High above the trees soared a lone eagle.

EXERCISE 13 **Varying Sentence Beginnings.** Rewrite the following paragraph, combining sentences and rearranging the structures within them to create a variety of sentence beginnings.

It was 1891. James Naismith invented a game. It would later become nationally popular. Naismith was a physical education teacher. He needed an indoor game for his class to play during the winter months. He used whatever equipment he could find. He nailed up two half-bushel peach baskets. There were at either end of the court. He borrowed a soccer ball from the supply room. Naismith then divided his class into two teams. He explained the rules. The players had to pass the ball down the court. They had to shoot it into their basket. This was to score a point. The game was soon under way. The players took many shots. Only one goal was scored during that first game. Everyone was enthusiastic about Naismith's creation. The sport of basketball began.

Varying Sentence Types

The following passage is made up only of statements:

> Most Americans say that they have no time to exercise. Yet if they looked at their busy schedules, they would probably find fifteen minutes each day that they could spend on some physical activity. Good health is worth at least that much of their time.

The revision that follows peppers the statements with questions and commands, making the writing more forceful and lively:

> Are you like most other Americans: Do you say that you have no time to exercise? Take a hard look at your busy schedule, and you will see that you can probably spare at least fifteen minutes each day. Spend that time on some physical activity. Isn't your good health worth it?

Vary your writing by using occasional questions and commands.

EXERCISE 14 **Varying Sentence Types.** Rewrite the following passage, combining the choppy sentences to create sentences of varying lengths, structures, and beginnings. Use at least one question and one command.

Many people in our society think nothing of using a product once. Then they throw the product away. Natural resources diminish. Waste and pollution continue to increase. We can help to solve these problems. We can replace our throwaway habits with the habit of recycling. This would be one positive step. Aluminum, tin, glass, or paper products are recycled. The material in them is not wasted. The material is reused. The material is processed by manufacturers into new containers and paper goods. Recycling can make a difference. Everyone should develop the recycling habit.

Using Parallelism for Effect

The following two-thousand-year-old bulletin will probably sound familiar. Why do you think people have remembered it?

> I came, I saw, I conquered.

This statement, coined by Julius Caesar to report his conquest of Gaul, is memorable because it repeats a particular structure: I came, I saw, I conquered (subject-verb, subject-verb, subject-verb). Of course, Caesar was writing Latin, not English, but the Latin version also contains the repetition of a particular structure. Using similar structures within a sentence or within a series of sentences helps to tie related ideas together. This technique is called *parallelism.*

Use parallelism to emphasize the links between related ideas.

After all your practice with writing concise and varied sentences, you may think that parallelism will make your writing sound monotonous. On the contrary, parallelism can add grace and fluency to your sentences. Just remember to use it with care, as Julius Caesar did. He did *not* say, "I came, I saw, I conquered. I ate, I wrote, I slept. I woke, I got up, I went home."

When you use parallelism, make sure that your structures truly match. Otherwise your writing will sound awkward:

NOT PARALLEL When you use a table saw, it is important that you **hold the wood** flush to the guide, **keep your fingers** from the blade, and **to wear goggles.**

PARALLEL When you use a table saw, it is important that you **hold the wood** flush to the guide, **keep your fingers** from the blade, and **wear goggles.**

You should use parallelism to present a series of related ideas:

NOT PARALLEL We were impressed by the clarity of the speaker's thought and **how brief her speech was.**

PARALLEL We were impressed by the clarity of the speaker's thought and **the brevity of her speech.**

You can also use it to balance or contrast ideas:

NOT PARALLEL Hold your head up, and **your shoulders should be straight.**
PARALLEL Hold your head up, and **keep your shoulders straight.**

NOT PARALLEL **Delicious muffins were there**, but the cocoa was tepid.
PARALLEL **The muffins were delicious**, but the cocoa was tepid.

EXERCISE 15 **Creating Parallelism Within Sentences.** Rewrite each of the following sentences to express related ideas in parallel structures.

SAMPLE I respect anyone who is honest in his actions and *what he says.*
REVISION I respect anyone who is honest in his actions and *words.*

1. She trained her dog to be obedient, loyal, and make friends easily.
2. They had more rain than sunny days during that vacation.
3. I was waxing my skis, adjusted their bindings, and I sharpened their edges.
4. Arching his back and with his arm extended, the spiker rose into the air to slam the volleyball into the opponents' court.
5. James Russell Lowell was an essayist, a critic, and he wrote poetry.

6. Use a map when deciding where to go and what you will see.
7. Many children learn to swim before walking.
8. Both sailors and people who climb mountains should know how to tie a variety of knots.
9. Sue wrote the music; the lyrics were written by Frank.
10. To err is human; forgiveness is divine.

EXERCISE 16 **Creating Parallel Constructions.** Assume that you are the captain of a team and you are giving a short pep talk at the beginning of the season. Rewrite the speech below to do the following: (a) Correct faulty parallelism within sentences. (b) Combine sentences by creating new parallel structures to connect related ideas. Feel free to rearrange words within most of the sentences here.

I am not merely hopeful about this season. I have excitement about this season. We have the things that make a great team. We have talent on our team. Our team is experienced. There is depth on our team. More important, we have the kind of attitude that makes a good team great. What goes into a great attitude? A great attitude does not mean practicing halfheartedly. It means constantly to push ourselves to improve. A great attitude does not mean hot-dogging as superstars. It is better to pull together as a team. Our attitude could make the difference between merely qualifying for the play-offs and whether or not we actually win the championship for the first time in our history. Let's kick off this season determined to give it our all, that we will perform our best, and quite simply, to be the greatest team we can be!

Writer's Choice #1

ASSIGNMENT To imitate the sentences used by a professional writer

LENGTH A paragraph of five sentences

AUDIENCE Readers of science fiction or fantasy

PURPOSE To portray an imaginary creature of your own choice

PREWRITING Read the following model, in which noted science-fiction and fantasy author Ursula K. Le Guin describes the flight of a dragon. Then imagine a creature of your own.

WRITING Write about the creature you have imagined, using the same sentence structures, in the same order, that Le Guin uses.

REVISING Make sure that your sentences echo those of the model. When you are satisfied, check your writing for errors.

MODEL Arren saw what might have been an eagle flying very high, but it was not an eagle. It circled and stooped, and down it came with that thunder and shrill whistle of outspread golden wings. It alighted with huge talons on the summit of the dune. Against the sun the great head was black, with fiery glints. The dragon crawled a little way down the slope and spoke.

Writer's Choice #2

ASSIGNMENT To revise the sentences in a sample of your own writing

LENGTH Your choice

AUDIENCE Your choice

PURPOSE Your choice

OPTIONS Choose a paragraph of your own of any length. Decide whether your sentences tend to be too short, too long, repetitious in their structures or in their beginnings.

Rewrite the paragraph, using some of the options that you have practiced in this chapter.

Writer's Choice #3

ASSIGNMENT To write a speech

LENGTH Your choice

AUDIENCE Your choice

PURPOSE Your choice

OPTIONS Find an idea in the Writer's Sourcebook, pages 353–383.

Follow the prewriting, writing, and revising steps you practiced in Chapters 1–4.

As you revise, pay special attention to your sentences.

Writer's Choice #4

ASSIGNMENT To write a friendly letter

LENGTH Your choice

AUDIENCE Your choice

PURPOSE Your choice

OPTIONS You may write about something that has happened in your life or something that you would like to happen.

Follow the prewriting, writing, and revising steps you practiced in Chapters 1–4.

As you revise, pay special attention to your sentences. Revise the letter in light of the sentence-combining techniques that you have studied in this chapter.

Writers on Writing

Born and raised in Colorado, Rachel Wright loves acting and writing; she says that she would like to be a writer or an actor "when I grow up." Rachel wrote the following passage and commentary as a student at Rangeview High School in Aurora, Colorado.

THE PRODUCT

Thousands of writers have scrawled out an existence for themselves ever since some anonymous scribe first wrote down the common tales of his people. Since then, many great English writers have left us part of their souls encased in paper and ink. Yet William Shakespeare, born so many years ago, is still considered the best English writer the world has ever seen. Why? The man never wrote a single original plot. Much of his writing is difficult for today's reader to understand. But one has only to begin to read one of the Shakespeare's masterpieces to be immersed in the mood, the life, the world he creates.

THE PROCESS

Writing should sound natural, like speech. I do not mean that I write things like "And then, the girl, like, asked me for the borrow of my pencil, like, I'm so sure!" Nevertheless, your writing should have the natural cadences of your speech. This means that sentence lengths should vary. For instance, the sentences in my paragraph are long/medium/medium/very short/short/medium/long.

The words you choose to put together in your sentences are very important too. No reader wants to grapple with a tongue twister like "Round and round the rugged rock the ragged rascal ran." I also try to avoid using the same word too often. I always keep a thesaurus close by when I write, for I've found that new words can add fresh images to my work. For instance, in my first sentence I wrote "Thousands of writers have scrawled out an existence. . . ." I could have used any number of words instead of "scrawled," but no other word so clearly evokes the picture of the writer's pen scratching across paper.

YOUR TURN   *Writing a Commentary About Your Style*

Reread one of the paragraphs that you wrote for this chapter. Then write a short commentary about this paragraph. As Rachel did, note the length of your sentences, and comment on your word choice.

CHAPTERS 5–6 STYLE

CHAPTER 5   CHOOSING WORDS

Writing Precisely and Writing Concisely   [pages 96–104]   Read the following passage, and indicate the letter of the item that correctly answers each question.

[1]Judd cowered just off stage, feeling as bad as usual before his first entrance. [2]He was cognizant of the fact that he was behaving like a dufoid. [3]He also knew that he was up to the demands of his role. [4]This knowledge, alas, did nothing to alleviate his disquietude. [5]Just as he was sinking into the depths of despair, the stage manager cued him. [6]Judd took a deep breath and walked onto the stage, smiling.

1. Which is a connotation of the word *cowered* in sentence 1?
   (a) fearful   (b) excited   (c) confident   (d) tired
2. Which would be a more specific word than *bad* in sentence 1?
   (a) yucky   (b) nasty   (c) awful   (d) jittery
3. Sentence 2 mixes which levels of diction?
   (a) formal/middle   (c) middle/informal
   (b) formal/informal   (d) middle/high
4. Which sentence contains an idiom?
   (a) sentence 1   (c) sentence 3
   (b) sentence 2   (d) sentence 4
5. How would you improve the inflated diction in sentence 4?
   (a) This knowledge did not make him feel any better.
   (b) This knowledge did not perk him up.
6. Which of the following is an example of jargon?
   (a) "depths of despair"   (c) "cued him"
   (b) "dufoid"   (d) "disquietude"
7. Which sentence contains a cliche?
   (a) sentence 1   (c) sentence 3
   (b) sentence 2   (d) sentence 4

Writing with Figurative Language   [pages 105–107]   Indicate the letter of the item that correctly answers each question.
8. Which of the following is a simile?
   (a) My heart is a hammer.
   (b) My heart pounds as hard as a hammer.
9. Which of the following is a metaphor for winter?
   (a) Winter is a steel wall.   (c) Winter is as cold as steel.
   (b) Winter is like steel.   (d) Winter is steely.

10. Why would a telephone be a good object to personify?
    (a) It is vital invention.   (c) Sometimes it speaks.
    (b) Its ring can be startling.   (d) It has many different parts.
11. Which of the following is a simile?
    (a) Little Mary is like a sweet budding flower.
    (b) Little Mary is a sweet budding flower.
12. Which of the following is a metaphor?
    (a) John is an ox.   (b) John is as strong as an ox.
13. Which of the following is a simile?
    (a) The tree was a groom sweeping the sky.
    (b) The tree was like a broom sweeping the sky.
14. Which of the following is a metaphor?
    (a) The train was like a dragon rumbling in its underground lair.
    (b) The train was a dragon rumbling in its underground lair.
15. Why would an umbrella be a good object to personify?
    (a) It is easy to use.   (c) It is inexpensive.
    (b) It is an old invention.   (d) It is helpful to people.

Writing for Review   Write a paragraph about your sensations just before lunch hour. Be sure to use concrete, specific words and at least one figure of speech. Read and revise your first draft.

CHAPTER 6   COMBINING AND VARYING SENTENCES

Combining Sentences with Coordination, Subordination, and Participles [pages 111–127]   Read the following passage, and indicate the letter of the item that correctly answers each question.

¹Karl Benz was the father of the modern car. ²In 1885 he learned something. ³Being an inventor can be hazardous. ⁴One fine day Benz unveiled his car to the world. ⁵He proudly drove his car around a public square. ⁶All was going well. ⁷Benz became excited about moving so fast. ⁸He forgot to steer. ⁹His vehicle collided with a brick wall. ¹⁰Thus, it can be said that Karl Benz gave us both the first car *and* the first car crash.

1. Which of these pairs of sentences would be *better* if combined?
    (a) 2 and 3   (b) 3 and 4   (c) 9 and 10
2. Which would be the best word to use to combine sentences 6 and 7?
    (a) after   (b) or   (c) until   (d) although
3. Which sentences could best be combined with a participle?
    (a) 1 and 2   (b) 4 and 5   (c) 9 and 10
4. Which sentences would you combine through coordination?
    (a) 3 and 4   (b) 2 and 3   (c) 8 and 9
5. Which sentence should probably *not* be combined with another?
    (a) 2   (b) 4   (c) 8   (d) 10

Writing Varied Sentences and Using Parallelism [pages 128–133]
Read the following passage, and indicate the letter of the item that correctly answers each question.

¹Personalized license plates, identifying the driver's hobby or that tell what the driver's profession is, have become quite popular. ²A French teacher in New York put LEPROF on his plates. ³A surfer in California chose SRFSUP for his plates. ⁴A farmer in New Jersey selected EIEIO for his plates. ⁵One may ask why these plates are popular. ⁶I think it may be because they provide people who are drivers with the chance to express an individuality that is their own.

6. Which sentence contains structures that should be parallel?
    (a) 1   (b) 4   (c) 5   (d) 6
7. Which sentences use the same kinds of beginnings and structures?
    (a) 1 and 2   (b) 2, 3 and 4   (c) 5 and 6
8. Which of the following sentences is the best one to turn into a question?
    (a) 1   (b) 3   (c) 4   (d) 5
9. Which sentence needs to be written more concisely?
    (a) 2   (b) 4   (c) 5   (d) 6
10. Which sentences sound better if combined?
    (a) 1 and 2   (b) 3 and 4   (c) 5 and 6

Writing for Review   Rewrite one of the paragraphs in the review for Chapter 6 to improve the sentences. Vary sentence length and structure.

The Modes of Writing

Thinking About Thinking: Recognizing Similarities and Differences

This unit presents four modes of writing—description, narration, exposition, and persuasion. Although each mode offers a different way of approaching a subject, all the modes involve the thinking process called critical analysis. To analyze is to take apart and examine the elements of a subject. Whether you are writing a descriptive paragraph or a persuasive speech, you need to examine your subject in detail.

Defining the Skill

Analyzing demands many different specific thinking skills. One very useful thinking skill is RECOGNIZING SIMILARITIES AND DIFFERENCES. Suppose you are writing an expository essay about parks. One of the most helpful approaches you may take is to identify the qualities parks have in common and the qualities that make them different. By analyzing parks in this way you and your reader will be able to think more clearly about parks.

Applying the Skill

Look at the photograph. List all the elements in the picture that are similar. Then list all the elements that are different. Based on your lists, do you think the purpose of this picture is to emphasize similarities or differences?

Descriptive Writing

My task . . . is, by the power of the written word, to make you hear, to make you feel—it is, before all, to make you see.

—Joseph Conrad

Louis Agassiz, a nineteenth-century zoologist, once gave a bright student a memorable lesson in descriptive writing. When the student appeared for a final interview before receiving his degree, Agassiz showed him a small dead fish. The following scene took place:

STUDENT: That's only a sunfish.

AGASSIZ: I know that. Write a description of it.

After a few minutes the student returned with the description *Ichthus Heliodiplodokus,* or whatever term is used to conceal the common sunfish from vulgar knowledge. . . .

Aggassiz again told the student to describe the fish.

The student produced a four-page essay. Agassiz told him to look at the fish. At the end of three weeks, the fish was in an advanced state of decomposition, but the student knew something about it.

—Ezra Pound, *ABC of Reading*

What did the student learn? He learned that description cannot be general or abstract, that *Ichthus Heliodiplodokus* does not describe anything. He learned that description must be exact and must appeal to the senses: Agassiz told him to *look* at the fish. He also learned that sometimes even a four-page essay is not enough to describe, truly, one small dead fish.

Descriptive writing creates a clear and vivid impression of a person, place, or thing.

In this chapter you will practice the following steps and varieties of descriptive writing:

prewriting: purpose and audience
prewriting: sensory details
prewriting: overall impression
writing: organization and coherence
writing descriptive language
writing a longer description
writing a character sketch
revising, editing, and **publishing** descriptive writing

In the following pages you will write descriptions of various objects, places, and people. Your purpose will be to portray your subject so exactly that your reader can see it—and possibly hear, smell, taste, and touch it as well—through the power of your words. This purpose should be uppermost in your mind whether your task is to write a single paragraph, several paragraphs, or—like Joseph Conrad—a long, spellbinding book.

Prewriting: Purpose and Audience

Obviously, the purpose of descriptive writing is to describe. You should, however, have a more specific purpose in mind when you set out to write a description. For example, you may want to describe what you saw under a microscope so that you can demonstrate your progress in biology. On another occasion you may want to describe a pair of running shoes so that your parents will understand why you positively must have them. At yet another time you may want to describe a new student so that a friend will appreciate why you feel the way you do about the new person. Unless you know specifically *why* you want to describe something or someone, you will not know the best way to put the description together.

You cannot think about a specific purpose without considering your audience, the person or persons whom you intend to read your work. You will select your words, sentence structure, and organization with your audience in mind. A biology teacher, a parent, a friend—each requires special consideration as the audience for your descriptive writing.

To define your purpose and audience, ask yourself the following set of questions:

Why do I want to write the description: to inform? to persuade? to gain sympathy? Do I have another purpose or combination of purposes?

Who is going to read the description? How much do my readers already know about my subject? Will they need special information to understand any part of my subject?

EXERCISE 1 **Identifying Purposes for a Description.** For each of the following subjects, list two specific purposes that a writer could have in mind during the prewriting stage of descriptive writing. Study the example.

SUBJECT OF DESCRIPTION   POSSIBLE PURPOSE OF DESCRIPTION
the Eiffel Tower

To inform readers about its history
To help readers appreciate its beauty

1. your face
2. an animal you know
3. a food you ate recently

EXERCISE 2 **Selecting an Audience for a Description.** First select one of the following subjects for descriptive writing. Then in two or three sentences state whether you would prefer to write the description for an expert audience or for a nonexpert audience, and explain the reason for your decision.

SUBJECT OF DESCRIPTION	EXPERT AUDIENCE	NONEXPERT AUDIENCE
a new baseball star	the manager of another team	someone who watches only two games a season
a broken ankle bone	a first-year medical student	the parent of the child with the broken bone
a flower	a gardener	a new homeowner who has never grown anything

Prewriting: Sensory Details

Details are concrete, specific features of a person, object, place, or experience. **Sensory details** are details that appeal to the sensations of sight, sound, smell, taste, touch, and motion.

You experience life through your senses. So do your readers. Therefore, bring your subject to life for your readers by describing it through as many senses as possible. When you tell your readers about a rainstorm, for example, try to make them actually see the rain streaming down. Better yet, try to make them *hear* the drumming rain, *smell* the wet earth, *taste* the fresh water, and *feel* the cool, pattering raindrops. Can you recall any written passages in which the author created a vivid sensory description?

In the following passage author E. B. White lovingly describes his return to a boyhood fishing spot. How many senses does White call up in this description?

> I guess I remembered clearest of all the early mornings, when the lake was cool and motionless, remembered how the bedroom smelled of the lumber it was made of and of the wet woods whose scent entered through the screen. The partitions in the camp were thin . . . and as I was always the first up I would dress softly so as not to wake the others, and sneak out into the sweet outdoors and start out in the canoe, keeping close along the shore in the long shadows of the pines. I remembered being very careful never to rub my paddle against the gunwale for fear of disturbing the stillness of the cathedral.
>
> E. B. White, "Once More to the Lake"

White refers to every sense except taste. Some details even combine senses: For example, one word, *stillness*, evokes the sensations of sight, sound, and motion.

The details here are not extras or frills; they are truly essential to White's meaning. Without them the passage would read something like this:

> I guess I remembered clearest of all the early mornings at the lake. As I was always the first up, I would try not to wake the others and would sneak out and start out in the canoe, keeping close along the shore.

What is missing? White's original passage made us see, hear, smell, and feel the mornings at the lake. More important, it shared with us White's deep and lasting love of the place. The second passage just tells us that White got up early each day and took out the canoe. In losing the details we have lost the whole experience.

EXERCISE 3 **Thinking About Sensory Details.** Read the following descriptive passage, and list the concrete sensory details that the author uses to describe the flight patterns of different kinds of birds. On your list note which sense each detail calls up.

The little ground doves fly as though uncertain of themselves, like apprentice birds learning the business. They take off with a whirring of tiny rose-lined wings, achieving the safety of the crepe myrtle [a southern tree] with a spasmodic effort. I perpetually expect them to miss the bough they have aimed for and topple indignantly to the ground, for they flutter nervously as they land. The large turtle doves on the contrary fly with such speed and directness that they seem like gray bullets shot from a long-range gun. They are hurled across space and when they light in the pecan trees it is as though the limbs had halted them abruptly and they are only caught and tangled there. A covey of quail explodes like a pan of popcorn popping and I can recognize the spasmic scattering far across the grove.

—Marjorie Kinnan Rawlings, *Cross Creek*

Collecting Sensory Details

In order to write effective description, you need to notice and remember as many sensory details as you can. Sharpen your powers of observation and your memory with questions like these:

1. What does my subject look like? What is its color, size, and shape?
2. What prominent or unusual features does it have? What do I notice first when I look at it?
3. What sounds can I associate with my subject?
4. What smells and tastes can I associate with it?
5. What does it feel like to the touch? It is warm or cool, rough or smooth, hard or soft?
6. How does my subject move?
7. How would I know my subject if I were blindfolded?

You can collect the answers to those questions on an observation table like the one shown here. In this chart details describing a high school corridor during the change of periods are listed sense by sense.

OBSERVATION TABLE

SUBJECT: *school halls between periods*			
SIGHTS	SOUNDS	SMELLS/TASTES	TOUCH/MOVEMENTS
• *posters peeling off walls* • *bobbing heads* • *blurred faces* • *colorful jackets.*	• *shuffling feet* • *clanging lockers* • *chatter* • *buzzer*	• *tomato soup* • *varnish* • *sawdust from industrial arts* • *formaldehyde from lab*	• *warmth from radiators* • *slippery floors* • *pressure of crowds* • *fresh air blowing from open windows*

You can use some of the details listed in an observation table when you write a description of your subject.

EXERCISE 4 **Prewriting to Collect Sensory Details.** Choose one of the places listed here or any other place that you would like to describe. Think about your specific purpose and a possible audience. Ask yourself any appropriate questions from the list above, and place the answers on an observation table. Fill in columns for three different senses. Then save the observation table for use in Exercise 6.

1. the inside of a school bus
2. an automobile
3. a clothing store
4. your room
5. a refrigerator
6. a garden

Prewriting: Overall Impression

The details in a description should add up to a single **overall impression** of the subject.

A description jells when the details belong together and create a single overall or dominant impression. Sometimes when you are thinking about describing something, a single strong impression of your subject might strike you. Other times, however, as you consider a subject, you will discover that its details lend themselves to several different impressions. It is up to you to decide which impression you want to present. Look, for instance, at the following list of details about an automobile.

large	twenty years old	gas guzzler
navy blue	snapped antenna	rust spots
gritty	broken windshield wiper	ten miles to gallon
legroom for six	eight-cylinder engine	

Which of these details would support the following overall impression?

It was a king-sized car.

Do you see that details such as legroom for six and gas guzzler indeed emphasize the largeness of the car? Do you also see that details such as broken windshield wiper and rust spots, although colorful and accurate, have absolutely nothing to do with the car's kingly size?

Which details does the following paragraph use to create the impression of the car's largeness?

> It was a king-sized car, a twenty-year-old relic from the days before the energy crisis. Hulking at the curb, it seemed to boast about its legroom for six passengers, its eight-cylinder engine, and its ability to guzzle gas to the tune of ten miles per gallon. It dwarfed the clever little modern cars parked around it; it made them look like flies buzzing around a hippopotamus.

Suppose, however, that you decide to emphasize the following impression of the car:

The automobile had seen better days.

Which details can you use to create this impression? In this case the details about the rust spots and the windshield wiper will create the picture you want, while the information about the car's size is beside the point. You might write a paragraph like the following one:

> The automobile had seen better days, twenty years ago. A once-stately dark blue, it was now blotched with rust and covered by a film of grit. Part of the antenna had snapped off, and one windshield wiper flopped out of control. All in all, it looked like a dignified person who has come down considerably in the world.

This is the same car as the gas guzzler described in the earlier paragraph, but the combination of different details creates an altogether different overall impression of it. In each paragraph that overall impression comes across clearly in the topic sentence, which is followed by supporting details. As you learned in Chapter 3, you can also present the supporting details first and then use the topic sentence to clinch the paragraph. You should choose the technique you should feel will be most effective.

EXERCISE 5 **Prewriting to Create an Overall Impression.** Look again at the observation table on page 146 listing details about a school corridor. On the basis of these details, decide on two different impressions of this scene that you could present to a general audience. For each overall impression write a sentence that could serve as the topic sentence of a paragraph. Then list details that will develop each impression. You may add appropriate details of your own. Save your sentences and details for Exercise 8.

EXERCISE 6 **Prewriting to Create an Overall Impression.** Look back at the details that you listed in Exercise 4. Now write a sentence expressing one overall impression of the place you chose. List any additional details that can develop that impression. Save your notes for Writer's Choice #3, on page 154.

EXERCISE 7 **Maintaining an Overall Impression.** Read the following paragraph, and identify the overall impression it conveys. Then rewrite the paragraph to eliminate any details that undercut the overall impression. You may replace those details with more appropriate ones.

As soon as we walked in the door, we knew that we had found a home. The house was sun-filled and smelled of apples. The old oak floorboards creaked pleasantly. The fireplace was filled with empty boxes and broken glass. We could see a tall maple tree sheltering the back yard. A homemade swing hung from one branch, and an eerie scar from a lightning bolt ran up the trunk.

Writing: Organization and Coherence

An effective description should be **organized** so that the details build on each other naturally and logically.

Depending on your subject, you may organize your description in any number of ways. Two ordering methods that work well for descriptive writing are spatial order and order of importance. Let us examine how each of these methods is used.

Spatial Order

Spatial order (see page 61) is a natural way of linking up the sensory details of a description, particularly a description of an object or a place. When you use spatial order to organize a description, you help to clarify the picture you are creating by using some of the common spatial transitions. These transitions, listed here, add coherence to your sentences:

above	down	near	parallel
ahead	far	next to	there
around	here	opposite	under
below	horizontally	outside	vertically
beneath	inside	over	within

Look, for example, at the following descriptive passage. It is organized spatially; the underlines highlight the expressions that clarify the spatial relationships:

> Grayness spread through the atmosphere. Just above the housetops a faint mist collected, and splotches of wetness fell to the ground. Down at ground level the blades of grass glimmered as the sun's brightness washed away the gray—as if to pull the coming morning from the night.
>
> —Amy Ho, Marlboro High School
> Marlboro, New Jersey

EXERCISE 8 **Writing a Description Using Spatial Order.** Choose one of the two topic sentences you wrote for Exercise 5 (about a school corridor at the change of periods), and write a descriptive paragraph that develops this topic sentence. As you write, use spatial order to arrange the details that support your topic sentence. After you have finished your first draft, be sure to revise and edit your paragraph. Then make a neat copy, and proofread the final version.

Order of Importance

Another effective way of ordering the details in a description is by arranging them according to the **order of their importance.** You might, for example, begin with the least important details and move on to the most important (or most interesting) ones. Sometimes it might be appropriate to make a strong start using the most important detail. When you organize the details in a description according to the order of their importance, you can clarify their relationship to one another by using transitions such as the following ones; they help to make your writing coherent:

at first	last	most of all
first	latter	primarily
former	most important	second

The following description is organized according to order of importance. Note the underlined words, which help the reader keep track of the details as the writer moves from less important ones to the more important ones:

> When you are sizing up a freshman in this school, you can begin by looking at shoes—for shoes can tell you a lot about how a student interprets the big transition to high school. One type of shoe that will catch your eye is the "four-incher." This shoe has a heel about four inches high that seems to find itself on its side every three or four steps as the result of a weak ankle giving way. Second, you will notice that this shoe is usually accompanied by a dress with clashing colors. Most important is the face whose make-up cannot be distinguished from a child's fingerpainting—the most obvious clues to the student's idea of high school. When you put all the clues together, you realize that the student wearing the shoes, dress, and make-up is a girl who feels that going to high school means being sophisticated but who hasn't yet got the hang of it.
>
> —Susan Anderson, Kentridge High School
> Kent, Washington

EXERCISE 9 **Writing a Description Using Order of Importance.** The following details refer to a record collection. Using at least four of the details, decide on an overall impression of the collection that you can present. Then write a short paragraph about it, arranging the details according to the order of their importance. Be sure to use transitions to connect your details. After you have written your first draft, revise and edit your paragraph. Then make a neat copy, and proofread the final version.

1. over nine hundred records in the collection
2. records piled up in stacks around the room
3. each stack holds about twenty records
4. many records warped and scratched
5. vintage records and new releases
6. records grouped according to color of the album cover
7. records all mixed together
8. rock, classical, big band, comedy, and sound effects records
9. collection begun in the 1950s, continued into the 1980s

Writing Descriptive Language

Effective descriptive writing uses exact and vivid **language.**

In order to pinpoint just how your subject looks, sounds, smells, and feels, you need to pick and place your words exactly. As a result, your writing will become vivid almost automatically, for precise language gives descriptive writing an individual spark and twist.

Keep in mind the following points when you are choosing between two similar words for descriptive writing. For more information about any of these points, see Chapter 5.

1. Always, always, always pick the most specific word.

> GENERAL   I would start out in the boat in the long shadows of the trees.
> MORE SPECIFIC   I would . . . start out in the canoe . . . in the long shadows of the pines.
>
> —E. B. White

2. Never use a boring word and a modifier when a single, powerful word expresses the same meaning more vividly.

> DULL   A covey of quail takes off noisily. . . .
> VIVID   A covey of quail explodes. . . .
>
> —Marjorie Kinnan Rawlings

3. Think about the connotations associated with a word.

> GOOD   They take off with a humming of tiny rose-lined wings. . . .
> BETTER   They take off with a whirring of tiny rose-lined wings. . . .
>
> —Marjorie Kinnan Rawlings

[Here the author chose *whirring* because it connotes the spinning of a mechanism.]

4. Use figures of speech to add an extra dimension to your subject.

> BLAND   I remembered being very careful [not to disturb] the stillness of the beautiful scene.
> SPECIAL   I remembered being very careful [not to disturb] the stillness of the cathedral.
>
> —E. B. White

[White creates a metaphor by saying that the beautiful scene is a cathedral. The metaphor adds a note of reverence to the scene. Note that White places his metaphor at a climactic point—the end of his paragraph.]

5. Just as you see with your *own* eyes, find your *own* way with words; avoid trite, overused expressions.

> CLICHÉ   . . . the sun's brightness washed away the gray—it was the crack of dawn.
> ORIGINAL   . . . the sun's brightness washed away the gray—as if to pull the coming morning from the night.
>
> —Amy Ho

A final note: Whenever you have a picture or a sound in your mind, you can be sure that the English language can supply words to capture that image. If necessary, use a thesaurus to find them. (See Chapter 33 for information about using a thesaurus.)

Using Descriptive Language. Rewrite the following paragraph using more exact and vivid language. Use figures of speech in at least one sentence. Feel free to combine any sentences as you see fit.

Our group climbed to the mountaintop. Fred and I moved ahead of the others, yelling our heads off when we caught sight of the moutaintop. The view that we saw at the top of the mountain was very colorful. The clouds below us looked nice. They sky around us was blue. We all enjoyed the experience a great deal.

Writing a Longer Description

An effective description of your subject may require **more than one paragraph**.

When a single paragraph cannot adequately convey your overall impression, it is usually because your subject is too rich and multi-faceted to describe briefly. Then you will want to develop your description over the course of several paragraphs much as an architect plans a large building, making sure all the facets fit together into one harmonious design. Naturally, you will need to give considerable thought to the way in which you want to divide your subject. Each paragraph should make a different but related contribution to your purpose and overall impression. For example, note in the following paragraphs from an essay, how the author organizes the description of his subject—the French cathedral of Arles and its surroundings—into separate paragraphs.

> The cathedral's interior is a harbor of peace. The portal was a song of hope and fear; it led into a vestibule of eternal silence. The central nave and the side naves are narrow, which gives an illusion of height, but not of vertical lines flying into infinity. The vault is a full arch, like a rainbow above a landscape. Day penetrates through small windows in the thick wall, but the cathedral is not gloomy. It possesses an inner light, seemingly independent of any exterior source.
>
> Abutting the cathedral there is a monastery with a central courtyard: A small boxwood garden, like a pond, surrounded by a cloister. It was built during the twelfth and fourteenth centuries, thus it is half Romanesque and half Gothic. Yet the Romanesque frame is so strong that at first one does not notice the mixture of styles.
>
> Above the delicately drawn arcades rise the massive walls of the cathedral and the graded roof of the monastery. According to all rules such surroundings should smother the monastery courtyard, deprive it of air, change it into a stone-faced well. And it is incomprehensible how the masters of living stone could transform this limited space into a garden full of delicate lightness and charm.
>
> —Zbigniew Herbert, *Barbarian in the Garden*

Herbert effectively uses spatial order in this excerpt to divide his subject into paragraphs. The first paragraph is devoted to the cathedral's interior; the second shifts our attention to the nearby monastery; and the last paragraph focuses our attention on the scene as a whole, giving us a broad view of both the cathedral and the monastery. Note that each paragraph serves Herbert's overall purpose: to show that Arles's buildings possess "a convincing and overwhelming unity" despite their varied styles and sizes (as Herbert states earlier in his essay). Herbert's exact and vivid language, such as "harbor of peace" and "like a rainbow above a landscape," also helps to create the single overall impression of tranquil beauty.

EXERCISE 11 **Writing a Longer Description.** Plan to write a three- or four-paragraph description about a particular landscape that stirs a strong emotional response in you. For example, you might consider writing about a large open meadow, an intimate backyard, a majestic mountain range, or a vibrant city skyline. Begin by writing a sentence that expresses your specific purpose and the overall emotional impression that you intend to convey. Then devise an organization in which you will treat each aspect of the landscape in a separate paragraph. List and assign sensory details to each paragraph. After you have completed your planning, write, revise, and edit your first draft. When you are satisfied that your draft fulfills your plan, make a neat final copy, and proofread it.

Writer's Choice #1

ASSIGNMENT   To describe briefly a familiar American landmark

LENGTH   A paragraph of six to eight sentences

PURPOSE   To describe the landmark so that anyone can recognize it

AUDIENCE   An English-speaking extraterrestrial being

PREWRITING   Choose your landmark, and decide on the features that the alien needs to know.

WRITING   Begin by identifying the landmark and pointing out its single most noticeable feature. Use spatial order to organize the subject's other important features.

REVISING   Can you visualize the subject from your writing? Make sure to edit and proofread carefully.

Writer's Choice # 2

ASSIGNMENT   To describe a group of people in a situation of your choice—for example, in a line at a movie

LENGTH   A paragraph of seven to nine sentences

PURPOSE   Either to show how the group acts as a unit or to focus on individual variety within the group

AUDIENCE   Your choice

PREWRITING   You might use an observation table to record sensory details. Decide on an overall impression of the group.

WRITING   Begin by stating your overall impression in a topic sentence. Then present your details, using either spatial order or order of importance. Try to use vivid, exact language to capture the scene.

REVISING   Does your paragraph truly support the topic sentence? Do you need to change the topic sentence or add details to the paragraph?

Writer's Choice #3

ASSIGNMENT   To describe a subject of your choice

LENGTH   Your choice

PURPOSE   Your choice

AUDIENCE   Your choice

OPTIONS   You might describe the subject for which you did prewriting in Exercises 4 and 6.

Be sure to revise and edit your first draft. Then copy and proofread the final draft.

Writing a Character Sketch

A **character sketch** is a description that portrays an individual's psychological traits and physical appearance.

When you describe a human being, you want to tell your reader about your subject's appearance, just as you do in describing an object or place. However, portraying a human being adds a new dimension to mere physical description; you want to suggest a connection between the outer and the inner person, between your subject's appearance and personality.

External appearance and behavior can often reveal someone's personality. For example, look again at the description of the student on page 135. This description begins by noting the student's four-inch-high heels and ends by pointing out the character trait that made her wear such shoes—her desire to appear more sophisticated than she actually is.

Read the following description of the great American dancer, Martha Graham, written by a fellow dancer, Agnes De Mille. Note that De Mille includes details that help us visualize Graham's face and imagine her voice and movement. More important, De Mille makes her description of these physical traits crackle with Graham's electric personality.

> It is the face that one sees first and last, the eyes and voice that hold one. . . . The shape of the face is Mongoloid with skin drawn taut over the bones. The cheeks are hollows. In the eye sockets, the great doelike orbs glow and blaze and darken as she speaks. Her eyes are golden yellow flecked with brown and on occasion of high emotional tension seem slightly to project from the lids while the iris glows like a cat's. . . . The skin of her cheeks and nose is all exposed and waiting with sensitive delight like the skin of an animal's face, or the surface of a plant as it bends toward light; every bit of surface breathing, listening, experiencing. . . .
>
> Her laughter is girlish and light—quite frequently a giggle. She has a sly wit that reminds one in its incisive perception of Jane Austen, or of Emily Dickinson whom she so greatly reveres. . . . Her speech—who shall describe Martha's speech? The breathless, halting search for the releasing word as she instructs a student, the miracle word she has always found. The gentle "you see it should be like this," as her body contracts with lightning, plummets to the earth and strikes stars out of the floor. "Now you try it. *You* can do it."
>
> —Agnes De Mille, *Dance to the Piper*

As you prepare to write a character sketch, ask yourself the following prewriting questions:

1. What can I say about my subject's height, weight, hair color, complexion, face, and clothing?
2. What can I say about the way my subject speaks and moves? About my subject's facial expressions?

3. What can I say about the way my subject behaves toward other people? How do other people treat my subject?
4. What can I say about my subject's character traits, likes, dislikes, strengths, and problems?
5. What specific examples or anecdotes can I offer to show these character traits in action?
6. What overall impression of my subject's appearance and personality do I want to convey? Can I focus on one basic quality?

When you actually write your character sketch, you may arrange your details according to the order of their importance. You may begin by describing a person's physical appearance and end by describing subtler, less obvious psychological traits.

EXERCISE 12 **Writing a Character Sketch.** Plan to write a character sketch about someone whom you know. Prewrite by answering the preceding questions, listing as many physical and psychological details as you can. Decide on an overall impression, and write a sentence expressing that impression. You may organize the details in your description by beginning with external qualities and moving to your subject's character traits. Be sure to revise and edit your first draft. When you are satisfied with what you have written, make a neat copy, and proofread it.

Revising, Editing, and Publishing

All the general questions to be asked when you revise paragraphs (Chapter 4) apply to descriptive writing, of course. In addition, descriptive writing requires you to ask special questions of the first draft—questions that will help you to revise it so that it will accomplish your purpose and be appropriate for your audience.

Checklist for Revising Descriptive Writing

1. What sensory details have I used? Which work best? Which could I do without? Which should I add?

2. What single, overall impression have I created through my choice of details? Is the impression stated in a sentence? Does this impression reflect all the details I use? How, if at all, should I change this impression to create a truer picture of my subject?

3. How many paragraphs do I need to adequately describe my subject? What kind of organization have I used to arrange my details? Would another kind of organization work better for this subject?

4. Which transitions add coherence to my description? Do I need more?

5. Which exact and vivid words help the reader to picture my subject? What words could I add to make that description even more precise and vivid? What figures of speech bring my subject to life?

6. For a human subject, which details portray the subject's physical traits? Which ones communicate psychological traits? What overall impression have I created of this person? What additional details does my reader need in order to see the subject as I do?

Writer's Choice #1

ASSIGNMENT To write a letter handing down a cherished possession to someone younger

LENGTH A paragraph of six to eight sentences

PURPOSE To describe the item so that the reader can understand why you cherish it

AUDIENCE A younger brother or sister, a favorite cousin, a special neighbor, or a close friend

PREWRITING List sensory details of the possession. Try to connect a few of these details to fond memories. Then decide on the overall impression you want to convey.

WRITING As you write, address your reader directly. You might start by announcing why you are bequeathing this precious item to the reader. Then describe the article in loving detail, pointing out the best memories that it calls up. You might explain in detail how this article is to be treated. Use either spatial order or order of importance to organize your description.

REVISING Check to see if your feeling for the possession comes across. Will the person receiving the article know something about your feeling for him or her? Make sure to edit and proofread also.

Writer's Choice # 2

ASSIGNMENT To write a character sketch

LENGTH A paragraph of seven to nine sentences

PURPOSE To describe someone by focusing on one item of his or her clothing

AUDIENCE A friend of yours who does not know your subject

PREWRITING Decide on your subject, and then decide on an article of clothing that seems characteristic of that person. Make a list of details about the item of clothing, always keeping in mind the connection of each detail to your subject's personality itself.

WRITING Begin by identifying your subject and describing the article of clothing. You might illustrate your comments by including a few anecdotes that relate the article of clothing to your subject's personality.

REVISING Remember that your reader does not know your subject. Would your reader be able to visualize the item of clothing and understand something about the person from what you have written? Remember to edit and proofread.

Writer's Choice #3

ASSIGNMENT   To write a description of a place that you never want to see again in your life

LENGTH   Your choice

PURPOSE   To create a mood so that your reader shares your feeling

AUDIENCE   Your choice

PREWRITING   Decide on your place and the reasons why you never want to see it again.

WRITING   Do not flatly state your feelings about the place. Rather, describe the place in vivid language that communicates your feelings about it.

REVISING   Have you written strongly enough? Have you overdone it? Is your purpose clear?

Writer's Choice #4

ASSIGNMENT   To write a character sketch based on a photograph in a newspaper or magazine or in the Writer's Sourcebook on pages 353–384

LENGTH   Your choice

PURPOSE   To describe someone in such a way that your reader will definitely want or not want to meet that person

AUDIENCE   Your choice

OPTIONS   Obviously you will make up the psychological details. These details, however, should seem to grow logically from the physical details in the photograph.

For prewriting you might ask yourself the questions on pages 155–156.

Writer's Choice #5

ASSIGNMENT   To describe a subject of your choice

LENGTH   Your choice

PURPOSE   Your choice

AUDIENCE   Your choice

OPTIONS   You might use material in the Writer's Sourcebook as a springboard for your description.

You might make an observation table to help you collect sensory details about your subject.

Writers on Writing

Ed Leman enjoys skiing, mountain climbing, and four-wheeling. After college he plans to open his own auto repair shop. Ed was a student at Rangeview High School in Aurora, Colorado, when he wrote the following description and commentary.

THE PRODUCT

Have you ever noticed a candle? I mean really noticed a candle? Have you ever noticed how the flame does not even appear to touch the wick? Or how the flame changes from blue at the base to yellow at the tip? Have you ever watched the little droplets of wax solidify as they roll down the candle? What about shape—have you ever wondered why almost every candle you buy is cylindrical? And the warm, waxy aroma: Have you ever noticed how many fragrances candles can have—cinnamon, mint, holly, evergreen, wintergreen . . . the list goes on. And finally the feel of the wax, the soft, smooth, almost velvety feel of warm candle wax. Now tell me, and be honest, had you ever really noticed a candle before?

THE PROCESS

My subject, the candle, came to me immediately when I found out that I was to write a descriptive paper. I felt that it was a perfect subject, for last year I spent an hour observing a candle in chemistry class. When I began my work on this paper, I simply jotted down everything I could think of that had to do with the appearance, smell, or texture of that candle. I listed these details without any semblance of logical order. Then, in later drafts, I grouped the details according to the senses used to detect them.

My main problem was that I wanted to take an object that would seem extremely ordinary to most people and make it interesting. I tried to do so by using vivid words instead of boring ones—for example, "the feel of the wax, the soft, smooth, almost velvety feel of warm candle wax." I also thought I could get people's attention if I asked questions rather than just stating facts. So, the whole process boiled down to choosing a subject I knew well, arranging the details, and then writing as vividly as I could.

YOUR TURN   *Describing an Ordinary Object*

As Ed Leman did, choose a very ordinary object that most people overlook, and write a descriptive paragraph about it.

CHAPTER 7 DESCRIPTIVE WRITING

Sensory Details [pages 144–146] Indicate which sense is called up in each sentence: (a) sight; (b) sound; (c) smell; (d) taste; (e) touch.

1. As we stood above the valley, the country stretched before us.
2. The never-ending rocking of the boat began to make her dizzy.
3. The aroma of lasagne was so inviting.
4. Thoreau said that a train whistle was like the cry of a hawk.

Organization [pages 148–150] Indicate whether each group of sentences uses (a) spatial order or (b) order of importance.

5. The music starts here, where you push the valve down. It goes round and round and comes out here.
6. I know him. Furthermore, I like him. Most of all, I admire him.
7. The red ceiling clashed with the pink walls and the blue floor.

Overall Impression and Descriptive Language [pages 147–148 and 150–152] Read the following paragraph written by Doris Lessing. Indicate the letter of the item that correctly answers each question.

She sat herself on a shaded bench; and on one side were the glittering plumes of the fountains, the roses, the lawns, the house, and beyond them the austere wind-bitten high veld [grassland]; on the other, at her feet, the ground dropped hundreds of feet sharply to the river. It was a rocky shelf thrust forward over the gulf, and here she would sit for hours, leaning dizzily outwards, her short gray hair blown across her face, lost in adoration of the hills across the river.

8. Which item states the overall impression created by the passage?
   (a) A lone woman sits sadly waiting for someone to join her.
   (b) A woman perched up high is dazzled by the beauty around her.
   (c) An old woman is lulled by a quiet natural scene.
   (d) A normally active woman is frustrated by inactivity.
9. "Plumes" is an excellent descriptive word because it suggests
   (a) swaying branches of trees   (c) featherlike spouts of water
   (b) feathers in the woman's hat   (d) birds flying overhead
10. Which of the following is a figure of speech?
    (a) "a shaded bench"   (c) "wind-bitten"
    (b) "at her feet"   (d) "hills across the river"

Writing for Review   Write a one-paragraph character sketch using order of importance. After you write, underline at least four sensory details, three vivid words, and one figure of speech.

Narrative Writing

At least a hundred times a year, you probably resort to narration. . . .
—X. J. Kennedy and Dorothy M. Kennedy

Narration, or story telling, shows us glimpses of real life that we might otherwise never share or that might otherwise go unnoticed. See, for example, how the following narrative pulls a small incident from life's random events to reveal the humanity and humor of the poet and biographer Carl Sandburg.

> Bernard Hoffman, who was a photographer for *Life* Magazine for some years, called on Sandburg at his Michigan home in order to do a story. The weather was so cold that even the goats were virtually freezing outside, recalls Hoffman. Whereupon, Sandburg called them into the house and about fifteen of the shivering animals crowded into one of the rooms. Sandburg did not stop with this hospitality. He took up his guitar and played for the visiting goats. "They listened politely," said Hoffman.
>
> —North Callahan, *Carl Sandburg, Lincoln of Our Literature*

Narration is the kind of writing that tells a story, real or imagined. A **nonfiction narrative** is factual prose writing that tells a true story. A **fiction narrative** is prose writing that is made up or imagined.

You are probably already a skilled storyteller. You use narration every time you tell someone what you have been doing, every time you tell a story, give a report, or record an event. Indeed, you may use narration well over a hundred times a year.

In this chapter you will practice the following skills and steps as you concentrate on writing narratives:

prewriting: the elements of a narrative
prewriting: subject, purpose, and audience
prewriting: a narrative outline
writing a narrative
writing dialogue in a narrative
writing: vivid verbs in a narrative
writing an anecdote as part of a longer narrative
revising, editing, and **publishing** narrative writing

As you master these skills, you will find that your writing becomes more focused and better organized. And, as a result of these improvements, your readers will find your work much more interesting and enjoyable to read.

Prewriting: The Elements of a Narrative

To maintain our interest, the author of a nonfiction, or true, narrative often uses techniques and elements of the short story as he or she presents the incident to us. These elements include a plot, a setting, and a point of view. The following brief narrative illustrates those elements:

> Communication can be a chancy thing at times. Not long ago I was returning home on a bus. I happened to be carrying something that contained liquid. As the bus went over a particularly bad stretch of road, I was forced to juggle frantically to avoid spilling the liquid. Then the bus moved onto a smoother stretch, and I could relax. With a sigh of relief, I turned to the woman next to me and remarked that the roads were just terrible. She nodded and replied that they were bad all over. We shook our heads at each other sympathetically. The next moment she turned back to me and announced that boric acid did wonders for them. I was naturally mystified by this comment, and so I could only respond by saying, "Oh, yes." We smiled at each other, she knowingly, I rather confusedly. Then I turned back to wonder how exactly boric acid was supposed to help the bad roads. At last it dawned on me. The woman thought I had said that the *roaches*—the cockroaches—were terrible. Relieved at having finally understood, I turned to her again, smiled, and assured her that she was quite right. Boric acid did do wonders for them!

The writer of the preceding narrative might have just told her story by saying, "This funny woman thought I was talking about a bad infestation of roaches when all I had remarked on was the bad condition of the roads." The writer would have communicated the same facts, but her audience would not have enjoyed the story as much. The version with a developed plot, setting, and point of view has much more impact.

The **plot** is the sequence of events that occurs in a narrative. Often at the center of a plot is a problem, or **conflict**. As a person in a narrative tries to solve the conflict, the plot builds to the point of highest interest, or the **climax**. The **resolution** brings the narrative to a satisfying and logical conclusion.

Not every short narrative has a conflict. For example, you can write a perfectly acceptable narrative about a summer vacation without ever introducing a conflict into the story line. Yet, as you know from your own reading experience, a narrative with a conflict, a problem, or even a misunderstanding, and an ultimate solution is usually more interesting to read.

The plot of an effective narrative—even that of a very short narrative—is arranged according to a meaningful and often dramatic or suspenseful sequence of action. For example, the plot of the model narrative begins with the author returning home. Then the narrator is confronted with a misunderstanding, or problem: the other passenger's puzzling remark about boric acid. The short plot builds to the climax as the narrator suddenly solves the puzzle. The resolution is simply the final communication between the narrator and the other passenger.

The **setting** of a narrative is the time and place in which the narrative occurs.

Setting includes the geographical area, the landscape, the season, the weather, the historical period, and the culture in which the action takes place. The setting can be drawn with great detail, or it can simply be suggested, as in the model narrative. There the setting is a bus traveling on bad roads.

Point of view represents the relationship of the narrator to the story.

Every narrative has a narrator who tells the story. A narrative told from the *first-person point of view* is related by the author, who speaks directly to the reader and uses the first-person pronoun *I*. The model narrative is told in this way. A narrative has a *third-person point of view* if the narrator stands back from the events and uses the third-person pronouns *he* and *she* to refer to the characters.

EXERCISE 1 **Recognizing the Elements of a Narrative.** Read the following narrative, and write your answers to each of the numbered questions:

Downing pitched ball one inside, and Henry Aaron watched impassively. Then came the second pitch, and this time Henry took his first cut of the night. The ball rose high toward left-center as the crowd came to its feet shouting, and as it dropped over the inside fence separating the outfield from the bullpen area, the skyrockets were fired and the scoreboard lights flashed in six-foot numerals: "715."

—Joseph Durso

1. Is this a nonfiction narrative? How do you know?
2. Briefly describe the plot of the narrative.
3. Where is the narrative set?
4. Is the story told from the first- or third-person point of view?

Prewriting: Subject, Purpose, and Audience

Subjects for narratives may be found in everyday occurrences, not just in dramatic events. To find a subject for a narrative, think about the people and events in your life. Use prewriting techniques that you have studied earlier—such as freewriting, brainstorming, and charting—to generate and explore ideas (see Chapter 2).

In the rest of this chapter, you will follow one student in the preparation of a narrative. At the time she was given the assignment to write a narrative, she had just witnessed the transformation of caterpillars into butterflies. She chose to narrate this real-life experience with the intention of conveying some of her own feelings and insights..

EXERCISE 2 **Prewriting for a Narrative.** Choose one of the subjects listed here or a subject of your own. Use one of the techniques of prewriting. Then ask the questions *Who? What? When? Where? Why?* and *How?* Work for ten minutes to generate and explore ideas for your subject. Save your notes for a narrative that you will write later.

1. something lost or found
2. an accident
3. helping a friend
4. a recital or play
5. learning a new skill
6. an accomplishment
7. having a job
8. a vacation

Defining Purpose and Audience

Narratives serve many general or specific *purposes*, or goals. A news narrative may inform. A sports narrative may entertain. A historical narrative may make a point, and an autobiographical narrative may present a truth about life or share insights about the past. Some narratives may serve several purposes.

Closely linked to purpose is *audience*, the person or persons whom you intend to read your work. As you shape your narrative, try to anticipate how your readers may react to it. Choose details and events that help them identify your reason for writing. Consider whether there are terms or concepts that need explanation.

Here is how the student who will write a narrative about butterflies defined her purpose and audience:

1. The purpose of the narrative is to make a point about nature: The instinct for survival is strong.
2. My teacher and my classmates are my audience. My readers are generally familiar with my subject—caterpillars changing into butterflies. I should define specific terms, such as *pupa* and *chrysalis*.

EXERCISE 3 **Defining Purpose and Audience.** Choose one of the subjects for which you generated ideas in Exercise 2, or choose a new subject, and define in writing the purpose and audience for the narrative you will write shortly. Be sure to save your notes for use later in the chapter.

Prewriting: A Narrative Outline

You may find it helpful to ask and answer some questions that will make your narrative more organized and to the point. The following questions will force you to think about all the events of the experience or incident and to focus on the critical ones. The sample answers on the right were formulated during prewriting by the student who is preparing to write about the caterpillars.

QUESTIONS TO EXPLORE THE EVENTS OF A NARRATIVE	SAMPLE ANSWERS
1. In what way did the experience or incident begin?	*The experience began when I noticed little brown worms on the parsley that was growing in the back yard.*
2. What problem, or conflict, did I or another character involved in the incident face?	*The little worms turned into large, yellow and green striped caterpillars, and my neighbor Angelo squashed them.*
3. What was my or another character's reaction to this problem?	*I was crushed.*
4. In what way did I or another character solve the problem?	*I solved the problem by bringing the pot of parsley--and the caterpillars--indoors.*
5. Did any obstacles prevent me or another character from solving this problem?	*The only obstacle I faced was that the caterpillars were nonstop eaters and quickly denuded the parsley. I then bought them parsley, which, after an elaborate display of finickiness, they devoured.*
6. What was my or another character's reaction to the solution?	*I was relieved and delighted with the solution because after about two weeks the caterpillars turned into chrysalises, or cocoons.*
7. What was the final outcome?	*The final outcome began about nine days later, when I held my hand out the window and the first of five eastern swallowtails flew away.*

Review the answers on your chart to be sure you have not omitted any important ideas or information.

EXERCISE 4 **Choosing Events for a Narrative.** Use one of the narrative subjects you worked with in Exercises 2 and 3 or another of your own choosing. List the events of your narrative by writing an answer for each of the seven questions on page 166. Add any other important events not covered by the questions. Save your notes for Exercise 5.

Eliminating Unnecessary Events

A successful narrative stresses only important events and does not get bogged down with insignificant details or sidetracked by irrelevant events. Therefore, eliminating unnecessary events is a crucial step in planning a narrative. You will probably find that some ideas generated by prewriting do not directly relate to the purpose of your narrative. For example, upon reviewing the list our student realized that some events were not directly enough related to her purpose; she drew a line through them.

> When I saw the hairy little brown worms on the parsley, I thought they were too small to do much damage, so I decided not to spray them with insecticide.
>
> ~~My tomatoes were beginning to blossom.~~
>
> A week later the hairy little brown worms had changed into big smooth green caterpillars.
>
> ~~My neighbor Angelo lost some of his tomatoes to red spiders.~~
>
> Angelo saw the biggest caterpillar on my parsley and squashed it. He thought he was being helpful.
>
> I was upset. I had found a picture of the caterpillar in a butterfly book. I wanted to see it change into a butterfly.
>
> Since the parsley was in a flower pot, I decided to bring it, along with the caterpillars, into the house.
>
> ~~One day I came home to find the biggest caterpillar on the kitchen floor. It was about to crawl under the refrigerator. Fortunately, my cat, Lance, called this to my attention.~~

EXERCISE 5 **Eliminating Unnecessary Events.** Look at the list of events you made in Exercise 4 for your narrative. Which, if any, are unnecessary or unrelated to the purpose and focus of your narrative?

Collecting Narrative Details

Think about how the people who were part of the situation looked, sounded, and acted. Picture the setting in which the experience occurred, and imagine the sensory details associated with this setting. Making charts like those that follow may help you to organize the details of your narrative.

PEOPLE IN A NARRATIVE

SUBJECT: *raising butterflies*			
PERSON	CHARACTER TRAITS	BEHAVIOR/ REACTION	WHAT THE CHARACTER LEARNED
Me	Determined, enthusiastic, hopeful	Distraught, harried, amazed	Nature adapts to its surroundings and carries on regardless.
Angelo	Vigilant	Well-intentioned, neighborly	

SETTING FOR A NARRATIVE

SUBJECT: *raising butterflies*			
PLACE	TIME OF DAY/YEAR	WEATHER	DETAILS OF SETTING
My backyard	An August evening, after dinner	Warm, balmy	Small back yard with a tiny vegetable garden in Queens, New York
Windowsill	August, various times of day	Sunny and warm	Houseplants, lace curtains, bright light, warm wood sill

EXERCISE 6 **Collecting Narrative Details.** Using the narrative subject you have worked with in preceding exercises or another of your own choice, make two charts like those shown above. Use the same, headings, modified if necessary, and fill in the information about the people and settings of your narrative. Save your notes.

Filling in the Narrative Outline

It is time to lay all your prewriting notes out in one place so that you will be able to write easily. Make an outline that corresponds to the example that follows. Notice that the outline starts by stating the purpose of the narrative and then lists the events in *chronological order*, or the order in which the events actually take place, with each part of the narrative leading clearly to the next (see pages 63–64). The outline also includes description of setting and characters. In other words, the outline brings together in one place all the prewriting work done up until this point:

NARRATIVE OUTLINE FOR RAISING BUTTERFLIES

I. Beginning
    A. State the purpose of your narrative in an introductory sentence.
        I want to write about one of the great strengths of nature--the ability of its creatures to adapt to new surroundings and survive.
    B. Describe the setting.
        One soft August evening last summer I tended my tiny vegetable garden, which is in my back yard, in Queens.
    C. Give important background information.
        This was my first garden.
    D. Begin to tell what happened.
        I saw several little brown hairy worms on some parsley that was growing in a flowerpot. At an eighth of an inch, they seemed too small to do much damage, so I ignored them. By the next week they were brightly colored, ten times bigger, and hard to miss.

II. Middle
    A. Introduce and briefly describe the other people involved.
        My next-door neighbor Angelo, who also had a garden, is a vigilant, generally helpful man. He often watered my garden. My mother had challenged me to do something constructive.
    B. Introduce a conflict, or problem.
        I was in the house. As soon as I heard Angelo's foot strike the cement, I knew what had happened.
    C. Show your reaction to the conflict with a direct statement.
        It was up to me to save them.
    D. Build toward a climax, the point of highest interest.
        I brought the caterpillars into the house, and they consumed what was left of my potted parsley. I bought them bunches of parsley, which they rejected with a vengeance at first. Finally they relented.

III. Ending
    A. Write a climax.
        They were ready to leave the parsley and attach themselves to the branch or stem of a larger plant to begin the pupal stage (the nonfeeding period in which they would undergo metamorphosis and become butterflies). I watched as each shed its caterpillar skin and was transformed into a motionless, pale green chrysalis, or cocoon. Would they all emerge as butterflies?
    B. Write a resolution.
        About nine days later the first of five butterflies emerged from its chrysalis, which was hanging on a ficus plant on the living room windowsill. There on a warm, sunny Saturday morning it rested on a branch waiting for its crumpled wings to unfurl. Half an hour later, with wings fully extended, it walked onto my outstretched hand. I pulled back the lace curtains, opened the screen, and the butterfly soared to freedom.

EXERCISE 7 **Preparing a Narrative Outline.** Using the subject you developed in preceding exercises or another subject of your choice, make a narrative outline. Use the narrative outline on page 169 as your model. Include as many of the categories in the outline as possible, and save your outline.

Writing a Narrative

If you have followed all the prewriting activities up until now, you should have all your ideas in note form in chronological order. To transform these notes into narrative writing, you will need to use *transitions*, words and phrases that help give writing coherence by connecting one sentence to another (see page 49). In narrative writing, transitions indicate the order in which events take place.

after	first	later	sometimes
always	following	meanwhile	soon
before	immediately	now	then
finally	last	preceding	until

EXERCISE 8 **Recognizing Transitions.** Reread the narrative paragraphs about the bad roads (page 163) and Hank Aaron (page 164). For each paragraph list at least two transitions that indicate time order.

A Model Narrative

The student whom you have been following in this chapter finally produced a five-paragraph narrative based on all her prewriting notes. Not all narratives need be five paragraphs long, however. To prove this point, a one-paragraph version of the caterpillar narrative follows the five-paragraph version.

FIVE-PARAGRAPH VERSION

Several months ago I witnessed firsthand one of the great strengths of nature—the ability of its creatures to adapt to new surroundings and survive. One soft August evening last summer I tended my tiny vegetable garden, which grows in Queens, a part of New York City. (This was my first garden, planted in response to my mother's challenge, "Why don't you do something constructive this summer?") As I was watering the plants, I saw several hairy little brown worms on the parsley that was growing in a flowerpot. At an eighth of an inch, they seemed too small to do much damage, so I decided not to blast them with bug spray. A week later they had evolved into six giant caterpillars with gaudy new neon yellow and green stripes.

My next-door neighbor Angelo, who also has a garden, is a vigilant, generally helpful man. He often watered my garden. One evening when I was in the house, I noticed Angelo in the back yard. As soon as I heard his foot strike the cement with a loud STOMP, I realized what had happened. In a flash I knew that it was up to me to save them.

I brought the five remaining caterpillars into the house, and they single-mindedly consumed what was left of the potted parsley. Then I bought them bunches of parsley, which they utterly and thanklessly rejected, crawling over and over the offensive store-bought greens, stubbornly refusing to eat.

Fortunately two days of hunger finally forced them to accept second best. After a week of pure gluttony, they were ready to begin the pupal stage (the nonfeeding period in which they would undergo metamorphosis and become butterflies). They left the parsley to hang by a silken thread from the branches of my largest, leafiest house plants. I watched as each shed its caterpillar skin and was transformed into a motionless, pale green chrysalis, or cocoon. Would they all emerge as butterflies?

Some nine days later the first of five eastern swallowtails clambered from its chrysalis, which was suspended from a plant on the living room windowsill. There on a warm, sunny Saturday morning the butterfly hung upside down waiting for its crumpled wings to unfurl. Half an hour later, with wings fully extended, it tottered onto my outstretched hand. I pulled back the lace curtains and slid open the screen; the butterfly soared to freedom. Now that I know nature will adapt to my hospitality, I will plant lots more parsley next year.

ONE-PARAGRAPH VERSION

One evening last summer while watering the plants in my first garden, I saw several hairy little brown worms on the parsley in a flowerpot. A week later the one-eighth-inch worms were six giant caterpillars. The drama really got underway one evening soon after, when I realized that my neighbor Angelo was stomping on a caterpillar. Immediately I brought the five remaining caterpillars into my house. A couple of days later they had adjusted to being indoors and eating store-bought parsley. After a week they were ready to begin the pupal stage. They hung by silken threads from the branches of my largest, leafiest house plants. Soon each shed its caterpillar skin and was transformed into a motionless pale green chrysalis, or cocoon. At this point I wondered if they would all emerge as butterflies. Some nine days later the first of five eastern swallowtails clambered from its chrysalis. Half an hour later, with wings fully extended, it tottered onto my outstretched hand and then soared through the window to freedom.

EXERCISE 9 **Writing from a Narrative Outline.** Write a narrative using the outline that you prepared in Exercise 7. Be sure to include all the elements of a narrative as well as specific details presented with descriptive language. Present your narrative in chronological order, using transitions to help your reader follow the sequence of events. Your narrative can be one paragraph or several paragraphs long. Review your first draft to see what kinds of improvements you can make.

Writer's Choice

Writer's Choice #1

ASSIGNMENT   An autobiographical sketch

LENGTH   A paragraph of six to ten sentences

AUDIENCE   Your classmates

PURPOSE   To narrate the outstanding events of your first day of high school

PREWRITING   List all the developments from the time you woke up until the time you got home. Use the questions on page 166. Then eliminate those events that do not seem significant. Put the remaining events in chronological order. Prepare charts for details of setting and descriptions. Put all your notes into a narrative outline.

WRITING   Begin by making an introductory statement about what kind of day it was. Then tell about the highlights.

REVISING   Make sure that you have developed your paragraph with specific details. If you presented a conflict, did you show how it was resolved? Edit your work. Prepare a final version to share with your audience. Proofread it.

Writer's Choice #2

ASSIGNMENT   A historical narrative

LENGTH   A paragraph of six to ten sentences

AUDIENCE   Your history class

PURPOSE   To write a brief account of a true event in which an obstacle is overcome or a challenge is met

PREWRITING   List the important events in chronological order. Use the exploring questions on page 166. Make a chart of narrative details. Fill in a narrative outline.

WRITING   In your introduction provide information about time and place. Show how the narrative unfolded. Tell how the plot is resolved.

REVISING   Be sure you have explained the obstacle or the challenge. Edit your work, prepare a final version, and proofread it.

Writer's Choice #3

ASSIGNMENT   A narrative of your own choice

LENGTH   A paragraph of six to ten sentences

AUDIENCE   Your choice

PURPOSE   To write a first-person account of an actual event

OPTIONS   Choose narrative details to make your account vivid. Select an event with a conflict and resolution.

Writing Dialogue in a Narrative

Dialogue is the conversation between individuals in a narrative, quoted word-for-word and enclosed in quotation marks.

In a nonfiction narrative, dialogue represents the real words actually spoken by the people in the narrative. (In a fiction narrative, dialogue is made up.) Dialogue adds reality to any narrative. When individuals in a narrative speak directly to the reader, they come to life. Dialogue can also give a narrative a sense of immediacy, an I-was-there quality. See, for example, how dialogue makes the following narrative real and believable:

> Down at the end of the bench is the drinking fountain. It works with a slight hum. Next to it, up against the wall, is the bullpen phone—the direct-line link with management far across the grass in the distant dugout and through which the orders come ("Okay, get so-and-so up"). Once, during last year's World Series, I was looking around before a game, and I lifted the phone off the set to see what would happen; almost immediately a voice answered from the Reds' dugout.
>
> "Yeah?"
> "Oh," I said, surprised.
> "Hello. *Yeah?*"
> "Who's this?" I asked.
> "Jack Billingham." The voice sounded testy. He was one of the Reds' first-rank pitchers.
> "No kidding!" I said, like a kid reaching for his autograph book.
> "Well, who's *this*?" he asked.
> "Just checking," I said vaguely. "Keep it up." I hung up the phone, crouching down in my embarrassment, so that if Billingham happened to look out of the Reds' dugout toward the bullpen he would probably only see an arm reaching up, poking at the hook to put the receiver back on.
>
> —George Plimpton, "Baseball Stories"

EXERCISE 10 **Changing Indirect Quotation to Dialogue**. The following passage, an adaptation of Dylan Thomas's autobiographical narrative "A Child's Christmas in Wales," relays dialogue indirectly. Rewrite the passage, changing the indirect quotations to dialogue. Hint: Thomas used dialogue five times in his version. For punctuation rules on the presentation of dialogue, consult Chapter 27. In class compare your version to Thomas's original.

> Mrs. Prothero cried that there was a fire as she beat the dinner gong. And we ran down the garden, with snowballs in our arms; smoke indeed was pouring out of the dining room. We bounded into the house, laden with snowballs, and stopped at the open door of the smoke-filled room. Something was burning all right; perhaps it was Mr. Prothero, who always slept

there after midday dinner with a newspaper over his face. But he was standing in the middle of the room saying something about its being a fine Christmas and smacking at the smoke with a slipper. Mrs. Prothero cried to us to call the fire brigade, as she beat the gong. Mr. Prothero said that the fire department wouldn't be there—it was Christmas. There was no fire to be seen, only clouds of smoke and Mr. Prothero standing in the middle of them, waving his slipper as though he were conducting. He told us to do something. And we threw our snowballs into the smoke—I think we missed Mr. Prothero—and ran out of the house to the telephone box.

Writing: Vivid Verbs in a Narrative

Vivid, precise verbs convey action. They help to re-create an experience or incident more exactly for the reader. Look, for example, at some of the verbs used in the first paragraph of the five-paragraph version of the butterfly narrative:

VERBS USED IN THE NARRATIVE	LESS PRECISE VERBS
witnessed	saw
tended	watched
evolved	changed
blast	spray

Do you agree that in each case the connotations of the words on the left are richer and more informative than those associated with the words on the right? (See Chapter 5 for more information on choosing words.)

EXERCISE 11 **Using Vivid Verbs and Narrative Details to Convey Action.** The following paragraph tells in a spare, straightforward, and unexciting way what happened on a mountain-climbing trip. Following the paragraph are a list of narrative details and transitions and a list of vivid verbs. Rewrite the narrative, and make it more exciting by filling in the blanks in the paragraph with items from the list of narrative details and transitions. Replace the underlined verbs in the paragraph with verbs from the verb list. In a sentence or two after the new paragraph, explain the effects of your revisions.

The assault on the mountain occurred in three stages. First the climbers went overland _____ to the base of the mountain, where they put Camp One. _____. The next day, _____, they left camp and started to climb. Two thirds of the way up, _____, they made Camp Two. _____. The next day, two thousand feet below the frozen summit, they established Camp Three. _____, a few hours before dark, they climbed the last two thousand feet and triumphantly put a flag on the summit. Later, _____, they began the descent.

through eight miles of deep, powdery snow
in a covelike area protected by two enormous boulders
at the first cold glint of dawn
as dusk began to settle around them
on the final day of their ascent
They stayed in camp for a full day and tested their equipment.
They put on heavy clothes and began to climb the steep slopes.
A well-earned night's sleep rewarded their efforts.

VIVID VERBS
plant   hike   scale   broke   pitch   struggle

Writing an Anecdote as Part of a Longer Narrative

An **anecdote** is a short narrative, or brief story, that is often used to illustrate a point within a longer piece of writing.

An anecdote may be about an historical character or event or about a personal incident. Though the primary purpose of an anecdote is usually to illustrate a point, anecdotes are often amusing as well. The use of anecdotes can be an effective means of supporting your ideas in expository and persuasive writing. For example, the following anecdote is but one of several that the author uses within an expository essay to illustrate the point that animal behavior can often mislead scientists.

The first paragraph introduces the main point of the essay.

Scientists who work on animal behavior are occupationally obliged to live chancier lives than most of their colleagues, always at risk of being fooled by the animals they are studying or, worse, fooling themselves. Whether their experiments involve domesticated laboratory animals or wild creatures in the field, there is no end to the surprises that an animal can think up in the presence of an investigator. Sometimes it seems as if animals are genetically programmed to puzzle human beings, especially psychologists.

The anecdote begins here.

The risks are especially high when the scientist is engaged in training the animal to do something or other and must bank his professional reputation on the integrity of his experimental subject. The most famous case in point is that of Clever Hans, the turn-of-the-century German horse now immortalized in the lexicon of behavioral science by the technical term, the "Clever Hans Error." The horse, owned and trained by Herr von Os-

Notice that the anecdote has many of the elements of a longer narrative, such as characters and a conflict, or problem.

Notice that the author uses transitions, such as "for several years" and "finally in 1911," to make order of events clear.

Pfungst's discovery and explanation serve as the climax and resolution of the anecdote.

The final paragraph clearly states the author's attitude toward his subject—he admires Clever Hans.

ten, could not only solve complex arithmetical problems, but even read the instructions on a blackboard and tap out infallibly, with one hoof, the right answer. What is more, he could perform the same computations when total strangers posed questions to him, with his trainer nowhere nearby. For several years Clever Hans was studied intensively by groups of puzzled scientists and taken seriously as a horse with something very like a human brain, quite possibly even better than human. But finally in 1911, it was discovered by Professor O. Pfungst that Hans was not really doing arithmetic at all; he was simply observing the behavior of the human experimenter. Subtle, unconscious gestures—nods of the head, the holding of breath, the cessation of nodding when the correct count was reached—were accurately read by the horse as cues to stop tapping.

Whenever I read about that phenomenon, usually recounted as the exposure of a sort of unconscious fraud on the part of either the experimenter or the horse or both, I wish Clever Hans would be given more credit than he generally gets. To be sure, the horse couldn't really do arithmetic, but the record shows that he was considerably better at observing human beings and interpreting their behavior than humans are at comprehending horses or, for that matter, other humans.

—Lewis Thomas, "Clever Animals"

EXERCISE 12 **Writing an Anecdote.** Write a three-paragraph narrative using an anecdote. Decide on the point of your anecdote; identify the characters, conflict, and resolution. Prepare a narrative outline, and then draft the introduction, anecdote, and conclusion of your narrative. Use the checklist on page 178.

Revising, Editing, and Publishing

All the general questions to be asked when you revise paragraphs (Chapter 4) apply to narrative writing as well. In addition, narrative writing requires you to ask special questions that will help you to revise your narrative so that it will accomplish your purpose and be appropriate to your audience.

 Checklist for Revising a Narrative

1. What makes my narrative either a nonfiction narrative or a fiction narrative?
2. What questions have I asked in order to define my purpose and audience?
3. What questions have helped me to choose the events.
4. Which events are not necessary to include in my narrative?
5. What conflict, if any, does my narrative contain? How is the conflict resolved?
6. What narrative details have I included?
7. Have I checked my first draft against my narrative outline to be sure that the first draft is complete?
8. What transitional words and phrases give my narrative coherence? Have I used chronological order?
9. Where can I add dialogue to my narrative?
10. Where and how have I used vivid verbs to convey action?
11. Where would the addition of an anecdote help to illustrate the main point of my narrative?

Writer's Choice

Throughout this chapter you have concentrated on skills that help you to write narratives. To give yourself practice in applying what you have learned about narration to writing compositions, try one or more of the following Writer's Choice assignments. Notice the broad range of subjects that are possible for narrative writing. If you already have a particular idea in mind, you will want to work on Writer's Choice #5.

Writer's Choice #1

ASSIGNMENT   A paragraph to read aloud in class

LENGTH   Six to ten sentences

AUDIENCE   Your classmates

PURPOSE   To tell about experiencing something for the first time, such as swimming, traveling, or public speaking

PREWRITING   Review the event in chronological order. Think about how those who were part of the situation looked, sounded, and acted.

WRITING   Begin by stating your subject—what it was that you did for the first time. Then, in as many sentences as is necessary, tell what happened. End with a comment explaining your reaction to the events you have just described.

REVISING   Make sure that you have used transitions to clarify the order of events and that you have included details that help your reader picture characters and setting. Edit your work, prepare a final version, and proofread it.

Writer's Choice #2

ASSIGNMENT   A paragraph that might be part of a letter

LENGTH   Six to ten sentences

AUDIENCE   A friend who is away at summer camp for a month

PURPOSE   To relate the plot of the latest episode of your friend's favorite television show.

PREWRITING   List the important events of the show. Eliminate from your list any events that are not crucial to the plot.

WRITING   Begin by describing the setting. Then tell how the plot of the show unfolds. End by telling how the episode is resolved and how you felt about this resolution.

REVISING   Be sure that you have included the conflict and climax of the episode in your narration. Edit your work, prepare a final version, and proofread it.

Writer's Choice #3

ASSIGNMENT   A historical narrative

LENGTH   Your choice

AUDIENCE   Your choice

PURPOSE   To recount an episode in the history of your town, county, or state

PREWRITING   Organize the details of people and setting in two charts. List the important events in chronological order.

WRITING   In your opening sentence identify the time and place of the episode. Then relate the important events, using as much vivid detail and characterization as possible.

REVISING   Make sure that you have explained any special information that your readers will need in order to understand your narrative. Edit your work, prepare a final outline, and proofread it.

Writer's Choice #4

ASSIGNMENT   A personal narrative

LENGTH   Your choice

AUDIENCE   Your choice

PURPOSE   To write a first-person account of one of the following topics or a topic of your own choosing.
a narrow escape
an act of bravery
leading a group
a journey

OPTIONS   You may want to include dialogue.
You may want to concentrate on using vivid verbs to make your narrative exciting.

Writer's Choice #5

ASSIGNMENT   A narrative of any kind

LENGTH   Your choice

AUDIENCE   Your choice

PURPOSE   Your choice

OPTIONS   Write on any subject you choose.

You may want to state your purpose.

You may want to base your narrative on a photograph in the Writer's Sourcebook, pages 360–361.

REVISING   Make sure you have used transitional words and phrases to give your narrative coherence. Did you try to include some dialogue or an anecdote?

Writers on Writing

In her senior year Stephanie Pallo moved to Richmond, Virginia, from Baltimore, Maryland. A student at Midlothian High School in Midlothian when she wrote this narrative and commentary, Stephanie plans to major in electrical engineering at Virginia Polytechnic Institute.

THE PRODUCT

I've always welcomed change, but changing high schools in my senior year was more change than I ever expected. Why did we move to Richmond, Virginia? It seemed so far away!

I dreaded the thought of the first day surrounded by strangers in a new school. As I entered the first class, I could feel my insides thrashing and my face turning a harsh red. I took a deep breath and tried to relax, but all the eyes in the room were fixed on me. Some friendly blurs managed to utter a small hello or a welcome, but these were outnumbered by piercing glares from indifferent faces.

For the first time I experienced real loneliness. There were no long telephone conversations with my best friend; as a matter of fact, there were no phone calls at all. I sat home on weekends watching reruns of *Fantasy Island*, thinking about what I might be doing if I were back home.

Amazingly, the days of loneliness ended as quickly as they came. Now party invitations are no longer a rarity. Just as before, my time is divided among study, friends, and work. Now I know I should have given things time to improve before deciding that my life was ruined!

THE PROCESS

In writing there is no substitute for real experience. So, before writing this piece, I thought about the ways in which my life changed after we moved. I wanted my audience to share my nervousness and loneliness, and so I decided to tell specifically how I felt on my first day in my new school. Because I wanted to make sure that my writing was realistic, I also included details about what I did—such as missing my friends and watching TV reruns. I hope other students recognize their own experiences in mine.

YOUR TURN   *Writing a Personal Narrative*

As Stephanie did, write a narrative about an experience that turned out better than you expected. Include realistic details.

CHAPTER 8   NARRATIVE WRITING

Answer the questions based on the following narrative paragraph.

¹The year was 1824, and the Vienna concert hall overflowed with people. ²Candles flickered; the air itself seemed charged with energy. ³Beethoven's Ninth Symphony would be conducted by the composer, a man who had grown totally deaf. ⁴Ludwig van Beethoven, his brow wrinkled, his eyes flashing, stepped to the podium. ⁵As the music poured forth, the audience sat spellbound. ⁶At the glorious conclusion the chorus and orchestra stopped. ⁷The audience broke out in a wave of applause. ⁸The composer, unaware of the sound behind him, still faced the players. ⁹Then came one of the most memorable moments in music history: One of the singers walked over to the composer and turned him around to face the audience. ¹⁰The man who had heard the performance only in his mind could only *see* the world's appreciation.

Narrative Elements and Details   [pages 163–168]
1. Which sentence identifies the setting?
    (a) sentence 1 (b) sentence 2 (c) sentence 3
2. From which point of view is the narrative told?
    (a) first-person point of view (b) third-person point of view
3. Which sentence identifies the conflict or central problem?
    (a) sentence 1 (b) sentence 2 (c) sentence 3 (d) sentence 4
4. Which sentence describes the climax of the narrative?
    (a) sentence 4 (b) sentence 5 (c) sentence 9 (d) sentence 10
5. Which sentence provides the resolution of the narrative?
    (a) sentence 7 (b) sentence 8 (c) sentence 9 (d) sentence 10
6. Which sentence contains details about the setting?
    (a) sentence 2 (b) sentence 3 (c) sentence 4 (d) sentence 5
7. Which sentence contains details about the main character?
    (a) sentence 2 (b) sentence 4 (c) sentence 6 (d) sentence 7

Chronological Order, Coherence, and Vivid Verbs   [pages 168–178]
8. Which of the following outlines the events in chronological order?
    (a) orchestra stopped, audience applauded, Beethoven turned around
    (b) orchestra stopped, Beethoven turned around, audience applauded
9. Which sentence contains a transition word that indicates time order?
    (a) sentence 3 (b) sentence 4 (c) sentence 9 (d) sentence 10
10. Which verb suggests the atmosphere in the concert hall?
    (a) flickered (b) sat (c) faced (d) turned

Writing for Review   Write a narrative paragraph with a definite climax.

Expository Writing

All good writing begins with information.
—Caroline D. Eckhardt and David H. Stewart

Read the following four passages, each of which represents a type of expository writing. What do they all have in common?

I do not hit the bricks; I do not break them. Rather, I take a deep breath, hold it for half a second, then *release* suddenly but smoothly, focusing on the energy line and allowing my arm to express it. My palm passes right through the place where the blocks were, but they have parted just before I get there, and there is no sensation of impact, no shock wave, no pain.

—Don Ethan Miller, "How the Bare Hand
Passes Through Bricks"

The novel *I Heard the Owl Call My Name* contrasts the older and younger generations of the Kingcome people [a native American tribe living in Canada]. The young believe that a good education is the key to a good life, while the older generation believe that working with their hands will provide for their needs. The older generation live for each day, while the young people live for tomorrow. In short, the old are unselfish, settled, and bound to the past, while the young are selfish, ambitious, and turned toward the future.

—Kyle Kirkpatrick, Irving High School
Irving, Texas

Sound has shaped the bodies of many beasts. . . . The rabbit has long ears to hear the quiet "whoosh" of the owl's wings, while the grasshopper's ears are on the base of his abdomen, the lowest point of his body, where he can detect the tread of a crow's foot or the stealthy approach of a shrew.

—Jean George, *That Astounding Creator, Nature*

A *spoonerism* is a slip of the tongue in which the speaker mixes up the letters in two or more words. It takes it name from Reverend William Archibald Spooner (1844-1930), who taught at Oxford University. Reverend Spooner amused his colleagues and students for years by creating such gems as "All hail the Kinquering Kong" (Conquering King) and "All of us have in our hearts a half-warmed fish to lead a better life" (half-formed wish). He reportedly once scolded a student in the following way: "You have hissed all my mystery lessons and completely tasted two whole worms."

—Nadine Bass, graduate of San Pedro High School
San Pedro, California

As different as these passages are, they have something important in common. Each passage is meant to *inform* you; each tells you something new about the world in which you live. For example, in the last few minutes you have learned how to slice through bricks barehanded, how young and old differ among the Kingcome, what a spoonerism is, and why rabbits have long ears.

Expository writing is meant to inform the reader by presenting facts and explaining ideas.

The word *expository* comes from a Latin word meaning "to set out"; expository writing sets out information for the reader. You might even say that expository writing *molds* information for the reader and, as the preceding four passages suggest, molds it in a great variety of ways. For instance, it may define a term (like *spoonerism*), explain a process (say, how to slice through bricks barehanded), or contrast two subjects (such as the younger and older generations of the Kingcome people).

This chapter will help you sculpt information expertly by giving you practice in the following expository skills:

determining purpose and audience in expository writing
explaining a process: **prewriting, writing, revising**
explaining causes and effects: **prewriting, writing, revising**
dividing and classifying: **prewriting, writing, revising**
defining: **prewriting, writing, revising**
comparing and contrasting: **prewriting, writing, revising**
using various strategies in longer exposition

As you shape information into each of the types of expository writing listed here, you will use the writing process you studied in Unit 1. Remember that although you will always begin with information, you will not end with it. You will end only when you have molded that information into writing that tells your audience something new—*and* worth remembering.

Purpose and Audience in Expository Writing

Division, classification, definition, comparison, contrast—these are some of the "molds" in which you can cast raw information when you do expository writing. Sometimes you will be told which mold to use when you write; other times the choice will be left to you. When the decision is yours, thinking about your purpose and audience will help you to choose well.

Suppose, for example, that you plan to inform your readers about a certain baseball pitcher. What is your purpose? What specifically do you want to say about him? Do you want to point out the factors that led to his success? If so, you probably want to write a *cause-and-effect* analysis. Do you want to evaluate his strengths and weaknesses? If so, *comparing* him with another pitcher will give you a good standard against which to measure him. Do you want to show how methodical he is? If so, you can present the painstaking *process* by which he warms up before a game. Each approach serves a different purpose; each determines which specific pieces of information you will select.

Keeping your audience in mind will also help you decide on a mold for your writing. For example, readers who know a great deal about baseball may be intrigued by the details of the pitcher's warm-up ritual. Less knowledgeable readers, on the other hand, may not appreciate your spending time on such fine points.

To define your purpose and audience, ask yourself questions such as the following:

> Why do I want to write this expository piece? To present a process? To link cause and effect? To divide a subject into parts or classify items into categories? To define something? To compare or contrast two items?

> Who is going to read my writing? How much do my readers already know about my subject? What approach is likely to interest them most?

EXERCISE 1 **Identifying Purposes for Expository Writing.** For each of the following subjects, list two specific purposes that a writer could have in mind for expository writing. Study the example shown here.

SUBJECT Solar energy

PURPOSES To explain the process by which solar energy is used to heat houses

To compare the cost of solar energy with the cost of another type of energy

1. a famous writer
2. your home state
3. a recent film
4. an invention

EXERCISE 2 **Selecting an Audience for Expository Writing.** First select one of the following subjects for expository writing. Then in two or three sentences state whether you would prefer to write for the expert or nonexpert audience given for the subject, and explain your choice.

SUBJECT OF EXPOSITION	EXPERT AUDIENCE	NONEXPERT AUDIENCE
1. a singing group	a record collector	your parent
2. Olympic free-style champion	a competitive swimmer	a beginners' swimming class
3. using a videocamera	a filmmaker	a group of your friends

Explaining a Process

Explaining a process means showing how something works or how one accomplishes a particular task.

Do you want to show how a plant converts carbon dioxide to oxygen? To tell someone how to interview for a job? To explain how a bare hand can slice through bricks? In each case you will be explaining a process. The best way to explain any process is to lead your readers, step by step, through the actions that make up the process. As you think through the steps of a process, you should also keep in mind the special needs of your audience.

Prewriting

Prewrite by listing the steps in a process in chronological, or time, order. Answering questions like the following ones will help you include all the information that you need in order to present a process—in this case, interviewing for a job.

LISTING STEPS IN A PROCESS

PROCESS: Interviewing for a job	
QUESTIONS	SAMPLE ANSWERS
1. Who is my audience?	*First-time job seekers*
2. What are the steps in the process?	• *Dress for business--NO JEANS!* • *Shake hands with the interviewer.* • *Make eye contact.* • *Answer questions firmly.* • *Speak well--watch grammar!* • *Ask questions.* • *Research the company beforehand.* • *Leave with a firm handshake.* • *Write a thank-you letter (remind interviewer of your phone number).*
3. Should the order of the steps be changed?	*Make researching the first step.*
4. Can any steps be mentioned together?	*Combine handshake and eye contact; also combine answering questions firmly and speaking well.*
5. Does my audience need any more information to understand the process?	• *For first-time job seekers, stress businesslike dress and behavior.* • *Explain why researching the company is a good idea.*

EXERCISE 3 **Prewriting: Ordering the Steps in a Process.** The items below represent the steps in the process by which dinosaur bones are recovered and assembled into models. These steps are out of order here. On your paper list the steps in what you think is the correct order. Then group together any steps that seem to belong together.

1. The completed model, made up of frame, real bones, and artificial bones, is ready to be displayed in a museum.
2. Rocks and bones are shipped to a laboratory for cleaning.
3. Rocks containing dinosaur bones are dug out from the earth.
4. Scientists attach the actual bones to the steel frame.
5. Making estimates from the cleaned bones, scientists at the laboratory design a steel frame that re-creates the dinosaur's body.
6. At the laboratory workers carefully separate bones from rocks with chisels and needles or dissolve the rock with acid.
7. Laboratory workers construct substitutes for the missing bones from plastic, plaster, or fiberglas.
8. Once they have attached the bones to the frame, the scientists can determine which bones are missing and need to be constructed.

EXERCISE 4 **Prewriting: Listing the Steps in a Process.** Choose one of the processes listed here or one of your own, and decide on an appropriate audience for an explanation of that process. Then fill out a chart like the one above. Save your notes.

1. how the space shuttle takes off
2. how Americans elect a president
3. how a team reaches the Super Bowl
4. how to lose weight
5. how to photograph a friend
6. how to tune a guitar
7. how a televison works
8. how to parallel park

Writing a First Draft

When you write your explanation of a process, you should choose language appropriate to your purpose and audience. If you are instructing your readers in a task, you should feel free to address them directly, using *you.* If you are explaining how something works, you may need to define technical terms.

As you write, use chronological order, and be sure to include appropriate transitions to make your explanation coherent. In explaining a process you would use the following transitions:

after	first	last	so that
always	following	meanwhile	then
before	immediately	now	until
finally	in order to	soon	

Read the following explanation of how to interview for a job. Note the way in which the author presents the steps, tying them together with appropriate transitions:

> Interviewing successfully for a job is not that difficult; all it takes is a little planning and a good supply of common sense. First prepare for your interview by going to the library to research the company that is interviewing you. You do this research in order to make yourself feel more in control during the interview; it will also help you to ask intelligent questions about the company. On the day of the interview, choose your clothes carefully. No matter *what* the job is, you should never wear casual clothes (such as jeans) to an interview. When you meet the interviewer, make eye contact and give a good, strong handshake. You should answer each of the interviewer's questions in a clear, concise manner, choosing your words carefully and avoiding careless grammar. Show that you are interested in the job by asking questions based on your research about the company. Remember, you are trying to "sell" yourself. When the interview is over, thank the interviewer briefly, and end with another handshake. The next day write a note thanking the interviewer for taking time with you. Include a phone number and a time when you can be reached so that the interviewer can call back to tell you if you got the job. If you have followed the advice given here, you stand a good chance of getting that call.
>
> —Melissa Dickerson, Kentridge High School
> Kent, Washington

Revising, Editing, and Publishing

When you finish your first draft, read it aloud, and use the following checklist to help you revise, edit, proofread, and publish your explanation of a process.

 Checklist for Explaining a Process

1. Which steps in the process should be added to my explanation? Which ones can be deleted or grouped together?
2. Are the steps presented in the most logical order?
3. What can I do to make this process clearer to my readers?
4. What transitions would add to the coherence of my writing?
5. Is each sentence a complete sentence? Have I avoided errors in verbs, pronouns, and modifiers?
6. Have I correctly capitalized and punctuated each sentence? Are all the words correctly spelled?
7. What might be a good way of presenting my writing to my intended audience? Writing a letter? Sending it to a newspaper?

Writing and Revising an Explanation of a Process. Working with the chart that you prepared for Exercise 4, write a paragraph explaining the process you chose. Use appropriate transitions. Be sure to add any information that you think your audience needs. Then use the preceding checklist to help you revise, edit, proofread, and publish your writing.

Explaining a Cause-and-Effect Relationship

A **cause** is an event or condition that produces a result, which is known as an **effect**.

You write about a cause-and-effect relationship when you want to explain the reasons behind or the results of a particular event or condition. For example, you will write about a cause-and-effect relationship if you want to explain why rabbits have long ears, why Romeo and Juliet came to a tragic end, or what happened to the English nobility as a result of the Norman Conquest in 1066.

Prewriting

In thinking about cause-and-effect relationships, you need to be sure that your events are related by cause and effect and not simply by time. In a simple time relationship one event merely comes after another. In a cause-and-effect relationship one event actually *causes* the other to happen.

Which of the following items presents a cause-and-effect relationship, and which presents a simple time relationship?

    A. Ben sat down at his desk. He studied for his biology exam.
    B. Ben studied for his biology exam. He got a good grade.

In item A the events are related by time alone: Sitting at this desk did not actually cause Ben to study. Item B presents a cause-and-effect relationship, since studying probably *did* enable Ben to do well on the exam.

When you write about cause-and-effect relationships, you should prewrite by choosing your topic and deciding whether you are looking for causes, effects, or both. Then you can brainstorm to show the causes and effects that are related to your topic.

If you are looking for *causes,* you can brainstorm by indicating the event or condition on which you are focusing and then listing the series of events that led up to it. You may want to use arrows to show how each event in this series caused another, and this event in turn caused another, and so on. If you want to focus on *effects,* you should list your chosen event or condition and then show results branching out from it.

For example, someone who is writing about how the pesticide DDT enters the food chain would be focusing on causes. He might make the following brainstorming notes:

BRAINSTORMING TO EXPLORE CAUSES

TOPIC: *How DDT enters the food chain*

DDT is sprayed on fields.

Rain washes DDT into streams, which feed into rivers, etc.

DDT does not dissolve in water; it settles to the bottom.

Organism 1 (plant or animal) absorbs DDT.

Organism 2 feeds on 1, absorbs DDT.

And so on, until —

DDT gets into my food!

EXERCISE 6 **Identifying True Cause-and-Effect Relationships.** On a separate sheet of paper, indicate whether each of the following pairs of sentences expresses a simple time relationship or a true cause-and-effect relationship.

1. Blanche walked up to the stage. She tripped.
2. Reg broke his flashlight. He could not find his way out of the cave.
3. Our region just endured a six-month drought. The farmers lost most of their crops.
4. I stared at the television. The picture began to roll horizontally.
5. Tyler spent today at the beach. Tonight his bed is filled with sand.

EXERCISE 7 **Prewriting: Explaining Cause-and-Effect Relationships.** Choose one of the subjects below or a subject of your own. Decide whether you want to focus on causes or effects, and make brainstorming notes like the preceding ones. Save your notes for a paragraph that you will write later.

1. an earthquake
2. laughter
3. increased life expectancy
4. any popular fashion
5. a victory or loss in a game
6. a headache
7. the energy shortage
8. popularity

Writing a First Draft

When you write your first draft, review your notes listing the causes and effects of your subject. Then write a topic sentence stating your main idea. From your chart choose those points that seem most important, and plan to use them as support.

Then write your explanation, following your chart and presenting the events in which you listed them there. You can use the following transitions to add coherence to your explanation:

TO INDICATE CAUSES AND EFFECTS

as a result	consequently	is the effect of	therefore
because	if . . . then	leads to	the reason for
causes	is due to	since	

TO INDICATE DEGREES OF CERTAINTY

possibly	likely	certainly	undoubtedly
maybe	probably	necessarily	unquestionably

The following paragraph explains how the chemical DDT enters the food chain. Note that the paragraph uses transitions that make the cause-and-effect relationships clear:

It is frighteningly easy for DDT to enter the food chain. When fields are sprayed with DDT, the residues remain in the soil. Then rains wash the DDT residues away. They run off into small streams, then into large rivers, and finally into lakes and oceans. Because DDT is not soluble in water, the residues settle to the bottom of those bodies of water. Consequently, they are easily absorbed by the plants and animals that live under water. Once these plants and animals absorb DDT, it remains in them for years to come. If DDT is absorbed by one organism, it becomes a threat to all organisms because it enters the food chain. When one organism eats another that has absorbed DDT, the second organism takes DDT into its system. Then that DDT-bearing organism is eaten, and so on up the chain. As a result, all organisms, including those that *we* eat, contain DDT.

—Michael Schiesl, Nathan Hale High School
West Allis, Wisconsin

Revising, Editing, and Publishing

When you finish your first draft, use the following checklist to help you revise your explanation. For further guidance, see page 188.

Checklist for Explaining a Cause-and-Effect Relationship

1. Where have I identified the causes or results related to the event or condition on which I am focusing?
2. Is the relationship that I present a true cause-and-effect relationship?
3. Which, if any, causes or effects should I add or delete?
4. What can I do to make clearer the connection between each cause and its effect? What transitions can I add?

Writing and Revising a Paragraph about a Cause-and-Effect Relationship. Using the notes that you made in Exercise 7, write a paragraph explaining a cause-and-effect relationship. Use appropriate transitions to clarify the relationship that you are presenting. Finally, use the preceding checklist to revise, edit, proofread, and publish your explanatory paragraph.

Dividing and Classifying

Division breaks up an item into its main parts. **Classification** groups items together into categories.

You can divide almost anything, and you can probably divide it in several different ways. You can divide the year into four seasons. You can divide a ping-pong ball into plastic and air. You can divide creativity, as Thomas Edison did, into one part inspiration and ninety-nine parts perspiration. Division is a good way of molding information when you are explaining a single, complex subject that is made up of several distinct parts—say, a machine, a space flight, an orchestra, or a novel.

You can classify all kinds of things, from jokes to jeans to the moons of Jupiter. You should consider using classification as a method of molding information when you are writing about many similar items that can be sorted into categories. For example, Shakespeare grouped great people into three categories: those who are born great, those who achieve greatness, and those who have greatness thrust upon them.

Remember: Like two sides of the same coin, division and classification face different ways. Division carves an item into its parts; classification glues items together into groups. Use the one that suits your subject and makes your point.

Prewriting: Division

You can divide anything. Begin with something easy: How can you divide a house? You could divide it by a number of methods. For instance, you can divide it by floors into a basement, first story, second story, and attic. What would be the point of such a division? Perhaps you want to show how the temperature and humidity vary throughout. If various sections were constructed at different times, you can also divide a house on the basis of age. In this case you could show how styles have changed over time.

If you are thinking of dividing a subject, make a chart like the following one. This chart experiments with several different methods of dividing the experience of riding a ski lift.

PREWRITING CHART FOR DIVISION

SUBJECT FOR DIVISION: Riding a ski lift	
METHOD OF DIVIDING	PARTS
METHOD 1: *skills needed to do it well*	1. *balance* 3. *alertness* 2. *coordination* 4. *levelheadedness*
METHOD 2: *stages of the experience*	1. *the wait* 3. *the ride* 2. *the liftoff* 4. *the landing*
METHOD 3: *emotions of a first-time rider*	1. *anticipation* 2. *anxiety* 3. *relief*

EXERCISE 9 **Prewriting: Division.** Choose one of the following items or an item of your own, and think of one method of dividing it. Then list the distinct parts that you will mention. Save your notes for a paragraph that you will write later.

SAMPLE ANSWER   school—divided on the basis of traditions for each grade: (1) freshman beanies, (2) sophomore sing, (3) junior prom, (4) senior trip

1. a sport
2. an automobile
3. a recent movie
4. your home town
5. your day
6. your school

Writing a First Draft: Division

When you are dividing a subject, you should choose a type of organization that suits both your topic and the method that you have used to divide it. For example, you can use *spatial* order to show your readers how a spaceship is divided into sections. You can use *chronological order* to show how a novel is divided into plot developments. You can use *order of importance* to show how a teacher's work is divided into various activities. In each case you should increase the coherence of your writing by using transitions.

The following passage divides riding a ski lift into the skills required to perform this activity well. Note that the paragraph is organized according to order of importance:

> The recipe for a successful ski lift ride is as follows: Mix one part balance with one part coordination, and add an extra dollop of alertness and levelheadedness. The physical gifts of balance and coordination are certainly helpful to anyone who rides a ski lift. The skier needs a fine sense of balance if he or she hopes to sit down easily on a moving, sometimes

slippery chair. Similarly, the skier must be coordinated enough to manage a swift series of actions: checking the location of the approaching chair, lifting the bar of the chair, gliding into the seat, hanging onto the ski poles, and so on. The equal importance of the skier's mental preparation is often overlooked, however. A skier must always be alert and ready to adapt to a change of wind, an unexpected jostle, or an unpredictable fellow rider. Furthermore, the skier must maintain a calm, levelheaded attitude toward the whole experience if he or she hopes to enjoy it *and* stay reasonably intact (if not upright) throughout.

EXERCISE 10   **Writing and Revising: Division.** Look back at your work for Exercise 9 and the method you used to divide your subject. Write a paragraph using that method of division, with appropriate transitions to show the relationships between the parts. Then revise your paragraph, keeping in mind what you have learned so far. For additional help look back at the checklist on page 188, and look ahead to the checklist that appears on page 196.

Prewriting: Classification

Classification is a technique that you have probably already used many times in the past. You know that various features of a particular group of items can be the basis of the classification categories. Try classifying a familiar example: houses. You can group them by type of architecture into colonial, split-level, ranch, and so on. You can also group them according to the type of material from which they are constructed. You can group them by size, age, or number of inhabitants. You can even group them according to their front doors.

When you are classifying, you must make sure that the categories you create are meaningful. That is, the categories must have the same basis and must not overlap. For instance, you would not classify one singer as a soprano and another as an opera singer. The category of sopranos is based on the singer's vocal range, and the category of opera singers is based on the type of music she sings. Besides, the categories overlap—many opera singers are sopranos. Instead, classify the singers either according to their vocal range (as sopranos, contraltos, and so on) or according to the type of singing they do (opera, rock, country and western, and so on). Note that although some singers cross from one category to another by singing different kinds of material, no singer can inhabit two meaningful categories at the same time.

When you are classifying a subject, making a chart like the one shown here will help you make sure that your categories are meaningful. The subject is the people at a ski lift, and the writer has found three different methods of classifying them:

PREWRITING CHART FOR CLASSIFICATION

SUBJECT FOR CLASSIFICATION: People at a ski lift	
METHOD OF CLASSIFYING	CATEGORIES
METHOD 1: *type and condition of skis*	1. *those with top-notch, new skis* 2. *those with used but well-cared-for skis* 3. *those with old, battered skis*
METHOD 2: *amount of experience*	1. *frightened beginners* 2. *nervous intermediates* 3. *relaxed experts*
METHOD 3: *personal identity*	1. *family groups* 2. *couples* 3. *singles*

EXERCISE 11 **Prewriting: Classification.** Each of the following items presents a set of categories. For each item indicate in writing whether or not the categories are meaningful. Then write a sentence explaining your answer.

1. breakfast foods, lunch foods, dairy foods
2. free-style races, butterfly races, backstroke races
3. villages, cities, seaports

EXERCISE 12 **Prewriting: Classification.** Choose one of the subjects listed here, and list three or four categories into which you can group its members. Make sure that your categories are meaningful ones.

1. actors		5. televison programs	
2. pets		6. U.S. presidents	
3. popular songs		7. jobs	
4. sandwiches		8. clothing	

Writing a First Draft: Classification

When you are grouping items into categories, you might arrange your categories according to the order of their importance—say, least to most significant, smallest to largest, most typical to most unusual. For example, Shakespeare's classification of great people begins with the most conventional category—those who are born great, and ends with the least conventional—those who have greatness thrust upon them. As you write, use the transitions listed on page 187. Look at the following paragraph, which classifies skiers approaching a ski lift:

At first glance the people at a ski lift may strike you as a diverse and motley crew. However, if you watch carefully, you will see that you can group them into several categories by the way in which they approach the chairlift. First, an inexperienced skier bumbles his way through. Tripping over his tangled skis, he gropes his way to the boarding spot. As the chair swoops him up into the air, his poles go clanging to the ground. Nearby is the intermediate skier, who likes to pretend that he is extremely advanced. He smirks at the bumbling inexperienced skier, but he is still unsure of himself and sometimes bumps his head on the chair or gets tangled in his poles. Finally we have the advanced skier. He is the one who looks truly relaxed and happy standing in line. He is so cool and collected that he casually removes a piece of beef jerky from his pocket as he prepares to get into the chair. He glides easily into place and settles in for a short nap as he rides confidently up to the slope.

—Kati Schnell, Kentridge High School
Kent, Washington

EXERCISE 13   **Writing and Revising: Classification.** Review your notes for Exercise 12, and write a paragraph classifying the members of the group that you chose. Be sure that your categories are meaningful and that you use appropriate transitions to link your sentences. When you have finished your first draft, revise your paragraph, keeping in mind what you have learned so far about revising. For additional help with revising, look back to the checklist on page 188, and consult the checklist on this page.

Revising, Editing, and Publishing

When you finish your first draft of a division or a classification, use the following checklist to help you revise your work. For additional guidance in editing, proofreading, and publishing your final version, see page 188.

 Checklist for Dividing and Classifying

1. *For division:* Into how many parts have I divided my subject? Are these enough? Too many? Are the divisions clear?
   For classification: Into how many categories have I grouped all the members of my subject? Are these categories meaningful and consistent, or do they overlap?
2. What can I do to clarify my reason for dividing or classifying my subject in this way?
3. How might I organize my division or classification more logically?

Defining

A **definition** explains the meaning of a term.

If you want to tell your readers what a spoonerism is, what an esthesiometer does, or how old a quinquagenarian is, you can write a definition. You can also write a definition if you want to tell your readers what a generally familiar term means to you in particular. For instance, you might write your own definition of the word *family* in order to explain how it means something different from the word *relatives*.

Prewriting: An Unfamiliar Term

When you define an unfamiliar term, you first identify the term as part of a group of items likely to be familiar to your readers. Then you explain how the term you are defining differs from the other items in the group. You might also include examples and comparisons to make the term's meaning clearer for your readers.

You can prepare to define an unfamiliar term by asking the kind of questions shown here. As you see, sample answers are shown for the term *disk drive*.

PREWRITING CHART FOR DEFINING AN UNFAMILIAR TERM

TERM TO BE DEFINED: Disk drive	
QUESTIONS	SAMPLE ANSWERS
1. In what class of items can I place the term?	*The parts of the computer*
2. What distinguishes this item from the other items in its class?	*Its function--the disk drive holds a magnetic disk with electronically recorded information and spins the disk so that the computer can read what is recorded on it.*
3. What examples or comparisons would help my readers?	*Compare the disk drive to a turntable spinning a record?*

EXERCISE 14 **Prewriting to Define an Unfamiliar Term.** From your reading, coursework, work experience, or hobbies, choose a term that may be unfamiliar to many people. For example, your recent reading might have acquainted you with the fairly new medical term *interferon*. Prepare to define the term by asking and answering questions like those shown in the preceding chart. Save your notes.

Writing a First Draft: An Unfamiliar Term

Your prewriting notes will guide you as you write your definition. The topic sentence should indicate the group of items to which the term belongs, as in this example:

> A disk drive is essential to the operation of a computer.

Your next sentences should spell out the features that distinguish the item from the other items in its group:

> The disk drive is that part of a computer that is designed to hold a software disk, a flat plastic object on which information has been recorded electronically. The disk drive spins the disk very rapidly, allowing the computer to "read" information on the disk.

Note that the definition of disk drive also includes a brief description of the term *disk*. The definition ends with an example to help the nonexpert.

> The disk drive acts like a turntable, which spins a record so that the stylus can transmit the recorded sounds. The disk drive spins the disk, allowing the computer to absorb the disk's information into its memory.

[EXERCISE 15] **Writing and Revising a Definition of an Unfamiliar Term.** Using your notes from Exercise 14, write a definition of the term you chose. Then revise, referring to the checklists on pages 188 and 200.

Prewriting: A Familiar Term

Why would you want to define a familiar term? You may want to explain what an abstraction, such as courage or joy, has come to mean to you. You may want to make readers think twice about something they may have taken for granted. For example, Robert Frost made people see home in a new light when he defined it in a poem as "the place where, when you have to go there, / They have to take you in."

You can prepare to define a familiar term by asking these questions:

PREWRITING CHART TO DEFINE A FAMILIAR TERM

TERM TO BE DEFINED: Fairy tale	
QUESTIONS	SAMPLE ANSWERS
1. What is the term's common meaning?	*Most people think fairy tales are simple, unbelievable stories about goblins, witches, and princesses.*
2. In what ways does my definition differ from the common one?	*I see fairy tales as much more significant--they are actually exaggerated expressions of real childhood concerns and emotions.*
3. What incidents and examples might clarify my definition?	*Compare fairy tales with myths. Also point out specific emotions that fairy tales work out.*

EXERCISE 16 **Prewriting to Define a Familiar Term.** Select one of the terms below, or choose a term of your own. Plan to write your own definition of this term. Prewrite by answering questions like those shown on the preceding chart.

1. common sense
2. nonconformist
3. legend
4. popularity
5. humor
6. practical joke
7. success
8. family
9. charm
10. friendship
11. solitude
12. leadership

Writing a First Draft: A Familiar Term

The fact that your readers already know the generally accepted meaning of a familiar term gives you much flexibility in defining it. You could mention the term's commonly accepted meaning and then present your own meaning. You might use examples, personal experiences, and figures of speech to make your definition clearer.

The writer of the following paragraph presents a personal definition of "fairy tale":

Far from being a simple childhood entertainment, a fairy tale actually expresses real concerns and conveys real truths about human life in a manner that reaches a child's uneducated mind. Like a myth, a fairy tale attempts to say something that would be impossible to state literally. Beneath the story's surface of princesses, palaces, elves, and witches, the fairy tale deals in the profoundest ways with the real emotional problems of childhood: the feelings of helplessness, the terrifying perceptions of danger, and the anxieties that possess children as they cope with the difficulties of growing up.

—Denise Stauffer, Marlboro High School
Marlboro, New Jersey

EXERCISE 17 **Writing and Revising a Definition of a Familiar Term.** Using the notes you made for Exercise 16, write your own definition of the term you chose. You should explain how your definition differs from the commonly accepted one. In addition, you may want to clarify your definition with examples or personal experiences. When you have finished your first draft, revise your definition. (See page 188 and below.)

Revising, Editing, and Publishing

When you finish your first draft, use the following checklist to help you revise your work. For additional guidance in editing, proofreading, and publishing your final version, see the checklist on page 188.

 Checklist for Defining

1. *For definitions of unfamiliar terms:* Have I indicated the group to which the term belongs? Have I explained what sets the term apart from the others in its group?
2. *For definitions of familiar terms:* How can I make even clearer my reasons for defining this term? What specific details and incidents can I add to clarify for my readers what the term means to me?

Comparing and Contrasting

When you **compare** items, you point out their similarities. When you **contrast** items, you point out their differences.

Whether you plan to emphasize similarities or differences, you must compare or contrast items that have something important in common—for example, two musicians, two kinds of engines, two generations in a family, or two historical eras. There would be no point in comparing and contrasting two items as mismatched as Oregon and oregano. Remember also that you compare and contrast two items for a *purpose.* You may, for instance, want to make the point that one item is better, funnier, or more economical than the other.

Prewriting

Whenever you examine two items, you should begin by listing *both* their similarities *and* their differences. Such a listing will help you decide whether you want to emphasize similarities or differences. The list will also help you organize your information when you begin to write.

One good way of prewriting for a comparison-contrast is to make a *comparison frame*. First determine the various points on which you want to compare and contrast the two items, and list these points. Then you can indicate whether the items are similar or different for each of these points, giving examples where possible.

The comparison frame shown here compares and contrasts a record system and a tape system for the purpose of determining which is better:

COMPARISON FRAME

BASIS FOR COMPARISON	RECORDS	TAPES
Cost	• *Record often costs less than cassette.* • *Turntable costs $200.*	• *Tape often holds more than record.* • *Tape deck costs $195.*
Sound quality	*Excellent*	*Excellent*
Selection	*Wide*	*Wide*
Durability	*Easy to scratch*	*Hard to damage*
Portability	*Must use turntable--not easily portable.*	*Can use portable player or tape deck in car.*

EXERCISE 18 **Prewriting: Making a Comparison Frame.** From the subjects listed below choose one, and identify the two specific items that you will compare and contrast. Write a reason for comparing and contrasting them. Then make a comparison frame for these items: List four points on which the two items can be compared and contrasted, and indicate specific similarities and differences between the items.

PARTIAL SAMPLE ANSWER

two colleges: Boston University and Trinity College
    reason: To decide which is more appropriate for me

1. two colleges
2. two movies
3. two courses in school
4. two professional teams
5. two cars

6. two members of your family
7. two styles of clothing
8. two singers
9. two politicians
10. two professions

Writing a First Draft

Once you have completed your comparison frame, you can decide whether you are more struck by the similarities or the differences between your items. You can then consider different ways of organizing your presentation of these similarities and differences.

You have the following options for organizing your presentation:

1. Order your information *item by item*. For example, in comparing records and cassettes, you will discuss all the points—cost, quality, selection, durability, and convenience—for records, and then present the same points *in the same order* for cassettes. This type of organization is labeled AAABBB since you present all your information for item A and then for item B.

2. Order your information *point by point*. In this case you will discuss relative cost for both records and tapes and then sound quality for both records and tapes, and so forth. This type of organization is labeled ABABAB.

The following paragraph compares and contrasts records and cassettes. The paragraph highlights the differences between these items, uses an ABABAB pattern, and includes transitions to add to its coherence:

> You are about to buy your first good sound system, but you are not able to purchase both a turntable and a tape deck. How do you decide which to choose? Economic considerations will not help you make up your mind, since the score seems to be even there. Prices of turntables and tape decks are about equal. Records are a little cheaper than cassettes, but cassettes often hold more material than records. Quality and selection will not help you either: The sound quality of both records and cassettes is excellent, and the selection is wide. What will tip the scales? You need to think in terms of your own particular needs. If you are likely to use your sound system a great deal, you may prefer cassettes because they are more durable than easily scratchable records. Furthermore, if you like to carry your music with you, you will definitely want cassettes. You can play tapes in a car or in a portable tape player; even the best turntable does not travel well.

EXERCISE 19 **Writing a Comparison-Contrast.** Using the comparison frame you made for Exercise 18, write a paragraph comparing and contrasting the items you chose. Follow either the AAABBB or the ABABAB type of organization for your paragraph.

Revising, Editing, and Publishing

When you finish your first draft, read it aloud, and use the following checklist to help you revise your work.

1. How can I make my comparison-contrast clearer?
2. Have I used the AAABBB type of organization or the ABABAB type? Would the other work better for my comparison-contrast?

Using Various Strategies in Longer Exposition

Longer forms of expository writing may require **more than one strategy** for presenting facts and exploring ideas.

To cover more complex subjects thoroughly in expository writing, you will often find that you need to use more than one strategy. In general, larger subjects can be divided into smaller parts. Each part may then be treated in one or more paragraphs. One aspect of your subject may require, for example, a cause-and-effect strategy to make your meaning clear, whereas another part may require the use of a comparison-and-contrast strategy. The kinds of strategies you choose will depend on the nature of your subject and on your overall purpose. In the following excerpt from a chapter about the building of London's first permanent theater by James Burbage in Shakespeare's day, the author uses several strategies to explore the various parts of her subject.

> As an actor, Burbage knew how much a theater was needed in London. The company he headed happened to be the first to get an official license and Burbage was well aware of the difficulties of moving from town to town with a skeleton company, with a constant packing and unpacking of theatrical properties and costumes. The greatest theater-going population in England was not in the provinces but in London, and there was an excellent profit to be made in London by any company that could establish itself with a permanent base of operations.
>
> At present, the arrangement in London was the same as in other English towns: the companies produced their plays in the open, rectangular court-yards of the inns. The system must have been fairly satisfactory, since an inn like the Cross Keys was still being used by major acting companies when there were new theaters all over London. The shape of the inn-yards made it easy for them to be used as theaters, with the actors working on a scaffold at one end of the inn-yard and part of the audience grouped around them while the more prosperous individuals used the seats in the surrounding galleries of the upstairs rooms; and the stage arrangements must have been elaborate since the Office of the Revels was willing to pay over twenty-four shillings to borrow a property well that had been in use by the actors in the Bell Inn in Gracechurch Street.

Nevertheless the inn-yards had their disadvantages. The actors had to share the yards with the carters, who brought freight and mail to London on weekly schedules. The carters used the inns on definite days of the week, so that their customers would know where to find them, and the arrangement made it difficult for the actors to use the inn-yards more than three days out of seven. It was difficult to collect admissions, the storage of properties was not easy, and since there was no permanent tiring-house the changing of costumes must have been extremely complicated. More-over the proprietors of the inns charged fairly high rentals, and there was every reason why an intelligent and prominent actor might decide to put up his own building and collect his own rentals.

By good fortune James Burbage had been apprenticed to a joiner in his youth and had practiced the trade of carpenter until he discovered there was much more money in acting. No man could have been better equipped to build the first theater in England, since as an actor he knew what actors needed and as a carpenter he had the technique to supply it.

—Marchette Chute, *Shakespeare of London*

Carefully study the preceding excerpt, and note how it fulfills the following plan.

EXPOSITORY PLAN USING SEVERAL STRATEGIES

SUBJECT	the situation just prior to the building of London's first permanent theater
AUDIENCE	general readers
PURPOSE	to explain why a permanent theater was built
DIVISION INTO PARTS	paragraph 1: Burbage's motivations paragraph 2: use of courtyards paragraph 3: disadvantages of courtyards paragraph 4: Burbage's expertise
INDIVIDUAL STRATEGIES	paragraph 1: **cause-and-effect strategy** to explain Burbage's motivations for building a theater
	paragraph 2: **reasons combined with description** to explain why performing in courtyards had advantages
	paragraph 3: **contrasting reasons** to explain the disadvantages of performing in courtyards
	paragraph 4: **cause-and-effect strategy** to explain why Burbage was particularly suited for building London's first theater

As you write longer expository papers, consider the variety of strategies that you may use to present your ideas effectively.

EXERCISE 20 **Using Several Strategies in Expository Writing.** Prepare to write a short expository paper of three or four paragraphs. Choose a subject that is large enough to divide into parts that can be treated in separate paragraphs. Begin by completing a plan like the preceding one. Pay particular attention to choosing the best strategies for presenting each part of your plan. After you write a first draft, use the appropriate checklists in this chapter for revising, editing, and publishing your work.

If you have trouble thinking of a topic you find interesting, you may wish to consider writing about one of the topics listed below.

1. The Origin of Baseball
2. How Compact Discs Are Made
3. Planning a Personal Budget
4. Acid Rain
5. Aerobics and Health

Writer's Choice #1

ASSIGNMENT To explain how to perform a simple task

LENGTH Two paragraphs, each approximately five sentences long

AUDIENCE Paragraph 1—a foreign exchange student; paragraph 2—an American teen-ager

PURPOSE To explain how to tie a square knot, tune in a radio station, or build a campfire

PREWRITING Choose one task, and make a list of the steps involved in performing that task. Then think about your two different audiences, and modify the list for each audience, adding or combining steps as appropriate.

WRITING As you write each paragraph, use language appropriate for your audience.

REVISING As you revise each paragraph, put yourself in the place of your reader. Would a foreigner understand the instructions you give in the first paragraph? Would a teen-ager find those in the second paragraph useful?

Writer's Choice #2

ASSIGNMENT To explain a cause-and-effect relationship

LENGTH Two paragraphs, each approximately six sentences long

AUDIENCE Paragraph 1—an adult; paragraph 2—a small child

PURPOSE To write two answers to *one* of the following questions:
Why is the sky blue?
What does lightning do?
Why do trees form rings?
What happens when the sun sets?
The first answer should be a logical, scientific explanation of the event directed at an adult; the second should be an imaginative, mythlike one that would satisfy a small child.

PREWRITING Choose your event, and make notes for your scientific explanation first. You may need to check in an encyclopedia or science text. Then plan your mythlike explanation; you may want to think of it as a magical story.

WRITING When you write your scientific explanation, be sure to lead logically from one event to the next and use transitions to add coherence to your writing. When you write your mythlike explanation, feel free to use the form of a children's story.

REVISING Does each explanation work for its audience? Is the tone of your writing appropriate for each?

Writer's Choice #3

ASSIGNMENT To define a term

LENGTH Your choice

PURPOSE To invent a term and write a reasonable definition of it

AUDIENCE Your choice

PREWRITING First invent your word. You might make up a new word based on parts of actual words; for example, a *minimall* could be a small shopping area; *ideable* could refer to a workable idea. Decide on the group of items to which your term belongs and the features that distinguish it from the other items in the group.

WRITING Follow the suggestions for writing a definition of an unfamiliar term. Include examples.

REVISING Does your definition create a good picture of the item?

Writer's Choice #4

ASSIGNMENT To compare and contrast two of your friends

LENGTH Your choice

PURPOSE To show that you like both for different reasons

AUDIENCE Your choice

PREWRITING Decide on the friends about whom you will write, and think of points that could serve as a basis for your comparison-contrast. Then make a comparison frame to highlight their similarities and differences.

WRITING Organize your comparison-contrast according to either the AAABBB pattern or the ABABAB pattern. Use transitions to add to the coherence of your writing.

REVISING From reading your comparison-contrast will someone who does not know you or your friends get a good picture of the two of them and understand why you like each?

Writer's Choice #5

ASSIGNMENT To write a short informative paper on any subject

LENGTH Your choice

PURPOSE Your choice

AUDIENCE Your choice

OPTIONS You might base your writing on one or more of the items presented in the Writer's Sourcebook, pages 362–363.

Be sure to decide on a purpose and audience and to choose an appropriate expository method.

Follow the appropriate steps for prewriting, writing, and revising your work.

Writers on Writing

Gina Griffin wrote the following paper and commentary while a student at Brandon High School in Brandon, Florida. She plans to study art and foreign languages in college.

THE PRODUCT

I have spent most of my teen-age years being "out." I don't mean unpopular—just not "in." Now, at last, I have discovered how to be "in." I report my findings as a public service:

1. *You must be named Jennifer* . . . or some other typically cute name. The name can be pert (like Missy), or exotic (like Mircea), or descriptive (like Cookie). If your name is Enid, Alma, or Florence, you can always say that your father used to call you Muffin.
2. *You must have your own car.* And not just any old car. It should be a late-model sports car (preferably European). At all costs, avoid driving your mother's station wagon.
3. *You must have your own boyfriend.* Of course, he must be handsome or at least disarmingly cute (like John McEnroe). He must also drive his own matching late-model sports car.
4. *Hair is everything.* You must have lots of hair. Always remember that hot curlers are your best friend.
5. *You must never, never, NEVER be seen without makeup.*
6. For further details see my forthcoming book, *How to Survive in a Large High School, or Life as the Perfect Teen-ager.*

THE PROCESS

I had just seen our school's new "Calendar Couples" calendar, and so I decided to write about being "in." I tried to think about all the things that bothered me about "in" people. Now, I enjoy satire, but if I'm not careful it can get out of hand. I try to mix it with humor and laugh at myself so that the person I am satirizing knows that this is written in fun. As I write, I try to picture who is speaking. Sometimes it is a version of someone I admire; this time it was me speaking to someone else, my glasses balanced on my nose.

From there on it's all rewriting, rewriting, rewriting. I never really know when I'm done—I just pass out from exhaustion.

YOUR TURN   *Writing a Personal Definition*

Follow Gina's example, and write down your own, tongue-in-cheek personal definition of a term, such as "being in."

CHAPTER 9 EXPOSITORY WRITING

Explaining a Process [pages 183–189]   The items here list the steps in parallel parking, out of order. Write the number of each item and next to it write *a* for the first step, *b* for the second step, and *c* for the third step.

1. When your front tires are next to the rear of the car ahead, turn the steering wheel sharply left and continue backing in.
2. Select your space, and stop alongside the car ahead of it.
3. Shift into reverse, turn your steering wheel right, and start to back into the space.

Division and Classification [pages 192–196]   Indicate the letter of the item that correctly answers the question.

4. Which item divides an automobile in the most meaningful way?
    (a) tires/trunk/radio (b) wheels/frame/body (c) seats/dashboard
5. Which item sorts automobiles into meaningful classes?
    (a) economy/luxury cars (b) foreign/used cars (c) new/sports cars

Definition [pages 197–200]   Read the following parts of a definition. Then indicate the letter of the item that correctly answers each question.
    (a) A fastback (b) is a type of automobile body (c) that curves without a break from windshield to rear fender.

6. Which words set the term off from other members of its group?
7. What term is being defined?
8. Which words indicate the group to which the term belongs?

Comparison/Contrast [pages 200–203]   Read the following passage. Indicate the letter of the item that correctly answers each question.

  Seatbelts work only when fastened; airbags work automatically. Seatbelts can cause internal injuries at high-speed impacts; airbags cushion against such injuries. On the other hand, seatbelts protect users from injuries at very low speeds, when airbags may not be activated. Furthermore, seatbelts protect users from injuries occurring from the side, while airbags protect only during head-on collisions.

9. Which type of organization does the passage follow?
    (a) AAAA/BBBB (b) ABABABAB
10. Which would be a good topic sentence for this passage?
    (a) Seatbelts protect more people than airbags.
    (b) Neither airbags nor seatbelts alone offer full protection.
    (c) Airbags are more cost-effective than seatbelts.

Writing for Review   Write a paragraph presenting either causes or effects for one of the following: (1) the rise of fuel-efficient cars (2) the 55-mph speed limit (3) car telephones.

Critical Thinking and Persuasive Writing

Clear thinking becomes clear writing: One can't exist without the other.

—*William Zinsser*

BUY NEW CRUNCHEROOS!

Why should you buy new Cruncheroos cereal? Well, let me give you five good reasons:

1. All crunchy cereals are better than any other kind, and Cruncheroos are the crunchiest cereal ever made!
2. Cruncheroos have the most colorful box on the market, with plenty of great pictures, so the cereal inside must be great too!
3. My sister tried Cruncheroos and really likes them. You will like them too!
4. Michael Wright had a bowl of Cruncheroos the morning he won the Olympic gold medal for pole vaulting. Think what they can do for you!
5. Everybody else is buying Cruncheroos. You should too!

After reading this advertisement, would you be persuaded to rush out and buy the new cereal, or would you stop to think more critically about the claims in the ad?

Critical thinking refers to analyzing and evaluating the information presented to you or that you plan to present to others in defense of an opinion.

If you apply critical thinking to the cereal advertisement, you will see that each of the five "reasons" for buying the cereal is misleading. It is not necessarily true that all crunchy cereals are better, that a great box makes a great cereal, that you will like what someone else likes, that a cereal will make you famous and successful, or that you should do something because everyone else is doing it.

Of course, no advertising writer would ever create an ad quite like the preceding one. Every day, however, you are required to respond to advertisements, editorials, political statements, and other kinds of writing that try to persuade you to do something. You are asked to buy or not buy something, vote one way or another, accept or reject an answer to a problem.

Persuasive writing is writing that tries to influence a reader to accept an idea, adopt a point of view, or perform an action.

In much of your own writing, you will try to persuade someone to do something, argue in support of a position, defend a statement in an essay or a test. This kind of writing demands clarity, and, as William Zinsser suggests in the opening quotation, writing clearly demands thinking clearly. This chapter is designed to help you think and write as clearly and persuasively as you can. Like descriptive, narrative, and expository writing, good persuasive writing grows out of the writing process—prewriting, writing, and revising. The writing process applies to persuasive writing of any length, although in this chapter you will be applying the process specifically to paragraphs. You must concentrate on the following areas if you are going to think critically and write persuasively:

> **prewriting**: purpose and opinion
> **prewriting**: audience
> **prewriting**: support
> **writing** an argument
> **writing** a multiparagraph argument
> **revising**, **editing**, and **publishing**: avoiding faulty methods of persuasion

Prewriting: Purpose and Opinion

In persuasive writing your purpose and your opinion are closely related to each other. Your *purpose* is to persuade your audience to accept your opinion. You must keep a clear vision of your purpose and your opinion. The sharper they are in your mind, the more success you will have. The more you concentrate on where you want your writing to go, the more likely you are to hit the bull's-eye in the center of the target.

When you set out to write persuasively, you must be sure that (1) your opinion is worth fighting for and (2) you have a reasonable chance for success. Some ideas are simply not appropriate material for persuasive writing. For example, a personal opinion such as "The weather in our country is the finest in the world" is inappropriate. On some subjects everyone is entitled to an opinion, and you could not possibly persuade an audience that your opinion is the right one. Someone living on the other side of the world undoubtedly believes that the weather *there* is the finest. On the other hand, a fact—for example, that water at sea level boils at 212 degrees Fahrenheit—does not allow for discussion at all. No one needs to be persuaded of a fact. In addition, when deciding on your purpose, you should not bite off more than you can chew. To try in a single paragraph to persuade Congress to abandon (or double) all social service programs is unrealistic; consider, for example, these three possible starting points:

1. A famine is a terrible disaster.
2. American relief programs are the best in the world.
3. You should contribute to the Famine Relief Fund today.

Statement 1 is a definition—a fact of sorts. What more could you possibly say about it in a persuasive paragraph? Statement 2 is too broad and too vague—"best" in what way? Statement 3, however, is specific and directed toward an action: You want to persuade people to contribute. It can be the basis for persuasive writing.

EXERCISE 1 **Selecting Appropriate Topics.** Number your paper from 1 to 10. Write *appropriate* next to the number of each statement that is appropriate as a basis for a single persuasive paragraph. Write *inappropriate* next to the number of each topic that is inappropriate.

1. This supermarket should provide more checkout lines.
2. Tofu is one of the healthiest foods you can eat.
3. I think that this is the greatest day of the year!
4. Everyone should wear seat belts because they save lives.
5. Albert Einstein was born in 1879.
6. Einstein had an enormous influence on many scientific fields.
7. We ought to pay special attention to this lesson.
8. Modern art is much more interesting than the art of other times.
9. I am sure I am going to win this tournament.
10. The democratic form of government is the best ever invented.

Selecting Suitable Topics. Choose a general topic of your own or one of the following. Then write one sentence stating an opinion about that topic that can be used as the basis for a single persuasive paragraph.

1. physical exercise
2. writing assignments
3. war and peace
4. American foods
5. advertising
6. self-control
7. positive thinking
8. honesty
9. vacations

Limiting Generalizations

The opinion you want to persuade others to accept is sometimes stated as a generalization.

A **generalization** is a statement that refers to a common characteristic of several items—people, places, animals, objects, or events.

You must consider your opinion carefully to make sure it is not an overgeneralization.

An **overgeneralization** is a statement that refers too broadly to people, places, animals, objects, or events.

If your opinion is an overgeneralization, your audience may reject it immediately. They will assume that your paragraph is simply not worth reading. For example, if your opinion is "Teen-agers today are not as responsible as teen-agers were ten years ago," you may lose your readers before you have hooked them. They may think, "Why should I subject myself to such a gross overstatement? I know that it's simply not true. I'm much more responsible than my older cousins ever were." On the other hand, if you state, "Some teen-agers today are not as responsible as teen-agers were ten years ago," you stand a better chance of holding your readers.

In the second statement about teen-agers, the word *some* has been introduced. *Some* is a limiting word. **Limiting words** account for exceptions. They are an important part of persuasive writing. Here is a list of some common limiting words:

almost never	in most cases	occasionally
a minority of	less than half	often
as a rule	many	rarely
certain	more than half	seldom
few	most	several
frequently	mostly	some
half	nearly all	sometimes
hardly ever	nearly always	the majority of
in general	not all	usually

| EXERCISE 3 | **Limiting Opinions.** Rewrite each of the following opinions so that it may be used as a basis for persuasive writing. Use limiting words wherever necessary.

1. Private cars should be banned from every street in the city.
2. Going to the circus is only for children.
3. Summer is the best time of year.
4. Catching birds is extremely difficult.
5. People should eat only fresh vegetables.

Prewriting: Audience

When political candidates campaign or when manufacturers introduce a new product, they often have public relations experts find out as much as possible about the audiences they will address. In your own way you too should have a mental picture, or profile, of the people you are addressing. A **profile** is a brief sketch providing basic facts and relevant information. Remember, the more you know about the people in your audience, the more likely it is that you will choose the supporting details that will have the greatest possible effect on them.

As part of prewriting, create a profile of your audience. Write down all the information you can about them, and decide which items of information are most relevant. You may find it useful to make a list of profile questions like this:

Why are they likely to listen to me in the first place?

What will catch and hold their attention?

What attitudes are they most likely to have regarding my topic?

What experiences have they had that relate to the topic?

Would they prefer plain speaking or more elegant language?

When you prewrite, you need to decide which supporting details will have the greatest effect on your audience. When you begin to write, these decisions about your audience—combined with a clear purpose—will determine much of what you say.

Knowing your audience also means being sure that you have a *possibility* of changing their minds. If your readers are likely to agree completely with your opinion, it is not necessary to try to persuade them. For example, you would not try to persuade an audience of steelworkers that the salaries of steelworkers should be raised.

If your readers are likely to be totally opposed to your opinion, it may be futile to try to change their minds. You may need to reconsider and revise the statement of your opinion. For example, you would have little success persuading an audience of sign painters that all roadside advertising should be eliminated from America's highways. You may, however, be able to persuade them that advertising signs should be placed in different locations or that billboards and other forms of advertising should conform to certain artistic standards.

EXERCISE 4 **Suiting Topic to Audience.** Number your paper from 1 to 5. For each audience and opinion listed, write *a*, *b*, or *c* to tell which statement applies.

    a. appropriate topic for this audience
    b. inappropriate; unnecessary to persuade this audience
    c. inappropriate; not likely to persuade this audience

1. *Audience:* movie fans. *Opinion:* A large new movie theater should be built on the vacant lot downtown.
2. *Audience:* movie fans. *Opinion:* Our new movie theater should show more classic movies than first-run movies.
3. *Audience:* your classmates. *Opinion:* No student passes should be accepted at our new movie theater.
4. *Audience:*your classmates. *Opinion:* A panel of students should be set up to recommend which movies should be shown at the theater.
5. *Audience:*your classmates. *Opinion:* No refreshments should be sold in the movie theater.

Prewriting: Support

    Good writers generally succeed in persuading their audience by showing *why* readers should believe a certain opinion or act in a certain way. You cannot simply state your opinion or repeat your opinion five different ways and expect your audience to listen to you. You have to give evidence in support of your opinion.

In persuasive writing **evidence** refers to the reasons that directly support your opinion. Usually the most effective reasons are facts.

    In a court a lawyer supports the client's position with the most reliable evidence. Reliable evidence is precise, accurate, and relevant. In the same way you persuade your audience by offering your readers reliable evidence to support your opinion.

    During prewriting note as much evidence as possible. Use brainstorming, freewriting, and charting to gather your evidence. Then determine which of it is the most reliable. To do this, apply the following question to each item: *Is it a fact, or is it an opinion?*

A **fact** is something that is known to be true.

The following statements are examples of facts:

> Water at sea level boils at 212 degrees Fahrenheit.
> The capital of Alabama is Montgomery.
> A soccer ball is shaped like a sphere, but a football is not.

Facts are reliable evidence to use in support of an opinion because everyone agrees that they are true. Facts can be checked either through direct personal experience or through a reliable source, such as an encyclopedia or a primary source.

An **opinion** is a personal judgment based on what one person believes or feels to be true.

People may disagree over opinion but not over facts. Compare the following opinions with the preceding list of facts:

> Ocean water is cold.
> My state has the most beautiful landscapes in America.
> A soccer ball is easier to throw than a football.

In some cases you *can* use certain types of opinions as evidence to support your main opinion. That is, you can at times employ sound opinions and authoritative opinions.

A **sound opinion** is one that is based on a sufficient number of accurate facts. An **authoritative opinion** is one that comes from a reliable source, such as an eyewitness or a recognized expert.

As you can see, sound opinions and authoritative opinions are based on facts; as such they are almost as good evidence as are hard facts themselves. For example, imagine that you are supporting the following statement: *The Wildcats are a better baseball team than the Raccoons.* Which of the following statements present the strongest support?

1. The Wildcats' outfielders have higher batting averages than those of the Raccoons' outfielders.
2. The Wildcats had a higher attendance total at their stadium this year than the Raccoons had at theirs.
3. I think the Wildcats are a better team because they have won more games than the Raccoons.
4. Every baseball writer in America says that the Wildcats are a better baseball team than the Raccoons.

The first statement is factual but inadequate because it does not supply enough information on which to judge a team's total performance. The second statement is factual but not relevant to the question of which team is better. The third statement is a sound opinion because it is based on facts that are directly relevant to the question of which team is better. The fourth statement is an authoritative opinion—a statement of experts based on facts. The third and fourth statements present the strongest support.

When you are gathering evidence for persuasive writing, remember that your audience is most likely to be persuaded by facts. Sound opinions and authoritative opinions are good evidence too, but they must be judged according to the reliability of the facts and the sources behind them.

EXERCISE 5 **Identifying Facts and Opinions.** Indicate in writing which of the following items are facts, unsound opinions, sound opinions, or authoritative opinions. Tell why the opinions are unsound, sound, or authoritative.

1. Richard Rodgers was an American composer.
2. Because many other composers were influenced by him, Richard Rodgers changed the course of American musicals.
3. Richard Rodgers must have been a great composer because I like him.
4. The Association of American Composers said that Richard Rodgers changed the course of American musicals.
5. Richard Rodgers wrote *Oklahoma!*
6. I think the Acme Widget Company is guilty of fraud because the widget I bought is defective.
7. The widget I bought is defective.
8. The Better Business Bureau has warned consumers that Acme widgets are not good products.
9. Acme produces faulty widgets; all of the different products that Acme makes are probably faulty.
10. Court records indicate that last June a consumer group filed a lawsuit against Acme.

Writing an Argument

An **argument** is an ordered presentation of support for an opinion that you want others to accept.

An argument is made up of your opening statement of opinion, any background information that your readers may need in order to follow you, the evidence that you will use to support your opinion, and a concluding statement.

When you begin to write, state your opinion clearly; do not antagonize your readers with immediate emotional outbursts. Then give your audience any background information they may need in order to understand your opinion. You may find it necessary to define a term, provide a name or date, or give an example to make sure that your readers understand exactly what you mean.

Present the evidence to support your opinion in a clear and straightforward way. If, for example, you have three facts or authoritative opinions, present them one at a time in order of importance or in some other logical order. Always let your readers know when you are stating a fact and when you are presenting someone else's opinion in support of your opinion.

As you write, lead your readers from one sentence to another by applying the methods of achieving coherence described in Chapter 3: repeated words, pronoun references, and transitions. Transitions are especially important in writing persuasively: You want your readers to follow each step you take so that at the end they will have arrived at exactly the opinion you hold. The following transitions are especially useful for persuasive writing:

TO PRESENT EVIDENCE	TO STATE YOUR OPINION
first, second, third	in my opinion
most importantly	I believe that
for example	from my point of view
for instance	in my experience
the facts show that	
according to	

TO DEAL WITH CONFLICTING OPINIONS
although
conversely
in opposition to
even though
in contrast to
still

Remember that in persuasive writing your strongest weapon is evidence. You need not, however, totally eliminate any personal expression in what you write. On the contrary, you want your readers to realize that you feel strongly about your topic. Without losing your control and resorting to unnecessary emotional outbursts, you can and should let your reader know the degree of your commitment to the topic under discussion.

If the critical thinking you engaged in during prewriting and your presentation of evidence have gone well, you will probably find a special satisfaction in stating your conclusion. A good conclusion to persuasive writing allows you to bring your work together in one statement and move the reader to action. The concluding statement to a one-paragraph piece of persuasive writing need be only one sentence long.

The following annotated model demonstrates how each of these parts of an argument work together in one paragraph:

Clear statement of opinion

Background information

Support clearly labeled, with transitions used

Most important point labeled

Authoritative opinion labeled

Concluding statement with call to action

The construction of the new industrial park on East Street was not well planned. This industrial park—the group of factories and corporate office buildings on East Street between North Avenue and South Boulevard—has been under construction for ten years. First, the companies continue to argue over who has the responsibility to build the access roads to the park. Second, no landscaping has been done, and the area looks like a huge field of mud. Finally, and perhaps most important, the area around the park is the site of huge traffic jams every weekday, making travel especially inconvenient for local residents. Even Mr. John Smith, the city commissioner for industrial development, believes that the planning was inadequate. The facts are clear. The park was badly planned, and it is up to each individual local resident to pressure the mayor to take immediate action.

EXERCISE 6 **Writing an Argument.** Write a one-paragraph persuasive argument on one of the following topics, or choose a topic of your own. State your opinion clearly, and include any necessary background information. Use transitions to help present your support. State your conclusion in one sentence, and, if you wish, make a statement moving the reader to action.

1. for or against adding one year to high school education
2. for or against televising courtroom trials
3. for or against changing the local speed limit
4. for or against spending more money on the space program

Writing a Multiparagraph Argument

The amount of evidence that you need in order to present your argument effectively will often require you to write more than one paragraph. Notice, for example, how each item of support in the preceding paragraph can be expanded with additional support to create a more convincing multiparagraph argument.

> The construction of the new industrial park on East Street was not well planned. This industrial park—the group of factories and corporate office buildings on East Street between North Avenue and South Boulevard—has been under construction for ten years. Several major problems that continue to delay completion of the site and inconvenience the public have become apparent over the years.
>
> First, the companies continue to argue with the city over who has the responsibility to build the access roads to the park. Acme Construction Corporation, the major developer, claims that the city should assume fifty percent of the cost. The city claims that Acme and the two other developers contractually agreed to provide the roads when they acquired the land from the city. Since these contracts are a matter of public record, the city should move in the courts to force the developers to fulfill their obligations with the utmost haste.
>
> Second, no landscaping has been done, and the area looks like a huge field of mud. Retailers adjacent to the site claim that their businesses have suffered because of this vast eyesore. Furthermore, municipal ordinances require all new developments to provide adequate landscaping that will preserve and enhance the quality of life in the city. Since the buildings are virtually complete, why doesn't the city act to make the construction companies comply with the law?
>
> Finally, and perhaps most important, the area around the park is the site of huge traffic jams every weekday, making travel especially inconvenient for local residents. There have been numerous reports over the years of cranes and other construction equipment left blocking public roadways for unreasonable lengths of time. Moreover, since curbside parking has been nonexistent around the site for a decade, drivers hunting for parking space contribute to the traffic problems. Obviously, this situation hurts local businesses.
>
> The people of this city have grown weary of this ten-year fiasco. Even Mr. John Smith, the city commissioner for industrial development, believes that the planning was inadequate. The facts are clear. The park was badly planned, and it is up to each individual local resident to pressure the mayor to take immediate action.

EXERCISE 7 **Writing a Multiparagraph Argument.** Expand the argument that you wrote in Exercise 6 into a multiparagraph argument. Consider adding the following:

1. additional information to your opening statement
2. further background information
3. more evidence to strengthen each item of support
4. an elaboration of your conclusion that urges your readers to take some specific action

Avoiding Faulty Methods of Persuasion

In persuasive writing the temptation is great to use any means available to achieve your purpose. Consequently, some false or faulty methods of persuasion may creep into an otherwise sound argument. As you revise your writing, look for these faulty methods in your own work, and be alert to them in the writing of anyone who attempts to persuade you.

When you have achieved a final draft, edit and proofread it, using the skills you mastered in Chapter 4. Then share your work with your intended audience.

Avoiding Stereotypes

One false method of persuasion that is commonly used is the stereotype.

A **stereotype** is an overgeneralization about someone or something that does not take into account exceptions. It usually refers to a belief that is held by many people who have not thoroughly examined the facts.

For example, the generalization *College professors are absentminded* is a stereotype because it does not take into account all of the college professors who are not absent-minded. A more accurate opinion would be *Certain college professors are absent-minded.*

Stereotypes are the result of faulty thinking or, more often, no thinking at all. Remember that *all* generalizations need to be tested. A good persuasive thinker—and writer—is careful to eliminate stereotypes completely.

EXERCISE 8 **Avoiding Stereotypes.** Explain in a few sentences why five of the following statements are stereotypes. Then rewrite each of those statements using limiting words to account for exceptions.

1. Artistic people are temperamental.
2. Poetry is difficult to understand.
3. Politicians are dishonest.
4. Big cities are dirty and noisy.
5. Business people dress conservatively.
6. Football players are tough and aggressive.
7. Actors are conceited.

Bandwagon

The **bandwagon** method attempts to persuade someone to do something because "everyone else is doing it."

The term *bandwagon* refers to the expression *jump on the bandwagon*, as in an old-fashioned political parade when jumping on the wagon that carried the band meant that you enthusiastically joined the crowd. The argument that "everyone" believes or wants or does something is an over-generalization, since it does not take exceptions into account. It is not logical, since reason tells us that it is not necessarily true that one person will like something simply because another person or a large group of persons likes it. Bandwagon persuasion is usually based on insecurity; the bandwagon approach appeals to those people who are unable or unwilling to think for themselves.

Testimonial

The **testimonial** is an attempt at persuasion that is based on the advice or testimony of a famous person.

This faulty method of persuasion is especially deceptive because it uses the glamour or prestige of famous people to give the impression that they are experts qualified to give good advice about almost anything. Here is an example:

> A famous hockey goalie says: "When it comes to protecting the goal, I do a great job. When it comes to protecting my home and family, I know that the Acme Insurance Company does a great job too."

The goalie may be an expert at his job, but that fact does not mean that he is qualified to judge insurance.

Apply your critical thinking to every testimonial. Ask yourself, *What is the logical connection between the person and what he or she is trying to persuade me to do?*

Red Herring

Often when a writer has a weak argument or no argument at all, the writer will throw in a red herring as a last resort.

A **red herring** is a second issue thrown in to distract attention from the first issue.

In other words, throwing a red herring into an argument is a way of changing the subject. The term comes from the practice of dragging a red herring (a strong-smelling fish) across a trail to make hunting dogs lose the trail and follow the scent of the herring. Here is an example:

> Yes, sir, these sales figures do seem to be lower than last year's figures, and there are many good reasons for that. However, I would like you to notice that we sold more SuperGizmos in January than we did in February and more Giant Whatchamacallits in December than we did in November of last year.

The unfortunate person in this example is desperately reaching for a subject that will take attention away from the lower overall sales figures. People introduce side issues when they feel that they can no longer persuasively argue the first issue or when they have no genuine evidence. A critical thinker, a critical writer, or a critical reader does not fall for a red herring.

EXERCISE 9 **Avoiding Bandwagon Persuasion, Testimonials, and Red Herrings.** Identify the faulty method of persuasion in each of the following statements. Then rewrite each statement, making whatever changes are necessary to make the statement genuinely persuasive.

1. Join the thousands who have found relief from backache pain with Back-Ease.
2. Before we decide how much money we are going to allocate for the completion of Highway 61, shouldn't we decide whether we want to continue funding a transportation system that daily adds to our pollution problem?
3. I'm a professional actor in front of the cameras, but when it comes to taking pictures of my friends, I need a camera that's as easy as 1-2-3. That's why I use the Simplex.
4. More and more people in this fine state of ours are recognizing that I truly understand what needs to be done. Join with your friends and neighbors on election day, and add your vote of support to theirs.
5. The team needs a new gym. There's no doubt about it. This one is ancient, and the floor is falling apart. But think how much good a new coach would do. He would reorganize the first squad, initiate new drills and better practice, and provide inspiration.

Either-Or Thinking

The **either-or error** is an oversimplification that takes only two choices into account.

This kind of faulty thinking forces you to say that someone is either completely right or completely wrong, kind or unkind, for you or against you. It falsely limits a situation to one extreme or another without any degrees or possibilities in between. Here is an example:

> Joseph did not volunteer to help me in my campaign for class president. Since he is not on my side, he must be campaigning for my opponent.

The writer mistakenly thinks that because Joseph is not helping him he must be helping the other side, that Joseph is either for him or against him. In fact, Joseph may not have wanted to campaign for anyone, or he may have forgotten to volunteer, or he may have wanted to campaign but not had the time.

When testing a statement for an either-or error, be sure to *consider other alternatives*. Ask yourself whether there may be possibilities other than the two limited ones before you.

Faulty Cause-and-Effect Thinking

Faulty cause and effect refers to establishing a false connection between a cause and an effect.

If you engage in faulty cause-and-effect thinking, you will lose the respect of your audience. Here is an example:

> Mayor Boast deserves to be reelected. He took office two years ago, and in two years this city's crime rate has dropped a full 10 percent.

The writer is asserting that the crime rate dropped *because* Boast took office. But are there no other possible causes? A new police commisioner? A new federally funded job program? Street lighting sponsored by businesses?

Review your writing for faulty cause-and-effect statements. Remember that if you do not do so, your argument will be weak at the core, and you will be less likely to persuade your audience.

EXERCISE 10   **Avoiding Either-Or Thinking and Faulty Cause-and-Effect Reasoning.** Identify the error in critical thinking in each of the following statements. Then rewrite the statement to eliminate the error.

1. We don't need to ask Ellen. She plays the flute and would not want to go to a rock concert.
2. If you have never enjoyed the well-being that running can bring, it's time you ran on Sound Footing, the shoe that gives you quiet joy.
3. The people of that country have complained about democracy for years. They are definitely becoming a socialist nation.
4. Miss Church has always wanted her class to win that award for academic excellence. It's clear that they won it for her this year.
5. I fell asleep trying to read that book. It must be one of the most boring stories ever written!

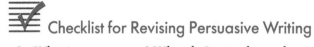 Checklist for Revising Persuasive Writing

1. What is my purpose? What do I want the reader to do?
2. Is my opinion an overgeneralization or a stereotype?
3. What qualities in my audience do I want to keep in mind as I write? What kinds of support are most likely to persuade them?
4. Which pieces of evidence are facts, which are sound opinions, and which are authoritative statements? Which unsound opinions, if any, need to be eliminated?
5. What revisions are necessary to make sure that my opening statement is clear, specific, and directed toward my purpose?
6. What method of organization have I used to present my argument? How many paragraphs do I need to present my argument fully and convincingly? Which transitions make my argument easy for readers to follow? Would another method of organization be preferable?
7. How clearly is my conclusion stated?
8. Have I used any faulty methods of persuasion—bandwagon, testimonial, red herring, either-or thinking, or faulty cause-and-effect thinking? What adjustments do I need to make to eliminate those faulty methods?

Writer's Choice

To practice writing persuasive paragraphs, choose from among these Writer's Choice assignments. Some are highly structured with specific ideas. Others indicate that you can determine your own direction. Whichever you choose, apply the skills learned in this chapter.

Writer's Choice #1

ASSIGNMENT   A one-paragraph fund-raising letter

LENGTH   Six or seven sentences

AUDIENCE   The general public in your state

PURPOSE   To persuade the reader of the letter to contribute to your favorite charity

PREWRITING   Freewrite for five minutes on the value of the charity. Then identify the points that would be most likely to persuade someone to contribute.

WRITING   State your opinion in the opening sentence. In four or five sentences give your evidence: facts, statistics, examples, reasons. End with a sentence that will move the reader to action.

REVISING   Apply all the questions on the checklist on page 225.

Writer's Choice #2

ASSIGNMENT   A one-paragraph advertisement for a product you admire

LENGTH   Your choice

AUDIENCE   Your choice

PURPOSE   To persuade the reader to buy the product

PREWRITING   List all the qualities of the product, and determine which qualities have the most appeal to your audience.

WRITING   Whatever method of organization you choose, be sure to avoid faulty methods of persuasion.

REVISING   Apply all the questions on the checklist on page 225.

Writer's Choice #3

ASSIGNMENT   A persuasive paragraph on a topic of your own choice

OPTIONS   Clearly identify your topic and your audience, and write out a statement of your purpose. State your opinion in one sentence, and provide any necessary definitions or background information. Organize your facts and opinions in any logical way, and use transitions to help present your support. State your conclusion in one sentence, and, if you wish, make a statement moving the reader to action.

Writers on Writing

A lifelong resident of Cincinnati, Ohio, Hugh Geier attended Indian Hill High School. Very active in student government, Hugh had to rely heavily on his skills of expression and persuasion. The following example of persuasive writing demonstrates those skills. Hugh plans to enter law and politics.

THE PRODUCT

Our nation's increasing reliance on high technology has affected practically every facet of our lives. It is not surprising that the high-tech craze has not passed by high schools. In many schools the personal system of class scheduling has been replaced by a less complicated and less time-consuming computer operation. Regrettably, computer scheduling has more disadvantages than advantages.

First, each teacher has a personal method of teaching. The computer is unable to take this factor into account. As a result, a student's education may be stifled by working with an incompatible teacher. For example, a student who works best in a structured environment can be arbitrarily placed in a class where the teacher does not emphasize structure.

Second, almost every student has "peak learning hours," specific times of the day during which the student is most capable of understanding new concepts. The computer cannot determine when a student is at a "peak" or a "low" and consequently can schedule a difficult class during a "low." Under the personalized scheduling system, the student can control the scheduling of difficult classes.

Third, a computer can schedule a student's most difficult courses back-to-back, making a student experience undue stress in one part of the day. The personalized scheduling system allows the student to even out the workload, placing less difficult courses or study halls in between challenging courses.

Of course the computer scheduling system has some advantages: It is quick and convenient. Unfortunately, the disadvantages outweigh the advantages. The computer system fails to account for individual student needs. Everyone connected with education should carefully consider this trend to computer scheduling by asking "What price are we paying for efficiency?"

THE PROCESS

Here Hugh explains the purpose and audience he had in mind when writing this piece.

When I was a freshman, our school decided to change its scheduling policy from the traditional personalized system to a more efficient computerized system. As a result, some students have experienced the problems of computer scheduling I mentioned in my paper. The arguments I presented are essentially the same ones I used when trying to lobby our administration to return to the personalized scheduling system.

However, this piece of persuasive writing is not meant to sway the opinion of any particular school administration. Rather it is directed to the mass of people who have not decided where they stand on the issue. The purpose of my paper is to create widespread public support for the idea of a personalized scheduling system.

YOUR TURN   *Writing Persuasively*

Write a persuasive paragraph on any subject you choose. Pay close attention to your purpose and audience, as Hugh's comment shows he did; write out a statement stating your purpose and identifying your audience. State your opinion clearly, and present your evidence in a logical fashion. End with a strong concluding sentence that restates your main idea and, if you wish, moves the reader to action.

CHAPTER 10   CRITICAL THINKING AND PERSUASIVE WRITING

Selecting Appropriate Topics [pages 211-213]

1. Indicate which topic is appropriate for persuasive writing.
   (a) Horseback riding is an Olympic sport.
   (b) Americans should devote more attention to horseback riding.
   (c) Horseback riding competition is elegant and exciting.

Limiting Opinions [pages 213–214]

2. Indicate which opinion is properly limited for persuasive writing.
   (a) In general, American factories today create fewer pollutants than ever before.
   (b) All American factories create fewer pollutants than ever before.
   (c) Factories today create fewer environmental pollutants than ever before in history.

Identifying Facts and Opinions [pages 215–217]   Indicate whether each of the following items is (a) a fact, (b) an unsound opinion, (c) a sound opinion, or (d) an authoritative opinion.

3. Twyla Tharp choreographed a ballet called *Push Comes to Shove.*
4. The panel of dance critics agreed unanimously that Twyla Tharp is one of the finest choreographers in the world.
5. Twyla Tharp is a brilliant choreographer because I have seen every one of her ballets.

Faulty Methods of Persuasion [pages 221–224]   Indicate whether each of the following statements demonstrates (a) a stereotype, (b) bandwagon or testimonial persuasion, (c) a red herring, (d) either-or thinking, or (e) faulty cause-and-effect thinking.

6. Your argument against reelecting the treasurer is certainly strong, but look at the terrible job done by the secretary.
7. Since she is not on that flight to Chicago, she must be going by car.
8. Home-cooked food tastes better than restaurant food.
9. Jennifer reads all the fashion magazines, and so she must have a great sense of style.
10. The trend these days is definitely toward polka-dot shoes, and so you ought to buy a pair immediately.

Writing for Review   Write a persuasive paragraph on a topic of your own choice. State your opinion clearly, organize and present your support in a logical way, and conclude with a statement moving the reader to action.

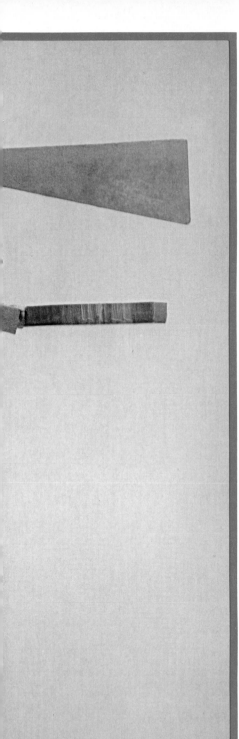

The Essay and the Research Report

Thinking About Thinking: Distinguishing Fact from Opinion

This unit applies the writing process to two longer forms of writing—the essay and the research report. Both are extended pieces of prose, but the essay emphasizes personal opinion, and the research report focuses on facts. In both cases, however, you engage in the thinking process of critical analysis to arrange and present information.

Defining the Skill

Analyzing a topic in an essay or research report often requires you to use the thinking skill called DISTINGUISH-ING FACT FROM OPINION. This skill is especially important when you are trying to think as objectively as possible. "Water at sea level boils at 212 degrees Fahrenheit" is a statement of fact. "This soup is hot" is an opinion.

Applying the Skill

Look at the photograph. As a class, list every fact you can about the sculpture. You may want to begin by precisely describing its size and shape. Question every fact, making sure no opinions are included. Then make a list of opinions about the sculpture, beginning by asking "What does it look like?" and "What is its purpose?"

CHAPTER *11*

Writing an Essay

So long as the emphasis is on revealing what the writer thinks—as opposed to what others think—it's an essay.

—*Mimi Schwartz*

What is the difference between a newspaper editorial about a forthcoming election and a page-one news story about the campaign? The answer is that the first tells readers what the writer thinks, whereas the second records the events but offers no opinions about them. The first is a kind of essay; the second in not.

An **essay** is a personal statement that contains an introductory paragraph, a body of supporting paragraphs, and a concluding paragraph, all of which concentrate on one particular topic.

The term *essay* can refer to news editorials, essay tests, magazine articles, college and job applications, advertising copy, autobiographies, biographies, movie reviews, and newspaper columns. The term *essay* applies to all these kinds of writing because they all reveal what the writer thinks.

These views can be expressed in many degrees of formality. Mimi Schwartz shows two excerpts from essays on the same topic—friendship— to illustrate how different their tones are. The essay on friendship written by a college student begins, "Boy, do I know someone who's a klutz."[1] The essay on friendship by Henry David Thoreau, the well-respected nineteenth-century writer, begins, "Friendship is evanescent in every man's experience and remembered like heat lightning in past summers." The tones are very different, but both authors let us know what they think.

Besides being a personal statement, an essay, according to the definition, contains several paragraphs. While all the paragraphs have to be on one particular topic, they can be different kinds of paragraphs—descriptive, narrative, expository, and persuasive.

In this chapter, within the context of the writing process, you will practice the various elements that make an essay:

    prewriting: generating, exploring, and focusing ideas
    prewriting: organizing an essay
    writing a first draft
    revising, editing, and publishing the essay

---

1. *Klutz,* deriving from the German word for "block," refers to a clumsy, awkward person. These examples are from Mimi Schwartz, "Essay Writing," in *Writing for Many Roles,* ed. Mimi Schwartz (Upper Montclair, N.J.: Boynton/Cook Publishers, 1985).

Prewriting: Generating, Exploring, and Focusing Ideas

Sometimes an essay topic will be assigned to you. In that case you have to invest time in making the topic "your own"—in finding the particular angle that you want to cover. Sometimes you will be told, simply, Write an essay. In that case you have to begin at the very beginning and first of all come up with a general subject for writing. Whichever situation you find yourself in, Chapter 2, "Prewriting," will help you to write more effectively. In this chapter you will find examples of the prewriting notes produced by the student whose essay on the movie *The Wizard of Oz* appears at the end of this chapter.

Where do you begin when you can write about anything in the world— or anything out of the world, for that matter? Most established writers will tell you to begin with yourself. Since an essay is a personal statement, it makes sense to explore your own likes and dislikes. The student who wrote an essay about the movie *The Wizard of Oz* was told to write an essay but was not given any particular direction in which to go. Here is how he began to generate, explore, and focus on ideas to use in his original essay.

Freewriting

Freewriting is writing done continuously for a specified, very brief period of time. In freewriting, someone jots down the ideas as they occur. Here is an example by the student:

> *What am I going to write about? They said I could write about anything. Somewhere I read that you should write about what's interesting to you because if it interests you, it'll interest your readers. Or if it doesn't interest you, why would anyone else want to read about it? Well, what interests me? The only interesting thing I did lately was watch* The Wizard of Oz, *which is on TV every year at this time. Actually it wasn't interesting so much as fascinating. Interesting is such a dumb word. Yes, the movie was fascinating. But I have to figure out why.*

The writer is off to a good start. At least he now has some ideas of a possible topic.

EXERCISE 1 **Freewriting for an Essay Topic.** Freewrite for five minutes in order to come up with a possible topic for an essay. Do not worry if after five minutes you still do not have an idea for writing. Just try the freewriting to see if it yields something worthwhile. When you have finished your freewriting activity, be sure to save your notes for use in Exercise 2 and in later exercises.

Brainstorming

Brainstorming can help you generate ideas by free association. Here is an example by the student who is working on an essay about *The Wizard of Oz*:

> The movie <u>The Wizard of Oz</u>—what's fascinating?
>
> plot has lots of fantasy in it—Dorothy mysteriously transported from Kansas to magical world of Oz
>
> fascinating characters: Munchkins, witches, and (of course) Tin Man, Scarecrow, Lion
>
> make-believe world, really unreal: speaking trees, flying monkeys, flowers with human faces, horse that changes color
>
> <u>color</u>: Oz is very colorful—the color makes Oz even more fantastic than it might be, ruby slippers glisten, importance of Yellow Brick Road and rainbow
>
> FASCINATING? NO, FANTASTIC! IT'S A FANTASY COME TO LIFE!

Through brainstorming, the student realizes that the film has much to do with fantasy—that it creates a fantasy world.

EXERCISE 2 **Brainstorming for an Essay Topic.** If the freewriting from Exercise 1 produced an idea that you may want to pursue, now is the time to brainstorm about it. If you still have not come up with an idea, try one of the following suggestions. Save your notes for Exercise 3 and for later exercises.

1. the last movie I saw
2. my favorite relative
3. oatmeal [or any other food]
4. my hair

Clustering

To check out his idea that much of the film has to do with fantasy, the writer tried the technique of clustering. He put one word—*fantasy*—in the center of the paper and let his mind wander to other words that clustered around that central word:

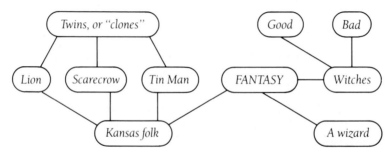

As a result of clustering, a few more details about fantasy occurred to the writer. For one thing, he remembered to add the wizard and the witches to his details about fantasy. He also began to recognize that Dorothy's friends and neighbors from Kansas appear as major characters in Oz.

EXERCISE 3 **Clustering for an Essay Topic.** If one word has emerged from Exercises 1 and 2 as a potential topic, place it in the center of a page, and draw a circle around it. Then write down other words that the central word calls to mind. You will have the most success with this exercise if you work quickly and if you write down specific, concrete words associated with the central word. Draw a circle around each new word, and use lines to show how one word leads to another. If you still do not have an idea to work with, put one of the following words in the center of a page, and begin clustering. Save your notes for Exercise 4 and for later exercises.

1. snow   3. lines
2. budgets   4. sunburn

Exploring Subjects and Focusing Ideas

Once you have a writing idea, whether you have generated it yourself or it has been assigned to you, you really have to dig into it so that you will have enough to fill an essay without endlessly repeating yourself. The remedy, as suggested in Chapter 2, is to ask yourself questions about the writing idea. Here are the answers produced by the student reacting to *The Wizard of Oz*.

INFORMATIONAL QUESTIONS TO EXPLORE A SUBJECT	ANSWERS
1. Who or what is my subject?	*The movie version of* The Wizard of Oz. *In particular, I'm going to concentrate on Dorothy's fantastic experience.*
2. What happened regarding my subject? What memorable incident can I relate about my subject?	*Dorothy gets transported to a world very different from her own. She has lots of adventures and misadventures along the way, but the real thrust of the film is her desire to get home to Kansas. Guess she'd rather have reality than fantasy.*
3. When did these events occur? In what way did my subject change over time?	*The events occur in a dream. Dorothy comes to appreciate her home.*
4. Where did all this happen?	*The beginning and end of the story take place in Kansas (black and white). The whole middle section takes place in Oz (blazing color). Just realized that these differences also emphasize the fantasy qualities of Oz: Kansas is plain in this film, and Oz is lush.*
5. How did it happen?	*Through the wonders of photography. I can't get into the psychological reasons for Dorothy's dream, but I can write about how the dream is communicated. Examples of unusual photographic effects: Glinda's bubble, the crystal ball, the talking trees, the dissolving witch.*

Now the student also has thoughts about the contrasts between Kansas and Oz and about the photographic effects in the film.

EXERCISE 4   **Exploring a Topic for an Essay.** Prepare a chart with questions that will help you dig into a topic from your work in Exercises 1–3. Base your chart on the sample charts in Chapter 2, pages 30, 31, and 32. If you still have not come up with an idea for an essay, use one of the following suggestions. Save your notes for use in Exercise 6 and in later exercises.

1. a character I admire in *Great Expectations* [or in some other work]
2. problems I have with personal computers
3. my reactions to human suffering
4. an adventure I'll never forget

You already know that you have to have enough to say. On the other hand, you must not have too much to say in an essay. That is, an essay must be *focused*. For example, the student whose notes we have been following now realized that he wanted to write only about the creation of a fantasy world in the film *The Wizard of Oz*. He realized that he does not have to discuss why Dorothy arrives in Oz or why she acts the way she does toward other characters or why she wants to get back to Kansas. All he has to explain is the fantasy that Oz turns out to be.

EXERCISE 5 **Focusing an Idea for an Essay.** For each pair tell whether you would prefer to write about *a* or *b*, and why. Save your notes for use in Exercise 7.

1. a. my love for movies
   b. my favorite movie
2. a. healthful diets
   b. the diet that works for me
3. a. what the circus meant to me
   b. clowns
4. a. the horrors of a toothache
   b. dental problems

EXERCISE 6 **Focusing an Idea for an Essay.** If you have successfully completed Exercises 1–4, state a focused topic that has grown out of all your prewriting activity. Save your response for Exercise 7.

Determining Your Purpose and Audience

Once you have focused your topic, you must identify the purpose of your essay. For example, you may want to persuade your readers to accept your opinion on a certain issue and to entertain them with a story at the same time. Here is the statement of purpose produced by the student we have been following:

> I want to explain the ways that a fantasy world is created in the film *The Wizard of Oz*.

A major factor to consider as you are establishing a purpose for your essay is your audience. For example, we know that the purpose of the essay about *The Wizard of Oz* is to explain how the movie creates a fantasy world. If the student had been writing for an audience of knowledgeable film students, he would have mentioned specific film techniques that help to create the fantasy, including a discussion of the types of shots and the cuts between shots. He would have used the specialized vocabulary of film-makers as well as other mature words and sentence structures. If, however, he had been writing for a group of young children, he would have kept his explanation, vocabulary, and sentence structure simple. He might have focused on the fanciful characters and the magical events of the movie.

EXERCISE 7 | **Selecting a Purpose and an Audience.** *If you were able to state a focused topic in Exercise 6,* now is your chance to tell for whom you want to write an essay about that topic and why. That is, state in writing a purpose and an audience for the limited topic you stated in Exercise 6. *If you did not state a limited topic in Exercise 6,* look back at your answers to Exercise 5. For one of the topics that you said you would prefer to write about, state in writing a possible purpose and a possible audience.

Prewriting: Organizing an Essay

Having generated this much prewriting material, some writers are ready to organize the material informally and then plunge right into writing a first draft. Other writers first prepare a formal outline based on their notes.

An **outline** is a writing plan that shows main points, the sequence in which they will be discussed, and their relation to one another.

Your teacher may suggest whether or not you should make a working outline or a formal outline before you begin your first draft. The student who worked on *The Wizard of Oz* essay first organized his prewriting notes loosely in a working outline, wrote a first draft, reviewed his first draft, and only then prepared a formal outline to guide him in writing his final draft. The working outline was sufficient at the first-draft stage. It helped him group together all the related ideas. It also helped him see which were his main ideas and which were details that supported main ideas. Each main idea was given a Roman numeral. Each detail that related to the main idea was given a capital letter:

WORKING OUTLINE
I. *Fantasy of the plot*
    A. *Dorothy arrives in Oz via cyclone*
    B. *Dorothy's adventures along Yellow Brick Road*
    C. *Dorothy clicks heels and returns to Kansas*
II. *Fantasy characters*
    A. *Lion, Scarecrow, and Tin Man who talk*
    B. *Witches—good and bad*
    C. *Wizard*
III. *Fantasy setting and photographic effects.*
    A. *Munchkinland*   E. *Talking Trees*
    B. *Emerald City*   F. *Dissolving witch*
    C. *Glinda's bubble*   G. *Winged monkeys*
    D. *Crystal ball*   H. *Flowers with human faces*
IV. *Oz vs. Kansas*
    A. *Kansas dreary: black-and-white film*
    B. *Oz magical: color film*

You might notice that the student added a few details to the preceding outline that were not in his other prewriting notes.

EXERCISE 8 **Making a Working Outline.** *If your work in Exercises 1–4 has yielded many notes,* now is the time for you to go through your notes and structure them into a working outline. Figure out what your main headings should be, and place details under each main heading. You may discard some notes along the way. *If you still do not have enough notes for an outline,* apply the prewriting techniques of freewriting, brainstorming, clustering, and asking questions to one of the limited topics in Exercise 5 or to another writing idea of your own choosing. One way or the other, you should develop a working outline with at least three main headings.

Writing a First Draft

The student started to write a first draft, closely following the working outline. The first draft of an essay is not intended to be a polished piece of writing. Its purpose is to allow a writer to get ideas down on paper in sequences of sentences and paragraphs.

Very often you will make the thesis statement the first or the last sentence in the introductory paragraph of your essay: Your reader will be sure to notice it there.

The **thesis statement** performs three important functions: (1) It states the main point of your essay. (2) It indicates your attitude toward the topic. (3) It suggests the organization that the essay will follow.

To write the thesis statement, review your working outline, and keep in mind the purpose of your essay and your chosen audience. Try to compose a single sentence that suggests most of the main topics on your outline. Look, for example, at the following thesis statement for the essay about *The Wizard of Oz.* Notice how it encompasses main topics I, II, III, and IV from the outline. Notice also that the thesis statement indicates the order in which the ideas will be developed:

> Through story line, characters, sets and photographic effects, and the contrast between Kansas and Oz, the film creates a fantasy world about a young girl's dream, a dream that you can relive as many times as you watch the film.

In addition to stating the thesis of your essay, the introductory paragraph should capture the reader's attention in an original way. You may consider the suggestions on page 240, or you may find other ways of appealing to your reader:

ASKING A QUESTION

The student writer in this chapter might have begun his first draft by asking, "Why has the film *The Wizard of Oz* captured the heart and imagination of generations of fans since it was released half a century ago?"

ADDRESSING THE READER DIRECTLY

The student writer might have begun by stating, "If you are like most people, you probably have wished that you could relive a special dream."

STATING AN INTERESTING FACT OR STATISTIC

The student writer might have begun by telling about the International Wizard of Oz Club, which publishes its own magazine called *Oziana*.

TELLING AN ANECDOTE

The writer might have begun with an amusing or interesting incident from his own life to support his topic. For example, he might have begun with "Now *I* know that there's no place like home—but sometimes we need to dream about another world."

QUOTING FROM A BOOK, POEM, OR SONG

The writer might have begun by quoting the line "Somewhere over the rainbow, skies are blue." Readers might respond positively, thinking, "That's such a familiar tune."

Besides capturing the reader's interest and stating the thesis, your introduction should also set the tone of the essay. *Tone* is the attitude that you express toward topic and your audience.

The tone of your essay may be formal or informal, humorous or serious, emotional or reflective. For example, you would probably use a serious, formal tone if you were explaining to the readers of your local newspaper the dangers of air pollution. You might use a light, humorous tone in describing to your classmates your dilemmas in a foreign country.

EXERCISE 9   **Evaluating Thesis Statements.** For each pair of statements, indicate in writing which is the better thesis statement, and tell why.

1. a. Basketball is an all-American sport.
   b. My enthusiasm for basketball can be traced to its pace and its grace.
2. a. Educational television is popular in my family.
   b. Three reasons account for why we subscribe to educational television: news, children's programming, and drama.
3. a. Travel is broadening in at least three ways.
   b. In recent years it has become more expensive to travel.

EXERCISE 10 **Stating a Thesis.** Based on your working outline (Exercise 8) and your statement of purpose and audience (Exercise 7), write a thesis statement. Your sentence should make clear to your reader what your main idea is, what your attitude toward that idea is, and how your essay will proceed. Save your thesis statement for Exercise 11.

EXERCISE 11 **Writing Introductory Paragraphs.** Write two different introductions for the essay for which you wrote a thesis statement in Exercise 10. Indicate in writing which version you prefer, and tell why. Save the preferred version for Exercise 12.

The Body and the Conclusion

The body paragraphs of an essay develop, or support, the thesis statement presented in the introduction. When you write the body paragraphs of your essay, it is generally wise to follow the order of your outline. In most instances each main heading in the outline should have a paragraph of its own.

As you are writing the body paragraphs, keep in mind the different modes of writing that you can use to develop a division or subdivision of your outline. At this point you may want to review Chapters 7–10 to remind yourself that you can use description, narration, exposition, and persuasion.

When you write an essay, you must make each paragraph connect smoothly with the paragraphs before and after it. The transitional devices discussed in Chapter 3 and again in Chapters 7–10 will help create coherence by connecting sentences within a paragraph and by providing bridges between paragraphs.

REPEATED WORDS AND SYNONYMS

By using the same word at the end of one paragraph and again at the beginning of the next paragraph, or by using words with the same meanings, you can forge strong connections between paragraphs, as the following excerpt from the student draft shows:

> . . . Oz is only a *fantasy world*.
>   In addition to the story line, the sets and photographic effects in the film create a visual *fantasy world*.

TRANSITIONS

Transitional words create coherence by making the movement from one paragraph to another clear, smooth, and easy to follow. Some of the most familiar transitions are listed at the top of page 242.

TIME	after	first	later	soon
	always	following	meanwhile	then
	before	immediately	now	until
	finally	last	sometimes	
PLACE	above	down	near	parallel
	ahead	far	next to	there
	around	here	opposite	under
	below	horizontally	outside	vertically
	beneath	inside	over	within
IMPORTANCE	at first	former	latter	second
	first	last	primarily	secondarily
CAUSE AND EFFECT	as a result	consequently	so that	
	because	so	therefore	
COMPARISON-CONTRAST	but	like	on the other hand	similarly
	however	likewise	on the contrary	unlike
EXAMPLES	for example	for instance	namely	that is

Here from the finished version of the essay on *The Wizard of Oz* is one example of a transition at work:

> The numerous special photographic effects contribute to our enjoyment of the fantasy. They include a witch materializing in a huge, floating bubble; another witch skywriting while riding her broom; and characters' faces magically appearing in a crystal ball.
>
> *Furthermore*, the image of Oz as a fantasy world . . .

The concluding paragraph closes and completes your essay. A well-written conclusion also adds to the force and appeal of your writing. Here are methods that you may use in your conclusion:

1. Summarize the important points that you have presented.
2. Restate the central idea of the essay.
3. Describe your personal reaction to the topic.
4. Relate an anecdote that supports the topic.
5. Suggest a solution to the problem that you have discussed.
6. Ask a question to draw the reader into your essay topic.

EXERCISE 12 **Writing a First Draft.** With your working outline and your preferred introduction from Exercise 11 close at hand, write the first draft of your essay. If you have three main headings on your working outline, you will probably have three body paragraphs. Do not worry about sentence structure at this point. Just try to cover all the main points and the supporting details on your outline. Save your first draft. Your assignment in Writer's Choice #1 on page 248 will be to revise the draft based on what you will study in the next few pages.

Revising, Editing, and Publishing the Essay

Revising a composition means reviewing and rethinking it. In examining your first draft you may find that you need to develop some ideas more or to eliminate other ideas that do not relate sufficiently to the topic. You may need to move a paragraph or to strengthen your conclusion. The following checklist will be helpful in discovering specific problems.

 ## Checklist for Revising an Essay

1. What am I trying to tell my audience? Will my audience understand my attitude toward the topic?
2. How do the points I discuss support the thesis?
3. Which points are most important to me? Do they need to be developed more or introduced earlier?
4. Which points can I discard?
5. What is strong and what is weak about my organization?
6. How well or poorly do my ideas connect with one another? Have I used transitions to create coherence?
7. How can my introduction and conclusion be improved?
8. What can I do to vary sentence structure and sentence length?
9. What adjustments should I make in grammar, usage, word choice, spelling, capitalization, and punctuation?

EXERCISE 13 **Revising a First Draft.** Begin to ask yourself the questions on the "Checklist for Revising an Essay" (above). Make notes on your first draft or on a separate page. These notes should indicate the kinds of changes you think you should make. Save your notes. You will write a formal outline and a revised version of your essay as Writer's Choice #1 on page 248.

The Formal Outline

As explained earlier, the student working on the essay about *The Wizard of Oz* wrote his first draft using a working outline. When he reviewed it by applying the preceding nine questions, he realized that he wanted to make some significant changes. At this point he was ready to prepare a formal outline. You will see differences from the earlier outline on page 238. Further, you will see that the formal outline is a bit more detailed. Note that the outline addresses just the body paragraphs—not the introduction and conclusion. If you or your teacher prefers, you can show the introduction and conclusion on your formal outline.

FORMAL OUTLINE

TOPIC: The fantasy world created in the film *Wizard of Oz*
I. The fantasy of the plot
    A. Arriving in Oz
    B. Meeting magical companions
        1. Munchkins
        2. Good witch and bad witch
        3. Scarecrow, Tin Man, Cowardly Lion
    C. Seeking the great wizard
        1. Example of troubles along the way
        2. Rewards for the four friends
II. The visual fantasy of sets and photographic effects
    A. Muchkinland
    B. Yellow Brick Road   E. Glinda's bubble
    C. Emerald City   F. Skywriting witch
    D. Wicked witch's castle   G. Crystal Ball
III. Fantasy emphasized by contrasts between Oz and Kansas
    A. Dry, flat Kansas versus lush, magical Oz
        1. Witches appearing in a puff of smoke
        2. Horse changing color
        3. Flying monkeys
        4. Speaking trees
    B. Kansas in black and white versus Oz in color

By comparing the working and the formal outlines you will see that the student decided to mention the characters as he discussed the plot: The first draft discussed the plot first and then discussed the characters; that was too artificial. Alongside the final version of the essay on pages 246–247, you will find notes that show you how the final version follows the formal outline.

Here is a summary of guidelines for writing a formal outline:

1. Place your topic at the top of the outline.
2. For each main idea use a heading that begins with a Roman numeral. You must have a *II* if you have a *I*.
3. Under each main idea list supporting details or subordinate ideas. For each of these use capital letters. You must have a *B* if you have an *A*.
4. Under each subordinate idea list any details that you want to remember to mention. For each of these, use an Arabic numeral. You must have a *2* if you have a *1*.
5. Follow the indentation scheme that you see in the preceding model.
6. Begin each entry with a capital letter. If your entries are sentences, end each with a period. Most of the time your entries can be phrases instead of sentences. The sample outline that precedes uses phrases, not sentences.

When you examine the final version of the essay, you will see that the thesis statement differs slightly from the thesis stated on page 239. As the student revised his thinking, he made corresponding changes in the wording of his thesis.

EXERCISE 14 **Preparing a Formal Outline.** Assume that you have written a first draft of an essay about your fascination with kites. Assume also that you are not satisfied with the first draft because it seems to wander from topic to topic too much. Apparently there is a weakness in your working outline. Now is the time for you to prepare a better outline, a formal outline. You realize from reading your first draft that the body of your essay should be organized into three main topics: *the history of kites, types of kites, and uses of kites.* Your job now is to organize all the details from your first draft under those three headings. Prepare a formal outline with three levels. Use all the notes on the following list in your formal outline.

three-sticker kites (hexagons)   scientific experiments
sporting uses   national sport, ancient Asia
observations of wind and weather   fancy kites (many shapes)
box kites (rectangles)   Malay kites (long diamonds)
Asia (no first record)   ceremonial uses
practical uses (before aircraft)   tournaments, many communities
Greece (500 B.C.)

The Title

Your title should reflect some aspect of the central idea of the essay as well as attract the reader's interest. For example, for an essay about the fantasy world created in the film *The Wizard of Oz,* the title "Why I Like *The Wizard of Oz*" is too dull. On the other hand, the title "A Wonderful Movie" is too general; it could refer to almost any movie that you have enjoyed. Furthermore, neither of these titles expresses the central idea of the essay. The titles "The Repeatable Dream" and "A Dream Come True" would be effective alternatives.

Model of a Finished Essay

On the following pages you will see the final essay produced by the student whose work we have been following throughout this chapter. The annotations in the margins indicate some of the points that have been raised in this chapter and show how parts of the essay correspond to parts of the formal outline on page 244.

A Dream Come True

How many times have you wished that you could relive your special dreams? Maybe you have thought that if you could only film your pleasant dreams you might experience them many times. The people responsible for making <u>The Wizard of Oz</u> must have had a similar thought in mind. <u>Through story line, sets and photographic effects, and the contrast between Kansas and Oz, the film creates a fantasy world about a young girl's dream, a dream that you can relive as many times as you watch the film.</u>

The film begins realistically, showing Dorothy's somewhat monotonous life on a farm in Kansas. <u>Soon,</u> however, Dorothy and her dog, Toto, are whirled by a cyclone "over the rainbow" to the wonderland of Oz. There Dorothy meets comical miniature people called Munchkins as well as two witches--a good witch, who guides and protects Dorothy, and another witch, who is terrifying and malicious. <u>Then</u> Dorothy begins a journey to meet the wizard of Oz, who she hopes can help her return to Kansas. <u>Before long</u> Dorothy encounters the Scarecrow, the Tin Man, and the Cowardly Lion, who each decide to ask the Wizard for what they want most in the world--a brain, a heart, and courage. <u>After</u> many predicaments, such as being lulled to sleep in a field of flowers through the powers of the wicked witch, the four friends <u>finally</u> reach the Emerald City and meet the Wizard. The great Oz gives the Scarecrow a degree in "thinkology," the Tin Man a heart, and the Cowardly Lion a medal for "conspicuous courage." <u>Then</u> Dorothy clicks her ruby slippers together, and returns to Kansas. <u>At</u>

NOTES ABOUT THE MODEL STUDENT ESSAY

A Notice that the introductory paragraph of this essay begins with a question to the reader.

B Notice the underlined thesis statement.

C Notice that this paragraph is developed as narration. The characters are mentioned as the plot is discussed. Transition words indicate when events in the narrative occurred. This paragraph corresponds to *I* on the writer's formal outline.

the _end_, as she wakes from a dream, we know that Oz is a fantasy world.

D   In addition to the story line, the sets and photographic effects in the film create a visual fantasy world. These wondrous sets include colorful Munchkinland; s spiraling Yellow Brick Road; the unusual Emerald City, where everything is green; and the sinister castle belonging to the wicked witch. The numerous special photographic effects contribute to our enjoyment of the fantasy. They include a witch materializing in a huge, floating bubble; another witch skywriting while riding her broom; and characters' faces magically appearing in a crystal ball.

E   Furthermore, the image of Oz as a fantasy world is made more powerful because it is _contrasted_ with Dorothy's life in Kansas. In the film Kansas has dry, flat plains, few trees, and simple houses. _Unlike_ Kansas, the land of Oz has lush forests, sparkling streams, and a castle in the Emerald City. Moreover, the people, animals, and plants of Oz are different from those in Kansas. For example, witches in Oz can disappear in a puff of smoke, horses can change into all the colors of the rainbow, monkeys can fly, and trees can speak. The contrast between the two worlds is emphasized by a photographic technique: The Kansas portions were filmed in black and white, _whereas_ the Oz portion was filmed in color.

F   If you have ever dreamed of a magical land like Oz, you can relive it again and again by watching _The Wizard of Oz_. A land where every story has a happy ending, Oz is surely a dream come true.

NOTES ABOUT THE MODEL STUDENT ESSAY

D Notice that this paragraph is developed as description. It contains details about the photographic effects in the film. This paragraph corresponds to _II_ on the formal outline.

E Notice that this paragraph is developed as contrast. Pay special attention to the transition words that help point out differences. This paragraph corresponds to _III_ on the formal outline.

F Notice that the concluding paragraph restates the thesis of the essay in a somewhat altered form.

Writer's Choice

Writer's Choice #1

ASSIGNMENT A formal outline and a final version of the essay you have been writing throughout this chapter

LENGTH Five to seven paragraphs

AUDIENCE As stated in Exercise 7 and reconsidered in Exercise 13

PURPOSE As stated in Exercise 7 and reconsidered in Exercise 13

PREWRITING You have already finished this stage in Exercises 1–8.

WRITING You have already finished this stage in Exercise 12.

REVISING Use the checklist on page 243 to review your first draft. Prepare a formal outline reflecting the changes you want to make in the organization of the essay. Follow the guidelines for a formal outline on page 244. Then use the formal outline and your first draft to write a final version of the essay. Be sure to edit and proofread the essay so that you can share your work with your readers.

Writer's Choice #2

ASSIGNMENT Your entry in an essay contest sponsored by the Chamber of Commerce on one of the following topics:
why it's great to live in [your town]
America's greatest contribution to the world
today's generation—our needs, our goals

LENGTH Five to seven paragraphs

AUDIENCE The leaders of your community

PURPOSE To describe, inform, or explain

PREWRITING Explore your subject with a series of informational, personal, or creative questions (see Chapter 2). Limit the topic, and organize the information, reasons, or opinions you wish to present into an informal outline.

WRITING State your thesis clearly, and write a first draft.

REVISING Refer to the revising checklist, and then prepare a formal outline. Write your final version. Carefully edit, proofread, and share your work with readers.

Writer's Choice #3

ASSIGNMENT An essay on any topic you choose

OPTIONS Determine and state in writing the length, audience, and purpose of the essay. Use the prewriting technique that best fits the topic. Follow these stages: Prepare a working outline, a first draft, a formal outline, and a final version. Edit, proofread, and share your work.

Writers on Writing

As a student at Encina High School in Sacramento, California, Leslie Wilcox wrote the following brief essay. A member of Future Farmers of America, Leslie also worked on the school yearbook and served as secretary of her class. She plans to become a veterinarian.

THE PRODUCT

Sitting on the steps of the quad, I can almost feel the school sigh with happiness and relief. Now that summer is over, it is no longer lonely, for the routine of school has begun.

Posters as well as class ring notices attest to the fact that students now occupy the premises. Despite the marks on the walls, despite the bits of gum wrappers left over from lunch, despite the path worn in the grass, the school has a comfortable feeling.

From peeling paint to cracking cement, the school has withstood the onslaught of twenty-eight graduating classes. As the school will stand for years, so will the pine cones drop to the ground year after year. Although the wind will still blow and the leaves will still die every autumn, there will be change. New students will come and go, noticing, yet not quite noticing, the "SWIMMING POOL CLOSED" sign.

THE PROCESS

While I was writing this essay, I sat on the school's quad and wrote down everything that I noticed—sights, smells, sounds, feelings. After doing that, I studied my list for any specific and interesting details to use in my paper. I decided that I wanted to convey the feelings of contentment and peace that I had felt.

I tend to be a "nonstructured" writer. I don't like having to keep to a specific format of five paragraphs when I write an essay. I feel limited to what I can do. I have recently begun outlining essays, but only analytical ones. For example, when writing about Shakespeare's *Hamlet*, I needed an outline to keep my mind on what each paragraph was going to be about. Without the outline, I might have wandered off to another topic!

YOUR TURN *Writing About Your School*

Write a brief essay describing your school at either the beginning of classes in the fall or the end of classes in the summer. As Leslie's essay does, your essay should express a definite attitude toward the school.

Writers on Writing

Cat Oliver wrote the following essay when she was a student at Waggener High School in Louisville, Kentucky. Cat plans to major in biology and minor in French in college. She hopes one day to become a pediatrician.

THE PRODUCT

When asked to describe the "American Dream," my stepmother was at a loss for words. Finally, she managed to come up with a very simple definition: "Health, wealth, and happiness." I was very surprised when she informed me that she is living her "American Dream."

Janice thinks it is good to have dreams, but most of the time reality is different. Her exact words were, "You have to walk between the dreams and reality." She also said that too many Americans feel they will be happy when they get something that they do not have yet. And people do not even attempt to be happy with the things they already have.

In order to give a better account of Janice's American Dream, I will describe her life a little. She lives in a typical suburban neighborhood. Her husband and one of her six children live with her. She has one grandson and one brother, and both of her parents are still living. She spends her days sewing. She is now a housewife, after being a medical supervisor for twenty-five years. Her one child at home will be leaving for college this summer. She is married to a man who loves her very much, as does everyone else who knows her.

Yes, now that I think this through, I can see why Janice feels that she is living her "American Dream."

THE PROCESS

When I sit down to write an essay, I make sure I have three things: a dictionary, a thesaurus, and a clear mind.

As soon as I am given my topic, I immediately begin thinking of ideas I will include in my essay. I obtain my best writing from a stream-of-consciousness technique. Since I write better in a freeform style, the first draft of my essay is usually very elementary in form.

After I have completed my rough draft, I go back and begin my revisions. I consult my thesaurus for the best words. My dictionary is close by so I can check for spelling mistakes. It is essential for me to concentrate. Television, music, and other noises distract me; therefore, I must be free of them.

It takes a lot of effort to turn out a good essay. However, if you just concentrate and write wherever you feel most comfortable, you will produce your best work.

YOUR TURN   *Writing About the American Dream*

Ask someone you respect to define the American Dream. Then write an essay, using that person's comments to personalize your writing.

CHAPTER 11   WRITING AN ESSAY

Topic [pages 233–238]   Indicate the letter of the item that correctly answers the question.

1. Which of the following is the most focused essay topic?
   (a) summer stock (b) what I learned in summer stock (c) theater

Outline, Introduction, and Thesis [pages 238–241]   Read the following working outline, and then indicate the letter of the item that correctly answers each question.

  I.   To my professional growth in summer stock
      A.   Playing different roles in a short time
      B.   Doing all kinds of jobs backstage
 II.   My personal growth in summer stock
      A.   Living away from home for the first time
      B.   Working with many different kinds of people
      C.   Accepting both successes and disappointments on my own
III.   My pleasure in working in summer stock
      A.   Sheer joy of performing for appreciative audiences
      B.   Friendships with people I would never have met otherwise

2. Where in this outline would you place a point about a friend you made?
   (a) in I under A (b) in II under C (c) in III under B
3. Which thesis statement best reflects this outline?
   (a) Performing in summer stock allowed me to develop as an actor.
   (b) I really enjoyed the summer I spent acting in summer stock.
   (c) Besides helping me grow as an actor and person, summer stock was just plain fun.

Body [pages 241–242]   Indicate the letter of the item that correctly answers each question.

4. What transition would best link the introductory paragraph to the first body paragraph of an essay based on the preceding outline?
   (a) furthermore (b) similarly (c) meanwhile (d) first
5. Which item would body paragraph #2 be most likely to discuss?
   (a) losing a coveted role   (c) hearing audiences sing along.
   (b) learning to build scenery   (d) learning how to fall down

Writing for Review   Write an essay about a topic of which you have some direct experience. Begin with a paragraph that engages your reader's interest and leads up to your thesis statement. Make sure that the paragraphs in the body of the essay discuss all the points raised in your thesis.

Writing a Research Report

The reason why research is like sculpting from memory is that in neither is there a concrete visible subject to copy directly. The subject—as sculptors themselves are fond of saying—is hidden in the block of material.

—Jacques Barzun and Henry Graff

When you write a research report, you sculpt a massive block of information into your own, original work.

A **research report** deals with a limited topic and is based on information from print sources, such as books and magazines, and from nonprint sources, such as personal interviews with experts.

Writing a research report involves finding out what experts have to say about a subject and then gaining the satisfaction of adding to your knowledge and opinions and becoming something of an expert yourself. In other words, a good research report provides your own analysis of the information you collect and includes opinions that you form as you research your topic.

This chapter will help you write a research report of a thousand words (about four typed pages), or of a length specified by your teacher. You will use at least five sources of information in researching the topic of your report. In writing the report you will use many of the skills discussed in earlier chapters of this book, such as prewriting, writing, and revising; writing topic sentences; and writing coherent paragraphs. To express your ideas, you will use one or more of the modes of writing covered earlier: description, narration, exposition, and persuasion. In addition, this chapter will give you practice in the following skills:

prewriting: selecting and limiting a topic
prewriting: beginning your research
prewriting: determining purpose, audience, and controlling idea
prewriting: preparing a working outline
prewriting: gathering sources and preparing a working bibliography
prewriting: taking notes
prewriting: writing a formal outline
writing the first draft
revising the first draft
publishing the final draft

Prewriting: Selecting and Limiting a Topic

Unless your teacher assigns a specific topic for your research report, selecting a topic will be your first step. Look for a general topic that interests you—one that you want to learn more about through reading and researching. Then use prewriting techniques that you studied in Chapter 2, such as freewriting, brainstorming, charting, and asking questions, to generate ideas for your topic.

Your major task in selecting your topic will probably be settling on a topic that is limited enough to be covered thoroughly in a four-page paper. For example, suppose you decide to write a research report on wildlife preservation. Such a topic is too general to be examined completely in a thousand words, and so you will have to focus on a more limited aspect of wildlife preservation. You could narrow the topic like this:

GENERAL   Wildlife preservation
LESS GENERAL   Preservation efforts concerning American wildlife
LESS GENERAL   Campaigns to save American bird species
LIMITED   The campaign to save the whooping crane

Also beware of choosing a topic that is *too* limited. If you write about how to apply for a driver's license, for example, you can do little more than list the steps in the application process.

The other main consideration in choosing a topic is the amount of research material available. When you have an idea for a topic, make a preliminary check at the library to see if you will be able to find enough information on it. Check the Subject Index of the catalog to see if there are enough books available on the topic. Check reference books like the *Readers' Guide to Periodical Literature* to see if there are magazine articles on the topic. Also consider newspaper articles and pamphlets in your library's vertical file.

For a thousand-word report (about four typed pages), you should use at least five sources (in addition to encyclopedias). Since some of the sources you identify in your preliminary check may prove unsuitable for your research later, it is thus a good idea to identify more sources now than the five now.

A **source** is anyone or anything that provides information on a topic.

Avoid topics that have been covered in only one or two sources. You may also have to avoid a topic based on very recent events or discoveries because you may find that not enough books or articles have thus far been written on the topic. However, you may often find sources beyond the library. Watching a TV news program or personally interviewing an expert in the field can provide you with valuable information on many topics. Pamphlets put out by businesses and government agencies can also be good sources of information. When you write a research report, you must sometimes engage in detective work to find a variety of sources.

In this chapter we will examine the writing process that one student followed in putting together a research paper on a topic of his own choosing. Randy Melick decided to write about Walt Disney World, the Florida amusement park, because he had recently vacationed there. In his preliminary check for sources, Randy found that his library carried only one book specifically about Walt Disney World, but it did have several other books on Walt Disney, American amusement parks, and travel in Florida, many of which would probably prove helpful. Randy also discovered that a number of articles on Walt Disney World had been published in newspapers and magazines. In addition, he already possessed a tourist brochure from Walt Disney World itself, mailed to his home at his family's request before the family visited Florida. Randy therefore felt that he would be able to find enough information to write a good report on the topic "The Making of Walt Disney World."

EXERCISE 1 **Limiting a Topic.** For five of the following general topics, suggest a limited topic that can be handled in a thousand-word report (about four typed pages). Then choose one of the limited topics (or another limited topic that interests you) for a thousand-word research report of your own.

GENERAL TOPIC Automobiles
  LIMITED TOPIC The Story of the Model T

1. Country Music
2. Detective Stories
3. U.S. Political Campaigns
4. Canada
5. Famous Painters
6. Early Days of Aviation

EXERCISE 2 **Checking the Library for Sources.** Go to the library, and consult the card catalog (or a computerized catalog system) to see how many books are available on the topic you chose in Exercise 1. Then consult the *Readers' Guide to Periodical Literature, The New York Times Index,* or similar sources for magazine and newspaper articles on your topic. (Consider only those articles in magazines and newspapers available at your library.) Third, check for pamphlets on your topic in your library's vertical file if it has one. At this point list at least ten sources with information on your topic, although some of them may prove unsuitable later. If you cannot identify at least ten sources, then you should choose another topic (see Exercise 1).

Prewriting: Beginning Your Research

Once you have chosen a limited topic for your research report, begin your actual research by reading one or two encyclopedia articles on the topic to gain an overview of basic factual material on all aspects of the topic. Your topic may have its own entry in the encyclopedia, or you may have to use the encyclopedia index to find information about your topic in a more general article. For example, to find a discussion of the painting *American Gothic*, the index may refer you to an article about the artist, Grant Wood, or to a general article, like one entitled "American Painting." If you cannot find enough information on your topic in an encyclopedia, get an overview of your topic by reading one or two magazine articles about it.

As you read the articles, make a list of the important aspects of your topic. This list will help you to prepare a working outline later.

Randy Melick consulted an encyclopedia and found information on Walt Disney World in an article entitled "Walt Disney." Walt Disney World also received brief mention in an article on Florida. To get a more complete overview of his topic, Randy read two magazine articles, one written about the amusement park soon after it opened, and one written more recently.

EXERCISE 3   **Finding General Information on a Topic.** Read one or two encyclopedia articles to learn general information about the topic for which you compiled your list of sources in Exercise 2. (If you cannot find encyclopedia articles on your topic, locate and read at least one magazine article that you identified in Exercise 2.) As you read the encyclopedia or magazine articles, jot down at least five important points about your topic.

Prewriting: Determining Purpose, Audience, and Controlling Idea

Once you have selected and limited your topic and examined some preliminary sources, you should define your **purpose** for writing your report. For example, if you were writing a report on a movie director, your purpose might be to persuade your readers to see his films. If you were writing a report on the French and Indian War, your purpose might be to present information about the causes and consequences of the war. You should be able to state your purpose in one sentence.

After you have defined your purpose, you should determine your **audience.** For example, the report on the movie director might be for an audience of both teen-agers and adults, while the report on the French and Indian War might be only for your history class. Your audience will determine how much detail and information you need to include.

The next step in prewriting is to state your controlling idea. The **controlling idea** is the central thought that you want to develop in your report. State the controlling idea as precisely as possible in a single sentence. Your statement of the controlling idea performs three important tasks: (1) It states the main point of the report; (2) it tells your reader your attitude toward the topic; and (3) it suggests the path that your report will follow. For example, Randy Melick developed this controlling idea for his report: "Walt Disney World was, for its creator and for thousands of tourists, a dream come true."

EXERCISE 4 **Determining Your Purpose, Audience, and Controlling Idea.** For the research report topic that you have been planning, write your purpose, describe your audience, and state your controlling idea.

Prewriting: Preparing a Working Outline

A **working outline** is a preliminary outline that will guide you in your reading and note taking.

Once you have an overview of your topic, you are ready to decide which aspects of the topic you want to cover in your report and how you want to organize them. Prepare a working outline to guide your note taking. As you take notes, you will probably revise your outline by adding subheadings, changing major headings, or even dropping some headings entirely.

To prepare a working outline, study the list of important aspects of your topic that you compiled in Exercise 3, and ask specific questions about these points. The questions you ask often will lead to the major headings of your working outline. For example, here are some of the questions Randy Melick asked after reading background articles on Walt Disney World:

1. Why did Disney want to open another amusement park when Disneyland was such a great success?
2. How is Walt Disney World different from Disneyland?
3. What do the two parks have in common?
4. Why does Walt Disney World appeal to so many people?

Randy then made a working outline based on his questions:

THE MAKING OF WALT DISNEY WORLD

I. Ideas behind Walt Disney World
II. Disneyland and Walt Disney World
III. Description of Walt Disney World
    A. Magic Kingdom
    B. EPCOT Center
IV. Reasons for Walt Disney World's success

EXERCISE 5 **Preparing a Working Outline.** Write specific questions about the important aspects of your topic. Then prepare a working outline using the one on page 256 as a model.

Prewriting: Gathering Sources and Preparing a Working Bibliography

Once you have made a working outline, you are ready to gather your sources of information for your report. Begin by obtaining copies of the books, magazine articles, and other sources that you identified when you first checked the library (Exercise 2). Remember to consider nonlibrary sources when you gather your sources of information. For example, to supplement his library sources, Randy Melick added a brochure that he had obtained from Walt Disney World.

A **working bibliography** is a list of books and other source materials that you will consult in researching your topic.

When you have located a source, skim it to decide whether it will be useful to you. If it will be, make it part of your working bibliography by recording the following information about the source on a **bibliography card,** a three-by-five-inch index card.

FOR A BOOK
1. the author(s) (or editor, labeled *ed.,* if no author is identified)
2. the complete title (put any subtitle after a colon)
3. the publisher
4. the place of publication (for large cities, only the city is necessary)
5. the edition (if specified in the book) (use abbreviations such as *rev. ed., 2nd ed., 3rd ed., 4th ed.,* and so on)
6. the copyright date (or most recent copyright date, if the book lists more than one)

FOR A SECTION OF A BOOK
Include the same information plus

1. the author of the section (if different from the main author or editor of the book)
2. the title of the section (if it has no specific title, use a descriptive title such as *introduction, essay,* or *afterword*)
3. the page number(s) of the section

FOR A MAGAZINE, NEWSPAPER, ENCYCLOPEDIA, OR OTHER ARTICLE

1. the author(s) of the article (if identified in the source)
2. the title of the article
3. the title of the source in which the article appears
4. the source's date of publication
5. the source's volume number (if given) (not needed for newspapers)
6. the page number(s) of the article (for newspapers, the section and page numbers if the paper has differently numbered sections)

FOR A PAMPHLET OR A BROCHURE

1. the author(s) or editor(s) (if identified)
2. the title
3. the company or organization that published the pamphlet or brochure
4. the location of the company or organization
5. the date of publication

Number each bibliography card in the upper left corner, in effect giving a number to each source. This numbering system gives you a simple and efficient way of identifying sources when you take notes later.

Here is one of Randy Melick's bibliography cards:

BIBLIOGRAPHY CARD FOR A BOOK

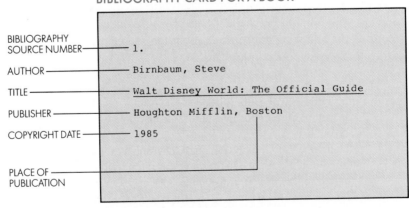

BIBLIOGRAPHY SOURCE NUMBER————— 1.

AUTHOR ————— Birnbaum, Steve

TITLE ————— Walt Disney World: The Official Guide

PUBLISHER ————— Houghton Mifflin, Boston

COPYRIGHT DATE ————— 1985

PLACE OF PUBLICATION

Gathering Sources and Preparing a Working Bibliography. Find the sources you identified in Exercise 2, or as many of those sources as you can. Skim the sources, and then write bibliography cards for those that you plan to use. Remember: For your thousand-word report, you will need to use at least five sources (not including encyclopedia articles); however, in case some sources prove unsuitable later, it is always a good idea to plan on gathering more than the minimum amount. In writing your bibliography cards, follow the format shown in the preceding sample. Also be sure to write bibliography cards for any encyclopedia or other articles that you consulted in Exercise 3, since those sources should also appear in your final bibliography.

Prewriting: Taking Notes

Once you have made a working outline, collected your source material, and prepared your working bibliography, you are ready to begin reading and taking notes. Keeping your working outline in front of you as you read and take notes will help you to focus on the points that you want to cover.

When you read a source, do not try to absorb all the information presented. Instead, skim the pages in search of material that is relevant to the headings on your outline. For full-length books, study the tables of contents and indexes to find the sections that apply to your outline.

When you find information that you think will be useful, take notes on that information. There are three ways of taking notes: paraphrasing, summarizing, and writing direct quotations.

Paraphrasing is restating an author's ideas in your own words.

Here is a passage from one of Randy Melick's sources:

In the summer of 1964, mysterious strangers from out of state began buying up large tracts of land on the outskirts of the small central Florida city of Orlando. All efforts to track down the identity of the buyers were unsuccessful.

Here is an example of a paraphrase of the preceding passage:

During the summer of 1964, unknown people started to purchase acres of land just outside Orlando, then a small city in central Florida. The buyers were not from Florida, and no one could discover who they were.

If you use paraphrased material in your report, you will need to give credit to the author whose ideas you are restating. Presenting someone else's words or ideas as your own is known as **plagiarism** and is illegal. (Later in this chapter you will learn the different means by which your report can give credit to authors for their words or ideas.)

Practicing Paraphrasing. For practice in paraphrasing when you take notes, try paraphrasing the following passages. If a passage contains an unfamiliar term, look it up in a dictionary.

1. Why is it so painfully hard for a computer to do what a small child can do so easily—understand human speech delivered in a natural way? The answer lies not only in the complexities of acoustics but in the mysterious properties of language itself.

   —Arthur Fisher, "Waddeesay?" *Popular Science* Dec. 1986

2. The father of *the epic*, and of all Western literature, is Homer. . . . Homer's *Iliad* and *Odyssey* came to be known and recited by every Greek. . . . Respected as fountains of wisdom, they provided succeeding Greek writers with countless plots, themes, and characters.

   —Thomas H. Greer, *A Brief History of the Western World*, 4th ed.

3 Checkers is *so called* only in the United States. In England and the British dominions, it is draughts. . . . The nature of checkers suggests that it had a common ancestor with chess and mill, but it has not been traced with certainty earlier than the fourteenth century.

   —Albert H. Morehead and Geoffrey Mott-Smith, eds.,
   Hoyle's Rules of Games, 2nd rev. ed.

4. The great burst of franchise growths began in the late 1940s and accelerated in the 1950s as the postwar generation migrated to the suburbs. There the chains found their national home, forming strips along the highways. In the 1960s franchises began invading the cities.

   —Stan Luxenberg, *Roadside Empires: How the Chains Franchised America*

5. Wyoming tips down as you head northeast; the highest ground—the Laramie Plains—is on the Colorado border. . . . From the clayey soil of northern Wyoming is mined bentonite, which is used as a filler in candy, gum, and lipstick.   —Gretel Ehrlich, *The Solace of Open Spaces*

Summarizing is restating only the main points and important supporting details.

The following example summarizes the same passage that was paraphrased on page 259. Notice that, unlike the paraphrase, this summary includes only the main points and details.

> In summer 1964 unknown buyers began purchasing large amounts of land near Orlando, Florida.

Summarizing demands that you decide which points are important enough to include in your summary. However, summarizing can save you a great deal of time, particularly when you are taking notes on a long article or section of a book.

Practicing Summarizing. For practice when you take notes, try summarizing each of the following passages. If a passage contains an unfamiliar term, look the term up in a dictionary.

1. Madison Avenue is going where no gray-flannel-suited executive has gone before: to the largest consumer market on earth. . . . The vastness of the Chinese market makes it appealing to American companies.

    —Annetta Miller, Katina Alexander, and Dorinda Elliott,
    "Advertisers Take on China," *Newsweek* 1 Dec. 1986

2. On March 2, less than two weeks after their return from America, the Beatles began working on their first feature film. . . . As shooting for *A Hard Day's Night* started in earnest, the Beatles found the pace of the six-week shooting schedule to be a snail's crawl compared to the frantic pace of their lives over the last six months.

    —Peter Brown and Steven Gaines, *The Love You
    Make: An Insider's Story of the Beatles*

3. Shakespeare's Juliet was . . . but a flimsy etymologist if she said, "What's in a name?" However, since she was referring to surnames, she may perhaps be forgiven, because their recent origin in comparison with given names entitles them to lesser respect. Strangely enough, it was the given name, today so little understood, that was created identical with the origin of language itself.

    —Flora Haines Loughead, *Dictionary of Given Names*

4. The outstanding critic of the British position was Mohandas K. Gandhi. Combining Western ideals, traditions from Hindu heritage, and the tactics of both ancient and modern politics, Gandhi built Indian nationalism into an explosive force. Ranking next to Gandhi in influence was Jawaharlal Nehru, an early convert to the nationalist cause. Together, Gandhi and Nehru succeeded in changing the goal of Indian nationalism from more Indian participation in government to complete independence for India.

    —Hyman Kublin, *India*, rev. ed.

5. Just twenty minutes short of midnight, April 14, 1912, the great new White Star Liner *Titanic*, making her maiden voyage from Southampton to New York, had a rendezvous with ice in the calm, dark waters of the North Atlantic. She brushed the berg so gently that many on board didn't notice it, but so lethally that she was instantly doomed.

    —Walter Lord, *The Night Lives On: New Thoughts,
    Theories and Revelations About the Titanic*

A **direct quotation** presents the exact words from a source.

In examining your sources, you will occasionally come across an especially relevant or powerful phrase, sentence, or passage that you may want to quote in your report. If so, copy it carefully into your notes, and enclose it within quotation marks. If you use a quotation in your report, you will need to give credit to the author; otherwise, you will be guilty of plagiarism.

At times you will find that some words should be omitted from a quotation, usually because they refer to information that the author provided earlier but that is not important to the quotation itself. If so, use **ellipses** (three dots) to indicate your omission. At other times, you may need to add a word or a phrase to make a quotation clear, usually because something in the quotation refers unclearly to something earlier that *is* important to the quotation. In that case, put the addition in **brackets** (square parentheses). Make such changes sparingly, and be careful not to tamper with the author's intended meaning.

The following example shows the use of ellipses and brackets in a direct quotation. Randy Melick copied a description that he wanted to quote in his report, omitting the information unrelated to the description and adding a phrase to clarify the description.

ORIGINAL PASSAGE

The territory stretched practically from horizon to horizon, and all Evans could see were great tracts of bald cypresses and saw grass, gashed every few hundred yards by drainage canals.

QUOTATION WITH ELLIPSES AND BRACKETS

"The territory [outside Orlando] stretched practically from horizon to horizon, . . . great tracts of bald cypresses and saw grass, gashed every few hundred yards by drainage canals."

Whether your note consists of a paraphrase, a summary, or a direct quotation, you need some way of recording it. Many students find that large (four-by-six-inch) index cards are best for taking notes:

1. In the upper left corner of the **note card**, write the number that you assigned to the source of the note when you prepared your working bibliography. That number will quickly refer you to the information you listed on your bibliography card for the source.
2. To the right of this bibliography source number, write a heading that identifies the information in your note. This will usually be one of the headings from your working outline.
3. In the upper right corner of each card, write a number to identify the note card.
4. In the center of the card, write the note itself—your paraphrase, your summary, or the direct quotation that you are recording.
5. Finally, at the bottom of the note card, briefly restate the source of the note, and write the number of the page on which the information for the note appears in the source.

Here is an example of one of Randy Melick's note cards with a direct quotation; however, the same format would be used for a paraphrase or a summary.

SAMPLE NOTE CARD

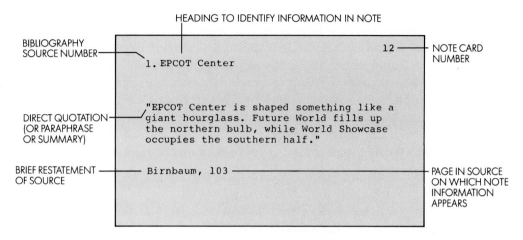

HEADING TO IDENTIFY INFORMATION IN NOTE

BIBLIOGRAPHY SOURCE NUMBER

NOTE CARD NUMBER

DIRECT QUOTATION (OR PARAPHRASE OR SUMMARY)

BRIEF RESTATEMENT OF SOURCE

PAGE IN SOURCE ON WHICH NOTE INFORMATION APPEARS

1. EPCOT Center

12

"EPCOT Center is shaped something like a giant hourglass. Future World fills up the northern bulb, while World Showcase occupies the southern half."

Birnbaum, 103

EXERCISE 9 **Taking Notes.** From the sources you listed in your working bibliography in Exercise 6, take notes on the information that you may use in writing your report. Use four-by-six-inch note cards, and model your notes on Randy Melick's note card shown above. Paraphrase or summarize most of the information you record; however, if you come across a phrase, a sentence, or a passage that you may want to quote in your report, include a direct quotation in your notes.

Prewriting: Preparing a Formal Outline

A **formal outline** is the final outline that will guide you in writing your first draft.

As you read and take notes, you will probably find that your working outline will require some revisions. To prepare your formal outline, read over your note cards carefully and group them into piles, one for each important aspect of your topic. If any of your cards do not seem to fit into your topics, set them aside. Compare your working outline with your piles of note cards, and ask yourself the following questions:

1. How do the headings on the note cards correspond to the headings in my working outline? What main headings should be added to the outline?

2. What other information do I need to cover the main headings in my working outline? Should I consider eliminating headings?
3. What logical subdivisions can I introduce for the main headings?
4. What is the best order for presenting my ideas?

Using these questions as a guide, make the appropriate changes and additions to your working outline. Draw up a final outline that presents your ideas in a logical order. If you need to review outlining, see Chapter 11.

During his reading, Randy Melick found so much descriptive material about Walt Disney World that he decided to devote more space to this part of his topic and less to a comparison of Walt Disney World and Disneyland. He also found two analyses of the reasons for Walt Disney World's success and decided to add subdivisions of that heading. Making these changes and adding details, he revised his working outline into the following formal outline:

THE MAKING OF WALT DISNEY WORLD

I. Ideas behind Walt Disney World
   A. Regrets about Disneyland
      1. Lack of insulating property
      2. Lack of revenue-producing hotels
   B. Ideas for new park
      1. Isolation
      2. Hotels
      3. Recreation
      4. Projects
   C. Follow-through by associates
II. Description of Walt Disney World
   A. The Magic Kingdom
      1. "Visual magnets"
      2. Theme parks
      3. Disney characters
      4. "Main Street" attractions
   B. EPCOT Center
      1. Theme parks
      2. Buildings and exhibits
III. Reasons for Walt Disney World's success
   A. "Service through people"
   B. Planned environment
   C. Controlled competition

EXERCISE 10 **Writing a Formal Outline.** Using your note cards, your working outline, and the four guide questions, prepare a formal outline for your research report. Follow the style shown in the preceding outline.

Writing the First Draft

Begin by arranging your note cards to correspond to the headings on your formal outline. Refer to your note cards as necessary when you write. Each time you include information from a note card in your draft, put the number of the note card right after the information. By doing so, you will quickly be able to credit the source of the information later.

As you prepare your first draft, skip lines so that you will later have plenty of room to make revisions and insertions. If you include any quotations, put them in quotation marks unless they are fairly long, in which case you may put them on separate lines set off from the body of the report. (You will learn more about the format of quotations in the section on publishing the final draft.) Remember to use ellipses if you delete any words in quotations and brackets if you add any words (see page 262).

At this point try to keep moving from one part of your outline to the next. Think of each section as a whole, and remember to link sections with logical transitions.

Above all, your writing should be in your own style. Strive to do more than simply expand your note cards into sentences and paragraphs, stringing together bits of information like mismatched beads in a necklace. Instead, decide exactly what you want each section of your report to tell your reader, and then express your own ideas in your own words.

Every research report needs an introduction and a conclusion, although neither of these sections needs to be listed on your formal outline. The **introduction** should present the topic and your controlling idea about it; the **conclusion** should restate and tie together the main points of your report.

EXERCISE 11 **Writing the First Draft.** Write the first draft of your thousand-word report on the topic you have been researching. Follow your formal outline, and keep in mind the purpose, audience, and controlling idea that you identified in Exercise 4. Be sure to include an introduction and a conclusion, although you may prefer to write these sections later.

Revising the First Draft

If you have put your first draft aside for a while, you will be able to revise it with a fresh and critical eye. Use the following questions to guide your thinking.

1. How effective is my introduction? Where does it clearly state my topic and controlling idea?
2. How closely does my report follow my outline?

3. What, if any, transitions do I need to tie together my ideas?
4. How can I make my sentences and terms clearer and easier to understand?
5. What details and examples have I included to support general statements?
6. Have I kept my audience in mind throughout? Where would a different approach, such as more pursuasion or more narration, help me in reaching my audience?
7. Where can I improve my language or vary my sentence structures to make reading my report more interesting?
8. How clear is my purpose, and how closely do I stick to my purpose?
9. How effective is my conclusion?
10. Is all my information accurate? Is my report free from errors in spelling, punctuation, capitalization, grammar, and usage?

EXERCISE 12   **Revising the First Draft.** After setting aside your report for a few hours or overnight, revise it with a fresh eye, according to the preceding list of questions.

Crediting Sources: Footnotes or Endnotes and a Bibliography

Your report must give credit to any ideas or direct quotations borrowed from other sources. For instance, suppose you are writing a report about medical research and include data from the *New England Journal of Medicine*. When the reader sees the source of the data, he or she will recognize that your information comes from a respected authority on medical research.

One method of crediting sources in your report is to use footnotes or endnotes and a bibliography.

A **footnote** is a note at the bottom of a page. It gives additional information, including source data, about a statement that occurs on that page.

Footnotes are numbered consecutively throughout a report. Within the body of the report, a raised footnote number called a *superscript* appears at the end of a sentence containing a quotation or a borrowed idea. The same raised number appears at the beginning of the footnote that gives credit to the source of the quotation or idea.

The following example shows part of a report containing two footnotes. Notice that each footnote is indented and that the footnotes, when typed, are singlespaced. Also notice that page numbers, which appear at the end of the footnotes, are not preceded by a *p*.

```
      To Walt Disney, the Magic Kingdom of Disney
characters and settings was not as important as
EPCOT Center, which he conceived as a model city of
the future.7 Because EPCOT was completed well after
his death, it is not quite what Disney had
envisioned. Nevertheless, it is a fascinating theme
park, or actually two theme parks--Future World and
World Showcase. "EPCOT Center is shaped something
like a giant hourglass. Future World fills up the
northern bulb, while World Showcase occupies the
southern half."8 Future World displays advances in
science, technology, and lifestyle that we may
expect in years to come; World Showcase focuses on
the customs and cultural contributions of the many
nations in the world today.
      7Leonard Mosley, Disney's World (Briarcliff
Manor, NY: Stein and Day, 1985) 287.
      8Steve Birnbaum, Walt Disney World: The
Official Guide, 1986 ed. (Boston: Houghton Mifflin,
1985) 103.
```

When you wrote the first draft, you included a note card number after each quotation or borrowed idea. To add footnotes, simply replace the note card numbers with superscripts in numerical order and a footnote with the same number. That footnote will give the page number for the item, which you get from your note card, plus other source information, which you get from your bibliography card.

The Style Chart for Footnotes and Endnotes, which appears on page 268, shows you the source information you should include in footnotes. It also shows you proper punctuation for footnotes. When a footnote credits the same source for a second time—like footnote 2 on the Style Chart—you need to provide only the author's last name and the page number (the earlier footnote contains the rest of the information). If two works by the same author appear, a repeated footnote for one of the works—like footnote 3 on the Style Chart—must include a short form of the title (so that readers know to which work you are referring).

Endnotes are just like footnotes, except that they are grouped together at the end of a report instead of being placed at page bottoms.

Endnotes are arranged in numerical order, with numbers that again correspond to the superscripts in the body of the report. They use the same style as footnotes, except that they are doublespaced if you type them.

STYLE CHART FOR FOOTNOTES AND ENDNOTES

FOR A BOOK (put any subtitle after a colon)

[1] JoAnn DiFranco, Walt Disney: When Dreams Come True (Minneapolis: Dillon, 1985) 60.

TO CREDIT THE SAME WORK AGAIN

When no other works by author appear in footnotes or endnotes, list only author's last name and page number(s):

[2] DiFranco 61.

When other works by author appear, include short form of title:

[3] DiFranco, Disney 61.

FOR A SPECIFIED EDITION OF A BOOK WITH TWO AUTHORS

[4] Jim Hill and Miriam Hill, Fabulous Florida, 2nd ed. (Clearwater, FL: Ambassador, 1976) 63-64.

FOR A SECTION OF A BOOK WITH AN EDITOR AND NO AUTHOR

[5] Paul J. Psychas, ed., "Disney World," Let's Go: The Budget Guide to the USA (New York: St. Martin's, 1986) 299.

FOR A BOOK WITH AN AUTHOR AND AN EDITOR

[6] Richard R. Beard, Walt Disney's EPCOT: Creating the New World of Tomorrow, ed. Lory Frankel (New York: Harry N. Abrams, 1982) 27.

FOR A MAGAZINE ARTICLE

[7] Horace Sutton, "Of Mouse and Man," Saturday Review 8 Apr. 1972: 12.

FOR A NEWSPAPER ARTICLE

[8] Paul Goldberger, "From English Pub to Chinese Pagoda: EPCOT'S Eerie but Endearing Sameness," New York Times 3 Feb. 1985, sec. 10: 1.

FOR AN UNSIGNED ARTICLE

[9] "Cinderella's Condos," Newsweek 4 Feb. 1985: 64.

FOR A BROCHURE WITH NO SPECIFIED AUTHOR

[10] "Do It All at Disney" (Lake Buena Vista, FL: Walt Disney World, 1986) 5.

FOR AN ENCYCLOPEDIA ARTICLE

[11] Roy Paul Nelson, "Walt Disney," World Book Encyclopedia, 1984 ed.: 193.

EXERCISE 13 **Practicing Footnote or Endnote Style.** Write footnotes based on the information provided in each numbered item. Use the number of the item as the number of the footnote.

1. You are crediting information that appeared on page 33 of the book *Arctic Manual* by Vilhjalmur Stefansson, published in Westport, CT, in 1974 by Greenwood.

2. You are crediting information from the article "A Forest Grows on Antarctica" by S. Weisburd, which appeared on page 148 of the March 8, 1986, edition of *Science News.*

3. You are crediting a quotation from "Polar Exploration" by A. F. Treshnikov. The selection appeared on pages 225–38 of *The Arctic World,* edited by William E. Taylor and published in San Francisco in 1985 by Sierra Club Books. The quotation appeared on page 227.

4. You are crediting information that appeared on page 44 of *Arctic Life,* subtitled *Challenge to Survive,* by Martina M. Jacobs and James B. Richardson III, published in Seattle in 1982 by the University of Washington.

5. You are crediting for a second time the same source that you credited in item 1, this time for information on page 17. You have also credited another book by Stefansson in your footnotes.

Whether you use footnotes or endnotes, you must also include a bibliography at the end of your report.

A **bibliography** is an alphabetical list of all the sources consulted in preparing a report.

To prepare your bibliography, you need only your bibliography cards. The Style Chart for Bibliography Entries, which appears on page 270, illustrates the order of the specific source information that should be included in bibliography entries for different kinds of sources. It also shows proper punctuation and indentation for bibliography entries.

Bibliography entries are arranged alphabetically by the first word to appear in each entry, excluding *a, an,* or *the.*

As you can see from the Style Chart on page 270, the first word to appear in each entry is usually an author's or editor's last name; however, if no author or editor is identified, the first word will be part of a title. If more than one work by the same author is listed, first group all entries for that author alphabetically by the author's last name; then, within the grouping, alphabetize the entries by the first words of titles, excluding *a, an,* or *the.* Instead of repeating the author's name, use a long dash, as in the second example on page 270.

EXERCISE 14 **Practicing Bibliography Style.** Write a bibliography that lists the sources in items 1–4 of Exercise 13 plus the following source: the book *Northwest to Fortune* by Vilhjalmur Stefansson, published in Westport, CT, in 1974 by Greenwood. Follow the Style Chart for Bibliography Entries, and remember to alphabetize your entries.

STYLE CHART FOR BIBLIOGRAPHY ENTRIES

FOR A BOOK (put any subtitle after a colon)

DiFranco, JoAnn. Walt Disney: When Dreams Come True. Minneapolis: Dillon, 1985.

FOR TWO BOOKS BY THE SAME AUTHOR

Smiley, Nixon. Florida: Land of Images. Miami: E. A. Seamann, 1977.
_____. Yesterday's Florida. Miami: E. A Seamann, 1974.

FOR A SPECIFIED EDITION OF A BOOK WITH TWO AUTHORS

Hill, Jim, and Miriam Hill. Fabulous Florida. 2nd ed. Clearwater, FL: Ambassador, 1976.

FOR A SECTION OF A BOOK WITH AN EDITOR AND NO AUTHOR

Psychas, Paul J., ed. "Disney World." Let's Go: The Budget Guide to the USA. New York: St. Martin's, 1986. 298-301.

FOR A BOOK WITH AN AUTHOR AND AN EDITOR

Beard, Richard R. Walt Disney's EPCOT: Creating the New World of Tomorrow. Ed. Lory Frankel. New York: Harry N. Abrams, 1982.

FOR A MAGAZINE ARTICLE

Sutton, Horace. "Of Mouse and Man." Saturday Review 8 Apr. 1972: 12-14.

FOR A NEWSPAPER ARTICLE (plus sign indicates continuation on nonconsecutive page)

Goldberger, Paul. "From English Pub to Chinese Pagoda: EPCOT's Eerie but Endearing Sameness." New York Times 3 Feb. 1985, sec. 10: 1 + .

FOR AN UNSIGNED ARTICLE

"Cinderella's Condos." Newsweek 4 Feb. 1985: 64.

FOR A BROCHURE WITH NO SPECIFIED AUTHOR

"Do It All at Disney." Lake Buena Vista, FL: Walt Disney World, 1986.

FOR AN ENCYCLOPEDIA ARTICLE

Nelson, Roy Paul. "Walt Disney." World Book Encyclopedia. 1984 ed.

Crediting Sources: Parenthetical Documentation and a Bibliography

Rather than using footnotes or endnotes, many students today are using parenthetical documentation to credit specific quotations and borrowed ideas within the body of their reports.

Parenthetical documentation provides brief source information in parentheses within the body of a report. For more complete source information, readers consult the alphabetized **bibliography** at the back of the report.

Parenthetical documentation may be brief but must (1) clearly identify only one source listed in the bibliography and (2) indicate from what page or pages of that source the borrowed idea or quotation comes.

FOR AN AUTHOR LISTED ONLY ONCE IN THE BIBLIOGRAPHY

Suppose a report includes an idea borrowed from page 387 of *Walt Disney: An American Original*. The book is listed in the bibliography as:

> Thomas, Bob. Walt Disney: An American Original. New York: Simon & Schuster, 1976.

If no other works by Bob Thomas are listed in the bibliography, the parenthetical documentation needs only the author's last name and the page number (Thomas 387). In the body of the report, it would look like this:

> EPCOT was Walt Disney's vision of the city of tomorrow (Thomas 387).

If the sentence containing the borrowed idea makes the author's name clear, the parenthetical documentation needs only the page number:

> According to Bob Thomas, Walt Disney envisioned EPCOT as the city of tomorrow (387).

Parenthetical documentation uses the same style for any author listed just once in the bibliography—whether the author wrote a book, a magazine article, a newspaper article, an encyclopedia article, or a section of a book. For example, suppose a report borrows a quotation from page 1 of a newspaper article listed in the bibliography as:

> Goldberger, Paul. "From English Pub to Chinese Pagoda: EPCOT's Eerie but Endearing Sameness." New York Times 3 Feb. 1985, sec. 10: 1 + .

If no other works by Paul Goldberger appear in the bibliography, the parenthetical documentation would again require only the author's name and the page from which the quotation was borrowed (Goldberger 1). In the body of the report, it would look like this:

> "Neither of the disparate parts of EPCOT is precisely what Walt Disney had in mind" (Goldberger 1).

Again, if the wording in the body of the report makes the author's name clear, the parenthetical documentation needs only the page number:

> As Paul Goldberger comments, "Neither of the disparate parts of EPCOT is precisely what Walt Disney had in mind" (1).

FOR A WORK WITH TWO AUTHORS

If a work has two authors, both authors' names should be used in the parenthetical documentation as follows:

> Employees at Walt Disney World are taught to provide "service through people" (Peters and Waterman 167-68).

Or the sentence might look like this:

> According to Peters and Waterman, employees at Walt Disney World are taught to provide "service through people" (167-68).

FOR A WORK WITH NO SPECIFIED AUTHOR

If a work has an editor but no specified author, use the editor's last name (without the *ed.* abbreviation) in the parenthetical documentation. If a work has no specified author or editor, use a short form of the title in the parenthetical documentation. For example, suppose a report borrows an idea from the unsigned magazine article listed in the bibliography as:

> "Cinderella's Condos," Newsweek 4 Feb. 1985: 64.

The parenthetical documentation might look like this:

> Plans are now in the works to develop the "buffer zone" around EPCOT Center ("Condos" 64).

If the wording in the body of the report makes the article's title clear, the parenthetical documentation requires only the page number:

> The Newsweek article "Cinderella's Condos" reports that plans are now in the works to develop the "buffer zone" around EPCOT Center (64).

FOR AN AUTHOR LISTED
MORE THAN ONCE IN THE BIBLIOGRAPHY

If a report's bibliography lists two or more works by the same author, the parenthetical documentation must include a short form of the work's title. Otherwise, readers will not know to which of the author's works the parenthetical documentation refers. For example, suppose *Walt Disney: An American Original* is not the only work by Bob Thomas listed in the bibliography. To credit page 387 of *Walt Disney: An American Original*, the parenthetical documentation has to include a short form of the work's title (separated from the author's name with a comma):

> EPCOT was Walt Disney's vision of the city of tomorrow (Thomas, Disney 387).

If the wording in the body of the report makes the author's name clear, the parenthetical documentation requires only the title and the page:

> According to Bob Thomas, EPCOT was Walt Disney's vision of the city of tomorrow (Disney 387).

PLACEMENT OF PARENTHETICAL DOCUMENTATION

The Modern Language Association recommends that you place the parenthetical documentation where a pause would naturally occur, preferably at the end of the sentence. Follow these guidelines:

1. Place the parentheses before the punctuation mark that concludes the sentence (or clause or phrase) that contains the material you are crediting.

   > Walt Disney envisioned EPCOT as a model city of the future (Mosley 287).

   > Walt Disney envisioned EPCOT as a model city of the future (Mosley 287), although his vision was modified when the actual construction of EPCOT began.

2. If the credited material is a direct quotation in quotation marks, close the quotation *before* the parenthetical documentation, and put the punctuation mark that concludes the sentence *after* the parenthetical documentation.

   > "Neither of the disparate parts of EPCOT is precisely what Walt Disney had in mind" (Goldberger 1).

3. If the credited material is a long direct quotation set off from the body of the report, put the parenthetical documentation *after* the closing punctuation of the set-off passage.

   > EPCOT is really two theme parks, Future World and World Showcase.

   > > Neither of the disparate parts of EPCOT is precisely what Walt Disney had in mind when he envisioned the Environmental Prototype Community of Tomorrow. . . . It was Disney's dream to create an actual town of the future—a full-time, living community. (Goldberger 1)

EXERCISE 15 **Practicing Parenthetical Documentation.** Rewrite the following report passages to include parenthetical documentation. Obtain the information for your parenthetical documentation from the source data provided below each passage.

1. While market research is important, most successful American companies think of those with whom they do business not as a "market," which implies a certain cynicism, but as customers who must be treated with courtesy and respect.

source: Information is summarized from page 41 of *A Passion for Excellence: The Leadership Difference* by Tom Peters and Nancy Austin, published in New York in 1985 by Random House. No other work by Peters and Austin appears in your bibliography.

2. Controversy continues to rage on the issue of colorization of old movies originally filmed in black and white. New York Times critic Vincent Canby joined others in the film industry when he condemned tampering with "The Maltese Falcon" and other classics.

   source: The paraphrase in the second sentence is from "Through a Tinted Glass, Darkly," by Vincent Canby. The article appeared in section 2 of the November 30, 1986, issue of *The New York Times*. The opinion being paraphrased appeared on page 19. No other work by Canby appears in your bibliography.

3. How do VCR magnetic tapes work? "When you record a program, the tiny particles on the tape are magnetized in a particular pattern."

   source: "Video Tapes: Standard, High Grade, Super High Grade, Hi-Fi, Professional." The quotation appeared in the November 1986 edition of *Consumer Reports,* page 730. No author is listed.

4. The plot in an Agatha Christie mystery usually centers around a simple circumstance that is then elaborately disguised. In The Mysterious Affair at Styles, for example,

   > the plot springs from the fact that in England somebody acquitted of a crime may not be tried for it again. Suppose, then, that a stumbling block against your committing a murder is the fact that you are an obvious suspect. You might . . . take advantage of this very situation by laying a trail of clues leading to yourself, which would cause your arrest. Once arrested and tried, you produce an alibi, and acquittal follows. . . . The Christie villain is foiled by Poirot, who sees what he is trying to do, manages to prevent his arrest, and even uncovers his alibi so that he is apparently cleared of suspicion. Poirot's maneuvering also deceives the reader.

   source: Set-off quotation is from "The Mistress of Complication" by Julian Symons, which appeared in *Agatha Christie: First Lady of Crime,* edited by H. P. F. Keating and published in New York in 1977 by Holt, Rinehart and Winston. The quotation appeared on pages 28–29; no other work by Symons appears in your bibliography.

EXERCISE 16 **Crediting Sources.** Now that you have learned the various means of crediting sources, go back to the report you have been preparing and provide credits where necessary. The note card numbers that you included after each borrowed idea or quotation in your report will remind you of each place that needs a specific credit. The note card numbers will also refer you to the note cards and bibliography cards that contain the source information you need to include in your credits. After you provide the credit, delete the note card number.

If your teacher has no preference, you yourself may decide whether you wish to use footnotes, endnotes, or parenthetical documentation to credit specific quotations or borrowed ideas in the body of your report. Use the same crediting method throughout your report.

Also write the bibliography of all the works you consulted in preparing your report. Remember to list the entries in alphabetical order.

Publishing the Final Draft

When you submit your report, you are publishing it, or offering it to the public. To prepare the final draft of your report for publication, you may use a word processor, a typewriter, or a pen, unless your teacher has a particular preference. If your teacher has no specific instructions on the following points, use these points as guidelines in preparing your final draft:

1. Begin your report with a **title page** that contains the report title, your name, your teacher's name, the name or number of the course, and the date. The title and your name should be centered in the middle of the page; the other information should be listed in the lower right corner.

2. In the **body** of your report, use one-inch margins on the left, right, top, and bottom. If you type the report, use double spacing except for set-off quotations and footnotes if you have any (see below). Indent the beginning of each paragraph about half an inch, or five typed spaces.

3. **Quotations** of under four lines should usually be placed within quotation marks and run into the body of your report. For longer quotations, instead of using quotation marks, set off the quotation from the body of the report with one space above and below it and *two*-inch margins on the left and right. If you type your report, use single spacing for set-off quotations.

4. **Footnotes,** if you use them, should also be single spaced. Indent the first line of each footnote, and follow the Style Chart for Footnotes and Endnotes on page 268. Remember to leave space for footnotes.

5. If you are using **parenthetical documentation** instead of footnotes or endnotes, follow the guidelines for Placement of Parenthetical Documentation on page 273.

6. If you are using **endnotes,** put them on a separate page after the body of the report, under the centered heading "Notes." Endnotes follow the same style as footnotes, except that they are double spaced if you are typing your report.

7. Make your **bibliography** the last page of your report, and list the entries under the centered heading "Bibliography." Begin each entry at the left margin; when an entry runs longer than one line, indent the additional line or lines. Follow the Style Chart for Bibliography Entries on page 270, and remember to alphabetize entries. If you are typing, use double spacing for your bibliography.

8. **Number** each page of your report except the title page. Place Arabic numbers (1, 2, 3, and so on) in the upper right corner of each page; do *not* precede the number with a *p*. However, it is always a good idea to precede each page number with your last name, in case of loss.

9. **Proofread** your final draft at least two times for errors in typing, spelling, grammar, capitalization, punctuation, and style. Make necessary corrections neatly.

EXERCISE 17 **Publishing the Final Draft.** Prepare the final draft of the thousand-word report on which you have been working. Use the method of crediting specific information that you employed in Exercise 16, and otherwise follow Randy Melick's model report and the guidelines on pages 275–276 (unless your teacher has other style requirements).

The following model report is the final draft of Randy Melick's report on Walt Disney World. Notice the lettered annotations, which we added to point out important features of the report. Notice, too, that Randy chose to use endnotes to credit sources of specific information in his report.

TITLE PAGE

A

B   The Making of Walt Disney World

C   Randy Melick

D   English 10-3
                                                     Mrs. Comba
                                                     May 26, 19--

NOTES ABOUT THE SAMPLE REPORT

A The title page is not given a page number.
B The title is centered but not underlined or put in quotation marks.
C The author's name—your name—is also centered.
D The course name, teacher's name, and date of submission are listed in the lower right corner.

E   More than fifteen years before the opening of
Disneyland in 1955, Walter Elias Disney had paid
several unsatisfying visits to local amusement
F parks with his young daughters.[1] He had wondered
why such parks could not be made as entertaining
for adults as they were for youngsters. Disney
imagined a park that would be not merely a
collection of rides and petty amusements but an
entire land of adventure, nostalgia, progress, and
the exotic. Disneyland, in Anaheim, California,
represented Disney's first attempt to fulfill his
ambitious dream. Not until 1971, however, with the
Walt Disney World in central Florida, did Disney
realize his dream by introducing creative,
innovative concepts, which he called "visual
magnets."

          To begin with, although Disneyland enjoyed
unparalleled success, Disney hoped to improve on
the Anaheim complex in the park he envisioned for
the East. He had several regrets about Disneyland
and had vowed not to make the same mistakes twice.[2]
The land surrounding Disneyland had been quickly
bought up by speculators hoping to capitalize on
the park's success; consequently, Disneyland was
completely hemmed in by unsightly motels and other
counterattractions.[3] Disney also regretted that no
hotels had been built on the park grounds. This
potential source of income had been disregarded
because of the inexperience of his staff.[4]

          Consequently, for his new park Disney had in
mind a complete vacationland, isolated from the
outside world. Campsites and hotel accommodations
would be provided along with a host of recreational
activities. Visitors to the Magic Kingdom, the
amusement section of Walt Disney World, would be
entertained by musical shows, strolling minstrels,
parades, and simulated cowboy shoot-outs, train

NOTES ABOUT THE SAMPLE REPORT

E The first paragraph is an introduction that states the topic and focus of the paper.

F Randy uses superscript numbers and endnotes to credit sources of borrowed ideas and quotations in his report.

robberies, and stagecoach holdups.[5] In his zeal Disney also planned to include in his wonderland an industrial park as a showcase for American business, a small community of vacation and permanent residences, and an "Experimental Prototype Community of Tomorrow" (EPCOT). EPCOT, Disney said, would be a place where "people actually live a life they can't find anywhere else in the world."[6]

Walt Disney had carefully planned the first stages of Walt Disney World and had set rigid guidelines for the follow-through.[7] Although he died six months before ground was broken for the park, his associates in the Disney organization carried out his ideas faithfully, and the project bears his unmistakable stamp.[8]

G   In addition to keeping Walt Disney World separate from other areas, Disney introduced innovative concepts. By the use of "visual magnets," visitors are kept moving throughout the complex. Cinderella's Castle, looming in the background from all points in the Magic Kingdom, is the major magnet.[9] The castle is located in the center of the Magic Kingdom, directly in front of a traffic circle from which roads lead to the six theme parks. Access to any point in the Magic Kingdom from one of the theme parks--Adventureland, Fantasyland, Frontierland, Liberty Square, Tomorrowland, or Main Street, U.S.A.--is convenient and simple.[10]

The Magic Kingdom is also filled with references to the many famous Disney cartoon characters. Costumed figures of Mickey Mouse, Donald Duck, and others roam freely within the park, greeting visitors and posing for pictures with delighted children.

NOTES ABOUT THE SAMPLE REPORT

G Notice that Randy's report closely follows his formal outline. After discussing the ideas behind Walt Disney World, including Disney's regrets about Disneyland and his ideas for a new park, Randy moves on to a description of Walt Disney World.

If Disney's associates altered his plans in any way, those alterations are most evident in EPCOT Center, the newer park that adjoins the Magic Kingdom and that Disney conceived as a model city of the future.[12] EPCOT, which opened in October of 1982, "is shaped something like a giant hourglass. Future World fills up the northern bulb, while World Showcase occupies the southern half."[13] Future World displays advances in science and technology; World Showcase focuses on the customs and cultural contributions of the many nations in the world today.

> Neither of the disparate parts of EPCOT is precisely what Walt Disney had in mind when he envisioned the Environmental Prototype Community of Tomorrow. . . . It was Disney's dream to create an actual town of the future--a full-time, living community.[14]

Nevertheless, though EPCOT is more of a world's fair than a living, working community, it does offer visitors fascinating glimpses of human progress. These include an impressive geosphere known as Spaceship Earth, a crescent-shaped building called Communicore West, and a wheel-shaped pavilion known as the World of Motion.

Furthermore, Disney's love for trains, which helped to inspire Disneyland, is evident in the physical format of Walt Disney World. A steam-powered railroad circles the perimeter of the park, and its quaint main station is situated at the main entrance. Beyond the station lies a small square with a firehouse and town hall. A small park covered with flowers leads the visitor onto Main Street, U.S.A., a reproduction of the main street of a typical midwestern town. Built on a slightly smaller than life-size scale to enhance the sense of friendliness and intimacy, the street serves as a base for concessions.[11] Visitors to Main Street can browse through Mlle. Antoinette's Parfumerie or investigate the local cinema.

What makes EPCOT different from an ordinary world's fair is its sense of oneness, its spirit of working together. In fact, that spirit pervades the entire Disney organization and is evident in the positive attitudes instilled in all employees of Walt Disney World. Visitors are treated as "guests," not customers, and staff members are encouraged to smile at all times and to be as helpful as they can be.[15] The desire to provide "service through people" had made Walt Disney Productions one of the most financially successful service companies in America today.[16]

With its attempt to correct the mistakes and problems of past ventures, Florida's Walt Disney World is the jewel in the Disney organization's crown. According to John Hench, a close associate of Disney, its success is closely related to the success of Disney's animated films.[17] Like an animated cartoon, Walt Disney World is a controlled environment in which every element is previously considered and carefully devised so that it complements all others. Unlike a typical world's fair, where exhibits attempt to outdo one another and ideas are constantly being introduced and then discarded, Walt Disney World has a noncompetitive format and a sense of progression and sequence.[18]

H   Thus Walt Disney World is a symbol of all that the name Disney represents. It is a fantasy world in which the past and the future, the unknown and the exotic, mingle harmoniously in the atmosphere of an animated cartoon. As one adult wrote about the sight of Mickey Mouse leading a marching band,

> there is a swell of joy in the part
> of one's heart that is still young,
> and the mind slips the shackles of
> reality, leaving one with naught to
> do but clutch the hand of a child
> and shout, "There's Mickey!"[19]

NOTE ABOUT THE SAMPLE REPORT

H   The final paragraph is a conclusion that sums up the report's main points.

A
B
C

Notes

[1]Christopher Finch, <u>The Art of Walt Disney</u> (New York: Harry N. Abrams, 1973) 383.

[2]Finch 396.

[3]Al Griffin, <u>"Step Right Up, Folks!"</u> (Chicago: Henry Regnery, 1974) 214.

[4]Finch 396.

[5]Griffin 67.

[6]Finch 396.

[7]Finch 398.

[8]Paul J.C. Friedlander, "What Has Mickey Mouse Wrought?" <u>New York Times</u> 21 Mar, 1971, sec. 10: 45.

[9]Finch 390.

[10]Peter Blake, "The Lessons of the Parks," <u>The Art of Walt Disney</u>, Christopher Finch 431.

[11]Finch 390.

[12]Leonard Mosley, <u>Disney's World</u> (Briarcliff Manor, NY: Stein and Day, 1985) 287.

[13]Steve Birnbaum, <u>Walt Disney World:The Official Guide</u>, 1986 ed. (Boston: Houghton Mifflin, 1985) 103.

[14]Paul Goldberger, "From English Pub to Chinese Pagoda: EPCOT's Eerie but Endearing Sameness," <u>New York Times</u> 3 Feb. 1985, sec. 10: 1.

[15]Sandra Gordon, "Working at Disney World Was No Mickey Mouse Job," <u>Seventeen</u> July 1985: 16.

[16]Thomas J. Peters and Robert H. Waterman, Jr., <u>In Search of Excellence: Lessons from America's Best-Run Companies</u> (New York: Harper & Row, 1982) 167-68.

[17]Finch 411.

[18]Finch 415.

[19]Horace Sutton, "Of Mouse and Man," <u>Saturday Review</u> 8 Apr. 1972: 12.

ABOUT THE ENDNOTES

A The endnotes page is numbered.

B The endnotes are listed in numerical order under the centered heading "Notes."

C Endnotes are double spaced, unlike footnotes.

A

B
Bibliography

C
Birnbaum, Steve. <u>Walt Disney World: The Official</u>
    <u>Guide</u>. 1986 ed. Boston: Houghton Mifflin,
    1985.

Blake, Peter. "The Lessons of the Parks. <u>The Art of</u>
    <u>Walt Disney</u>. Christopher Finch. New York:
    Harry N. Abrams, 1973. 423-48.

Christensen, David E., Judy Hamilton, and R.W.
    Patrick. "Florida." <u>World Book Encyclopedia</u>.
    1984 ed.

"Do It All at Disney." Lake Buena Vista, FL: Walt
    Disney World, 1986.

Finch, Christopher. <u>The Art of Walt Disney</u>. New
    York: Harry N. Abrams, 1973.

Friedlander, Paul J.C. "What Has Mickey Mouse
    Wrought?" <u>New York Times</u> 21 Mar. 1971,
    sec. 10: 45.

Goldberger, Paul. "From English Pub to Chinese
    Pagoda: EPCOT's Eerie but Endearing Sameness."
    <u>New York Times</u> 3 Feb. 1985, sec. 10: 1+.

Gordon, Sandra. "Working at Disney World Was No
    Mickey Mouse Job." <u>Seventeen</u> July 1985: 16.

Griffin, Al. <u>"Step Right Up, Folks!"</u> Chicago: Henry
    Regnery, 1974.

Mosley, Leonard. <u>Disney's World</u>. Briarcliff Manor,
    NY: Stein and Day, 1985.

Nelson, Roy Paul. "Walt Disney." <u>World Book</u>
    <u>Encyclopedia</u>. 1984 ed.

Peters, Thomas J., and Robert H. Waterman, Jr. <u>In</u>
    <u>Search of Excellence: Lessons from America's</u>
    <u>Best-Run Companies</u>. New York: Harper & Row,
    1982.

Sutton, Horace. "Of Mouse and Man." <u>Saturday Review</u>
    8 Apr. 1972: 12-14.

Thomas, Bob. <u>Walt Disney: An American Original</u>. New
    York: Simon & Schuster, 1976.

ABOUT THE BIBLIOGRAPHY

A The bibliography page is numbered.

B Entries are listed alphabetically under the centered heading "Bibliography."

C The bibliography is double spaced.

CHAPTER 12   WRITING A RESEARCH REPORT

Limiting a Topic and Beginning Research   [pages 253–255]

1. Which is probably the best topic for a research report?
   (a) why I love *E.T.*   (b) *E.T.*'s special effects   (c) film fantasy
2. Which controlling statement could best guide research on this topic?
   (a) The most inventive of *E.T.*'s special effects is E.T. himself.
   (b) *E.T.* is a wonderful blend of humor, pathos, and excitement.
   (c) *E.T.*'s most remarkable feature is its characterization of childhood.
3. Which of these information sources is more relevant to this topic?
   (a) a book on science fiction   (b) an article on the making of *E.T.*

Gathering Information   [pages 257–263]   Read the following note card, and then answer each question.

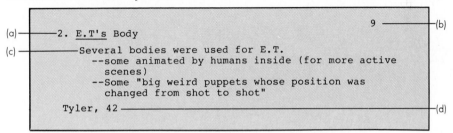

4. Which item identifies the source of the information?
5. Which has information from the source in the note taker's own words?
6. Which item locates the information within the source?
7. Which item identifies the note card?

Footnotes and Bibliography [pages 266–270]

8. Which item represents the correct footnote form for crediting the same source a second time?
   (a) [4]Kael, Pauline, *Reeling* , p. 56.   (b) [4]Kael p. 56.

9. Which item represents the correct form for a bibliography entry?
   (a) Champlin, Charles. "Steven Spielberg." *The World Book Encyclopedia.* 1984 ed.
   (b) "Steven Spielberg" by Charles Champlin. *The World Book Encyclopedia.* 1984 ed.

10. In your bibliography how would you list an unsigned news item?
    (a) after the signed items   (b) integrated alphabetically by title

Writing for Review   Choose a topic, find one source about it, and then take notes from that source on two note cards.

Writing Across the Curriculum

Thinking About Thinking: Recognizing Relationships

Writing across the curriculum means writing in the subject areas you study in school. You engage in the thinking process called invention when you have no idea what to write about. You also engage in invention when you write about a specific topic in social studies, science, or literature.

Defining the Skill

Inventing ideas about a topic often involves the specific thinking skill called RECOGNIZING RELATIONSHIPS. A relationship is a connection. For example, an airplane has different relationships to a pilot and to a landscape painter. To one it is a precision machine; to the other it is part of a scene. If you can recognize many relationships, you can open up possibilities for writing.

Applying the Skill

Look at the photograph. Tell what relationship, or connection, the dwellings in the photo might have

>   to the people who live in them
>   to a visiting anthropologist
>   to the photographer who took the photo
>   to the history of their country
>   to you

Now write a sentence in which you invent another completely different relationship for the dwellings.

CHAPTER 13

Writing About Social Studies

Nothing human is foreign to me.

—*The Roman playwright Terence*

About the year 1300 the Venetian traveler Marco Polo wrote about his amazing experiences in China. He wrote about the vast, barren land of the Gobi Desert and about the architecture of Chinese cities. He wrote about China's government, its wars, history, trade, neighbors, and the personality of its ruler Kublai Khan. He recorded details of Chinese arts, scientific experiments, customs, inventions—everything from coal to currency. His attempt to provide a portrait of Chinese society made Polo one of the earliest and best-known writers of *social studies*.

Social studies is the study of people living in groups and their ways of life. It includes history, geography, civics, economics, and sociology. In fact, because social studies is about people and their cultures, some writers believe that "nothing is foreign" to it, that it includes everything human. In this chapter you will apply the following writing skills to writing about social studies:

> **prewriting**: topic, audience, and purpose
> **prewriting**: evidence, sources, and documentation
> **prewriting**: making generalizations
> **writing** objectively
> **writing** chronologically
> **writing** about cause and effects
> **writing** with comparison and contrast
> **revising**, **editing**, and **publishing**

Prewriting: Topic, Audience, and Purpose

Writing about social studies, like writing in any subject area, demands that you carefully focus your topic and clearly define your audience and purpose. In most cases you can focus a social studies topic by thinking specifically about the *who, what, when, where, how,* and *why* of the topic. Suppose, for example, that you were to plan an essay about ancient Egypt. The subject of Egypt is so huge that your paper would be vague and rambling unless you focused the topic. By thinking specifically about the *what* and *when* of the topic, however, you might narrow it this way:

ancient Egypt [*What?*]

↓

government in ancient Egypt [*When?*]

↓

government during the Old Kingdom of Egypt
(2700 B.C.–2200 B.C.)

Usually at this point in your life, your audience for social studies writing will be your teacher. No matter who the audience is, however, ask yourself two questions during prewriting:

1. What does the audience need to know? (You must think about any basic information the audience needs in order to understand you, including any terms you need to define.)
2. What is the audience's point of view—biased in favor, biased against, or neutral? (You must think about what kind of statements, what method of organization, and what level of diction will be most appealing to your audience.)

During prewriting you should also identify your purpose. Clarifying your purpose will not only make the writing more accessible for your audience, it will also make the writing task much easier for you. State your purpose in writing: Do you intend to inform, explain, persuade, amuse, narrate, or describe? Do you have a combination of purposes, such as to describe something in order to explain it? Whatever your purpose, make sure you know what it is.

EXERCISE 1 **Focusing a Topic in Social Studies.** On your paper state questions the writer asked in order to focus the following topic.

the Crusades

↓

the Third Crusade

↓

Richard the Lion-Hearted during the Third Crusade

↓

victories of Richard the Lion-Hearted during the Third Crusade

strategies used by Richard the Lion-Hearted
to achieve victories during the Third Crusade

EXERCISE 2 **Focusing a Topic in Social Studies.** Choose a social studies topic of your own, or select one of the following general topics. Ask yourself *who? what? when? where? how?* and *why?* so that you can focus the topic into a manageable one for a three-paragraph paper.

modern communications	France	industrialism
romanticism	Printing	the year 1984
fashion	pyramids	space travel

Prewriting: Evidence, Sources, and Documentation

In 490 B.C. the Greeks defeated the Persians at Marathon. This statement is accepted by historians as a fact because over many years a vast amount of *evidence* has been assembled to support it. In writing about social studies, probably no question is more important than *What is your evidence?*

If you are stating a fact—a statement about an event that actually happened—decide whether the fact is common knowledge. For example, you do not need to prove that the pyramids are in Egypt or that the Spanish Armada was defeated in 1588. No one will argue with you; these facts are generally known to be true. If, however, you are stating a fact that is not generally known—such as the height of a pyramid or the number of ships in the Armada—you need to provide your *sources* of information.

A **primary source** states the words of a person actually involved in the event described. It may be a document, a diary, a letter, or an autobiography. A **secondary source** states the words of a person who, like a historian, has examined a primary source and comments on it. For example, in 1543 Copernicus published his theory that the earth moves around the sun. You can find this information in one of Copernicus' *own* books—a primary source. You can also find this information in a biography or a book *about* the scientist—a secondary source. A primary source usually carries greater authority than a secondary source: It is closer to the event and is not secondhand information.

As a general rule, **documentation** means providing the information necessary so that the reader can find the source that you used. This procedure allows the reader to determine what degree of authority to give your sources. If you consult any sources during prewriting, keep complete and accurate records of them for future reference and citation. Whether you use footnotes or endnotes when you write, follow the proper form described in Chapter 12, "The Research Report."

Evaluating Evidence. Indicate whether each of the following items is a statement of fact, an opinion, a quotation from a primary source, or a statement from a secondary source.

1. a page from the logbook of Christopher Columbus
2. a paragraph from *Queen Victoria*, by Lytton Strachey
3. World War I broke out in 1914.
4. World War I was the worst war in history.

Prewriting: Making Generalizations

Writing about social studies often begins with facts and leads toward **generalizations**—broad statements that are based on facts and may or may not be true in all cases. By examining information, synthesizing details, and making general statements, we can often make clear the common elements that unite the people of a community, the citizens of a nation, or the peoples of the world.

In prewriting the simplest way to form a generalization is to closely examine the facts and ask yourself, What element do these facts have in common? For example, suppose you assembled these statements in prewriting about the fall of the Roman Empire:

> The Roman Empire spread to so many distant provinces that it became tremendously expensive to govern them efficiently.
>
> By the end of the second century A.D., many of the distant borders of the empire came under frequent attack.
>
> More money had to be devoted to military purposes.
>
> The Roman economy became less productive, businesses failed, and the number of poor people increased.
>
> Romans lost faith in their ability to govern efficiently.

You notice that three statements are concerned with money, and you generalize: *Economic crisis was the cause of the fall of the Roman Empire.* Does this generalization account for all of the evidence? The second statement suggests that there may have been other causes for the collapse: Were the border attacks *only* an economic matter? Perhaps they also distracted Romans from solving important social problems. The last statement also opens other possibilities: Was the economic crisis the *only* reason people lost faith in the government? Perhaps the emperors were incompetent. Your generalization needs to be revised: *Economic crisis was one of the causes of the fall of the Roman Empire.*

You revised the generalization by adding *one of*—a qualifying word or phrase that defines a statement more precisely and makes it conform more closely to all the facts. In social studies qualifying words are vital because they account for exceptions, and a field as wide and various as social studies includes many exceptions. Beware of absolute, or all-inclusive, statements, and do not hesitate to use qualifying words, such as *in most cases, some,* and *sometimes.*

EXERCISE 4 **Making Generalizations.** Assume that you have gathered these five facts during prewriting on the subject of the Chou dynasty in China. Form a generalization and use qualifying words.

During the Chou dynasty many neighboring lands were added to the Chinese domain.

The inhabitants of these lands adopted Chinese customs and culture.

During this period agriculture and metalworking were improved.

Poetry, history, and philosophy were written during this period, including the works of Confucius and Mencius.

Confucius, Mencius, and their followers thought and wrote about improving the quality of government and society.

Writing Objectively

In January 1793 King Louis XVI of France was guillotined. Imagine that you were to find four letters describing this event, each one written by a different eyewitness. Each letter presents a different account of what actually happened and describes the meaning of the event from a different point of view. For example:

Robespierre, revolutionary leader: "a necessary, inevitable act"

Marie Antoinette, queen of France: "an unnecessary, tragic act"

Francois, radical citizen of Paris: "a just, reasonable act"

Jean, member of the aristocracy: "an unjust, unreasonable act"

If they really existed, each of these letters would be an important primary source. None of them, however, would be *objective.*

Writing objectively means writing without bias or prejudice. When you write about social studies, it is important for you to recognize the biases and prejudices of your sources and to make sure that your own writing is as objective as possible. Several rules may help you to write objectively:

1. Give the facts in clear, straightforward language.
2. If you are quoting someone, quote *exactly* what he or she says.
3. If you are giving an opinion, clearly label it as an opinion.
4. Use adverbs sparingly. One adverb can change a statement of fact into an opinion. For example, "The Loyalists fought during the Spanish

Civil War" is a fact. "The Loyalists fought bravely [or desperately, or furiously, or heroically]" is a value judgment that may or may not be justified by evidence.

5. Avoid loaded words, words intended to evoke strong emotions in the reader—for example, "the *villainous* Prince John," or "the *noble* King Richard."

These rules do not mean that you should not use vivid words to make your writing lively and interesting. Be careful, however, not to choose words that unnecessarily manipulate the emotions or the biases of your reader.

EXERCISE 5 **Writing Objectively.** Imagine that the following paragraph is intended to be an objective account of Hannibal's attack on Rome. Rewrite the paragraph, rewording any statements that are not objective.

The Second Punic War (218–201 B.C.) was the most terrible war in ancient history. Led by their overconfident general, Hannibal, the Carthaginians believed that they could completely defeat the Romans. Unfortunately, they made too many stupid mistakes. Crossing the Alps to attack Rome from the north was a fine idea, but the price Hannibal had to pay was too great. He probably said to himself, "The Romans will never expect us to attack from the north." Everyone now thinks of that march with elephants across the Alps as a brilliant military achievement. The truth is that Hannibal lost many thousands of men on that journey and totally exhausted those who survived. It was too cold in the mountains to try something like that! Hannibal was able to keep going as long as he did, winning the battles of Trasimene and Cannae, only because of his tremendous skill as a general. Ultimately he was defeated by a lack of supplies from his own government and by the delaying tactics of the Roman general Fabius.

Writing Chronologically

Much of your social studies writing will require you to describe events or processes in **chronological,** or time, **order.** Biographical sketches, essays on historical events, and explanations of processes, such as the passage of bills in Congress, demand clear chronological writing. In many cases it is important for your reader to know whether one event takes place before or after another because the *order* of events often makes a difference in determining their *significance.* For example, it is important that a civil war occurred among the Incas in 1524, *before* the conquistador Pizarro attacked in 1531. The civil war weakened the Incan Empire and helped make Pizarro's victory possible.

Review what you learned about chronological order in Chapter 3, "Writing the Paragraph," and in Chapter 8, "Narrative Writing." As you write, pay special attention to transitions that show the sequence of time, such as *before, after, then,* and *at the same time.*

EXERCISE 6 **Writing Chronologically.** Write a paragraph based on the time line in the Writer's Sourcebook (pages 368–369). Describe the events in chronological order, using appropriate transitions.

Writing About Causes and Effects

Writing about causes and effects is one of the most common and most significant kinds of social studies writing. Identifying and relating the causes and effects of events will provide the major focus for much of the writing you will be asked to do in the study of history and world cultures.

If you are writing a scientific analysis of a process—the boiling of water, for example—you may say with certainty that one event causes another event: *The temperature reached 212 degrees Fahrenheit, and therefore the water boiled.* In writing about social studies, however, you are writing about *people in action.* Human events usually have more than one cause and more than one effect. For example, it would be inadequate to write *World War I broke out because of the assassination of the Archduke Ferdinand.* You also need to recognize other causes of the war, such as trade competition, intense nationalism, an armaments race, and a system of alliances.

When writing about causes and effects, consider your topic from different angles. Questions like these may help you:

PERSONAL Who was directly responsible? Who was directly affected? A single person? A group of persons?

SOCIAL What general beliefs or attitudes of the society made the event possible? In what way did the event change people's beliefs or attitudes? What system of government made the event possible?

ECONOMIC What economic factors made the event possible? Who profited or lost financially because of the event?

Finally, remember that causes and effects can be both short-term and long-term. A short-term, or immediate, cause or effect is usually a specific event that can be pinpointed. A long-term cause or effect is often more difficult to identify but eventually more important to a greater number of people.

EXERCISE 7 **Writing About Causes and Effects.** Write a paragraph about the causes or effects of a cultural or historical event. Choose an event of your own, or use one of the following. Be sure to consider the wide variety of possible causes or effects.

1. the invention of printing
2. the coronation of Henry Tudor of England
3. the changing role of women in the work force
4. the increasing use of home computers

Writing with Comparison and Contrast

Comparison is writing that describes similarities; **contrast** is writing that describes differences. Writing with comparison and contrast is a useful social studies skill, especially because historical and cultural events do not occur in isolation. They are part of the continuing movement of history and are often best understood by relating them to other events.

Writing a paragraph or an essay with comparison and contrast (Chapter 3, "Writing the Paragraph") will be easier for you and clearer for your reader if during prewriting you decide on the points of comparison and contrast. Make a chart that identifies the similarities or differences between your subjects. For example:

ELIZABETH I OF ENGLAND	CATHERINE THE GREAT OF RUSSIA
SIMILARITIES	
• highly intelligent and cultured • strong-willed and shrewd • considered major historical figure	
DIFFERENCES	
• presided over cultural renaissance • secretly allowed piracy against Spain • peaceful and prosperous reign	• made peasantry even poorer • openly sought war with Turks • despotic, aggressive reign

When you write, begin by identifying your subjects and telling the reader that you are going to compare or contrast them. Organize your paragraph or paper in one of two ways: *AAABBB,* in which all the *A*s are statements about Elizabeth and all the *B*s are statements about Catherine; or *ABABAB,* in which you alternate statements about each of the subjects. Either way, be sure to make your points of comparison clear. At the end you may want to add a general statement that sums up your subject and unites all your points of comparison or contrast in one observation. A chart like the preceding one for Elizabeth and Catherine might grow into the following social studies paragraph:

> Elizabeth I of England and Catherine the Great of Russia were both highly intelligent, cultured women. These two major historical figures were also both strong-willed, shrewd rulers. Their reigns, however, differ in significant ways. While Elizabeth gave her name to the Elizabethan Age, a time of tremendous cultural achievements by all levels of the English people, Catherine actually increased the number of serfs in her country and made the poor even poorer. Elizabeth slyly permitted piracy against Spain while avoiding war, but Catherine openly sought war with the Turks so that Russian lands could be increased. Elizabeth's reign was basically peaceful, and she was known as Good Queen Bess; Catherine's reign was aggressive, and she was fundamentally a despot. These rulers demonstrate how two multitalented women can lead their countries down different paths.

EXERCISE 8 **Writing with Comparison and Contrast.** Write a paragraph comparing or contrasting two social studies subjects. You may use the information given in the following chart to compare and contrast living standards in the United States and the Soviet Union. If you prefer, you may use one of the other pairs of subjects provided, or you may choose a subject of your own. Think carefully about your intended audience and about whether you can summarize your points in a general statement.

LIVING STANDARDS	UNITED STATES	SOVIET UNION
Daily calorie supply per person	3,450	3,328
Grain production (pounds per person)	1,960	1,405
Meat production (pounds per person)	236	130
Automobiles (per 1,000 persons)	538	35
Refrigerators (per 1,000 persons)	349	268
Telephones (per 1,000 persons)	791	84
Physicians (per 1,000 persons)	2	4
Infant mortality (per 1,000 births)	11	32
Life expectancy at birth (years)	75	69

Source: *U.S. News and World Report,* February 4, 1985

Other subjects for comparison and contrast:

1. the golden age of India and the golden age of China
2. Alexander the Great and Napoleon Bonaparte
3. art of the Renaissance and art of the Romantic age
4. an African kingdom and a European kingdom

Revising, Editing, and Publishing

Revising a paragraph, essay, or paper in social studies calls for using all the basic revising skills described in Chapter 4, "Revising the Paragraph." You will also want to revise your writing with special attention to the particular social studies writing skills you learned in this chapter. The following checklist may help as you revise. Remember to edit and proofread the final version so that you can share your work with readers. Use the rules of standard manuscript form to make your final copy.

If you are writing an essay, review the special section on revising the essay in Chapter 11, "The Essay." If you are writing a research report, review the section on revising in Chapter 12, "The Research Report."

Checklist for Revising a Social Studies Report

1. What questions can I apply to the social studies topic to define and focus it—*who? what? when? where? how?* and *why?*
2. What basic social studies facts or definitions does the audience need? What statements or word choices, if any, are inappropriate to the audience? What is the purpose of this piece of writing?
3. Is any source, primary or secondary, incorrectly or insufficiently identified? Is the proper format for documentation used in all cases?
4. What qualifying words should be used to revise any generalizations?
5. Which statements are not as objective as possible? Which, if any, use unclear language, inexact quotations, unlabeled opinions, unnecessary adverbs, or loaded words?
6. Which transitions that show time can be used to make chronological statements absolutely clear?
7. Which causes and effects, if any, are not clearly identified? Which personal, social, or economic causes and effects need to be reconsidered and expanded?
8. Are any points of comparison or contrast unclear? Should any changes be made in the organization so that the point-by-point comparison or contrast will be easier for the reader to follow?

Writer's Choice

Writer's Choice #1

ASSIGNMENT Answer this social studies examination question: Which of the following inventions do you think had the greatest effect on world history, and why: Farming, gunpowder, printing, the telephone, space flight?

LENGTH One paragraph

AUDIENCE Your teacher

PURPOSE To inform and explain

PREWRITING Make a list of the short-term and the long-term effects of the invention and a list of reasons for your opinion.

WRITING Begin by identifying your choice. Then give the short-term effects, followed by the long-term effects. You may want to write about the effects in order of importance. End with a general statement about the invention.

REVISING Refer to the checklist on page 295 to revise your paragraph. Edit your first draft, prepare a final copy, and proofread it.

Writer's Choice #2

ASSIGNMENT Compare or contrast any two of the following historical figures: Hammurabi, Pericles, Julius Caesar, Confucius, Hernando Cortes, George Washington, Queen Victoria, Winston Churchill, Golda Meir, Lech Walesa.

LENGTH Your choice

AUDIENCE Your choice

PURPOSE To inform and explain

PREWRITING Make a chart of the similarities or the differences between the two historical figures.

WRITING Order your paragraph according to the *AAABBB* or the *ABA-BAB* structure. End with a general statement about the two figures. Use appropriate qualifying words.

REVISING Refer to the checklist on page 295.

Writer's Choice #3

ASSIGNMENT A paragraph or brief essay about social studies

OPTIONS Determine your own length, audience, and purpose. Write on any social studies topic you choose. You may want to refer to the Writer's Sourcebook (pages 366–369) for an idea. Limit and focus your topic during prewriting, and clearly identify it at the beginning of your paragraph or essay. Use the checklist on page 295 to make revisions.

Writers on Writing

Arica Allen, whose interests include music and creative writing, wrote the following paragraph and commentary as a student at Yorktown High School in in Yorktown Heights, New York. Arica is considering a career in psychology.

THE PRODUCT

American history has seen many examples of the doctrine of checks and balances. One of the first was the case of Marbury vs. Madison. President Jefferson ordered Secretary of State James Madison not to issue letters of appointment to judges who had been appointed by President Adams a term earlier. This act, if enforced, would have rendered the Supreme Court judges practically powerless. Subsequently, William Marbury, a Supreme Court justice appointed by President Adams, sued Madison before the Supreme Court. Marbury asked the court to issue a mandamus, a written order, to Madison so that Jefferson's instruction to Madison would be invalid. The court ruled against Marbury, claiming that the Judiciary Act of 1789, which gave the court power to issue writs of mandamus, was unconstitutional. This decision illustrates the concept of checks and balances, in that the judiciary branch established its power to interpret the law and decide what is constitutional and what is not.

THE PROCESS

The preceding paragraph comes from an assignment in my social studies class. I had heard of the doctrine of checks and balances before, but I really did not know enough to write a paper about it. Luckily, most of the information I needed was in my textbook. If I had not had this textbook, I would have had to do some research in other sources. The first thing I would have done would be to look up "checks and balances" in the *American Political Dictionary,* to see how the term is used and what it refers to. Next, I would look up the particular case of Marbury vs. Madison in an encyclopedia, a book about Jefferson's presidency, and similar sources.

YOUR TURN   *Keeping a Research Log*

As Arica did, choose a brief paper that you wrote for a social studies assignment and explain how you gathered the information for the paper. Indicate what outside sources you used or could have used.

CHAPTER 14

Writing a Scientific or Technical Report

Scientists and engineers today produce far more written material than do novelists and poets, and may, in their way, be more influential.

—Deborah C. Andrews and Margaret D. Blickle

In her book *Technical Writing* Maxine T. Turner relates the following anecdote:

> Late on a Sunday afternoon as a team of engineers worked to meet a deadline for a technical recommendations report, the project manager threw his pen across the room, buried his face in his hands, and sobbed "*@#%&*! I hate to write *sooo Bad!*"

Perhaps if the project manager had known more about scientific or technical writing, he would have realized that his task was not so difficult after all. In fact, it is relatively easy to put together a scientific report once you have done the research.

Scientific papers or technical reports follow a set format to present in clear, accurate, and concise language factual information based on research.

In this age of advanced technology, legions of scientists all over the world share their work by writing every day. Not all technical writing is for specialists, however. Major technical corporations, such as AT&T, IBM, and Atari, hire writers who specialize in translating scientific data, or information, into terms that the average person can understand.

This chapter will cover the various conventions for scientific and technical reports and will present these conventions in terms of the writing process:

> prewriting: finding a suitable topic
> prewriting: purpose and audience
> prewriting: gathering information
> writing a scientific or technical report
> revising, editing, and publishing a report

Learn how to write about science and technology, and your writing, as Andrews and Blickle suggest, may be influential.

Prewriting: Finding a Suitable Topic

A reader looking for scientific or technical information will be interested in your report only if it has a serious, objective tone and presents information or conclusions and recommendations not readily available in other reports. In other words, a reader looking for scientific or technical data is not interested in your feelings about a topic, nor does a reader want to find information that already is reported elsewhere. With such a reader in mind, you can begin to generate and explore ideas for a topic about which you will do research and write a report. Here are some examples of suitable and unsuitable topics for a scientific paper or technical report:

SUITABLE	UNSUITABLE
the effects of tetracycline	why students study biology
the place of robots in industry	my feelings about robots

In this chapter you will follow the course of a high school student who eventually wrote a paper entitled "Industrial Robots: A Study of Their Impact on Human Labor." At the start the student was generally interested in robotics, and he used various prewriting techniques until he narrowed his topic to the use of industrial robots to replace human workers.

EXERCISE 1 **Evaluating the Suitability of Topics.** Read the following list of topics. On your paper write *Suitable* if the topic is suitable for a scientific paper or technical report. Write *Unsuitable* for each topic that is unsuitable, and explain why it is inappropriate.

1. the relationship between humans and machines
2. human intelligence versus machine intelligence
3. my reasons for banning computers
4. my opinion of home banking
5. some special languages of science and technology

EXERCISE 2 **Selecting a Topic.** From the following list of broad topics, select one, and begin to generate and explore ideas. (See Chapter 2.) If you wish, you may select another general topic. The purpose of this exercise is to help you find a topic to develop into a scientific or technical report for Writer's Choice #1 on page 310.

1. passive solar heating
2. burn clinics
3. alternative energy sources: wind and water power
4. cholesterol reduction
5. hydroponics

Prewriting: Purpose and Audience

The general purpose of scientific or technical writing is to inform. The specific purpose of a scientific or technical report may be one of the following:

1. *to explain a process:* for example, to show how a machine operates
2. *to analyze causes and effects:* for example, to predict long-term consequences
3. *to divide and classify items:* for example, to divide a problem into its logical parts and relate the problem to a larger problem or to a general scientific or technical concern
4. *to define terms:* to explain technical terminology, or jargon
5. *to compare and contrast items:* for example, to point out similarities and differences among processes, operations, or problems

(For more specific information about these types of expository writing, see Chapter 9.)

As in all kinds of writing, once you have determined your purpose, you must next turn your attention to addressing an audience. Before writing, ask yourself the following questions:

1. Who is my audience?
2. How much do these readers know about my topic?
3. How interested are they in my material?

EXERCISE 3 **Determining a Purpose.** For the topic that you selected in Exercise 2, state your specific purpose. Think about the five kinds of purposes listed just above. Try to apply each of those purposes to your topic. Which would you like to develop in a scientific paper or technical report? Write your purpose in a single sentence. Save your statement for Writer's Choice #1.

EXERCISE 4 **Matching Audience and Writing.** Read the following short paragraphs. On your paper write *Expert* if you think the paragraph is suitable for an audience of experts. Write *Nonexpert* if you think the paragraph is better suited for readers without specialized knowledge of the topic. Use specific examples from each paragraph to explain your answer.

1. This report presents a comparative feasibility study of two alternatives for the product warehousing operations of Piedmont Mills. Limited to an evaluation of economic factors, the study compares the current system and a new conventional system on the basis of after-tax cash flow, present worth, and rate-of-return calculations.

2. This report analyzes the economic factors of two alternatives to the current warehousing operation of Piedmont Mills. The purpose of this report is to describe these alternatives and to evaluate them in terms of economics. The report will show that a new warehousing system would have several advantages.

EXERCISE 5 **Identifying Your Audience.** Decide what kind of audience you think will read the report you have been considering in Exercises 2 and 3. In a written sentence or two describe this audience, indicating whether it is expert or nonexpert. Tell how much your intended readers know about your topic and whether or not they will be interested in reading your report. Save your comments for Writer's Choice #1.

Prewriting: Gathering Information

Prepare a list of questions based on your purpose and the needs of your audience in order to decide what you will need to include in your report. The following general questions can guide you:

1. What problem or idea am I trying to solve or present?
2. What is the best way to solve or present it?
3. What does my audience need to know?
4. What questions do I need to answer in my report?
5. Where will I go to find the answers?
6. How do my ideas relate to and build upon previous research?

With these questions in mind, a good next step is to consult a general reference book and scan the entry for your topic. For example, you might consult one of the following:

> *McGraw-Hill Encyclopedia of Science and Technology,*
>   5th ed. New York: McGraw-Hill, 1982. 15 volumes.

> *Van Nostrand's Scientific Encyclopedia,* 6th ed. New York:
>   Van Nostrand Reinhold Co., 1983.

Once you have scanned a general reference work, try to find a major reference book for your particular topic. For example, if you are going to write about ecology, you might consult the following reference work:

McGraw-Hill Encyclopedia of Environmental Science, 2d ed.
New York: McGraw-Hill, 1980.

Having consulted general and major reference works, you will be able to prepare a *working outline* to guide the rest of your research. (See Chapter 12 for a review of how to prepare a working outline for a research report.) Below is the working outline that the student prepared for his paper on industrial robots.

INDUSTRIAL ROBOTS: THEIR IMPACT ON HUMAN LABOR
 I. Use of industrial robots to replace human factory workers
 II. Advantages and disadvantages of industrial robots
 III. Advantages and disadvantages of human factory workers
 IV. Recommended uses of industrial robots.

Locate additional books and articles to read in detail. You may have found leads to such books and articles in the general reference works you first checked. The fields of science and technology are constantly being updated, however, so you cannot rely heavily on older reference books. Look through the card catalog and indexes to periodicals in order to find current sources of information. For each promising source first fill out a bibliography card. Then begin to read or scan the assembled materials and take notes. Eventually you will be ready to write a *formal outline.* (For more information about these research techniques, see Chapter 12.)

To research the report on industrial robots, the student consulted the *Readers' Guide to Periodical Literature,* which includes listings of articles in magazines such as *Science* and *Scientific American.* Then, to find more articles for his topic, he consulted the *Applied Science and Technology Index.* If he had lived near factories that use industrial robots and human workers, he would have gained firsthand knowledge of his topic by conducting interviews with union leaders and factory workers and owners.

EXERCISE 6 **Gathering Information.** Follow the steps indicated here as you begin to research the scientific or technical topic for your report.

1. Ask general questions about the topic to guide your early research.
2. Check a general reference work to gather background information.
3. Prepare a working outline.
4. Locate specific sources, and begin reading and taking notes.
5. Decide whether your report would benefit from interviews and information that you would have to request by mail or phone.
6. Prepare a formal outline.

Writing a Scientific or Technical Report

To give an accurate, logically developed, and unbiased presentation, the writer of a scientific or technical report should use precise language, including appropriate technical terms. In addition, the writer of such a report should sound serious, objective, and impersonal. While *I* and *me* might be fine in more personal writing, third-person pronouns are more appropriate to scientific or technical writing.

APPROPRIATE Robot arms are strong mechanisms made up of three parts.

INAPPROPRIATE I'm going to stress that robot arms are strong mechanisms made up of some parts.

All writing that is well thought out has a noticeable beginning, middle, and end. A scientific or technical report actually carries labels for its three sections. This labeling is one of the conventions of scientific or technical writing. Here is a description of each of the three parts:

INTRODUCTION

The purpose of the introduction is to explain to the reader what general problem you intend to discuss in the paper or report. Here you can give background information about the problem. In the introduction you will also state clearly your specific purpose.

DISCUSSION (OR BODY)

The discussion (or body) is the major section of the report and contains the results of your research. It focuses on facts, their relationships, and their importance.

CONCLUSIONS AND RECOMMENDATIONS

Since a technical report often discusses a problem, your readers will appreciate clear and simple recommendations for the actions that should be taken in the future to solve the problem.

In addition to its three major divisions, a scientific paper or technical report has several other features and elements. Scientists consider these other conventions important to follow:

TITLE PAGE

Include the following information on the title page: the title of the report, your name, your teacher's name, and the date.

TABLE OF CONTENTS

The table of contents lists in sequence all the parts of the report, including the introduction, discussion (the body), conclusions and recommendations, and bibliography.

BIBLIOGRAPHY

Put the bibliography on a separate page with its own heading. To style the items in the bibliography, use the formats suggested in Chapter 12.

The word **mechanics** refers to the uses of punctuation, capital letters, and abbreviations. In a scientific or technical report mechanics allow you to express your thoughts more precisely and help your readers to understand your writing.

ABBREVIATIONS

Writers may use abbreviations in scientific or technical reports, especially to express units of measurement (for example, *ft, lb, km*). Always write a word in full the first time you use it, and write its abbreviation in parentheses. Thereafter you may use only the abbreviation.

NUMBERS

Here is a list of conventions relating to the use of numbers in scientific or technical writing:

1. Write out numbers from one to ten (*nine rooms*).
2. Use Arabic numerals for all numbers above ten (*14 offices*), except when writing small numbers in a mathematical expression (*4 times 8*).
3. Write round numbers above a million as a combination of Arabic numerals and words (*11 billion*).
4. Use numerals to express fractions, percentages, decimals, page numbers, figures, monetary units, and exact measurements.
5. Never begin a sentence with a number, either spelled out or written as numerals.

DOCUMENTATION

Unlike other research reports, scientific papers or technical reports do not include footnotes or end notes. Instead, an author-date-page-number system is used to give information about the sources you use. In this system you present the author's last name, the year of publication, and the page reference in parentheses when you cite the source, as in this example: (*Jones, 1983, p.41*). If you use the same reference more than once, omit the date after the first citation. Cite these sources in the bibliography.

ILLUSTRATIONS

Most scientific or technical reports use sketches, tables, and diagrams to aid complex explanations. Number each sketch, table, and diagram, and refer to it by number in the body of the paper, as in this example: (*see Figure 1*). Place each sketch, table, and diagram on a separate page, and place its number, title, and source, if there is one, below it: (*Figure 1: A Capillary*).

EXERCISE 7 **Analyzing a Scientific or Technical Report.** In order to see how the preceding advice can be followed, examine the sample report beginning on page 306, and write the answers to the following questions:

1. How does the introduction differ from the discussion? How does the conclusions and recommendations section differ from the discussion?
2. How does the first acknowledgment of the D'Ignazio source differ from the other acknowledgments of that source?
3. Find one instance in which an idea rather than a direct quotation is attributed to a source.
4. What is the purpose of Figure 1?

Revising, Editing, and Publishing

All the general questions to be asked when you revise a paragraph (see Chapter 4) apply to scientific or technical writing. In addition, scientific or technical writing requires you to ask some special questions.

 Checklist for Revising a Scientific or Technical Report

1. What, if anything, distracts from the serious, impersonal tone of my report? Have I removed any references to personal experiences or opinions? Have I used third-person pronouns throughout?
2. What does the introduction provide in terms of background information? How well does the introduction state my general purpose and my specific purposes?
3. What, if anything, can I do to present my findings concisely and objectively in the discussion?
4. What conclusions and recommendations have I stated? Are the conclusions and recommendations consistent with the facts presented in the introduction and the discussion?
5. What corrections, if any, do I need to make in the other elements of the report—on the title page, in the table of contents, and in the bibliography? Have all elements of mechanics been handled correctly?
6. What can I do to improve the precision of my language?
7. What other editing should I do on a sentence-by-sentence basis?
8. How carefully have I proofread the final version?

Once you have revised your report, you are ready to share it with your audience. Whether your audience is your class, your teacher, a science club publication, or a community group, you will be presenting a report that may be very influential.

Model of the Finished Report

Industrial Robots:
A Study of Their Impact on Human Labor

Brian Meyers*

Science 10-3
Mrs. Ackley
April 25, 19--

Introduction

Since the creation of the first industrial robot in 1961 by a company called Unimation, public concern over the use of robots to replace human workers has been growing. In the early 1960s only a few robots were built each month, and many were used by General Motors in its automobile assembly plants. By the early 1980s more than 20 thousand industrial robots will exist in the world, and according to one source, "The applications of robots already run into the hundreds, and the list is growing" (Collier's Encyclopedia, 1980 ed., "Robot"). Another source states that "by 1990, as many as 200,000 robots will be at work" (D'Ignazio, 1984, p.57). These modern robots, controlled by high-speed electronic computers, will be working not just on an automated assembly line. Instead, they will be used for a large number of routine factory operations, such as moving stock and cleaning, thereby replacing thousands of human workers. Many of

---

*This paper is based on research done by Brian Meyers of Indian Hill High School, Cincinnati, Ohio.

the jobs that these robots will be taking are too dangerous, fatiguing, or boring for human workers.

It is the general purpose of this paper to examine whether industrial robots will be a benefit or a threat to human labor. The specific purposes of this report are as follows:

1. To analyze the positive and negative impact of industrial robots on human labor
2. To compare and contrast the abilities of industrial robots and human factory workers
3. To suggest recommendations that will lessen the negative impact of industrial robots on human labor

Discussion

Since the 1960s a controversy between factory owners and union leaders has arisen over the use of robots in industry. Because of their desire to lower the cost of production, factory owners have spent large sums of money to develop and install new robots in their plants. Concerned about the loss of many jobs, union leaders and workers believe that industrial robots should be used in factories only to do work that is too dangerous (such as the handling of toxic substances) or too dull for human workers. Factory owners feel that robots should be used to perform many different types of jobs (not just those that are dangerous or repetitive) because robots are more efficient and more reliable than their human counterparts. Therefore, in spite of the high price of an industrial robot (about 40 thousand dollars), owners believe that robots are cheaper and more economical in comparison with the skyrocketing cost of human labor.

One well-known computer and robotics consultant says,

> Over the last twenty years, the average salary
> for a factory worker has gone from $3.80 an hour
> to over $16.00 an hour. During that same period,
> the total cost of a robot-hour (including instal-
> lation, maintenance depreciation, and energy) has
> increased from $4.00 to only $4.80. (D'Ignazio, p.58)

In addition, a robot can work multiple shifts without becoming fatigued or without complaining about working conditions. Also robots never show up late for work or take coffee breaks or vacations. One computer engineer points out that "the 'up time' of a robot on the job averages around 95 percent, compared with 75 percent or less for the average blue-collar worker" (Logsdon, 1984, p. 29).

Unlike human workers, who must be retrained to take a new job, robots are easily reprogrammable. That is, robots can be programmed to do one thing and then reporgrammed to do something else. This reprogramming may take only two to four weeks. Therefore, in just a short time an industrial robot can go from "being a welder" to being "a painter or an assembler" (D'Ignazio, p. 58). By contrast, it might take several months or even years for a human worker to master new skills.

Despite these advantages over humans, most of today's industrial robots are inferior to human workers. Almost all present-day robots cannot see or hear, and they have little or no sense of touch or intelligence. These limitations make it especially difficult for robots to recognize and match parts, tasks at which they are "notoriously bad" because of their inability to see (D'Ignazio, p. 59).

For certain jobs--those that require the use of a powerful arm--robots are clearly supervisor to human workers. Unlike the mechanical men of science faction, such as R2D2, robots are really nothing more than arms mounted on boxes (see Figure 1). In the book Robots and Robotology, which outlines how robots are made. R. H. Warring explains that robot arms are strong mechanisms made up of three parts. These parts--the manipulator (a mechanical arm), the power supply (often an electrical system that drives the arm), and the controller, or brain (usually a computer)--equip the robot with the capacity to perform tiresome, repetitive tasks (Warring, 1984, pp. 40, 47, 99). Unlike the human arm, the robot arm, because of its structure, is well equipped for doing jobs such as welding, drilling, spray painting, and wrapping food, since it never tires and has much more power.

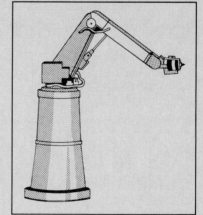

Figure 1. The Robot's Arm

In spite of many comparisons, industrial robots and human workers do not have to be in competition with each other. In fact, in more ways than one both groups can work side by side. Today more companies are creating teams of robots and humans to work together to do certain jobs. Such cooperation is often seen in Japan, where one third of the workers keep their jobs for life and the fear of losing a job is not as great as it is in the United States. For example, in a large watch factory in Japan, robots and humans work side by side. While the robots insert "the delicate hairlike mainspring," the "mainspring adjustments are . . . handled by human craftsmen" (Logsdon, p. 99). Such cooperative efforts are regarded so highly in Japan that "when a new robot is put on the payroll, factory workers have a celebration and give it a suitable nickname--often that of a popular baseball player or a movie star" (Logsdon, p. 27). By working together "humans and robots can pool their talents and offset each other's weaknesses" (D'Ignazio, p. 89). In other words, humans can deal with unexpected situations, apply common sense, and make decisions, while robots can handle jobs that are beyond the human workers' ability or strength.

Conclusions and Recommendations

A study of the impact of robots on industry has shown that robots can be a benefit to human labor. Although industrial robots have replaced factory workers, many of the jobs they have taken have been either too dangerous or too dull for human workers. Despite the fact that many workers have taken an unfavorable attitude toward industrial robots, when jobs have been introduced that require teamwork between humans and robots, workers have responded more favorably.

This report recommends that industrial robots should be used largely to perform jobs that are too dangerous or fatiguing for human workers. This study further recommends that to create a better environment in the work place, more efforts should be made to develop teams of human workers and industrial robots.

Bibliography

D'Ignazio, Fred. Working Robots. Hasbrouck Heights, NJ: Hayden Book Co., 1984

Logsdon, Tom. The Robot Revolution. New York: Simon & Schuster, 1984.

Malono, Robert. "Robot" Collier's Encyclopedia, 1980 ed.

Warring, R. H. Robots and Robotology, Blue Ridge Summit, PA: Tab Books, 1984.

Writer's Choice

Writer's Choice #1

ASSIGNMENT   A scientific or technical report based on the work you did in Exercises 2, 3, 5, and 6

LENGTH   500 to 1,000 words

AUDIENCE   As you stated in Exercise 5

PURPOSE   As you stated in Exercise 3

PREWRITING   You have already finished this stage by completing Exercises 2, 3, 5, and 6.

WRITING   Prepare a first draft. Begin with the discussion, which should follow your formal outline. Then prepare an introduction and conclusions and recommendations. Add illustrations if you think they will help. Prepare the other parts of the paper: title page, table of contents, and bibliography.

REVISING   Use the checklist on page 305 to make sure that you have followed the conventions of scientific and technical writing. Be sure to consider large issues such as organization as well as matters of editing and proofreading. When your final draft is ready, share it with your audience.

Writer's Choice # 2

ASSIGNMENT   To write a brief operating manual for a machine or a computer program of your choice

LENGTH   Two pages for the discussion

AUDIENCE   Your classmates who are not familiar with the operation of the machine or program

PURPOSE   To describe one operation of the machine or one application of the program so completely and clearly that your readers will have no problem using it

PREWRITING   Select a machine or program about which you want to write, and prepare a working outline so that you can begin to research the problems of using that machine or program. (Try to select a machine or program about which you can also do research. That is, try to find reports such as an operating manual prepared by the manufacturer of the machine or program, an advertising brochure prepared by the manufacturer, or reviews of the machine or program in magazines. For example, for a particular personal computer, you might look in magazines such as *Consumer Reports, PC World,* and *InfoWorld.* Other magazines specialize in stereo equipment, in VCRs, in farm machinery, and so on.)

Prepare a bibliography card for each source, and take notes as you read.

Consider talking to people who use the machine or program. You might interview them about problems they have had and solutions that they have developed to aid them in operating the machine or program smoothly.

WRITING   Prepare a first draft. Begin with the discussion, which should follow your formal outline. Then prepare an introduction and conclusions and recommendations. Add illustrations if you think they will help. Prepare the other parts of the paper: title page, table of contents, and bibliography.

REVISING   Use the checklist on page 305 to make sure that you have followed the conventions of scientific and technical writing. Be sure to consider large issues such as organization as well as matters of editing and proofreading.

Writer's Choice #3

ASSIGNMENT   To write about an environmental problem in your part of the country

LENGTH   Two to three pages for the discussion

AUDIENCE   The chamber of commerce or a similar organization

PURPOSE   To present all sides of an environmental issue and to suggest a solution

PREWRITING   Use prewriting techniques from Chapter 2 to develop and explore a specific idea. You may get an idea by looking at the illustrations in the Writer's Sourcebook on pages 370–373. Do general reading so that you can prepare a working outline, and then locate sources for more detailed reading and note taking. Prepare a formal outline.

WRITING   Prepare a first draft. Begin with the discussion, which should follow your formal outline. Then prepare an introduction and conclusions and recommendations. Add illustrations if you think they will help. Prepare the other parts of the paper: title page, table of contents, and bibliography.

REVISING   Use the checklist on page 305 to make sure that you have followed the conventions of scientific and technical writing. Be sure to consider large issues such as organization as well as matters of editing and proofreading.

CHAPTER *15*

Writing About Literature

Literature is the property of all; its appeal is to all. But literature, as an art, employs techniques and offers problems that can be understood only thorugh analysis, and analysis means work.

—Edgar V. Roberts

The poet John Ciardi tells this story about Robert Frost's exchange with a woman at a poetry reading:

> "But Mr. Frost," she cried, "surely when you are writing one of your beautiful poems, surely you can't be thinking about . . .technical tricks."
>
> Mr. Frost put his hands together, the spread fingers touching tip to tip, looked owlish for a moment, and leaned forward into the microphone and said in a playfully, gravelly bass: "I revel in 'em!"

Like the woman at Frost's reading, many people think of literature as an elevated enterprise, far removed from such humble matters as "technical tricks." They imagine novelists, playwrights, and poets as explorers launching forth on grand and mysterious journeys. In a sense, they are right, but they forget that writing a story, play, or poem is also deliberate, technical work. Writers need all the technical tricks they can muster if they are to fly to unknown worlds—*someone* must think about building the launch pad, fueling the rockets, steering the ship.

When you write about a literary work, you will be thinking about both the writer's destination and the craft that enabled the writer to get there. This means that you will focus on both the insight that the writer presents in the work and the literary techniques that he or she uses to express this insight.

This chapter will give you practice in the following:

> **writing** about a short story
> **writing** about a dramatic scene
> **writing** about a poem

In each case you will be writing for an audience that is thoroughly familiar with the work. Your purpose will be to explain what you think the work really means and what literary techniques the writer used to convey that meaning.

As you write about what writers say and how they say it, you may discover what the woman at the poetry reading did not know—that writers cherish the technical tricks that enable them to do their difficult work. After all, the flying ship is no less wonderful than the flight itself.

Writing About a Short Story

Part of the enjoyment of reading a story comes from interpreting it—understanding what the story says and how its parts work together to say it. Use the following suggestions to help you interpret and write about a story.

Prewriting: First Responses to a Story

Read the story over a few times. On your first reading concentrate on the characters and action. As you read the story again, decide on your basic reaction, and think about what the author may have intended to say.

Next freewrite or brainstorm about your first reaction to the story. You will see here some freewriting based on "The Open Window," a story by the British author Hector Hugh Munro, who was known by the pen name Saki. You will find "The Open Window" on page 374 in the Writer's Sourcebook. Read the story before you look at the freewriting.

> *Loved the roller-coaster combination of horror and humor—I was fooled along with Nuttel—was a little disappointed to find that everything is normal, except that the last part is so funny! I can see why Vera makes up her story, why Nuttel swallows it, why we like ghost stories—they spice up our lives.*

Prewriting: Exploring a Story

Once your first impression of the story is on paper, you can begin to analyze *why* you reacted as you did and what the author might have been saying. Here is a brief review of the main elements of short stories:

1. The **plot** is the sequence of events in the story. The plot revolves around a **conflict**—a problem or struggle of some kind. The plot builds to a **climax**, or high point; after the climax the conflict is resolved.
2. We understand the **characters** in a story through their actions, words, the comments of other characters, and the comments of the narrator.
3. The **setting** is the time and place of the story's action. The setting often creates an **atmosphere**, or mood.
4. The **point of view** of a story is the relationship between the narrator, or storyteller, and the story. Some stories are told from a **first-person point of view**—through the voice of a character in the story. Other stories are told from a **limited third-person point of view**, in which the narrator relates the thoughts of only one character but speaks in the third person. Still other stories use an **omniscient point of view**, in which the narrator knows the thoughts of all the characters.
5. The **tone** is the author's attitude toward the events and characters.
6. The **theme** of the story is the underlying idea about life that is conveyed by the events, characters, setting, point of view, and tone.

You can explore a particular story by focusing on each of its elements with questions like the following ones. There may be other questions that will occur to you. The sample answers presented below are based on "The Open Window." Note the types of details that are included in these sample answers.

QUESTIONS TO EXPLORE A STORY	SAMPLE ANSWERS FOR "THE OPEN WINDOW"
1. What is the main conflict in the story?	*At first the conflict seems to be over the aunt's "delusion" that the hunters will return. But the real conflict is actually between Vera's "romance" and the ordinary truth.*
2. What is the climax?	*The arrival of the ghostly hunters.*
3. How is the conflict resolved?	*Vera's second "romance" and the narrator's final comment reveal that Vera likes to invent stories.*
4. How would I describe the main characters? Are they sympathetic? Why or why not?	*Nuttel is young, self-centered, nervous, ultrasensitive. Vera is younger, cleverer, poised, overimaginative. Neither is really sympathetic, but they are a funny pair. Nuttel is so vulnerable, and Vera is so ready to manipulate people.*
5. Describe the story's setting and atmosphere.	*The story takes place in an English country house a while ago. At first the atmosphere seems peaceful, but Vera's story makes it seem creepy--until we learn the truth.*
6. From what point of view is the story told?	*Omniscient, but the narrator concentrates on Nuttel's thoughts. We see as he does and so believe Vera.*
7. What tone, or attitude, does the author take toward the characters and events?	*Seems drily amused most of the time but changes when the hunters appear "noiselessly," singing in a "hoarse voice." Ghostly details create a hushed tone.*
8. How would I state the theme, or underlying idea, of the story?	*(1) The power of suggestion makes us accept an outlandish explanation for an ordinary situation. (2) The story proves the appeal of farfetched "romance" over the dull truth.*

Prewriting: Main Idea and Support

After answering your exploring questions, you are ready to decide on the main idea that you will present. You should state the story's theme and indicate the elements that most clearly convey it, as in this example:

> The plot, characters, and tone of "The Open Window" show that an exciting untruth is often more appealing than the ordinary truth.

EXERCISE 1 **Prewriting for a Paper About a Short Story.** Plan to write a paper about a short story of your own choosing. Begin by reading the work several times. Freewrite or brainstorm about your response to the story. Then write your answers to exploring questions like those shown on page 314. Finally, use your answers to these questions to help you state in writing your main idea.

Writing About a Story: Structure

You will probably want to organize your response to a story (or any other literary work) into several paragraphs. You might write your paragraphs in the following way.

INTRODUCTION AND THESIS STATEMENT

Begin with an introductory paragraph containing your thesis statement, which states the main idea of your paper. Your thesis statement should indicate what you think is the story's theme and which elements you think contribute most to that theme.

BODY

Then write the body of your paper. Here you should focus on the elements that you feel contribute most to the story's theme. Each paragraph should discuss a single element and should have its own topic sentence stating the main idea of that paragraph. Each paragraph should also have unity, clear organization, and coherence. Add to the coherence of your writing by using transitions such as *however, in addition, similarly,* and *as a result.*

SUPPORT AND QUOTATIONS

You should use incidents, details, and quotations from the story to support your statements. Integrate quotations shorter than five lines into your text, enclosing them in quotation marks. Set quotations of five lines or more apart from the text by skipping a line, indenting, and single-spacing the quotation. You should not use quotation marks when you set a quotation apart in this way.

CONCLUSION

Conclude your paper with a paragraph that refers once more to your main idea. You might end with a clincher that expresses your response to the story in a satisfying and memorable way.

You can also apply these suggestions to responses that are only a paragraph long. If you are limited to a paragraph, begin with a strong topic sentence. Each of your subsequent sentences should develop and support one aspect of the topic sentence.

Model of a Paper About a Short Story

The following paper discusses "The Open Window." Note how the writer's freewriting, exploring answers, and main idea fed into this analysis.

"The Open Window"

A   "The Open Window" by Saki is as full of thrills and illusions as an amusement park. However, in addition to chilling us and tricking us, this story says something true about real life. The plot, characters, and point of view prove that an exciting untruth often has more appeal than the dull, ordinary truth.

B   The story's plot is like a roller-coaster ride. It begins on a normal plane as Nuttel waits for his hostess to appear. Then the plot takes a strange turn when Vera starts to unfold her aunt's "tragedy" to Nuttel. When the "ghosts" appear, the plot seems to leave normality entirely. After Nuttel flees, the plot plunges back into the everyday world, a world in which ghosts do not exist except in our imaginations and in the "romances" of people like Vera.

C   The characterization of Vera and Nuttel help create this roller-coaster ride from normality to "romance" and back. Vera, extremely poised for her age, is a convincing actress and has a wild imagination. She finds her ideal victim in Nuttel, a nervous person who is among strangers and so likely to accept her word.

D   The omniscient narrator turns us into Vera's victims as well by concentrating on Nuttel's view of things. Just like Nuttel, we believe Vera because we have no reason not to. As Vera piles up the eerie details of the hunters' disappearance, her incredible story seems more

convincing. Finally we see the returning hunters through
Nuttel's terrified eyes: "In the deepening twilight
three figures were walking. . . . Noiselessly they
neared the house. . ." We quake along with Nuttel. Then
the omniscient narrator lets us in on the trick Vera and
he played on us.

       When we learn that there are no such things as
ghosts, those of us who are disappointed prove Saki's
point: Many people are quick to accept a bizarre untruth
over the dull truth. So we understand why the Veras of
this world develop the specialities they do.

E

F

NOTES ABOUT MODEL PAPER ON A SHORT STORY

A The thesis statement expresses the main idea and identifies three elements.

B Body paragraph 1 discusses plot. Note the transitions that highlight time sequence.

C Body paragraph 2 discusses the characters.

D Body paragraph 3 discusses point of view.

E Note the format for short prose quotations.

F The concluding paragraph restates the main idea and ends with a clincher.

Revising, Editing, and Publishing

Set your first draft aside for a while. Then answer the following questions as you revise, edit, proofread, and publish your work:

1. Which sentence is my thesis statement? In what way can it state the story's theme more clearly? On which elements of the story does my thesis focus?

2. Are the ideas expressed in my thesis statement taken up in the following paragraphs? Does each paragraph have a topic sentence?

3. Each time I discuss one of the story's elements, what details from the story do I use? According to my paper, how does each element contribute to the theme?

4. What transitions and other techniques do I use to create more effective, clearer movement from sentence to sentence and from paragraph to paragraph?

5. How might I rewrite the ending to wrap up the paper in a more satisfactory, memorable way?

6. Is each sentence a complete sentence? Have I avoided errors in the use of verbs, pronouns, and modifiers?

7. Is the final draft neatly copied? Are all the sentences correctly capitalized and punctuated? Are all the words correctly spelled?
8. Am I ready to share this paper with my intended audience? In what ways can I present this paper: For example, could I read it aloud, send it to the school newspaper, or mail it to a journal that publishes student writing?

EXERCISE 2 **Writing and Revising a Paper About a Short Story.** Using the work you did for Exercise 1, write a paper about the story you have chosen. Include a thesis statement expressing your idea about the story's theme and identifying the elements that you think contribute most to that theme. Be sure to discuss each element that you mention in your thesis statement and to tie your writing together with transitions and other devices. End by restating your main idea in an interesting way.

Writing About a Dramatic Scene

A **drama** is a play, a work meant to be performed for an audience. One way of interpreting a play is to focus on a single scene.

Prewriting: First Responses to a Dramatic Scene

Freewrite or brainstorm about your first reaction to the scene. The following freewriting was based on Act II, Scene ii, of William Shakespeare's *Julius Caesar.* The play as a whole portrays the assassination of the Roman leader and its aftermath. Read the scene, which begins on page 377 of the Writer's Sourcebook. Then see one writer's first reaction to it.

> *A quiet scene compared with the rest of the play, but really the only private view we get of Caesar. What a clear picture of Mr. Big—vain, power-loving, shrewd, changeable! Wants everyone to love him but he always comes first. Yet I feel sorry for him—he's going to be killed in an hour by people he thinks are his friends. Does he deserve it?*

Prewriting: Exploring a Dramatic Scene

Now you can explore what is going on in the scene and what the scene contributes to the whole play. Here is a review of the basic elements of drama.

1. A play is made up of **dialogue**—the speeches—and **stage directions**—descriptions of the characters, setting, and action.
2. Like a story, a play presents a **plot**, or series of events.
3. We understand the **characters** in a drama through their words and behavior and through others' treatment of them.

4. Each scene involves a **conflict** either between characters or within a character.
5. The **setting** is the time and place in which the scene occurs.
6. A play usually presents several **themes**, or ideas about life.

You can explore a particular scene by asking questions like the following ones. The answers shown here for Act II, Scene ii, of *Julius Caesar* show how one reader probed the characters and action of this scene.

QUESTIONS TO EXPLORE A SCENE	SAMPLE ANSWERS FOR *JULIUS CAESAR*
1. What happens in the scene?	*Fearing for Caesar's safety, Calpurnia tries to keep him from going to the Capitol. He gives in to her. Then Decius, sent by the conspirators, persuades C. to change his mind and go out. C. is killed in an hour.*
2. What is each character like? What is the goal of each?	*Calpurnia: loyal, protective wife. She calls on C.'s love and good sense to make him stay. Decius: clever, wants C. to go to the Capitol to be killed. Plays on C.'s pride. Caesar: central character, complex--rational, resigned, proud, vain, indulgent. Has opposed goals--wants power, wants to soothe Cal.; wants to be safe and yet seem brave.*
3. What conflict occurs between characters? How is it resolved? Does conflict occur within a character?	*C. and Cal. argue about his going to the Capitol. Then Decius argues against Cal. and wins. Caesar is in conflict, but his love of power wins over his concern for wife and safety.*
4. What is the scene's setting? How might the setting affect the characters?	*C.'s home, where he is safe--he will be killed once he leaves there. Also, the night's strange events have made Cal. (and maybe C.) uneasy. This is ancient Rome--people believe in omens.*
5. Does the scene develop any of the themes of the whole play?	*The play concerns power; the scene shows Caesar's hunger for it. Also, the play focuses on whether it was right to kill C. The scene shows that C. is no monster but simply flawed.*

Prewriting: Main Idea and Support

After answering your exploring questions, you are ready to decide on the main idea for your paper. You will be stating how the scene contributes to the play as a whole, as in this example:

> Act II, Scene ii, of *Julius Caesar* is important for what it reveals about Caesar as a man and leader.

EXERCISE 3 **Prewriting for a Paper About a Dramatic Scene.** Plan to write a short paper about another scene from *Julius Caesar* or about a scene from a play of your own choosing. Begin by reading the whole work; then read the scene aloud. Freewrite or brainstorm about your response to the scene. Then write your answers to exploring questions like those shown on page 319. Finally, use your answers to these questions to help you state in writing your main idea about the scene. If you follow these steps, you should be ready to begin writing.

Writing About a Dramatic Scene: Structure

When you write about a dramatic scene, your opening paragraph should identify the scene and the play from which it comes. You should end your introductory paragraph with a thesis statement indicating why you think the scene is significant.

In your first body paragraph, summarize the action of the scene and briefly sketch the characters. Then zero in on the most important character in the scene, noting statements or actions that reveal the character's traits, goals, conflicts, and so on.

When you are quoting the words of one character, integrate the quotation into your text. If the quotation is in prose, follow the format illustrated on page 281. If the quotation is in verse, follow the format illustrated on page 290. When you are quoting an exchange involving several characters, use the following format:

> The following exchange shows both Calpurnia's belief in omens and Caesar's desire to be (or seem) brave:
>
> CALPURNIA. The heavens themselves blaze forth the
>   death of princes.
> CAESAR. Cowards die many times before their deaths;
>   The valiant never taste of death but once.

Conclude your paper with a paragraph that relates the scene to the play. You might end by saying what you think is the scene's most important contribution to the play.

Model of an Essay About a Dramatic Scene

The following paper discusses Act II, Scene ii, of *Julius Caesar*. Note how the writer used her freewriting, exploring questions, and main idea in writing this paper:

Julius Caesar, Act II, Scene ii

A   Shakespeare's Julius Caesar portrays the assassination of the Roman leader Julius Caesar and the violent aftermath of that event. The play as a whole explores the nature of political power and leadership. In Act II, Scene ii, Caesar decides to leave his home and go to the Capitol, where he will be killed. The scene is important not only because of this fatal decision but also for what the decision reveals about Caesar as a man and leader.

B   The scene begins as Caesar's wife, Calpurnia, who has been frightened by recent strange events, tries to persuade Caesar not to go to the Capitol. He boasts about his bravery and also tries to reason with his wife, but he finally gives in to her. They are joined by Decius, one of the conspirators, who has come to make sure that Caesar goes to the Capitol. Caesor tells Decius to inform the Senate that he refuses to come, confiding that Calpurnia had been disturbed by a dream in which she saw his statue spouting blood. Cleverly, Decius interprets the dream to flatter Caesar. The dream

C   he says, "Signifies that from you great Rome shall suck/ Reviving blood." He baits his trap with news that the Senate plans to crown Caesar that day. As a result, Decius persuades Caesar to go to his doom.

D   The scene creates the best portrait of Caesar in the entire play. The conspirators claim that he is a tyrant. His desire for the crown and his lordly statements show that there may be a germ of truth in the conspirators' claim. For example, Caesar displays his autocratic side when he says, "Cannot, is false; and that I dare not, falser:/I will not come today." Caesar

NOTES ABOUT MODEL ESSAY ON A DRAMATIC SCENE

A The thesis statement explains what the scene contributes to the play's themes.
B Body paragraph 1 summarizes the scene and describes the characters.
C Note the format for short dramatic quotations.
D Body paragraph 2 presents a more detailed discussion of Caesar's character.

is also vain and easily flattered. Yet he shows other
sides. For one thing, he can be moved by his wife. For
another, he seems to be both brave and resigned, as when
he says, "death, a necessary end,/Will come when it
will come." Behind the bold front he might even be a
little afraid; he may have given in to Calpurnia partly
to allay his <u>own</u> fears of death.

     In short, Caesar shows himself to be a complex,
flawed human being, swayed one way and another by
conflicting emotions. His flaws--vanity, foolhardiness,
desire for power--are common to many people; they are
far from monstrous. He may not deserve to be king, but
neither does he deserve to be killed. As the rest of the
play shows, his murder and its bloody aftermath do Rome
much more harm than the Caesar we see in Act II, Scene
ii, is likely to do.

NOTES ABOUT MODEL ESSAY ON A DRAMATIC SCENE

E The concluding paragraph restates the main idea and ends with a clinching
sentence.

Revising, Editing, and Publishing

The following questions focus on revising a paper about a dramatic
scene. For additional reminders for revising a paper about any literary
work, see pages 317–318.

1. Where do I mention the scene's contribution to the play? How might I
   state this idea more clearly?
2. How might I summarize the action more clearly and succinctly?
3. How can my introduction and conclusion be improved?
4. When I discuss each character, what examples do I use of that character's speech and behavior?
5. What corrections should I make in grammar, usage, word choice,
   spelling, capitalization, and punctuation?

EXERCISE 4 **Writing and Revising a Paper About a Dramatic Scene.**
Using your work for Exercise 3, write a short paper about the scene you
chose from *Julius Caesar* or from another play. Be sure to include a thesis
statement that expresses your idea about how the scene fits into the play.
Summarize the action in the scene, and discuss the characters, quoting
their significant statements. End by restating your main idea in an interesting way.

Writing About a Poem

For some people writing about a poem is an act akin to stuffing a bird of paradise. Perhaps you too have wondered how you can write about a poem without losing the wonder you felt when you first read it. Remember that the best reason for writing about a poem is to discover what sparked your wonder in the first place. Does understanding a poem automatically destroy its magic? Not at all—just as understanding a friend does not necessarily destroy a friendship. Respond to the poem thoughtfully, and you will keep its magic alive.

Prewriting: First Responses to a Poem

You should begin to think about a poem by reading it several times out loud. A poem is meant to be heard. As you read aloud the poem, think about what it means.

Next, try freewriting or brainstorming about the poem. Here is a sample of freewriting about a poem by Philip Booth entitled "First Lesson." Before you read the sample, look at the poem itself, which appears in the Writer's Sourcebook on page 379. Read the poem several times before you read the prewriting notes below.

> *A father talks to his daughter, teaching her how to float. He reassures her, speaks calmly, simply (repeats words to soothe her?) so that she will never be afraid of the ocean. "First Lesson"—could it be more than a swimming lesson? Sounds like he's talking about more than swimming—maybe life itself. Is he telling her to trust life, accept it, not to fear it? Is he right?*

Prewriting: Exploring a Poem

Once you have expressed your first thoughts about a poem's meaning, you can think specifically about how the poet created that meaning and prompted your response. Here is a brief review of the techniques poets use to shape meaning and response:

1. The **speaker** of the poem is the special voice that the reader hears in the poem.
2. The poet may use any number of **sound effects**, including the **repetition** of certain words or phrases; **rhyme**—the repetition of similar sounds; **rhythm**—the pattern of stressed and unstressed syllables; **onomatopoeia**—imitation of a sound by a word or phrase; **alliteration**—the repetition of initial consonant sounds; **consonance**—the repetition of internal consonant sounds; and **assonance**—the repetition of vowel sounds.

3. A poem's **images** are its concrete sensory details.
4. A poet may also create meaning by using **figures of speech**. A **simile** compares two unlike items using the word *like* or *as*. A **metaphor** compares two unlike things without using these words. **Personification** describes an animal or object as if it had human traits.

You can explore a poem by asking questions like the following ones. The answers shown here for the poem "First Lesson" help explore the poet's use of various techniques to create meaning:

QUESTIONS TO EXPLORE A POEM	SAMPLE ANSWERS FOR "FIRST LESSON"
1. Who is the speaker in the poem? What is the speaker doing?	*He is a father speaking to his daughter. They are in a tidal basin as he teaches her to float.*
2. What words or phrases are repeated? What ideas or feelings does the poet emphasize with this repetition?	*Lie, hold (held), let, back, wide--all create a feeling of trust and calm, reassure the daughter of her father's protection and love.*
3. What rhymes do I notice? what effects do these rhymes have?	*"I told you"/"sea will hold you"-- emphasizes that the daughter should trust the sea; also links father with sea (IMPORTANT?)!!!!*
4. How can I describe the rhythm? What effect does it create?	*Short lines, mostly short words, conversational rhythm. Soothing without being singsongy.*
5. What other sound devices do I notice? What do these add to the poem's meaning?	*Use of i sounds--lie, side, high, I, survive, light-year--assonance; open sound--idea of being open to life?*
6. What do the poem's images make me see, hear, smell, taste, touch? What do the images add to the meaning?	*I see the seashore, gulls, water, stars; I feel the hand cupping the head, the water supporting the girl, the cramp of fear. Mixture of tranquil and menacing images.*
7. What figures of speech do I notice? What might they mean?	• *"dead-/man's float"--metaphor for despair?* • *"cup of my hand"—metaphor, comforting* • *"light-year stars"—metaphor suggesting vastness, eternity of nature (including the sea)*

Prewriting: Main Idea and Support

After answering your exploring questions, you are ready to decide on the main idea that you will present. The statement of your main idea will announce how various poetic techniques create the poem's meaning, as in the following example:

> In "First Lesson" the speaker, images, and figures of speech all suggest that it is best to accept life calmly and without fear.

EXERCISE 5 **Prewriting for a Paper About a Poem.** Plan to write about a poem of your own choosing. Begin by reading the poem several times. Freewrite or brainstorm about your first response to the poem. Then write answers to exploring questions like those shown above. Using your freewriting and your answers to exploring questions like those shown on page 324, write your main idea about the poem's meaning.

Writing About a Poem: Structure

The suggestions given here apply specifically to writing a paper about a poem. For additional help in writing a paper about a literary work, refer to pages 315–316.

When you write about a poem, your thesis statement should indicate what you think the poem means and should identify the techniques that you think contribute most to that meaning. The body of your paper should discuss each of the techniques that you mention in your thesis statement.

Be sure to quote exactly from a poem and to use the poet's original capitalization and line breaks. Integrate poetry quotations of three lines or less into your text, enclosing such short quotations in quotations marks and marking ends of lines with a slash, as in this example: "You will dive/ and swim soon enough. . . . " Set quotations of four or more lines apart from the text by skipping a line and indenting and single-spacing the quotation. Quotation marks are not used when you do this.

Conclude your paper with a paragraph that refers once more to your thesis. You might end by stating your overall feeling about the poem.

Model of an Essay About a Poem

The following paper discusses "First Lesson." Note how the writer used his freewriting, exploring questions, and main idea in writing this paper:

"First Lesson"

A Philip Booth's poem "First Lesson" seems to be a simple lesson about swimming, but it actually turns out to be a lesson in living. In particular, the speaker, **images**, and figures of speech suggest the poem's deeper meaning: that we survive by accepting life, by being open to it rather than fearing it.

B The speaker is a father teaching his daughter to float. He begins by supporting her gently in the water, but by the poem's end he has let go with the words "As you float now, where I held you/and let go." He speaks to her gently, lovingly, and soothingly.

C As he gives his lesson, the speaker uses tranquil images of nature--the stream, the gulls, the sea, the "light-year stars"--to make his daughter feel easy in the water. Yet he also warns her with menacing images of human experiences in the sea: the dead-man's float, the long thrash, the heart cramped with fear. On one level these menacing images warn the daughter against making fatal mistakes when she is in the water: She should not give up, exhaust herself, or be afraid.

D In addition, the speaker means for his daughter to take his words figuratively, as metaphors for aspects of living. For example, the dead-man's float seems to be a metaphor for despair, and the "long thrash to your island" could refer to the long, hard struggle through life. In contrast, the stream and gulls can be seen as representing some of the best things in life--beauty, peace, and harmony. The speaker is using figurative language to tell his daughter that while many experiences will pain her, she should remember that there is more to life than suffering, and this knowledge will sustain her.

E This idea is reinforced by the moving figures of speech in the poem's last lines:

F . . . remember when fear cramps your heart what I told you: lie gently and wide to the light-year stars, lie back, and the sea will hold you.

In "the light-year/stars" the speaker suggests an
eternal calm, high above passing human trouble. In the
poem's last line he personifies the sea, turning it into
a parent cradling the girl. He is saying that she must
learn to trust the sea--that is, life itself--just as
she now trusts her father. Life will always be with her;
he will not.

G   Together the speaker, images, and figurative
language of "First Lesson" create the poem's special
lesson about living: As the speaker held his daughter,
so life will always hold her. And whenever she is
lonely, unhappy, or afraid, she will survive if she
remains open to life and accepts its support, just as
she rested in her father's hand one day by the sea.

NOTES ABOUT MODEL ESSAY ON A POEM

A The thesis statement expresses the poem's central idea and identifies three elements.

B Body paragraph 1 discusses the poem's speaker. Note the format for short quotations of poetry.

C Body paragraph 2 discusses the poem's imagery.

D Body paragraph 3 discusses the poem's figurative language.

E Body paragraph 4 expands on this discussion.

F Note the format for longer quotations of poetry.

G This paragraph restates the thesis and ends with a clinching sentence.

Revising, Editing, and Publishing

The following questions focus on revising a paper about a poem. For reminders about revising a paper on a literary work, see pages 317–318.

1. Where do I state my idea about the poem's meaning?
2. What specific poetic techniques do I discuss? How does each technique contribute to the poem's meaning and my response?
3. When I quote from the poem, do I write the words and lines exactly as the poet did?

EXERCISE 6 **Writing and Revising a Paper About a Poem.** Using the work you did for Exercise 5, write a short paper about the poem you chose. Be sure to include a thesis statement that expresses your idea about what the poem means and identifies the techniques that you think contribute most to that meaning. Include one body paragraph for each technique. End by restating your main idea in an interesting way.

Writer's Choice

Writer's Choice #1

ASSIGNMENT   To write a letter about a short story, scene, or poem

LENGTH   Your choice

AUDIENCE   The author of the work

PURPOSE   To explain your interpretation of the work and ask about an aspect of the work that intrigued or confused you

PREWRITING   Freewrite or brainstorm about the work, and ask exploring questions about it.

WRITING   Write your interpretation, and end by setting forth your question for the author.

REVISING   Be sure that your view of the work is clear and that you have made no mistakes in grammar, usage, word choice, spelling, or punctuation.

Writer's Choice #2

ASSIGNMENT   To write a paper about a story, dramatic scene or poem

LENGTH   Your choice

AUDIENCE   The editor of a high school literature textbook

PURPOSE   To persuade the editor to include the work in a literature textbook

OPTIONS   You may want to write further about one of the works you have read or written about in this chapter. You may want to write about an original story, scene, or poem of your own.
Be sure that your persuasive paper expresses your interpretation of the work and mentions why you think other students would enjoy it and benefit from reading it.

Writer's Choice #3

ASSIGNMENT   To compare two stories, scenes, or poems

LENGTH   Your choice

AUDIENCE   Your choice

PURPOSE   Your choice

OPTIONS   You may want to compare a work of your own choosing with one of the works you have already read or written about in this chapter. Or you may wish to choose two entirely different literary works to compare.
Be sure to choose two works that have something in common. For example, you might compare "First Lesson" with another poem in which a parent speaks to a child.

Writers on Writing

Helen Prior was a student at Conway High School in Conway, South Carolina, when she wrote this analysis of Nathaniel Hawthorne's story "Young Goodman Brown." Helen enjoys biking, reading, fashion design, and writing poetry.

THE PRODUCT

Here are the first two paragraphs from Helen's paper on "Young Goodman Brown."

> The short story "Young Goodman Brown" by Nathaniel Hawthorne contains extremely vivid descriptions of settings. The settings help depict the story's environment, but, more important, they provide information about Young Goodman Brown's emotional state. The story focuses on three significantly different settings: the path Brown takes, the Witches' Sabbath, and the calm woods. These settings represent the various stages Young Goodman Brown goes through on his journey from sin to evil to overpowering guilt.
>
> As Goodman Brown begins his journey down the path of evil, "darkened by all the gloomiest trees of the forest . . .," the story's ominous tone is set. Goodman Brown feels as if he is trapped within sin and evil. He wonders "if the devil himself should be at his very elbow." As he is led down this path by the devil and temptation, all of Goodman Brown's faith is lost. He soon finds himself "deep into the heathen wilderness." This path leads him through "the heart of the dark wilderness" to the core of evil within himself.

THE PROCESS

When I first read "Young Goodman Brown," its symbolism intrigued me. I was also very interested in Young Goodman Brown's personal experience of evil and its relation to the changing scene of the story. I wanted to show how the setting was symbolic of Brown's emotions as he experienced evil.

After I chose my topic, I began rereading the story and selecting phrases that Hawthorne used to describe the setting and Brown's emotions. Then I began constructing my paper in an outline and planning the order in which I would present the changes in setting. I also began incorporating into my outline the quotations that I extracted from the story. I feel that these are extremely important. When I began writing the paper, it was much simpler to refer to my outline and elaborate on it than it would have been to just begin writing without these notes.

YOUR TURN *Writing About Setting*

Choose a short story or novel in which the setting is very important, and show how the setting helps to express the work's theme or affects its outcome. Be sure to include quotations from the literary work in your essay.

Writers on Writing

While attending Socastee High School in Myrtle Beach, South Carolina, Sonja Kerby wrote the following analysis of John Steinbeck's novel The Pearl. *Sonja plans to study journalism and become a professional writer.*

THE PRODUCT

In the following short essay, Sonja discusses the development of the character of Kino in *The Pearl*.

Throughout *The Pearl* Kino experiences numerous emotions, coming out a different man by the novel's end. In the beginning of the book, Kino is satisfied with life. The Song of the Family flows strong and true through him. Each part of the whole of his life—the rhythm of the grinding stone, the flicker of the cooking fire, the smell of the corncakes, the creak of his son's cradle, the safety, the warmth—plays its role in the Song of the Family; each makes life happy and good.

Then the evil of the "Pearl of the World" that Kino finds begins to destroy his happiness. The pearl creates hope and determination in Kino, but it also leads to greed and hatred in him and in other people. The pearl instills want in Kino. He wants everything the pearl can give him, his wife, and his son. He is determined to let nothing stand in his way. When someone tries to steal his pearl, Kino feels hate, and the Song of Evil becomes intermixed with the Song of the Pearl. Because of the pearl, Kino kills a man, sees his house burn down, and is forced to flee from the village with his family. Then the final evil occurs. Kino's son, Coyotito, for whom Kino wanted to use the pearl to create a better life, dies because of the pearl.

Kino emerges from this final evil a new man. He has created a shell around himself. He is immune to emotion. Both he and his wife, having passed through pain and emerged whole, seem to be set apart from human experience. They toss the pearl and its evil back into the sea. As Kino has changed, so too has the Song of the Family changed. Where it once was a joyful harmony made of several parts, it has become a fierce battle cry.

THE PROCESS

I chose to write about John Steinbeck's *The Pearl* because it tells of a person going through an ordeal and coming out a wiser man. I decided to approach the composition about Kino chronologically, relating Kino's emotions before the change in his life, during the change, and after the change.

When I write, I find it easiest to go directly into the drafting stage in order to get my ideas flowing. I may jot down a few ideas beforehand, but most of my ideas come during the writing itself. When my thoughts come to a standstill, I return to the beginning and read and revise what I have already written. In this way I get my ideas flowing again.

This method requires writing many drafts, but the rewriting and revising help to produce a better final draft. At times I throw out whole sentences and write new ones. Because of all my rewording, my final draft looks very different from my rough draft, but this usually means that it is better, too.

YOUR TURN *Writing About Change in a Character*

As Sonja did, choose a short story or novel in which a character undergoes a significant change of some kind. After making your selection, write an essay explaining how and why that character changes. Be sure to use examples and quotations from the short story or novel.

CHAPTER *16*

Creative Writing

It begins with a character, usually, and once he stands up on his feet and begins to move, all I do is trot along behind him with a paper and pencil trying to keep up long enough to put down what he says and does.

—*William Faulkner*

Creative writing is writing in which an author invents characters, situations, images, and emotions and puts these inventions into stories, novels, plays, and poems.

What makes your imagination—or Faulkner's or anybody's—begin to create? Sometimes seeing a photograph in a magazine sparks you to imagine a story or scene; other times you see the photograph but just turn the page. Sometimes seeing stark November trees makes you think of candles whose flames have just been blown out; other times you see only bare branches.

You may already have your own way of encouraging your imagination to create characters, situations, and images, or you may simply trust to luck and the accidents of art. Either way, the following pages will provide you with a few options and methods for sparking your imagination throughout the writing process.

This chapter will focus on these types of creative writing:

    prewriting, writing, and revising a short story
    prewriting, writing, and revising a dramatic scene
    prewriting, writing, and revising a poem

As you use the writing process to create stories, scenes, and poems, you may find that you are becoming less dependent on luck to fire up your imagination. Strangely enough, the more creative writing you do, the more quickly your imagination will seem to take off on its own.

Writing a Short Story

Like William Faulkner you might start to write a story by imagining a character, or you might begin by picturing an intriguing place or problem. Your story might also grow from a small moment in your own life—a gesture, a comment, a smile—that somehow tugs at your imagination and makes it invent a story.

No matter how you write, you will be constructing your story from the following elements, which are present in all stories:

1. a **plot**—a sequence of events that build to a **climax**, or high point. Your plot will develop a **conflict**, or problem. Conflict may occur between an individual and an outside force such as nature or society, between two people, or within one individual.
2. one or more **characters**, who should have believable personalities and clear motivations for their actions
3. a **setting**—a specific time and place in which the story occurs
4. a **narrator** through whom you tell your story. A **first-person narrator** is a character in the story; a **limited third-person narrator** relates the thoughts of only one character; an **omniscient narrator** relates the thoughts of several characters.
5. a **theme**—an idea about life or an impression of life suggested by the specific situation, people, and environment of your story

Prewriting: Generating Ideas for a Story

Begin to write your story by generating story ideas. Conjure up interesting people, places, and situations. Page through magazines for photographs, and create ministories around them. Sift through your own experiences for moments worth expanding into stories. Then make a chart like the one shown here:

CHART OF STORY IDEAS

SITUATION/PROBLEM	CHARACTER(S)	SETTING
Crossing a street alone	Small boy	City neighborhood
Watching young players	Former football star	High school field
A camping trip	Two inexperienced campers	Woods at night
A writing contest	Two rivals	Classroom after school
Culture shock	Alien	Suburban shopping mall
A faulty computer	Three astronauts	Space shuttle
A poisonous snake	Two hunters	Jungle
Stepping into a movie	Shy young man	Theater showing Raiders

EXERCISE 1   **Prewriting: Generating Ideas for a Story.** Generate ideas for a story by making the kind of chart shown just above. You can use the Writer's Sourcebook (pages 380–383) as one source of ideas.

Prewriting: Exploring Ideas for a Story

You are now ready to explore one of your story ideas. Imagine how the characters look and behave; picture their environment. You can use questions like the ones shown here to prompt you as you explore your ideas. Note how the writer applied these questions to the third idea on the chart.

STORY IDEA: *Two inexperienced campers in the woods on a camping trip*	
QUESTIONS TO EXPLORE A STORY IDEA	SAMPLE ANSWERS
1. Why would I like to explore this idea?	*Could use bits of my own experience; also could be funny*
2. What is the *conflict?*	*Individuals against nature? Also, one character could be gung-ho about camping and the other unenthusiastic.*
3. Who are my main *characters?* How old are they?	*Marggy and her friend Liz, both 16*
4. What do they look like—height, weight, coloring, features, clothing?	*Liz: short, thin, dark; short, curly black hair; large eyes; glasses.* *Marggy: tall, a bit stocky, fair with freckles; long blond hair, conservative clothes*
5. What are their personalities like? How do they speak and act?	*Liz: energetic, lively; seeks adventures; speaks and moves impulsively; often interrupts Marggy.* *Marggy: more reflective, slower-moving, sedentary; likes to read*
6. What is the *setting*--locale, season, weather?	*Marggy's suburban home; then woods for campout; late summer--hot*
7. What *point of view* would work well for this story?	*Try first-person narrator--Marggy*
8. What *theme* might this story express? How?	*The story might show why opposite types of people (Liz and Marggy) need each other in spite of (or because of?) their differences.*

Prewriting: Developing a Story Outline

You may want to organize your thoughts by writing an outline of the main events in your story's plot. This will help you to clarify your plot and identify your main characters. The writer planning the story about the camping trip followed a standard outline:

I. Beginning
   A. Introduce the main characters.
      Marggy, the first-person narrator, introduces herself and her more adventurous friend Liz.
   B. Describe the setting.
      It is late summer in a suburban community near the woods; the weather is hot, the atmosphere oppressive.
   C. Establish the basic situation.
      In search of adventure, Liz persuades reluctant Marggy to join a group on a hiking and overnight camping trip although neither girl has ever camped before.

II. Middle
   A. Introduce the conflict or problem.
      Exhausted from the hike, the girls struggle unsuccessfully to pitch their tent and cook.
   B. Show the characters in action reacting to the problem.
      Marggy blames Liz for getting her into "this mess." She is uncomfortable in the tent. Liz, uncomfortable herself, becomes defensive.
   C. Lead up to the climax.
      Rain begins to fall, flooding the tent and adding to Marggy's misery. The girls leave the tent to huddle under a tarp on a picnic table. Then it begins to thunder and lightning.

III. End
   A. Present the climax.
      Marggy discovers that Liz is petrified of lightning.
   B. Wind down the action.
      Marggy reassures Liz, who falls asleep.
   C. Present the final outcome.
      Marggy realizes that Liz can be vulnerable underneath her bold front; she values Liz's friendship more.

EXERCISE 2 **Prewriting: Exploring and Outlining a Story Idea.**
Choose one story idea from the chart that you created in Exercise 1. Decide on the kind of reader that you think might enjoy a story based on this idea. Explore your story idea by asking questions like those shown on page 334. Then outline the main events of your story. Make sure that you include information about the main characters as well as the plot.

Writing the First Draft of a Story

Use the following suggestions to help you write your first draft.

BEGINNING

Let your narrator introduce the characters and place them in the setting in a way that catches your reader's attention. If the narrator is a character, make the narrator's words convey his or her personality. For first-person narrators, use first-person pronouns (*I, me*) throughout; for third-person or omniscient narration, use third-person pronouns (*he, she, it, they*).

In the following lines the writer developing the idea about the camping trip gets her story off to a good start.

> I am not the adventurous type. My idea of a wilderness experience would be sleeping in my own bedroom with all the windows open. My friend Liz is another story—Liz craves adventure.
>
> This is Liz: short and dark with curly black hair and huge aviator glasses. She's superactive—eats a lot and never gains weight. I (my name is Marggy, pronounced MAR-ghee) am tall, blond, and slow moving. I eat a lot and *do* gain weight. We've been friends forever, but we are totally different. Last summer I learned to appreciate our differences.
>
> One hot day in August, Liz barged into my house.

CHARACTERIZATION AND DIALOGUE

Let your characters' words and actions speak for themselves. Instead of saying "Liz was impatient," let Liz *show* her impatience by interrupting or gesturing.

Including **dialogue**, or conversation between characters, makes a story more vivid because it presents the characters' own words. Remember:

1. Place all words spoken by characters within quotation marks. A direct quotation can come at the beginning or end of a sentence.
2. Begin a direct quotation with a capital letter. If you interrupt the quotation in midsentence, begin the second part with a small letter.

3. Begin a new paragraph each time you switch speakers.
4. Set off direct quotations with commas.

Here is an example of dialogue:

> Liz bubbled, "Sheila's mother is taking some girls on a campout and she's asked us to go—isn't that *great?*"
>
> "But Liz—"
>
> "Oh, Marggy, don't tell me you don't want to," Liz raced on. "It would do us good. It'll be an adventure."
>
> Wrong, I thought. But what I said was, "Hey, can't we just *imagine* that we did it?"
>
> Liz shook her head. "Marggy," she asked solemnly, "do you want to grow old *before your time?*"

SUSPENSE, CLIMAX, AND RESOLUTION

Build **suspense**, or tension, as your story develops the conflict and rises to the point of highest interest. Try to make each character's behavior consistent with his or her personality. As your story nears its end, present the climax, the story's peak. Then wind down by resolving the conflict. You might conclude by showing what each character has learned:

> The sky ripped with lightning and roared with thunder. Liz jumped.
>
> "What's the matter?"
>
> "Nothing," said Liz, closing her eyes tightly. "Nothing."
>
> There was another lightning flash, and she jumped again. I realized that she was afraid of lightning but was trying not to show it. So I went on casually, "You know, you can tell how close lightning is by counting the seconds between the flash and the thunder. Five seconds equals a mile. I usually count seconds by chimpanzees."
>
> Liz still had her eyes squeezed shut. There was a new flash. I began to count, "*One* chimpanzee, *two* chimpanzees, *three* chimpanzees—" thunder. I said, "That's threefifths of a mile. It's going away."
>
> Liz opened her eyes and looked at me. "Really, Marggy?" she asked. She seemed to relax a little.
>
> We "chimpanzeed" together through a few more flashes, and then she fell asleep. As she slept, I wondered how many other terrors my friend had kept hidden, and I felt a new respect for her craving for adventure. And Liz was right: We *had* had an adventure. Although I'd been miserable most of the time, I would probably look back on it fondly. Strange. I must have drifted off myself just after the sun rose.

TITLE

Write a title that sparks readers' interest. It might refer to an important event, character, place, or theme in the story. For example, the author of the story about Liz and Marggy chose the title "The Call of the Wild."

Revising, Editing, and Publishing a Story

Once you have finished your first draft, you need to take time to improve your story until it satisfies you. Read your story out loud, and then use this checklist to help you revise, edit, proofread, and publish your writing:

Checklist for Revising, Editing, and Publishing a Story

1. What details describe the setting?
2. What phyisical details depict the characters? What personality traits do they display, and what words and actions convey these traits? What motives lie behind each character's actions?
3. What point of view does the story use? Does the story stay within that point of view?
4. What conflict does the story present, develop, and resolve?
5. How is each event connected to what happens before and after?
6. Where do I use dialogue? How can I make it sound more true to life? Do I use the correct format for each quotation?
7. What is the climax of the story? How is the conflict resolved?
8. Is the language concrete and vivid?
9. Is each sentence a complete sentence? Have I avoided errors in verbs, pronouns, and modifiers?
10. Have I correctly capitalized and punctuated each sentence? Are all the words correctly spelled?
11. What might be a good forum for sharing my finished story—showing it to friends and teachers? Entering it in a contest?

EXERCISE 3 **Writing, Revising, and Sharing a Story.** Write a short story using the notes and outline that you created for Exercise 2. Then use the preceding checklist to revise and edit your first draft. Make a finished copy of your story, proofread it, and present it to an audience.

Writing a Dramatic Scene

A *dramatic scene* consists entirely of dialogue and action. You might think of a scene as a story minus the narrator. For example, the following passage dramatizes part of "The Call of the Wild":

> [*Lightning and thunder. Liz jumps.*]
> MARGGY. What's the matter?
> LIZ. Nothing. [*Closing her eyes tightly.*] Nothing.
> [*Lightning and thunder again. Liz jumps again. Marggy realizes that Liz is frightened but is trying to hide it.*]

As you see, Marggy no longer functions as a narrator, telling us what happened; instead, we see the action as it occurs. The narration is either dropped or written in the form of stage directions.

Although a scene follows a format that is different from that of a story, it consists of most of the same elements:

1. The **plot** of a scene pivots on a **conflict** of some kind, most often a conflict between individuals. As the characters work through their conflict, the scene builds to a **climax**.

2. You need at least two **characters** for a dramatic scene. These characters reveal themselves entirely through their dialogue and behavior. **Stage directions** describe the characters' actions and sometimes their motives.

3. The **setting** of the scene is also described in the stage directions. Stage directions provide more detailed information about the scenery, furniture, and lighting. Stage directions also specify the **props**, or items used by the characters in the scene.

Prewriting: Generating Ideas for a Scene

When you generate ideas for a dramatic scene, remember that you will need at least two characters. Look for contrast—people who are strikingly different. Record potential scene ideas:

CHART OF SCENE IDEAS

FIRST CHARACTER	SECOND CHARACTER	CONFLICT
Candidate	Makeup artist (disagrees with candidate)	Preparation for television debate
Quiet college student	Noisy roommate	Studying vs. playing music
Robot worker	Human partner	Communication gap
Famous woman from literature or history	Famous man from literature or history	Blind date
Nervous young man	Woman with a cat	Trapped in an elevator
High school student	High school teacher	Deciding whether to go to college or not
Rock guitarist	Symphony violinist	Mistaken identity

EXERCISE 4 **Prewriting: Generating Ideas for a Scene.** Generate ideas for a scene by making a chart. Photographs in the Writer's Sourcebook (pages 380–383) might be a source of ideas.

Prewriting: Exploring Ideas for a Scene

Look over your chart, choose the idea that appeals to you most, and begin to explore it. Imagine your characters in the situation that has created their conflict. You can use questions like the ones shown here to help you explore an idea for a scene. These questions are applied to the fourth idea from the preceding chart:

SCENE IDEA: *Two famous people from history on a blind date*	
QUESTIONS TO EXPLORE A SCENE IDEA	**SAMPLE ANSWERS**
1. Who are the characters? How old are they?	*Emily Dickinson: nineteenth-century American poet; in her thirties Cyrano de Bergerac: seventeenth-century French writer and soldier; in his forties*
2. What do they look like—height, weight, coloring, features, clothing?	*Emily: small; light-brown hair in a bun; intelligent face; wears a simple white dress with a lace collar Cyrano: tall; dark; huge nose; sword; shabby, once-elegant black velvet cape*
3. What are their personalities like?	*Emily: intelligent, witty, very shy Cyrano: brilliant, romantic, flamboyant*
4. How do they speak and act?	*Emily: speaks softly, hesitantly; makes small movements; looks away often Cyrano: speaks boldly; moves grandly*
5. What does each want in the scene?	*Emily: to run away Cyrano: to break through Emily's shyness*
6. Where does the scene take place? How is it lit? What props do the characters use?	*In a library: bookshelves, table. Dim, warm lighting. As identification Emily carries a handkerchief; Cyrano carries a black hat with a white plume.*

Prewriting: Developing a Scene Outline

You may want to organize your thoughts by writing an outline of the main events in your scene. The writer planning the scene about Emily Dickinson and Cyrano de Bergerac wrote the following outline. Notice that it follows the same sequence as the story outline on page 335.

I. Beginning
   A. Establish your characters' identities and their relationship to one another.
      Emily and Cyrano meet and identify each other.
   B. Introduce the problem or conflict.
      Emily's shyness and Cyrano's contrasting flamboyance emerge through dialogue; each is lonely and wants to meet a kindred spirit.

II. Middle
   A. Present the characters' reactions to the conflict.
      Emily, uncomfortable, wants to end the meeting; Cyrano, intrigued, tries to prolong it.
   B. Build toward the point of highest interest, or climax.
      Cyrano charms Emily, but she becomes more intent on escaping.

III. Ending
   A. Reach the point of highest interest.
      As Emily tries to leave, Cyrano gallantly saves her from some toppling books.
   B. Show the characters' reactions at the climax.
      Cyrano is knocked unconscious; Emily is moved and grateful; Cyrano recovers.
   C. Present the final outcome.
      Emily bandages Cyrano's head with her kandkershief; she agrees to go with him to a poetry reading.

EXERCISE 5 **Prewriting: Exploring and Outlining a Scene Idea.**
Choose one of the scene ideas that you generated in Exercise 4, and think of an audience to whom that scene might appeal. Then explore your idea with questions like those shown on page 340. Finally, outline the scene's action.

Writing the First Draft of a Scene

You can use the following suggestions to help you write your first draft.

CAST OF CHARACTERS

List your characters in the order of their appearance with some identification of each, as in this example:

    EMILY DICKINSON Nineteenth-century American poet
    CYRANO DE BERGERAC Seventeenth-century French poet and soldier

SETTING THE STAGE

As the beginning of the scene, write stage directions describing what the audience sees on stage: the scenery, furniture, and lighting. Explain which characters are on stage, and describe them briefly. Write the stage directions in brackets, as shown on the following page.

[*A public library. There is a long table center stage with empty chairs on one side of it and bookshelves on the walls. The lighting is dim, except for the area around one end of the table. Emily Dickinson stands here. She seems to be in her thirties; she is small and intelligent looking. She wears a long white dress and carries a letter along with a white handkerchief, which she twists nervously. She starts to leave, heading left. Suddenly Cyrano de Bergerac bounds in, almost knocking her over. He appears to be in his forties. He is tall and thin, with a prominent nose. He wears a sword and a shabby black cape. He also carries a letter and a black hat with a long white plume.*]

DIALOGUE AND ACTION

On the next line write the name of the first character to speak and that character's first line of dialogue. Use stage directions to indicate how the character speaks and moves. Then begin the other character's first speech on a new line:

> CYRANO. A thousand pardons! [*He leans on the table to catch his breath and then spots Emily's handkerchief. He checks his letter.*] Ah! You are Mademoiselle Dickinson? [*He has a slight French accent.*]
>
> EMILY. [*Sees the plumed hat and checks her letter.*] And—you—[*Clearing her throat.*] you are [*Looking away.*] Mister—de Bergerac?

CONFLICT AND CLIMAX

Follow your outline, using dialogue and stage directions to introduce the problem or conflict. Clearly develop the sequence of events. Build interest as your scene leads to its high point, or climax. Then present the climax:

> EMILY. Mister de Bergerac, I, really must, ah, leave—so sorry—[*She looks around her, determined to go.*]
>
> CYRANO. [*Shaking his finger at Emily but smiling.*] No, Mademoiselle, you cannot go yet. You promised in your letter that you would read me some of your charming poetry, and so far I have heard no poetry. You are a lady of your word, no?
>
> EMILY. [*Charmed in spite of herself, with a little smile.*] Yes, but, well, you see— [*Twists the handkerchief.*] I—cannot—utter my poetry. I, ah, write it down. Hardly anyone has ever seen my—work. It is so difficult for me.
>
> [*Unable to say any more, she suddenly bolts, knocking over an unsteady bookcase. Just in time, Cyrano pulls her aside and is hit himself. He crashes to the floor.*]

RESOLUTION

Show the characters' reactions to the climax. Then wind down the action, and present the ending. Write final stage directions at the end.

> [*Horrified, Emily rushes to Cyrano's aid, dabbing at his head with her handkerchief. He opens his eyes.*]
>
> EMILY. [*Startled.*] Oh, Mister de Bergerac, you are so brave! Are you—your head is—oh dear!

CYRANO. [*Smiling weakly.*] It is the merest nothing. A tiny wound. I would have endured a thousand more for the sake of so charming a lady. [*A pause. They smile at each other. She bandages his head.*]

CYRANO. *Merci,* Mademoiselle. And now I suppose I must let you go. "Parting is such sweet sorrow." That is Shakespeare. Regrettably, I cannot at the moment recall an opportune line of my own.

EMILY. [*Looks down shyly and whispers.*] "Parting is all we know of heaven/And all we need of hell."

CYRANO. [*Looks at her closely.*] So sad. But so brilliantly expressed. May I ask who is the poet?

EMILY. I . . . it is a line of my own.

CYRANO. [*Delighted.*] So! You have spoken your poetry to me at last. [*They smile again. Emily helps Cyrano to his feet.*] My dear Miss Dickinson, may I presume to invite you to accompany me to a poetry reading at a place not far from here?

EMILY. Oh, my dear Mister de Bergerac, I think—I think it is the least I can do for so—*gallant* a gentleman! [*Cyrano offers his arm to Emily. She hesitates, then smiles and accepts it. They walk slowly out of the light.*]

TITLE

Choose a title for your scene. The title may refer to the situation, characters, setting, or a line of dialogue. For example, the author of the scene involving Cyrano de Bergerac and Emily Dickinson decided to emphasize their relationship by entitling the scene "Kindred Spirits."

Revising, Editing, and Publishing

Once you have finished your first draft, you need to revise and edit your scene until it satisfies you. Read your scene out loud. If possible, do a dramatic reading with friends. Then use the following checklist to revise and edit your writing.

✔ Checklist for Revising, Editing, and Publishing a Scene

1. At the beginning of the scene, have I clearly listed and identified each character and described the scenery?
2. What personality traits does each character display in the scene? How can the dialogue and stage directions convey these traits more clearly?
3. What conflict does the scene present, develop, and resolve? How can I sharpen the presentation of this conflict?
4. What moment is the climax of the scene? How is the conflict resolved?
5. Have I used the correct format for dialogue and stage directions?
6. Have I avoided errors in verbs, pronouns, and modifiers?
7. Are my capitalization, punctuation, and spelling correct?
8. What might be the best way of presenting my scene to an audience— an informal reading? A full staging with costumes?

EXERCISE 6 **Writing, Revising, and Publishing a Scene.** Write a dramatic scene, using the notes and outline that you created for Exercise 5. Use the checklist to edit your first draft. Make a finished copy of your scene, and proofread it. Present the scene in a reading or a performance.

Writing a Poem

A poem can be slight or profound, simple or intricate. Still, no matter what you might think a poem is, you can usually recognize one when you see it, for poetry has its own distinct qualities:

1. A poem communicates its meaning largely through **images**—specific, concrete details appealing to the senses of sight, hearing, smell, taste, and touch.
2. Poetry can also use **figures of speech** to go beyond the literal facts. A **simile** compares two seemingly unlike items by using the words *like* or *as*. A **metaphor** links two unlike things without using such words. **Personification** lends human qualities to animals, objects, or ideas.
3. A poem puts together special **sound effects**. Not every poem uses all of these sound effects, but most use at least some of them. They can include **repetition, rhyme,** and **rhythm**. They also can include **onomatopoeia**, the imitation of a sound by a word; **alliteration**, the repetition of initial consonant sounds; **consonance**, the repetition of internal consonant sounds; and **assonance**, the repetition of vowel sounds.
4. Every poem has an overall pattern, or **form**. Some poems are divided into **stanzas**, or groups of lines.

Prewriting: Generating Ideas for a Poem

Anything can give you an idea for a poem. In the following section you will generate ideas for a poem by experimenting with imagery, figures of speech, and sound effects.

IMAGERY

Images are sensations expressed in words. Practice using concrete, vivid images by listing different images for one item, such as an apple:

ITEM	SENSE	IMAGE
An apple	Sight	Shiny red globe
	Sound	A soft crunch
	Smell	Fresh
	Taste	Sweet, tangy
	Touch	Crisp, smooth skin; juicy

FIGURATIVE LANGUAGE

Figurative language stretches literal reality in a vivid, memorable way. Notice what the following figures of speech do for summer:

SIMILE   In March summer shimmers in the distance like a mirage.

METAPHOR   Summer is an oven in which we bake happily.

PERSONIFICATION   On a warm May day summer seems to dance with spring.

SOUND EFFECTS

You might be inspired to write a poem simply because you like the way certain words sound together. For example, you might experiment with **alliteration**, as in the following example:

Fran *phoned*—she *found* a *freckled fritata* in her *fridge*.

You might also try echoing the sound of an item with **onomatopoeia**, as the following sentence does:

The chick *cheeped* and *skittered* in the nest; the hen *clucked* and *squawked* at him.

You can create more subtle sound effects with **consonance**, which repeats internal consonant sounds, and **assonance**, which repeats vowel sounds. Consonance and assonance make the words sound as if they belong together. Note how the following sentence is knit together by consonance (here, the repetition of *d*, *n*, and *l* sounds) and assonance (the repetition of *i* sounds):

Hidden in the box, the little tin soldier jingled still.

EXERCISE 7   **Generating Ideas for a Poem with Imagery.** Choose one of the following items or an item of your own. Make a chart like the preceding one, listing images to describe your item. Appeal to at least three different senses. Save your notes.

1. soup   3. ice   5. a watermelon
2. leather   4. the ocean   6. a coin

EXERCISE 8   **Practicing with Figurative Language to Generate Ideas.** Choose one of the following numbered sets of items, or invent a set of your own. Write a simile for the item in the left-hand column and a metaphor using the middle item. Then personify the item in the righthand column. Save your notes.

1. the wind   the rain   the sun
2. an antique chair   a grandfather's clock   an old house
3. sadness   joy   love

EXERCISE 9   **Practicing with Sound Effects to Generate Ideas.** Choose two of the following items, or supply two items of your own. Then write a sentence about each. Use onomatopoeia and alliteration in one sentence and consonance and assonance in the other. Save your notes for a poem that you may write later on.

1. an out-of-tune piano   3. sleet   5. a motorboat
2. popcorn   4. leaves   6. a schoolyard

Charting to Generate Ideas for a Poem

If you have difficulty finding a subject for a poem, you could make a chart like the following one. As you see, each entry in the right-hand column represents a potential subject for a poem:

CHART OF IDEAS FOR A POEM

GENERAL CATEGORY	SPECIFIC SUBJECT FOR A POEM
A person (you, a friend, a star)	*King Tut*
An animal (real or imaginary)	*My cats, Lance and Lola*
An object (natural or artificial)	*Glass paperweight with falling snow*
A scene (remembered or invented)	*First view of the Rockies*
An event (remembered or invented)	*A day in the life of a genie*
An emotion	*Regret*

EXERCISE 10 **Charting to Generate Ideas for a Poem.** Make a chart like the one shown here. For each general category fill in one specific item about which you could write a poem. You might find ideas in the Writer's Sourcebook (pages 380–383). Save your notes.

EXERCISE 11 **Compiling Your Ideas for a Poem.** Review the notes you created in Exercises 7–10. Star six ideas that you would like to use when you write poetry.

Prewriting: Exploring Ideas for a Poem

Decide on a subject for your poem, and then explore that subject by asking questions like the ones shown in this chart:

POEM IDEA: *Glass paperweight with falling snow*	
QUESTIONS TO EXPLORE AN IDEA FOR A POEM	SAMPLE ANSWERS
1. Why do I want to write about this subject?	*The paperweight was special to me as a child; I still have it.*
2. What do I see, hear, smell, taste, and touch when I imagine the subject?	*Clear crystal ball fits in my palm; filled with water; drifting snow; smiling snowman.*
3. What emotions does the subject evoke in me?	*Remembrance of childhood; sense of loss; intense nostalgia*
4. What figures of speech could I use?	*Compare it to something that traps the past in the present; snowman--myself as a child, maybe?*
5. What alliteration, onomatopoeia, and other sound effects could I use?	• *"Smiling snowman, swirling snow"--alliteration* • *"I see a child whose smile I know"--assonance, consonance*
6. What word or phrases could I repeat?	*"turn and turn and turn again; make the snowflakes fall"*

EXERCISE 12 **Exploring an Idea for a Poem.** Plan to write a poem of any length. You may use rhyme if you like, but you need not. You can work with one of the ideas that you starred in Exercise 11 or a new idea altogether. Think about who you want to read your poem. Then explore your idea using questions like those shown above.

Writing the First Draft of a Poem

In your first line identify your subject, using concrete language and sensory details. Try to choose words that sound as if they belong together. This poem uses rhyme and a regular rhythm, but your poem need not:

> A childhood friend: an old glass ball,
> A smiling snowman, sighing snow.
> Turn, and turn, and turn again—
> Make the snowflakes fall.

In the lines that follow your first lines, use ideas, images, figures of speech, sound effects, and patterns that you discovered as you generated and explored ideas for your poem.

> Sealed inside the old glass ball
> I see a child whose smile I know.
> Turn, and turn, and turn again—
> Make the snowflakes fall.
> I feel time bend and make me tall;
> I feel my childhood sigh and go.
> Turn, and turn, and turn again—
> Make the snowflakes fall.

When you have finished writing, choose an appropriate title. The author of the poem about the paperweight decided on the title "Snowboy."

Revising, Editing, and Publishing

Read your poem out loud, and ask yourself these questions:

 Checklist for Revising, Editing, and Publishing a Poem

1. To what senses do the images in my poem appeal? Which images can I sharpen or intensify?
2. What figures of speech have I used? Which sound effects?
3. Which words or phrases do I repeat? Should I repeat any?
4. What form have I used? Have I followed it consistently?
5. Do the words of my poem seem to belong together?
6. Have I used correct spelling and punctuation in my poem?
7. How should I present my poem?

EXERCISE 13 **Writing, Revising, and Publishing a Poem.** From the notes that you created in Exercise 12, write a poem. You may use any form; you can use rhyme if you like, but you are not required to do so. Read your first draft aloud, and revise it.

Writer's Choice

Writer's Choice #1

ASSIGNMENT To write a short story or dramatic scene

LENGTH Your choice

PURPOSE To re-create an actual event, altering that event

AUDIENCE Your choice

PREWRITING Choose an event, either from your own life or from history. Decide whether you want to convert it into a story or scene, and follow the appropriate prewriting suggestions presented in this chapter. When you write your plot outline, decide the specific ways in which you will alter the actual event.

WRITING Follow the suggestions for writing a story or a scene. If you are writing about a historical event, be sure to identify that event for your reader.

REVISING Have you altered the actual event? Does your story or scene hang together on its own? Proofread your final copy. Then share your work with your audience.

Writer's Choice #2

ASSIGNMENT To write a poem of three to five stanzas

LENGTH Your choice

PURPOSE To express an emotion

AUDIENCE Your choice

PREWRITING Decide on the emotion that you want to express and decide on the form that your poem will follow. Think about the images, figures of speech, and sound effects that you will use.

WRITING Write your poem, using notes made during prewriting.

REVISING Read your poem aloud. Does it evoke the emotion you had in mind? Be sure to proofread your final copy; then present it to your chosen audience.

Writer's Choice #3

ASSIGNMENT To write a story, scene, or poem

LENGTH Your choice

PURPOSE Your choice

AUDIENCE Your choice

OPTIONS You might use a story, scene, or poem idea that you generated but did not explore in this chapter. You might also use the Writer's Sourcebook (pages 380–383) as a source of material.

Whatever you write, follow the prewriting, writing, and revising steps presented in this chapter.

Writers on Writing

Susan Appel feels lucky to have attended schools that encouraged her passion for writing. As a student at Indian Hill High School in Cincinnati, Ohio, Susan wrote the following poem and commentary.

THE PRODUCT

Walk with me
Through the web
of eternity.
For it is a maze
5 as
Time has no pattern.
It is
shapeless
planeless
10 infinite.
All that once was
is
and
will be.

There is no past
no present
no future.
They are the same,
just carbon copies
20 given different names.
The light slowly recedes
Into the deep ocean of the sky
Taking with it
Warmth and sound
25 And, suddenly, it is
cold and clear and
Silent.
Then, the night noises come.
Darkness creeps quietly in.

THE PROCESS

I'd never thought much about the concept of time until last year when I read Arthur C. Clarke's *Childhood's End,* but now my thoughts often drift back to time. At first I tried to write a paragraph, but structured sentences didn't seem to express my view of time.

Once I began the poem, it just flowed from me—almost as though someone were writing it through me. I did have a few problems, though. Originally, I did not include the lines "For it is a maze/as." In revising I saw that the first three lines didn't fit the rest of the poem. Yet line 6 wasn't a proper beginning. So I came up with a hook, which is now lines 4 and 5. Also, when I first added line 4, I'd repeated the word *web.* But a web is precise, and I was trying to describe clutter. I finally came up with *maze*— which is still not perfect, but does suit my purpose.

I am reasonably pleased with this draft of the poem. However, I don't want to call it a "final draft." It is as final as I can make it right now, but eventually I'll be able to go back and improve it.

YOUR TURN *Writing a Poem*

As Susan Appel did, choose an abstract subject such as time, love, or joy, and write an unrhymed poem about it.

CHAPTERS 13–16
WRITING ACROSS THE CURRICULUM

CHAPTER 13   WRITING ABOUT SOCIAL STUDIES

Focusing a Topic [pages 286–287]

1. Which of the following topics is most narrowly focused?
   (a) Cultures of West Africa: The Benin People (b) West African Kingdoms (c) Art and Sculpture of the Benin People

Evidence and Sources [pages 288–289]   Tell whether the item is (a) a primary source, (b) a secondary source, (c) a fact, or (d) an opinion.

2. A biography of Queen Elizabeth II of England
3. A letter in Queen Elizabeth's handwriting
4. It is a fact that Queen Elizabeth is loved by all her subjects.
5. Queen Elizabeth II began her reign in 1952.

Making Generalizations   [pages 289–290]

6. Which of the following statements is properly qualified?
   (a) Prince Henry dominated the Age of Exploration.
   (b) Prince Henry supported all the major voyages of exploration.
   (c) Prince Henry of Portugal, a major figure in the Age of Exploration, supported many of the most important voyages.

Organization [pages 291–295]   Tell whether the statement demonstrates (a) chronological order, (b) cause and effect, (c) comparison, or (d) contrast.

7. Garibaldi's vision was a strong force leading to a united Italy.
8. Unlike those in power, Garibaldi took strong and swift action.
9. Two weeks after landing in Sicily, Garibaldi set up a government.
10. Nationalism was growing in Germany just as it was in Italy.

Writing for Review Write a paragraph about a social studies topic of your own choice. Follow the complete writing process.

CHAPTER 14   WRITING A SCIENTIFIC OR TECHNICAL REPORT

Topic and Purpose [pages 299–230]   Indicate the letter of the item that correctly answers each question.

1. Which topic is more suitable for a scientific or technical report?
   (a) how holographs are made
   (b) visiting the Museum of Holography
2. Which purpose would probably suit this topic best?
   (a) to contrast (b) to classify (c) to explain a process

Structure [pages 304–305] Match each part of a scientific or technical report in the left column with the appropriate phrase in the right.

3. Introduction   (a) This report recommends . . .
4. Bibliography entry   (b) For example, Alpha Centauri, . . .
5. Conclusion   (c) This paper will discuss . . .
6. Discussion   (d) (Jameson, 1983, p.96)
7. Internal source citation   (e) Sagan, Carl, *Cosmos* . . .

Style, Tone, and Mechanics [pages 304–305] Indicate which form is correct for items 8, 9, and 10—the *a* form or the *b* form.
Earwigs (*usually, I guess*) grow to a length of between
        8. (a)   8. (b)
(*six-tenths and one, .6 and 1*) centimeters (cm). A few ear-
   9. (a)   9. (b)
wigs grow as long as (*1.5 cm, one and a half centimeters*).
         10. (a)   10. (b)

Writing for Review   Write an introductory paragraph for a paper about a scientific or technical subject of your own choosing.

CHAPTER 15   WRITING ABOUT LITERATURE

Writing About a Story and Scene [pages 313–322] Indicate the letter of the item that correctly answers each question.

1. Which is the best topic for a paper about "The Open Window"?
   (a) Why I hate all horror stories   (c) the narrator's change of tone
   (b) Nuttel as narrator   (d) Saki's life
2. If you were writing a paper about "The Open Window," what term would you use to describe Vera?
   (a) courageous (b) pretty (c) truthful (d) self-possessed
3. If you were planning a paper about Act II, Scene ii, of *Julius Caesar,* which question would you ask about Caesar?
   (a)Why does he go to the Capitol?   (b) What battles did he win?
4. Whom or what could you contrast in a paper about Act II, Scene ii, of *Julius Caesar*?
   (a) Caesar and Brutus   (c) ancient Rome and modern America
   (b) Calpurnia and Decius (d) Brutus' and Anthony's speeches

Writing for Review   Write a short essay about "First Lesson" or about a poem of your own choosing. Follow the writing process.

CHAPTER 16   CREATIVE WRITING

Writing for Review   Write a story, scene, or poem about something that you would like to happen. If you choose to write a story or scene, decide on your setting and characters, and outline your plot. If you choose to write a poem, decide on the poetic techniques that your poem will use.

WRITER'S SOURCEBOOK

The Writer's Sourcebook is a collection of illustrations and assignments that correspond to many of the chapters in Part 1: Composition. For example, as shown in the contents below, the Writer's Sourcebook opens with a section called "The Writing Process and Style," which presents paintings, photographs, and assignments coordinated with the first two units of the book.

Using the Writer's Sourcebook

You may work with the Writer's Sourcebook in a variety of ways:

> Just looking through the Writer's Sourcebook may help you generate ideas for writing.

> You may respond to specific material in the Writer's Sourcebook by completing the assignment suggested for each illustration.

> Illustrations from the Writer's Sourcebook will help you to complete certain Writer's Choice assignments, which appear regularly throughout Part 1: Composition.

For instance, in responding to Writer's Choice #5 in the chapter on narrative writing, you may choose the option that refers you to the photographs headed "Narrative Writing" in the Writer's Sourcebook. You may then write a narrative based on the action you see in the photographs.

Writer's Sourcebook Contents

THE WRITING PROCESS AND STYLE

1

2

3

Winslow Homer (1836–1910), detail, *Long Branch, New Jersey*, 1868.
Oil on canvas. H. 16 in. W. 21¾ in.

4

ASSIGNMENTS

Generating Ideas in Prewriting (*pages 23–32*). Choose three illustrations on pages 354–355 and use techniques of prewriting, such as freewriting, brainstorming, and charting, to generate several writing ideas for each. Write down all your prewriting thoughts and writing ideas.

Writing a Variety of Topic Sentences (*page 49*). Choose a new topic or use one based on the writing ideas that you developed in the assignment above, and write two different topic sentences for a paragraph.

Using Order of Importance (*pages 65–66*). Write a paragraph about painting 4 using order of importance to organize the paragraph. Make sure your paragraph is unified and coherent.

5

The illustrations on these two pages complement the instruction in Chapters 1–6.

1

Winslow Homer (1836–1910). *Long Branch, New Jersey*. 1868. Oil on canvas. H. 16 in. W. 21 34 in.

2

3

ASSIGNMENTS

Revising Support, Development, and Organization *(pages 77–78)*. If you wrote a paragraph based on painting 4 on page 355, rewrite it now. Base your revisions on the painting as it is shown in illustration 1, page 356. Revise for correct support, sufficient development, and logical organization.

Using Vivid and Precise Words to Evoke a Mood or Atmosphere *(pages 102–106)*. Write a descriptive paragraph that uses colorful and concise words to evoke the mood of one of the illustrations on pages 354–357. Include sensory language and figures of speech.

Writing Concise Sentences *(pages 127–128)*. Write one compact and direct sentence for each of five illustrations on pages 354–357. Make your sentences concise by removing unnecessary or repetitious language and by simplifying long structures.

4

The illustrations on these two pages complement the instruction in Chapter 1–6.

1

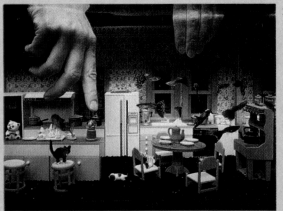

2

Francisco de Goya (1746–1828). *Don Manuel Osorio Manrique de Zuniga.* Oil on canvas. H. 50 in. W. 40 in.

3

4

He Dog (*Sunka Bloka*), a subchief. Cut Meat District. 1900. (John A. Anderson Collection #918.)

ASSIGNMENTS

Using Spatial Order (*page 149*). Write a descriptive paragraph about the fish tank pictured in photograph 2. Begin with a topic sentence, and then use spatial order to arrange the details that support your topic sentence. Be sure to use spatial transitions to add coherence to your sentences.

Using Descriptive Language (*pages 150–152*). Use exact and vivid language to write a paragraph that describes painting 3. Make an observation table (page 146), and fill in columns for at least three different senses. Bring the subject to life by including in your paragraph a variety of sensory details and figures of speech.

Creating an Overall Impression (*pages 147–148*). Write a paragraph about the impression created in photograph 1. Freewrite for one minute. Then write a topic sentence stating the overall impression, and develop the paragraph by discussing specific supporting details. Use vivid, exact language to capture the scene.

Describing a Person (*pages 155–156*). Write a character sketch of the person in photograph 4. Begin with a topic sentence in which you express an overall impression. Then describe the individual's physical traits. Finally, discuss the psychological traits that the picture suggests. Try to show a connection between the inner and the outer person.

The illustrations on these two pages complement the instruction in Chapter 7.

NARRATIVE WRITING

1

ASSIGNMENTS

Prewriting for a Narrative *(pages 163–165).* Study one of the two sequences on pages 360–361. Then use the questions *Who? What? When? Where? Why?* and *How?* to generate and explore ideas for writing a nonfiction narrative about the sequence.

Preparing a Narrative Outline *(pages 166–170).* Make a narrative outline for one of the sequences on pages 360–361. First state the purpose of the narrative. Then list the events in chronological order. Be sure to include descriptions of characters and setting.

Writing a Narrative in Chronological Order *(pages 168–169).* Write a narrative about one of the sequences on pages 360–361. Include all the elements of a narrative (plot, setting, and point of view), as well as specific details presented with descriptive language. Write your narrative in chronological order, using transitions to help your reader follow the sequence of events.

Using Vivid Verbs and Narrative Details to Convey Action *(pages 175–176).* Revise the narrative you wrote for the assignment above. First, replace any weak verbs with vivid, precise verbs. Then add narrative details that will make your narrative richer and more informative.

The illustrations on these two pages complement the instruction in Chapter 8.

2

EXPOSITORY WRITING

John Sloan, *Backyards, Greenwich Village*, 1914. Oil. H. 26 in. W. 32 in. Collection of Whitney Museum of Modern Art.

Thomas Birch (1779–1851). Skating. Oil on canvas. H. 20 in. W. 30 in.

1

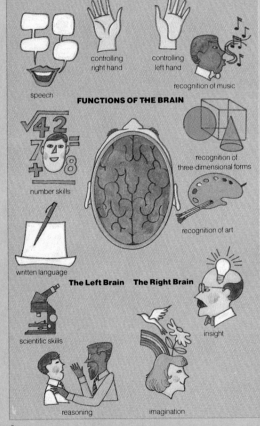

FUNCTIONS OF THE BRAIN

controlling right hand

controlling left hand

recognition of music

speech

number skills

recognition of three-dimensional forms

recognition of art

written language

The Left Brain   The Right Brain

insight

scientific skills

reasoning

imagination

2

3

ASSIGNMENTS

Writing About Cause and Effect *(pages 189–192).* Write a paragraph about the causes and effects shown in illustration 3.

Dividing Items *(pages 192–194).* Use spatial order to show in a paragraph how the diagram in illustration 2 has been divided into sections.

Comparing and Contrasting Items *(pages 200–203).* Using a comparison frame (p. 201), write a comparison-contrast based on illustration 1.

The illustrations on these two pages complement the instruction in Chapter 9.

CRITICAL THINKING AND
PERSUASIVE WRITING

1

2

3

4

ASSIGNMENTS

Selecting a Topic and Suiting Topic to Audience (*pages 211–215*). Study the photographs on pages 364–365, and write down an opinion to use as the basis for a persuasive paragraph. Next, determine your audience by responding to the profile questions on page 214.

Identifying Facts and Opinions (*pages 215–217*). Gather evidence about your topic. Then make a list of facts and a list of opinions that directly support your opinion about the environment. Eliminate any inadequate and unreliable evidence.

Writing an Argument (*pages 217–221*). First state your opinion clearly. Then give your audience any background information necessary to understand your opinion. Present your evidence in order of importance or in some other logical order. Use transitions to help your readers follow each step you take. State your conclusion in one sentence.

The illustrations on these two pages complement the instruction in Chapter 10.

WRITING ABOUT SOCIAL STUDIES

THE INDUSTRIAL REVOLUTION IN EUROPE ABOUT 1870

MILES 0 — 300
KILOMETERS 0 — 480

★ MAJOR INDUSTRIAL CITIES

■ IRON ORE DEPOSITS

● COAL FIELDS

NORWAY

SWEDEN

NORTH SEA

DENMARK

★ Glasgow

★ Newcastle

★ Manchester

IRELAND

★ Liverpool

NETHERLANDS

★ Hamburg

GREAT BRITAIN

★ Birmingham

GERMANY

★ Berlin

London

BELGIUM

★ Dresden

RUSSIA

ATLANTIC OCEAN

Brussels

RUHR

Paris ★

SAAR

★ Frankfurt

AUSTRIA-HUNGARY

FRANCE

★ Vienna

SWITZERLAND

Lyons ★

★ Turin

ROMANIA

SERBIA

PORTUGAL

SPAIN

ITALY

OTTOMAN EMPIRE

MEDITERRANEAN

GREECE

The illustrations on these two pages complement the instruction in Chapter 13.

2

A Family Working Together to Make Cloth Before the Industrial Revolution

ASSIGNMENTS

Making Generalizations About Information in a Map (*pages 289–290*). Study the map shown in illustration 1, and form at least three generalizations based on the information it presents. Write a paragraph about your generalizations. Begin by stating the topic of the map. Then discuss the generalizations. Be sure to use appropriate qualifying words, such as *in most cases, some,* and *sometimes.*

Writing with Comparison and Contrast (*pages 293–295*). Write a paragraph contrasting illustrations 2 and 3. Base your writing on a list of differences (page 293). End with a general statement that unites your points of contrast in one observation.

3   Courtesy of Victoria and Albert Museum, London.

Cotton Made on a Cotton Mill During the Industrial Revolution.

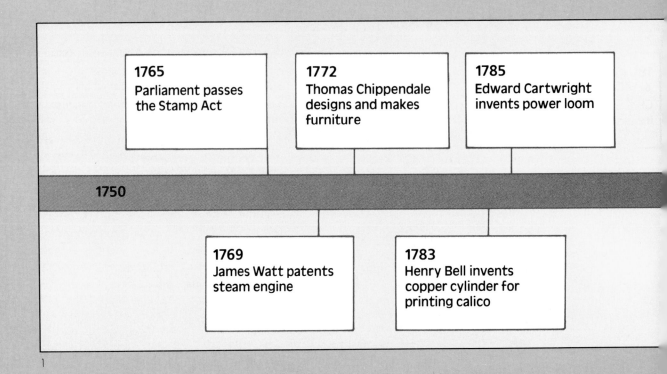

1

ASSIGNMENTS

Writing Chronologically About Events in a Time Line (*pages 291–292*). Study the time line in illustration 1, and, as prewriting, list the events that helped to advance the industrial revolution in Europe. Then write a paragraph about these events in chronological order, using transitions that show the sequence of time.

Writing About Causes and Effects (*pages 292–293*). Study both the graph shown in illustration 2 (page 369) and the map shown in illustration 1 (page 366). As prewriting, answer the following questions: Which countries have the greatest amount of railroad track? Which countries have the most coal and iron deposits? Do countries without coal and iron ore deposits have railroads? Using your answers, write a paragraph about the cause-and-effect relationship between amount of track and amount of coal and iron ore deposits.

The illustrations on these two pages complement the instruction in Chapter 13.

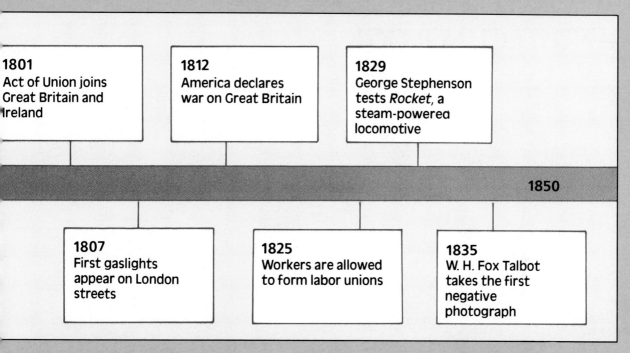

1801
Act of Union joins Great Britain and Ireland

1812
America declares war on Great Britain

1829
George Stephenson tests *Rocket*, a steam-powered locomotive

1850

1807
First gaslights appear on London streets

1825
Workers are allowed to form labor unions

1835
W. H. Fox Talbot takes the first negative photograph

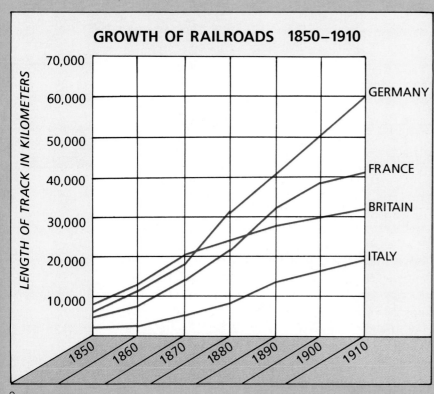

GROWTH OF RAILROADS   1850–1910

LENGTH OF TRACK IN KILOMETERS

70,000
60,000
50,000
40,000
30,000
20,000
10,000

GERMANY
FRANCE
BRITAIN
ITALY

1850 1860 1870 1880 1890 1900 1910

2

WRITING ABOUT SCIENCE AND TECHNOLOGY

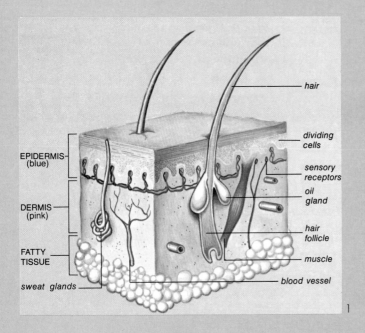

EPIDERMIS (blue)

DERMIS (pink)

FATTY TISSUE

sweat glands

hair

dividing cells

sensory receptors

oil gland

hair follicle

muscle

blood vessel

1

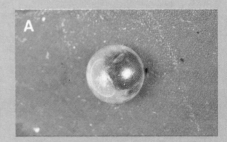

A

B

2

The illustrations on these two pages complement the instruction in Chapter 14.

ASSIGNMENTS

Writing a Description for the Discussion Section of a Scientific Report (*page 303*). Assume that you are writing a short report about the body's largest single organ, skin. You have written the introduction to your report, and you are ready to begin the discussion (or body). Your outline calls for a description of a section of human skin.

Write a paragraph that describes concisely the section of skin shown in illustration 1. As prewriting, list the components of the epidermis, dermis, and fatty tissue. You may want to use spatial order to organize your paragraph. The tone of your paragraph should be serious, objective, and impersonal.

Explaining a Process in a Scientific Report *(page 300)*. Illustration 2 shows the complete metamorphosis of a butterfly: A. egg, B. larva, C. pupa, and D. adult. Assume that you are writing a brief report on insects that experience complete metamorphosis (beetles, butterflies, flies, and bees). You have reached the point on your outline where it calls for an explanation of the four stages in a butterfly's life.

As prewriting, list the stages in chronological order. Then fill out a chart like the one on page 186. You may also want to prepare definitions of *complete metamorphosis, larva,* and *pupa* as a part of prewriting. Finally, write a paragraph explaining the process. Use transitions to make your explanation coherent.

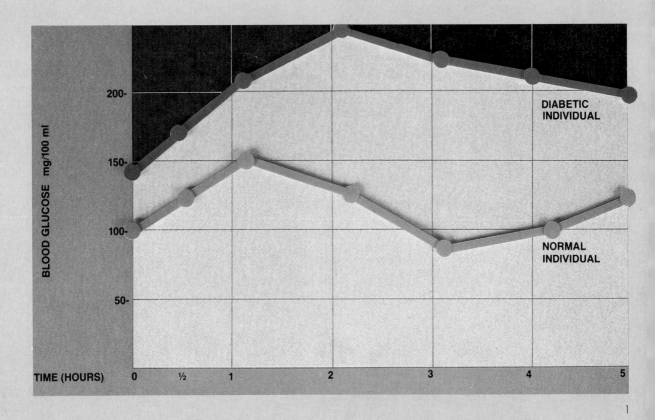

BLOOD GLUCOSE mg/100 ml

200-

150-

100-

50-

TIME (HOURS) 0   ½   1   2   3   4   5

DIABETIC INDIVIDUAL

NORMAL INDIVIDUAL

1

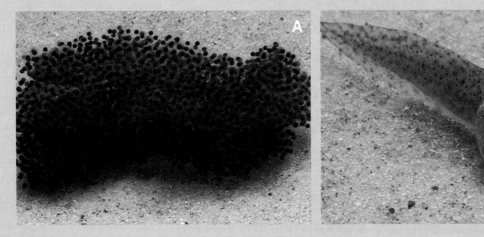

A

B

2

The illustrations on these two pages complement the instruction in Chapter 14.

ASSIGNMENTS

Writing About Causes and Effects (*page 300*). Say that you are writing a report about diabetes mellitus and are discussing the graph shown in illustration 1. Study the graph. The blue line represents a normal individual, and the purple line represents an individual with diabetes mellitus. Each was given 50 g of glucose in 200 mL of water before eating anything that day.

As prewriting, make notes on what happens to the blood glucose concentration in each person. Where on the graph does each person's insulin begin to affect the blood glucose concentration? Use your notes to write a paragraph about the cause-and-effect relationship shown in the graph.

Comparing and Contrasting Items (*page 300*). As prewriting, briefly explain the process shown in illustrations 2A, B, C, and D. Then compare and contrast this process with the butterfly metamorphosis shown in illustrations 2A, B, C, and D on pages 370–371. Write a paragraph about your findings.

WRITING ABOUT LITERATURE

Saki

The Open Window

"My aunt will be down presently, Mr. Nuttel," said a very self-possessed young lady of fifteen. "In the meantime you must try and put up with me."

Framton Nuttel endeavored to say the correct something which should duly flatter the niece of the moment without unduly discounting the aunt that was to come. Privately he doubted more than ever whether these formal visits on a succession of total strangers would do much towards helping the nerve cure which he was supposed to be undergoing.

"I know how it will be," his sister had said when he was preparing to migrate to this rural retreat; "you will bury yourself down there and not speak to a living soul, and your nerves will be worse than ever from moping. I shall just give you letters of introduction to all the people I know there. Some of them, as far as I can remember, were quite nice."

Framton wondered whether Mrs. Sappleton, the lady to whom he was presenting one of the letters of introduction, came into the nice division.

"Do you know many of the people round here?" asked the niece, when she judged that they had had sufficient silent communion.

"Hardly a soul," said Framton. "My sister was staying here, at the rectory,[1] you know, some four years ago, and she gave me letters of introduction to some of the people here." He made the last statement in a tone of distinct regret.

"Then you know practically nothing about my aunt?" pursued the self-possessed young lady.

"Only her name and address," admitted the caller. He was wondering whether Mrs. Sappleton was in the married or widowed state. An undefinable something about the room seemed to suggest masculine habitation.

"Her great tragedy happened just three years ago," said the child; "that would be since your sister's time."

"Her tragedy?" asked Framton. Somehow in this restful country spot tragedies seemed out of place.

"You may wonder why we keep that window wide open on an October afternoon," said the niece, indicating a large French window[2] that opened on to a lawn.

"It is quite warm for the time of the year," said Framton; "but has that window got anything to do with the tragedy?"

"Out through that window, three years ago to a day, her husband and her two young brothers went off for their day's shooting. They never came back. In crossing the moor[3] to their favorite snipe-shooting[4] ground they were all three engulfed in a treacherous piece

---

1. **rectory:** house of a clergyman.
2. **French window:** floor-length hinged window that opens outward.
3. **moor:** area of open, often marshy land.
4. **snipe-shooting:** Snipe is a popular game bird.

The literary works presented here complement the instruction in Chapter 15.

of bog.[5] It had been that dreadful wet summer, you know, and places that were safe in other years gave way suddenly without warning. Their bodies were never recovered. That was the dreadful part of it." Here the child's voice lost its self-possessed note and became falteringly human. "Poor aunt always thinks that they will come back some day, they and the little brown spaniel that was lost with them, and walk in at that window just as they used to do. That is why the window is kept open every evening till it is quite dusk. Poor dear aunt, she has often told me how they went out, her husband with his white waterproof coat over his arm, and Ronnie, her youngest brother, singing, 'Bertie, why do you bound?' as he always did to tease her, because she said it got on her nerves. Do you know, sometimes on still, quiet evenings like this, I almost get a creepy feeling that they will all walk in through that window—"

She broke off with a little shudder. It was a relief to Framton when the aunt bustled into the room with a whirl of apologies for being late in making her appearance.

"I hope Vera has been amusing you?" she said.

"She has been very interesting," said Framton.

"I hope you don't mind the open window," said Mrs. Sappleton briskly. "My husband and brothers will be home directly from shooting, and they always come in this way. They've been out for snipe in the marshes today, so they'll make a fine mess over my poor carpets. So like you menfolk, isn't it?"

She rattled on cheerfully about the shooting and the scarcity of birds, and the prospects for duck in the winter. To Framton it was all purely horrible. He made a desperate but only partially successful effort to turn the talk on to a less ghastly topic. He was conscious that his hostess was giving him only a fragment of her attention, and her eyes were constantly straying past him to the open window and the lawn beyond. It was certainly an unfortunate coincidence that he should have paid his visit on this tragic anniversary.

"The doctors agree in ordering me complete rest, and absence of mental excitement, and avoidance of anything in the nature of violent physical exercise," announced Framton, who labored under the tolerably widespread delusion that total strangers and chance acquaintances are hungry for the least detail of one's ailments and infirmities, their cause and cure. "On the matter of diet they are not so much in agreement," he continued.

"No?" said Mrs. Sappleton, in a voice which only replaced a yawn at the last moment. Then she suddenly brightened into alert attention—but not to what Framton was saying.

"Here they are at last!" she cried. "Just in time for tea, and don't they look as if they were muddy up to the eyes?"

Framton shivered slightly and turned towards the niece with a look intended to convey sympathetic comprehension. The child was staring out through the open window with dazed horror in her eyes. In a chill shock of nameless fear Framton swung round in his seat and looked in the same direction.

In the deepening twilight three figures were walking across the lawn towards the window. They all carried guns under their arms, and one of them was additionally

---

5. bog: marsh.

burdened with a white coat hung over his shoulders. A tired brown spaniel kept close at their heels. Noiselessly they neared the house, and then a hoarse young voice chanted out of the dusk: "I said, Bertie, why do you bound?"

Framton grabbed wildly at his stick and hat. The hall door, the gravel drive, and the front gate were dimly noted stages in his headlong retreat. A cyclist coming along the road had to run into the hedge to avoid imminent collision.

"Here we are, my dear," said the bearer of the white mackintosh,[6] coming in through the window; "fairly muddy, but most of it's dry. Who was that who bolted out as we came up?"

"A most extraordinary man, a Mr. Nuttel," said Mrs. Sappleton; "could only talk about his illness, and dashed off without a word of good-by or apology when you arrived. One would think he had seen a ghost."

"I expect it was the spaniel," said the niece calmly. "He told me he had a horror of dogs. He was once hunted into a cemetery somewhere on the banks of the Ganges[7] by a pack of pariah[8] dogs, and had to spend the night in a newly dug grave with the creatures snarling and grinning and foaming just above him. Enough to make any one lose their nerve."

Romance at short notice was her specialty.

---

6. **mackintosh:** raincoat worn in England, named for the inventor Charles Macintosh (1766–1843).
7. **Ganges** (gan'jez): river in northern India.
8. **pariah** (pari'a): outcast; here, wild.

William Shakespeare

from Julius Caesar

The literary works presented here complement the instruction in Chapter 15.

from Act II, Scene ii. CAESAR's house. Rome, 44 B.C.

> [It is early morning. CAESAR, an ambitious military leader and politician and the most powerful man in Rome, appears in his dressing gown. He intends to go to the Capitol soon. Like many other Romans who were awakened by a violent storm, he has spent a restless night. He is in an agitated state and paces about the room. There are still flashes of lightning and rumbles of thunder from the storm that raged during the night. CALPURNIA, CAESAR's wife, enters from her bedroom, alarmed at CAESAR's activity.]

CALPURNIA. What mean you, Caesar? Think you to walk forth?
You shall not stir out of your house today.

CAESAR. Caesar shall forth. The things that threatened me
Ne'er looked but on my back; when they shall see
5   The face of Caesar, they are vanished.

CALPURNIA. Caesar, I never stood on ceremonies,[1]
Yet now they fright me. There is one within,
Besides the things that we have heard and seen,
Recounts most horrid sights seen by the watch.[2]
10   A lioness hath whelped[3] in the streets,
And graves have yawned, and yielded up their dead;
Fierce fiery warriors fought upon the clouds
In ranks and squadrons and right form of war,
Which drizzled blood upon the Capitol;...
15   O Caesar, these things are beyond all use,[4]
And I do fear them...

CAESAR. Yet Caesar shall go forth; for these predictions
Are to the world in general as to Caesar.[5]

CALPURNIA. When beggars die, there are no comets seen;
20   The heavens themselves blaze forth the death of princes.

CAESAR. Cowards die many times before their deaths;
The valiant never taste of death but once.
Of all the wonders that I yet have heard,
It seems to me most strange that men should fear,
25   Seeing that death, a necessary end,
Will come when it will come....

---

1. **stood on ceremonies:** believed in omens.
2. **watch:** night watchman.
3. **whelped:** given birth.
4. **use:** normal experience.
5. **Are...Caesar:** apply to everyone else as much as they apply to me.

CALPURNIA. Alas, my lord,
　　Your wisdom is consumed in confidence.
　　Do not go forth today. Call it my fear
30　That keeps you in the house and not your own.
　　We'll send Mark Antony to the Senate House,
　　And he shall say you are not well today.
　　Let me, upon my knee, prevail in this. *[She kneels.]*

CAESAR. Mark Antony shall say I am not well,
35　And for thy humor[6] I will stay at home.

　　[CAESAR helps CALPURNIA rise as the conspirator DECIUS enters. He has been sent to
　　make certain that CAESAR goes to the Capitol.]

　　Here's Decius Brutus, he shall tell them so.

DECIUS. Caesar, all hail! Good morrow, worthy Caesar;
　　I come to fetch you to the Senate House.

CAESAR. And you are come in very happy time
40　To bear my greeting to the senators,
　　And tell them that I will not come today.
　　Cannot, is false; and that I dare not, falser:
　　I will not come today. Tell them so, Decius.

CALPURNIA. Say he is sick.

CAESAR.　　　　　　　Shall Caesar send a lie!
45　Have I in conquest stretched mine arm so far
　　To be afeard to tell graybeards the truth?
　　Decius, go tell them Caesar will not come.

DECIUS. Most mighty Caesar, let me know some cause,
　　Lest I be laughed at when I tell them so.

50　**CAESAR.** The cause is in my will: I will not come.
　　That is enough to satisfy the Senate.
　　But for your private satisfaction,
　　Because I love you, I will let you know.
　　Calpurnia here, my wife, stays me at home.
55　She dreamt tonight she saw my statue,
　　Which, like a fountain with an hundred spouts,
　　Did run pure blood, and many lusty Romans
　　Came smiling and did bathe their hands in it.
　　And these does she apply for warnings and portents....

60　**DECIUS.** This dream is all amiss interpreted;
　　It was a vision fair and fortunate:
　　Your statue spouting blood in many pipes,
　　In which so many smiling Romans bathed,

---

6. humor: whim.

Signifies that from you great Rome shall suck
65   Reviving blood,...
This by Calpurnia's dream is signified.

CAESAR. And this way have you well expounded it.

DECIUS. I have, when you have heard what I can say;
And know it now, the Senate have concluded
70   To give this day a crown to mighty Caesar.
If you shall send them word you will not come,
Their minds may change. Besides, it were a mock
Apt to be rendered, for someone to say
"Break up the Senate till another time,
75   When Caesar's wife shall meet with better dreams."
If Caesar hide himself, shall they not whisper
"Lo, Caesar is afraid"?
Pardon me, Caesar, for my dear dear love
To your proceeding bids me tell you this,
80   And reason to my love is liable.[7]

CAESAR. How foolish do your fears seem now, Calpurnia!
I am ashamèd I did yield to them.
Give me my robe, for I will go.

---

7. liable: subservient: Decius is saying that his love of Caesar makes him speak the truth, even if he is overstepping himself.

Philip Booth

First Lesson

Lie back, daughter, let your head
be tipped back in the cup of my hand.
Gently, and I will hold you. Spread
your arms wide, lie out on the stream
5 and look high at the gulls. A dead-
man's-float is face down. You will dive
and swim soon enough where this tidewater
ebbs to the sea. Daughter, believe
me, when you tire on the long thrash
10 to your island, lie up, and survive.
As you float now, where I held you
and let go, remember when fear
cramps your heart what I told you:
lie gently and wide to the light-year
15 stars, lie back, and the sea will hold you.

CREATIVE WRITING

1

2

ASSIGNMENTS

Exploring and Outlining a Story Idea (*pages 334–335*). Select a photograph from pages 380–383, and use it to answer the questions for exploring a story idea (page 334). Then write an outline of the events in the story's plot.

Writing a Story (*pages 336–338*). Write a story based on your work for the assignment above. Your story should include the following elements: characterization, dialogue, suspense, climax, resolution, and a title.

Generating Ideas for a Scene (*page 339*). Complete a chart of scene ideas (page 339) using three photographs from pages 380–383. You will need at least two characters, since a scene consists entirely of dialogue and action.

3

The illustrations on these two pages complement the instruction in Chapter 16.

The illustrations on these two
pages complement the instruction
in Chapter 16.

3

ASSIGNMENTS

Exploring and Outlining a Scene Idea *(pages 340–341)*. Look over the chart you made for the previous assignment, and choose the idea that you like best. Explore your idea with questions like those on page 340. After exploring your idea, outline the scene's action.

Writing a Dramatic Scene *(pages 341–344)*. Write a dramatic scene based on your work for the assignment above. Your scene should include setting, dialogue and action, conflict and climax, resolution, and a title.

Exploring Ideas for a Poem *(page 347)*. Select a photograph on pages 380–383, and use it to answer the questions for exploring ideas for a poem (page 347). Think about the audience you expect to read your poem. Your poem need not rhyme.

Writing a Poem *(page 348)*. Write a poem of any form and any length from the notes you created for the assignment above.

4

Identification of Writer's Sourcebook Illustrations

Pages 354–355—The Writing Process and Style: 1. Walking through wet city streets at dusk. **2.** Frankie and Johnnie, from the play *Him* by E. E. Cummings. **3.** Robots. **4.** Detail, Winslow Homer, *Long Branch, New Jersey,* 1868. Museum of Fine Arts, Boston. **5.** Sandstone pinnacles, Bryce National Park, Utah. **6.** Jackson Hole Airport, Wyoming. **Pages 356–357—The Writing Process and Style (continued): 1.** Winslow Homer, *Long Branch, New Jersey,* 1868. Museum of Fine Arts, Boston. **2.** Pandas at play. **3.** Mount Rushmore, South Dakota. **4.** Three young people playing Scrabble. **Pages 358–359—Descriptive Writing: 1.** Photograph by Walker Evans. **2.** Fully furnished fish tank. **3.** Francisco Goya, *Don Manuel Osorio Manrique de Zuniga.* Metropolitan Museum of Art, New York. **4.** He Dog (Sunka Bloka), a subchief, Cut Meat District, 1900. Nebraska Historical Society. **Pages 360–361—Narrative Writing: 1.** Collision of Mary Decker and Zola Budd at the 1984 Olympics in Los Angeles. **2.** Sand castle, perhaps of U.S. Capitol. **Pages 362–363—Expository Writing: 1. Top:** John Sloan, *Backyards, Greenwich Village,* 1914. H. 26. W. 32. Whitney Museum of American Art. **Bottom:** Thomas Birch, *Skating,* c. 1830. Museum of Fine Arts, Boston. **2.** Diagram of functions of the brain. **3.** Cyclone funnel. Paired with photo of wreckage caused by cyclone. **Pages 364–365—Critical Thinking and Persuasive Writing: 1.** Automobile dump. **2.** Monument Valley, Utah. **3.** Girl with antipollution mask. **4.** Bald eagle. **Pages 366–367—Writing About Social Studies: 1.** Map: The Industrial Revolution in Europe About 1870. **2.** A family working together to make cloth before the industrial revolution. **3.** Cotton made on a cotton mill during the industrial revolution. **Pages 368–369—Writing About Social Studies (continued): Top:** Time line—1750–1850. **Bottom:** Graph—Growth of Railroads 1850–1910. **Pages 370–371—Writing About Science and Technology: 1.** Cross section of human skin. **2.** Palamedes swallowtail—A. egg, B. larva, C. pupa, D. adult. **Pages 372–373—Writing About Science and Technology (continued): 1.** Graph—Blood Glucose Concentration. **2.** Leopard frog—A. egg mass underwater, B. tadpole, C. tadpole in metamorphosis, D. adult. **Pages 374–379—Writing About Literature:** Selected pieces of literature. **Pages 380–381—Creative Writing: 1.** Dramatization of *Anne of Green Gables* by L. M. Montgomery. **2.** Urban street scene: rainy day. **3.** Scene from the film *Mr. Deeds Goes to Washington,* starring Jimmy Stewart. **Pages 382–383—Creative Writing: 1.** Students building with playing cards. **2.** Three boys with schoolbooks and flowers. **3.** Trees and fences in mist. **4.** NASA drawing of a space center interior constructed from ore mined from the moon and designed to hold 10,000 people.

Grammar, Usage, and Mechanics

*Using our language: an assortment of lead type
for setting text by hand*

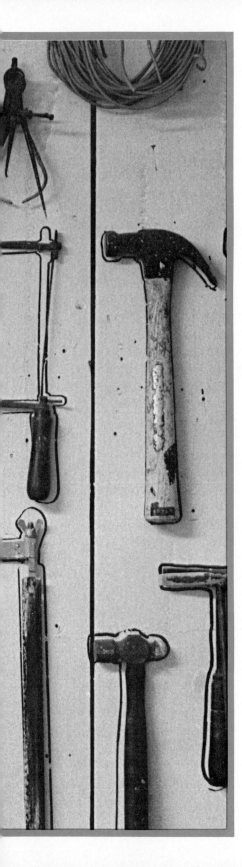

Grammar

Thinking About Thinking: Classifying Information

Suppose that you look at a group of words and you notice that some words perform one function (like naming a thing) and other words perform a different function (like describing a thing). You may say that therefore it would be logical to divide the words into two different groups. Grammar provides a useful structure for this kind of orderly thinking about words.

Defining the Skill

A specific thinking skill that is built into the study of grammar is CLASSIFYING INFORMATION. Classifying involves dividing information into groups, and it also reveals the relationships that hold the groups together.

Applying the Skill

Look at the photograph, and list on the board all the objects in the picture. Then divide the list into parts, grouping the objects that seem to share the same function. If you are not sure, guess according to what the objects look like. Then indicate which groups you would probably use at the same time.

Parts of Speech

The eight different kinds of words, or *parts of speech,* that you use every day are nouns, pronouns, verbs, adjectives, adverbs, prepositions, conjunctions, and interjections. Learning more about these parts of speech will be of great practical value to you.

The more you know about the parts of speech, the fewer errors you will make in speaking and writing. The more you know about what a particular part of speech can do, the more likely you are to build up your vocabulary of that kind of word. You will see that you can keep adding nouns, verbs, adjectives, and adverbs to your vocabulary. (It may surprise you to learn that you probably already know all the words that make up the other parts of speech.)

The following pages explain how to recognize each part of speech. Use this section when you are revising your writing to get quick, simple explanations of how the parts of speech work.

Nouns

A **noun** is a word that names a person, a place, a thing, or an idea.

A noun can name a person, place, or thing (living or nonliving) that occupies space.

PERSON	woman, man, boy, girl, baby, parent
PLACE	planet, island, farm, kitchen
LIVING THING	dolphin, parrot, ivy, hand
NONLIVING THING	book, calendar, telephone, stapler

A noun can also name something that does not occupy space. Not only can we say, "We know about that *city,*" but we can also say, "We know about *loyalty.*" In other words, some nouns allow us to take an aspect of experience—such as being loyal—and talk about it as though it were a thing to which we could actually point. Here are some other examples of nouns that do not occupy space:

Wednesday is my **birthday.**
We learned about Greek **philosophy.**
The **state** of her **health** is a **cause** of **anxiety.**
The **past** belongs to **memory.**

As you will learn in the subsections that follow, nouns may be divided into several different classes.

Recognizing Nouns

As you have just seen, you can classify a word as a noun if it names something. In addition, you can identify a word as a noun if it satisfies one of the following tests.

1. A word is a noun if it makes sense in one of the blanks in the following sentences.

    I have a(n) _____.
    We know about (the) _____.
    (The) _____ is (are) interesting.

2. The following suffixes almost always signal that a word is a noun: *-acy, -age, -cy, -dom, -ee, -ence, -ency, -er, -ery, -ess, -et, -ette, -hood, -ian, -ics, -ion, -ism, -ite, -ity, -let, -ment, -ness, -or, -ship, -tion.*

supremacy	marionette
marriage	robotics
excellence	communism
dependency	armament
eaglet	boldness

Nouns can be singular or plural, depending on whether they name *one* person, place, thing, or idea or *more than one.*

SINGULAR desk, bench, sky, wife, man
PLURAL desks, benches, skies, wives, men

(For rules on making the plural forms of nouns, see Chapter 29.)

Nouns have a form to show possession, ownership, or the relationship between two nouns.

SINGULAR	PLURAL
the girl's coat	the girls' coats
a prince's crown	the princes' crowns
a man's voice	men's voices

EXERCISE 1 **Identifying Nouns.** On your paper list the twenty nouns that appear in the following passage. Identify the nouns by finding the words that name something, by testing the words to see whether they make sense in any of the blanks in the sentences above, and by looking for words that end with noun-forming suffixes from the above list.

¹The British queen, Victoria, the very symbol of the empire for over sixty years, died in the first year of this century. ²Gradually, the British colonies gained independence and formed a federation of nations united under the merely symbolic powers of the monarchy. ³The national wealth and international influence that had been a British way of life were quickly becoming memories of the past. ⁴This decline was hastened by the two great wars.

EXERCISE 2 **Completing Sentences with Nouns.** On your paper complete each sentence by filling the blanks with nouns. Be sure that your completed sentences make sense. Try to use a variety of nouns to complete the sentences.

1. The two _____ bought new _____.
2. This green _____ comes from the _____.
3. The _____ watched a(n) _____.
4. Her _____ seems to be her worst _____.
5. Seven _____ sat on the _____.

Proper and Common Nouns

A **proper noun** is the name of a particular person, place, thing, or idea.

A **common noun** is the general—not the particular—name of a person, a place, a thing, or an idea.

The word *proper* comes from the Latin word *proprius,* which means "one's own." Therefore, a word that is "one's own"—such as a person's name—is considered *proper.* The important words in proper nouns are capitalized. (For rules on capitalizing proper nouns, see Chapter 26.) Common nouns are not capitalized.

PROPER NOUNS

PERSON   Dr. Gonzales, Aunt Shirley, Joan of Arc

PLACE   Mars, the Atlantic Ocean, the Bar-R-Ranch

THING   Black Beauty, the *Mona Lisa,* Flako soap, Thanksgiving Day, Scribner Educational Publishers

IDEA   Republicanism, Romanticism, the New Deal

EXERCISE 3   **Matching Proper Nouns with Common Nouns.** On your paper match the numbered proper nouns on the left with the lettered common nouns on the right.

1. Houston
2. *National Geographic*
3. Wheaties
4. Shakespeare
5. Barbra Streisand
6. Cadillac
7. Africa
8. the Grand Canyon
9. World Trade Center
10. Muhammad Ali

a. automobile
b. continent
c. landmark
d. magazine
e. skyscraper
f. author
g. athlete
h. city
i. cereal
j. singer

Collective Nouns

A **collective noun** names a group.

army	(the) public
team	(the) clergy
(a) pride (of lions)	committee
(the) staff (of a company)	choir

A collective noun may be considered either singular or plural. You consider a collective noun singular when you talk about a group as a whole. You consider a collective noun plural when you talk about the individual members of a group. (For help with subject-verb agreement with collective nouns, see Chapter 22.)

SINGULAR The **committee** wants our attention.
          The **class** likes to read plays.
PLURAL   The **committee** have gone their separate ways.
          The **class** take their seats.

EXERCISE 4 **Identifying Collective Nouns.** On your paper list the five collective nouns in the following paragraph.

¹After the crew of the merchant ship had finished their chores, they loved to watch the sea. ²Once at night a swarm of plankton made the ocean glow softly. ³A young sailor watched in amazement as a pod of feeding whales suddenly broke the calm surface. ⁴At another time, along the coast of California, the sailor spotted a herd of sea lions frolicking in the waves. ⁵The varied population of the sea never ceased to delight the young sailor.

EXERCISE 5 **Using Collective Nouns.** On your paper complete each sentence by filling the blank with a collective noun from the five below.

faculty   team   class   club   audience

1. The debate _____ held its first match in the school's auditorium.
2. All of the _____, even substitute teachers, were on hand to see how their students would perform.
3. The members of the _____ had been chosen from the upper grades.
4. Parents of the debaters sat in the _____ and watched proudly.
5. After the debates were over, our _____ stood up to applaud the winners.

Compound Nouns

A **compound noun** is a noun that is made up of more than one word.

housekeeper	ice cream	mother-in-law
bookmark	high school	great-grandfather
necklace	dining room	kilowatt-hour

Sometimes two words are written as one to form a compound noun; sometimes a compound noun is written as two separate words, and sometimes it is written with hyphens. Check a dictionary if you are not sure of the way a compound noun should be written.

Proper nouns that name particular people or places may be compound: Geraldine Ferraro, John Glenn, Niagara Falls, the Empire State Building.

EXERCISE 6 **Forming Compound Nouns.** Match the nouns in column 1 with the nouns in column 2 to form as many compound nouns as you can. (At least thirty possibilities exist.)

1	2
air	work
eye	power
house	hole
field	boat
iron	glasses
stage	sparrow
pigeon	hand
water	door
lace	craft
fire	wings

Concrete and Abstract Nouns

A **concrete noun** names an object that occupies space or that can be recognized by any of the senses.

> thorn   stars   thunder
>
> gas   milk   Iowa

An **abstract noun** names an idea, a quality, or a characteristic.

> softness   acidity   innocence
>
> mustiness   harmony   excitement

Nouns may be classified as concrete or abstract, common or proper.

EXERCISE 7 **Supplying Abstract and Concrete Nouns.** For each concrete noun in item 1, write an abstract noun that names an idea with which the concrete noun can be associated. For each abstract noun in item 2, write a concrete noun that possesses the quality of the abstract noun.

SAMPLES 1. *dancer*—grace

2. *redness*—tomato

1. quarterback, scream, perfume, pepper, bruise
2. intelligence, friendliness, darkness, aroma, stupidity

SENTENCE WRITING **Creating Sentences with Nouns.** Write five sentences about one of your favorite places. Rely especially on concrete nouns to convey a vivid picture of the place.

REVIEW EXERCISE **Nouns.** On your paper complete each sentence by filling the blanks with the kinds of nouns specified in italics.

1. _____*proper*_____ left her ____*compound*____ in the ____*concrete*____.
2. The practice of ____*common*____ has become popular with the ____*collective*____.
3. The ____*collective*____ proved its ____*abstract*____.
4. Near the ____*compound*____ I saw three ____*common*____ run across the ____*concrete*____.
5. ____*proper, compound*____ wrote a famous ____*concrete*____.
6. Environmental ____*abstract*____ is a serious ____*abstract*____ for anyone who cares about the ____*abstract*____ of humankind.
7. A ____*collective*____ of zebras and a ____*collective*____ of ostriches are only two of the spectacular sights on the plains of East ____*proper*____.
8. I was thrilled to be able to watch ____*proper*____ practice ____*compound*____ before the game.

Revising Your Writing

In the following sentence from *To the Lighthouse,* Virginia Woolf uses nouns effectively to convey a picture of darkness swallowing up the daytime world.

> Nothing it seemed could survive the flood, the profusion of darkness which, creeping in at the keyholes and crevices, stole round window blinds, came into bedrooms, swallowed up here a jug and basin, there a bowl of red and yellow dahlias, there the sharp edges and firm bulk of a chest of drawers.

Study the passage above closely, and try to apply some of Woolf's techniques when you write and revise your own work.

1. Try to balance concrete nouns with abstract nouns, as Woolf does in the phrase "the *flood,* the *profusion* of darkness." By itself the abstract noun *profusion* means "an abundant outpouring." However, when it is balanced by the concrete noun *flood,* it takes on the connotations of that noun: Like a flood, Woolf is saying, the profusion of darkness is both fluid and destructive as it fills the room and obliterates the daytime world.

2. Try to choose nouns for the effect of their sound as well as for their meaning. For example, notice the *k* sounds in Woolf's phrase "creeping in at the keyholes and crevices."

3. Try to replace general words with precise concrete nouns. Notice that Woolf does not merely say that the darkness swallowed up the furniture. Instead, she makes the scene vivid by selecting particular items: a jug and basin, a bowl of dahlias, a chest of drawers. By using such precise concrete nouns, Woolf stirs our imaginations and gives us a clearer picture of the room.

4. Try to expand single nouns into longer word groups that are more specific and detailed. Woolf expands the noun *chest* into "the sharp edges and firm bulk of a chest of drawers." This expansion helps Woolf make her original point that the darkness is a flood washing away the shapes of things.

Practice these techniques by revising the following passage on your paper. Pay particular attention to the italicized words.

> When the sun rises above the harbor, *everything* turns into shades of *various colors*. Gradually the *water* appears ribboned with *light*. Next, the shore emerges from under the night's *cover*. Only at *this time* can a *person walking* fully enjoy the *beauties* of the *harbor*.

In the following exercise, each sentence contains an italicized abstract or general noun that could be improved by being either balanced or replaced with a concrete noun. Revise each sentence on your paper by adding or substituting a suitable concrete noun.

> SAMPLE   Nothing it seemed could survive the *profusion* of darkness.
> REVISION   Nothing it seemed could survive the flood, the profusion of darkness.
> REVISION   Nothing, it seemed, could survive the flood of darkness.

1. Few citizens fully appreciate the *responsibility* of the Presidency.
2. The audience were startled by the massive *volume* of the conclusion of the symphony.
3. The *gentleness* of the paramedic's voice soothed the distraught accident victim.
4. No listener remained untouched by the *emotionalism* of the keynote speaker.

Pronouns

A **pronoun** is a word that takes the place of a noun, a group of nouns, or another pronoun.

Pronouns allow you to avoid unnecessary repetitions when you speak or write. The word or group of words that a pronoun replaces is called its *antecedent*.

> When Sylvia Plath was still a young girl, **she** decided to become a writer. [The pronoun *she* takes the place of the noun *Sylvia Plath*.]

> George Orwell wrote *Animal Farm* and *Nineteen Eighty-Four* in the 1940s. **Both** remain immensely popular today. [The pronoun *both* takes the place of the nouns *Animal Farm* and *Nineteen Eighty-four*.]

> After Elizabeth Barrett was married to the poet Robert Browning, **she** continued to write poetry **herself**. [The pronouns *she* and *herself* take the place of the noun *Elizabeth Barrett*.]

The English language has about seventy-five pronouns, which fall into one or more of the following categories: personal pronouns, reflexive and intensive pronouns, demonstrative pronouns, interrogative pronouns, relative pronouns, and indefinite pronouns.

Personal Pronouns

A **personal pronoun** refers to a specific person or thing by indicating the person speaking (the first person), the person being addressed (the second person), or any other person or thing being discussed (the third person). Personal pronouns also express **number;** they are singular or plural.

	SINGULAR	PLURAL
FIRST PERSON	I, me	we, us
SECOND PERSON	you	you
THIRD PERSON	he, him, she, her it	they, them

FIRST PERSON	Thomas went with **me** to the game. [*Me* refers to the person speaking.]
SECOND PERSON	Ask Gina to show **you** the article. [*You* refers to the person being addressed.]
THIRD PERSON	**He** gave **them** a poor excuse. [*He* and *them* refer to the persons being discussed.]

Third-person pronouns express **gender.** *He* and *him* are masculine; *she* and *her* are feminine; *it* is neuter (neither masculine nor feminine.)

The personal pronouns include several forms that indicate possession or ownership. These **possessive pronouns** take the place of the possessive forms of nouns.

	SINGULAR	PLURAL
FIRST PERSON	my, mine	our, ours
SECOND PERSON	your, yours	your, yours
THIRD PERSON	his	their, theirs
	her, hers	
	its	

Some possessive forms are used before nouns. Other possessive forms can be used by themselves.

USED BEFORE NOUN	This is **her** radio.
	Its battery is new.
USED ALONE	This radio is **hers.**

EXERCISE 8 **Using Personal and Possessive Pronouns.** Improve the following paragraph by replacing the underlined words or groups of words with personal or possessive pronouns. Write your answers on your paper.

¹In the late twentieth century eight riders and the riders' horses retraced the Santa Fe Trail, once a major route for pioneers going west. ²The trip's leader, Allan Maybee, made sure that the riders planned carefully. ³Maybee asked Maybee's friend, Ms. Evelyn Vinogradov, to drive Vinogradov's truck ahead of the riders. ⁴The truck carried groceries, and Vinogradov had filled the truck with jugs of water as well. ⁵Vinogradov also arranged for places where the group could stay overnight. ⁶Would the reader of this passage be interested in planning the reader's own trip along the Santa Fe Trail?

Reflexive and Intensive Pronouns*

Reflexive and intensive pronouns are formed by adding *-self* or *-selves* to certain of the personal pronouns.

	SINGULAR	PLURAL
FIRST PERSON	myself	ourselves
SECOND PERSON	yourself	yourselves
THIRD PERSON	himself	themselves
	herself	
	itself	

*Reflexive and intensive pronouns are also called *compound personal pronouns.*

A **reflexive pronoun** refers to a noun or another pronoun and indicates that the same person or thing is involved.

I almost exhausted **myself** working for her in the campaign.

Today, for the first time in months, she is **herself**.

As a team, they have no faith in **themselves.**

   Note that the reflexive pronoun refers to the subject and describes the subject doing something to itself.

An **intensive pronoun** adds emphasis to another noun or pronoun.

You **yourself** told me to stop.

Rita **herself** met us.

I baked that bread **myself.**

EXERCISE 9   **dentifying Reflexive and Intensive Pronouns.** On your paper write the reflexive or intensive pronoun that appears in each sentence of this paragraph.

   [1]It is uncertain when or how people began to cook for themselves. [2]Prehistoric people may have cooked meals over a fire that started itself naturally. [3]In ancient Rome the woman of the house herself lifted large, heavy kettles onto iron tripods that stood over fires. [4]If you had lived during the Middle Ages, you yourself would have broiled meat on a spit, which turned over an open flame. [5]Today, technological improvements, such as the microwave oven, make it simple for us to prepare meals for ourselves.

EXERCISE 10   **Using Reflexive and Intensive Pronouns.** Supply the appropriate reflexive or intensive pronoun for each blank. Write your answers on your paper.

1. Many of us have transformed _____ from Saturday joggers into serious runners.
2. Running _____ is not a difficult sport.
3. If you are new to running, be sure to pace _____ carefully, or your body may rebel.
4. Some runners use a stopwatch to time _____.
5. I _____ enjoy a morning run most of all.
6. Marcia _____ prefers swimming to running.
7. We _____ are responsible for our own physical fitness.

SENTENCE WRITING **Creating Sentences with Reflexive and Intensive Pronouns.** Write one sentence using each pronoun listed below as a reflexive pronoun and one sentence using each as an intensive pronoun.

1. himself   2. itself   3. ourselves

Demonstrative Pronouns

A **demonstrative pronoun** points out a person, place, thing, or idea.

SINGULAR this   that   PLURAL these   those

This is the hat I want.   Show me **that** again.
These were left over after last night's dinner.   My old shoes are more
                                                comfortable than **those**.

EXERCISE 11 **Identifying Demonstrative Pronouns.** On your paper write the demonstrative pronoun in each sentence.

1. This is one of the area's largest farmers' markets.
2. These are the freshest vegetables.
3. That is the farmer with the best variety of vegetables.
4. Buy these because they are the freshest.
5. Those are Mr. Gray's prize melons.

Interrogative and Relative Pronouns

An **interrogative pronoun** is used to form questions.

These are the interrogative pronouns:
    who?   whom?   whose?   what?   which?

Who are those strangers?   **Whom** should I invite?
Whose did you borrow?   **What** did you say?
Which of these personal computers shall I buy?

A **relative pronoun** is used to begin a special subject-verb word group called a subordinate clause (see Chapter 20).

These are the relative pronouns:

who   which
whom   that
whose

The pilot **who** landed the plane is my cousin. [The relative pronoun *who* begins the subordinate clause *who landed the plane.*]

That plane, **which** landed late, carried our equipment. [The relative pronoun *which* begins the subordinate clause *which landed late.*]

The baggage **that** we checked is not on the carousel. [The relative pronoun *that* begins the subordinate clause *that we checked.*]

The passengers **whom** we left on the plane are going on to another destination. [The relative pronoun *whom* begins the subordinate clause *whom we left on the plane.*]

The passenger **whose** baggage was put on the wrong flight complained loudly. [The relative pronoun *whose* begins the subordinate clause *whose baggage was put on the wrong flight.*]

Note that all the relative pronouns except *that* can also be used as interrogative pronouns to ask questions.

EXERCISE 12 **Distinguishing Between Interrogative and Relative Pronouns.** On your paper list the interrogative or relative pronouns in each of the following paragraphs. Next to each pronoun, indicate whether it is used as a relative or an interrogative pronoun.

A. [1]Joan of Arc, who was born in 1412, led the French army to victory at Orleans. [2]Visions, which Joan felt sure were from heaven, led her to believe she was chosen to liberate her country. [3]Charles VII, then the uncrowned King of France, asked Joan to command the French army that was fighting the English. [4]After many victories Joan fell into the hands of the enemy, whose leaders sentenced her to death. [5]Keeping Joan of Arc's exploits in mind, who else acted heroically in wartime?

B. [1]Which of these colorful paintings appear on countless greeting cards every year? [2]They are the work of Anna Mary Robertson, the amazing American artist whom we know as Grandma Moses. [3]Grandma Moses, who lived to be 101 years old, did not even begin to paint until she was 76! [4]Generally, her paintings, which are praised for their freshness and simple humanity, depict realistic scenes of rural life. [5]With her reputation, who has not heard of Grandma Moses?

Indefinite Pronouns

An **indefinite pronoun** refers to persons, places, or things in a more general way than a noun does.

Some indefinite pronouns do not have clear antecedents.

> Jacob seems to know **everyone** at school. [The indefinite pronoun *everyone* refers to people in general.]

> I'm going to bake you **something** special for your birthday. [The indefinite pronoun *something* does not tell to what it specifically refers.]

Other indefinite pronouns often have specific antecedents.

> When we served the bread, we discovered that **some** was stale. [The indefinite pronoun *some* has the specific antecedent *bread.*]

Some indefinite pronouns are listed in the following chart.

all	either	most	other
another	enough	much	others
any	everybody	neither	plenty
anybody	everyone	nobody	several
anyone	everything	none	some
anything	few	no one	somebody
both	many	nothing	someone
each	more	one	something

EXERCISE 13 **Identifying Indefinite Pronouns.** On your paper list the eight indefinite pronouns in the following paragraph.

¹Everyone cheered as *Friendship 7* rose from the launching pad, beginning John Glenn's historic space flight. ² During the first orbit everything went well. ³Then someone realized that the spacecraft was swinging to the right. ⁴Obviously, something was wrong, and the tracking stations could do little to help. ⁵ Glenn quickly reviewed all he had learned. ⁶ Taking several of the controls off automatic, he "flew" the craft manually through the final two orbits. ⁷Nobody had ever done anything like this before. ⁸ Nor had any of the earlier American astronauts orbited the earth.

SENTENCE WRITING **Following Models.** Each of the following quotations has pronouns in it. Using each quotation as a model, write your own version of the quotation with the same pronouns in the same positions. A sample response is provided for each item.

1. He who does not enjoy his own company is usually right.

—Coco Chanel, French Designer

SAMPLE ANSWER He who enjoys his own cooking is probably overweight.

2. I think continually of those who were truly great. . . .

—Stephen Spender, British poet

SAMPLE ANSWER   I avoid invariably those who talk too much.

3. The most I can do for my friend is simply to be his friend.

—Henry David Thoreau, American writer

SAMPLE ANSWER   The least I can do for my student is merely to be his
tutor.

4. We are all poets when we read a poem well.

—Thomas Carlyle, British essayist

SAMPLE ANSWER   We are all ambassadors when we travel abroad.

REVIEW EXERCISE **Pronouns.** (a) On your paper list in order the twenty-five pronouns contained in the following paragraph. (b) Identify each pronoun as personal, possessive, reflexive or intensive, demonstrative, interrogative, relative, or indefinite.

¹The Sphinx is a mythical monster that has the body of a lion but the head of a woman. ²The people of Thebes were under her control, and anyone who met her had to answer a riddle correctly or die. ³This is the riddle: What walks on four legs in the morning, two legs at noon, and three legs at night? ⁴Many tried, but none could solve the riddle. ⁵Then Oedipus, himself a Greek hero, confronted her. ⁶When he correctly answered the riddle, the enraged Sphinx threw herself from a cliff. ⁷The people of Thebes, whose deliverance Oedipus had won, were so grateful that they made him king. ⁸In our time everyone knows the answer to the riddle. ⁹It is you and I and all of humankind. ¹⁰We crawl on all fours as babies, travel on two legs in our youth, and use a cane to support ourselves in old age.

Verbs

A **verb** is a word that expresses action or a state of being and that is necessary to make a statement.

The verb is the part of speech that is essential to the formation of the sentence. The nouns and pronouns in sentences name people, places, or things, and the verbs tell what those people, places, or things *do* or *are*.

Business people **work.**	Artists **are** creative.
The curtain **closed** too soon.	The street **appears** empty.

In the subsections that follow, you will learn about the different classes of verbs.

Recognizing Verbs

You can test whether a word is a verb by seeing if it makes sense in one of the blanks in the following sentences:

The group _____.
It _____ on the farm.
They _____ them there.
We _____ it to you.
The cold water _____ good.

Certain suffixes signal that a word is a verb. These suffixes include *-ate*, *-en*, *-esce*, *-fy*, and *-ize*.

coordinate   convalesce   characterize
quicken   magnify

The primary characteristic of a verb is its ability to express time—present, past, and future. Verbs express time by means of *tense* forms. (For rules on forming and using the tenses of verbs, see Chapter 21.)

PRESENT TENSE   We **hear** a car outside.
PAST TENSE   We **heard** a car outside.
FUTURE TENSE   We **will hear** a car outside.

EXERCISE 14   **Adding Verbs to Make Sentences.** Complete the sentences by supplying a verb for each of the blanks below.

1. The hawk _____ above the valley.
2. It _____ black against the blue sky.
3. Sensing the hawk's presence, the rodents _____ in the grass.
4. Riding air currents, the hawk barely _____ its wings.
5. Its flight _____ effortless
6. With its piercing eyes, the hawk _____ the countryside.
7. A hawk _____ eight times more acutely than a human being.
8. Some hawks even _____ at night, catching bats on the wing.
9. Hawks are territorial birds that _____ their nests from other hawks.
10. Most hawks _____ their nests high in trees.

Action Verbs

An **action verb** tells what someone or something does.

Some action verbs express physical action; others express mental action:

PHYSICAL ACTION   The huge linemen **lead** the charge through the defense.
MENTAL ACTION   The coaches **plan** the team's strategy.

Identifying Action Verbs. On your paper write the action verb that appears in each of the following sentences.

1. Frisbee disks soar through the air as gracefully as birds.
2. Their path and speed depend on the player's grip, the force of the throw, and the wind.
3. The manufacturers make Frisbee disks in different weights and several bright colors.
4. The lighter disks fly farther and faster than the heavier ones.
5. Players still prefer the heavier ones for team sports.
6. Heavier disks keep a steadier course on windy days.
7. In championship games contestants obey formal rules just as in any other sport.
8. Ordinarily players set their own rules.
9. Frisbee players practice their tosses anywhere and anytime.
10. They need only the disk, an open space, and a partner.

SENTENCE WRITING **Creating Sentences with Action Verbs.** Choose five of the action verbs that you identified in Exercise 15. For each verb write one sentence.

Transitive and Intransitive Verbs

A **transitive verb** is an action verb that is followed by a word or words that answer the question *what?* or *whom?*

The word that answers the question *what?* or *whom?* after the action verb is called the *direct object,* or *object of the verb.* (For more information about direct objects, see Chapter 18.)

Fleas **bite** people. [The action verb *bite* is followed by the direct object *people,* which answers the question *bite whom?*]

Hawks **see** their prey from far away. [The action verb *see* is followed by the direct object *prey,* which answers the question *see what?*]

Many action verbs are not transitive. That is, they are not followed by words that answer the question *what?* or *whom?*

An **intransitive verb** is an action verb that does not have a direct object.

Intransitive verbs simply tell what someone or something does, or they are followed only by words that tell *when, where,* or *how* an action occurs.

Fleas **bite.** [The action verb works alone.]

Hawks **see** well in most weather conditions. [The action verb is followed by words that tell *how* and *when.*]

Many action verbs can be transitive or intransitive, as you can see by comparing the two preceding sets of examples. Some action verbs, however, are either always transitive or always intransitive. That is, some action verbs make sense only with a direct object, and some make sense only without a direct object.

ALWAYS TRANSITIVE
Astronomers **view** Neptune by telescope.
The clouds of Jupiter **contain** ammonia.

ALWAYS INTRANSITIVE
Occasionally large meteorites **fall** to earth.
Meteoroids **glow** brightly and briefly.

EXERCISE 16 **Recognizing Transitive and Intransitive Verbs.** Write on your paper the action verb in each of the following sentences. Indicate whether each action verb is used as a transitive or an intransitive verb.

1. Anteaters prefer the warmer regions of the world.
2. Anteaters possess no teeth whatsoever.
3. On the whole, anteaters live rather peacefully.
4. Like other toothless animals, anteaters often hide from their enemies for self-protection.
5. When fearful, though, anteaters react fiercely.
6. In general, they attack only insects.
7. With their razor-sharp claws anteaters slash the nests of ants and termites.
8. A long, sticky tongue darts from a dime-sized mouth at the end of a twelve-inch nose.
9. Within seconds the tubelike nose captures hundreds of insects.
10. In captivity some anteaters reach an age of fourteen years.

SENTENCE WRITING **Creating Sentences with Transitive and Intransitive Verbs.** For each of the following action verbs, write two sentences. First use the word as a transitive verb. Then use it as an intransitive verb.

1. drove
2. developed
3. attacked
4. hid
5. shouted
6. stopped
7. froze
8. walked

Linking Verbs

A **linking verb** links a noun or pronoun (the subject of a sentence) with a word or expression that identifies or describes that noun or pronoun.

Be in all its forms—*am, is, are, was, were, will be, has been, was being*—is the most commonly used linking verb.*

That singer **is** an artist.
The days **were** hot.
Those **are** mosquitoes.

Several other verbs besides the forms of *be* can act as linking verbs:

look	remain	sound	stay
grow	appear	become	smell
feel	seem	taste	

EXERCISE 17 **Identifying Action and Linking Verbs.** Identify each verb in the following paragraph as either action or linking.

¹"I am just a reporter." ²Winslow Homer, nineteenth-century American painter, made that statement about his role as an artist. ³Homer's work is a blend of naturalistic and impressionistic painting styles. ⁴For most of his life he was a resident of the New England countryside and seashore. ⁵He used the ordinary people, the land, and the choppy ocean as his subject matter. ⁶Homer's people seem natural, active, and informal. ⁷His delightful farm and resort scenes display American country life authentically. ⁸Homer's most famous paintings portray the rugged life of sailors and fishermen. ⁹*The Gulf Stream, The Fog Warning,* and *Eight Bells* are examples of these dramatic seascapes. ¹⁰Their realism reflects Homer's familiarity with sailors and their lives at sea.

Linking Verb or Action Verb?

Except for the forms of *be* and *seem,* all the words listed above as linking verbs can also be action verbs. Each of the following sentence pairs shows a word first used as a linking verb and then as an action verb:

LINKING Bird lovers **look** overjoyed upon spotting rare species.
ACTION Bird lovers **look** for rare bald eagles.

LINKING Farmers **grow** concerned about taxes.
ACTION Farmers **grow** corn.

LINKING Some companies **appear** responsive to consumer complaints.
ACTION Consumer specialists often **appear** [make an appearance] on news shows.

LINKING Earl Grey tea **tastes** different from oolong tea.
ACTION Tea tasters **taste** tea.

---

*Sometimes rather than acting as a linking verb, the forms of *be* are used to state *where* something exists (*Ice is on the lake.*) or *when* something happened (*Vacation is over.*). These uses of the verb *be* are usually considered purely intransitive constructions.

If you are unsure of whether a word is a linking verb, substitute the word *seem* in the sentence. If the sentence still makes sense, the word in question is probably a linking verb.

> Small airplanes **grow** [seem] more popular every year. [Here *grow* is a linking verb.]
>
> Some pilots **grow** beards. [Here *grow* is not a linking verb. *Seem* cannot be substituted for *grow*.]

EXERCISE 18 **Distinguishing Between Action Verbs and Linking Verbs.** For each of the following sentences, write the verb. Then indicate whether it is an action verb or a linking verb.

1. People outdoors often grow sick of insects.
2. Insect colonies grow quite quickly.
3. Perhaps the noises of insects sound an alarm or another message to other insects.
4. To Chinese people, crickets sound cheerful.
5. Many insects feel through their antennae.
6. Some insects probably taste good to people.
7. Some people regularly taste grasshoppers.
8. Insects appear in all corners of the world.
9. Insects appear entirely adaptable to extreme climates.
10. Insects remain the most widespread creatures on earth (to many people's dismay).

SENTENCE WRITING **Changing Linking Verbs to Action Verbs.** Look again at the words in the preceding exercise that you identified as linking verbs. For each one, write an original sentence using the word as an action verb.

Verb Phrases

The verb in a sentence may consist of more than one word. The words that accompany the main verb are called **auxiliary,** or helping, **verbs.**

A **verb phrase** consists of a main verb and all its auxiliary, or helping, verbs.

The verb phrase functions in a sentence as a single unit. A main verb may have as many as three auxiliary verbs coming before it. The most common auxiliary verbs are the forms of *be* and *have*.

BE am, is, are, was
    were, be, being, been
HAVE have, has, had

These auxiliary verbs help the main verb to express the various tenses. (For more information about using auxiliary verbs to form tenses, see Chapter 21.)

> I **am walking.**
> I **have walked.**
> I **had been walking.**

The following auxiliary verbs are used for other purposes in addition to expressing time. They are called modal auxiliaries.

do, does, did	should
may, might	must
can, could	will
would	shall

All of the auxiliary verbs on the preceding list, with the exception of the forms of *do,* can be used with the forms of *be* and *have* and the main verb.

> She **might have waited.**   We **would have played.**
> He **could be told.**   I **must be going.**

EXERCISE 19   **Identifying Verb Phrases.** On your paper write the verb phrase in each of the following sentences. Put parentheses around the auxiliary verbs in each phrase. (Words that interrupt a verb phrase are not considered part of the verb phrase.)

1. For a long time now, the April Fiesta has been the highlight of the year in San Antonio, Texas.
2. The Fiesta may be the world's most enchanting party.
3. For years now, people have flocked to the area to enjoy Spanish and Mexican food and music.
4. Tourists can often hear country swing, country rock, and Dixieland.
5. The Fiesta must begin in front of the Alamo on a Saturday.
6. The Fiesta may last ten days.
7. Always the highlight, the Battle of Flowers parade has been attracting people since 1891.
8. All San Antonio's diverse cultures can brilliantly display themselves during the Fiesta.
9. The pomp and lavishness of the Fiesta could have humbled the royalty of Europe.
10. Tourists will long remember the lights, the flowers, the costumes, and the music.

SENTENCE WRITING   **Creating Sentences with Vivid Verbs.** Write five sentences about one of your favorite sports. Choose specific action verbs to convey a vivid sense of the sport.

Verbs. On your paper complete each sentence in the following paragraph by supplying the kind of verb specified in the blanks. Be sure that your completed sentences make sense.

Because people (1) ___*action verb (transitive)*___ more leisure time than ever before, hobbies (2) ___*verb phrase*___ in popularity. Hobby preferences (3) ___*action verb (intransitive)*___ greatly from person to person. While some people (4) ___*action verb (transitive)*___ sculpture, others (5) ___*linking verb*___ most content when they (6) ___*verb phrase*___ on an old car. Photography (7) ___*action verb (intransitive)*___ to many people, some of whom (8) ___*action verb (transitive)*___ darkrooms where they (9) ___*verb phrase*___ their own film. Hobby stores (10) ___*action verb (transitive)*___ model planes that actually (11) ___*action verb (intransitive)*___even though they (12) ___*verb phrase*___ very fragile. People who (13) ___*action verb (intransitive)*___ for a hobby (14) ___*linking verb*___ quite pleased when they (15) ___*verb phrase*___ their work at an art show. Anyone (16) ___*verb phrase*___ a philatelist, which (17) ___*linking verb*___ the term for a person who (18) ___*action verb (transitive)*___ stamps. The more a philatelist's collection (19) ___*action verb (intransitive)*___, the more valuable it (20) ___*linking verb*___.

Poets are particularly skillful at using verbs to crystallize images in their readers' minds. Here are some guidelines that poets—and prose writers, too—keep in mind as they write and revise their work.

1. Try to reduce a group of words to one action verb. For example, instead of writing "It looks like powder in the woods" to describe falling snow, Emily Dickinson wrote "It powders all the Wood." Dickinson's choice of the verb *powders* conveys a vivid action, not merely appearance.

2. Instead of beginning sentences with "there is" or "there were," begin with a noun and follow up with a colorful action verb. E. A. Robinson began one of his poems, "War shook the land where Levi dwelt." How flat the beginning would have been had Robinson started, "There was a war where Levi dwelt."

3. Whenever possible, use action verbs rather than linking verbs. In describing a cold day, W. H. Auden wrote, "The mercury sank in the mouth of the dying day." The action verb *sank* is stronger than any linking verb. Compare the power of Auden's line to "The mercury was low in the mouth of the dying day."

4. Try to replace general verbs with more precise action verbs. For example, instead of writing "a boat adrift touches the pier," the poet Denise Levertov wrote "a boat adrift nudges the pier." *Nudges* is both less commonly used and more precise than *touches.*

Practice the writing techniques listed on the preceding page by revising the following passage. Pay particular attention to the italicized words.

The four of us *walked* with our gear along the winding trail. After two hours we *were* finally at our destination. Jon and I *took* the water tank to the stream while Mike *looked* for firewood and Bob *set up* the tent. After our chores we *began to take in* our surroundings. *There were* three tall pines above our campsite, casting their cool shadows. Birds *sang their songs* in the highest branches. Nearby, the stream *became a wide* pool, deep enough for swimming. All in all, Farnham Woods *was* an ideal setting for a weekend with nature.

In the following passage, the italicized verbs are general and overused. Revise the passage on your paper by replacing each italicized verb with a vivid verb that conveys a more precise action.

[1]When I entered my room, I carelessly *put* my new hat on the bed. [2]I did not realize that my young dog Samson *was* in the corner. [3]To my sudden horror, I saw Samson *get* up onto the bed and *take my hat*. [4]I shouted in vain as Samson *ran* out the door with me in close pursuit.

Adjectives

An **adjective** is a word that modifies a noun or pronoun by limiting its meaning.

Adjectives modify, or change, the meaning of a noun or pronoun by making it more specific. As the following examples show, adjectives can modify nouns and pronouns in any of four ways. The arrows point to the modified words.

1. Some adjectives *describe;* they answer the question *what is it like?*

   rainy afternoon   It seems **heavy.**   **smooth** surface

2. Some adjectives *classify;* they answer the question *what kind is it?*

   female spiders   **Siberian** winters   **governmental** regulations

3. Some adjectives *identify;* they answer the question *which one?*

   this book   **those** horses   **our** party   **his** car*

4. Some adjectives *quantify;* they answer the question *how much* or *how many?*

   an apple   **three** cents   **several** pounds   **no** water

Adjectives that identify or quantify nouns or pronouns are sometimes called determiners.

Recognizing Adjectives

The vast majority of adjectives can be used either before a noun or after a noun and a linking verb. That is, the vast majority of adjectives fit in both blanks in the following.

   The _____ table is _____.
   The _____ candidate seems _____.
   The _____ opinion is _____.

Certain suffixes signal that a word is an adjective. These suffixes include *-able* and *-ible, -al, -esque, -ful, -ic, -ish, -less,* and *-ous.*

serviceable	picturesque	childish
invisible	sorrowful	humorless
gigantic	virtuous	scenic

---

*Possessive pronouns, such as *our* and *his,* can be considered adjectives because they modify nouns in addition to their usual function as pronouns. Similarly, possessive nouns can be considered adjectives: *John's* car.

Many adjectives have different forms to indicate *degree of comparison*. (For the rules regarding the degrees of comparison, refer to Chapter 24.)

POSITIVE	COMPARATIVE	SUPERLATIVE
slow	slower	slowest
healthy	healthier	healthiest
strenuous	more strenuous	most strenuous

Adjectives appear in various positions according to the word they modify.

Beautiful, the tulips gleamed on the piano.
How **beautiful** the tulip is!
That **beautiful** tulip won first prize.
The tulip is **beautiful**.
The florist considered the tulip **beautiful**.
The tulips, **beautiful** in the sunlight, danced in the wind.

EXERCISE 20 **Finding Adjectives.** On your paper list the twenty adjectives in the following passage. Count possessive pronouns as adjectives in this exercise, but do not count the words *a, an,* and *the*.

[1]There was a bright, full moon in the clear sky, and the sunset was still shining faintly in the west. [2]Dark woods stood all about the old . . . farmhouse, save down the hill, westward, where lay the shadowy fields which John Hilton, and his father before him, had cleared and tilled with much toil—the small fields to which they had given the industry and . . . affection of their honest lives.

[3]John Hilton was sitting on the doorstep of his house. [4]As he moved his head in and out of the shadows, . . . one could see his good face, rough and somewhat unkempt, as if he were indeed a creature of the shady woods and brown earth, instead of the noisy town.

—Sarah Orne Jewett

Completing Sentences with Adjectives. On your paper, complete the following sentences by replacing each blank with the kind of adjective named in the parentheses. You may want to review the various types of adjectives as listed on page 412.

1. There are _____ basic kinds of stereo systems: the component and the compact. (quantifying)
2. In the component system each part can be bought separately, and the sound is very _____. (describing)
3. Some people prefer the component system because they can buy the best parts from _____ manufacturers or American manufacturers. (classifying)
4. Other people like the compact system because _____ system is easier to carry back to the stereo store for repairs. (identifying)
5. Compact disk players, developed in the late 1970s, use laser technology to produce nearly _____ sound. (describing)

Articles

Articles are the adjectives *a, an,* and *the. A* and *an* are called indefinite articles. *The* is called the definite article.

INDEFINITE	We camped near **a** river.
	She ate **an** orange.
DEFINITE	We camped near **the** river.
	She ate **the** orange.

The definite and indefinite articles show how much you think the person to whom you are speaking or writing knows about whatever you are discussing. If Sheila says to Mark, "I was at *the* party last night," the definite article *the* shows that she thinks Mark can identify which party she is talking about. If she does not think he can, she will use the indefinite article and say, "I was at *a* party last night."

EXERCISE 22 **Identifying Articles.** Find the articles in the following pairs of sentences. On your paper explain the differences in meaning between each pair.

1. Janet, do you have a hammer?
   Janet, do you have the hammer?
2. The eagle is soaring above Cobb's Field.
   An eagle is soaring above Cobb's Field.
3. A tiger is a dangerous animal.
   How old is the tiger at the zoo?

Proper Adjectives

A **proper adjective** is formed from a proper noun and begins with a capital letter.

Proper adjectives classify; they answer the question *what kind?*

Allan Pettersson was a **Swedish** composer.
The **Victorian** era refers to the years 1837 to 1901.

The following suffixes are often used to create proper adjectives: *-an, -ian, -n, -ese,* and *-ish.*

PROPER NOUNS	PROPER ADJECTIVES
Queen Elizabeth I	Elizabethan
Australia	Australian
Japan	Japanese
Britain	British

EXERCISE 23 **Forming Proper Adjectives.** Write a proper adjective that is formed from each of the following proper nouns. Consult a dictionary if you need help.

1. American
2. George Washington
3. Ireland
4. Greece
5. France
6. Mars
7. Portugal
8. Charles Dickens
9. Paris
10. China

SENTENCE WRITING **Creating Sentences with Adjectives.** Write five sentences about one of your favorite foods. Be sure you include the origin, method of preparation, appearance, aroma, and flavor in your description. Choose adjectives that are especially descriptive to convey a vivid image of the food.

REVIEW EXERCISE **Adjectives.** On your paper write the twenty adjectives, including articles, that appear in the following paragraph.

[1]Hawaii consists of a chain of 132 islands. [2]These islands extend northwest for 1,523 miles. [3]Main islands of Hawaii include Maui, Lanai, Kahoolawe, Molokai, Oahu, Kauai, Niihau, and Hawaii, an island that is quite large and famous for active volcanoes. [4]Although there are a number of islands, Hawaiian people live only on major ones. [5]Kahoolawe, for example, had no inhabitants and is used only for naval purposes. [6]Minor islands, only as big as great rocks, are too small and infertile to support human life.

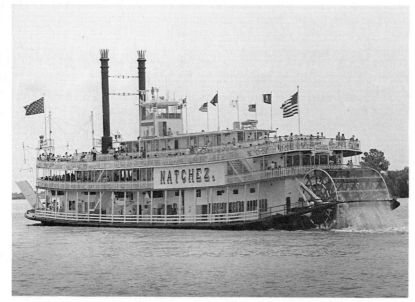

Examine the following description of the Mississippi River written by Mark Twain. Notice especially the effective use of the italicized adjectives.

> A *broad* expanse of the river was turned to blood; in the *middle* distance the *red* hue brightened into gold, through which a *solitary* log came floating, *black* and conspicuous; in one place a *long, slanting* mark lay *sparkling* upon the water; in another the surface was broken by *boiling, tumbling* rings that were as *many-tinted* as an opal; where the *ruddy* flush was *faintest* was a *smooth* spot that was covered with *graceful* circles and *radiating* lines, ever so delicately traced. . . .

Here are some of Twain's techniques that you can apply when you write and revise your work:

1. Try to use adjectives that will make nouns more specific. Twain makes his nouns more specific by using vivid adjectives that describe color (*red, black, many-tinted, ruddy*), shape or position (*broad, middle, solitary, conspicuous, long, slanting*), and other visual characteristics (*faintest, smooth, graceful*). These adjectives appeal to our senses.

2. Try to use adjectives that suggest action. Notice Twain's lively *-ing* words: *sparkling, boiling, tumbling, radiating*. All of these give us the picture of a river in motion.

3. Try to determine where adjectives are helpful and where they are not needed. Notice the beginning of Twain's description. Twain uses *broad* to specify the size of the expanse, but he leaves the nouns *river* and *blood* unmodified. Do not feel that every noun needs an adjective.

Here is the rest of Twain's description, but without his adjectives. Revise the passage, adding your own adjectives in the places indicated by the carets (∧).

> The shore on our left was densely wooded, and the∧shadow that fell from this forest was broken in one place by a∧∧trail that shone like silver; and high above the forest wall a∧tree waved a∧bough that glowed like a flame in the∧splendor that was flowing from the sun.
>
> —from *Life on the Mississippi*

Here is a passage from *Roughing It*, also by Mark Twain, describing Lake Tahoe on the Nevada-California border. The excerpt, however, has been altered to include many unneeded adjectives in addition to the adjectives that Twain actually wrote. Revise the passage on your paper. Decide which adjectives contribute to the effectiveness of the description and which are unnecessary and can be deleted.

> Thus refreshed, we presently resumed the invigorating march with renewed vigor and steadfast determination. We plodded on, two or three wearisome hours longer, and at last the beautiful lake burst upon us—a noble sheet of blue water lifted six thousand three hundred feet above the flat level of the sea, and walled in by a perfect rim of snow-clad mountain peaks that towered aloft full three thousand feet higher still! It was a vast oval, and one would have to use up eighty or a hundred good miles in traveling around it. As it lay there with the dark shadows of the high mountains brilliantly photographed upon its still surface, I thought it must surely be the fairest picture the whole earth affords.

Adverbs

An **adverb** is a word that modifies a verb, an adjective, or another adverb by making its meaning more specific.

Like adjectives, adverbs are modifiers. Adjectives modify nouns and pronouns; adverbs modify verbs, adjectives, and other adverbs. Adverbs modify by answering the questions *when? where? how?* and *to what degree?* The following sentence illustrates the use of adverbs to modify an adjective (*few*), a verb (*nest*), and an adverb (*successfully*).

Extremely few eagles **now** nest **very** successfully in the area.

Recognizing Adverbs

You can test whether a word is an adverb by seeing if it makes sense in one of the following sentences:

He did it _____.
She has _____ done it.
He is feeling _____ tired.
We did it _____ well.

Certain suffixes signal that a word is an adverb. The most widely used is *-ly* when it is added to an adjective. Others include *-ward* and *-wise*.

logically   skyward   clockwise
totally   upward   likewise

Like adjectives, some adverbs have different forms to indicate degree of comparison. (For rules on forming and using the degrees of comparison, see Chapter 24.)

POSITIVE	COMPARATIVE	SUPERLATIVE
arrived **late**	arrived **later**	arrived **latest**
speaks **properly**	speaks **more properly**	speaks **most properly**
works **well**	works **better**	works **best**

When an adverb modifies a verb, it may be placed in various positions in relation to the verb. When an adverb modifies an adjective or another adverb, it immediately precedes the modified word.

MODIFYING A VERB	**Eventually** the train will arrive at the station.
	The train will **eventually** arrive at the station.
	The train will arrive at the station **eventually.**
MODIFYING AN ADJECTIVE	The train is **very** late.
MODIFYING AN ADVERB	**Only** rarely does the train arrive on time.

EXERCISE 24 **Identifying Adverbs.** Write down the adverb in each of the following sentences. Then write the word or words each adverb modifies. (Remember that adverbs modify an entire verb phrase.)

1. Diamonds are very valuable stones.
2. They have always been prized as gems.
3. Diamonds are used for practical purposes here.
4. One spacecraft was handsomely equipped with a diamond window.
5. Diamond is the one material that could easily withstand the extremes of temperature and pressure.
6. Eye surgeons can now remove cataracts with diamond knives.
7. Diamonds often are associated with romance and superstition.
8. The beautifully cut Hope Diamond is reputed to have brought disaster to its owners.
9. A diamond ring is usually given for engagements and weddings as a symbol of everlasting love.
10. This mysterious and highly desirable gem is crystallized carbon.

EXERCISE 25 **Completing Sentences with Adverbs.** On your paper complete the following sentences by replacing each blank with the kind of adverb named in parentheses.

1. Years ago, ships did not sail ____*(to what degree)*____ ____*(where)*____ from land.
2. Mariners _____*(how)*_____ beached their craft at night, rising _____*(when)*_____ the next morning to continue their voyage.
3. _____*(when)*_____, as ships became larger, mariners became ____*(to what degree)*____ more daring.
4. Using the polestar, which _____*(when)*_____ points northward, as a guide, mariners could navigate _____*(how)*_____ at night.
5. Today, ____*(to what degree)*____ sophisticated equipment has _____*(how)*_____ simplified navigation.
6. But modern technology has not lessened ____*(to what degree)*____ _____*(how)*_____ the joy of sailing.
7. For many ancient and modern mariners, sailing the seas is ____*(to what degree)*____ more important than _____*(how)*_____ reaching a destination.
8. _____*(when)*_____, it is the search for adventure that _____*(how)*_____ steers the course.
9. _____*(when)*_____ outer space offers new unexplored seas of a _____*(how)*_____ new kind.
10. The new ships can navigate _____*(how)*_____ while their crews sleep _____*(how)*_____.

Positioning Adverbs. (a) On your paper, add an appropriate verb-modifying adverb to each of the following sentences. (b) Rewrite each sentence, placing the adverb in a different position.

SAMPLE Sir Edmund Hillary reached the top of Mount Everest.

ANSWER (a) Sir Edmund Hillary triumphantly reached the top of Mount Everest.

(b) Triumphantly, Sir Edmund Hillary reached the top of Mount Everest.

1. The mountaineers approached the foot of the mountain.
2. They gazed upward toward the pinnacle.
3. They remembered their long training and painstaking preparations.
4. The mountaineers climbed up the steep slope.
5. Around them the cold wind blew.
6. The climbers watched for signs of avalanches.
7. They had listened to all the weather reports.
8. At one point the climbers considered turning back.
9. Then the slope leveled out.
10. The climbers had reached the top of the mountain.
11. They planted their country's flag on the peak.
12. They celebrated their achievement.
13. Then they rested before they began their descent.
14. The mountaineers climbed down the now familiar slope.
15. They were greeted by the villagers who lived at the foot of the mountain.

Kinds of Adverbs

An **adverb of time** *tells when.*

Some adverbs of time tell about a particular point in time (*now*). Some tell about duration (*continually*). Some tell about frequency (*seldom*).

> Young eagles **now** fly.
> The baby cries **continually.**
> The baby **seldom** cries.
> The baby **often** cries.

An **adverb of place** tells *where.*

Some adverbs of place tell about position (*there*). Some tell about direction (*forward*).

> The mother eagle perches **here.**
> Young eagles fly **there.**
> The offense charged **forward.**

An **adverb of degree** tells *to what degree* or *to what extent.*

When adverbs of degree are used with adjectives or other adverbs, they are sometimes called *intensifiers,* because they indicate the degree of intensity of the adjective or the other adverb.

> **Very** young eagles fly **quite** eagerly. [The adverbs tell the degree of youth and of eagerness.]
>
> He **somewhat** accepts their argument. [The adverb tells the degree of acceptance.]
>
> She was **completely** content. [The adverb tells the degree of contentment.]

An **adverb of manner** tells *how* or *the means by which* an action is done.

Adverbs of manner generally answer the question *how?* or *by which means?* Sometimes adverbs of manner modify adjectives:

> HOW **carefully** wired, agrued **effectively**
>
> BY WHICH MEANS **electrically** wired, treated **radioactively**
>
> MODIFYING
> AN ADJECTIVE **ridiculously** funny

Most, but not all, adverbs of manner end in *-ly* (for example, *closely, happily*). The *-ly* is added to an adjective to form the adverb of manner. Be aware of other common words that do not end in *-ly* but that are also adverbs of manner (for example, *alone,* as in *walked alone*).

NEGATIVE WORDS AS ADVERBS

The word *not* and the contraction *-n't* are considered adverbs. Other negative words can function as adverbs of time, place, and degree.

> The cow is **not** in the barn.
> The cow is **nowhere** in sight.
> I **never** saw a purple cow.
> The cow **scarcely** chews her cud.

EXERCISE 27   **Classifying Adverbs.** Identify each italicized adverb in the following sentences as: (a) an adverb of time, (b) an adverb of place, (c) an adverb of degree, (d) an adverb of manner, or (e) a negative adverb.

1. *Very* intense heat and pressure crystallize carbon into diamonds *underground.*
2. Diamonds vary *rather widely* in value.
3. Experts *usually* determine diamond value *quite simply* by evaluating carat, cut, clarity, and color.
4. A high weight in carats *definitely* raises a diamond's value.
5. The carat weight of a rough diamond may be *greatly* reduced when the diamond is cut.

6. If a diamond is polished and shaped *expertly*, it is *more* valuable than a diamond of the same weight that is *not* polished.
7. Fifty-eight facets sparkle *brilliantly* from the *most* popular diamond cut.
8. Well-cut diamonds are *breathtakingly* beautiful.
9. Diamonds that are *heavily* flawed *almost always* cost less than flawless stones.
10. Colorless diamonds are the *most highly* valued for use in precious jewelry.

SENTENCE WRITING **Following Models.** A "Tom Swifty" is a sentence in which an adverb comments in a humorous way on an action or object mentioned in a quotation. Note the relationship between each adverb and quotation in the following examples:

"I cleaned my room," Craig said *tidily*.
"This picture has no color," complained Andrea *drably*.

(a) Write each of the following Tom Swifties on your paper, completing each with an adverb that comments in a humorous way on the quotation. (b) Write five Tom Swifties of your own, using the adverbs provided. Consult a dictionary if necessary.

1. "Don't burn yourself!" Meg warned _____.
2. "Nice job of sanding that board," said the carpenter _____.

3. "These flowers were just picked," the florist said _____.
4. "Is the pond frozen yet?" asked Brent _____.
5. "That lemon made my mouth pucker!" Robin
   exclaimed _____.
6. dully   7. crisply   8. softly   9. blandly   10. coolly

REVIEW EXERCISE   **Adverbs.** On your paper write each of the twenty adverbs in the following paragraph. Then write the word or words that each adverb modifies.

[1]As a child Pearl Primus came north to the United States from Trinidad. [2]Later, she attended college in New York and apparently planned to be a doctor. [3]She never expected to be a dancer. [4]Her obvious talent very quickly distinguished her: Soon she won a scholarship and was studying dance exclusively. [5]Subsequently she worked with Martha Graham, Doris Humphrey, and other masters of modern dance. [6]When she performed professionally, she received rave reviews everywhere for her beautiful dancing. [7]Critics justifiably called her the outstanding new dancer of 1943. [8]Primus was greatly interested in African dance and is widely credited with the introduction of African motifs into American dance. [9]Her quite frequent trips to the Caribbean and Africa helped her substantially, and she translated African dances meaningfully for all audiences. [10]At age sixty Primus had hardly slowed her pace. [11]She developed programs for the handicapped and worked persistently on her doctoral degree. [12]In 1978 she finally received it.

Revising Your Writing

Notice the italicized adverbs in the following sentence from a story by Dorothy Canfield Fisher:

> The Elwells were *not consciously* unkind to their aunt—they were *even* in a vague way fond of her; but she was so *utterly* insignificant a figure in their lives that they bestowed no thought whatever on her.

Try reading the sentence without the adverbs, and you will see how important they are to Fisher's meaning. The negative adverb *not* is essential. The other adverbs "fine-tune" the sentence's meaning; they either add subtlety or emphasis. Keep in mind the following techniques when you write and revise your work:

1. Add subtlety to an expression by balancing a negative adverb with a negative adjective or verb. For example, Fisher does not say outright that the Elwells are unkind. She understates the situation by modifying *unkind* with *not consciously.*

2. Use adverbs to emphasize a point. Notice how Fisher uses *even* and *utterly* to stress the irony of the Elwells' fondness and the extreme hopelessness of the aunt's position.

Apply these techniques in revising the following passage. Employ the first technique to the italicized adjective. Add adverbs in the places indicated by carets (∧).

> The Patersons were ∧ *ungenerous* to their dinner guests. They ∧ set out their finest china, but the meats they served, although ample, were ∧ unchewable. ∧ the vegetables were stringy and ∧ unpalatable. A dinner with the Patersons was ∧ forgotten.

One problem that you may discover as you revise your writing is unnecessary adverbs. When an adverb does not add precision, subtlety, or emphasis to a sentence, it is meaningless and should be deleted:

I felt rather tired after raking leaves all afternoon.

In addition, you should delete any adverb that duplicates an idea implied by another word in the sentence. For example, in the following sentence, *again* duplicates the meaning of *repeat*:

The reporter asked the speaker to repeat her answer again.

Apply these guidelines by revising the following sentences on your paper. Each sentence contains two adverbs. Decide which adverb is unnecessary, and delete it.

1. I immediately returned the defective appliance back to the store where I had purchased it.
2. As North America's only marsupial, the exeedingly timid opossum is very unique among our wildlife.
3. At low tide we curiously watched the crabs sidle across the rocks sideways.
4. At the very first sound of the alarm, the soldiers dashed quickly for cover.

Prepositions

A **preposition** is a word that shows the relationship of a noun or pronoun to some other word in a sentence.

Prepositions express space, time, and other relationships among words.

The garage is **behind** the house. [*Behind* shows the spatial relationship of the house and the garage.]

The engine purred **after** the adjustment. [*After* tells the time relationship between the purring and the adjustment.]

The car started **with** ease. [Here, *with* does not cover a spatial or time relationship, but it does relate *started* and *ease*.]

As with pronouns, there are only a limited number of prepositions in English. Here are some common ones.

aboard	beneath	in	since
about	beside	inside	through
above	besides	into	throughout
across	between	like	to
after	beyond	near	toward
against	but*	of	under
along	by	off	underneath
among	concerning	on	until
around	down	onto	up
at	during	outside	upon
before	except	over	with
behind	for	past	within
below	from	regarding	without

A **compound preposition** is a preposition that is made up of more than one word.

according to	because of	instead of
ahead of	by means of	next to
along with	in addition to	on account of
apart from	in front of	on top of
aside from	in spite of	out of

Recognizing Prepositions

You can test whether a word is a preposition by seeing if it makes sense in one of the following sentences:

No one talked _____ me.
We put them _____ the freight cars.
The march proceeded _____ the early afternoon.

---

*meaning "except"

Prepositions begin phrases that generally end with a noun or pronoun, called the *object of the preposition.*

> He gave me a book **of poetry.**   Susan sat **next to me.**
> I was talking **with Susan.**

(For more information about the function of prepositional phrases, see Chapter 19.)

Unlike nouns, pronouns, verbs, adjectives, and adverbs, prepositions never undergo spelling changes. Every preposition has just one form.

The word *preposition* means "placed before." In general, a preposition comes before the noun or pronoun that ends the phrase.

EXERCISE 28   **Identifying Prepositions.** On your paper list the prepositions in each of the following sentences. Remember that some prepositions are made up of more than one word. (The numeral in parentheses at the end of each item indicates the number of prepositions in that sentence.)

1. Wills O'Brien, a creator of special effects for the early film industry, pioneered the use of rubber and clay models in movies   (4)
2. Shooting the film frame by frame and changing the position of the model slightly between shots, he created illusionary movement.   (3)
3. By means of this method, O'Brien shot an experimental film with a clay dinosaur that "roamed" through a miniature set.   (3)
4. Since the dinosaur's movements looked too choppy in this first attempt, O'Brien shot a second version, using dinosaurs made from rubber and metal instead of clay and wood.   (3)
5. Six years after this film, which was distributed throughout the United States, O'Brien worked on a full-length movie concerning dinosaurs in a South American jungle.   (5)
6. During one scene a brontosaurus is brought across the ocean to London, where it escapes and runs around the city.   (4)
7. In addition to his dinosaur models, O'Brien used scenery painted onto glass panes that he positioned in front of the action.   (3)
8. Because of O'Brien's skill, models and sets turned into believable monsters and jungles on the movie screen.   (3)
9. Years later another movie showed a giant gorilla on top of the Empire State Building, high above the frightened crowds.   (2)
10. This giant gorilla, which we now know as King Kong, was created by O'Brien.   (2)

SENTENCE WRITING   **Creating Sentences with Prepositions.** Choose five prepositions from the lists on page 426. Use each one in a sentence. Add adjectives and adverbs wherever necessary.

Conjunctions

A **conjunction** is a word that joins single words or groups of words.

Conjunctions are very important because they clarify the relationship between parts of a sentence. English has four kinds of conjunctions: *coordinating conjunctions, correlative conjunctions, subordinating conjunctions,* and *conjunctive adverbs.*

Here we will study the first two in detail and cover the second two briefly. The last two will come up again in Chapter 20.

Coordinating Conjunctions

A **coordinating conjunction** joins words or groups of words that have equal grammatical weight in a sentence.

The coordinating conjunctions are *and, but, or, nor, for,* and *yet.* All the coordinating conjunctions except *for* can join words, phrases, or clauses. *For* joins only clauses and nothing else.

> She serves **and** volleys. [joins words]
>
> He writes in French **but** not in English. [joins phrases]
>
> Practice writing, **or** you will never improve. [joins clauses]
>
> She had no homework, **nor** did she have basketball practice. [joins clauses]

EXERCISE 29 **Identifying Coordinating Conjunctions.** Write the coordinating conjunction in each of the following sentences.

1. Atop Mount Washington, winds have hit 231 miles per hour, and temperatures have fallen to minus 47° Fahrenheit.
2. Station WMTW-TV maintains transmitting facilities on Mount Washington, for the high altitude increases transmitting range.
3. The U.S. Weather Bureau has a year-round station on the summit, and meteorologists spend the winter there.
4. The meteorologists and the television technicians say that they have sensed an invisible presence on Mount Washington.
5. These people are not superstitious, nor do they believe in ghosts.
6. The Kennebec-Abnaki tribe considered Mount Washington the home of "the great spirit," and so they named it Agiocochook.
7. Three men spent the winter on Mount Washington, but S. A. Nelson was the first to endure a summit gale there alone.
8. In May of 1871 Nelson wrote in his journal that a dead calm followed the winds and that he felt he was not alone.
9. Al Oxton of the Mount Washington Observatory watched a curtain being lifted off its hooks and dropped around his neck.
10. Do you think there is a ghost or a great spirit on Mount Washington?

Correlative Conjunctions

Correlative conjunctions work in pairs to join words and groups of words of equal weight in a sentence.

both . . . and   neither . . . nor   though . . . yet
either . . . or   not only . . . but (also)   whether . . . or
just . . . so

You use the first part of the correlative conjunction before one word or group of words and the second part before the related word or group of words. Correlative conjunctions make the relationship between words or groups of words a little clearer than do coordinating conjunctions.

COORDINATING CONJUNCTIONS	CORRELATIVE CONJUNCTIONS
You and I must go.	**Both you and I** must go [*You* and *I* are of equal value: They are related words. The correlative conjunction *both . . . and* makes the relationship clearer and stronger than does the coordinating conjunction *and.*]
You or I must go.	**Either you or I** must go.
	Neither you nor I must go.
We saw **Paris and Rome.**	We saw **not only Paris but also Rome.**

EXERCISE 30 **Identifying Correlative Conjunctions.** On your paper write both parts of the correlative conjunctions in the following sentences.

1. Countries issue special stamps either to honor a famous person or to commemorate an important event.
2. Some countries print specially priced stamps that both celebrate an event and generate extra funds.
3. Either original art or reproductions of famous paintings may decorate special stamps.

4. The special 1893 stamp not only celebrated the discovery of America but also was the first U.S. commemorative stamp.
5. Other stamps have honored both famous leaders and important occasions.
6. Neither the Apollo space flight nor the Bicentennial passed without a special stamp.
7. During the International Year of the Child, children's art appeared on both postage stamps and holiday seals.
8. Neither the American Lung Association nor the design sponsors chose the themes for the seals.
9. Each school decided whether to tell its children exactly what to draw or simply to suggest a holiday theme.
10. Just as these U.S. holiday seals celebrated children's art, so did the postage stamps from many other countries.

EXERCISE 31 **Completing Sentences with Coordinating and Correlative Conjunctions.** On your paper supply the coordinating or correlative conjunctions that make the most sense in each of the following sentences.

1. In colonial America both secondary school and college were open to men, but _____ secondary school _____ college was open to women.
2. For their education women relied on _____ private tutors ____ family members.
3. Most women were not encouraged to study at all, _____ they were considered to be better suited for domestic concerns.
4. Women were believed to have three common traits—patience, perseverance, _____ neatness.
5. Secondary schools for women first appeared in the 1820s, _____ Mount Holyoke, the first women's college, did not open until 1837.
6. The early women's colleges took science education very seriously, making use of scientific apparatus, books, _____ teachers.
7. _____ science was considered important to the development of the mind, _____ it was not thought to be a suitable career for a woman.
8. Most women were naturally incapable of serious scientific work— _____ so it was argued.
9. Clearly this charge did not apply to Ellen Swallow, _____ she became the first woman to attend a graduate school of science.
10. She _____ became a special student in chemistry at the Massachusetts Institute of Technology _____ played an important role in the growth of ecology.

Subordinating Conjunctions

A **subordinating conjunction** joins two clauses, or ideas, in such a way as to make one grammatically dependent upon the other.

The idea, or clause, that a subordinating conjunction introduces is said to be "subordinate," or dependent, because it cannot stand by itself as a complete sentence. You will learn more about these conjunctions when you study clauses (Chapter 20). Here are examples of subordinating conjunctions in use:

> We cheered the tall ships **because** they were exciting.
> We cheered the tall ships **when** they arrived.
> **Whenever** the ships sail again, we will want to see them.
> We will want to see them **if** they sail again.

Here is a list of common subordinating conjunctions:

after	as soon as	inasmuch as	unless
although	as though	in order that	until
as	because	since	when
as far as	before	so long as	whenever
as if	considering (that)	so that	where
as long as	if	than	while

EXERCISE 32 **Identifying Subordinating Conjunctions.** Write the subordinating conjunction in each of the following sentences. Remember that some subordinating conjunctions are made up of more than one word.

1. Considering that Harold Krent was totally blind by his eighth birthday, his achievements are extraordinary.
2. Life is not easy when you are visually handicapped.
3. When he was in high school, Harold was elected president of his school by his classmates.
4. Because Krents was brilliant, he was accepted at Harvard.
5. Before he went to Harvard, Krents spent the summer as a music and dramatics counselor at a camp.
6. Since he could find his way among the tents in the dark, Krents easily kept the campers quiet after taps.
7. As soon as he had graduated *cum laude* from Harvard College, Krents ws accepted at Harvard Law School.
8. Harold Krents became acquainted with his future wife while she was reading for blind law students.
9. Harold Krents was very surprised when his draft board mistakenly classified him 1-A.
10. After he had heard Krents's story, Leonard Gershe wrote the Broadway hit *Butterflies Are Free*.

Conjunctive Adverbs

A **conjunctive adverb** is used to clarify the relationship between clauses of equal weight in a sentence.

Conjunctive adverbs are usually stronger and more precise than coordinating conjunctions. Consider the difference in emphasis between the following two sentences.

COORDINATING CONJUNCTION The ships sailed away, **but** they left us with many happy memories.

CONJUNCTIVE ADVERB The ships sailed away; **however,** they left us with many happy memories.

Note that a semicolon comes before the conjunctive adverb and that the adverb is usually followed by a comma.

There are many conjunctive adverbs, and they have several uses:

TO REPLACE *AND* also, besides, furthermore, moreover
TO REPLACE *BUT* however, nevertheless, still, although
TO STATE A RESULT consequently, therefore, so, thus
TO STATE EQUALITY equally, likewise, similarly.

EXERCISE 33 **Identifying Conjunctive Adverbs.** Each of the following sentences has one conjunctive adverb. Write it on your paper.

1. It has never been easy to harness the energy of the sun; nevertheless, people have tried since ancient times.
2. The ancient Greeks may have ignited Roman ships by bouncing sunlight onto them with mirrors; also, an eighteenth-century French chemist created an effective solar furnace.
3. Solar energy is spread out; furthermore, its strength depends on the season, time of day, and number of clouds in the sky.
4. Scientists have developed solar energy collectors and furnaces; consequently, it has become possible to heat buildings with solar energy.
5. Solar-heating systems are costly; however, they eventually pay for themselves.
6. Solar-heating systems can cut fuel costs by 70 percent; moreover, they require little maintenance.
7. A solar heater for a swimming pool can pay for itself in three years; similarly, a home solar heater can pay for itself in seven years.
8. Solar panels serve only to collect the sun's heat; therefore, another medium must be installed to transfer that heat to the house.
9. No solar-heating system can completely eliminate reliance on coal or gas; still, the system does save a considerable amount of fuel.
10. Today, solar energy fuels satellites in space; likewise, it will be used in the future to generate electricity for industrial purposes.

Following Models. Each of the following quotations has conjunctions in it. Using each quotation as a model, write your own version with the same conjunctions in the same position. A sample response is provided for each item.

1. If we ever see how we got here, we may know a little better where we are.

—Robert M. Adams, critic

SAMPLE ANSWER If you knew how a file should be organized, you would know where to look for your records.

2. Either war is obsolete, or men are.

—R. Buckminster Fuller, American engineer

SAMPLE ANSWER Either I will marry her, or someone else will.

3. I don't know whether Churchill enjoyed making speeches, but he looked as if he did.

—Prince Philip

SAMPLE ANSWER The actors were not sure whether the performance was a success, but they acted as if it had been.

4. Not only did he not suffer fools gladly, but he did not suffer them at all.

—Lester Pearson, Canadian politician

SAMPLE ANSWER Not only did the senators pass the resolution, but they passed it unanimously.

REVIEW EXERCISE **Conjunctions.** On your paper replace the blank in each of the following sentences with a conjunction that makes sense. The kind of conjunction you should use is stated in parentheses.

1. The Flathead River lies mostly in the United States; _____ its headwaters are in Canada.   (conjunctive adverb)
2. The lands drained by the Flathead River are forests, _____ they are populated by about two-thirds of the remaining grizzly bears.   (coordinating conjunction)
3. _____ the threatened grizzly _____ the Rocky Mountain wolf inhabit the Flathead wilderness.   (correlative conjunction)
4. The North Fork of the Flathead River is eventually joined by _____ the Middle Fork _____ the South Fork.   (correlative conjunction)
5. _____ you visit the North Fork valley, you may meet Mary McFarland, a retired veterinarian. (subordinating conjunction)
6. From Mary McFarland's window you can see mountains _____ you turn. (subordinating conjunction)

7. Luckily, _____ a Dolly Varden trout _____a rare cut-throat trout is a likely catch along the Flathead River. (correlative conjunction: Pay attention to the form of the linking verb.)
8. Otters play along the Flathead River _____ bald eagles soar overhead. (subordinating conjunction)
9. _____ it leaves the wild country, the Flathead River meanders through rich farmlands into Lake Flathead, just west of the Mississippi. (subordinating conjunction)
10. _____ the Flathead emerges from the lake, it turns west to join the mighty Columbia River. (subordinating conjunction).

Revising Your Writing

Revise the paragraph below by replacing some of the coordinating conjunctions with more precise connectives. Use the following guidelines to help you.

1. Try to improve your writing by stressing the relationship between words with correlative conjunctions instead of relying on coordinating conjunctions.

   SAMPLE   He won a gold medal and a cash prize.
   REVISION   He won not only the gold medal but also a cash prize.

2. Try to replace coordinating conjunctions with conjunctive adverbs to state a result or to state equality.

   SAMPLE   The play was poor, but I sat through it.
   REVISION   The play was poor; nevertheless, I sat through it.

3. Try to make the relationship between two ideas clearer by replacing coordinating conjunctions with subordinating conjunctions.

   SAMPLE   The play was poor, but I sat through it anyway.
   REVISION   Although the play was poor, I sat through it.

As you revise, pay particular attention to the italicized words and the places marked by carets (∧).

> ∧I coax my dog Bruno into the tub, *and then* I use the hose to fill it with water. Bruno∧dislikes baths *and* he even dislikes water. *And so* lathering him up is a challenge.∧He keeps trying∧to shake himself dry *and* leap out of the tub. ∧Bruno gets his bath, *and* I get one, too!

As you revise the following paragraph on your paper, find the coordinating conjunctions for yourself, and decide which of them should be replaced with correlative conjunctions, conjunctive adverbs, or subordinating conjunctions. Aim not only for precision of expression in your revision but also for variety in the kinds of conjunctions you use.

[1]Collecting postage stamp errors is a major area of philately, and it is interesting more and more collectors worldwide. [2]By far the most popular errors to collect are those involving missing colors, and these occasionally result from a mishap during the printing process. [3]Such errors remove certain details from the stamps, and they may produce startling effects, such as headless figures or missing denominations. [4]Other errors involve mistakes in perforation. [5]The sheet of stamps slips, and the perforator may cut into the stamps' design, but the most sought-after perforation errors have no perforations at all. [6]Called imperforates, these errors may cost the collector hundreds or even thousands of dollars, and they are exceedingly rare. [7]Errors can be found to suit almost every stamp collector's budget. [8]Many dealers stock the more common kinds of errors, and these involve double impressions, wrong paper or gum, or mistakes in the stamp's phosphor coating.

Interjections

An **interjection** is a word or phrase that expresses emotion or exclamation. An interjection has no grammatical connection to any other words.

An interjection can be part of a sentence, or it can stand alone.

Oh, didn't you know?
Ah, your father knows the recipe.
Oops! I slipped.
Why, Harry!

Interjections are used more often in informal speech than in writing.

EXERCISE 34 **Using Interjections.** On your paper fill the blanks in the following sentences with an appropriate interjection from the list below.

wow   ssh   good luck   help   hi

1. _____, the movie is about to begin.
2. _____! The sink is overflowing.
3. _____! We hope to see you at the finish line.
4. _____, we just moved into the house next door.
5. _____! How did you manage to catch that pass?
6. _____! I'm glad that test is over.
7. _____! What an incredible view there is from here!
8. _____, I wish you'd told me that sooner.
9. _____! Where do you think you're going with my bicycle?
10. _____, what a fantastic picture that would make!

Words as More Than One Part of Speech

A word's part of speech is directly related to how the word is used in a sentence.

Many words can be more than one part of speech. Notice, for example, how the word *down* is a different part of speech in each of the following sentences:

NOUN	My pillow is stuffed with **down.**
VERB	Can a hurricane **down** an oak tree?
ADJECTIVE	Marcia bought a **down** jacket.
ADVERB	The baby fell **down.**
PREPOSITION	The boulder rolled **down** the hill.

The following sections will explain how words normally considered one part of speech may often act as another part of speech.

Noun or Adjective?

Many words commonly listed as nouns in a dictionary may act as adjectives by modifying other nouns.

NOUNS   The couple pledged their **love** to each other.
         The wall was made of **concrete.**
ADJECTIVES   They read a **love** poem.
              They built a **concrete** wall.

Some combinations of nouns become so common that they are often thought of, to varying extents, as compound nouns.

city council   dog biscuit   summer squash

EXERCISE 35   **Using Nouns as Adjectives.** Use each noun below as an adjective by having it modify another noun.

SAMPLE   shirt   ANSWER   shirt button

1. kitchen kitchen sink   5. beach beach blanket
2. hat hat tree   6. flower flower basket
3. farm farm team   7. bread bread knife
4. ocean ocean beach   8. telephone telephone cord

Pronoun or Adjective?

Many pronouns may be used like adjectives. Possessive pronouns, demonstrative pronouns, interrogative pronouns, and indefinite pronouns can all be used as adjectives when they modify a noun.

The following possessive pronouns by their very nature modify nouns by answering the question *which one?*: *my, your, his, her, its, our, their.*

POSSESSIVE PRONOUN   The book is **his.**
POSSESSIVE ADJECTIVE   **His** book is lost.

This and *that* may modify singular nouns. *These* and *those* may modify plural nouns.

DEMONSTRATIVE PRONOUN   **This** is the one I want.
DEMONSTRATIVE ADJECTIVE   **This** book is my choice.

The interrogative pronouns *whose, what,* and *which* may be used as adjectives.

INTERROGATIVE PRONOUN   **Whose** are you playing?
INTERROGATIVE ADJECTIVE   **Whose** symphony are you playing?

Many indefinite pronouns function as adjectives.

INDEFINITE PRONOUN   **Some** grew tired.
INDEFINITE ADJECTIVE   **Some** swimmers grew tired.

EXERCISE 36 **Distinguishing Between Pronouns and Adjectives.** List on your paper the twenty-five italicized words from the following sentences. Then write whether each word is used here as a pronoun or an adjective.

"Affinities" is a game (1) *that* challenges players to make a list of words commonly joined by "and." The player (2) *whose* list is longest wins. "Day and night," "bread and butter," "meat and potatoes," and (3) *many* (4) *more* would qualify as affinities. In (5) *another* game, called "Hidden Words," the leader gives (6) *several* words of ten or (7) *more* letters. From the long words players make a list of shorter words. The game (8) *"What* Did the Person Wear?"* tests how (9) *much* people notice about (10) *other* people. In (11) *this* game, (12) *one* person leaves the room and the (13) *other* players answer questions such as, (14) *"What* color shirt was (15) *that* person wearing?" and "Would you say (16) *his* were suede or canvas shoes?" A (17) *little* creativity is needed for "Alphabet Tale." For (18) *this* game players write a story twenty-six words in length; (19) *each* of the words must begin with a successive letter of the alphabet. (20) *This* is an excellent way to learn new words.

(21) *These* brain teasers are sure to challenge (22) *your* powers of thinking. (23) *All* can be played without (24) *much* difficulty, and (25) *several* are as educational as they are entertaining.

Preposition or Adverb?

Many of the words listed as prepositions on page 426 can, in some sentences, be adverbs. If the word stands alone and answers a question such as *where?* or *when?* and if it does not connect a noun or pronoun to the rest of the sentence, consider the word an adverb. Otherwise consider it a preposition.

ADVERB The players assembled **inside.** [answers the question *where?*]
PREPOSITION The players assembled **inside** the auditorium. [connects the noun *auditorium* to the rest of the sentence]

EXERCISE 37 **Distinguishing Between Prepositions and Adverbs.** Decide whether the italicized word in each sentence is a preposition or an adverb. Write the answer on your paper.

1. An upholstered chair has springs and padding *inside.*
2. Springs and padding *inside* a chair make it comfortable.
3. Furniture makers upholster a chair by stretching strips of heavy cloth *across* the bottom of the frame.

4. These strips are placed *across* to give good support.
5. Upholsterers then put coil and zigzag springs *throughout* the chair.
6. Lighter springs may also be used *throughout*.
7. Next, furniture makers put padding *over* the springs.
8. Upholsterers use padding to give comfort all *over*.

Preposition or Conjunction?

The words *after, as, before, since,* and *until* can function in sentences as either prepositions or subordinating conjunctions. As prepositions these words connect a noun or pronoun to the rest of the sentence. As subordinating conjunctions these words will be followed by a word group that, without the conjunction, could stand alone as a sentence.

PREPOSITIONS Turn left **before** the park.
The car has been in the repair shop **since** yesterday.
CONJUNCTIONS We asked for directions **before** we drove to the park.
The car has been in the repair shop **since** I bought it.

EXERCISE 38 **Distinguishing Between Prepositions and Conjunctions.** List on your paper the ten italicized words from the following sentences. Identify each word as a preposition or a conjunction.

The ancient city of Pompeii once prospered (1) *as* an important commercial center in southern Italy. Then, in A.D. 79, nearby Mount Vesuvius erupted, raining ash and pumice onto Pompeii (2) *until* everything but the rooftops was buried. (3) *After* that famous eruption, the city remained buried and almost forgotten (4) *until* 1748, when excavation work began. (5) *Since* the layers of ash had protected Pompeii from the elements, excavators found an ancient city that looked much (6) *as* it had (7) *before* the disaster struck. Excavation was rather haphazard (8) *before* 1860, but (9) *after* archaeologists realized the city's immense value, they developed more systematic methods. Excavators have continued to work (10) *since* that time, revealing this ancient city to modern eyes.

SENTENCE WRITING **Using Words as Various Parts of Speech.** Write a sentence for each of the following words, using it as the part of speech indicated.

1. paper (noun)
2. paper (adjective)
3. this (pronoun)
4. this (adjective)
5. round (noun)
6. round (adjective)
7. along (preposition)
8. along (adverb)
9. before (preposition)
10. before (conjunction)

CHAPTER 17   PARTS OF SPEECH

Nouns [pages 388–393]   Identify each of the ten underlined nouns as (a) proper, (b) common and concrete, (c) common and abstract, (d) collective, or (e) common and compound.

Have you heard of a (1) land called (2) Thule (thoo lē)? The ancient (3) Greeks and Romans gave the name Thule to the northernmost land on the face of the (4) earth. An explorer named Pytheas supposedly sailed to Thule about (5) 300 B.C. Pytheas and his (6) crew reported that Thule was a land of great (7) beauty where summer nights were long and as bright as day. (8) Historians now think that Thule, the land of evening (9) sunshine, was probably (10) Scandinavia.

Pronouns [pages 396–402]   For each sentence, indicate whether the underlined pronoun is (a) personal or possessive, (b) reflexive or intensive, (c) demonstrative, (d) relative or interrogative, or (e) indefinite.

11. Who traveled with you?
12. Who traveled with you?
13. You yourself took the books that were on the table.
14. You yourself took the books that were on the table.
15. I did not know those were his.
16. I did not know those were his
17. She turned herself into a successful business executive in a very short period of time.
18. No one denies it.
19. Who said, "It is either all or nothing"?
20. Who said, "It is either all or nothing"?

Verbs [pages 402–409]   Indicate whether each of the ten underlined verbs is (a) a transitive action verb, (b) an intransitive action verb, (c) a linking verb, (d) an auxiliary, or (e) a verb phrase.

The electronic synthesizer (21) has changed music making tremendously. A synthesizer (22) is a machine that uses electronic impulses. Filters, oscillators, and special amplifiers (23) work together inside the synthesizer and (24) turn those impulses into sounds. By using a keyboard and a series of dials and switches, a musician (25) can control and shape the sounds. Synthesizers (26) are able to imitate almost any traditional instrument. The sounds (27) seem so authentic that few people (28) can tell that they are synthesized. Synthesizers (29) have been growing in popularity because they (30) give any musician the ability to "play" all the instruments of an entire orchestra.

Adjectives [pages 412–415] Match the underlined adjective in the left column with the correct identification in the right column.

31. They had made a date.
32. They liked Italian food.
33. The choice was obvious
34. It was the best restaurant.
35. The others were more expensive.

(a) comparative degree
(b) superlative degree
(c) definite article
(d) indefinite article
(e) proper adjective

Adverbs [pages 418–423] Match the underlined adverb in the left column with the correct identification in the right column.

36. She fully understood.
37. They would ride together.
38. He could not be found.
39. She went out.
40. Eventually he arrived.

(a) adverb of time
(b) adverb of place
(c) adverb of degree
(d) adverb of manner
(e) negative adverb

Prepositions, Conjunctions, and Interjections [pages 426–434, 437] Indicate whether each of the ten underlined words as used here is (a) a preposition, (b) a coordinating conjunction, (c) part of a correlative conjunction, (d) a subordinating conjunction, or (e) an interjection.

The Pulitzer Prize is named (41) after Joseph Pulitzer, a newspaper owner who died in 1911. In his will Pulitzer donated several million dollars to found the Columbia School of Journalism (42) and create a fund for annual awards. (43) When the prizes are given, they are divided into many categories. The categories include (44) both journalism and literature. Just as prizes are given (45) for reporting and editorials, (46) so they are also given for editorial cartoons. (47) Because Pulitzer wanted to support the arts, prizes are also awarded (48) to the best novel, play, and poetry. (49) Indeed, a prize is also given (50) in music.

Writing for Review Write one paragraph on any subject you choose. Underline and identify in your paragraph at least one example of each of the following parts of speech: noun, pronoun, verb, adjective, adverb, preposition, and conjunction.

Parts of the Sentence

Simple Subjects and Simple Predicates

In this chapter you will learn about different parts of sentences and how these parts work together. Once you understand these important concepts, you will be able to apply them to help you write more clearly and more effectively.

A **sentence** is a group of words that expresses a complete thought.

Every sentence has two basic parts, a *subject* and a *predicate*.

The **simple subject** is the principal noun or pronoun that tells what the sentence is about.

The **simple predicate** is the verb or verb phrase that tells something about the subject.

SIMPLE SUBJECT	SIMPLE PREDICATE
Condors	soar.
Spring	will come.
Coretta Scott King	is speaking.
Class	was canceled.

The simple subject is found by asking *who?* or *what?* about the verb. For example, in the first sentence above, the noun *condors* answers the question *what soar?*

Complete Subjects and Complete Predicates

In most sentences the meaning of the simple subject and the simple predicate is expanded or modified by the addition of other words and phrases.

The **complete subject** consists of the simple subject and all the words that modify it.

The **complete predicate** consists of the simple predicate and all the words that modify it or complete its meaning.

COMPLETE SUBJECT	COMPLETE PREDICATE
The condors of California	soar gracefully in the sky.
A welcome spring	will come after a cold winter.
Coretta Scott King	is the first speaker.
Our last class	suddenly was canceled.

Identifying Subjects and Predicates. Copy each of the following sentences, and indicate with a vertical line the division between the complete subject and the complete predicate. Next underline the simple subject once and the simple predicate twice.

SAMPLE ANSWER   <u>Mark Twain</u> of Hannibal, Missouri,/<u><u>used</u></u> his own life as material for his writing.

1. The characters in *The Adventures of Tom Sawyer* and *The Adventures of Huckleberry Finn* resemble real people.
2. Tom's Aunt Polly was modeled on Mark Twain's own mother.
3. The model for Huck Finn was Tom Blankenship, Mark Twain's best friend in Hannibal.
4. The hamlet of Hannibal, Missouri, was Mark Twain's home.
5. This little town on the Mississippi has a Tom Sawyer festival every July.
6. The funniest event of the festival is the fence-painting contest.
7. Children between the ages of ten and thirteen may enter this contest.
8. Each contestant must have a costume, a frog, and a weed to chew.
9. Soon the local fences are covered frantically with whitewash.
10. The contestants are judged on their costumes and on the speed and quality of their work.

Compound Subjects

A **compound subject** is made up of two or more simple subjects that are joined by a conjunction and that have the same verb.

Eagles and **owls** hunt for food.
Neither the two **eagles** nor the lone **owl** is hunting.
Eagles, owls, and **vultures** are birds of prey.

EXERCISE 2   **Identifying Compound Subjects.** Write on your paper the compound subject in each of the following sentences.

SAMPLE   Cars and musical instruments age differently.
ANSWER   cars, instruments

1. On leaving the showroom, cars and motorcycles lose a third of their value.
2. Years of use and added mileage further reduce their resale price.
3. Your job, your savings, and your credit are considered when you buy a new car.
4. Age and use, however, do not reduce the market value of all articles.
5. Works of art and musical instruments may increase in value with age.
6. Your first violin or painting is likely to increase in value.

7. Not only this rise in value but also other factors make art a good investment.
8. Good paintings and sculpture become more valuable but not actually better.
9. Most violins, violas, and cellos do actually improve with use and age.
10. Eventually yours and mine will achieve a richer tone.

Compound Predicates

A **compound predicate**, or **compound verb**, is made up of two or more verbs or verb phrases that are joined by a conjunction and that have the same subject.

> Eagles **soar** and **plunge**.
> We **have lost** or at least **misplaced** the map.
> Sandy **will buy** a stamp, **mail** the letter, and **hurry** home.
> Linda either **is** here already or **will be** here momentarily.

A sentence may have both a compound subject and a compound predicate. The terms *compound subject* and *compound predicate* always refer to a compound *simple* subject and a compound *simple* predicate.

> S   S   P   P
> **Eagles** and **condors soar** and **plunge** in the sky.

EXERCISE 3 | **Identifying Compound Predicates.** Write on your paper the compound predicate in each of the following sentences.

SAMPLE   These facts may startle and amaze your friends.
ANSWER   may startle, amaze

1. The following list of sports oddities will surprise athletes and perplex sports fans but amuse readers.
2. Land crabs sometimes grab golf balls and scamper to their holes.
3. Dogs often bury golf balls or swallow them.
4. During an extra-point kick in one football game, the ball exploded and split in half.
5. The ball hung in shreds but cleared the crossbar.
6. The fans neither believed their eyes nor accepted the score.
7. Notre Dame football players either practice ballet or shadowbox.
8. According to Knute Rockne, both activities maintain strength and develop grace.
9. During one high school basketball game four of the five players fouled out and sat on the bench.
10. The remaining player not only scored three points but also won the game.

Identifying Subjects and Predicates. On your paper copy the following sentences. Then underline simple subjects once and simple predicates twice. Some of the subjects and predicates are compound.

1. Neither football nor tennis originated in the United States.
2. The ancestor of football, "Dane's Head," was played first in the early Middle Ages in Europe.
3. The game of Dane's Head began halfway between two villages.
4. Each team maneuvered and kicked a ball toward the other team's village.
5. Soon towns and villages were neglecting archery practice and were playing football instead.
6. The government therefore issued a ban on football and maintained it until the seventeenth century.
7. By then archery was no longer necessary for the country's defense.
8. In football's early development players could kick but could not throw the ball.
9. Players of Rugby football, a later development, carried and threw the ball.
10. The forerunner of American football was introduced in 1823 in Rugby, England.

SENTENCE WRITING **Expanding Subjects and Predicates.** (a) Write five sentences, each with one subject and one predicate. (b) Expand each by making both the subject and the predicate compound.

SAMPLE ANSWER (a) Fred Astaire acted in movies in the 1930s.
(b) Fred Astaire and Ginger Rogers acted and danced in movies in the 1930s.

Order of Subject and Predicate

In most sentences in English, the subject comes before the verb. There are exceptions to this normal word order. Study the examples given below.

1. In the case of commands or requests, the subject *you* is not expressed; it is "understood."

> [You] **Jump!**
> [You] **Tear** it down.
> [You] **Ask** her.
> [You] **Please** come here.

2. At times a sentence is written in inverted order—that is, with the predicate before the subject. This reversal of the usual order is done to add emphasis. In the following examples the simple predicates and the simple subjects are in bold type.

PREDICATE	SUBJECT
Over the mountain **soared**	the two **eagles.**
Beyond the eagles **was**	a **condor.**

3. The words *there* and *here* are sometimes used as expletives. An *expletive* is a word used to introduce or to fill out a sentence. In sentences with expletives, the subject generally comes after the predicate. Very often the expletive is followed by a form of the verb *be*.

PREDICATE	SUBJECT
There **are**	three **owls** in the nest.
Here **is**	my **sister.**

Remember, to find the subject of a sentence, begin by finding the verb and then ask *who* or *what* of the verb. The answer to these questions will be the subject of the sentence.

[EXERCISE 5] **Recognizing Word Order.** Copy each of the following sentences, and draw a vertical line between the complete subject and the complete predicate. Next underline each simple subject once and each simple predicate twice. Some sentences are in normal subject-predicate order.

SAMPLE ANSWER   Below is a/brief history of farm machinery.

1. America has been the leader in the production of farm machinery since the last century.
2. There long had been many small farms in the East.
3. Heavy machinery was necessary there.
4. Only large-scale cultivation was profitable in the Midwest, however.
5. Large-scale cultivation demanded machines.

6. John Deere's invention of the steel plow was the first major development in farm implements.
7. There are many advantages to a steel plow.
8. Wet soil clings less to a steel plow.
9. After the steel plow came the invention of the mechanical reaper by
   McCormick in 1834.
10. There eventually were mechanical harvesters and combines to help
    farmers with their daily chores.

EXERCISE 6 **Writing Inverted Sentences.** Rewrite each of the following
sentences as an inverted sentence with the predicate first.

1. Her voice echoed through the empty hallways.
2. A dark cat crept up the rickety stairway.
3. The mournful cry of a dog came from far away.
4. Her three friends rushed into the room.
5. Their laughter echoed through the empty hallways.
6. The bright summer sunlight streamed past the lacy curtains.
7. The four girls darted from room to room.
8. The oldest of the girls bounded toward the open doors.
9. A soft breeze floated across the threshold.
10. Suddenly, the sharp command "Cut!" dropped from the director's
    chair overhead.

Complements

A **complement** is a word or group of words that complete the meaning of
the verb.

A complement is anything that helps to make something else complete.
A painting, for example, can be complemented by a frame. Similarly, a
subject and a verb often need a *complement* in order for the meaning of a
sentence to be complete. Note that the following sentences sound incomplete even though they include a subject and a verb:

> Roberto bought _____.
> That house looks _____.
> Parents often give children _____.

What complements would help complete the meaning of each of the
preceding items?

The next four sections will discuss four kinds of complements that can
be used to complete sentences: *direct objects, indirect objects, object complements,* and *subject complements.*

Direct Objects

A **direct object** answers the question *what?* or *whom?* after an action verb.

The subject of a sentence usually performs the action indicated by the verb. That action may be directed toward or received by someone or something: the direct object. Nouns, pronouns, or words acting as nouns may serve as direct objects. Only transitive verbs have direct objects; an intransitive verb never takes a direct object.

> Roberto bought **lunch**. [Roberto bought *what?*]
> Sandra likes **me** very much. [Sandra likes *whom?*]
> Ralph reported **what you had said**. [Ralph reported *what?*]

Like other sentence parts, direct objects may be *compound.*

> Roberto bought **lunch** and **dinner.** [Roberto bought *what?*]

EXERCISE 7 **Identifying Direct Objects.** On your paper write the action verb in each of the following sentences. Then list any direct objects. (One sentence has a compound object.)

1. In 1885 English immigrants founded a little town in North Dakota.
2. The settlers named it after their home town in England—Rugby.
3. The English town previously had given its name to Rugby football, a sport similar to soccer.
4. The American town never attracted a large industry or population.
5. Even today fewer than three thousand people make their home there.
6. Nevertheless, Rugby, North Dakota, enjoys a unique importance.
7. It occupies the exact center of the North American continent.
8. Imagine Rugby as the hub of a huge wheel.
9. Approximately fifteen hundred miles separate Rugby from the four borders of the continent.
10. Do Rugbyites have a longer trip to the seashore than anyone else in North America?

EXERCISE 8 **Adding Direct Objects.** On your paper complete the following subjects and verbs by adding a direct object. You may also add any other words that you need to make a sentence that makes sense.

1. Pioneers settled _____.
2. Every pioneer carried _____.
3. For the journey west, families needed _____.
4. Ahead of them, settlers drove _____.
5. Settlers built _____.

6. First they cleared _____.
7. A pioneer family mainly ate _____.
8. Women used spinning wheels to make _____.
9. Parents as well as schoolteachers educated _____.
10. Neighbors helped _____.

SENTENCE WRITING **Creating Sentences with Direct Objects.** Write five sentences describing how to make or do something. Use action verbs. Identify the subjects, verbs, and direct objects in these sentences.

Indirect Objects

An **indirect object** answers the question *to whom?* or *for whom?* or *to what?* or *for what?* after an action verb.

A sentence may have an indirect object only if it has a direct object. The indirect object will always come between the verb and the direct object, never after a preposition. Indirect objects are usually nouns or pronouns.

Engineers gave **students** awards. [Engineers gave awards *to whom?*]

Roberto bought **me** lunch. [Roberto bought lunch *for whom?*]

Trisha gives **homework** her full attention. [Trisha gives her full attention *to what?*]

Indirect objects may be *compound*.

Roberto bought **Flo** and **me** lunch. [Roberto bought lunch *for whom?*]

EXERCISE 9 **Identifying Indirect Objects.** First write on your paper the direct objects in each of the following sentences. Then list any indirect objects. (Not all sentences will have indirect objects.)

1. The Winchester Mystery House guarantees San Jose, California, a mention in any guidebook.
2. Sarah Winchester never finished the costly mansion.
3. In 1881 her husband left her a bequest of twenty million dollars.
4. Sarah bought herself an eight-room farmhouse.
5. With the best craftspeople available, Sarah began converting the farmhouse into an enormous Victorian mansion.
6. Sarah spent the next thirty-eight years enlarging the house.
7. Today the Winchester house has 158 rooms, 10,000 windows, 2,000 doors, and 40 staircases.
8. The Winchester House offers its many visitors some strange sights.
9. For example, the house has a door that opens onto a wall.
10. In 1973 California granted this house the status of a landmark.

Object Complements

An **object complement** answers the question *what?* after a direct object. That is, it *completes* the meaning of the direct object by identifying or describing the direct object.

Object complements occur only in sentences with direct objects and only in sentences with action verbs like the following.

appoint	consider	find	render
call	elect	make	think
choose	prove	name	voted

An object complement follows a direct object. An object complement may be an adjective, a noun, or a pronoun.

Engineers find plans **essential**. [adjective]
Nations often make their bridges **symbols**. [noun]
The citizens call that privilege **theirs**. [pronoun]
Geri considers me her **friend** and **adviser**. [nouns]

Object complements may also be *compound*, as in the last example.

EXERCISE 10 **Identifying Object Complements.** Write the object complement (or complements) in each of the following sentences.

1. Do you call money the root of all evil?
2. Does early to bed and early to rise make you healthy, wealthy, and wise?
3. Do you find honesty the best policy?
4. Do you call silence golden?
5. Will you make the future yours?

6. Does absence really make the heart fonder?
7. Do you call life a bowl of cherries?
8. Do you consider all history a lie?
9. Have airplanes rendered ocean liners useless?
10. Do you name your conscience your guide?
11. Is any place you hang your hat home?
12. Will they consider me an enemy?
13. Do you call your dog Lassie?
14. Has television made books obsolete?
15. Did you find the story interesting?

Subject Complements

A **subject complement** follows a subject and a linking verb and identifies or describes the subject.

A linking verb almost always needs one or more additional words in the predicate to complete its meaning. After all, a linking verb *links* a subject to something else. The "something else" is the subject complement, and there are two kinds: *predicate nominatives* and *predicate adjectives.*

A **predicate nominative** is a noun or pronoun that follows a linking verb and points back to the subject to identify it further.

Engineers are **scientists.**

The engineer on this project is **she.**

Predicate nominatives are usually found in sentences that contain forms of the linking verb *be.* Often these are sentences that classify things. A few other linking verbs (for example, *become* and *remain*) can be followed by a predicate nominative.

San Francisco is a **city.**
You became a **student** in my school.
Monday remains a **holiday** for us.

Like other sentence parts, predicate nominatives may be *compound.*

Nancy became a famous **singer** and **dancer.**
Jerry was neither a **friend** nor a **colleague** of mine.

A **predicate adjective** follows a linking verb and points back to the subject and further describes it.

Engineers are **inventive.**

Engineers must be highly **responsible.**

Predicate adjectives may follow any linking verb and may be *compound*.

The hikers had become very **weary**.
The team looks **ready** for the game.
Sheila seems **eager** and **determined**.
I feel quite **tired**.
These plums taste **sweeter**.

EXERCISE 11 **Identifying Subject Complements.** Write on your paper all the subject complements in the following sentences. Identify each as a predicate nominative or a predicate adjective. (Some sentences have more than one subject complement; others have none.)

[1]A farmer's market is a place where local farmers sell their produce. [2]In many communities these markets have become quite popular. [3]With the eager crowds, colorful stands, and shouting vendors, a farmer's market seems festive. [4]Locally grown fruit and vegetables, artfully arranged on open stands, look crisp and fresh. [5]Breads and rolls, often still warm from the oven, smell delicious. [6]To get their stands ready, the farmers must be early risers. [7]Many of them sell preserves or craft items as well as produce. [8]Their shouted sales pitches always sound persuasive. [9]Spend a morning at a farmer's market. [10]You will be a regular customer before you know it.

SENTENCE WRITING **Using Complements.** Write four sentences about a natural phenomenon, such as an eclipse, a thunderstorm, or a sunset. In each sentence use at least one of the four kinds of complements: direct object, indirect object, object complement, and subject complement. Label the complements in your sentences.

REVIEW EXERCISE **Complements.** On your paper write the complements that appear in the following paragraph. Next to each complement, write what kind of complement it is: direct object, indirect object, object complement, predicate nominative, or predicate adjective. (One sentence has a compound complement.)

[1]Lightning was mysterious to the ancient Greeks. [2]In fact, for them lightning was a weapon used by their chief god, Zeus. [3]According to mythology, the Greeks gave Zeus the thunderbolt and scepter. [4]Many persons today still consider lightning something to be feared. [5]Of course, the reasons for this fear seem sound. [6]During a storm lightning strikes the earth about one hundred times a second. [7]Sometimes, lightning strikes the tallest tree in a field. [8]Often lightning causes fire. [9]In addition, in the United States alone lightning kills approximately one hundred people every year. [10]Lightning can be both mysterious and dangerous.

Basic Sentence Patterns

You regularly combine the parts of the sentence in ways that produce recurring patterns. You can express these patterns in a kind of shorthand using capital letters. Most sentences in the English language fall into one of the following patterns:

1. **Subject + Action Verb (Intransitive)**

   S   AV(I)
   Eagles soar.

2. **Subject + Action Verb (Transitive) + Direct Object**

   S   AV(T) DO
   Eagles build nests.

3. **Subject + Action Verb (Transitive) + Indirect Object + Direct Object**

   S   AV(T) IO DO
   The parents are feeding the eaglets fish.

4. **Subject + Action Verb (Transitive) + Direct Object + Object Complement**

   S   AV(T) DO OC
   Ornithologists consider eagles predators.

5. **Subject + Linking Verb + Subject Complement (Predicate Nominative)**

   S   LV SC(PN)
   Eagles are predators.

6. **Subject + Linking Verb + Subject Complement (Predicate Adjective)**

   S   LV SC(PA)
   Eagles are powerful.

You may expand each of these basic patterns by adding modifiers, such as adjectives and adverbs.

S   AV(I)
The three eagles commonly soar above the valley.

Another common method of expanding basic sentence patterns is by compounding. Sentences may have various combinations of compound subjects, verbs, and complements.

S   S   AV(T) DO AV(T)
Either the male or the female may hatch the eggs and feed
DO
the young.

Identifying Sentence Patterns. On your paper write the basic sentence pattern of each sentence.

1. Fires are terrible.

2. In a forest flames cover the ground.

3. Firefighters use hoes, shovels, and rakes in their struggle.

4. They consider these fires difficult and dangerous.

5. Firefighters battle fires in homes, offices, and factories.

6. All fires are very dangerous.

7. Firefighters also rescue people trapped in cars or trains.

8. They aid victims of natural disasters such as floods and tornadoes.

9. Most fires are results of carelessness.

10. You and I should work to prevent fires.

SENTENCE WRITING **Creating Sentences with Various Patterns.** Write one sentence for each of the following sentence patterns. You may need to add modifiers to your subjects, verbs, and complements.

1. S + S + AV(T) + DO
2. S + AV(T) + DO + OC
3. S + LV + SC(PA)
4. S + AV(I) + AV(I)
5. S + AV(T) + IO + DO

Diagraming Basic Sentence Patterns

Diagraming is a method of showing the relationship of various words and parts of a sentence to the sentence as a whole.

The following examples show the traditional method of diagraming the six basic sentence patterns. The examples also show how to diagram modifiers, such as adjectives and adverbs, and compound sentence parts, such as compound subjects and predicates.

To diagram a sentence, find the simple subject; keep in mind it may be a compound subject. Then find the action or linking verb that goes with it. Write the subject and the verb on a horizontal line. Separate them with a vertical line that bisects the horizontal, dividing the complete subject from the complete predicate of the sentence.

Additional sentence elements are added as indicated in the following examples:

1. Subject + Action Verb (Intransitive)

Senators meet.

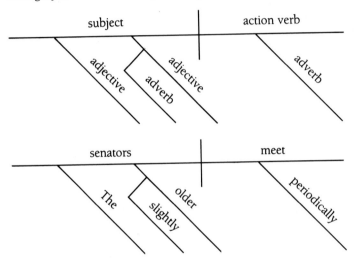

2. Subject + Action Verb (Intransitive), including adjectives and adverbs

The slightly older senators meet periodically.

3. Subject + Action Verb (Transitive) + Indirect Object + Direct Object

Experts give senators advice.

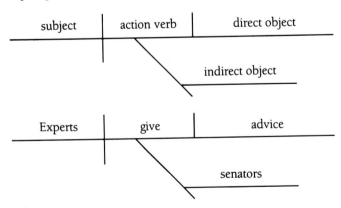

4. Compound Subject + Action Verb (Transitive) + Direct Object + Object Complement

Staff and supporters considered her important.

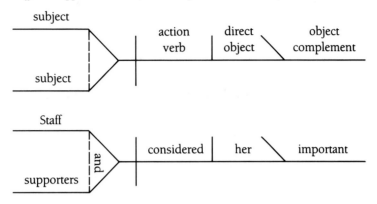

5. Subject + Linking Verb + Subject Complement (Predicate Nominative)

Senators are legislators.

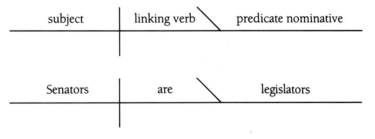

6. Subject + Compound Linking Verb + Subject Complement (Predicate Adjective)

Senators are busy but should be helpful.

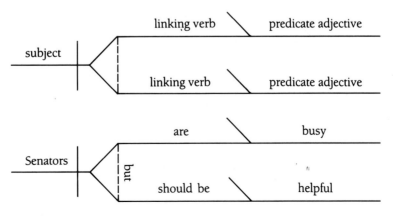

EXERCISE 13 **Diagraming Basic Sentence Patterns.** Use the preceding models as you diagram the following sentences.

1. The show ended.
2. A very enthusiastic audience applauded.
3. People handed the performers flowers.
4. The public and the critics considered the play successful.
5. The play was a comedy.
6. The plot seemed realistic but was very funny.
7. The actors and the orchestra members gave the audience their best performance.
8. Everyone was tired but felt very happy.
9. They had worked hard.
10. They considered that performance their best.

Revising Your Writing

As you read from "Through the Tunnel" by Doris Lessing, notice how effectively she varies the length of her sentences and their word order.

> Under him, six or seven feet down, was a floor of perfectly clean, shining white sand, rippled firm and hard by the tides. Two grayish shapes steered there, like long, rounded pieces of wood or slate. They were fish. He saw them nose toward each other, poise motionless, make a dart forward, swerve off, and come around again. It was like a water dance.

Study Lessing's techniques and try to use them when you write and revise.

1. Vary the length of your sentences. A series of sentences of similar length has a numbing effect. Notice that the length of Lessing's sentences varies greatly—from three words to twenty-three.

2. Occasionally use a very short sentence to accent a point, indicate a change of thought, or clinch a paragraph. Lessing's third sentence, "They were fish," gives the effect of a sudden realization.

3. Achieve variety in your writing by occasionally inverting a sentence's word order, as Lessing does in the first sentence.

Apply these techniques by revising the following passage adapted from "Through the Tunnel." Try to imagine how Lessing would have combined ideas to create a pleasing variety of sentence lengths. In addition, decide which sentence would be most effective in inverted order.

> He put on his goggles. He fitted them tight. He tested the vacuum. His hands were shaking. Then he chose the biggest stone. He slipped over the edge of the rock. He looked up once at the empty sky. He filled his lungs once, twice. Then he sank fast to the bottom with the stone. He let it go. He began to count. No strain was on his lungs.

Review

CHAPTER 18   PARTS OF THE SENTENCE

Subjects and Predicates   [pages 443–448] For each of the following sentences, identify the underlined word or words as (a) a complete subject, (b) a complete predicate, (c) a simple subject, (d) a simple predicate, or (e) a compound subject.

1. The Allies divided Berlin into four sectors after World War II.
2. The French, British, and American sectors have become West Berlin.
3. The Russian sector is known as East Berlin.
4. Millions of East Germans fled to the West through West Berlin.
5. Since 1961 a wall and barbed wire have separated the two Berlins.

Complements   [pages 448–453]   For each of the following sentences, identify the underlined word or words as (a) a direct object, (b) an indirect object, (c) an object complement, (d) a predicate nominative, or (e) a predicate adjective.

6. The person credited with first uniting Germany is Otto von Bismarck.
7. Bismarck's speeches won him the attention of Frederick William IV.
8. The king made Bismarck prime minister of Prussia in 1862.
9. By 1871 Bismarck had united Germany through conquest and diplomacy.
10. In 1888 the new emperor grew envious of Bismarck and dismissed him.
11. Prince von Metternich of Austria was another famous statesman of the nineteenth century.
12. Metternich guided the Congress of Vienna after Napoleon's downfall in 1815.
13. This congress restored the monarchies in existence before the French Revolution.
14. For many years Metternich's conservative policies gave Europe political stability.
15. By 1848, however, revolutions again made Europe a battleground, and the "Age of Metternich" ended.

Basic Sentence Patterns   [pages 454–455]   Match the sentence in the left column with the sentence pattern in the right column. *Code:* S = subject, AV = action verb, LV = linking verb, IO = indirect object, DO = direct object, OC = object complement, SC = subject complement

16. Hamburg is an attractive modern city.   (a) S + AV + DO
17. Tourist boats explore the city's many canals. (b) S + AV + IO + DO
18. A large lake makes the downtown area
    pleasant.   (c) S + AV + DO + OC

19. Clean buses and subways run throughout
    the city.   (d) S + LV + SC
20. A flourishing harbor guarantees this German
    city its prosperity.   (e) S + S + AV

Diagraming Basic Sentence Patterns [pages 455–458] Indicate the
letter of the position that each numbered word in the following sentence
should occupy in the diagram below.

   The many <u>canals</u> and the old <u>town hall</u> <u>give</u> <u>Hamburg</u> its Old World
<u>charm</u>.   21   22   23   24
   25

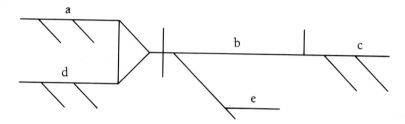

Writing for Review   Write a paragraph on a topic of your choice. Demonstrate your knowledge of sentence parts by using a variety of sentence
patterns. Underline and identify in your paragraph at least five of the
following: simple subject, simple predicate, direct object, indirect object,
object complement, predicate nominative, predicate adjective.

Phrases

A **phrase** is a group of words that acts in a sentence as a single part of speech.

You have already learned about verb phrases (Chapter 17). In this chapter you will learn about three other kinds of phrases: *prepositional phrases, appositive phrases,* and *verbal phrases.*

Prepositional Phrases

A **prepositional phrase** is a group of words that begins with a preposition and usually ends with a noun or pronoun, which is called the *object of the preposition.*

> I voted **against the idea**. [*Idea* is the object of the preposition *against.*]
> The elevator is necessary **for us**. [*Us* is the object of the preposition *for.*]

(For lists of common prepositions, see page 426.)

Adjectives and other modifiers may be placed between the preposition and its object. In addition, a preposition may have more than one object.

> The elevator goes **to the cool, dark basement**. [adjectives added]
> This elevator goes **to the basement and the penthouse**. [two objects]

A prepositional phrase normally acts in the same way that an adjective or an adverb does. Used as an adjective, a prepositional phrase is called an *adjectival phrase*; it modifies a noun or a pronoun. Used as an adverb, a prepositional phrase is called an *adverbial phrase*; it modifies a verb, an adjective, or an adverb.

> Take the elevator **on the right**. [adjectival phrase modifying the noun *elevator*]
> Which **of these elevators** is working? [adjectival phrase modifying the pronoun *which*]
> **After the meeting** you should take this elevator **to the lobby**. [adverbial phrases modifying the verb phrase *should take*]
> The elevator is helpful **to us**. [adverbial phrase modifying the adjective *helpful*]
> You are walking too much **for your own good**. [adverbial phrase modifying the adverb *much*]

EXERCISE 1 **Identifying Prepositional Phrases.** Copy the following sentences. Underline the prepositional phrase in each sentence.

1. Omaha business leaders formed a civic group in 1895.
2. Ak-Sar-Ben, the name of Omaha's civic group, is Nebraska spelled backward.
3. Omaha's Ak-Sar-Ben has encouraged the citizens' sense of pride and accomplishment.
4. Omaha has benefited greatly from Ak-Sar-Ben's many civic projects.
5. Omaha now prospers because of many new industries.
6. Many people are involved in the huge meat-packing organizations.
7. In addition to numerous insurance companies, the city has food processing and construction firms.
8. Many downtown Omaha skyscrapers are connected by walkways.
9. Ak-Sar-Ben is a model for civic groups.
10. Omaha's Ak-Sar-Ben is very proud of the city's achievements.

EXERCISE 2 **Identifying Adjectival and Adverbial Phrases.** Look again at the prepositional phrases you underlined in Exercise 1. Write the word each phrase modifies. Then indicate whether each prepositional phrase is *adjectival* or *adverbial*.

SENTENCE WRITING **Expanding Sentences with Prepositional Phrases.** Expand the following sentences by adding at least one adjectival phrase and one adverbial phrase to each.

1. The lake glimmers.
2. No one told me.
3. The horse galloped.
4. The workers piled up the bricks.
5. The dancers rehearsed.

Appositives and Appositive Phrases

An **appositive** is a noun or pronoun that is placed next to another noun or pronoun to identify or to give additional information about it.

An **appositive phrase** is an appositive plus any words that modify the appositive.

> My friend **Rick** sent me a postcard from England. [The appositive *Rick* identifies the noun *friend*.]
>
> Joanne rode a hydrofoil across the English Channel, **the body of water between England and France**. [The appositive phrase, in bold type, identifies *English Channel*.]

(For rules about using commas with appositives and appositive phrases, see Chapter 27.)

Identifying Appositives and Appositive Phrases. On your paper write the appositive or appositive phrase in each sentence below.

1. The first female doctor in the United States was Elizabeth Blackwell, a determined woman.
2. The young Algonquian princess Pocahontas married a settler.
3. Pocahontas, a young Algonquian princess, married an English settler.
4. In 1964 Dorothy Hodgkin, a British chemist, became the fifth female scientist to receive the Nobel Prize.
5. The labor organizer Mary Harris was nicknamed "Mother Jones."
6. Harriet Tubman, the most famous leader of the underground railroad, helped hundreds of slaves escape to freedom.
7. The American anthropologist Margaret Mead wrote the famous book *Coming of Age in Samoa*.
8. A highly regarded actress in America today is Meryl Streep, an unusually gifted performer.
9. Jane Austen, author of *Pride and Prejudice* and *Emma*, is generally considered the first great woman novelist.
10. My favorite singer is the operatic soprano Leontyne Price.

Adding Appositive Phrases to Sentences. Rewrite each of the following sentences, incorporating into the sentence as an appositive phrase the words in parentheses that follow the sentence. Use a comma or commas to set off the appositive phrase from the rest of the sentence.

SAMPLE Rotterdam handles more cargo than any other port in the world. (a city in the Netherlands)

ANSWER Rotterdam, a city in the Netherlands, handles more cargo than any other port in the world.

1. Sweden was formed by Ice Age glaciers. (a country that borders Norway and Finland)
2. Argentina is proud of Buenos Aires. (its cosmopolitan capital)
3. In Australia voting is compulsory. (a member of the Commonwealth of Nations)
4. Damascus is the capital of Syria. (probably the oldest continuously inhabited city in the world)
5. Sudan is bigger than Alaska and Texas combined. (the largest country in Africa)

Verbals and Verbal Phrases

A **verbal** is a form of a verb that works in a sentence as a noun, an adjective, or an adverb.

While working in sentences as nouns, adjectives, and adverbs, verbals retain some of the qualities of verbs. For example, verbals can show action and can have complements and modifiers.

A **verbal phrase** contains a verbal plus any complements and modifiers of the verbal

There are three kinds of verbals: *participles, gerunds,* and *infinitives.* All three types can be expanded into verbal phrases.

Participles and Participial Phrases

A **participle** is a form of a verb that works in a sentence as an adjective.

Present participles end in *-ing. Past participles* often end in *-ed,* but they can also take other forms. Many of the adjectives that you commonly use in sentences are actually participles.

The **freezing** rain slowly turned to hail.

Frozen switches delayed all the trains.

The **heated** argument occurred among the **losing** players.

When a participle is part of a verb phrase in the predicate of a sentence, it is not acting as an adjective.

PARTICIPLE AS ADJECTIVE   The **married** couple have jobs.
PARTICIPLE IN VERB PHRASE   The minister **has married** the young couple.

(For more information about forming present and past participles, see Chapter 21.)

A **participial phrase** contains a participle plus any complements and modifiers.

A participial phrase can have a present participle or a past participle. Participial phrases act as adjectives and can be placed in various positions in a sentence.

> We saw John McEnroe **playing tennis.**
>
> **Disappointed with his first serve**, McEnroe then served an ace.
>
> You rarely see fans **sitting quietly during one of McEnroe's games.**
>
> **Graciously accepting a trophy from the sponsors**, he grinned at the crowd.

(For practice in avoiding dangling participles, see Chapter 24.)

EXERCISE 5 **Identifying Participles and Participial Phrases.** Write the participle or the participial phrase in each of the following sentences. Then identify the word each modifies.

1. American women, looking for variety, often adopt the fashions of other countries.
2. The demand for goods imported from other lands is great.
3. Chinese textile mills export silk decorated by hand.
4. A wool scarf woven in Ecuador is warm and colorful.
5. Brides prize lace veils made by French nuns.
6. Thin bracelets, shining with gold threads, come from India.
7. Embroidered cloths from Eastern Europe make beautiful scarves.
8. Freshwater pearls imported from Japan are set in necklaces and ear-earrings.
9. Czechoslovakian garnets glittering in a gold ring flatter American fingers.
10. Italy exports gold hoops for pierced ears.

Gerund and Gerund Phrases

A **gerund** is a form of a verb that ends in *-ing* and that is used in the same ways a noun is used.

> **Reading** is my favorite pastime. [as subject]
>
> Dana enjoys **eating**. [as direct object]
>
> Joseph gives **studying** top priority. [as indirect object]
>
> How much time do you give to **exercising**? [as object of preposition]
>
> My preference is **dancing**. [as predicate nominative]
>
> Her hobbies, **skiing** and **hiking**, are strenuous and healthful. [as appositives]

A **gerund phrase** contains a gerund plus any complements and modifiers.

A gerund phrase can vary in length, depending on how many complements and modifiers are added to the gerund.

> **Making a success of your career** requires hard work.
> **Very diligent studying** is required in college.
> Success in any field demands **planning well**.

The difference between a present participle and a gerund, both of which end in -*ing*, is that a present participle is used as an adjective and a gerund is used as a noun.

> **Listening** to the radio, Dean worked much faster. [present participle]
> **Listening** to the radio helps Dean work faster. [gerund]

EXERCISE 6   **Identifying Gerunds and Gerund Phrases.** List on your paper the gerunds and gerund phrases in the following sentences. The number of gerunds or gerund phrases is given in parentheses.

1. Studying abroad has always been popular with Americans. (1)
2. Planning is important in order to obtain a proper program of study. (1)
3. Relaxing and sightseeing should not take up a student's time. (2)
4. Attending classes and doing assignments take as much time abroad as in America. (2)
5. Students in foreign countries should enjoy learning the language of their host country. (1)
6. Understanding foreign customs is often difficult. (1)
7. Methods of teaching are sometimes very different abroad. (1)
8. Lecturing is more common than conducting seminars. (2)
9. The professor's responsibility is not counseling students or initiating class discussion. (2)
10. Students are responsible for mastering the subject. (1)

EXERCISE 7   **Identifying the Uses of Gerunds.** Look again at your answers for sentences 5, 6, 9, and 10 in Exercise 6. On your paper identify in which way each gerund or gerund phrase is used: subject, direct object, complement, or object of preposition.

SAMPLE   1. Studying abroad
ANSWER   subject

SENTENCE WRITING   **Creating Sentences with Gerunds.** Choose five of the gerunds that you identified in Exercise 6, and write one original sentence for each. Make sure that you use the -*ing* words as a gerund.

Infinitives and Infinitive Phrases

An **infinitive** is a form of a verb that is usually preceded by the word *to* and is used as a noun, an adjective, or an adverb.

When you use the word *to* before a verb, the *to* is not a preposition but is part of the infinitive form of the verb. Infinitives can be used in the same ways that nouns, adjectives, and adverbs are used.

> **To sleep** is relaxing. [infinitive as subject]
> Everyone needs **to sleep**. [as direct object]
> Her wish is **to succeed**. [as predicate nominative]
> I had a tendency **to drowse**. [as adjective]
> He was eager **to rest**. [as adverb]

An **infinitive phrase** contains an infinitive plus any complements and modifiers.

> They wanted **to eat quickly**.
> My baby brother loves **to nap holding his toy bear**.
> We decided **to dress for the party**.
> The committee voted **to appoint Jennifer president of the drama club**.

EXERCISE 8   **Identifying Infinitives and Infinitive Phrases.** Write the infinitive or infinitive phrase in each of the following sentences. One sentence has two infinitive phrases.

1. One of the most remarkable figures to join the American labor movement was Mary Harris Jones.
2. In 1880, at fifty, Jones decided to change her life.
3. After abandoning her work as a teacher and dressmaker, she proceeded to become a union organizer.
4. Her custom was to travel around the country in a black gown and bonnet.
5. She worked in the cotton mills of the South to gather evidence for her campaign against child labor.
6. Later she worked in New York City to help the garment and streetcar workers.
7. While she was in Pittsburgh to support a steel mill strike, Jones was asked who had permitted her to speak publicly.
8. Jones, quick to reply, said, "Patrick Henry, Thomas Jefferson, John Adams!"
9. Mary Jones helped workers to organize the great steel strike of 1919.
10. Mother Jones, as she was sometimes called, was able to make a vigorous speech on her hundredth birthday.

EXERCISE 9
Identifying the Uses of Infinitives. Look again at your answers to the first five items in Exercise 8. Write whether each infinitive phrase is used as (a) a noun, (b) an adjective, or (c) an adverb.

SENTENCE WRITING
Writing Sentences with Infinitives. Jot down five action verbs. Use each in an infinitive phrase in an original sentence. Underline the infinitive phrases.

REVIEW EXERCISE
Verbal Phrases. On your paper write each of the verbal phrases in the following sentences. Tell whether each is a participial phrase, a gerund phrase, or an infinitive phrase.

1. Searching for gold has always been a favorite activity of avid treasure seekers.
2. The story behind the Lost Dutchman Mine in Arizona's Superstition Mountains has succeeded in fascinating many listeners.
3. The story began in 1887 when Jacob Walz used gold nuggets to pay a bill in Phoenix, Arizona.
4. Jacob Walz claimed he had found a gold mine and intended to keep the location a secret.
5. Most people, assuming the theft of the gold nuggets, did not believe the man.
6. Miners began to follow him everywhere but without success.
7. Jacob Walz, predicting that no one would ever find his mine, died in 1891.
8. Proved right so far, Walz must have covered his tracks well. participial
9. Each summer, however, treasure hunters, looking for Walz's mine, search the Superstition Mountains.
10. Finding the lost gold would be quite an achievement.

Diagraming Phrases

This section is a continuation of Diagraming Basic Sentence Patterns at the end of Chapter 18. Review those six diagrams before proceeding.

7. Prepositional Phrases

Place the preposition on a slanted line that comes down from the word modified by the prepositional phrase. Then draw a horizontal line from the slanted line. Place the object of the preposition on the horizontal line.

Carpenters of today use tools with electric power in their work.

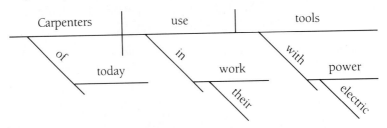

8. Appositives and Appositive Phrases

Place the appositive in parentheses after the noun or pronoun it identifies. Add any words that modify the appositive beneath it.

Argentina is proud of Buenos Aires, its cosmopolitan capital.

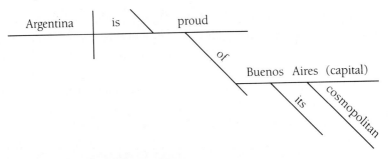

9. Participles and Participial Phrases

Curve the participle as shown below. Add modifiers and complements.

Pounding nails carelessly, the carpenter bruised his thumb.

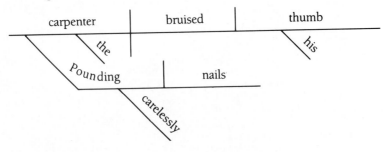

10. Gerunds and Gerund Phrases

Place the gerund on a step as shown below. The phrase in the subject position is placed on a "stilt" so that it will fit.

Using an electric saw is a quick way of cutting wood.

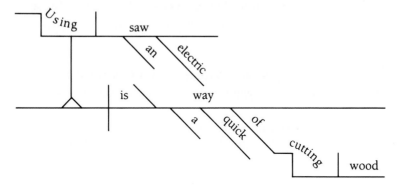

11. Infinitives and Infinitive Phrases Used as Adjectives or Adverbs

These infinitives are diagramed like prepositional phrases. Place "to" on the slanted line descending from the word being modified and the rest of the infinitive on the horizontal line.

Carpenters strive to build carefully.

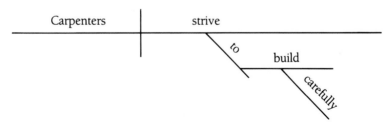

12. Infinitives and Infinitive Phrases Used as Nouns

Here you have to use stilts again.

To love work is to know satisfaction.

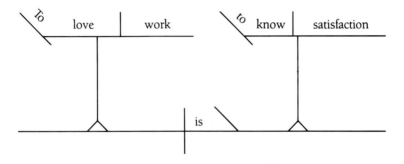

EXERCISE 10 **Diagraming Prepositional Phrases.** Using Diagram 7 as a model, diagram the five example sentences preceding Exercise 1 of this chapter.

EXERCISE 11 **Diagraming Appositives and Appositive Phrases.** Using Diagram 8 as a model, diagram the first five sentences in Exercise 3 of this chapter.

EXERCISE 12 **Diagraming Participles and Participial Phrases.** Using Diagram 9 as a model, diagram Sentences 6–10 in Exercise 5 of this chapter.

EXERCISE 13 **Diagraming Gerunds and Gerund Phrases.** Using Diagram 10 as a model, diagram Sentences 1, 5, 6, and 10 in Exercise 6 of this chapter.

EXERCISE 14 **Diagraming Infinitives and Infinitive Phrases.** Using Diagrams 11 and 12 as models, diagram Sentences 1, 2, 6, and 9 in Exercise 8.

Revising Your Writing

Phrases are versatile. Because they can act as various parts of speech—as nouns, adjectives, or adverbs—phrases allow writers to expand the basic sentence patterns by adding precise description and detail. Writers can control the rhythm of their prose by carefully positioning phrases at particular points in their sentences. Try to use the following techniques when you write and revise your work.

1. Use prepositional phrases to add precise description and detail to your sentences. For example, the following sentence from "The Red-Headed League," by Sir Arthur Conan Doyle, has a basic subject-verb-object pattern ("I had called and found him"). The italicized prepositional phrases expand the basic pattern and bring the author's meaning into sharp focus.

   > I had called *upon my friend,* Mr. Sherlock Holmes, one day *in the autumn of last year,* and found him *in deep conversation with a very stout, florid-faced, elderly gentleman, with fiery red hair.*

2. When you revise, see if adding prepositional, appositive, or verbal phrases enhances the flow of your sentences or creates an appropriate pause. For example, try reading aloud the following sentence from "Shaving" by Leslie Norris. Notice that you must pause before the italicized phrases and your voice tends to emphasize them. These phrases give the sentence an overall balance and pleasing rhythm.

   > He lay back on his pillow, *knowing his weakness and his mortality,* and looked at his son with wonder, *with a curious humble pride.*

The balanced effect would not have been achieved if Norris had composed the sentence as follows without the carefully positioned phrases.

> He lay back on his pillow and knew his weakness and his mortality and looked at his son with wonder and a curious humble pride.

Apply these techniques when revising the following passage adapted from "Thirteen" by Jessamyn West. Follow the numbered directions below to try to reconstruct the sentences as West actually wrote them.

> Someone brought out the fish grotto proprietor. He came in his white apron and tall chef's hat.

1. Add the appositive phrase *a worthy man dedicated to service* to the first sentence so that it creates a noticeable pause in midsentence.
2. Add the participle phrase *brandishing a long-handled ladle* to the second sentence.
3. Add the phrase *happy at first to see his fish arousing so much interest* to the second sentence.

Review

CHAPTER 19   PHRASES

Identifying Phrases [pages 462–469]   In each of the following sentences, tell whether the underlined phrase is (a) a prepositional phrase, (b) an appositive phrase, (c) a participial phrase, (d) a gerund phrase, or (e) an infinitive phrase.

1. Clara Schumann was one of the world's greatest pianists.
2. She performed works by her husband, the composer of *Carnaval.*
3. Playing the piano was only one of her musical abilities.
4. She also taught students to understand and interpret music.
5. Inspired by her husband, she composed her own beautiful songs.

Prepositional Phrases [pages 462–463]   In the following sentences, tell whether the prepositional phrase is (a) adjectival or (b) adverbial.

6. The Hohokam once flourished in the Southwest.
7. The Pima, descended from the Hohokam, call them "the people who have gone."
8. The Hohokam built a system of canals to irrigate the desert.
9. Scholars believe the Hohokam reached their peak about A.D. 1000.
10. The mystery of the Hohokam's decline has not been solved.

Gerund Phrases [pages 466–467]   In each of the following sentences, tell whether the gerund phrase is used as (a) a subject, (b) a direct object, (c) an object of a preposition, (d) a predicate nominative, or (e) an appositive.

11. Analyzing soil is an important skill for geologists.
12. Data gained by studying soil samples is useful for farmers.
13. Farmers appreciate knowing the needs of the soil.
14. Their concern remains using the soil efficiently.
15. The result, managing the soil wisely, means great productivity.

Infinitive Phrases [pages 468–469]   In each of the following sentences, tell whether the infinitive phrase is used as (a) a noun, (b) an adjective, or (c) an adverb.

16. Have you ever wondered when people first learned to ice skate?
17. Historians are able to state that skating began about A.D. 800.
18. The first skaters to glide over ice used reindeer bones.
19. They had the ingenuity to shape and tie the bones to their feet.
20. If you want to see ancient skates, look in European museums.

Writing for Review   Write a paragraph on any subject you choose. Include and underline at least one example of each kind of phrase—prepositional phrase, appositive phrase, participial phrase, gerund phrase, and infinitive phrase.

CHAPTER *20*

Clauses and Sentence Structure

A **clause** is a group of words that has a subject and a predicate and that is used as a part of a sentence.

There are two kinds of clauses: *main clauses,* also called *independent clauses,* and *subordinate clauses,* also called *dependent clauses.*

Main Clauses

A **main clause** has a subject and a predicate and can stand alone as a sentence.

Every sentence must have at least one main clause. A sentence may have more than one main clause. Both of the clauses in the following example are main clauses because both can stand alone as a sentence:

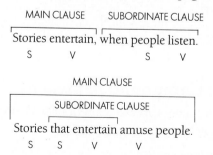

Subordinate Clauses

A **subordinate clause** has a subject and a predicate, but it cannot stand alone as a sentence.

A subordinate clause must be attached to a main clause in order for it to make sense. Subordinate clauses frequently begin with subordinating conjunctions (see page 431) or relative pronouns (see pages 399–400).

In the first example the subordinating conjunction *when* placed before *people listen* creates a word group—*when people listen*—that cannot stand alone as a main clause. In the second example the relative pronoun *that* begins a subordinate clause that comes between the subject and the verb of the main clause. *That* also serves as the subject of the subordinate clause.

In the following pages you will see how various combinations of main clauses and subordinate clauses form the four kinds of sentence structures: *simple sentences, compound sentences, complex sentences,* and *compound-complex sentences.* You will also see how subordinate clauses act in sentences as adverbs, adjectives, or nouns.

EXERCISE 1 **Identifying Main and Subordinate Clauses.** In each of the following sentences, the first clause appears in italics. On your paper write whether that clause is a main clause or a subordinate clause. (Remember that a subordinate clause cannot stand alone as a sentence.)

1. *Margaret Fogarty Rudkin had never baked a single loaf of bread* before she was forty years old.
2. *When she was forty-one years old,* Rudkin was the head of her own baking company.
3. *Margaret Rudkin started making bread* after her family settled in Connecticut.
4. *Although she initially baked only for her family and neighbors,* she later began selling bread to local stores.
5. *Rudkin opened her own baking company in 1939* because her bread was selling so well.
6. *She and her husband named the company Pepperidge Farm for the old pepperidge tree* that grew in their front yard.
7. *While most companies were baking with commercial shortening and bleached flour,* Rudkin insisted on using only high-quality ingredients.
8. *Although high-quality ingredients were more costly,* their use gave Pepperidge Farm a reputation for fine baked goods.
9. *The company grew even larger* when it added sweet baked goods to its list of products.
10. *Today Pepperidge Farm is a highly successful company,* largely because Margaret Rudkin insisted on maintaining her high standards of excellence.

Simple and Compound Sentences

Two kinds of sentences are made up of main clauses only: *simple sentences* and *compound sentences.*

A **simple sentence** has only one main clause and no subordinate clauses.

A simple sentence may have a compound subject or a compound predicate or both (see Chapter 18). The simple subject and the simple predicate may also be expanded in many other ways. Adjectives, adverbs, prepositional phrases, appositives, and verbal phrases may make some simple sentences seem anything but simple. Yet as long as the sentence has only one main clause, it remains a simple sentence.

Stories entertain. [simple sentence]

Stories and riddles entertain. [simple sentence with compound subject]

Stories entertain and amuse. [simple sentence with compound predicate]

Stories and riddles amuse and entertain. [simple sentence with compound subject and compound predicate]

Stories about the Old West entertain adults and children alike. [simple sentence expanded]

A **compound sentence** has two or more main clauses.

As the following examples show, each main clause of a compound sentence has its own subject and predicate. Notice that the main clauses of a compound sentence are usually joined by a comma and a coordinating conjunction, such as *and, but, or, nor, yet,* or *for.*

MAIN CLAUSE 1   MAIN CLAUSE 2

Stories entertain, and riddles amuse.
S   V   S   V

MAIN CLAUSE 1   MAIN CLAUSE 2   MAIN CLAUSE 3

Stories entertain, and riddles amuse, but poems delight.
S   V   S   V   S   V

Two main clauses may also be joined to form a compound sentence by means of a semicolon (see Chapter 27).

MAIN   MAIN
CLAUSE 1   CLAUSE 2

She pushed; he pulled.

EXERCISE 2 **Identifying Simple and Compound Sentences.** On your paper write whether each of the following is a simple or a compound sentence. (Remember that a single main clause can have a compound subject and a compound predicate.)

1. Nineteenth-century American scenes and customs were recorded and preserved by the firm of Currier & Ives.
2. Nathaniel Currier was a printer, and James Ives was an executive.
3. The two men produced "engravings for the people."
4. Currier favored current events; he produced drawings of ships, battles, and news events.
5. Ives had broader interests and favored country scenes.

6. Together they published color engravings depicting every facet of American life.
7. Currier & Ives produced thousands of engravings, and each print was rich in color and detail.
8. Many drawings showed city life, but most depicted life in the country.
9. In the last century most Americans lived in the country, and many events happened outdoors.
10. Currier & Ives's engravings show Americans at work and at play in the late nineteenth century.

Complex and Compound-Complex Sentences

When subordinate clauses are added to simple sentences and compound sentences, they form complex sentences and compound-complex sentences.

A **complex sentence** has one main clause and one or more subordinate clauses.

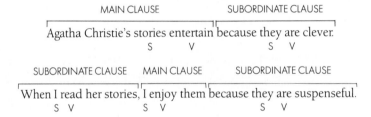

A **compound-complex sentence** has more than one main clause and at least one subordinate clause.

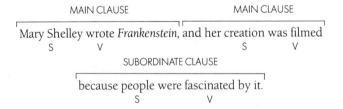

EXERCISE 3 **Identifying Complex and Compound-Complex Sentences.** Write on your paper the subordinate clause in each of the following sentences. Indicate whether each sentence is a *complex* sentence or a *compound-complex* sentence.

1. Although everyone talks about the weather, no one can affect it.
2. People usually talk about the temperature, which is only one aspect of the weather.

3. People need to understand temperature, air pressure, and wind, since all these factors make up the weather.
4. Unless people learn more about these factors, they can discuss the weather, but they cannot predict it.
5. Because communications, industry, farming, and space exploration depend on the weather, everyone must learn more.
6. When weather conditions are dangerous, people need to take precautions; they can then avoid disasters.
7. If weather instruments could accurately predict a hurricane, people could be warned, and lives might be saved.
8. When the weather changes, people's moods often change.
9. Some people are sluggish whenever it rains.
10. As soon as the sun shines, many people feel happy, and they go outdoors.

SENTENCE WRITING **Writing Sentences with Various Structures.**
Write a simple sentence. Next rework it and make it a compound sentence. Rework it again, but now make it part of a complex sentence. Finally, rework your compound sentence into a compound-complex sentence.

SAMPLE ANSWER The baseball field became a vast sea of mud.
It rained so much, and the baseball field became a vast sea of mud.
It rained so much that the baseball field became a vast sea of mud.
It rained so much that the baseball field became a vast sea of mud, but we continued to play.

Complex and Compound-Complex Sentences 479

Adjective Clauses

An **adjective clause** is a subordinate clause that modifies a noun or a pronoun.

An adjective clause normally follows the word it modifies.

> The horror story **that has always been my favorite** is "The Black Cat."
> The writer **whom I like best** is Katherine Anne Porter.
> I like a writer **who surprises me.**

In addition to the relative pronouns *(who, whom, whose, that,* and *which),* the adverbs *where* and *when* may introduce adjective clauses.

> The Elizabethan Age spans the time **when Elizabeth I ruled.**
> That is the house **where I was born.**

An adjective clause is sometimes essential to the sentence; that is, it is needed to make the meaning of the sentence clear. This kind of adjective clause is called an *essential clause,* or a *restrictive clause.* Without the essential adjective clause, the sentence would not make complete sense.

> Edgar Allan Poe is the only American writer **who always fascinates me.** [essential clause]
> "The Black Cat" is the story **that I like best.** [essential clause]

In the first example the meaning of the sentence would change without the essential clause *who always fascinates me.* Edgar Allan Poe is certainly not the only American writer. In the second example the adjective clause is needed because the sentence seems incomplete without it. The essential adjective clause *that I like* limits or restricts the meaning of the noun *story* and helps the reader recognize *which* story is being discussed.

An adjective clause that is *not* needed to make the meaning of the sentence clear is called a *nonessential clause,* or a *nonrestrictive clause.* It may add information to the sentence, but the sentence would be perfectly logical without the clause.

> Edgar Allan Poe, **who is my favorite author,** wrote "The Black Cat." [nonessential clause]
> "The Black Cat," **which was written by Edgar Allan Poe,** is my favorite short story. [nonessential clause]

You can use either *that* or *which* to introduce an essential clause, but you must always use *which* to begin a nonessential clause. Never use *that* before a nonessential clause.

> "The Black Cat," **which I like best,** is thrilling. [nonessential clause]
> I like a story **that thrills me.** [essential clause]

(For rules about punctuating clauses, see Chapter 27).

EXERCISE 4 **Identifying Adjective Clauses.** On your paper write the adjective clause in each of the following sentences. Then write the word that the clause modifies.

1. William Sydney Porter wrote stories under a pseudonym, which is another word for pen name.
2. Porter, who lived from 1862 to 1910, used the pseudonym O. Henry.
3. Porter contributed articles to a humor magazine, which he had founded in Texas in 1894.
4. He wrote a daily column that was humorous and witty.
5. As O. Henry, Porter published many stories that were sympathetic and touching.
6. He created unusual plots that ended in surprising ways.
7. *The Four Million,* which is a collection of O. Henry's short stories, was published in 1906.
8. "The Gift of the Magi" is a story that many people enjoy.
9. Another O. Henry literary creation that is very popular is "The Third Ingredient."
10. Readers who enjoy the unusual and the humorous will delight in O. Henry's stories.

EXERCISE 5 **Recognizing Essential and Nonessential Clauses.** Here are five pairs of sentences. For each pair write the adjective clause and then identify it as an essential or nonessential clause.

1. a. The 1983 U.S. space mission that received the most public attention was the *Challenger* space shuttle.
   b. The Challenger space shuttle, which went on a six-day mission in 1983, received much public attention.
2. a. Sally Ride, who was flight engineer on the Challenger mission, became the first U.S. woman to enter outer space.
   b. The U.S. woman who first entered outer space was Challenger flight engineer Sally Ride.
3. a. The background that Ride had in astrophysics helped her qualify for the space program.
   b. Ride's doctorate in astrophysics, which she earned from Stanford University, helped her qualify for the space program.
4. a. Sally Ride used a remote-control mechanical arm, which was fifty feet in length, to retrieve a satellite in space.
   b. Sally Ride used the remote-control mechanical arm that she had helped design to retrieve a satellite in space.
5. a. Today's astronauts are people who have training in specific fields.
   b. Today's space program is using missions specialists, who are astronauts with training in specific fields.

Adverb Clauses

An **adverb clause** is a subordinate clause that modifies a verb, an adjective, or an adverb. It tells *when, where, how, why, to what extent, or under what condition*.

> **Whenever it is quiet**, I study hard. [The adverb clause modifies the verb *study*. I tells *when*.]
>
> I remained calm **as long as you were nearby**. [The adverb clause modifies the adjective *calm*. It tells *under what condition*.]
>
> She can swim faster **than I can run**. [The adverb clause modifies the adverb *faster*. It tells *to what extent*.]

Subordinating conjunctions such as those listed on page 431 introduce adverb clauses. Knowing those conjunctions will help you recognize adverb clauses. Remember that an adverb clause may either precede or follow the main clause. The first example above might have been written as follows:

> I study hard **whenever it is quiet**.

Occasionally words may be left out of an adverb clause. The omitted words can easily be supplied, however, because they are understood, or implied. Such adverb clauses are called *elliptical adverb clauses*.

> She can swim faster **than I [can swim]**.
> The dish made Joe sicker **than [it made] me [sick]**.

EXERCISE 6 | **Identifying Adverb Clauses** Write the adverb clauses in each sentence. (Some sentences have more than one adverb clause.)

1. Wherever he went, Henry David Thoreau made an impression.
2. Although Thoreau died in 1862, his writings still excite readers.
3. Thoreau earned his place in history because he believed in the power of the individual.
4. As Thoreau saw it, life would be richer if we were self-reliant.
5. Thoreau did not favor selfishness, however, since he believed in harmonious cooperation among people.
6. If someone needed help, Thoreau gave it because that was the moral thing to do.
7. He sympathized when anyone, even an animal, was hurt or suffering.
8. Although Thoreau believed in human cooperation, he lived alone during an important part of his life.
9. Thoreau wrote essays while he was living alone at Walden Pond.
10. If he had not lived at Walden Pond, Thoreau might not have written *Walden*.

Noun Clauses

A **noun clause** is a subordinate clause used as a noun.

You can use a noun clause as a subject, a direct object, an object of a preposition, or a predicate nominative.

NOUN

Farmers enjoy home-grown food.
S

NOUN CLAUSE

Whoever lives on a farm enjoys home-grown food.
S

NOUN

Weather affects crops.
DO

NOUN CLAUSE

Weather affects **whatever grows outdoors**.
DO

In the preceding examples notice that each noun clause forms an inseparable part of the sentence's main clause. In the second sentence, for example, the noun clause *Whoever lives on a farm* is the subject of the main clause. In the last sentence the noun clause *Whatever grows outdoors* is the direct object of the main clause. Notice also that the examples with the nouns are simple sentences because each contains only one subject and one predicate. The examples with the noun clauses are complex sentences because each has a main clause (the entire sentence) and a subordinate clause (the noun clause).

Some of the words that can be used to introduce noun clauses follow:

how	which
that	whichever
what	who, whom
whatever	whoever
when	whose
where	why

Here are additional examples of noun clauses:

Do you know **why farmers are hard workers?** [as direct object]

This is **how most farmers plant their crops.** [as a predicate nominative]

Crops are fertilized with **whatever will make them grow faster and stronger.** [as an object of a preposition]

Identifying Noun Clauses. Write the noun clauses in each sentence. (Four of the sentences have two noun clauses each.)

1. Whoever is interested in mountain climbing should read *Mountaineering* by Alan Blackshaw.
2. That mountain climbing requires strength and courage is well known.
3. What makes mountain climbing exciting is that it is dangerous and demanding yet satisfying.
4. Whatever happens during the climb can endanger the climber.
5. Until a climb is finished, no one knows how it will end.
6. Why someone would want to climb a mountain is easy to understand.
7. What many mountain climbers say is that the existence of a mountain is reason enough to want to climb it.
8. Whoever questions such an answer would never be found on the side of a mountain.
9. What challenges climbers is whatever seems dangerous yet immensely rewarding.
10. Where no one has been is where daring people want to go.

SENTENCE WRITING **Using Subordinate Clauses in Sentences.** Write four original sentences. In the first use an adverb clause. In the second use an adjective clause. In the third use a noun clause as a subject. In the fourth use a noun clause as a direct object.

REVIEW EXERCISE **Clauses.** On your paper write each subordinate clause in the following sentences. Then write whether the subordinate clause is (a) an adverb clause, (b) an adjective clause, or (c) a noun clause.

1. Books on how you should rear children are very popular.
2. *The Common Sense Book of Baby and Child Care,* which was written by Dr. Benjamin Spock, revolutionized child care.
3. This book has sold over thirty million copies since it was published in 1946.
4. What accounts for Dr. Spock's success is a combination of events.
5. There were few child-rearing guides before Spock wrote his book.
6. Most parents previously used a book that had been published in 1894.
7. Although this book was useful, it advised a rather harsh approach to rearing children.
8. A factor that made Dr. Spock's book popular was the rising interest in child psychology.
9. Psychological studies, which were becoming more common, raised many questions about the best way to discipline children.
10. Whereas earlier books advised parents not to spoil a child, Dr. Spock approved of tenderness and love.

Four Kinds of Sentences

Sentences may be classified according to their purpose. The four types of sentences are *declarative, imperative, interrogative* and *exclamatory.*

A **declarative sentence** makes a statement.

> A lion is chasing the ostriches.
> The huge birds run fast.

A declarative sentence normally ends with a period. It is the type of sentence used most frequently in speaking and writing.

An **imperative sentence** gives a command or makes a request.

> Look at the fleeing ostriches.
> Please take pictures of them.

An imperative sentence usually ends with a period. The subject "you" is understood (see Chapter 18).

An **interrogative sentence** asks a question.

> What did the lion chase?
> Is the lion chasing the ostriches?

An interrogative sentence ends with a question mark. If often begins with an interrogative pronoun (see Chapter 17) or with an auxiliary verb.

An **exclamatory sentence** expresses strong emotion.

> The lion sees us!
> Watch out!
> How can we escape!
> How ferocious the lion looks!

An exclamatory sentence is a declarative, imperative, or interrogative sentence expressed with strong emotion. The exclamation point at the end of the sentence conveys the strong emotion to the readers.

EXERCISE 8 **Identifying Kinds of Sentences.** On your paper write whether each of the following sentences is (a) declarative, (b) imperative, (c) interrogative, or (d) exclamatory.

1. Have you read a very exciting book called *The Man Who Rode the Thunder?*
2. What a hair-raising tale it is!
3. The man who wrote about his own experiences was William H. Rankin.
4. He had joined the U.S. Marines seeking travel and adventure.
5. For two years Rankin served as a squadron leader.

6. He first met adventure on a routine flight over South Korea.
7. What would you do if your engine suddenly went dead 47,000 feet above the ground?
8. Imagine bailing out into a thunderstorm and taking forty minutes to reach the ground.
9. How terrified he must have been!
10. Put yourself in his place.

SENTENCE WRITING **Using Four Kinds of Sentences.** Write four sentences about a recent news story. Use one declarative, one imperative, one interrogative, and one exclamatory sentence.

Sentence Completeness

Unless you are mimicking conversation in your writing, your sentences should be complete. They should have at least one subject and one predicate and express a complete thought (see Chapter 18). Incomplete sentences, or sentence fragments, are considered a serious error because they confuse readers. Another kind of sentence error occurs when two or more sentences run on in such a way that readers cannot tell where one ends and the next begins.

Sentence Fragments

In general, avoid sentence fragments in your writing. A **sentence fragment** lacks a subject or a predicate or does not express a complete thought.

Sentence fragments are usually phrases or subordinate clauses that have mistakenly been capitalized and punctuated as if they were complete sentences. Often you can correct a sentence fragment by joining it to an idea that comes before or after the fragment. Sometimes, however, you may need to add missing words to form a complete sentence.

FRAGMENT **The large bird with blue feathers at the feeder.** It is a jay.

COMPLETE SENTENCE The large bird with blue feathers at the feeder is a jay.

FRAGMENT I filled the feeder with sunflower seeds. **Which the jays seem to like.**

COMPLETE SENTENCE I filled the feeder with sunflower seeds, which the jays seem to like.

FRAGMENT **Sometimes used suet in the winter.** Woodpeckers are particularly fond of that.

COMPLETE SENTENCE Sometimes I have used suet in the winter. Woodpeckers are particularly fond of that.

Identifying Sentence Fragments. Indicate in writing whether each of the following numbered items is a complete sentence or a sentence fragment.

¹Consumers in America are protected from dishonest selling practices. ²Before 1977 poorly made products, no warranties, and angry customers. ³A warranty states that a product is guaranteed to last a certain length of time. ⁴The Magnuson-Moss Warranty Act of 1977 gave customers more rights. ⁵By requiring warranties not only for expensive products but also for items costing as little as fifteen dollars. ⁶Even without a written warranty, consumers protected. ⁷A product broken upon arrival can be returned for a full refund. ⁸Because all companies behind their products. ⁹Satisfaction for all customers. ¹⁰The new act also gives consumers more power in court.

SENTENCE WRITING **Correcting Sentence Fragments.** Revise the preceding paragraph by correcting each fragment that you identified in Exercise 9. Whenever possible, combine the fragments with other sentences in the paragraph.

Run-on Sentences

Avoid run-on sentences in your writing. A **run-on sentence** occurs when main clauses are run together without proper punctuation. Do not use a comma alone to separate two main clauses.

Such errors are also called *comma splices* or *comma faults*.

RUN-ON   Horror stories are thrilling, most people enjoy them.

You may correct run-on sentences in any of four ways:

1. A comma *and* a coordinating conjunction may be used to combine the two clauses.

   Horror stories are thrilling, **and** most people enjoy them.

2. A semicolon may be used to separate the two clauses when their meaning is closely related.

   Horror stories are thrilling; most people enjoy them.

3. Turn the clauses into two separate sentences. Use a period and a capital letter.

   Horror stories are thrilling. Most people enjoy them.

4. Turn one of the main clauses into a subordinate clause or into a phrase.

   Because horror stories are thrilling, most people enjoy them.
   Most people enjoy horror stories, **which are thrilling**.

Identifying Run-on Sentences. Indicate on your paper whether each of the following numbered items is a complete sentence or a run-on sentence.

[1]Architects design and build many different kinds of buildings, they also design monuments. [2]Architects must be artists, but they must also be engineers. [3]A building should look beautiful; it should also be a place where people can live or work comfortably. [4]Architecture is unlike most other arts, in the first place, an architect must work with many other people. [5]Architecture is among the oldest art forms, it appears even in prehistoric times.

EXERCISE 11 **Correcting Run-on Sentences.** Rewrite each of the following run-on sentences. Use each of the four methods for correcting run-on sentences at least once in this exercise.

1. American artist Georgia O'Keeffe became famous for her paintings of natural objects, her canvases are stunning and vibrant.
2. Her painted objects become huge and overwhelming, her enlarged flowers and stones seem unique.
3. Her paintings are equally realistic, however, most of them have an abstract quality.
4. O'Keeffe's colors are bold and startling, a patch of blue and green on a field of white looks stark and compelling.
5. Most of O'Keeffe's paintings remain popular with art lovers, her work is intense, realistic, and unique.
6. She was greatly influenced by the landscape of the American Southwest, there are many recognizable images in her pictures.
7. O'Keeffe was married to the American photographer Alfred Stieglitz in 1924.
8. Stieglitz operated two art galleries in New York City, he often displayed his wife's work.

REVIEW EXERCISE **Sentence Completeness.** Rewrite the following paragraph, correcting all sentence fragments and run-on sentences.

[1]The word *laser* from the expression "light amplification by stimulated emission of radiation." [2]Both radio waves and light waves are forms of energy, however, neither weak radio waves nor weak light waves affect us. [3]Producing and transmitting intense light being the basic purpose of a laser. [4]Either a rare metal or a rare gas used for the intensification of light waves. [5]Chromium and helium were used in early lasers, today various kinds of

lamps or the sun produces the light that a laser intensifies. [6]Electrons and light waves interacting to make the light extremely intense. [7]Intricate eye surgery not possible without lasers, astronauts depend on them, too.

Diagraming Clauses

This section is a continuation of Diagraming Basic Sentence Patterns (Chapter 18) and Diagraming Phrases (Chapter 19). Review the twelve diagrams in those sections before proceeding.

13. Compound Sentences

To diagram a compound sentence, you must place each main clause in a diagram of its own. If the main clauses are connected by a semicolon, use a vertical dotted line to connect the verbs of each main clause. If the main clauses are connected by a conjunction, place the conjunction on a solid horizontal line.

Mechanics like to fix objects, but carpenters must learn to build.

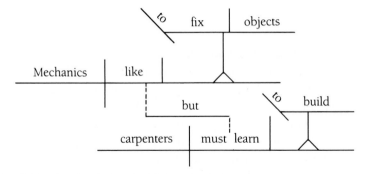

14. Complex Sentences: Adjective Clauses

To diagram a complex sentence with an adjective clause, place the main clause in one diagram and the adjective clause beneath it in another diagram. Use a dotted line to connect the relative pronoun or other introductory word in the adjective clause to the modified noun or pronoun in the other clause.

The carpenter whom you hired fixed the shelves that were uneven.

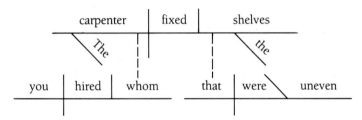

15. Complex Sentences: Adverb Clauses

To diagram a complex sentence with an adverb clause, place the main clause in one diagram and the adverb clause beneath it in another diagram. Place the subordinating conjunction on a diagonal dotted line connecting the verb of the adverb clause to the modified verb, adjective, or adverb of the other clause.

Before they cut the wood, carpenters make a design.

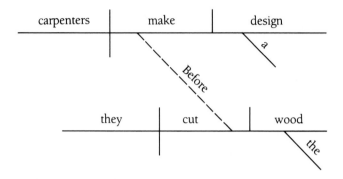

16. Complex Sentences: Noun Clauses

To diagram a complex sentence with a noun clause, first decide what role the noun clause plays within the main clause of the sentence: subject, direct object, predicate nominative, or object of preposition. Then diagram the main clause with the noun clause on a stilt rising out of the appropriate position. Place the introductory word of the noun clause as the subject, object, or predicate nominative within the noun clause itself. If the introductory word merely begins the noun clause, simply place it on a line of its own.

AS SUBJECT

What the carpenter builds is sturdy.

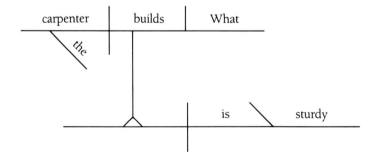

AS DIRECT OBJECT

We know that the mechanic fixes machines.

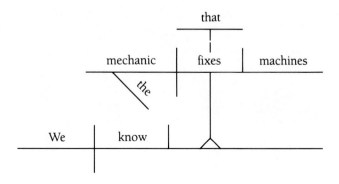

EXERCISE 12 **Diagraming Compound Sentences.** Using Diagram 13 as a model, diagram Sentences 2, 4, 7, 8, and 9 in Exercise 2 in this chapter.

EXERCISE 13 **Diagraming Adjective Clauses.** Using Diagram 14 as a model, diagram Sentences 1, 2, 4, 8, and 10 in Exercise 4 in this chapter.

EXERCISE 14 **Diagraming Adverb Clauses.** Using Diagram 15 as a model, diagram Sentences 1, 2, 3, 8, and 9 in Exercise 6 in this chapter.

EXERCISE 15 **Diagraming Noun Clauses.** Using Diagram 16 as a model, diagram the second and fourth examples on page 483.

Revising Your Writing

In the following paragraph from "Her First Ball," Katherine Mansfield uses a variety of sentence structures not only to maintain reader interest but also to develop an appropriate rhythm and mood.

> Exactly when the ball began Leila would have found it hard to say. Perhaps her first real partner was the cab. It did not matter that she shared the cab with the Sheridan girls and their brother. She sat back in her own little corner of it, and the bolster on which her hand rested felt like the sleeve of an unknown young man's dress suit; and away they bowled, past waltzing lampposts and houses and fences and trees.

Notice that the structure of each of Mansfield's sentences is different: complex, simple, complex, compound-complex. Try to apply techniques like Mansfield's when you write and revise your work.

1. Vary your sentence structures to keep your readers interested.
2. Complex and compound-complex sentences can form patterns of sound that subtly reinforce the meaning of your words. Notice, for example, how perfectly suited the sound of Mansfield's last sentence is to the unfolding meaning of the paragraph. As Leila gradually becomes lost in her daydream, the sound and the duration of the long compound-complex sentence mirror the action and mood.

Apply these techniques in revising the following series of simple sentences: The first sentence will be compound and the second sentence will be complex.

> At that moment the music stopped. They went to sit on two chairs against the wall. Leila tucked her pink satin feet under. She fanned herself. She blissfully watched the other couples. They were passing and disappearing through the swing doors.

CHAPTER 20   CLAUSES AND SENTENCE STRUCTURE

Clauses and the Sentences They Form   [pages 475–479]   Indicate whether each of the following sentences is (a) simple, (b) compound, (c) complex, or (d) compound-complex.

1. Liechtenstein is a tiny principality between Switzerland and Austria.
2. The country takes its name from the Liechtenstein family, who have ruled the area since about 1700.
3. In 1866 Liechtenstein fought in the Seven Weeks' War and since then has remained neutral.
4. Until recently most Liechtensteiners were farmers, but now many work in factories that make appliances and precision instruments.
5. A parliament governs the country, but the prince approves all laws.

Kinds of Clauses   [pages 480–484]   Identify the underlined clauses in each of the following sentences as (a) a main clause, (b) an adjective clause, (c) an adverb clause, or (d) a noun clause.

6. San Marino is a small republic that is entirely surrounded by Italy.
7. By tradition, San Marino has been independent since Marinus fled there from Roman persecution during the 300s.
8. That San Marino is the world's oldest republic is seldom disputed.
9. The people elect a council, which selects two members as leaders.
10. These captains-regent, who serve for six months, appoint the heads of the various government departments.

Kinds of Sentences   [pages 485–486]   For each sentence write (a) declarative, (b) imperative, (c) interrogative, or (d) exclamatory.

11. Bavaria became part of Germany in 1871.
12. Who ruled Bavaria before then?
13. The Wittelsbach family had ruled since 1180.
14. What a long time that is for one family to rule!
15. Look for information about King Ludwig's castles.

Sentence Completeness   [pages 486–488]   Identify each of the following as (a) a fragment, (b) a run-on, or (c) a complete sentence.

16. Andorra, one of the smallest countries, between Spain and France.
17. The country is ruled by two princes, one is the president of France, the other is the bishop of Urgel, Spain.
18. This system of joint rule has existed by treaty since the 1200s.

Writing for Review   Write a paragraph containing a variety of clauses. Identify in your paragraph at least one each of the following sentence types: simple, compound, complex, and compound-complex.

Usage

Thinking About Thinking: Recognizing Appropriateness

As you use language, you make decisions. In fact, usage is the result of an uncountable number of decisions that people have made as they found themselves speaking and writing. We all still participate in the making of English usage—and in the thinking process of decision making—whenever we speak or write.

Defining the Skill

A specific thinking skill that will help you make decisions about using words is RECOGNIZING APPROPRIATE-NESS. After you have identified the context for your words—the topic, the form, the purpose, the audience—you will have to make decisions about which words fit that context. The best writers choose words and arrangements of words that are most appropriate to topic, form, purpose, and audience. They have learned to master conventions—usages that most people agree are appropriate in certain situations.

Applying the Skill

Look at the photo. Identify the context, or the situation, shown in the photo. What type of apparel is appropriate to the context? What other conventions can you name that are appropriate to this situation?

CHAPTER 21

Verb Tenses and Voice

Principal Parts of Verbs

All verbs have four **principal parts**—a *basic form,* a *present participle,* a *simple past form,* and a *past participle.* All the verb tenses are formed from these principle parts.

BASIC FORM	PRESENT PARTICIPLE	PAST FORM	PAST PARTICIPLE
sail	sailing	sailed	sailed
soar	soaring	soared	soared
work	working	worked	worked
sing	singing	sang	sung
be	being	was, were	been
hit	hitting	hit	hit

The basic form is sometimes called the *present form* because it is the principal part used to form the present tense. The basic form is also called the *infinitive form* because it is the form that is used with *to.* The present participle is always formed by adding *-ing* to the basic form of the verb.

The basic form and the past form can be used by themselves as main verbs. To function as the simple predicate in a sentence, the present participle and the past participle must always be used with one or more auxiliary verbs.

> Eagles **soar**. [basic or present form]
>
> Eagles **soared**. [past form]
>
> Eagles **are soaring**. [present participle with auxiliary verb *are*]
>
> Eagles **have soared**. [past participle with auxiliary verb *have*]

Regular and Irregular Verbs

Verbs are regular or irregular depending on how their past form and their past participle are formed.

A **regular verb** forms its past and past participle by adding *-ed* to the basic form.

BASIC FORM	PAST FORM	PAST PARTICIPLE
soar	soared	soared
climb	climbed	climbed
guess	guessed	guessed

Some regular verbs undergo spelling changes when a suffix beginning with a vowel is added.

regulate + **-ed** = regulat**ed**
try + **-ed** = tri**ed**
stop + **-ed** = stop**ped**

An **irregular verb** forms its past and past participle in some way other than by adding *-ed* to the basic form.

Some of the oldest and most common verbs in English are irregular. Study the following list and refer to it whenever you are in doubt about a form of one of the verbs.

BASIC FORM	PAST FORM	PAST PARTICIPLE
be	was, were	been
bear	bore	borne
beat	beat	beaten *or* beat
become	became	become
begin	began	begun
bite	bit	bitten
blow	blew	blown
break	broke	broken
bring	brought	brought
burst	burst	burst
cast	cast	cast
catch	caught	caught
choose	chose	chosen
come	came	come
creep	crept	crept
dive	dived *or* dove	dived
do, does	did	done
draw	drew	drawn
drink	drank	drunk
drive	drove	driven
eat	ate	eaten
fall	fell	fallen
feel	felt	felt
find	found	found
fling	flung	flung
fly	flew	flown
freeze	froze	frozen
get	got	got *or* gotten
give	gave	given
go	went	gone
grow	grew	grown
hang	hanged *or* hung	hanged *or* hung

Regular and Irregular Verbs 497

BASIC FORM	PAST FORM	PAST PARTICIPLE
have, has	had	had
know	knew	known
lay*	laid	laid
lead	led	led
lend	lent	lent
lie*	lay	lain
lose	lost	lost
put	put	put
ride	rode	ridden
ring	rang	rung
rise*	rose	risen
run	ran	run
say	said	said
see	saw	seen
set	set	set
shake	shook	shaken
shine	shone *or* shined†	shone *or* shined
shrink	shrank *or* shrunk	shrunk *or* shrunken
sing	sang	sung
sink	sank *or* sunk	sunk
sit*	sat	sat
slay	slew	slain
speak	spoke	spoken
spring	sprang *or* sprung	sprung
steal	stole	stolen
sting	stung	stung
swear	swore	sworn
swim	swam	swum
swing	swung	swung
take	took	taken
tear	tore	torn
tell	told	told
think	thought	thought
throw	threw	thrown
wear	wore	worn
win	won	won
write	wrote	written

*For more detailed instruction on *lay* versus *lie*, *raise* versus *rise*, and *sit* versus *set*, see Chapter 25.

†*Shone* is intransitive. (The sun *shone*.) *Shined* is transitive. (I *shined* my shoes.)

Supplying the Correct Principal Part. On your paper complete the following sentences by filling the blanks with the principal part indicated in parentheses.

1. The number of words in the English language has been _____ for centuries. (present participle of *grow*)
2. Most words in our language have _____ through changes in spelling or meaning. (past participle of *go*)
3. Etymologists, who study the history of words, have _____ interesting clues to the present meanings of words. (past participle of *find*)
4. Two Latin words meaning "not speaking" _____ the word *infant.* (past form of *become*)
5. An ancient word meaning "blood" has _____ down as the word *red.* (past participle of *come*)
6. The word *ketchup* comes from the Chinese name for a fish sauce that sailors _____ to England in the seventeenth century. (past form of *bring*)
7. Long ago people sometimes _____ their last names on the basis of their profession; it is easy to understand why the names *Baker, Carpenter, Miller, Taylor,* and *Smith* were often selected. (past form of *choose*)
8. Celtic families often _____ their last name with *Mac* or *Fitz,* meaning "son of." (past form of *begin*)
9. The name *John* has _____ various forms in different languages around the world, including *Jean, Giovanni, Juan, Hans,* and *Ivan.* (past participle of *take*)
10. The Spanish have _____ the American language such words as *brocade, mosquito, sombrero, poncho,* and *vanilla.* (past participle of *give*)

Tense of Verbs

The **tenses** of a verb are the forms that help to show time.

Depending on which principal part of a verb you use and which, if any, auxiliary verbs you put before the principal parts, you can show *when* the action or condition you are describing occurred.

There are six tenses in English: *present, past,* and *future* and *present perfect, past perfect,* and *future perfect.* In the subsections which follow each of these tenses will be studied in detail. To be a good writer, it is important to learn how to use each of these tenses correctly and effectively.

The Present Tense

The present tense of any action verb and of every linking verb other than *be* is the same as the verb's basic form. The following is a *conjugation*, or list of forms, for the present tense of action verb *play*:

	SINGULAR	PLURAL
FIRST PERSON	I **play.**	We **play.**
SECOND PERSON	You **play.**	You **play.**
THIRD PERSON	She, he, or it **plays.**	They **play.**
	Ronnie **plays.**	The children **play.**

Note that in the present-tense forms of the third-person singular, an -s is added to the basic form. In the following conjugation note that the present tense of *be* has three forms:

	SINGULAR	PLURAL
FIRST PERSON	I **am** happy.	We **are** happy.
SECOND PERSON	You **are** happy.	You **are** happy.
THIRD PERSON	She, he, or it **is** happy.	They **are** happy.

The **present tense** expresses a constant, repeated, or habitual action or condition. It can also express a general truth.

> The Hudson River **flows** into the Atlantic. [not just now but always—a constant action]
>
> Jesse **plays** the flute well. [now and always—a habitual action]
>
> Uranium **is** radioactive. [a condition that is always true]

The **present tense** can also express an action or condition that exists only now.

> Ronnie **feels** sick. [not always but just now]
>
> I **declare** these games over. [at this very moment.]

The **present tense** is sometimes used in historical writing to express past events and, more often, in poetry, fiction, and reporting—especially sports reporting—to convey to the reader a sense of "being there."

> Above the spectators the *Hindenburg* suddenly **bursts** into flames.
>
> The wild pitch **gets** away from the catcher and **bounces** into the fence behind home plate.

EXERCISE 2 **Using the Present Tense.** On your paper write your answer to each of the following questions in a complete sentence, beginning with *Yes.* (This exercise will help you practice using singular present-tense action verbs that end in *s*, *es*, and *ies*.)

SAMPLE Does the wholesaler supply goods?
ANSWER Yes, the wholesaler supplies goods.

1. Does a physical therapist enjoy good job opportunities?
2. Does the police force expect expansion?
3. Does an urban planner face difficulties in the job market?
4. Does a bank officer anticipate a good future?
5. Does new technology multiply the job opportunities for a computer technician?
6. Does the future carry risks even for a highly qualified petroleum engineer?
7. Does the job market impress dental hygienists?
8. Does the scientific world search for more geologists?
9. Does the business world hope for more well-trained secretaries and word processors?
10. Does the nursing profession attract its fair share of well-educated young people?

SENTENCE WRITING **Expressing the Present Tense in Sentences.**
Write a sentence using each of the following verb forms. Make the content of your sentence express the kind of present time indicated in parentheses.

SAMPLE   does (now and always)
ANSWER   He does his laundry on Saturday.

1. works (now and always)
2. sound (just now)
3. is (always true)
4. says (at this moment)
5. sing (always)

The Past Tense

Use the **past tense** to express an action or condition that was started and completed in the past.

The team **defeated** its opponent.
The rivalry **seemed** fierce.
Victory **tasted** sweet.

All regular and irregular verbs—except *be*—have just one past-tense form, such as *soared* or *began*. When you use *be*, you must choose *was* or *were*, depending on whether the person or thing you are talking about is first, second, or third person, singular or plural.

PAST TENSE OF *BE*

I **was** happy.   We **were** happy.
You **were** happy.   You **were** happy.
He, she, or it **was** happy.   They **were** happy.

Using the Past Tense. Complete each of the following sentences by writing on your paper the correct past-tense form of the verb in parentheses.

1. Ambrose Bierce _____ as a journalist in San Francisco in the 1860s. (begin)
2. He _____ for those "enlightened souls who prefer . . . clean English to slang." (write)
3. Bierce _____ a cutting humorist. (be)
4. He once _____ a young writer to "cultivate the good opinion of squirrels." (tell)
5. In 1906 he _____ *The Cynic's Word Book.* (publish)
6. He later _____ the title of that book to *The Devil's Dictionary.* (change)
7. Bierce _____ *alone* as "in bad company." (define)
8. A *coward*, he _____, was "one who in a perilous emergency thinks with his legs." (say)
9. He _____ any "person who talks when you wish him to listen" to be a *bore.* (find)
10. Bierce _____ *discussion* as "a method of confirming others in their errors." (interpret)

The Future Tense

You form the future tense of any verb by using *shall* or *will* with the basic form: *I shall study, you will go.*

Use the **future tense** to express an action or condition that will occur in the future.

Brad **will mail** the application.
I **shall write** my essay tonight.

The following are other ways to express future time besides using the words *shall* or *will.*

1. Use *going to* with the present tense of *be* and the basic form of a verb.

   Brad **is going to** mail the application.

2. Use *about to* with the present tense of *be* and the basic form of a verb.

   Brad **is about to** mail the application.

3. Use the present tense with an adverb or an adverbial phrase that shows future time.

   Brad **sails tomorrow.**
   Brad **sails on the fifteenth of next month.**

EXERCISE 4 **Identifying Expressions of Future Time.** Write on your paper the words that express future time in each of the following sentences.

SAMPLE Next spring we plant grass.
ANSWER Next spring, plant

1. The people in our neighborhood are going to build a community park.
2. It will provide a safe play area for children.
3. We shall work on the park for most of the summer.
4. We are about to unload our tools from the truck.
5. Tomorrow we clear the property.
6. Construction on the park is about to begin.
7. Obviously, everyone is going to get wet if it rains.
8. However, we will not postpone the ground-breaking ceremony.
9. Construction begins next week regardless of the weather.
10. We shall prepare ourselves for any kind of weather.

SENTENCE WRITING **Expressing Future Time in Sentences.** Write five statements or predictions about the future. Your sentences can be as realistic or as imaginary as you wish. Try to use at least two other ways of expressing future time besides with *shall* or *will*.

SAMPLE ANSWER The film companies are going to produce all-day movies.

The Perfect Tenses

In this section you will study the three perfect tenses—the *present perfect tense*, the *past perfect tense*, and the *future perfect tense*. The term *perfect* comes from the Latin word *perfectus*, meaning "completed," and all of these tenses refer to actions or conditions that are or will be completed.

To make the perfect tenses you must use a form of the auxiliary verb *have* with the past participle of the main verb.

Present Perfect Tense

You form the present perfect tense by using *has* or *have* with the past participle of a verb: *has stopped, have waited.**

Use the **present perfect tense** to express an action or condition that occurred at some *indefinite* time in the past.

> She **has listened** to the recording.
> They **have bought** a new home.

---

*Do not be confused by the term *present perfect*; this tense expresses *past* time. *Present* refers to the tense of the auxiliary verb *has* or *have*.

The present perfect can refer to completed action in past time only in an indefinite way. Adverbs such as *yesterday* cannot be added to make the time more specific.

He **has arrived** from Nebraska. [indefinite past]

To be specific about completed past time, you would normally use the simple past tense:

He **arrived** from Nebraska yesterday.

The present perfect can also be used to communicate the idea that an action or a condition *began* in the past and *continues* into the present. This use normally involves adverbs of time or adverbial phrases:

He **has spoken daily** from his prison cell.

Special guards **have remained** at the embassy **around the clock**.

She **has been** class president **for three months**.

Past Perfect Tense

You form the past perfect tense by using *had* with the past participle of a verb: *had loved, had written*.

Use the **past perfect tense** to indicate that one past action or condition began *and* ended before another past action started.

PAST PERFECT   PAST
She **had worked** as manager before I **took** the job. [She worked; she stopped working; I worked.]

        PAST   PAST PERFECT
When I **arrived**, several actors **had auditioned**. [They auditioned; they finished auditioning; I arrived.]

Future Perfect Tense

You form the future perfect tense by using *will have* or *shall have* with the past participle of a verb: *will have walked, shall have walked*.

Use the **future perfect tense** to express one future action or condition that will begin *and* end before another future event starts.

By June I **will have worked** here two months. [The two months will be over by the time another future event—the coming of June—occurs.]

By the time those children reach high school, they **will have watched** many years' worth of television.

EXERCISE 5 **Identifying the Perfect Tenses.** On your paper write the tense of the italicized verbs in each of the following sentences.

1. For too long people *have seen* their problems in birds and beasts.
2. Writers from the earliest times *have given* animals human traits.
3. After people *had attributed* to animals the defects of the human race, perhaps they felt better about themselves.
4. One says, for example, that the beast in a person *has awakened*.
5. People *have associated* wildcats with strikes, crocodiles with tears, and kangaroos with courts.
6. Cowardice *has brought* chickens to mind, and stupidity *has reminded* people of turkeys.
7. Sometimes, however, animals *have received* praise.
8. People respect a colleague who *has worked* as hard as a beaver or who *has been* as busy as a bee.
9. Throughout history one person who *had outfoxed* another was thought of as wise as an owl.
10. By the time humans realize their mistake, they *will have ascribed* every human trait to animals.

SENTENCE WRITING **Expressing the Present Perfect Tense in Sentences.** (a) Rewrite each of the following sentences, changing the tense of the verb from past to present perfect. (b) Add appropriate adverbs or adverbial phrases to each of your new sentences to communicate the idea that an action or condition began in the past and continues into the present.

SAMPLE We looked for a new car.
ANSWER (a) We have looked for a new car. (b) We have looked for a new car for over two weeks.

1. He taught swim classes.
2. Movie critics praised the film.
3. The state highway was under repair.
4. Our art class studied portrait painting.
5. The towering waves cascaded over the craggy shore.

The Perfect Tenses   505

The Progressive and Emphatic Forms

Each of the six tenses has a **progressive** form that expresses a continuing action.

You make the progressive forms by using the appropriate tense of the verb *be* with the present participle of the main verb:

PRESENT PROGRESSIVE	They *are* listening.
PAST PROGRESSIVE	They *were* listening.
FUTURE PROGRESSIVE	They *will be* listening.
PRESENT PERFECT PROGRESSIVE	They *have been* listening.
PAST PERFECT PROGRESSIVE	They *had been* listening.
FUTURE PERFECT PROGRESSIVE	They *will have been* listening.

The present and past tenses of verbs have additional forms, called **emphatic**, that add special force or emphasis to the verb.

You make the emphatic forms by using *do* or *did* with the basic form of the verb:

PRESENT EMPHATIC	I **do listen.**
PAST EMPHATIC	I **did listen.**

EXERCISE 6 **Identifying Progressive and Emphatic Forms.** Write the form of the italicized verb in each of the following sentences.

1. Even today remarkable trees *are growing* everywhere.
2. Giant sequoias and redwoods *have been living* for thousands of years.
3. Traveler's trees *do store* nearly a pint of water in the base of each leaf stalk.
4. The tough ombu tree *will be thriving* a century from now no matter how many droughts, fires and windstorms attack it.
5. That banyan tree, which now covers acres, *was spreading* trunklike roots even when I was a child.

EXERCISE 7 **Using the Present Progressive.** For each of the following sentences, write the present progressive form of the verb that appears in parentheses.

1. Large parks (get) more important to people in large cities.
2. Nowadays San Fransisco's Golden Gate Recreation Area (bustle) with activities like hiking, hang gliding, and surfing.
3. San Franciscans (discover) forest and mountain trails only an hour's ride from Market Street.
4. Urban parks (bring) the wilderness to the city.
5. Nearly three thousand miles east, New York City (enjoy) the Gateway National Recreation Area.

EXERCISE 8   **Using the Past Progressive.** For each of the following sentences, write the past progressive form of the verb in parentheses.

1. The crew of a sailing canoe (retrace) an ancient sea route when they sailed from Hawaii to Tahiti.
2. The replica of a twelfth-century canoe (carry) no navigational instruments when it sailed on May 1, 1976.
3. Navigator Mau Piailug (study) to become a navigator when he was only six years old.
4. Piailug (travel) an unfamiliar route when he guided the canoe through the rapid currents.
5. Thousands of Tahitians (shout) a welcome when the canoe triumphantly sailed into Papeete Harbor on June 4, 1976.

SENTENCE WRITING   **Expressing Past Time in a Paragraph.** Write a paragraph of at least five sentences about an important event in your past. Underline five verbs or verb phrases that you have used, and identify the tense of each underlined item.

REVIEW EXERCISE   **Verbs.** On your paper complete the following sentences by filling the blank with the verb form indicated in parentheses.

1. Soon scientists _____ robots with a sense of vision and touch. (future tense of *equip*)
2. Robots _____ machines programmed to perform tasks that previously only humans could perform. (present tense of *be*)
3. Some scientists already _____ robots for industry. (present perfect tense of *build*)
4. Other scientists _____ to work on all-purpose housekeeping robots. (present progressive of *plan*)
5. These robots _____ your apartment by the time you get home from work. (future perfect tense of *clean*)
6. A robot inventor _____ to complete his watchdog robot by the end of this decade. (past emphatic of *promise*)
7. By the year 1995 you _____ more household robots than you can now imagine. (future perfect tense of *see*)
8. In the past some new inventions sometimes _____ hazardous and unsafe. (past tense of *prove*)
9. People _____ such products before they learned of their dangers. (past perfect tense of *buy*)
10. The government and industry _____ a joint responsibility to ensure the safety of new products for all consumers. (present emphatic of *have*)

The Progressive and Emphatic Forms   507

Compatibility of Tenses

The various verb tenses enable you to show whether two or more events occur at the same time and whether one event precedes or follows another.

Do not shift tenses when two or more events occur at the same time.

INCORRECT	During the storm the dam **broke**, and the river **reaches** flood level. [The tense shifts from the past to the present.]
CORRECT	During the storm the dam **broke**, and the river **reached** flood level. [Now it is clear that both events happened at nearly the same time in the past.]

Shift tenses only to show that one event precedes or follows another.

INCORRECT	By the time the game **ended**, she **bowled** six strikes. [The two past-tense verbs give the mistaken impression that both events happened at the same time.]
CORRECT	By the time the game **ended**, she **had bowled** six strikes. [The shift from the past tense (*ended*) to the past perfect tense (*had bowled*) clearly indicates that the bowling of six strikes happened before the game ended.]
INCORRECT	Since they **moved** to Dallas, the Davilas **lived** in the same house. [It is not clear which event came first.]
CORRECT	Since they **moved** to Dallas, the Davilas **have lived** in the same house. [The past tense (*moved*) indicates a completed action. The present perfect (*have lived*) indicates another past action, one that has continued into the present.]

EXERCISE 9 **Making Tenses Compatible.** Rewrite each sentence by making the tenses of the verbs compatible.

A. [1]The apartment was vacant when our moving van arrives. [2]We changed the lock because the former tenants took a key. [3]After the superintendent padded the freight elevator, we started to move in our belongings. [4]Since we have lived here, we have no problems. [5]We had moved to this building four years ago, when I was twelve.

B. [1]People have celebrated Valentine's Day since the ancient Romans were holding a festival called *Lupercalia*. [2]An old English legend has claimed that birds choose their mates on February 14. [3]When a French duke was captured by the English, he writes the first Valentine's Day message from the Tower of London! [4]In the 1700s, friends met to draw names from a jar, and for days afterward people had worn their valentine's name on their sleeves. [5]Since commercial valentines became popular in the 1800s, many artists designed beautiful and charming cards.

Tense. On your paper explain the difference in meaning between the sentences in each of the following pairs. (The sentences are all correct and are labeled for time and tense.)

1. (a) Did she live in Washington long? (past)
   (b) Has she lived in Washington long? (present perfect)
2. (a) They went to Utah for two weeks. (past)
   (b) They have gone to Utah for two weeks. (present perfect)
3. (a) He said that his parents had been in Virginia for three months. (past; past perfect)
   (b) He said that his parents have been in Virginia for three months. (past; present perfect)
4. (a) What happened in Oklahoma when you arrived? (past; past)
   (b) What had happened in Oklahoma when you arrived? (past perfect; past)
5. (a) She was working in New Mexico. (past progressive)
   (b) She worked in New Mexico. (past)
6. (a) What has she seen in Texas? (present perfect)
   (b) What had she seen in Texas? (past perfect)
7. (a) He will have traveled through all of Colorado when the summer is over. (future perfect; present tense with future meaning)
   (b) He will travel through all of Colorado when the summer is over. (future; present tense with future meaning)
8. (a) We took the children to Arizona. (past)
   (b) We have taken the children to Arizona. (present perfect)
9. (a) Have the students been to Hawaii? (present perfect)
   (b) Had the students been to Hawaii? (past perfect)
10. (a) How long has he been in Indiana? (present perfect)
    (b) How long was he in Indiana? (past)

Voice of Verbs

An action verb is in the **active voice** when the subject of the sentence performs the action.

> The trainer **teased** the lion.

An action verb is in the **passive voice** when its action is performed on the subject.

> The lion **was teased** by the trainer.

Both the preceding examples say the same thing, but in the first sentence the *trainer* (the subject of the sentence) performs the action. In the second sentence the *lion* (now the subject of the sentence) takes center stage, and the trainer is reduced to something called an *agent*.

As a writer you often have a choice between using a verb in the active or passive voice. It is often a question of whom you want to place in center stage—the trainer or the lion, for example.

Generally the active voice is stronger, but there are times when the passive voice is preferred or, in fact, necessary. If you do not want to call attention to the performer, or if you do not know the performer, use the passive voice, as in the following examples:

> The milk **was spilled**. [You may not want to identify the culprit.]

> The diamond **was stolen**. [You may not know who the culprit is.]

You form the passive voice by using a form of the auxiliary verb *be* with the past participle of the verb. The tense of a passive verb is determined by the tense of the auxiliary verb.

> The lion **is teased** by the trainer. [present tense, passive voice.]

> The lion **was being teased**. [past progressive tense, passive voice]

> The lion **will have been teased** by the trainer. [future perfect tense, passive voice]

When a verb is in the passive voice, the performer of the action may be stated as the object of the preposition *by*.

> The elephants are fed **by the children**.

EXERCISE 10 **Changing the Voice of Verbs.** In each of the following sentences, change the active voice to the passive or the passive voice to the active.

1. Some of today's drive-in movie theaters have been changed by new technology.
2. In the earliest drive-ins the sound was transmitted by loudspeakers above the screen.
3. Those speakers were replaced by smaller window receivers.
4. Now radio sound replaces the window receivers.
5. In this new system the car radio transmits the sound.
6. The sound is greatly improved by the new system.
7. Theater owners expect drive-in audiences to grow.
8. One other big advantage is offered by the radio systems: channels with two languages.
9. An audience in Los Ángeles can choose an English or a Spanish sound track.
10. Owners of drive-ins see a great future for bilingual sound.

Revising Your Writing

No. 2310. **CUP AND BRUSH** $7 50
[MALACOLITE]
Satin, bright cut.

No. 35 **CUP AND BRUSH** ... $7 50
[MALADY]
Satin, beaded.

The overuse of the passive voice can often rob writing of its vigor, causing sentences to sound awkward and sapping action verbs of their vitality. If Leslie Norris had relied on the passive voice in the following passage from "Shaving," his prose would have sounded like this:

> . . . the razor *was placed* delicately against his father's face, setting the head [of the razor] accurately on the clean line near the ear where the long hair ended. The razor *was held* by him in the tips of his fingers and the blade *was drawn* sweetly through the lather.

Notice how flat and wordy the writing in the preceding sentences is in comparison to Norris' actual prose:

> Barry . . . *placed* the razor delicately against his father's face, setting the head accurately on the clean line near the ear where the long hair ended. He *held* the razor in the tips of his fingers and *drew* the blade sweetly through the lather.

Notice also that the active voice clearly identifies Barry as the person performing each action involved in the shaving—*placed, held, drew*. Moreover, the active voice allows the readers to imagine the character moving through time—an important element in any narrative. Whenever a story is "fast-moving," it is likely that the writer is using active-voice verbs.

Revise the following passage adapted from "Shaving" by restoring verbs to the active voice.

> Inside, on the bottom, a few dark bristles were lying, loose and dry. They were shaken out by Barry. Then the cup was held in his hand, and its solidness was felt. Methodically everything was set by him on a tray, razor, soap, brush, towels. The hot water was tested with a finger, the mug was filled by him, and that was put, too, on the tray.

CHAPTER 22

Subject-Verb Agreement

In this chapter you will study how to use verbs correctly in sentences. The agreement of the verb with the subject of the sentence is the central topic that will be studied. Sometimes, intervening phrases, linking verbs, inverted word order, or the use of special nouns may confuse you. Study the examples in each subsection to help you remember the rules for correct subject-verb agreement.

A verb must agree with its subject in person and number.

With most verbs the only change in form to indicate agreement occurs in the present tense: An *s* (or *es*) is added to the basic verb when its subject is third-person singular. The linking verb *be* changes in both the present and the past tense.

SINGULAR	PLURAL
She **learns.**	They **learn.**
He **is** here.	They **are** here.
It **was** sour.	They **were** sour.

In verb phrases the auxiliary verbs *be, have,* and *do* change in form to show agreement with third-person subjects.

She **is learning.**	They **are learning.**
She **has gone** home.	They **have gone** home.
Does he **live** here?	**Do** they **live** here?

Making a verb agree with its subject involves not only recognizing subjects and verbs but also telling whether a subject is singular or plural. In some sentences it may be easy to mistake another word for the actual subject. In other sentences determining whether the subject is singular or plural may be difficult.

Intervening Prepositional Phrases

Do not mistake a word in a prepositional phrase for the subject of a verb.

The simple subject is never within a prepositional phrase. Make sure the verb agrees with the actual subject, not with the object of a preposition.

The ***price*** of the houses we saw **amazes** us. [The subject *price* is singular; *of the houses* is a prepositional phrase; the verb *amazes* is thus singular.]

The ***designs*** for the house **are** pretty. [The subject *designs* is plural; *for the house* is a prepositional phrase; the verb *are* is thus plural.]

Making Subjects and Verbs Agree When Prepositional Phrases Intervene. First find the simple subject in each of the following sentences. Then write on your paper the verb in parentheses that agrees with the subject of each sentence.

1. Trees with paper-thin bark (belong/belongs) to the birch family.
2. Some shrubs in North America also (come/comes) from this family.
3. The bark of birch trees (peel/peels) off in horizontal sheets.
4. The light, strong bark of *canoe birches* (serve/serves) as raw materials for handmade canoes.
5. Silver and gray birches, with their distinctive white bark, (grow/grows) primarily in the eastern and southern parts of North America.
6. The scaly spikes of the birch (contain/contains) small flowers.
7. The precise name for these spikes (is/are) *catkins*.
8. The leaves of a birch tree (appear/appears) alternately on the twig.
9. The flexibility of birch trees (make/makes) it possible to swing from the top of the tree to the ground.
10. One of Robert Frost's poems (describe/describes) a boy's pleasure in swinging from birch trees.

Agreement with Linking Verbs

Do not be confused by a predicate nominative that is different in number from the subject. Only the subject affects the number of the linking verb.

> The last **course was** strawberries with cream. [The singular verb *was* agrees with the singular subject *course*, not with the predicate nominative *strawberries*.]

> **Baskets** of flowers **were** the decoration at the banquet. [The plural verb *were* agrees with the plural subject *baskets*, not with the predicate nominative *decoration*.]

Making Linking Verbs Agree with Their Subjects. First find the simple subject in each of the following sentences. Then write on your paper the verb in parentheses that agrees with the subject of each sentence.

1. Before the invention of clocks, shadows (was/were) a way of telling the time of day.
2. The changing lengths of shadows (was/were) an indication of time passing.
3. Over four thousand years old, sundials (was/were) the first method of measuring time.
4. Hourglasses (was/were) another early device for keeping track of time.
5. A thirteenth-century development (was/were) clocks powered by mechanical devices such as weights.
6. When only the wealthy could afford clocks, mechanical timepieces (was/were) a sign of prosperity.
7. For many eighteenth-century Americans a favorite topic of conversation (was/were) cuckoo clocks from Germany.
8. An innovation in the 1940s (was/were) atomic-powered clocks.
9. Today chiming clocks (is/are) a decoration in many homes.
10. A popular feature in many modern homes (is/are) digital clocks.

Agreement in Inverted Sentences

When a subject follows its verb, carefully locate the simple subject and make sure that the verb agrees with the subject.

Inverted sentences are those in which the subject follows the verb. Inverted sentences often begin with prepositional phrases. Do not mistake the object of the preposition for the subject.

SINGULAR Over the mountains **soars** the *eagle*.

PLURAL Over the mountain **soar** the *eagles*.

Inverted sentences may also begin with the expletive *there* or *here*. An expletive is never the subject of a sentence.

SINGULAR There **is** an *eagle* on the mountain.

Here **goes** the last *match*.

PLURAL There **are** *eagles* on the mountain.

Here **go** the last two *matches*.

In questions an auxiliary verb may come before the subject. Look for the subject between the auxiliary verb and the main verb.

$$\overset{V}{} \overset{S}{} \overset{V}{}$$
SINGULAR   **Does** that *eagle* **live** in the mountains?

$$\overset{V}{} \overset{S}{} \overset{V}{}$$
PLURAL   **Do** those *mountains* **contain** eagles?

EXERCISE 3   **Making Subjects and Verbs Agree in Inverted Sentences.** First find the simple subject in each of the following sentences. Then write the verb in parentheses that agrees with the subject of each sentence.

1. There (are/is) two ice-skating rinks on the east side of town.
2. Over the entrance of one (hang/hangs) a sign with admission prices.
3. (Don't/Doesn't) the owner of the rink rent skates by the hour?
4. Onto the ice (glide/glides) the eager skaters in their long scarves.
5. Here (come/comes) the machines that smooth the ice.

EXERCISE 4   **Making Verbs Agree with Their Subjects.** Complete the following inverted sentences by supplying the *present-tense* form of the verb in parentheses.

1. Here _____ the basic rules for a sport called *curling*. (be)
2. On a flat sheet of ice _____ teams of players. (stand)
3. Across the ice _____ heavy stones which are thrown in turns by players from the opposing team. (slide)
4. _____ the number of stones thrown affect the score? (do)
5. No, here _____ the way to keep score: one point is awarded for every stone that lands close to the opponent's target. (be)

Agreement with Special Subjects

Some subjects require careful attention when you select a verb to agree with them.

Collective Nouns

A **collective noun** names a group. (See Chapter 17.) Consider a collective noun singular when it refers to a group as a whole. Consider a collective noun plural when it refers to each member of a group individually.

SINGULAR	PLURAL
The *squadron* of planes soars.	The *squadron* **protect** one another.
The *crowd* **cheers.**	The *crowd* **fight** for seats.
The *New York Yankees* **is** a fine team.	The *New York Yankees* **are** in first place.

Special Nouns

Certain nouns that end in *s*, such as *mumps*, *measles*, and *mathematics*, take singular verbs.

SINGULAR   **Measles is** a disease.
Mathematics interests many people.

Certain other nouns that name one thing but that end in *s*, such as *scissors*, *pants*, *binoculars*, and *eyeglasses*, take plural verbs.

PLURAL   The **scissors were** defective.
Your **pants need** cleaning.

Many nouns that end in *ics* may be singular or plural depending on meaning.

SINGULAR   **Politics is** often exciting. [one subject of interest]
PLURAL   His **politics are** shameless. [more than one action of a political nature]

Nouns of Amount

Some nouns are singular or plural depending on how they are used in the sentence. When the noun of amount refers to a total considered as one unit, it is singular. When the noun refers to a number of individual units, it is plural.

SINGULAR   Five **dollars is** a fair price. [one amount]
PLURAL   Five **dollars are** on the table. [five individual bills]
SINGULAR   Three **months is** the waiting period. [one unit of time]
PLURAL   Three **months have gone** by already. [three individual periods of time]

Titles

A title is always considered singular even if a noun within the title is plural.

SINGULAR   **The Life and Adventures of Nicholas Nickleby delights** readers of all ages.

The Number, A Number

The number is considered singular. *A number* (meaning "some") is considered plural.

SINGULAR   The **number** of guests **is** astounding.
PLURAL   A **number** of guests **are** late. [meaning "some" guests]

Making Verbs Agree with Special Subjects. First find the subject in each of the following sentences. Then write on your paper the verb in parentheses that agrees with the subject of each sentence.

1. During the mid-nineteenth century a large number of clipper ships (was/were) carrying goods and passengers across the ocean in record-breaking time.
2. The crew of a clipper ship (was/were) an important factor in the success of the sailing vessel's voyage.
3. If the crew (was/were) working well with one another, the clipper ship had a better chance of making a speedy passage.
4. Eighty-nine days (was/were) the record time for one of these slender vessels to make the trip from New York City to San Francisco.
5. The number of fast clipper ships (was/were) impressive.
6. The economics of the clipper trade (is/are) an interesting subject.
7. A number of traders (was/were) using clipper ships to transport goods between the United States and China, Australia, and Europe.
8. Molasses (was/were) one of the products clipper ships transported.
9. High-powered binoculars (was/were) not yet in existence, but the captain could scan the horizon with a telescope.
10. *Two Years Before the Mast* (was/were) written by Richard Henry Dana about the exciting era of the clipper ships.

Agreement with Compound Subjects

When the subject of a sentence is compound (Chapter 18), you must pay attention to the conjunction that joins the compound parts and to the meaning of the entire subject. Only then can you know which verb form agrees with a particular compound subject.

1. Compound subjects joined by *and*

Usually compound subjects joined by *and* or by *both . . . and* are considered plural. However, when the parts of the compound subject are actually parts of one unit or when they refer to the same person or thing, the subject is considered singular.

PLURAL The *eagle* and the *owl* **are** soaring.
Both *sailing* and *swimming* **are** fun.

SINGULAR *Ham* and *eggs* **costs** two dollars. [Compound subject is one unit.]
Sitting and *waiting* **is** boring. [Compound subject is one unit.]
Her *friend* and *teacher* **helps** her. [One person is both the friend and the teacher.]

2. Compound subjects joined by *or* or *nor*

With compound subjects joined by *or* or *nor* (or by *either . . . or* or *neither . . . nor*), always make the verb agree with the subject nearer the verb.

PLURAL   *Neither the **eagle** nor the **owls** **are soaring.***
SINGULAR   *Either the **eagle** or the **owl** **is soaring.***
*Neither the **eagles** nor the **owl** **soars.***

3. *Many a, every,* and *each* with compound subjects

When *many a, every,* or *each* precedes a compound subject, the subject is considered singular.

SINGULAR   *Many a **man, woman,** and **child** **knows** hunger.*
*Every **eagle, owl,** and **parrot** **scares** me.*
*Each **eagle** and **owl** **is soaring.***

Intervening Expressions

Certain expressions, such as *accompanied by, as well as, in addition to, plus,* and *together with,* introduce phrases that modify the subject but do not change its number. Although their meaning is similar to that of *and,* these expressions do not create compound subjects.

If a singular subject is linked to another noun by an intervening expression, such as "accompanied by," the subject is still considered singular.

SINGULAR   ***Wind,** in addition to rain, **is expected** for today.*
*The **father** as well as his daughter **is arriving.***

EXERCISE 6   **Making Verbs Agree with Their Subjects.** On your paper write the appropriate form of the verb in parentheses.

1. Many a worker and shopper (makes/make) use of mass transit.
2. Every city resident and commuter (knows/know) about public transportation.
3. The bus as well as the subway (is/are) used by many people.
4. Neither you nor the typical commuter (thinks/think) of elevators as public transportation.
5. Yet a person, together with his or her belongings, (rides/ride) elevators as often as trains and buses.
6. Of course, huffing and puffing up a stairway to the twentieth floor (does/do) not appeal to most of us.
7. Both passenger and freight elevators (moves/move) by either hydraulic power or electric traction.

8. Compressed oil or water (pushes/push) the hydraulic elevator.
9. Each traction passenger elevator and freight elevator (has/have) at least three steel cables that lift the car.
10. Not surprisingly, the average passenger elevator or service lift (travels/travel) about 10,000 miles a year.

SENTENCE WRITING **Using Compound Subjects.** Write sentences using each of the following compound subjects. Make the compound subject agree with a present-tense verb.

SAMPLE bread and butter
ANSWER Bread and butter is on the plate.

1. peanut butter and jelly
2. neither the plaintiff nor the defendants
3. both the *Times* and the *Chronicle*
4. Mother or her cousin
5. many a soldier and sailor

Indefinite Pronouns as Subjects

A verb must agree in number with an indefinite pronoun subject.

Indefinite pronouns can be divided into three groups: those that are always singular; those that are always plural; and those that can be either singular or plural, depending upon the nouns to which they refer.

The following are the indefinite pronouns that are always singular:

each	everyone	nobody	anything
either	everybody	nothing	someone
neither	everything	anyone	somebody
one	no one	anybody	something

These are the indefinite pronouns that are always plural:

several	few	both	many

These indefinite pronouns may be singular or plural:

some	all	any	most	none

The verb used with an indefinite pronoun from the third group often shows whether you are assigning the pronoun a singular or a plural meaning.

SINGULAR When we checked, **all was** as it should be. [*All* is used here in the sense of "everything," which is singular.]

PLURAL ***All*** in my class **are** good in Spanish. [*All* is used here to refer to *students*, which is plural.]

Making Verbs Agree with Indefinite Pronoun Subjects. Write sentences using each of the following indefinite pronouns as the subject. Use present-tense verbs that agree with each subject.

SAMPLE   Each
ANSWER   Each of the teachers has a master's degree.

1. one
2. several
3. both
4. nobody
5. everyone

SENTENCE WRITING **Using Indefinite Pronoun Subjects.** Write two sentences, using each of the following indefinite pronouns as the subject of both sentences. Write the first sentence of each pair with a singular present-tense verb and the second sentence with a plural present-tense verb.

SAMPLE   None
ANSWER   None of the pudding is for me.
         None of the fans are happy with the call.

1. some   2. all   3. any   4. most

Agreement in Adjective Clauses

The verb in an adjective clause must agree with its subject, which is often a relative pronoun. (See Chapter 20.) The number of the relative pronoun subject depends on the number of its antecedent in the main clause.

The eagle is one of the **birds that are endangered.** [The antecedent of *that* is *birds*, a third-person plural noun.]

The eagle is the only **one** of the birds of prey **that is recognized by many people.** [The antecedent of *that* is *one*, a third-person singular pronoun.]

If the expression "one of" appears in the main clause, you must take care to determine if the antecedent is "one" as in the second example above or the noun that follows it, such as "birds" in the first example. (The word *the* before *one* indicates that *one* is the antecedent.)

The verb in an adjective clause with a relative pronoun subject must agree with the antecedent to which the relative pronoun refers.

EXERCISE 7 **Making Subjects and Verbs Agree in Adjective Clauses.** Complete each sentence on the following page by choosing the correct form of the verb.

SAMPLE   John Curry is one of the figure skaters who (has won/have won) Olympic gold medals.
ANSWER   have won

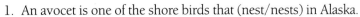

1. An avocet is one of the shore birds that (nest/nests) in Alaska.
2. The oboe is one of the wind instruments that (was/were) first developed in Egypt.
3. Before 1896 the *New York World* was the only one of the nation's newspapers that (was printing/were printing) a full-color comic strip.
4. Gottlieb Daimler was one of two nineteenth-century inventors who (was/were) successful in producing a workable automobile.
5. A singer named Elizabeth Tible was the only one of the eighteenth-century balloonists who (was/were) a woman.
6. Rod Laver is one of only two men in tennis history who (has won/have won) the Grand Slam.
7. Buster Keaton is the only other film comic who (is/are) comparable to Charlie Chaplin.
8. Vladimir Nabokov is one of the few great writers in English who (was/were) not native English speakers.
9. The golden eagle is one of the two members of the animal kingdom that (is/are) capable of outracing the cheetah.
10. Sympathy is one of the characteristics of human beings that (distinguish/distinguishes) them from other species.

REVIEW EXERCISE **Subject-Verb Agreement.** The following paragraph contains ten errors in subject-verb agreement. Locate the sentences with errors, and rewrite those sentences with the verb form that agrees with the subject. (Some of the sentences will have more than one subject-verb combination.)

[1]In the center of the field are a large circus tent as well as cages of animals. [2]The crowd buy their tickets, and soon every one of the cages are deserted. [3]One little boy, accompanied by his parents, stare in astonishment at a large bear. [4]A number of people sits on the grass, eating picnic lunches. [5]There is dishes piled with chicken. [6]Bread and butter seems to be a part of everyone's meal. [7]In most cases, the dessert course of these lunches are made with fruit. [8]Suddenly, someone shouts, "Here comes the performers!" and this nineteenth-century American circus begins. [9]The originator of modern circuses was the Englishman Philip Astley. [10]In eighteenth-century Europe neither traveling troops of acrobats nor the traditional county fair were able to compete with Astley's circus. [11]The number of acts were amazing to the audience. [12]Gymnastics was one of Astley's most popular spectacles. [13]A large number of Astley's circuses were established during his lifetime. [14]Although much has changed, circuses remain a major event in most towns today. [15]Many a young boy and girl have been delighted by the exotic animals and amazing performers of a circus.

Revising Your Writing

When you revise, part of your purpose is to take what is already good and make it better. Changes such as combining simple sentences into more complex structures involve choices of style rather than matters of accuracy. However, revising also often involves checking for correct usage. For example, lack of subject-verb agreement will jar the reader and weaken the writer's credibility. If Alexander Pope had written "And the smooth stream in smoother numbers **flow**," his readers would probably have doubted his competence as a poet.

Keep the following guidelines in mind as you check your work for subject-verb agreement.

1. Be alert to intervening prepositional phrases and other expressions that fall between a subject and its verb. Mentally block out this intervening material when you check for agreement.

   > All the complicated **details**
   > of the attiring and
   > the disattiring **are** completed!
   >
   > —William Carlos Williams, "Winter Trees"

2. Take time to determine whether special subjects, such as collective nouns, are singular or plural. Sometimes personal pronouns elsewhere in the sentence will help you decide whether the subject is intended to be singular or plural.

   > The so-called debtor **class** . . . **are** not dishonest because *they* are in debt.
   >
   > —Grover Cleveland

Apply these guidelines in revising the following excerpt; adapted from Lord Byron's poem "Destruction of Sennacherib." Imagine that the excerpt is a near-final draft. Correct any errors in subject-verb agreement.

> The Assyrian came down like the wolf on the fold,
> And his cohorts were gleaming in purple and gold;
> And the sheen of their spears were like stars on the sea,
> When the blue wave rolls nightly on deep Galilee.
>
> Like the leaves of the forest when Summer is green,
> That host with their banners at sunset was seen:
> Like the leaves of the forest when Autumn hath blown,
> That host on the morrow lay withered and strown.

CHAPTER 23

Using Pronouns Correctly

Several pronouns change their form depending on how they function in a sentence. Consider the following sentences:

Marion invited Sara.
She invited her.

Notice that the nouns in the first sentence can be reversed (*Sara invited Marion*) but that the pronouns in the second sentence cannot. *Her invited she* is simply not normal English. This chapter will explain why pronouns such as *she* and *her* can fill only certain functions in sentences and not others. The last part of this chapter will discuss the relationship between pronouns and their antecedents and will give you guidelines for making them agree. It will also alert you to problems that may arise as a result of unclear pronoun references.

Case of Personal Pronouns

Personal pronouns have three **cases,** or forms. The case of a personal pronoun depends on the pronoun's function in a sentence (whether it be a subject, object, etc.). The three cases are called **nominative, objective,** and **possessive.**

The following chart lists the case forms of personal pronouns according to the pronouns' function in sentences. You should become thoroughly familiar with these forms and their functions to avoid errors in your speech and writing.

	SINGULAR	PLURAL	FUNCTION
NOMINATIVE CASE	I, you, she, he, it	we, you, they	subject or predicate nominative
OBJECTIVE CASE	me, you, her, him, it	us, you, them	direct object, indirect object, or object of preposition
POSSESSIVE CASE	my, mine, your, yours, her, hers, his, its	our, ours your, yours, their, theirs	replacement for possessive noun(s)

You and *it* rarely cause usage problems because they have the same form in both the nominative and the objective case. Learn to recognize the forms and functions of the other pronouns according to their case.

You can avoid errors involving the case of personal pronouns if you keep the following rules in mind:

1. Be sure to use the nominative case for a personal pronoun in a compound subject.

> Ann and **I** made a Ping-Pong table. [*not* me made]
> **She** and Tom bought the paddles. [*not* Her and Tom bought]
> **He** and **I** bought the net. [*not* Him and me bought]

2. Be sure to use the objective case for a personal pronoun in a compound object.

> Tom's serve challenged Juan and **her**. [*not* Juan and she]
> This match is between you and **me**. [*not* between you and I]

When you have to choose the correct pronoun in a sentence with a compound subject or object, it is helpful to say the sentence to yourself without the conjunction and the other noun or pronoun subject.

3. In general, use the nominative case of a personal pronoun after a form of the linking verb *be*.

> The best Ping-Pong player was **he**. [*not* was him]
> Tom said that the best player was **I**. [*not* was me]
> Ann hoped that it would be **she**. [*not* would be her]

In speaking, people often use the objective case after a form of the linking verb *be*: they say "It's me," and "It was him." In writing, however, you should use the nominative case after the linking verb *be*.

> It was **I**. [*not* me]
> It was **he**. [*not* him]

4. Be careful not to spell possessive pronouns with apostrophes.*

> This paddle is **hers**. [*not* her's]
> The table is **theirs**. [*not* their's]

It's is a contraction for *it is*. Do not confuse it with the possessive pronoun *its*.

> **It's** my watch. [contraction for *it is*]
> **Its** band is broken. [possessive pronoun]

5. Be sure to use possessive pronouns before gerunds (-*ing* forms used as nouns).

> **Your** singing relaxes the baby. [*not* You singing relaxes the baby.]
> He is amused by **my** talking. [*not* by me talking]

My, yours, his, her, its, our, and *their* are sometimes called possessive adjectives because they modify nouns: *This is her serve*, for example.

Choosing the Correct Case Form. Write the personal pronoun that correctly completes each sentence.

1. My sister and (I/me) are just learning to play bridge.
2. Mother gave my sister and (I/me) a book on how to play bridge.
3. (Its/It's) explanation about bidding is easy to understand.
4. (You/Your) remembering what cards have been played is important.
5. My friends say canasta is their favorite game. What is (yours/your's)?
6. Hearts is much easier for my sister and (I/me).
7. Cribbage is the two-handed game that my brother and (I/me) like best.
8. (She/Her) and I call combinations that add up to fifteen.
9. I enjoy (our/us) teaching friends how to play cards.
10. Maybe my sister and (I/me) can play bridge with our parents.

Pronouns in Appositive Phrases

Pronouns often appear with nouns in appositive phrases that follow other nouns or pronouns. (See Chapter 19.)

> The best spellers, **Louis and I**, should compete. [The pronoun *I* is part of a phrase that is in apposition to the noun *spellers*.]

Use the nominative case for a pronoun that is in apposition to a subject or predicate nominative.

> The girls, **she and Joan**, won the tournament. [*Girls* is the subject.]
>
> They were the winners, **Joan and she**. [*Winners* is the predicate nominative.]

Use the objective case for a pronoun that is in apposition to a direct object, indirect object, or object of a preposition.

> The crowd favored the local pair, **Hilda and her**. [*Pair* is a direct object.]
>
> I gave my friends, **Tom and him**, a ticket. [*Friends* is an indirect object.]
>
> The officials talked to both teams, **them and us**. [*Teams* is the object of the preposition *to*.]

In appositive phrases with *we* and *us*, such as *we sisters* or *us brothers*, choose the case of the pronoun on the usual basis of its function in the sentence.

> **We sisters** go the same high school. [*We* is the correct form because *we* is the subject of the sentence.]
>
> My aunt gave presents to **us brothers**. [*Us* is the correct form because *us* is the object of the preposition *to*.]

It is often helpful in choosing the correct pronoun to say the sentence without the noun.

Choosing the Correct Pronoun in Appositive Phrases.
Choose the pronoun that correctly completes each sentence.

1. My parents told (we/us) teen-agers to clean up after the party.
2. The guests of honor, my sister Ashley and (she/her), were surprised.
3. The hosts were my best friends, (Cora and he/ Cora and him).
4. We all chipped in and gave a set of encyclopedias to our cousins, (Heather and he/Heather and him).
5. (We/Us) classmates had schemed for weeks to arrange this party.
6. Give my notes to the absent students, (he and she/him and her).
7. The boys, John and (he/him), were the last to leave.
8. (My father and he/My father and him) play tennis together.
9. (We/Us) sophomores are leading the league in basketball this season.
10. We felt that our success had been the work of (we/us) friends.

Pronouns After *Than* and *As*

In elliptical adverb clauses using *than* and *as* (see Chapter 20), fill in the missing words to find the correct case of the pronoun.

> You finished the puzzle faster than **he** [finished the puzzle].

The nominative pronoun *he* is the subject of the adverb clause *than he finished the puzzle.*

> The movie frightened John as much as [it frightened] **me**.

The objective pronoun *me* is the direct object of the adverb clause *as much as it frightened me.*

Using Pronouns After *Than* and *As*. Expand each expression into a complex sentence containing an elliptical adverb clause. End each sentence with a personal pronoun other than *you* or *it*.

SAMPLE more surprised than
ANSWER No one at the party was more surprised than I.

1. happier
2. as friendly as
3. more intelligent than
4. more than
5. as much as

Using *Who* and *Whom* Correctly

The pronoun *who* can function as an interrogative or a relative pronoun. (See Chapter 17.) It has these case forms:

NOMINATIVE who
OBJECTIVE whom
POSSESSIVE whose

When *who* is used as a relative pronoun to introduce a subordinate clause, its case is determined by its function in the subordinate clause.

Use the nominative pronoun *who* for subjects.

> **Who** did you say called me? [*Who* is the subject of the verb *called*.]

> Tell me **who is in charge here**. [*Who* is the subject of the noun clause *who is in charge here*.]

In questions with an interrupting expression, it is often helpful to drop the interrupting phrase to determine whether to use *who* or *whom*.

Use the objective pronoun *whom* for the direct or indirect object of a verb or verbal or for the object of a preposition.

> **Whom** are you telling? [*Whom* is the direct object of the verb *telling*.]

> They asked her **whom** she had seen at the party. [*Whom* is the direct object of the verb *had seen* in the noun clause *whom she had seen at the party*.]

> Harding is a President about **whom** I know very little. [*Whom* is the object of the preposition *about* in the adjective clause *about whom I know very little*.]

In informal speech, people generally use *who* in place of *whom* in sentences like this one: *Who did you ask?* In writing and in formal speech, people are expected to make the distinctions between *who* and *whom*.

EXERCISE 3   **Choosing *Who* or *Whom*.** Write the appropriate form of the pronoun in parentheses in each of the following sentences.

A. ¹(Who/Whom) did the Greeks honor as the goddess of agriculture? ²Hades, (who/whom) ruled the underworld, admired Persephone, the daughter of Demeter, and he kidnapped her. ³Persephone, (who/whom) Hades made queen of the underworld, could not escape. ⁴Demeter, (who/whom) had grown angry at the loss of her daughter, refused to allow any crops to grow. ⁵Hades was persuaded by Zeus, (who/whom) the gods must obey, to let Persephone return for part of each year so that the crops would grow.

B. ¹According to Greek mythology, there once lived a man named Daedalus, (who/whom) was the supreme architect and inventor of his time. ²King Minos of Crete, (who/whom) kept a terrible monster called the Minotaur, commanded Daedalus to build a labyrinth where Minos could safely keep the Minotaur. ³King Minos was delighted with Daedalus, (who/whom) he would not allow to leave Crete. ⁴So Daedalus used feathers and wax to build wings for himself and his son, Icarus, (who/whom) Daedalus warned not to fly too close to the sun. ⁵Icarus, (who/whom) was a vain and foolish boy, flew too near the sun, melting the wax in his wings and causing him to fall to his death in the sea.

Pronoun-Antecedent Agreement

An *antecedent* is the word or group of words to which a pronoun refers or which a pronoun replaces.

Agreement in Number and Gender

A pronoun must agree with its antecedent in number (singular or plural) and gender (masculine, feminine, or neuter).

A pronoun's antecedent may be a noun, another pronoun, or a phrase or clause acting as a noun. In the following examples the pronouns appear in bold type and their antecedents in bold italic type.

> *Emily Bronte* published **her** novel, *Wuthering Heights*, in 1847. [singular, feminine pronoun]
>
> *Emily, Charlotte,* and *Anne Bronte* published **their** collected poems in 1845. [plural pronoun]
>
> *Henry James* published **his** novel *The American* in 1877. [singular, masculine pronoun]
>
> *Henry James* and *William James* are highly respected for **their** writing. [plural pronoun]
>
> The *spruce*, because of **its** soft wood, is used to make paper. [singular, neuter pronoun]
>
> *Spruce* and *aspen* are economical to raise because of **their** rapid growth. [plural pronoun]

Usually, a masculine pronoun is used when the gender of the antecedent is not known or may be either masculine or feminine.

> A *skier* must keep **his** legs strong and limber.

If you do not wish to use a masculine pronoun, you can frequently reword the sentence so that the pronoun is plural or eliminated entirely.

> *Skiers* must keep **their** legs strong and limber.
> Skiers must have strong, limber legs. [no pronouns]

EXERCISE 4 **Making Pronouns and Antecedents Agree.** On your paper complete the following sentences by filling the blank with an appropriate possessive pronoun. Also write the antecedent of each pronoun that you supply.

1. Animated cartoons can reproduce anything that we can imagine in _____ minds.
2. An animated cartoon achieves _____ effects through a simple technique.
3. Cartoon artists draw _____ pictures on a large board.
4. The camera operator films these individual pictures repeatedly in _____ proper sequence.
5. As you view the animated cartoon, _____ eyes seem to see the figure's eyelashes flutter.

Agreement in Person

Personal pronouns must agree with their antecedents in person. Personal pronouns are in the first person, second person, and third person. (See Chapter 17.)

Do not use the second-person pronoun *you* to refer to an antecedent in the third person. Either change *you* to an appropriate third-person pronoun, or replace it with a suitable noun.

POOR   Richard and Harriet are going to the Bavarian Alps, where you can see King Ludwig's castle.

BETTER   Richard and Harriet are going to the Bavarian Alps, where **they** can see King Ludwig's castle.

BETTER   Richard and Harriet are going to the Bavarian Alps, where **tourists** can see King Ludwig's castle.

EXERCISE 5 **Making Pronouns and Antecedents Agree in Person.** On your paper rewrite each of the following items, eliminating the inappropriate use of *you* by substituting a third-person pronoun or a suitable noun.

1. The ancient Greeks ate only two meals a day. You ate in the midmorning and at sunset.
2. Men and women in ancient Greece wore tunics. You wore a brown one for work and a bleached one for special occasions.
3. There were three social classes in Athens, where you might be a citizen, a slave, or a resident alien.
4. Women in ancient Greece led a more restricted life than men. You spent a great deal of time in the home.
5. Children in Athens attended school, where you learned to run, wrestle, handle weapons, and sing, as well as read and write.

Agreement with Indefinite Pronoun Antecedents

In general, use a singular personal pronoun when its antecedent is a singular indefinite pronoun, and use a plural personal pronoun when the antecedent is a plural indefinite pronoun. (See page 519 for lists of singular and plural indefinite pronouns.)

> *Each* of the men on our block makes **his** own holly wreath for the front door.
>
> *Each* of the women lights **her** candles one by one.
>
> *Several* of the neighbors make **their** own plum pudding.

Notice that the plural nouns in the prepositional phrases—*of the men, of the women*—do not affect the number of the personal pronouns. *His* and *her* are singular because *each*, their antecedent, is singular. In speaking, however, people often use the plural pronoun *their* in such sentences.

> INFORMAL   *Neither* of the men made **their** own holly wreaths.

Writers traditionally make a masculine pronoun agree with an indefinite antecedent when no gender is specified.

> *Everyone* should make **his** own decorations.

If you do not want to use a masculine pronoun when the indefinite pronoun may refer to a female, try rewording your sentence. You might substitute a plural indefinite pronoun for the singular one or eliminate the personal pronoun entirely. Although some people use two pronouns *(he or she, him or her, his or her)*, many writers consider such wording awkward.

> *All* should make **their** own decorations.
>
> Everyone should make decorations. [no pronoun]

EXERCISE 6   **Making Pronouns Agree with Indefinite Pronoun Antecedents.** On your paper supply the missing possessive personal pronoun in each of the following sentences. Then write the antecedent of each pronoun that you supply.

1. In Shakespeare's time all of the female characters, regardless of _____ age or importance, were portrayed by men.
2. Each of the main female characters in Shakespeare's *Twelfth Night* finds _____ true love in the last act.
3. Everything in the plot gets _____ impetus from Viola's masquerade as a man.
4. Many of the funniest lines in *Twelfth Night* derive _____ puns from the gender mix-up.
5. Any of today's actresses would probably choose the character of Viola as _____ role.

6. Both of the male leads in *Twelfth Night* proclaim _____ love for the character Olivia.
7. Neither of the male leads has _____ meeting with Olivia until the play is nearly over.
8. One of the male characters is famous for _____ pomposity.
9. Some of the scenes have Olivia's garden as _____ setting.
10. All of the play has as _____ setting a city in Illyria, a region north of Greece.

Clear Pronoun Reference

Make sure that the antecedent of a pronoun is clear and that a pronoun cannot possibly refer to more than one antecedent.

To correct unclear pronoun reference, either reword the sentence to make the antecedent clear or eliminate the pronoun.

UNCLEAR ANTECEDENT When the apples fell among the leaves, **they** were hidden. [Which word is the antecedent of *they*? Were the apples or the leaves hidden?]

CLEAR ANTECEDENT The apples were hidden when **they** fell among the leaves.

NO PRONOUN When the apples fell among the leaves, the apples were hidden.

NO PRONOUN The fallen apples were hidden by the leaves.

Do not use the relative pronoun *which* without making certain that it has a clearly stated antecedent.

NO ANTECEDENT In 1765 Harvard Hall burned, **which** started from an overheated fireplace. [What started from an overheated fireplace? A fire started, but *fire* does not appear in the sentence.]

CLEAR ANTECEDENT In 1765 a fire, **which** started from an overheated fireplace, burned Harvard Hall.

EXERCISE 7 **Making Pronoun Reference Clear.** On your paper rewrite each of the following sentences, making sure that all pronoun references are clearly stated.

1. Nellie Bly was the journalist Elizabeth Cochrane, which she took from the title of a popular song by the famous American composer Stephen Foster.
2. This daring journalist once investigated the treatment of patients by their custodians in a New York City mental hospital, where she interviewed them.

3. She also got arrested as a thief, which she used to write an exposé on how the police treated female prisoners.
4. In 1889 her editor told Nellie Bly that she would attempt to travel around the world in less than eighty days.
5. A record was set, which took seventy-two days, six hours, and eleven minutes.

REVIEW EXERCISE **Pronoun Usage.** Rewrite each of the following sentences, eliminating any mistakes in the use of pronouns. Each sentence has one error.

1. Me and my sister have collected stamps ever since we were seven years old.
2. I enjoy collecting because you learn many facts about little-known parts of the world.
3. Karen collects American stamps, but it was her who first introduced me to the stamps of the Ascension Island.
4. This island in the Atlantic is tiny, which accounts for the small number of stamps it issues.
5. The profile of Queen Elizabeth II (whom, I understand, collects stamps) appears on almost every one of Ascension's recent issues.
6. Many of its inhabitants work at the United States air base and tracking station.
7. Karen has many more unusual stamps in her collection than her friend Sara or me.
8. Karen's friend Elizabeth says her stamp collection is much more valuable than mine.
9. Each of our outstanding collections has their own value and special philatelic attractions.
10. Stamp collecting gives my sister and I many enjoyable hours together.

Revising Your Writing

The distinction between *who* and *whom* is rarely made in casual speech today or in dialogue in contemporary fiction or drama; nevertheless, the correct use of *whom* is still expected in all but the most informal levels of writing. Writers who ignore the distinction risk losing the respect of their readers. (Review the uses of *who* and *whom* on pages 526–527.

Apply your knowledge of this area of pronoun usage by proofreading the following quotations, some of which have been altered and no longer use *who* or *whom* correctly. Revise any that are incorrect.

1. Who I had looked for, I don't know. I had not looked for him.
   —Charles Dickens, *Great Expectations*

2. I know about thirty people who one might call friends.
   —Anne Frank, *Diary of a Young Girl*

3. I had the hint from Holmes that this smooth-faced pawnbroker's assistant was a formidable man—a man who might play a deep game.
   —Sir Arthur Conan Doyle, *"The Red-Headed League"*

4. On entering his room I found Holmes in animated conversation with two men, one of whom I recognized as Peter Jones. . . .
   —Sir Arthur Conan Doyle, *"The Red-Headed League"*

5. Framton wondered whether Mrs. Sappleton, the lady to who he was presenting one of the letters of introduction, came into the nice division.
   —Saki, *"The Open Window"*

Remember that you should always check for correct usage of *who* and *whom* in your own writing.

CHAPTER 24

Using Modifiers Correctly

This chapter will discuss how adjectives and adverbs are used to make comparisons. In addition, it will show you how to avoid certain errors in making comparisons and how to correct misplaced and dangling modifiers.

The Three Degrees of Comparison

Most adjectives and adverbs have three degrees: the positive, or base, form; the comparative form; and the superlative form. A modifier in the **positive** degree is the form used as the entry word in the dictionary; it does not make a comparison. A modifier that shows two things being compared is called **comparative.** A modifier that shows three or more things being compared is called **superlative.**

POSITIVE	The mechanic's hands are **rough.**
	The canary sang **happily.**
COMPARATIVE	The mechanic's hands are **rougher** than mine.
	The parakeet sang **more happily** than a canary.
SUPERLATIVE	Of the three, his hands are **roughest.**
	The orange canary sang **most happily** of all.

The following are rules to guide you in forming the comparative and superlative degrees of adjectives and adverbs.

In general, add -er to form the comparative and -est to form the superlative of modifiers with one syllable.

> fast, fast**er,** fast**est**
> She walks **faster** than I do.
> sweet, sweet**er,** sweet**est**
> This is the **sweetest** apple I have ever tasted.

In some cases, there will be spelling changes when you add -er and -est. (See Chapter 29.)

> hot, hot**ter,** hot**test**
> blue, blu**er,** blu**est**
> weary, wear**ier,** wear**iest**

Sometimes it may sound more natural to use *more* and *most* with some one-syllable modifiers,

> sour, **more** sour, **most** sour

Add *-er* to form the comparative and *-est* to form the superlative of most two-syllable adjectives.

> gentle, gentl**er**, gentl**est**
> The black dog is **gentler** than the brown one.

If *-er* and *-est* sound awkward with a two-syllable adjective, use *more* and *most*.

> helpful, **more** helpful, **most** helpful
> No one was **more helpful** than Rita.

Always use *more* and *most* to form the comparative and superlative degrees of adverbs ending in *-ly*.

> quickly, **more** quickly, **most** quickly
> I am able to run **more quickly** in cold weather.

> tightly, **more** tightly, **most** tightly
> This knot was tied the **most tightly** of all.

Always use *more* and *most* to form the comparative and superlative degrees of modifiers of three or more syllables.

> delicious, **more** delicious, **most** delicious
> I think pears are **more delicious** than apples.

> sentimentally, **more** sentimentally, **most** sentimentally
> Dana writes the **most sentimentally** of all my friends.

Less and *least,* the opposite of *more* and *most,* can also be used with most modifiers to show comparison.

> Amanda is **less talkative** than Buddy.
> Bea is the **least talkative** person I know.

Irregular Comparison

A few modifiers have irregular forms:

POSITIVE	COMPARATIVE	SUPERLATIVE
good	better	(the) best
well	better	(the) best
bad	worse	(the) worst
badly	worse	(the) worst
ill	worse	(the) worst
far	farther	(the) farthest
far	further	(the) furthest
little (amount)	less	(the) least
many	more	(the) most
much	more	(the) most

Irregular Comparison   535

EXERCISE 1 **Identifying Degrees of Comparison.** On your paper write the degree of comparison of the italicized modifier in each of the following sentences.

SAMPLE His drawings are *more imaginative* than mine.
ANSWER comparative

1. Drawing is one of our *oldest* art forms.
2. Prehistoric people drew *colorful* images on rock or clay.
3. Parchment was the *most common* drawing surface of the Middle Ages.
4. Eastern artists were *more likely* to use silk as their drawing surface than Western artists.
5. Since the 1400s artists have preferred using paper, which is *less expensive* than parchment.
6. Artists in every century have created *wonderful* drawings.
7. Leonardo and Michelangelo were among the *finest* draughtsmen of the High Renaissance.
8. Later Rembrandt and Goya produced many *powerful* drawings.
9. In our century Picasso was the *most versatile* of modern artists.
10. Also let's not forget Walt Disney, whose cartoon characters are *better known* than most of the subjects of these great artists.

EXERCISE 2 **Making Correct Comparisons.** Complete each sentence by filling the blank with the correct form of the modifier in parenthesis.

SAMPLE Belinda is the _____ cyclist in our school. (fast)
ANSWER fastest

1. Many people consider Mildred ''Babe'' Didrikson Zaharias the _____ all-around athlete of the twentieth century. (good)
2. Babe Zaharias excelled in _____ sports than any other athlete, male or female. (many)

3. She not only was _____ in basketball, track and field, golf, skating, and lacrosse, but she also designed sportswear that won awards. (outstanding)
4. Zaharias rose to national fame _____ than most athletes. (quickly)
5. In high school she held numerous track and field records and was the _____ female basketball player in the country. (fine)
6. During the 1932 summer Olympics, Zaharias broke three world records that she herself had set _____ in her career. (early)
7. From 1940 to 1950 she established herself as the country's _____ golfer, winning every possible golf title. (successful)
8. Zaharias could drive a golf ball _____ than most golfers. (far)
9. Despite a major operation, Zaharias still played _____ than any other competitor in the 1953 National Women's Open. (skillfully)
10. Her health _____ declined, however, and in 1956 Babe Didrikson Zaharias died. (finally)

SENTENCE WRITING **Creating Sentences That Make Comparisons.** Select five of the irregular modifiers from the list on page 535. Write a sentence for each, using the positive and comparative degrees of the modifier to make a comparison. Underline your modifiers.

SAMPLE far
ANSWER Chuck can throw the ball quite *far*, but Belle can throw it *farther*.

Double Comparisons

Do not make a double comparison by using both -er or -est and more or most.

INCORRECT Texas is more bigger than Oklahoma.
CORRECT Texas is bigger than Oklahoma.

EXERCISE 3 **Correcting Double Comparisons.** Rewrite each of the following sentences, correcting the double comparison.

1. Today we recognize Sir Winston Churchill as one of the most ablest statesmen in world history.
2. Churchill's star shone most brightest when he was Great Britain's Prime Minister during World War II.
3. His courage, eloquence, and faith in victory inspired the British to endure more greater hardships than they had ever known.
4. One of the more happier sights during the war was Churchill himself, a cigar in his mouth and two fingers raised in a victory salute.

5. Although he had stuttered as a boy, Churchill gave more clearer speeches than any other leader of his time.
6. Churchill was also one of the most liveliest writers of the day.
7. Yet, as a schoolboy, he had been the least carefulest student in the class.
8. Physically, Churchill was one of the most fittest leaders of the war.
9. He loved the rough, active life of a soldier, but he also had a more quieter side, which expressed itself in some excellent paintings.
10. No other British leader is regarded with more higher esteem.

Incomplete Comparisons

Do not make an incomplete or unclear comparison by omitting *other* or *else* when you compare one member of a group to the other members.

> UNCLEAR Alaska is closer to Russia than any state.
> CLEAR Alaska is closer to Russia than any **other** state.

> UNCLEAR She had more luggage than everyone.
> CLEAR She had more luggage than everyone **else**.

Be sure your comparisons are between like things.

> UNCLEAR The population of Texas is greater than Oklahoma. [One state's population is being compared illogically to a whole state.]
> CLEAR The population of Texas is greater than **Oklahoma's**. [The word *population* is understood after *Oklahoma's*.]
> CLEAR The population of Texas is greater than **that of Oklahoma**.

EXERCISE 4 **Making Complete Comparisons.** Rewrite each of the following sentences to correct the incomplete comparison.

1. Birds travel faster than any animal.
2. Their ability to fly makes them seem freer than any living thing.
3. The ostrich can run faster than any bird.
4. The duck hawk flies faster than the ostrich runs, yet the bar-headed goose flies higher than any bird.
5. The migration of the Arctic tern—halfway around the world—is farther than geese.
6. The common loon can dive to a depth of about 160 feet, deeper than any waterfowl can dive.
7. However, the diving speed of the peregrine falcon—180 miles per hour—is faster than the common loon.
8. The size of the bee hummingbird is not much greater than a butterfly.
9. I think a parakeet is more affectionate than any feathered pet.
10. In my bird-watching club I have spotted more birds than anyone.

Good or *Well*; *Bad* or *Badly*

In choosing a modifier, you must often decide if you need an adjective or an adverb. Two pairs of words frequently cause confusion.

Always use *good* as an adjective. *Well* may be used as an adverb of manner telling how ably something was done or as an adjective meaning ''in good health.''

> The child is a **good** speaker. [adjective]
>
> The child looks **good** in that coat. [adjective after linking verb]
>
> The child speaks **well**. [adverb of manner]
>
> The child is not **well** right now. [adjective meaning "in good health"]

Always use *bad* as an adjective. Therefore, *bad* is used after linking verbs. Use *badly* as an adverb. *Badly* usually follows action verbs.

> The machine made a **bad** copy. [adjective]
>
> The potato smelled **bad**. [adjective following linking verb]
>
> I felt **bad** about your poor grades. [adjective following linking verb]
>
> His cut is bleeding **badly**. [adverb following action verb]

EXERCISE 5 **Choosing the Correct Modifier.** On your paper complete the following sentences correctly by filling the blank with either *good, well, bad,* or *badly.*

1. A person who can speak _____ can make a lasting impression on the audience.
2. On the other hand, a poor speaker can make an audience feel _____.
3. _____ organization is important in a speech.
4. A speech that is _____ written or organized will usually confuse the audience.
5. A _____ delivery is just as important as the content of the speech.
6. Even a speaker who is not feeling _____ should speak forcefully and with conviction.
7. Although it often helps to use humor in a speech, speakers look _____ if their jokes are in poor taste.
8. If a speech begins _____, an audience may immediately lose interest.
9. A speaker can promote a _____ relationship with an audience by making eye contact.
10. A speaker must know the content of a speech very _____ in order to be comfortable and relaxed in front of an audience.

Double Negatives

In general do not use a **double negative**, two negative words in the same clause. Use only one negative word to express a negative idea.

INCORRECT I didn't see no accident.
CORRECT I didn't see any accident.

INCORRECT He hasn't received no letters.
CORRECT He hasn't received any letters.
CORRECT He has received no letters.

INCORRECT She never tells no lies.
CORRECT She never tells any lies.
CORRECT She tells no lies.

EXERCISE 6 **Avoiding Double Negatives.** On your paper rewrite each of the following sentences, eliminating the double negative.

1. Boa constrictors do not inject no venom into their prey.
2. Still, I would not want no boa constrictor for a pet.
3. They kill birds and rodents by not allowing them no air.
4. Once captured in the boa constrictor's coils, a bird or rodent cannot do nothing.
5. Although the boa constrictor is big, it cannot be compared to no anaconda, python, or king cobra.
6. Boa constrictors cannot swallow no cows, horses, or people, as legends have it.
7. After a meal these snakes do not eat nothing for a week or more.
8. Often they do not do nothing; they just sleep and digest their food.
9. Like other snakes, boa constrictors can survive for many months without no food at all.
10. Unlike many snakes, boa constrictors never lay no eggs.

Misplaced and Dangling Modifiers

Place modifiers as close as possible to the words they modify in order to make the meaning of the sentence clear.

Misplaced modifiers modify the wrong word or seem to modify more than one word in a sentence. To correct a sentence with a misplaced modifier, move the modifier as close to the word it modifies as possible.

MISPLACED The mountains delight many visitors **in their autumn splendor.** [prepositional phrase]

CLEAR The mountains **in their autumn splendor** delight many visitors.

MISPLACED The search party found the lost child **using binoculars.** [participial phrase]

CLEAR **Using binoculars,** the search party found the lost child.

Dangling modifiers seem to modify no word at all. To correct a sentence with a dangling modifier, you must supply a word the dangling phrase can sensibly modify.

DANGLING **Digging in the field,** an Indian village was found. [participial phrase]

CLEAR **Digging in the field,** archaeologists found an Indian village.

Be sure to place the modifier *only* close to the word you wish it to modify, or the meaning of your sentence may be unclear.

UNCLEAR Sharon **only** has breakfast on Saturday. [Does she have one meal on Saturday or no breakfast on any day but Saturday? Or is Sharon the only person (in a group) who has breakfast on Saturday?]

CLEAR Sharon has **only** breakfast on Saturday. [not lunch or dinner]

CLEAR Sharon has breakfast **only** on Saturday. [not on any other day of the week]

EXERCISE 7 **Identifying Misplaced and Dangling Modifiers.** On your paper rewrite each sentence that contains a misplaced or dangling modifier. If the sentence does not contain a misplaced modifier or a dangling modifier, then write *correct*.

1. I saw two squirrels riding my bike in the park.
2. Searching for gold, fossils were found instead.
3. Driving carefully down the narrow country road, Mom was able to avoid an accident.
4. Stuck inside the coin slot, I tried to remove the quarter.

5. Because of their huge size and strength, many backpackers fear the grizzly bear.
6. Crashing into a thousand tiny pieces, Vanessa dropped the crystal chandelier onto the floor.
7. We caught the butterfly using a net.
8. Roberta only dreams of winning the tennis championship; she knows she can do it, and nothing else interests her.
9. Alex and Maria saw two birds making a nest in the tree behind the main post office building.
10. Only Bill knows the combination to the company safe; he won't tell anyone else what it is.

EXERCISE 8 **Correcting Misplaced and Dangling Modifiers.** On your paper rewrite the following sentences, correcting the misplaced or dangling modifiers.

1. As its eighth congresswoman, the Eighty-ninth Congress received Patricia Takemoto Mink.
2. Interested in politics from an early age, her high school elected Mink president of the student body.
3. Obtaining her law degree from the University of Chicago in 1952, law firms were not interested in hiring a woman.
4. The lawyer opened a one-person law firm undaunted by her situation.
5. Learning to organize young politicians, her efforts began to pay off in 1954.
6. Ringing doorbells and handing out leaflets, the 1954 campaign introduced Patricia Mink to politics.
7. Running successfully for a position in the Hawaiian House of Representatives, encouragement was given to her by her husband.
8. Well qualified for the Congress in Washington, four years in the Hawaiian Congress were Patricia Mink's credentials.
9. Recognized as a champion of women's rights, an early equal rights bill was sponsored by Mink.
10. Advising young female politicians to develop a specialty, expertise in politics was encouraged by Mink.

REVIEW EXERCISE **Modifiers.** The following paragraph contains ten errors in the use of modifiers. Rewrite the paragraph to correct these errors.

[1]Going to college is a good way to train for some kinds of work but not for all kinds. [2]Apprenticeship is probably a more better way to train to be a carpenter, for example. [3]Apprentices never gain no practical skill without on-the-job experience. [4]As their training progresses, they become han-

dyer at various job skills. [5]After about four years—more longer for some trades and not so long for others—they become experts. [6]Then these skilled workers can receive better wages than the unskilled. [7]The construction industry is more crowded with registered apprentices than any field. [8]There are 450 different occupations that require apprenticeship. [9]Most people find some fields attractiver than other fields. [10]Apprenticeship programs have entrance exams and minimum age and education requirements. [11]If you want to become an apprentice, the most brightest thing you can do is to find out about your chosen field while you are still in school. [12]Sometimes you will find that the most good thing to do is to finish college first. [13]A biger percentage of artists and craftspeople are trained in colleges today than before. [14]However, many people believe that a close relationship between master and apprentice only can provide suitable training.

Revising Your Writing

Make sure your modifiers, especially participial phrases, are positioned correctly. Often there are two or more "correct" options, and you must decide which option seems the most logical and reads best. Consider, for example, the placement of the italicized participial phrase in the following sentence from "Through the Tunnel" by Doris Lessing.

> He rushed to the bathroom, *thinking she must not see his face with bloodstains, or tearstains, on it.*

Lessing had another "correct" option; she could have placed her participial phrase at the beginning of the sentence. Why do you suppose she did not choose the following version?

> *Thinking she must not see his face with bloodstains, or tearstains, on it,* he rushed to the bathroom.

In the second version—the one Lessing did not choose—the boy first thinks, then rushes. This ordering of events implies forethought on the boy's part, a definite clear-headedness. In Lessing's actual version, however, the thinking and the rushing are simultaneous, suggesting panic rather than cool deliberation.

Below are two other sentences adapted from "Through the Tunnel." Revise each sentence by choosing the most logical and most effective position for each participial phrase in parentheses.

1. He flung himself on his bed and slept. (waking at the sound of feet on the path outside)
2. After a long time, the boy came up on the other side of a big dark rock. (letting the air out of his lungs in a spluttering gasp and a shout of triumph)

CHAPTER 25

Glossary of Specific Usage Items

The glossary that follows presents some particularly troublesome matters of preferred usage. The glossary will give you guidance, for example, in choosing between two words that are often confused. It will also make you aware of certain words and expressions that you should avoid completely when speaking or writing for school or business purposes.

a, an Use the article *a* when the word that follows begins with a consonant sound, including a sounded *h: a ticket, a hurricane*. Use *an* when the word that follows begins with a vowel sound or an unsounded *h: an umbrella, an hour*. Use *a* before a word that begins with the "yew" sound: *a eulogy, a uniform*.

a lot, alot This expression is always written as two words and means "a large amount." Some authorities suggest avoiding it altogether in formal English.

> **A lot** of television programs show too much violence.

a while, awhile *A while* is made up of an article and a noun. *In* and *for* often come before *a while*, forming a prepositional phrase. *Awhile* is an adverb.

> She'll speak in **a while.**
> She'll speak for **a while.**
> She'll speak **awhile** before showing the filmstrip.

accept, except *Accept* is a verb that means "to receive" or "to agree to." *Except* may be a preposition or a verb. As a preposition it means "but."

> Miki decided to **accept** the invitation to lunch.
> The restaurant is open every day **except** Monday.

affect, effect Although *affect* and *effect* sound nearly the same, they should not be confused. *Affect* is a verb that means "to cause a change in, to influence." *Effect* may be a noun or a verb. As a noun it means "result." As a verb it means "to bring about or accomplish."

> Daily exercise will **affect** your health.
> Daily exercise will have a good **effect** on your health. [noun meaning "result"]
> Daily exercise will effect a positive change in your health. [verb meaning "bring about"]

ain't   Ain't is unacceptable in speaking and in writing unless you are quoting somebody's exact words. se *I am not, she is not,* and so on.

> "I ain't going to leave this place," said the old prospector.

all ready, already   The two words *all ready* should not be confused with the adverb *already.* *All ready* means "completely ready." *Already* means "before or by this time."

> David was **all ready** to go at seven o'clock, but his so-called friends had **already** left without him.

all right, alright   Write this expression as two words. Although often seen in print as one word, most authorities prefer *all right.*

> I hope that the baby is **all right.**

all the farther, all the faster   These are regional expressions. Use *as far as* and *as fast as* in writing.

> Is this **as fast as** you can walk?
> I will drive **as far as** Reno and then travel by plane.

all together, altogether   Use *all together* to mean "in a group." Use the adverb *altogether* to mean "completely" or "on the whole."

> The actors joined hands and took a bow **all together.**
> **Altogether** it was a very good play.

EXERCISE 1   **Making Usage Choices.** For each of the following senten-ces, write the correct choice of the two expressions in parentheses.

1. George Washington fought for (a/an) independent United States.
2. As leader of the Continental Army, Washington tried to make sure that his troops were (alright/all right).
3. Washington's courage and determination to win (affected/effected) his soldiers, improving their morale.
4. After his victory Washington rested (a while/awhile) at home.
5. When the delegates from the states met (all together/altogether) to write the Constitution, they chose Washington as their leader.
6. Washington was pleased to (accept/except) the office of President after the vote of the first Electoral College.
7. President Washington was (all ready/already) widely known and re-spected when he took office.
8. As the first President of the United States, Washington did (a lot/alot) to shape the duties of that office.
9. Washington certainly went (all the farther/as far as) he could go to mold the young nation into a strong republic.
10. It (ain't/is not) surprising that the capital of the nation was named in honor of Washington.

amount, number   *Amount* and *number* both refer to quantity. Use *amount* when referring to nouns that cannot be counted. Use *number* when referring to nouns that can be counted.

> A huge **amount** of lava spurted from the erupting volcano.
> A **number** of volcanoes are still active today.

bad, badly   See Chapter 24.

being as, being that   These expressions are sometimes used instead of *because* or *since* in informal conversation. In formal speaking and writing always use *because* or *since*.

> **Because** bears are hibernators, they sleep during the winter.
> **Since** the movie has already started, let's come back later.

beside, besides   These are two different words, so use them carefully. *Beside* means "located at the side of." *Besides* means "in addition to."

> The cat sat **beside** the refrigerator.
> I lost two buttons from my coat **besides** losing my gloves.

between, among Use *between* with two persons or things, or use it to compare one person or thing to other persons or things. *Between* may also be used with more than two persons or things when they are considered in a close relationship.

> It was difficult to chose **between** the two desserts.
> What is the difference **between** this opera and others by Verdi?
> One result of the meeting was the establishment of a trade agreement **between** the Western Allies and the Eastern bloc nations.

Use *among* with groups of three or more.

> The moment I walked into the room and saw the smiling faces, I felt that I was **among** friends.
> Tim's great-grandfather had lived **among** the Iroquois.

borrow, lend, loan   *Borrow* and *lend* have opposite meanings. *Borrow* is a verb meaning "to take something with the understanding that it must be returned." *Lend* is a verb meaning "to give something with the understanding that it will be returned." *Loan* is a noun. It may be used as a verb, but most authorities prefer *lend*.

> Charlene wants to **borrow** Cliff's bicycle.
> Cliff will **lend** her the bicycle if she puts air in the tires.
> Charlene may ask her parents for a **loan** to buy a bicycle.

bring, take   Use *bring* to mean "to carry to" or "to go with." Use *take* to mean "to carry away" or "to go with." *Bring* is related to *come* as *take* is to *go*.

> **Bring** the dog when you come to our house for dinner on Saturday.
> Don't **take** the dog when you go to the Bradleys'.

can, may   *Can* indicates the ability to do something. *May* expresses permission to do something.

>You **may** go skiing if you **can** find a place to rent good equipment.

can't hardly, can't scarcely   These terms are considered double negatives because *hardly* and *scarcely* by themselves have a negative meaning. Therefore, avoid using *hardly* and *scarcely* with *not* or *n't.*

>Amy **can hardly** believe that she is taller than both her mother and brother.

>I **can scarcely** hear my television when my neighbor plays the drums.

could of, might of, must of, should of, would of   After *could, might, must, should,* or *would,* you need another verb form, not the preposition *of.* Use the helping verbs *have* after *could, might, must, should,* or *would.*

>I **could have** danced all night.

>I **might have** won the singing award if I had not lost my voice the day before.

EXERCISE 2   **Making Usage Choices.** For each of the following sentences, write the correct choice of the two expressions in parentheses.

1. As a young man Lincoln had to (borrow/lend) money in order to open a store.
2. (Because/Being that) Lincoln always dealt fairly with people, he earned the nickname Honest Abe.
3. As President, Lincoln (could of/could have) isolated himself, but instead he spent many hours listening to the people's problems.
4. If I had to choose (between/among) the Gettysburg Address and Lincoln's Second Inaugural Address, I would choose the Second Inaugural Address as the better speech.
5. Other issues (beside/besides) slavery divided the North and the South.
6. Toward the end of Lincoln's first term, the Civil War was going (badly/bad) for the North.
7. A large (amount/number) of memorials have been dedicated to this great President.
8. I (can't hardly/can hardly) believe that a great man like Lincoln was assassinated.
9. (Can/May) I borrow this biography of Lincoln?
10. Ann will (bring/take) the biography with her to my house on Sunday.

different from   Use *different from* before a noun or a pronoun.

>Ice dancing is **different from** figure skating.
>These cloud formations are **different from** those.

doesn't, don't These are different contractions. *Doesn't* is a shorter form of *does not,* which is used with *she, he, it,* and singular nouns. *Don't* is a shorter form of *do not,* which is used with *I, you, we, they,* and plural nouns.

My mom is one commuter who **doesn't** mind long bus rides.
Most subway riders **don't** expect comfortable conditions.

emigrate, immigrate Use *emigrate* to mean "to go from one country to another to live." Use *immigrate* to mean "to come to a country to settle there." Use *from* with *emigrate* and *to* or *into* with *immigrate.*

Graham will **emigrate** from England this spring.

He will **immigrate** to the United States, where he will teach courses in English literature.

farther, further *Farther* should be used in reference to physical distance. *Further* should be used in reference to degree or time.

Compact cars can go **farther** on a gallon of gasoline than big cars can.

Argue no **further**—I will do as you suggest!

fewer, less Use *fewer* when referring to nouns that can be counted. Use *less* when referring to nouns that cannot be counted. *Less* may also be used with figures that are seen as a single amount or quantity.

Buy **fewer** apples than you did last week.

We cooked **less** rice last night.

The rent was **less** than $400. [The money is treated as a single sum, not as individual dollars.]

good, well See Chapter 24.

had of Do not use *of* between *had* and a past participle.

I Wish **I had known** that you were ill.

hanged, hung *Hanged* and *hung* are the past-tense and past-participle forms of the verb *hang.* Use *hanged* when you mean "to put to death by hanging." Use *hung* in all other instances.

The British government **hanged** Guy Fawkes in 1606.
Joe **hung** his shirts on the clothesline.

in, into Use *in* to mean "inside" or "within" and *into* to indicate movement or direction from the outside to a point within.

The baby was **in** the bassinet. Gillian put the rabbit **into** the basket.

irregardless, regardless Use *regardless.* The prefix *ir-* and the suffix *-less* both have negative meanings. When used together, they produce a double negative, which is incorrect.

Regardless of the snow, Robby always jogs.

EXERCISE 3 **Making Usage Choices.** For each of the following sentences write the correct choice of the two expressions in parentheses.

1. Theodore Roosevelt's ancestors (emigrated/immigrated) from Holland during the 1640s.
2. Roosevelt fought so (good/well) in the Spanish-American War that he
   gained national attention.
3. Many of President Roosevelt's policies were different (from/than)
   those of his predecessor, William McKinley.
4. Roosevelt's conservation efforts went (farther/further) than those of
   previous Presidents.
5. The Roosevelts moved (in/into) the White House at the beginning of
   the twentieth century.
6. (Regardless/Irregardless) of his faults, he was a good President.
7. If I (had/had of) lived during the time of President Roosevelt, I might
   not have seen the merit in so much that he did.
8. Even Roosevelt's critics (doesn't/don't) deny his great determination.
9. Theodore Roosevelt wrote no (less/fewer) than forty books.
10. Hunting trophies (hanged/hung) on the walls of his home.

this kind, these kinds *Kind* is singular. Therefore, the singular form *this* or
that modifies it. *This* and *that* should also be used with *sort* and *type* (*this
type, that type, this sort, that sort*). *Kinds* is plural. Therefore, the plural form
these or *those* modifies it. Also use *these* and *those* with *sorts* and *types*.

> **This kind** of injury is serious. **These kinds** of injuries are not serious.
> **That sort** of fruit is delicious. **Those sorts** of fruit are delicious.

lay, lie People often confuse these two words in both writing and speaking. *Lay* means "to put" or "to place"; it takes a direct object. *Lie* means "to
recline" or "to be positioned"; it never takes an object.

> **Lay** the bar of soap on the edge of the sink.
> I like to **lie** under a shade tree in the summer.

Problems arise particularly in using the principal parts of these verbs. Notice, for example, that the past tense of *lie* is *lay.* Learn all the principal parts of these verbs.

BASIC FORM	lay	lie
PRESENT PARTICIPLE	laying	lying
PAST FORM	laid	lay
PAST PARTICIPLE	laid	lain

He **laid** the bar of soap on the edge of the sink.
Yesterday I **lay** under that tree and wrote letters.

learn, teach   These words have different meanings. *Learn* means "to receive knowledge," and *teach* means "to give knowledge.

I **learned** how to find the hypotenuse of a triangle.
My sister is going to **teach** history at Yale.

leave let   *Leave* means "to go away," and *let* means "to allow" or "to permit." Some people use the expressions *leave alone* and *let alone* to mean the same thing, but they have different meanings. *Leave alone* means "to go away from," and *let alone* means "to permit to be alone" or "to refrain from disturbing."

The speaker threatened to **leave** the meeting.
Let him try to open the door by himself.
Do not **leave** me alone while I have this high fever.
Let your sister alone so she can do her homework.

like, as   *Like* is a preposition and introduces a prepositional phrase. *As* is a subordinating conjunction and introduces a subordinate clause. Therefore, many authorities say that it is incorrect to use *like* before a clause.

He drives **like** a maniac.
She thinks **as I** do in this matter.

loose, lose   Use *loose* to mean "free," "not firmly attached," or "not fitting tightly." Use *lose* when you mean "to have no longer," "to misplace," or "to fail to win."

My watch is so **loose** that I'am afraid I will **lose** it.

passed, past   *Passed* is the past-tense form and the past participle of the verb *to pass. Past* may be an adjective, a preposition, an adverb, or a noun.

The challenger in the race **passed** the leader. [verb]
This **past** year has been very difficult for me. [adjective]
Make a sharp right turn **past** the bank. [preposition]
A school bus drove **past**. [adverb]
Dale is a woman with a mysterious **past**. [noun]

precede, proceed   Use *precede* when you mean "to go or come before." Use *proceed* when you mean "to continue" or "to move along."

> In a dictionary the entry *airplane* **precedes** *airship*.
> *An airplane can* **proceed** *at a faster speed than an airship.*

raise, rise   The verb *raise* means "to cause to move upward" or "to lift up" and always takes an object. *Rise* means "to get up" or "to go up"; it is an intransitive verb and does not take an object.

> We will **raise** the flag at sunrise.
> She **raised** her hand in class.
> A helium-filled balloon will **rise** high into the air.
> Did you **rise** from your chair to greet the visitor?

reason is because   *Because* means "for the reason that." Therefore, do not use *because* after *reason is*. *Reason is because* is repetitive. Use *that* after *reason is* or simply use *because* alone.

> The **reason** Nan entered the marathon **is that** she enjoys long-distance running.
> Nan entered the marathon **because** she enjoys running.

EXERCISE 4   **Making Usage Choices.** For each of the following sentences, write the correct choice of the two expressions in the parentheses.

1. One reason that John F. Kennedy is still admired is (because/that) he showed exceptional leadership qualities.
2. As a young man Kennedy toured Europe, talking to heads of state to (learn/teach) their political views.
3. (These kind/These kinds) of situations prepared Kennedy for the presidency.
4. When Kennedy took office, he (raised/rised) the nation's morale with his inaugural address.
5. Kennedy declared that "the torch has been (passed/past) to a new generation of Americans."
6. Much of Kennedy's charm (lay/laid) in his fine speaking ability.
7. (Like/As) you would expect from a couple interested in the arts, the Kennedys invited performers to come to the White House.
8. During the missile crisis Kennedy refused to (leave/let) the Soviet Union keep missiles on the island of Cuba.
9. Kennedy's decision to (precede/proceed) with a naval blockade of Cuba was very difficult to make.
10. It was painful for Americans to (loose/lose) such a young and vibrant leader.

respectfully, respectively   Use these two words carefully. *Respectfully* means "with respect." *Respectively* means "in the order named."

> The man shook the President's hand **respectfully.**
> Ann and Arlene are my aunt and cousin, **respectively.**

says, said   *Says* is the third-person singular of *say. Said* is the past tense of *say.* Be careful not to use *says* when you mean *said.*

> She always **says** that she is ill so no one will know she is afraid of the water.
> Last week Ruth **said** she knew how to swim.

sit, set   *Sit* means "to place oneself in a sitting position." *Sit* rarely takes an object. *Set* means "to place" or "to put" and usually takes an object. *Set* may also be an intransitive verb when it is used with *sun* to mean the sun is "going down" or "sinking out of sight." When *set* is used in this way, it does not take an object.

> **Sit** down and stop talking.
> **Set** the flowers on the mantelpiece, please.
> The sun **set** in a blaze of color.

than, then   *Than* is a conjunction used to introduce the second element in a comparison; it also shows exception.

> Aaron is more athletic **than** Carl.
> It is none other **than** our Japanese friend Tamotsu!

Then is an adverb that means "at that time," "soon afterward," "the time mentioned," "at another time," "for that reason," "in that case," and "besides."

> I remember it was hot **then.**
> You bowl first, and **then** it will be my turn.
> He will be there by **then.**
> First Jane is happy, **then** she is sad.
> If you get that job, **then** you can buy a new car.
> If you won't tell him, **then** I will.
> The ski trails are too difficult for me, and **then** there are too many people on the slopes.

this here, that there   Avoid using *here* and *there* after *this* and *that.* Use only *this* and *that.*

> I want to look at **this** newspaper.   Please hand me **that** lantern.

where at   Do not use *at* after *where.*

> **Where** are you going to stay?

who, whom   See Chapter 23.

Making Usage Choices. For each of the following senten-ces, write the correct choice of the two expressions in parentheses.

1. Many people (said/says) that Franklin Roosevelt was one of the great-est Presidents.
2. After being stricken with polio in 1921, Roosevelt had to work harder (than/then) ever to maintain his active life.
3. (This/This here) paralysis struck Roosevelt when he was thirty-nine.
4. It was Warm Springs, Georgia, (where/where at) he took treatments to recover from his illness.
5. Roosevelt did not (set/sit) idly while the nation faced the Depression.
6. People (who/whom) had lost everything looked to Roosevelt for hope.
7. The Tennessee Valley Authority and the Works Progress Administra-tion were, (respectively/respectfully), a natural resources corporation and an employment program.
8. In 1945 Roosevelt, (then/than) in his fourth term, met with Allied leaders to plan the final stages of the war.
9. (Who/Whom) do you think was Roosevelt's most trusted ally?
10. After World War II did the sun really (set/sit) on the British Empire?

REVIEW EXERCISE   **Usage (Part 1).** For each of the following sentences write the correct choice of the two expressions in parentheses.

1. (Because/Being that) miniature objects have fascinated people since early times, it is no wonder that doll houses are very popular today.
2. The first doll house might (have/of) been the one constructed for the Duke of Bavaria in 1558.
3. Most lovers of miniatures think that the doll house presented to Queen Mary of England in 1924 is (all together/altogether) the most interest-ing structure of its kind.
4. It took four years of work before the house was (all ready/already) to present to the Queen.
5. Collectors (who/whom) want to meet other collectors may join the National Association of Miniature Enthusiasts.
6. Most of the doll houses put together today are furnished in styles from the (passed/past).
7. In Victorian England collectors (hanged/hung) wallpaper on the walls of their doll houses.
8. The success of miniatures (lays/lies) in how closely they duplicate the original objects.
9. (A/An) original miniature is more valuable than a reproduction.
10. (Beside/Besides) good tweezers, a would-be miniature maker needs pliers, a metal ruler, and a contour marker.

11. Along with (this kind/these kinds) of tools, the doll-house maker must have agile fingers and a careful nature.
12. Handling of miniatures should be done (respectfully/respectively) in order not to break delicate pieces.
13. Collectors are careful to repair any (loose/lose) parts or pieces.
14. (Irregardless/Regardless) of the funds a person has available, collecting miniatures can be a rewarding hobby.
15. There are (fewer/less) miniature makers (then/than) collectors.

REVIEW EXERCISE   **Usage (Part 2).** For each of the following sentences, write the correct choice of the two expressions in parentheses.

1. The hobby of collecting photographs is different (from/than) that of taking photographs.
2. The reason some people hesitate to collect photographs is (because/that) they believe the prints will be easy to duplicate.
3. (This/This here) belief is mistaken since many prints are quite rare.
4. Some photographers keep their negatives only for (a while/awhile) and then destroy them.
5. A person who (can scarcely/can't scarcely) pay more than $100 for a collectible photograph should probably find a cheaper hobby.
6. (A lot/Alot) of collectors find unusual prints at auctions.
7. The auctioneer will (leave/let) the highest bidder claim the print.
8. Care should be taken to protect prints from the (affects/effects) of light and humidity.
9. A photograph should not be pressed (among/between) two other photographs.
10. The discovery of a rare photograph will (raise/rise) the spirits of any collector.

Review

CHAPTER 21   VERB TENSES AND VOICE

Principal Parts of Verbs [page 496]

1. Which of the following items uses the underlined participle correctly?
   (a) Pheasants <u>nesting</u> along the river.
   (b) The hen <u>been</u> on her nest for days.
   (c) Ring-neck pheasants were <u>brought</u> to America in the 1800s.

Regular and Irregular Verbs [pages 496–499]   Which of the following sets of principal parts is correct?

2. (a) climb, climbed, clumb (b) begin, began, begun (c) break, broke, broke (d) bring, brung, brung, (e) go, gone, gone

3. (a) ring, rung, rung (b) see, seen, seen (c) set, sat, sat (d) shake, shaked, shaken (e) sing, sang, sung

Tense of Verbs [pages 499–507]   Indicate whether the underlined verb in each of the following sentences is (a) present, (b) past, (c) future or future perfect, (d) present perfect, or (e) past perfect.

4. Since 1790 Pitcairn Island <u>has been</u> the home of mutineers from the *Bounty* and of their descendants.
5. Polynesians <u>had inhabited</u> Pitcairn before people kept records.
6. When the British <u>discovered</u> Pitcairn in 1767, it was deserted.
7. in 1990 the Pitcairn islanders <u>will celebrate</u> their bicentennial.

Compatibility of Tenses [pages 508–509]

8. In which of the following sentences are the tenses compatible?
   (a) After the mutineers took control of the *Bounty*, Captain Bligh is set adrift in a small open boat.
   (b) When nine of the mutineers settled on Pitcairn, they had brought nineteen Polynesians with them.
   (c) When an American ship arrived at Pitcairn in 1808, all but one of the mutineers had died.

Voice of Verbs [pages 509–510]   Indicate whether the verb in each of the following sentences is (a) in the active voice or (b) in the passive voice.

9. Captain Bligh and eighteen sailors were cast adrift by the mutineers.
10. The group eventually landed 4,000 miles away in the East Indies.

   Writing for Review   Write a paragraph relating an incident that happened to you in the past. Be sure that you have used verbs correctly.

CHAPTER 22   SUBJECT-VERB AGREEMENT

Agreement in Number [pages 512–521]   Indicate the verb that agrees with the subject in each of the following sentences.

1. The staple food of the South Pacific and other parts of the world (a) is/ (b) are the breadfruit.
2. There (a) is/(b) are two distinct kinds: seedless and seeded.
3. A few pounds of breadfruit (a) makes/(b) make a family meal.
4. Cool winters or frost (a) kills/(b) kill breadfruit trees.
5. Not one of my classmates (a) know/(b) knows that Captain Bligh introduced breadfruit to Central and South America.

Writing for Review   Write a short description on a topic of your choice. Demonstrate your mystery of subject-verb agreement by including in your description various compound subjects and intervening phrases.

CHAPTER 23   USING PRONOUNS CORRECTLY

Personal Pronouns [pages 523–526]   Indicate the correct case of the personal pronoun in each sentence.

1. Pat and (a) I/(b) me started a vegetable garden.
2. Mother helped Pat and (a) I/(b) me plant the seedlings.
3. Pat announced that the hardest worker was (a) he/(b) him.
4. (a) We/(b) Us gardeners grow the best vegetables in town.
5. The tomato plants grew as tall as (a) I/(b) me!

Who* and *Whom [pages 526–527]   Indicate the correct pronoun

6. Tell me (a) who/(b) whom the best gardeners in town are.

Pronoun-Antecedent Agreement [pages 528–529]   Indicate the correct pronoun.

7. A gardener must guard (a) their/(b) his plants against insects.

Agreement in Person [page 529]

8. In which item does the personal pronoun agree in person with its antecedent?
   (a) Mara bought a hat that you can wear with casual clothes.
   (b) Not too long ago people almost always wore hats. They would have felt uncomfortable with uncovered heads.

Agreement with Indefinite Pronoun Antecedents [pages 530–531]

9. Which of the following sentences has correct agreement between pronouns?
   (a) Each of the actors forgot some of their lines.
   (b) Only one of the actresses applied her own make-up correctly.
   (c) Both of the female leads gave her best performance on Friday.

Clear Pronoun Reference [pages 531–532]

10. In which sentence is the pronoun reference clear?
    (a) When the celebrities mingled with the fans, they were bashful.
    (b) The guest of honor entered the room, which started the crowd cheering.
    (c) The host gave his speech, which no one was able to hear.

Writing for Review   Write a paragraph describing what you and your family do together to have a good time. Demonstrate your mastery of pronoun usage by including a variety of personal and indefinite pronouns in your paragraph.

CHAPTER 24   USING MODIFIERS CORRECTLY

The Three Degrees of Comparison [pages 534–535]   Indicate the correct comparative or superlative form in each sentence.

1. I feel (a) iller/(b) worse today than I did yesterday.
2. Balsa wood is (a) lighter/(b) more light than birch.
3. They are the (a) attractivest/(b) most attractive couple I know.

Double Comparisons [pages 537–538]   Indicate the correct form of the modifier in each sentence.

4. The train arrived (a) more earlier/(b) earlier than I or my parents had expected.
5. My friend Bob has more clothes than (a) anyone/(b) anyone else I know.
6. A cheetah can run faster than (a) any other/(b) any cat.

Double Negatives [page 540]   Indicate the correct usage.

7. Koala bears (a) eat/(b) never eat nothing but eucalyptus leaves.

Misplaced and Dangling Modifiers [pages 541–542]   For each pair indicate the sentence in which modifiers are placed correctly.

8. (a) Collecting rare coins, Janet's hobby became a career.
   (b) Janet's hobby of collecting rare coins became a career.
9. (a) The woods with their varied wildlife attract many campers.
   (b) The woods attract many campers with their varied wildlife.
10. (a) Searching the beach at low tide, many shells were found by the girls.
    (b) Searching the beach at low tide, the girls found many shells.

Writing for Review   Write a paragraph in which you compare one thing with another, such as a dog with a cat. In your paragraph use modifiers to make comparisons.

CHAPTER 25   GLOSSARY OF SPECIFIC USAGE ITEMS

Preferred Usage [pages 545–555]   Indicate the preferred usage of the choices given in each sentence.

1. Thunder has a startling (a) affect/(b) effect on my dogs: They howl.
2. They howl until the storm is (a) all together/(b) altogether over.
3. Hearing them howl makes me feel (a) bad/(b) badly.
4. They cower (a) besides/(b) beside the bed in my room.
5. On sunny days I (a) take/(b) bring my dogs for walks in the park.
6. People (a) can't hardly/(b) can hardly believe how many wrinkles bloodhounds have.
7. Basset hounds have (a) less/(b) fewer wrinkles than bloodhounds.
8. (a) Regardless/(b) Irregardless of their name, bloodhounds are gentle.
9. My dogs like to (a) lay/(b) lie in the shade.
10. One is two years older than the other. They are named Sneaker and Snooper, (a) respectfully/(b) respectively.

Writing for Review   Demonstrate your knowledge of the distinction between the words in each of the following pairs by writing a sentence for each term.

a while, awhile   accept, except
like, as   sit, set

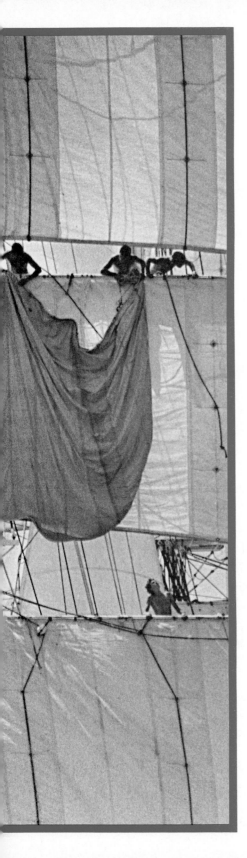

Mechanics

Thinking About Thinking:
Recognizing Ambiguity

Capitalization and punctuation—often called mechanics—are symbols we use to solve problems in language. To solve the problem of letting the reader know when a sentence ends, we use a period. To clarify a name or a title, we use a capital letter. These symbols are useful devices for achieving clear, unambiguous communication.

Defining the Skill

An ambiguous message—one that says two different things at the same time—can be confusing. **RECOGNIZING AMBIGUITY** is a thinking skill essential to the proper use of mechanics. For example, in the sentence "John, Jo and Jill graduated," how many people graduated? Is someone telling John that Jo and Jill graduated? Or did all three graduate? A comma after Jo would solve the problem.

Applying the Skill

Look at the picture. Identify the subject of the picture. Is there more than one subject? What message do you think this picture communicates? What message about ambiguity does it communicate?

CHAPTER 26

Capitalization

Capitalization of Sentences

Capitalize the first word of every sentence, including the first word of a direct quotation that is a complete sentence.

> **T**raditionally a comedy ends with a marriage between the principal characters.
>
> **R**obert E. Lee once wrote, "**D**uty is the sublimest word in our language."

Capitalize a sentence in parentheses that stands by itself.

> Webster's first dictionary encouraged a distinctive American spelling of British words. (**F**or instance, the British *honour* was replaced by the American *honor*.)

Do not capitalize a sentence within parentheses that is contained within another sentence.

> A major cotton-producing state in the antebellum South (*antebellum* means "before the war") was Georgia.

Do not capitalize the first word quoted unless the entire quotation can stand as a complete sentence.

> The ecologist reminded the audience to save "**t**he air, the water, the animals, and the trees."

Do not capitalize an indirect quotation. (An indirect quotation gives the meaning of an original statement without repeating it word for word. It is often introduced by the word *that*.)

> Amendment VI of the U.S. Constitution states that **a**ccused persons have the right to a speedy trial.

EXERCISE 1　**Capitalizing Sentences.** Rewrite correctly any of the following sentences that have errors in capitalization. Write on your paper the word *Correct* if a sentence has no errors.

1. one line of Langston Hughes's poem "Harlem" asks, "what happens to a dream deferred?"
2. Thomas Jefferson wrote that all people have the right to "Life, liberty, and the pursuit of happiness."
3. Helen Keller said that One can never consent to creep when one feels an impulse to soar.

4. Ralph Waldo Emerson argued, "Nothing is at last sacred but the integrity of your own mind."
5. in her diary Ann Frank wrote, "laziness may appear attractive, but work give satisfaction."
6. Abraham Lincoln said that Frederick Douglass was "the most meritorious man of the nineteenth century."
7. Golda Meir (She was premier of Israel) said, "to deny oneself various comforts is also easier in talk than in deed."
8. Marian Anderson once said that when there is money, there is fighting. (she meant that greed encourages conflict.)
9. The complete line from Edna St. Vincent Millay's poem is "My candle burns at both its ends."
10. Anais Nin wrote, "one handles truths like dynamite."

Capitalization of Proper Nouns

Capitalize a proper noun.

In reviewing the following sections, remember to capitalize only the important words (excluding articles, coordinating conjunctions, and prepositions of under five letters) in proper nouns composed of several words.

1. Names of individuals

John F. Kennedy	Grandma Moses
Babe Ruth	Athena
Katharine Hepburn	Sandra Day O'Connor
Uncle Sam	Jesse Jackson

2. Titles of individuals

Capitalize titles used before a proper name and titles used in direct address (naming the person or persons to whom one is speaking).

President Lincoln	Congresswoman Rankin
Queen Elizabeth II	Cardinal Cooke
Chief Tecumseh	Yes sir, General [direct address]

Capitalize titles used after a proper name or titles that replace a proper name when you wish to show respect or to indicate a high official. (For example, when referring to the President of the United States, always capitalize the title.) Do not capitalize titles used as common nouns to refer to a general class or type.

the Republican Senator from Wyoming	*but*	the life of a senator
Tecumseh, Chief of the the Shawnees	*but*	the chiefs bargained with each other

In general, capitalize the title of a family relationship used with or in place of a proper name. Do not capitalize the title if a possessive is used before it (unless the title is considered part of the name).

Dear Cousin Jenny,	*but*	My cousin Jenny sews.
Did you ask Mother?	*but*	my husband's mother
Won't you write, Uncle?	*and*	Uncle Carlos visited.

3. Names of ethnic groups, national groups, and languages

Americans	Apache
Chinese	Latin
Afro-Americans	Russian

4. Organizations, institutions, political parties and their members, and firms

Knights of Columbus	the Republican party
Ohio State University	a Democrat
the Senate	General Motors

The word *party* is not capitalized. Do not capitalize common nouns such as *court* or *university* unless they are part of a proper noun.

She visited two members of the Supreme Court.
Lawyers spend a great deal of time in court.

5. Monuments, bridges, and buildings

Tomb of the Unknown Soldier	Empire State Building
Golden Gate Bridge	Sears Tower

6. Trade names

a Ford	Kraft cheese
Gleem toothpaste	Sanka

7. Documents, awards, and laws

Declaration of Independence	an Oscar
Treaty of Versailles	Sherman Antitrust Act
Nobel Prize	Civil Rights Act of 1968

8. Geographical terms

Capitalize the names of continents, countries, states, counties, and cities, and of specific bodies of water, topographical features, regions, and streets.

Asia	Rocky Mountains	United States
Grand Canyon	Kentucky	Mojave Desert
Essex County	Long Island	Denver
Tropic of Cancer	Pacific Ocean	Southeast Asia
Snake River	Pennsylvania Avenue	Lake Erie

9. Planets and other heavenly bodies

Jupiter	Milky Way
Venus	Big Dipper
Pluto	Pisces

Do not capitalize the words *sun* and *moon*. *Earth* is capitalized only when it is used in conjunction with the names of the other planets. It is never capitalized when used with the definite article *the*.

Mercury, Venus, and Earth are the planets closest to the sun.

We looked from the sky above to the earth below.

10. Compass points

Capitalize the words *north*, *east*, *south*, and *west* when they refer to a specific area of the country or of the world, or when they are part of a proper name. Do not capitalize them when they merely indicate direction.

the South	*but*	south Florida
the East Coast	*but*	the east coast of Maine
North Dakota	*but*	north Texas

11. Ships, planes, trains, and spacecraft

U.S.S. *Constitution*	*Air Force One*
Philadelphia Flyer	*Apollo I*
Lusitania	*Voyager I*

12. Historical events, eras, and calendar items

Boston Tea Party	Renaissance
Korean War	Thanksgiving Day
World War I	Labor Day

Do not capitalize a historical period when it refers to a general span of time.

the fifteenth century   the sixties

Capitalize the days of the week and the months of the year, but do not capitalize the names of the seasons (*spring, summer, autumn, fall, winter*).

13. Religious terms

Capitalize names of deities, religions, denominations, and their adherents; words referring to a supreme deity; and religious books and events.

Judaism	Koran
Protestantism	Bible
the Catholic Church	Easter
the Lord	Yom Kippur

14. School courses

Capitalize only those school courses that are languages or that are titles of specific courses rather than general names of subjects.

English	*but*	**mathematics**
The Twentieth Century	*but*	**history**
Economics 101	*but*	**economics**

15. Titles of works

To the Ligthhouse	the *Washington Post*
"Bartleby the Scrivener"	"America the Beautiful"

Capitalize articles (*a, an, the*) at the beginning of a title only when they are part of the title itself. It is preferred practice not to capitalize (nor to italicize) articles preceding the title of a newspaper or a periodical. In general, do not capitalize (or italicize) the word *magazine* following the title of a periodical.

"The Open Boat"	*but*	the *Post-Dispatch*
"A Christmas Carol"	*but*	She has a *Time* magazine.

EXERCISE 2 **Capitalizing Proper Nouns.** Rewrite the following sentences correctly, adding or dropping capital letters as necessary.

1. The puritans, a group of protestants, felt that the church of england followed practices that were not approved by the bible.
2. A group from a Village named scrooby emigrated to holland and, unhappy there, decided to travel to north America.
3. Although they received permission from the london company to settle in virginia, their ship, the *mayflower*, was blown North and landed on cape cod.
4. The Settlers, now called pilgrims, named their settlement plymouth and drew up the document known as the mayflower compact.
5. In the Fall of 1621, the pilgrims held a celebration to give thanks to god; this became the Holiday called thanksgiving.
6. At the beginning of the Nineteeth Century, france owned a vast territory from the Mississippi river to the Rocky mountains.
7. The Area, called louisiana after king Louis XIV of france, was controlled by emperor napoleon bonaparte.
8. Although the U.S. constitution did not explicitly authorize such a purchase, president jefferson wanted to buy the land.
9. Although the federalist party objected, the purchase was finally approved, and the house of representatives appropriated the money.
10. Notes taken during the Louisiana exploration were later published as *Original journals of the Lewis and clark expedition 1804-1806.*

Capitalization of Proper Adjectives

Capitalize proper adjectives (adjectives formed from proper nouns).

Most proper adjectives fit into the following categories:

1. **Adjectives formed from names of people**

Elizabethan literature	Jeffersonian principles
Machiavellian character	Newtonian physics
Shakespearean actor	Aristotelian philosophy

2. **Adjectives formed from place names and names of national, ethnic, and religious groups**

Roman candle	Afro-American leaders
Canadian bacon	Chicano heritage
Jewish history	Irish linen

Many proper nouns do not change form when used as adjectives.

Senate majority	Oscar-winning performance
New York debut	Rembrandt exhibit
Vietnam War	White House statement

EXERCISE 3 **Capitalizing Proper Adjectives and Proper Nouns.** Rewrite the following sentences correctly, adding capital letters as necessary.

1. In the central mediterranean sea is the tiny island of malta.
2. Malta's strategic location has caused it to be occupied by many foreign peoples, including the phoenicians, the greeks, and the french.
3. The isle of tonga in the pacific ocean is the last polynesian monarchy.
4. Tonga's economy is based on agriculture, and tongan children are taught early to cultivate the land.
5. Vatican city is located in the heart of rome, near the west bank of the tiber river.
6. Vatican city attracts both roman catholic pilgrims and italian tourists interested in great art.
7. The vatican railroad line, only three hundred yards long, is the shortest in the world.
8. The land of tibet lies in south-central asia.
9. Tibet's capital city and religious center is lhasa.
10. Many tibetans live in nearby chinese provinces.
11. The people of tibet practice lamaism, a form of the buddhist religion.
12. Mount everest, the highest mountain in the world, is located on the border of tibet and nepal.

13. Belize occupies the southeast corner of the yucatan peninsula.
14. Before the arrival of europeans, belize was the site of several mayan ceremonial cities.
15. Liechtenstein is nestled between austria and switzerland.

SUMMARY OF CAPITALIZATION RULES

CAPITALIZE:	DO NOT CAPITALIZE:
He told us to turn to page 506 for the rules of capitalization. (There was no page 506.)	He told us to turn to page 506 (there was no page 506) for the rules of capitalization.
She said, "He liked it very much."	She said that he liked it very much.
Grandma Moses	My grandmother is eighty-five years old.
the Surgeon General	My surgeon advised me.
Ohio State University	a university in Ohio
Joslyn Art Museum	the art museum in the city.
Dial soap; Crest toothpaste	Buy soap and toothpaste.
the U.S. Constitution	Our club drew up a constitution.
Atlantic Ocean; Times Square; Eighth Street	the square at the end of the streetlife
Jupiter; Venus; Mars	sun; the earth, moon
the Midwest; the South	south of this midwestern city
the Civil War	The country was on the verge of a civil war.
Koran; Easter Sunday	sacred book; holidays
German; Art History II	foreign languages; history

SENTENCE WRITING **Using Capitalized Words.** (a) Write a sentence in which you include a quotation by a famous author. Be sure to mention the author's name. (b) Revise your first sentence by adding the nationality of the author. (c) Write a third sentence including the name of the work from which you originally quoted.

SAMPLE ANSWER (a) Herman Melville wrote, "Call me Ishmael."

(b) The American author Herman Melville wrote, "Call me Ishmael."

(c) The American author Herman Melville began *Moby Dick* with the words "Call me Ishmael."

Capitalization. Write the letter of the one item that is correctly capitalized in each of the following pairs.

1. (a) Countee cullen said, "good poetry is a lofty thought beautifully expressed."
   (b) Countee Cullen said, "Good poetry is a lofty thought beautifully expressed."
2. (a) Yale university
   (b) Yale University
3. (a) General Douglas MacArthur
   (b) general Douglas MacArthur
4. (a) Abigail Adams was the mother of John Quincy Adams.
   (b) Abigail Adams was the Mother of John Quincy Adams.
5. (a) Andrew Wyeth's famous painting is called *Christina's world.*
   (b) Andrew Wyeth's famous painting is called *Christina's World.*
6. (a) *Death Of A Salesman*
   (b) *Death of a Salesman*
7. (a) American History II and mathematics
   (b) American History II and Mathematics
8. (a) a Buddhist temple
   (b) a buddhist temple
9. (a) If spring is here, can summer be far behind?
   (b) If Spring is here, can Summer be far behind?
10. (a) East of the Hudson River
    (b) east of the Hudson River

CHAPTER 27

Punctuation, Abbreviations, and Numbers

Period

Use a period at the end of a declarative sentence or a polite command.

DECLARATIVE SENTENCE   At first Bartleby did an extraordinary quantity of
writing.
—Herman Melville

POLITE COMMAND   Look in the book for ten quotations from Melville.

Exclamation Point

Use an exclamation point to show strong feeling and to indicate a forceful command.

That woman looks exactly like me!
What a colorful garden!
How gracefully the couples are dancing!
Don't you ever say that again!

Question Mark

Use a question mark to indicate a direct question.

Was Benjamin Franklin born in 1706 or 1707?
Should I ask my history teacher?

Do not place a question mark after an indirect question (one that is reworded as part of a statement).

My friend asked whether Benjamin Franklin was born in 1706 or 1707.
I wondered if I should ask my history teacher.

In general, do not place a question mark after a polite request.

Will the assembly please be seated.

EXERCISE 1   **Using End Punctuation.** Rewrite the following sentences correctly, adding periods, exclamation points, and question marks where they are needed.

1. Baseball fans are forever arguing about who was the greatest baseball player. Which player would you choose
2. Many people would name Willie Mays as an all-time great player

3. In 1951 Mays entered major league baseball as a center fielder for the New York Giants and quickly became a hero to the fans

4. For years there was a spirited rivalry in New York involving Mays, the Yankees' Mickey Mantle, and the Dodgers' Duke Snider

5. When the Giants moved to San Francisco, Mays electrified the fans there as well

6. He will always be remembered as a fearless base runner and an exceptionally gifted fielder. What a fantastic catch he made in the 1954 World Series

7. Many people wonder if there will ever be another outfielder as spectacular as Mays

8. Mays's hitting statistics were also impressive. Do you know that he hit 660 home runs and had a career batting average of .302

9. How many players have hit more homers than Mays did Only Babe Ruth and Hank Aaron have.

10. In 1979 Mays was elected to the National Baseball Hall of Fame. Some still wonder why the vote was not unanimous

Colon

COLONS TO INTRODUCE

1. Lists

Use a colon to introduce a list, especially after a statement that uses such words as *these, the following,* or *as follows.*

To make a real Italian spaghetti sauce, you will need these ingredients: celery, onions, ground beef, tomato sauce, olive oil, and seasonings.

Perform the following operations to start a car with a stick shift: (1) Step on the clutch, (2) put the car into first gear, (3) turn the ignition key, and (4) slowly press down the accelerator as you take your foot off the clutch.

Do not use a colon to introduce a list if the list immediately follows a verb or a preposition.

Actor and director Woody Allen has written plays, screenplays, monologues, and comedy sketches. [The list follows the verb phrase *has written,* and therefore is not preceded by a colon.]

2. Illustrations or restatements

Use a colon to introduce material that illustrates, explains or restates the preceding material.

You can see how bitterly cold the winters are in Wainwright, Alaska: On a windy morning your breath freezes into ice crystals in front of your face.

COLONS BEFORE QUOTATIONS

Use a colon to introduce a long or a formal quotation. A formal quotation is often preceded by such words as *these, the following,* or *as follows.*

> Lincoln began the Gettysburg Address with these famous words: "Four score and seven years ago our fathers brought forth on this continent a new nation, conceived in liberty, and dedicated to the proposition that all men are created equal."

Poetry quotations of more than one line and prose quotations of more than several lines are generally written below the introductory statement (and indented on the page).

> Stephen Crane makes this admission in his poem "Truth":

> For truth was to me
> A breath, a wind,
> A shadow, a phantom,
> And never had I touched
> The hem of its garment.

OTHER USES OF COLONS

Use a colon between the hour and the minute in writing the time, between the chapter and the verse in making biblical references, and after the salutation of a business letter.

5:45 P.M.	1 Kings 11:1-13
8:30 A.M.	Madam:
Proverbs 8:22-31	Dear Sir:

EXERCISE 2   **Using the Colon.** Rewrite the following sentences correctly, adding colons where they are needed.

1. There are two times in a man's life when he should not speculate when he can't afford it and when he can.

   —Mark Twain

2. Among the natural rights of the colonists are these firstly, a right to life; secondly, a right to liberty; thirdly, to property.

   —Samuel Adams

3. There are three faithful friends an old wife, an old dog, and ready money.

   —Benjamin Franklin

4. Poet Karl Shapiro and composer Aaron Copland have something in common Each won a Pulitzer Prize in 1945.

5. Dorothy Parker asked to have this epitaph engraved on her tombstone "Excuse my dust."

6. A famous haiku by Ezra Pound follows

   The petals fall in the fountain
   the orange-colored rose-leaves,
   Their ochre clings to the stone.

7. These famous words are engraved on the Statue of Liberty "Give me your tired, your poor. . . ."

8. The following quotation appeared in Eleanor Roosevelt's autobiography, *This Is My Story* "No one can make you feel inferior without your consent."

9. In "The Still Voice of Harlem" Conrad Kent Rivers writes "I am the hope of your unborn."

10. In reading Genesis 21 1–21, keep in mind that *Sarah* means "princess" and *Isaac* means "laughter."

Semicolon

SEMICOLONS TO SEPARATE MAIN CLAUSES

Use a semicolon to separate main clauses that are not joined by the coordinating conjunctions *and, but, or, nor, yet* and *for*.

> The acting and directing ability of Orson Welles is considered phenomenal, **and** his film *Citizen Kane* is still studied and appreciated.

> The acting and directing ability of Orson Welles is considered phenomenal; his film *Citizen Kane* is still studied and appreciated.

Use a semicolon to separate main clauses joined by conjunctive adverbs (such as *however, therefore, nevertheless, moreover, furthermore,* and *consequently*) or by such expressions as *for example* and *that is*.

In general, a conjunctive adverb or an expression such as *for example* is followed by a comma.

> In her youth Mary Cassatt was strongly discouraged from any artistic endeavors; nevertheless, she later became one of America's foremost painters.

> All the trees were conifers; that is, they were cone-bearing evergreens.

SEMICOLONS AND COMMAS

Use a semicolon to separate the items in a series when these items contain commas.

> Notable transcendentalists were Ralph Waldo Emerson, who wrote *Nature*; Henry David Thoreau, who wrote *Walden*; and Margaret Fuller, who wrote *Women in the Nineteenth Century*.

Use a semicolon to separate two main clauses joined by a coordinating conjunction when such clauses already contain several commas.

> Leonardo da Vinci pursued a wide range of subjects, including mathematics, music, astronomy, and engineering; but he always returned to his primary interest, which was, of course, art.

EXERCISE 3 **Using the Semicolon.** Rewrite the following sentences correctly, adding semicolons where they are needed. Remember to use a semicolon when items in a series contain internal commas.

1. Persons attempting to find a motive in this narrative will be prosecuted persons attempting to find a moral in it will be banished persons attempting to find a plot in it will be shot.
2. Mark Twain attached the preceding notice to *Huckleberry Finn* he felt that too much analysis of art made it less enjoyable.
3. The trouble with music appreciation in general is that people are taught to have too much respect for music they should be taught to love it instead.
   —Igor Stravinsky
4. Among Stravinsky's numerous compositions are the operas *Oedipus Rex, the Rake's Progress,* and *Mavra* the ballets *Petrouchka, The Firebird,* and *Pulcinella* and three symphonies.
5. Stravinsky lived and worked in Leningrad, Russia Paris, France and the United States.
6. Oscar Wilde agreed with Twain and Stravinsky he said that art should be pleasurable rather than instructive.
7. Art does not reproduce the visible rather, it makes visible.
   —Paul Klee
8. Art and politics rarely go together nevertheless, art sometimes gets support from the state.
9. Painting, sculpture, and photography, which are visual arts, please the eye and music, which is a temporal art, pleases the ear.
10. We must never forget that art is not a form of propaganda it is a form of truth.
    —John F. Kennedy

Comma

As you study the rules for comma usage, keep in mind that to "separate" elements means to place a comma between two equal elements. To "set off" an element means to put commas *before* and *after* it. Of course, if the element that is set off occurs at the beginning or end of a sentence, only one comma is needed—either after it (for a beginning element) or before it (for a final element).

COMMAS AND COMPOUND SENTENCES

Use a comma between the main clauses in a compound sentence.

Place a comma before a coordinating conjunction (*and, but, or, nor, yet,* or *for*) that joins two main clauses.

> I told Sue what he said, and she advised me to forget it.
> I carefully picked up the vase, yet it crashed to the floor.

You may omit the comma between very short main clauses that are connected by a coordinating conjunction unless the comma is needed to avoid confusion.

> I opened the door and Fritz ran out. [clear]
> I opened the door for the dog and the cat ran out. [confusing]
> I opened the door for the dog, and the cat ran out. [clear]

COMMAS IN A SERIES

Use commas to separate three or more words, phrases, or clauses in a series.

> Alaska, Texas, and California are our three largest states.
> The movie was long, dull, and humorless.
> He can throw, catch, and hit as well as anyone else.
> They have traveled on land, by sea, and in the air.
> I enjoy reading stories, writing articles, and listening to poetry.
> Preheat the oven, beat the eggs, and sift the flour.

No commas are necessary when all of the items are connected by conjunctions.

> The movie was long and dull and humorless.

Nouns used in pairs (*pen and ink, ham and eggs, bread and butter*) are considered single units and should not be divided by commas. The pairs themselves must be set off from other nouns or groups of nouns in a series.

> The short-order cook prepared ham and eggs, bacon and eggs, and French toast.

COMMAS AND COORDINATE ADJECTIVES

Place a comma between coordinate adjectives preceding a noun.

Adjectives are coordinate if it would sound right to reserve their order or to put the word *and* between them.

> It was long, hard work.
> It was long, hard, boring work.

Do not use a comma between adjectives preceding a noun if they sound unnatural with their order reversed or with *and* between them. Adjectives that do not need commas between them usually describe different aspects of the word to which they refer—for example, size, age, and material.

> The big old oak desk stood in one corner of the room.

Commas may be needed between some of the adjectives in a series but not between others.

> A noisy, dusty British truck roared down the street.

In this sentence *and* would sound natural between *noisy* and *dusty*, but it would not sound natural between *dusty* and *British*.

EXERCISE 4 | **Using the Comma (Part 1).** Rewrite the following sentences correctly, adding commas where they are needed.

1. The American Film Institute is continually trying to popularize old films to discover new talent and to encourage innovative films.
2. Actors actresses and filmmakers greatly value the institute's Life Achievement Award.
3. The institute's annual award ceremony is publicized in newspapers in trade publications and on television.
4. The 1977 Life Achievement Award went to Bette Davis and many film stars applauded the decision.
5. This famous talented screen actress was the first woman to receive the award.
6. Celebrities retraced evaluated and praised Davis' career.
7. Davis was one of the first film actresses to play hard ambitious sometimes villainous women.
8. In *Mr. Skeffington* Davis played a selfish vain character.
9. She was convincing and powerful she was always vibrant and she appeared in more than eighty films.

COMMAS AND NONESSENTIAL ELEMENTS

1. Participles, infinitives, and their phrases

Use commas to set off participles, infinitives, and their phrases if the words are not essential to the meaning of the sentence.

> My brothers, having eaten, ran out to play. [participle]
>
> She sat there by the window, watching silently. [participial phrase]
>
> I have not received the money, to be perfectly honest. [infinitive phrase]

Do not set off participles, infinitives, and their phrases if they are essential to the meaning.

> The girl watching us is my sister. [participial phrase tells us *which* girl]
>
> She said it to sound intelligent. [infinitive phrase tells *why*]
>
> To study my notes would not help you much. [infinitive phrase used as subject]

2. Adjective clauses

Use commas to set off a nonessential adjective clause.

A nonessential (nonrestrictive) clause can be considered an *extra* clause because it gives additional information about a noun. An *extra* clause does not change, but adds to, the basic meaning of the sentence. Therefore, it is set off by commas.

> Jackson Pollock, who was an American painter, was greatly influenced by Zen Buddhism. [nonessential clause: *who was an American painter*]

Do not set off an essential adjective clause. An essential (restrictive) clause gives necessary information about a noun. It is needed to convey the exact meaning of the sentence.

> The only American writer whom she read was Ernest Hemingway. [essential clause: *whom she read*]

3. Appositives

Use commas to set off an appositive if it is not essential to the meaning of the sentence.

A nonessential (nonrestrictive) appositive can be considered an *extra* appositive; it calls for commas.

> Lionel Trilling, a famous literary critic and teacher, was also a novelist.
>
> Two major cultural centers are Boston and New York, cities with large populations.

A nonessential appositive is sometimes placed before the word to which it refers.

> A historic city, New Orleans was originally settled by French colonists.

An essential (restrictive) appositive gives necessary information about a noun and is not set off.

The *Iliad* and the *Odyssey* are traditionally attributed to the poet Homer. [The appositive *Homer* is needed to identify the poet.]

COMMAS WITH INTERJECTIONS AND CONJUNCTIVE ADVERBS

Use commas to set off interjections (such as *yes, no,* and *well*), parenthetical expressions (such as *on the contrary, on the other hand, in fact, by the way, to be exact,* and *after all*), and conjunctive adverbs (such as *however, moreover,* and *consequently*).

Yes, I hope to build my own home one day.

After all, I did my best.

Philadelphia, on the other hand, is three centuries old.

We drank two bottles of orange juice last night; consequently, we did not have enough left to make the punch today.

She intended to use the money to buy a stereo, however.

EXERCISE 5 **Using the Comma (Part 2).** Rewrite the following sentences correctly, adding commas where they are needed. For the three sentences that do not need commas, write *Correct.*

1. Bette Davis could not afford tuition for drama school; nonetheless she dreamed of studying to be an actress.
2. She came to New York and won a scholarship that paid for her tuition.
3. Davis having also studied modern dance left school to act.
4. Davis made her New York debut in 1928 performing in the stage play *The Earth Between.*
5. It was as a screen actress however that she achieved lasting fame.
6. Charlie Chaplin who was once a vaudeville comedian became an extremely popular silent-film star.
7. The role that Chaplin made famous of course was that of a tramp.
8. The modern-day film comedian who is most similar to Chaplin is Woody Allen.
9. *Nashville* a film that deals with the lives of country singers in Tennessee was directed by Robert Altman.
10. The screenwriter Joan Tewkesberry wrote the screenplay for *Nashville.*

COMMAS AND INTRODUCTORY PHRASES
1. Prepositional phrases

Use a comma after a short introductory prepositional phrase if the sentence would be misread without the comma.

Among those running, women were well represented. [comma needed]
Beside the soldiers an unarmed man was standing. [comma not needed]

Do not use a comma if the phrase is immediately followed by a verb.

Among those running were three women.

Use a comma after a long prepositional phrase or after the final phrase in a succession of phrases.

In the dead of winter, she caught a bad cold.

2. Participles and participial phrases

Use commas to set off introductory participles and participial phrases.

Galloping, the horses headed for the barn.
Running after my sister, I sprained my ankle badly.

COMMAS AND ADVERB CLAUSES

Use commas to set off introductory adverb clauses. Use commas to set off internal adverb clauses that interrupt the flow of a sentence.

Because it was a beautiful day, we decided to eat outdoors.
Elizabeth, because she knew the way, acted as our guide.

In general, do not set off the adverb clause at the end of a sentence unless the clause is parenthetical or the sentence would be misread without the comma.

COMMAS AND ANTITHETICAL PHRASES

Use commas to set off an antithetical phrase.

An *antithetical phrase* uses a word such as *not* or *unlike* to qualify what precedes it.

Alaska, not Texas, is the largest state in the United States of America.
Australia, unlike New Zealand, is an island that is considered a continent.
Tornadoes, never hurricanes, cause damage in this part of the country.

EXERCISE 6 **Using the Comma (Part 3).** Rewrite the following sentences correctly, adding commas where they are needed.

1. Throughout the history of art only a few artists can be said to have changed the course of painting.
2. One candidate might be Jasper Johns as many critics consider him to be the most influential of modern artists.
3. Because Jasper Johns and Robert Rauschenberg have influenced each other both artists are significant.

4. Putting aside their traditional training both artists preferred to work with abstract images.
5. Their finished works although they were carefully planned and executed look haphazard.
6. In the middle of a splash of paint and beside a scrap of newspaper Rauschenberg placed a light bulb.
7. Confused by such unusual combinations art critics have disagreed ever since they first attempted to interpret Rauschenberg's work.
8. Although the critics were puzzled at first they eventually realized that the everyday objects Rauschenberg used took on new meanings in his work.
9. The use of everyday objects by both artists was meant to be symbolic not absurd.
10. Articles like light bulbs and brooms became mysterious and beautiful things unlike ordinary light bulbs and brooms.

COMMAS AND SPECIFYING WORDS AND PHRASES

Use commas to set off specifying words and phrases.

Specifying words and phrases add specific information about what precedes them.

1. Titles of People

Use commas to set off titles when they follow a person's name.

Maria Lopez, Ph.D.   Bill Clinton, Governor of Arkansas
Henry James, Sr.   Alberta Picconi, D.D.S., will address us.

2. Addresses, geographical terms, and dates

Use commas to separate the various parts of an address, a geographical term, or a date.

Lancaster County, Pennsylvania, is known for its farms.
Send my mail to 51 South Spring Lane, Valley Forge, Pennsylvania 19460, until next month.
Friday, August 21, 1984, was my sixteenth birthday.

Use the following forms for letter writing:

51 South Spring Lane
Valley Forge, Pennsylvania 19460
August 21, 1984

Do not use commas if only the month and the day or only the month and the year are given:

July 4   July 1776

3. References

Use commas to set off the parts of a reference that direct the reader to the exact source.

> These ideas are stated in *The End of the Road*, pages 114–118.
>
> We performed Act III, Scene i, of Shakespeare's *Macbeth*.

COMMAS AND DIRECT ADDRESS

Use commas to set off words or names used in direct address.

> Carlos, are you sure that you can get tickets for the game?
>
> Remain in your seats, students, until the lecture is over.
>
> Please don't forget to call me tomorrow, Cindy.

COMMAS AND TAG QUESTIONS

Use commas to set off a tag question.

A tag question, such as *shouldn't I?* or *have you?*, emphasizes an implied answer to the statement preceding it.

> You handed in your paper, didn't you?
>
> You haven't read that book, have you?

COMMAS IN LETTER WRITING

Place a comma after the salutation of an informal letter and after the closing of all letters.

> Dear Juan,   Dear Aunt Miriam,
>
> Sincerely,   Love,

MISUSE OF COMMAS

Do not use a comma before a conjunction that connects a compound verb having only two parts.

> INCORRECT   The quarterback threw the ball, and then slipped.
>
> CORRECT   The quarterback threw the ball and then slipped.
>
> CORRECT   The quarterback stopped running, threw the ball, and then slipped.

The same rule applies to other compound elements, such as subjects, direct objects, and objects of the preposition.

> INCORRECT   The clothes that we needed, and the clothes that we did not want were packed together.
>
> CORRECT   The clothes that we needed and the clothes that we did not want were packed together.

Do not use a comma alone to join two main clauses that are not part of a series. A sentence with this error is called a *run-on sentence* (or a *comma splice* or *comma fault*). Use a coordinating conjunction with the comma, or use a semicolon.

INCORRECT The Pennsylvania state flag is blue and gold͓the state flower is the mountain laurel.

CORRECT The Pennsylvania state flag is blue and gold, **and** the state flower is the mountain laurel.

CORRECT The Pennsylvania state flag is blue and gold; the state flower is the mountain laurel.

Do not use a comma between a subject and its verb or between a verb and its complement.

INCORRECT What she thought fit to do͓was beyond my comprehension.

CORRECT What she thought fit to do was beyond my comprehension.

INCORRECT The ingredients for the turkey stuffing are͓bread crumbs, eggs, sausage, and spices.

CORRECT The ingredients for the turkey stuffing are bread crumbs, eggs, sausage, and spices.

EXERCISE 7 **Using the Comma (Part 4).** Rewrite the following letter, adding commas where they are needed and dropping the incorrect ones.

714 Williams Road
Charlottesville, Virginia 22901
September 12, 1985

Dear Greta,

I am enclosing a copy of the famous speech you requested. You haven't already found a copy of it have you Greta? The original speech was published in the September 9 1963 edition of *Newsweek* page 21. You can use it for your English assignment can't you?

On August 23 1963 there was an important civil rights march in Washington D.C. The march was led by Dr. Martin Luther King Jr. who was a church leader͓and a political activist. Dr. King believed in nonviolent protest͓and put his beliefs into practice. He organized a boycott of the segregated bus system of Montgomery Alabama in December 1955.

I hope the speech and this information͓will help you Greta.

Your friend
Eileen

Dash

Indicate the dash in typing by two hyphens (--). Do not place a comma, semicolon, colon, or period before or after a dash.

DASHES TO EMPHASIZE

Use a dash to set off and emphasize supplemental information or parenthetical comments.

> Louis Cyr—using one finger—once lifted 588 pounds off the floor.

DASHES TO SIGNAL HESITATION

Use a dash to indicate an abrupt change in thought within a sentence or to show a hesitation or faltering in dialogue.

> "You're—you're not taking me to the police station?" she stammered.
>
> —Katherine Mansfield

Parentheses

Use parentheses to set off extra material.

Commas and dashes are also used for this purpose; the difference between the three marks is one of degree. Use commas for extra material that is fairly closely related to the rest of the sentence. Use parentheses for material that is not intended to be part of the main statement but is nevertheless important enough to include. Use dashes for material that more abruptly interrupts the sentence and that you wish to emphasize.

> Minnesota (from the Dakota Sioux word meaning "cloudy water") was first explored by French scouts.

A complete sentence within parentheses is not capitalized and needs no period if it is contained within another sentence. If a sentence in parentheses stands by itself, both a capital letter and a period are needed.

> As gold and silver mining waned (mining declined in the 1870s), cattle became Nevada's principal source of revenue.
>
> Nebraska contains two of the widest and flattest rivers in the country: the Missouri River and the Platte River. (The name *Nebraska* comes from the Indian word *Nibrathka*, meaning "flat water.")

PARENTHESES WITH OTHER MARKS OF PUNCTUATION
1. With a comma, semicolon, or colon

Always place a comma, semicolon, or colon *after* closing parentheses.

> Although Death Valley may appear barren (it is often called a desert), many plants and animals flourish there.
>
> Pioneer towns had few women (more than half the population of Seattle were bachelors); however, in 1864 a settler brought a group of widows and orphans to Seattle.
>
> Washington State is the site of these fur-trapping posts (all built before 1833): Spokane, Walla Walla, and Nisqually.

2. With a question mark or exclamation point

Place a question mark or an exclamation point *inside* parentheses if it is part of the parenthetical expression.

> There is a city named Clinton (named after American statesman De Witt Clinton?) in almost every state.

> Many names have been suggested for the Black Hills of South Dakota (they were almost named the Purple Mountains!).

Place a question mark or an exclamation point *outside* parentheses if it is part of the entire sentence.

> Did you visit the famous "cowpoke capitals" of the Old West (Dodge City, Cimarron, Wichita, and Abilene)?

> How surprised I was to find out that a Franciscan mission was the site of the Alamo (Antonio de Valero Mission)!

EXERCISE 8 **Using the Dash and Parentheses.** Rewrite the following sentences correctly, adding dashes and parentheses where needed.

1. Anne Frank wrote a remarkable diary about her life in Amsterdam during World War II. She and her family were born in Germany but had moved to Holland before the war.
2. The diary—addressed to an imaginary friend named Kitty has been published in over thirty languages including Esperanto!
3. Anne, her parents, an older sister, and four friends—eight persons in all went into hiding during the Nazi occupation of the Netherlands.
4. Their hiding place for two years was an unused section of an old office building. In Dutch, their small, secret apartment was called *het achterhuis,* which means "the house in the back.")
5. The eight persons hidden in the apartment had to avoid making any noise.   How could they be so quiet for so long?)
6. The diary begun in June 1942 and ended in August 1944) covers Anne Frank's life from the age of thirteen to the age of fifteen a significant period in a girl's life.
7. One entry tells how pleased she was (who wouldn't be? to find out that a boy she liked very much also liked her.
8. Another entry tells that she felt her ideals, dreams, and hopes could not compete with "the ever approaching thunder" the misery and destruction that was sweeping Europe.
9. When Anne and the others were eventually discovered and taken prisoner, the diary was left behind. The diary was later found—along with some short stories and sketches and was published in 1947.
10. Anne Frank died in the concentration camp at Bergen-Belsen in March 1945. She was not even sixteen.

Quotation Marks

QUOTATION MARKS FOR DIRECT QUOTATIONS

Use quotation marks to enclose a direct quotation.

Place quotation marks around *only* the quoted material, not around purely introductory or explanatory remarks. Generally, separate such remarks from the quotation by using a comma.

> Socrates wisely said, "As for me, all I know is that I know nothing."
>
> "I celebrate myself, and sing myself," wrote Walt Whitman.

Do not use a comma after a quotation that ends with an exclamation point or a question mark.

> "Learn how to cook!" advises culinary artist Julia Child.

(For the use of colons to introduce quotations, see page 572.)

When a quotation is interrupted by explanatory words such as *he said* or *she wrote,* use two sets of quotation marks.

Separate each part of the quotation from the interrupting phrase with two marks of punctuation, such as two commas or a comma and a period. If the second part of the quotation is a complete sentence, begin it with a capital letter.

> "Poets alone," wrote Dorothy Parker, "should kiss and tell."
>
> "I never think of the future," wrote Albert Einstein. "It comes soon enough."

Do not use quotation marks in an indirect quotation (a quotation that does not repeat the person's exact wording).

> ORIGINAL QUOTATION "I never intended to become a run-of-the-mill person," said Barbara Jordan.
>
> INDIRECT QUOTATION Barbara Jordan said that she had determined never to become a run-of-the-mill person.

Use single quotation marks for a quotation within a quotation.

> My instructor smiled and replied, "It was Sarah Bernhardt who said, 'An *artiste* with short arms can never, never make a fine gesture.'"

In writing dialogue, begin a new paragraph and use a new set of quotation marks every time the speaker changes.

> Mr. Blakely smiled pleasantly. "I was looking out of the window a minute ago," he said, "and I saw a dog run across the street and turn the corner."
>
> "What kind of a lookin' dog was it?" Penrod inquired, with languor.
>
> "Well," said Mr. Blakely, "it was a—it was a nice-looking dog."
>
> —Booth Tarkington

QUOTATION MARKS FOR TITLES OF SHORT WORKS

Use quotation marks to enclose titles of short works, such as short stories, short poems, essays, newspaper and magazine articles, book chapters, songs, and single episodes of a television series.

"To Build a Fire" [short story]   "Self-Reliance" [essay]
"The Road Not Taken" [poem]   "America the Beautiful" [song]

(For the use of italics with titles, see page 588.)

QUOTATION MARKS FOR UNUSUAL EXPRESSIONS

Use quotation marks to enclose unfamiliar slang and other unusual or original expressions.

My roommate used to call clumps of dust "dust bunnies."

QUOTATION MARKS WITH OTHER MARKS OF PUNCTUATION

1. With a comma or period

Always place a comma or a period *inside* closing quotation marks.

"Everything had its wonders, even darkness and silence," wrote Helen Keller, who was blind and deaf from birth.

Billie Jean King has said, "Women can be great athletes."

2. With a semicolon or colon

Always place a semicolon or a colon *outside* closing quotation marks.

A male swan is a "cob"; a female is a "pen"; a baby is a "cygnet."

There are two Spanish verbs that mean "to be": *ser* and *estar.*

3. With a question mark or exclamation point

Place the question mark or exclamation point *inside* the closing quotation marks when it is part of the quotation.

My friend asked, "How did you persuade your mother?"
My father kept saying, "That's incredible!"

Place the question mark or exclamation point *outside* the quotation marks when it is part of the entire sentence.

Why did he say, "This is only the beginning"?
How wonderful that she will print your story "Winter"!

If both the sentence and the quotation at the end of the sentence need a question mark (or an exclamation point), use only *one* question mark (or exclamation point), and place it *inside* the quotation marks.

When did he say, "Will the car be fixed in time?"
Don't you dare say to me, "That's enough out of you!"

Using Quotation Marks. Rewrite the following sentences correctly, adding quotation marks where they are needed. For the one sentence that needs no changes, write *Correct.*

1. Albert Einstein's uncle taught him algebra. It is a merry science, he told the boy. When the animal that we are hunting cannot be caught, we call it *x.*
2. The young Einstein, although a genius, was often called oddball!
3. The great physicist was once told, You will never amount to anything, Einstein.
4. It is sad that his teacher said, Your presence in this class destroys the respect of the students.
5. I am a horse for a single harness, Einstein later said, not cut out for tandem or teamwork.
6. In 1911 Einstein published a paper entitled The Influence of Gravity on the Propagation of Light.
7. If Einstein's theory should prove correct, said physicist Max Planck, he will be considered the Copernicus of the twentieth century.
8. In 1915 Einstein published his paper General Theory of Relativity. Its effect was revolutionary.
9. Einstein believed that time and space could disappear!
10. The most incomprehensible thing about the world is that it is comprehensible, said Einstein.

Italics (Underlining)

Italic type is a special slanted type that is used in printing. (*This is printed in italics.*) Indicate italics in typing or in handwriting by underlining. (<u>This is underlined.</u>)

ITALICS FOR TITLES

Italicize (underline) titles of novels and other books, lengthy poems and plays, film and television series, paintings and sculptures, and long musical compositions. Italicize the names of newspapers and magazines, ships, trains, airplanes and spacecraft.

Wuthering Heights [novel]	*The People, Yes* [long poem]
Macbeth [play]	*On the Waterfront* [film]
Venus de Milo [sculpture]	*Newsweek* [magazine]
U.S.S. *Constitution* [ship]*	*Congressional Limited* [train]
Air Force One [airplane]	*Sputnik I* [spacecraft]
the *Baltimore Sun* [newspaper]	*Appalachian Spring* [musical work]

Italicize (underline) and capitalize articles (a, an, the) written at the beginning of a title only when they are part of the title itself.

The Red Desert	*but*	the *Boston Globe*
A Farewell to Arms		a *Reader's Digest* article

ITALICS FOR FOREIGN WORDS

Italicize (underline) foreign words and expressions that are not used frequently in English.

Do not italicize such words if they are commonly used in English.

Because Einstein was unconventional as a child, he was considered an *enfant terrible*.

The menu included spaghetti and lasagne.

ITALICS FOR WORDS AND OTHER ITEMS USED TO REPRESENT THEMSELVES

Italicize (underline) words, letters, and numerals used to represent themselves.

Why does the author use the word *essence* instead of *life?*
The *i* and the *t* were reversed in the title.
The *5* was crossed out and replaced by a *6.*

EXERCISE 10 **Using Italics.** Rewrite the following sentences correctly, underlining the parts that should be italicized.

1. The first black newspaper, Freedom's Journal, was started in 1827.
2. Writer Zora Neale Huston, acclaimed for her use of black folklore, criticized the play Emperor Jones by Eugene O'Neill.

---

*Do not italicize *U.S.S.* in name of a ship.

3. Composer Scott Joplin, whose ragtime music was used in the 1973 movie The Sting, used black folklore in his opera Treemonisha.
4. Jacob Lawrence's painting Vaudeville is based on his memories of the famous Apollo Theater in the twenties.
5. Cicely Tyson, who appeared in the television series Roots, learned her craft in the New York theater.
6. In Jules Verne's 1865 science-fiction novel From the Earth to the Moon, space travelers were launched from southern Florida.
7. It was just over a century later that the Apollo XI astronauts were launched from the U.S. space center in southern Florida.
8. The astronauts were hoisted onto the deck of the carrier U.S.S. Hornet after their splashdown.
9. There are craters, mountains, and maria (flat areas) on the moon. The term maria is Latin for "seas."
10. The word seas is not an accurate description for these areas, however, because there is no water on the moon.

Apostrophe

APOSTROPHES FOR POSSESSIVES

1. Pronouns

Use an apostrophe and s for the possessive of an indefinite pronoun that is singular.

Do not use an apostrophe with other possessive pronouns.

everyone's time	**his** duty
somebody else's clothes	**its** paws

2. Nouns not ending in s

Use an apostrophe and s to form the possessive of a singular or plural noun not ending in s, whether common or proper.

Dickinson's poetry   Colorado's mountains   women's rights

3. Plural nouns ending in s

Use an apostrophe alone to form the possessive of a plural noun ending in s, whether common or proper.

purple mountains' majesty	the Hawaiian Islands' exports
the bosses' demands	the Ladies' Home Journal

4. Singular nouns ending in s

The possessive of a singular noun, common or proper, ending in s (or an s or z sound) depends on the number of syllables in the noun.

If the noun has only one syllable, use an apostrophe and *s*. If the noun has more than one syllable, you can usually use an apostrophe alone.

my boss's instructions	Socrates' teachings
Sandy Glass's party	the countess' horse
Groucho Marx's humor	Confucius' sayings

5. Compound nouns

Put only the last word of a compound noun in the possessive form.

my father-in-law's camera	the heir apparent's throne
the sergeant-at-arms' order	the Surgeon General's warning

6. Joint possession versus separate possession

If two or more persons (or partners in a company) possess an item (or items) jointly, use the possessive form for the last person named.

Bill and Kristen's home
Gilbert and Sullivan's operettas
Strawbridge and Clothier's prices

If two or more persons (or companies) possess an item (or items) individually, put each one's name in the possessive form.

Newman's and Streisand's screen roles   Ford's and General Motors' cars

7. Expression of time and money

Use a possessive form to express amounts of money or time that modify a noun.

The modifier can also be expressed as a hyphenated adjective. In that case no possessive form is used.

one minute's time	*but*	a one-minute break
five cents' worth		a five-cent package

APOSTROPHES IN CONTRACTIONS

Use an apostrophe in place of letters omitted in contractions.

A *contraction* is a single word made up of two words that have been combined by omitting letters. Common contractions combine a subject and a verb or a verb and an adverb.

I'm	*formed from*	I am
you're		you are
it's		it is, it has
doesn't, don't		does not, do not

Use the apostrophe in place of omitted numerals in such expressions as the "the class of '82" and "the '76 election results."

APOSTROPHES FOR SPECIAL PLURALS

Use an apostrophe and *s* to form the plural of letters, numerals, symbols, and words used to represent themselves.

Italicize (underline) the letter, numeral, or word but not the apostrophe and the *s*.

> Your *a*'s are indistinguishable from your *o*'s.
> All of the *8*'s had been typed as *3*'s,
> Please replace your *&*'s with *and*'s.
> While editing my paper, I changed all the *till*'s to *until*'s.

EXERCISE 11 **Using the Apostrophe.** Rewrite the following sentences correctly, adding apostrophes where they are needed.

1. Whos to control the ocean floor, and whose rights supersede everyone elses?
2. Time-lapse photography of six months duration revealed much activity miles below the Pacifics surface.
3. Exploration of the worlds ocean floors has revealed vast mineral deposits containing important metals.
4. In addition to thousands of years worth of copper and nickel, there are over a trillion tons of manganese ore.
5. Various industries interest in gathering these riches is obvious.
6. Many products rely on coppers unique properties.
7. Back in 59 John Mero wrote one of the first articles in favor of deep-sea mining. The article contained few *ifs*, *ands*, or *buts*.
8. Meros line-bucket system is probably the simplest method of mining.
9. The right to mine the seabed beyond a nations territorial limits hasnt yet been fully defined.
10. The third-world countries belief is that these resources are everyones.

Hyphen

HYPHENS FOR PREFIXES AND SUFFIXES

A hyphen is not ordinarily used to join a prefix or a suffix to the beginning or end of a word. There are a few exceptions, however.

1. Prefixes

Use a hyphen after any prefix joined to a proper noun or proper adjective. Use a hyphen after the prefixes *all-*, *ex-* (meaning ''former'') and *self-* joined to any noun or adjective.

un-American	ex-governor
all-inclusive	self-admiration

Use a hyphen after any prefix joined to a proper noun or proper adjective. Use a hyphen after the prefixes *all-, ex-* (meaning ''former'') and *self-* joined to any noun or adjective.

anti-inflationary   vice-consul

Use a hyphen to avoid confusion between words that look alike but are different in meaning and pronunciation.

re-count the ballots	*but*	recount a story
re-lay the tiles		relay the message
re-mark the papers		remark about her condition

2. Suffixes

Use a hyphen to join the suffix *-like* to a proper noun or a word ending in *ll*.

Miami-like weather	*but*	a ghostlike apparition
a bell-like sound		a pearllike shine

HYPHENS IN COMPOUND ADJECTIVES

Use a hyphen in a compound adjective that precedes the noun.

A compound adjective that follows a noun is usually not hyphenated.

up-to-date reference	*but*	The references are up to date.
a sixteen-year-old boy		The boy was sixteen years old.
a well-educated girl		The girl is well educated.

An expression made up of an adverb ending in *-ly* and an adjective is not hyphenated.

a happily married couple   a mainly green interior

HYPHENS IN NUMBERS
1. Compound numbers

Hyphenate any spelled-out cardinal or ordinal compound numbers up to ninety-nine and ninety-ninth.

forty-five   eighty-eighth

2. Fractions used as adjectives

Hyphenate a fraction used as an adjective or adverb (but not one used as a noun).

a two-thirds majority   *but*   two thirds of the members

3. Connected numerals

Hyphenate two numerals to indicate a span.

pages 354-392   1884-1903

HYPHENS TO DIVIDE WORDS AT THE END OF LINES

Words are generally divided between syllables or pronounceable parts. Because it is frequently difficult to determine where a word should be divided, check your dictionary.

In general, if a word contains two consonants occurring between two vowels or if it contains a double consonant, divide the word between the two consonants.

rep-resentative	bat-tle
impor-tant	skip-per
insig-nificant	big-gest

If a suffix such as *-ing* or *-est* has been added to a complete word that ends in two consonants, divide the word after the two consonants.

track-ing	roll-ing
black-est	full-est

EXERCISE 12 **Using the Hyphen.** Rewrite the following sentences correctly, adding hyphens where they are needed. If no hyphens are needed, write *Correct*. Then make a list of the italicized words showing where each would be divided if it had to be broken at the end of a line.

1. The children are self reliant *because* they were taught to be.
2. Even pro American countries *sometimes* receive criticism from our government for their warlike behavior.
3. A previously *unknown* collection of pre Columbian pottery was uncovered by archaeologists.
4. One half of the *lettuce* is wilted.
5. One of the all American *players* came from Arizona, the forty eighth state to join the Union.
6. He came up with a totally silly notion that left us *baffled*.
7. The store specialized in *selling* hard to find items.
8. We *spotted* a yellow bellied sapsucker.
9. The exmayor has been cultivating a *number* of belllike flowers.
10. There will be a three fifths reduction in the work force at the *beginning* of the next year.

Abbreviations

Abbreviations are shortened forms of words. Abbreviations save space and time and prevent unnecessary wordiness. For instance, "800 B.C." is more concise and easier to write than "800 years before the birth of Christ." Most abbreviations take periods. If you are unsure about how to write a particular abbreviation, check a dictionary.

Use only one period if an abbreviation occurs at the end of a sentence that would ordinarily take a period of its own. If an abbreviation occurs at the end of a sentence that ends with a question mark or an exclamation point, use both the period and the second mark of punctuation.

She arrived at 7 P.M.
Did she arrive at 7 P.M.?
She arrived at 7 P.M.!

CAPITALIZATION OF ABBREVIATIONS

Capitalize abbreviations of proper nouns.

St. Louis, Missouri
Washington, **D.C.**
U.S. Department of Labor

Abbreviations of organizations and government agencies are often formed from the initial letters of the complete name. Such abbreviations omit periods.

NAACP   **UNESCO**   **IBM**
YMCA   **FBI**   **RCA**

State names used in addressing mail may be abbreviated as shown in the following list. The official ZIP-code form consists of two capital letters with no periods.

Alabama **Ala. AL**		Michigan **Mich. MI**	
Alaska **AK**		Minnesota **Minn. MN**	
Arizona **Ariz. AZ**		Mississippi **Miss. MS**	
Arkansas **Ark. AR**		Missouri **Mo. MO**	
California **Calif. CA**		Montana **Mont. MT**	
Colorado **Colo. CO**		Nebraska **Nebr. NE**	
Connecticut **Conn. CT**		Nevada **Nev. NV**	
Delaware **Del. DE**		New Hampshire **N.H. NH**	
Florida **Fla. FL**		New Jersey **N.J. NJ**	
Georgia **Ga. GA**		New Mexico **N.Mex. NM**	
Hawaii **HI**		New York **N.Y. NY**	
Idaho **ID**		North Carolina **N.C. NC**	
Illinois **Ill. IL**		North Dakota **N.Dak. ND**	
Indiana **Ind. IN**		Ohio **OH**	
Iowa **IA**		Oklahoma **Okla. OK**	
Kansas **Kans. KS**		Oregon **Oreg. OR**	
Kentucky **Ky. KY**		Pennsylvania **Pa. PA**	
Louisiana **La. LA**		Rhode Island **R.I. RI**	
Maine **ME**		South Carolina **S.C. SC**	
Maryland **Md. MD**		South Dakota **S.Dak. SD**	
Massachusetts **Mass. MA**		Tennessee **Tenn. TN**	

Texas **Tex. TX**	Washington **Wash. WA**
Utah **UT**	West Virginia **W.Va. WV**
Vermont **Vt. VT**	Wisconsin **Wis. WI**
Virginia **Va. VA**	Wyoming **Wyo. WY**

Capitalize the following abbreviations related to dates and times.

A.D. (*anno Domini*), "in the year of the Lord" (since the birth of Christ); place before the date: A.D. 66

B.C. (before Christ); place after the date: 336 B.C.

B.C.E. (before the common era); place after the date: 1000 B.C.E.

C.E. (common era); place after the date: 60 C.E.

A.M. (*ante meridiem*), "before noon"

P.M. (*post meridiem*), "after noon"

ABBREVIATIONS OF TITLES OF PEOPLE

Use abbreviations for some personal titles.

Titles such as *Mrs., Mr., Sr.,* and *Jr.* and those indicating professions and academic degrees (*Dr., M.D., B.A.*) are almost always abbreviated. Titles of government and military officials and members of the clergy are frequently abbreviated when used before a full name.

Mrs. Ethel Kennedy	**Dr.** Melo
Mr. Fred Astaire	**Gov.** William A. O'Neill
Ms. Simone Yang, **B.S.**	**Sen.** Bill Bradley
Sammy Davis, **Jr.**	**Col.** June E. Williams
Consuelo Melo, **M.D.**	**Rev.** Billy Graham

ABBREVIATIONS OF UNITS OF MEASURE

Abbreviate units of measure used with numerals in technical or scientific writing but not in ordinary prose.

The abbreviations that follow stand for plural as well as singular units.

ENGLISH SYSTEM		METRIC SYSTEM	
ft.	foot	**cg**	centigram
gal.	gallon	**cl**	centiliter
in.	inch	**cm**	centimeter
lb.	pound	**g**	gram
mi.	mile	**kg**	kilogram
oz.	ounce	**km**	kilometer
pt.	pint	**L**	liter
qt.	quart	**m**	meter
tbsp.	tablespoon	**mg**	milligram
tsp.	teaspoon	**ml**	milliliter
yd.	yard	**mm**	millimeter

Using Abbreviations. Write the abbreviations for the italicized words or phrases in the following sentences.

1. *Governor* Mario Cuomo called for increased aid to the homeless.
2. Among the guests were *Mister* Diaz and his daughters.
3. In 1976 *Doctor* Christiaan Barnard made medical history by performing the first human heart transplant.
4. The powerful Roman statesman Julius Caesar ruled until the middle of the first century *before the birth of Christ.*
5. The city of Rome was destroyed by fire (*anno Domini* 64).
6. The ZIP code for that area in *New York* 10028.
7. Add 20 *milliliters* of water to the formula.
8. The bus leaves the depot at exactly 11 *ante meridiem.*
9. The *Central Intelligence Agency* gathers information for the government.
10. My friend belongs to the *Young Women's Christian Association.*

Numbers and Numerals

In nontechnical writing some numbers are spelled out, and some are expressed in figures. Numbers expressed in figures are called *numerals.*

NUMBERS SPELLED OUT

In general, spell out cardinal and ordinal numbers that can be written in one or two words. Spell out any number that occurs at the beginning of a sentence.

> The Senate consists of one hundred members—**two** senators from each of the **fifty** states.
> The building is **sixty-eight** feet tall.
> Wisconsin was the **thirtieth** state to join the Union.
> **Two thousand twenty-eight** people were at the concert.

NUMERALS

In general, use numerals to express numbers that would be written in more than two words.

> There were **2,028** people at the concert.
> The Homestead Act allowed each farmer to claim **160** acres.
> The area of the United States is **3,615,122** square miles.

Very large numbers are often written as a numeral followed by the word *million* or *billion:*

> The population of the United States is roughly **237 million.**

If related numbers appear in the same sentence, use all numerals, even though you might spell one out if it appeared alone.

> Of the **435** members of the House of Representatives, **50** were newly elected.

1. Money, decimals, and percentages

Use numerals to express amounts of money, decimals, and percentages.

> **$398,000,000** or **$398** million
> **$19.50**
> **2.5** kilograms
> **6.25** million
> **57** percent

Amounts of money that can be expressed in one or two words, however, should be spelled out.

> **Eighty-six** cents
>
> **six thousand** dollars

2. Dates and times

Use numerals to express years and days in a date and for specific references to A.M. or P.M. time.

> The First Continental Congress met on September **5, 1774**.
> The President was to meet the ambassador at **3:15** P.M.

Spell out references to time used without the abbreviations A.M. or P.M. Spell out centuries and decades. Decades may be expressed as numerals if the century is included.

> The President was scheduled to meet the ambassador at approximately **three** o'clock.
>
> The greatest decade of the twentieth century was the **twenties** [*or* **1920s**].

3. Addresses

Use numerals for streets and avenues numbered above ten and for all house, apartment, and room numbers. Spell out numbered streets and avenues with numbers of ten or under.

> **526** West **111th** Street   **52** South **Ninth** Street
> Apartment **6D**   Room **8**
> **18** East **12th** Avenue   **866** Third Avenue

4. References

Use numerals to express page, line, act, and scene numbers.

> Look on pages **9** and **24** for references to André Watts.
> Read lines **360-414** in Book **IV** of the poem.
> We performed Act **5**, Scenes **i** and **ii**, of the school play.

EXERCISE 14 **Using Numbers and Numerals.** Rewrite the following sentences correctly by making any necessary changes in the use of numbers and numerals. If a sentence is correct as is, write *correct.*

1. Professional athletes are well paid. Many earn over two hundred thousand dollars a year.
2. Baseball players were on strike from June twelfth until August tenth, 1981.
3. 700,000 admission tickets were sold to the San Francisco Giants' fans during a losing year.
4. In a winning year one point seven million fans came to see the Giants play ball.
5. According to the U.S. Bureau of Labor Statistics for nineteen eighty four, six point two percent of America's dentists are women.
6. 16 percent of all physicians in the United States are women.
7. In 1980 there were ninety-four point five males for every one hundred females.
8. In 1985 about seven hundred thousand Native Americans were living on reservations in the United States.
9. About twenty million Native Americans live in Latin America.
10. Native Americans and other nonwhite groups make up about 10 percent of the total population of the United States.
11. 1 out of every 10 Americans is 65 or over.
12. In nineteen eighty five baseball's 5-game league championship series was expanded to seven games.

13. The expansion of the championship series increased baseball's revenue by nine million dollars.
14. Four out of every one hundred Americans are 75 or over.
15. The population of the world increased to approximately four point seventy five billion in 1985.
16. About three of every 5 persons in the world are between the ages of 15 and 64.
17. About six percent of the people in America were born in other nations.
18. In the 1980s the world experienced a one point seven percent yearly rate of population growth.
19. The playing time in professional football games is sixty minutes.
20. The Los Angeles Raiders won the 1984 Super Bowl with a 38 to nine victory over the Washington Redskins.

Review

CHAPTERS 26–27   MECHANICS

CHAPTER 26   CAPITALIZATION

For each numbered item indicate the correct capitalization.

Agatha Christie wrote many [1]Detective Stories. During her long career, [2]dame Agatha wrote plays as well as novels. Popular movies, such as [3]*Witness For The Prosecution*, have been made from her plays. One of her plays, *The Mousetrap*, was the longest-running play in the history [4]british theaters. "I get most of my story ideas," she once said, [5]"While I am doing some boring chores."

1. (a) Detective Stories (b) Detective stories (c)detective stories
2. (a) dame Agatha (b) Dame Agatha (c) dame agatha
3. (a) *Witness For The Prosecution* (b) *Witness For the Prosecution*
   (c) *Witness for the Prosecution* (d) *Witness for The Prosecution*
4. (a) *british theaters* (b) *British theaters* (c) *British Theaters*
5. (a) *while I am doing* (b) *While I am doing*

Writing for Review   Demonstrate your knowledge of capitalization by writing a paragraph that includes several different kinds of proper nouns, proper adjectives, titles, and quotations.

CHAPTER 27   PUNCTUATION, ABBREVIATIONS, AND NUMBERS

For each numbered item indicate the correct punctuation or usage.

Agatha Christie [1]1891 1976 wrote mysteries. In addition to novels and short [2]stories she wrote [3]17 plays some of which became movies. Christie said [4]that she got the idea when her sister said the [5]following you can always tell who committed the crime before the end of the [6]story I could write a [7]mystery answered [8]Christie that you [9]couldnt figure out." She wrote the story [10]The Mysterious Affair at Styles

1. (a) —1891—1979— (b) (A.D. 1891 to A.D. 1976), (c) (1891-1976)
2. (a) stories (b) stories, (c) stories; (d) stories—
3. (a) 17 plays, (b) seventeen plays, (c) seventeen plays
4. (a) that she (b) that: She (c) "that she
5. (a) following. "You (b) following: You (c) following: "You
6. (a) story. "I (b) story". "I (c) story." "I
7. (a) mystery"! (b) mystery," (c) mystery"
8. (a) Christie. "That (b) Christie, "that (c) Christie that
9. (a) couldn't (b) could'nt (c)couldnt (d) could n't
10. (a) *The Mysterious Affair at Styles*. (b) The Mysterious Affair at Styles.
    (c) "The Mysterious Affair at Styles."

Writing for Review   Write a paragraph that includes a short dialogue.

Skills and Resources

A computer's store of information: a resource for the future

Skills

Thinking About Thinking:
Making Associations

In this unit you will be developing your skills in spelling, vocabulary, listening, speaking, and test taking. Each of these uses of language engages you in the process of problem solving. As you solve problems with words, you practice the thinking skills required to solve problems of all kinds.

Defining the Skill

An effective problem solver is often skilled at MAKING ASSOCIATIONS. In language the associations that words have for you can be useful in helping you to remember the meanings of those words. Making associations is a way to build vocabulary. If you associate, or connect, a word with an object or experience that is especially meaningful to you, the word itself may become just as meaningful.

Applying the Skill

Look at the photograph. What associations can you make with the scene so that details of the scene will still be clear to you after you close your book? Identify at least two associations that may help you remember a specific detail.

CHAPTER *28*

Vocabulary Skills

A good vocabulary is an important tool of effective communication. The more words you know, the more clearly you will be able to express yourself. This chapter looks at ways to build your vocabulary. It focuses especially on improving the vocabulary you use in your writing.

Words in Context

Probably the most natural way of building your vocabulary is by reading. When you read, you are likely to come across many new words. Often you understand the meanings of these new words because the words occur in sentences and in paragraphs—that is, they occur in *context*.

The **context** is the setting or surroundings in which a word appears.

By examining the context of an unfamiliar word, you can often figure out its meaning. You can also get an idea of how to use the word in your own writing. Look at this line from a poem by the British poet Lord Byron:

And the sheen of their spears was like stars on the sea . . . .

The word *sheen* may be unfamiliar to you, but the context gives you a strong clue to its meaning. Since *sheen* is applied to spears and compared to stars on the sea, you can figure out that *sheen* must mean "brightness."

When you are trying to determine a word's meaning from its context, look for the following different types of context clues: restatement, illustration or example, and comparison and contrast. Each of these context clues will be taken up in detail on the following pages.

RESTATEMENT

Sometimes the context clarifies the meaning of an unfamiliar word by restating it in other, simpler words. Here is an example:

Most people should visit an ophthalmologist, or eye doctor, about every two years.

The context clarifies the meaning of *ophthalmologist* by restating it in the simpler words "eye doctor." Notice that in this example the restatement interrupts the sentence and is set off with commas.

Not all restatements are set off with commas. Look at this example:

Many American children visit pediatricians. These children's doctors have offices in most cities.

Here the restatement is a bit less obvious because it occurs in a second sentence. Yet you can still figure out that a *pediatrician* is a children's doctor.

ILLUSTRATION OR EXAMPLE

Sometimes the context helps you understand an unfamiliar word by giving you one or more examples that illustrate the meaning of the word. Look at this sentence from Mark Twain's satiric novel *A Connecticut Yankee in King Arthur's Court*:

> My raiment was of silks and velvet and cloth of gold, and by consequence very showy, also uncomfortable.

Raiment may be unfamiliar, but a series of examples—silks, velvet, and cloth of gold—helps you figure out that *raiment* is clothing.

One long example can also clarify the meaning of an unfamiliar word, as the following sentence illustrates:

> Debbie Allen is the award-winning choreographer who directs the dance sequences of the television show *Fame*.

Here the single example about directing dance sequences for *Fame* gives you a strong clue to what a *choreographer* is. A *choreographer* is a person who directs dances.

Sometimes the unfamiliar word is one of the examples given:

> Before the creation of synthetic fabrics, most clothing was made of cotton, wool, silk, and linen.

Linen may be unfamiliar, but it is listed along with three familiar examples of fabrics—cotton, wool, and silk. You can therefore figure out that *linen* is also a type of fabric.

COMPARISON AND CONTRAST

Sometimes the context compares an unfamiliar word with a familiar word or phrase:

> George Eliot was the pseudonym for Mary Ann Evans.
> Mark Twain was also a pen name; the writer's real name was Samuel Clemens.

Although you may not know what a *pseudonym* is, the word *also* suggests that a comparison is being made. By examining the comparison you can figure out that a *pseudonym* is a pen name.

Sometimes the context contrasts an unfamiliar word with a familiar word or phrase:

> At the beginning of *A Christmas Carol*, Ebenezer Scrooge is a miser, but by the story's end he changes into a generous person.

Miser may be unfamiliar, but the word *but* suggests that a contrast is being made. By examining the contrast you can figure out that a *miser* is the opposite of a generous person. A *miser* is therefore a stingy person.

Determining Meanings from Context. Each of the following ten passages contains an italicized word that may be unfamiliar to you. Write the italicized word and its meaning. Determine the meaning by examining the context, or surroundings. Look for the different types of context clues—restatement, illustration or example, and comparison and contrast.

1. Following the fall of Rome, *anarchy*, or complete disorder, prevailed throughout most of western Europe.
2. Among America's tallest *edifices* are the World Trade Center and the Empire State Building in New York City and the Sears Tower in Chicago.
3. Most early tribes were *nomadic*, but, because of the development of agriculture, some tribes were able to stay in one place.
4. Sol Hurok's skill in organizing and managing live entertainment made him one of the most famous and successful *impresarios* of his time.
5. Hardwoods make durable furniture. Among the woods commonly used are oak, maple, and *mahogany*.
6. A person with a broken *femur* has to wear a leg cast until the fracture heals.
7. In making a cake, beat the milk and eggs until they are *homogeneous*. Then mix the dry ingredients until they, too, are uniform throughout.
8. The heir to the estate lived in great wealth, while his disinherited brother was reduced to *penury*.
9. From the top of the mountain, Celia admired the lovely *panorama*. "What a beautiful view!" she exclaimed.
10. *Myths* and legends are both traditional folk tales, but while *myths* focus on a people's spiritual beliefs, legends attempt to record a people's history.

SENTENCE WRITING **Using Words in Context.** To show that the italicized words in Exercise 1 have become part of your writing vocabulary, use each word in an original sentence of your own.

Word Parts

Another important way to build your vocabulary is to learn the meanings of the parts, or elements, that many English words contain. For example, when you look at the parts of the word *unsinkable*, you find *un-* ("not") + *sink* ("lower") + *-able* ("capable of"). You can therefore figure out that *unsinkable* means "not capable of being lowered."

When you write, you can put word parts together to make useful longer words. For instance, instead of writing "Molly Brown's spirits were not capable of being lowered," you can write "Molly Brown's spirits were unsinkable." Notice how much stronger and clearer the second sentence is.

Prefixes

A **prefix** is a word part that is attached to the beginning of a word or another word part.

Many English words contain prefixes. For example, *unsinkable* contains the prefix *un-*, meaning "not." Knowing the meanings of common prefixes can help you figure out the meanings of words in which the prefixes appear. A knowledge of prefixes can also help you build new words to use in your writing.

Study the following chart of common prefixes.

PREFIX	MEANING	EXAMPLE
a-	without, lacking, not	amoral
anti-	against, opposite	antisocial
circum-	around	circumnavigation, circumscribe
co-	together with, joint	coauthor
counter-	going against, opposite	counterproposal, counteract
de-	to reverse an action, to remove, to deprive of	deactivate, defrost, dethrone
dis-	not, opposite of, to remove, to reverse an action	dissimilar, discredit, disentangle
en-	to put into, to make	encase, enlarge
ex-	previous, former	ex-soldier, ex-wife
in-, il-, im-, ir-	not, without, lacking	incapable, illegal imbalance, irrelevant
in-, im-	in, into	insight, immigrate
inter-	between, among	interstate
intra-	within	intracity
mal-	bad, wrongful, ill	malfunction, malnourished
mid-	in the middle of	midsection, mid-April
mis-	wrongly, bad, astray	mistreat, misquote, mistaken

PREFIX	MEANING	EXAMPLE
non-	not	nonexistent
out-	going beyond better than	outnumbered, outdo
over-	excessively, outside, beyond	overeat, overcoat
post-	after	postgame
pre-	before	preseason
pro-	in favor of, for	pro-European, prounion
re-	again, back	reconsider, reestablish
sub-	under, beneath, less than	subcellar, subcommittee
trans-	across	transatlantic
un-	not, opposite of, to reverse an action, to deprive of	uninvolved, uncover, unroll
under-	too little, lower, beneath	underplay, undergarment

EXERCISE 2 **Using Prefixes.** Rewrite each of the following fifteen sentences by replacing the awkward underlined phrase or clause with a single word that uses a prefix. Make sure the new word is placed so that your revision reads smoothly.

SAMPLE Proofread your essays for words <u>that are not spelled correctly.</u>
REVISION Proofread your essays for misspelled words.

1. The automobile industry is attempting to end practices <u>that are not efficient.</u>
2. If you feel uncomfortable with one doctor's diagnosis, you should be <u>examined again</u> by another doctor.
3. The boxer won because he <u>fought better than</u> his opponent.
4. Some advertisements <u>state excessively</u> the advantages of products.
5. Most parents scold children <u>who are the opposite of courteous.</u>
6. Many workers are allowed a coffee break <u>in the middle of the morning.</u>
7. Some politicians favor spending <u>that is in favor of the military.</u>
8. Navy ships are often equipped with guns <u>to fight enemy aircraft.</u>
9. Some psychologists emphasize the importance of thoughts <u>below the conscious level.</u>
10. Lack of certain vitamins results in <u>nutrition that is bad.</u>
11. A good balance of trade occurs when a country does not <u>ship into port</u> more than it exports.
12. Because of excessive wartime spending, nations often have recessions <u>after a war.</u>
13. Some people feel that too many polls <u>taken before an election</u> interfere with the democratic process.

14. In some tests students are asked to <u>put a line under</u> misspelled words and other errors.

15. It is important to be pleasant to <u>workers with whom people work</u>.

Suffixes

A **suffix** is a word part that is attached to the end of a word or another word part.

A suffix has a grammatical function as well as a specific meaning. For example, the suffix *-able* is an adjective-forming suffix. In the word *sinkable* the suffix *-able* turns the verb *sink* into an adjective. In addition, the specific meaning of *-able* is "capable of." Thus, *sinkable* is an adjective meaning "capable of being sunk."

Study the following chart of common suffixes. The chart has been divided into sections that show the grammatical function of each suffix. Notice that a spelling change sometimes accompanies the addition of a suffix, as in the first example, where the *e* in *conspire* is dropped when the suffix *-acy* is added.

SUFFIXES THAT FORM NOUNS

SUFFIX	MEANING	ORIGINAL WORD	NEW NOUN
-acy, -cy	state, condition	conspire	conspiracy
-age	result, process	drain	drainage
-al	action	portray	portrayal
-ance, -ence	state, quality	comply prefer	compliance, preference
-ant, -ent	agent, doer	occupy, depend	occupant, dependent
-ation, -ition, -ion	action, state, result	expect, compose, perfect	expectation, composition, perfection
-dom	condition, state	bore	boredom
-ee	one receiving action	train	trainee
-eer	doer, worker, agent	auction	auctioneer
-er, -or	doer, maker, resident	invent, New York	inventor, New Yorker
-hood	state, condition	child	childhood
-ism	system	symbol	symbolism
-ity	state, quality	real	reality
-ment	action, result	govern	government
-ness	quality, state	stubborn	stubbornness
-ship	state, condition	leader	leadership
-ure	act, result, means	expose	exposure
-y	result, action	inquire	inquiry

SUFFIXES THAT FORM ADJECTIVES

SUFFIX	MEANING	ORIGINAL WORD	NEW ADJECTIVE
-able, -ible	able, capable of	break, convert	breakable, convertible
-al	characteristic of	region	regional
-ant, -ent	doing, showing	defy, emerge	defiant, emergent
-en	made of, like	lead	leaden
-ful	full of, having	hope	hopeful
-ic	characteristic of	history	historic
-ive	tending to, given to	express	expressive
-less	lacking, without	joy	joyless
-like	simliar, like	dog	doglike
-ly	like, characteristic of	friend	friendly
-ous	full of, marked by	glory	glorious
-y	like, showing	dirt	dirty

SUFFIXES THAT FORM NOUNS AND ADJECTIVES

SUFFIX	MEANING	ORIGINAL WORD	NEW NOUN AND ADJECTIVE
-an, -ian, -ese	(one) belonging to (something or someone) of a place or a style	America, Vienna	American, Viennese
-ish	(something) characteristic of	Scot	Scottish
-ist	doer, believer, related to	capital	capitalist

SUFFIXES THAT FORM VERBS

SUFFIX	MEANING	ORIGINAL WORD	NEW VERB
-ate	become, form, treat	active	activate
-en	make, cause to be	weak	weaken
-fy, -ify	cause, make	pure	purify
-ize	make, cause to be	crystal	crystallize

EXERCISE 3 **Using Suffixes.** Rewrite each of the following fifteen sentences by replacing the awkward underlined phrase or clause with a word that uses a suffix. You may have to make other changes so that the new sentence reads smoothly. Remember that you sometimes have to make small spelling changes when you add suffixes. Also remember that suffixes have different grammatical functions as well as specific meanings.

SAMPLE   When you buy appliances to take overseas, check <u>how many volts</u> they use.

REVISION When you buy appliances to take overseas, check the voltage they use.

1. When offered second helpings, dieters must avoid <u>what is tempting</u>.
2. Public television airs many science programs <u>that tend to instruct</u>.
3. Many laws were <u>made into codes</u> in ancient Rome.
4. Olympic medalists should be proud of <u>what they have achieved</u>.
5. Beverly Sills and Placido Domingo have both helped to <u>make popular</u> opera.
6. <u>People who export goods</u> suffer economically when the dollar is high.
7. Adam Smith helped set down the principles of <u>the system involving capital</u>.
8. Presidential debates allow us to examine the candidates' ideas <u>that show a tendency to differ</u>.
9. Attitudes <u>characteristic of a nationalist</u> need not prevent agreement among nations.
10. When we are frightened, our heartbeats usually <u>are made quick</u>.
11. Many television series portray brave police officers and detectives <u>without fear</u>.
12. Recent space probes have explored planets, moons, and other bodies <u>characteristic of the heavens</u>.
13. <u>The state of being jealous</u> is sometimes called the green-eyed monster.
14. Some companies encourage input from <u>people whom they employ</u>.
15. Modern art often points out humorous <u>qualities that are absurd</u> in modern life.

Roots

A **root** is the central part, or core element, or a word, to which other word parts may be attached.

In the word *unsinkable* the prefix *un-* and the suffix *-able* have been attached to the root *-sink-*.

While prefixes and suffixes can give you hints to a word's meaning, the real clue is the word's root. Some roots, like *-sink-*, are also English words; others are not. For instance, the word *illegible* contains the prefix *il-* ("not') and the suffix *-ible* ("able"), but the key to its meaning is its root, *-leg-*, which is not an English word. Only if we know that *-leg-* is a Latin root meaning "read" can we figure out that *illegible* is an adjective meaning "not able to be read."

Many roots come to English from Latin, like -leg-, or from Greek. A knowledge of Greek and Latin roots can therefore help build your vocabulary. Study the following chart of Greek and Latin roots:

ROOT	MEANING	EXAMPLES
-aqu-	water	aqueduct, aquarium
-astro-, -aster-	star	astrology, asteroid
-audi-	hear	audience, inaudible
-ben-	good, well	benign, benefactor
-bio-	life	biography, biology
-cent-	hundred	century, centipede
-chron-	time	synchronize, chronic
-cred-	believe	credit, incredible
-duc-	lead	conduct, educate
-fac-, -fec-	do, make	manufacture, infect
-frag-, -frac-	break	fragment, fracture
-gen-	race, kind, origin	generate, gene
-geo-	earth	geography, geodesic
-graph-, -gram-	write, writing	biography, grammar
-hom-	same	homonym, homogenize
-hydr-	water	hydrant, dehydrate
-leg-, -lect-	read	legible, lecture
-log-	word, study	logical, biology
-man-	hand	manipulate, manual
-metr-, -meter-	measure, instrument	metric, barometer
-milli-	thousand	millimeter, million
-mor-	die	mortal, mortuary
-nym-	name	synonym, homonym
-ped-	foot	pedal, biped
-phil-	love	philospher, philanthropy
-phon-	sound	telephone, phonic
-phot-	light	photography, photogenic
-port-	carry	portfolio, import
-psych-	soul, mind	psychiatry, psychic
-sci-	know	science, omniscient
-scop-	examine, instrument	scope, telescope
-scrib-, -scrip-	write	scribe, script
-son-	sound	sonic, resonant
-spect-	sight	perspective, spectacle
-tele-	far, distant	telegraph, telepathy
-therm-	heat	thermos, thermometer
-tract-	draw, pull	extract, traction
-uni-	one	universe, unique
-ven-, -vent-	come	convene, prevent
-vid-, -vis-	see	evident, invisible
-vit-	life	vitality, vitamin

EXERCISE 4 **Using Word Parts.** Using your knowledge of prefixes, suffixes, and Greek and Latin roots, write the meanings of the following fifteen words.

1. unify	6. telegram	11. credence
2. retract	7. geology	12. genetic
3. thermal	8. inaudible	13. revitalize
4. inspector	9. chronological	14. dissonance
5. portable	10. metrical	15. subscript

SENTENCE WRITING **Using Vocabulary.** Write an original sentence for each word in Exercise 4.

Word Origins

Latin and Greek are not the only languages that have influenced English. Many other languages have contributed words to the English vocabulary. Here are some examples:

FRENCH	rouge, menu, bureau, deluxe, mystique
SPANISH	canyon, patio, plaza, ranch
ITALIAN	balcony, opera, umbrella, cello
GERMAN/YIDDISH	kindergarten, delicatessen, bagel
ALGONQUIAN	skunk, moccasin, tomahawk
IRISH/GAELIC	shamrock, slogan
NORSE/SCANDINAVIAN	skate, ski
DUTCH	cookie, shore
BANTU	gumbo, marimba
ARABIC	alcohol, algebra

Most dictionaries give the origins of a word in brackets or parentheses before or after the word's definitions (see Chapter 33).

EXERCISE 5 **Examining Word Origins.** Use a dictionary to help you identify and write the meanings and origins of the following fifteen words.

1. bazaar	6. gauche	11. schwa
2. corral	7. kowtow	12. slalom
3. fiasco	8. maraca	13. taboo
4. furlough	9. parka	14. tariff
5. galore	10. poltergeist	15. trek

SENTENCE WRITING **Using Words with Unusual Origins.** Write an original sentence for each word in Exercise 5.

In addition to borrowing words, English speakers have borrowed many expressions from foreign languages, especially from French and Latin. For example, we call the headwaiter in a restaurant the *maître d'*, and if a menu lists prices for main dishes and side dishes separately, we say our meal is *à la carte*. *Maître d'* is short for *maître d'hotel*, which in French originally meant "master of the house." Also originally French is *à la carte*, which literally means "according to the menu."

EXERCISE 6 | **Using Foreign Expressions.** Rewrite each of the following ten sentences by replacing the awkward underlined phrase or clause with one of the listed foreign expressions. Be sure to position the expression so that your revision reads smoothly. Use a dictionary to check the meanings of unfamiliar expressions. Use each expression only once.

FOREIGN EXPRESSIONS		
a cappella	coup d'etat
al dente	ex post facto
avant-garde	faux pas
bona fide	non sequitur
carte blanche	savoir-faire

1. Few architects are given freedom to do whatever they wish in designing buildings.
2. Realtors often have to separate offers made in good faith from those that are not serious.
3. Many people prefer spaghetti cooked so that it is firm to the teeth.
4. The Constitution forbids Congress to enact laws with a retroactive effect.
5. Your ignorance of a subject will be obvious if you make a remark that is unrelated to what has just been said.
6. The advanced and unconventional style of the Impressionist painters shocked most of their contemporaries.
7. After his return to France following military campaigns in Italy and Egypt, Napoleon arranged for a sudden overthrow of the government.
8. You can often avoid embarrassment by turning a tactless social blunder into a joke.
9. Folk songs are often sung without instrumental accompaniment.
10. The knowledge of what to do or say in every situation is a basic qualification for a successful diplomat.

Words from Proper Names

Some English words and expressions come from place names or from the names of people, fictional characters, or characters in Greek and Roman mythology. For example, we use the word *pasteurization* to name the

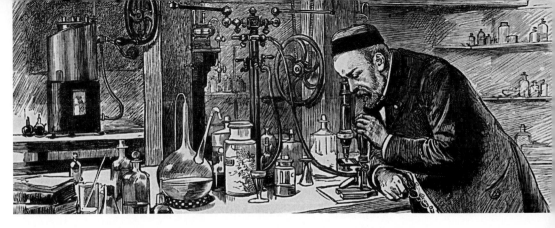

process by which we remove harmful bacteria from milk. The word comes from the name of the man who discovered the process, the French scientist Louis Pasteur. The word *madras* comes from a place name: The checked cloth we call *madras* originally was made in Madras, India.

EXERCISE 7 **Examining Words from Proper Names.** Use a dictionary to find out and write the meanings and origins of the following fifteen words.

1. bedlam	6. magnolia	11. paean
2. boycott	7. mausoleum	12. paisley
3. braggadocio	8. maverick	13. quixotic
4. canter	9. mecca	14. tantalize
5. gerrymander	10. narcissism	15. vulcanize

SENTENCE WRITING **Using Words from Proper Names.** Write an original sentence for each word in Exercise 7.

Synonyms

Synonyms are words that have the same or nearly the same meanings.

Loud and *noisy* are synonyms. A knowledge of synonyms can help you improve your writing vocabulary. Instead of repeating the same word over and over, you can use a synonym. For instance:

> WEAK REPETITION Because noisy conditions make concentration difficult, you should not play noisy music when you are studying.
>
> REVISED WITH A SYNONYM Because noisy conditions make concentration difficult, you should not play loud music when you are studying.

The first sentence sounds repetitious because *noisy* is used twice. In the revised sentence the second use of *noisy* is replaced with a synonym, *loud.* Notice how much better the revised sentence sounds.

EXERCISE 8 **Using Synonyms.** Rewrite each of the following fifteen sentences by replacing the awkward underlined word with its synonym. Choose the appropriate synonym from the list below. Use each word only once.

admonitions	impede	reluctant
affliction	irritated	respond
bereavement	pertinent	routine
enmeshed	portents	shackles
evident	remnants	signify

1. Ancient peoples often saw ominous <u>omens</u> in the flights of birds.
2. The loss of a loved one is difficult to endure, but friends and relatives can offer comfort at a time of <u>loss</u>.
3. Many clothing manufacturers try to find profitable ways to use cloth <u>remainders</u>.
4. In some tests you lose more points if you answer incorrectly than if you fail to <u>answer.</u>
5. Parked cards and other obstructions can <u>obstruct</u> a driver's view when he or she is making a turn.
6. Some people are <u>hesitant</u> to speak unpleasant truths, while others do not hesitate to say what is on their minds.
7. Characters in suspense novels are often <u>entangled</u> in tangled situations beyond their control.
8. In colonial times many indentured servants had to wear heavy chains around their necks, while African slaves were often forced to wear leg <u>chains.</u>
9. To a dentist, some cavities are immediately obvious, but others become <u>obvious</u> only from the patient's X-rays.
10. Literary symbols often have more than one meaning and can <u>mean</u> different things to different readers.
11. Some people are easily <u>annoyed</u> by the small but annoying habits of others.
12. Holistic medicine considers not only the physical disease from which a patient may be suffering but also any mental <u>suffering</u> that can contribute to the physical ailment.
13. A good reporter seeks all information <u>relevant</u> to a story and does not waste time exploring irrelevant details.
14. To find out the <u>habitual</u> habits of the Samoan people, anthropologist Margaret Mead lived in Samoa for some time.
15. People often reprimand their dogs for running into the road, but some dogs do not heed their owner's <u>reprimands.</u>

Antonyms

Antonyms are words that have opposite or nearly opposite meanings.

Noisy and *quiet* are antonyms. A knowledge of antonyms can help you improve your writing vocabulary. Often you can strengthen statements by using an antonym for a word expressed with a weak negative. For instance:

WEAK NEGATIVE   Libraries are not noisy places.
REVISED WITH AN ANTONYM   Libraries are quiet places.

Instead of using *not* + *noisy*, the revised sentence uses an antonym for *noisy, quiet*. Notice that the revision is more direct and precise.

EXERCISE 9   **Using Antonyms.** Rewrite each of the following fifteen sentences by replacing the awkward underlined phrase or clause with an antonym for the italicized word. For example, in the first sentence, provide an antonym for *stubborn*. Make sure to place the antonym so that your revision reads smoothly. Choose the appropriate antonym from the list below. Use each word only once.

abstain (from)	aggressive	beneficial	deplored	indisputable
abstract	articulate	benign	flexible	loathsome
accede (to)	assent	congested	fruitful	strife

1. A person who is not *stubborn* often makes an effective leader.
2. Dieters should generally not *indulge* in eating fried foods.
3. When the facts are not *doubtful*, a jury will reach a quick decision.
4. Some tumors are not *malignant*.
5. Studying is often not *unrewarding*.
6. Before a treaty is signed, the Senate must give its opposite of *dissent*.
7. Exercise can be not *disadvantageous* to your health.
8. Even after police officers are assigned to control traffic, some city thoroughfares remain not *unclogged*.
9. To sell products, a person must often be the opposite of *timid*.
10. British taxes were not *admired* by many of the rebelling colonists.
11. Internal lack of *harmony* often accompanies business mergers, especially if some workers lose their jobs.
12. Things that are not *concrete* cannot be perceived by the senses.
13. A democratic government usually must not *refuse* the demands of the majority.
14. When Charles Dickens visited America in the 1800s, he found the slums of New York City not *delightful*.
15. A speaker who is not *unclear* will usually be more persuasive than a speaker who mumbles.

Word List for Writers

The following list contains words that you will find useful in your writing. Try using each word in a sentence. If you have trouble at first, look up the meanings of unfamiliar words in a dictionary.

NOUNS

adjunct	diversity	populace
aftermath	elite	preconception
aggregate	entrant	prelude
amenity	entrenchment	proponent
analogy	exuberance	realm
aplomb	fanfare	reputation
attribute	fervor	riddle
aura	festoon	solitude
berth	grandeur	surveillance
buffer	implement	tendency
chagrin	mentor	texture
clique	morass	totality
columnist	onset	traditionalist
commentary	parallel	trend
commitment	penalty	watershed
confluence		weaponry
crucible		

ADJECTIVES

anonymous	impromptu	simplistic
awed	indiscriminate	singular
bombastic	indistinguishable	tense
canny	infantile	tolerant
causative	infectious	uncontrollable
caustic	influential	underlying
ceremonial	insuperable	unimpressed
curative	insurmountable	uninhabited
egoistic	marginal	unique
faceless	merciful	unrelated
gallant	orthodox	unreliable
grandiose	overwrought	unremarkable
honorific	paramount	unspeakable
identifiable	peevish	unthinkable
imminent	pointed	vengeful
immodest	puritanical	vested
impermissible	ruinous	vintage
implausible	rustic	virtual

VERBS

abide
afford
allay
assuage

compel
couch

deem
delve
detect
disengage
disgruntle
distinguish
dote

emerge
encase

encrust
engross
engulf
enrage
ensue
entail
entwine
exceed

formulate

impart
imperil
invalidate
invoke

menace
mull

orchestrate
override

reappear
reconcile
rely
resolve

salvage
savor
simulate

underscore
understate

wrest

CHAPTER 29

Spelling Skills

Spelling is a vital element in writing. Correct spelling is never noticed, but even one spelling error jars a reader and spoils a sentence. This chapter looks at some of the ways in which you can improve your spelling.

The spelling of many English words can be mastered with the help of the following spelling rules. Learning these rules and their exceptions will help you to improve your spelling.

Spelling Compound Words

When joining a word that ends in a consonant to a word that begins with a consonant, keep both consonants.

> book + case = bookcase
> room + mate = roommate

EXERCISE 1 **Spelling Compound Words.** Combine the following words, and write the resulting compound words.

1. back + ground
2. bath + house
3. bill + board
4. book + keeper
5. ear + ring
6. hand + kerchief
7. lamp + post
8. night + time
9. team + mate
10. with + hold

Adding Prefixes and Suffixes

When adding a prefix to a word, retain the spelling of the original word.

> dis- + appoint = disappoint
> im- + migrate = immigrate

EXERCISE 2 **Adding Prefixes.** Combine the following prefixes and words, and write the resulting words.

1. dis- + satisfied
2. im- + mature
3. ir- + regular
4. ir- + resistible
5. mis- + spell
6. out- + take
7. re- + commend
8. un- + natural
9. un- + necessary
10. under- + rated

When adding *-ness* to a word that ends in *n,* keep the *n.*

keen + -ness = keenness
mean + -ness = meanness

When adding a suffix that begins with *e* or *i,* or the suffix *-y* pronounced *e,* to a word that ends in a vowel + *c,* add a *k* after the *c* to retain the hard *c* sound. Do not add a *k* if the sound changes to soft *c.*

final + -ly = finally   subtle + -ly = subtly
full + -ly = fully   natural + -ly = naturally

When adding a suffix that begins with *e* or *i,* or the suffix-*y* pronounced *e,* to a word that ends in a vowel + *c,* add a *k* after the *c* to retain the hard *c* sound. Do not add a *k* if the sound changes to soft *c.*

panic + -y = panicky
public + -ity = publicity (changes to soft *c*)
traffic + -ing = trafficking

EXERCISE 3 | **Adding Suffixes.** Combine the following suffixes and words, and write the resulting words.

1. able + -ly
2. beautiful + -ly
3. brown + -ness
4. comfortable + -ly
5. dull + -ly
6. horrible + -ly
7. incidental + -ly
8. picnic + -ing
9. shellac + -ed
10. thin + -ness

Words That End in *y*

When adding a suffix to a word that ends in a consonant +*y,* generally change the *y* to *i.* Do not change the *y* to *i* when the suffix begins with *i.*

cry + -ed = cried   worry + -ed = worried
cry + -ing = crying   worry + -ing = worrying

Exceptions include certain one-syllable words combined with certain suffixes; *spry + -ness = spryness,* for example. When you are in doubt, check a dictionary.

When adding a suffix to a word that ends in a vowel + *y,* generally keep the *y.*

destroy + -ed = destroyed
employ + -er = employer

Exceptions include *day + -ly = daily, gay + -ly = gaily.*

Adding Suffixes to Words That End in y. Combine the following words and suffixes, and write the resulting words.

1. baby + -ish
2. betray + -al
3. bully + -ed
4. carry + -ing
5. crazy + -ness
6. gray + -ness
7. library + -an
8. luxury + -ous
9. necessary + -ily
10. ninety + -eth

Words That End in Silent *e*

When adding a suffix that begins with a consonant to a word that ends in silent *e*, generally keep the *e*.

advertise + -ment = advertisement
nine + -ty = ninety

Exceptions include a number of one-syllable words and words that end in *dge* or two vowels; for example, *argue + -ment = argument, awe + -ful = awful, judge + -ment = judgment, true + -ly = truly, whole + -ly = wholly.* When you are in doubt, check a dictionary.

When adding a suffix that begins with a vowel (including *-y* pronounced *e*) to a word that ends in silent *e*, generally drop the *e*. However, when adding a suffix that begins with *a* or *o* to a word that ends in *ce* or *ge*, keep the *e* so that the word will retain the soft sound of the *c* or the *g*.

mouse + -y = mousy
notice + -able = noticeable
move + -able = movable
manage + -able = manageable

Exceptions include certain one-syllable words and words that end in two vowels; for instance, *canoe + -ing = canoeing, mile + -age = mileage, shoe + -ing = shoeing.* A few one-syllable words that end in *i* + silent *e* change the *ie* to *y* when adding *-ing;* for example, *tie + -ing = tying.* When in doubt, check a dictionary.

Adding Suffixes to Words That End in Silent *e*. Combine the following words and suffixes, and write the resulting words. If you think that a word may be an exception, check its spelling in a dictionary.

1. approve + -al
2. argue + -ing
3. care + -less
4. change + -able
5. excite + -ment
6. ice + -y
7. like + -ly
8. live + -ly
9. pursue + -ing
10. sincere + -ly

Words That End in Consonants

When adding a suffix that begins with a vowel to a word that ends in a single vowel + a single consonant, double the final consonant if (a) the original word is a one-syllable word, (b) the original word has its accent on the last syllable and the accent remains there after the suffix is added, or (c) the original word is a prefixed word based on a one-syllable word.

top + -ed = topped   re•fer ′ + -ed = re•ferred ′
outfit + -ed = outfitted   (prefix + one-syllable word)

Do not double the final consonant if the accent is not on the last syllable or if the accent shifts when the suffix is added.

ben ′e•fit + -ed = benefited (accent not on last syllable)
re•fer ′ + -ence = ref ′er•ence (accent shifts)

Do not double the final consonant if it is preceded by two vowels or by another consonant.

retreat + -ing = retreating
exist + -ence = existence

When adding a suffix that begins with a consonant to a word that ends in a consonant, do not double the final consonant.

daunt + -less = dauntless
equip + -ment = equipment

EXERCISE 6   **Adding Suffixes to Words That End in Consonants.** Combine the following words and suffixes, and write the resulting words.

1. admit + -ed
2. annul + -ed
3. annul + -ment
4. bag + -age
5. develop + -ed
6. equip + -ed
7. expel + -ed
8. label + -ing
9. pamphlet + -eer
10. quiz + -ed

Spelling Plurals

RULES	EXAMPLES
To form the plural of most nouns, including proper nouns, add *s*. If the noun ends in *ch, s, sh, x,* or *z*, add *es*.	bat, bats Shaw, Shaws dash, dashes Lopez, Lopezes
To form the plural of common nouns ending in a consonant + *y,* change *y* to *i* and add *es*.	bully, bullies factory, factories sky, skies

RULES	EXAMPLES
To form the plural of common nouns ending in a vowel + *y* and of all proper nouns ending in *y*, add *s*.	play, plays Courtney, Courtneys Mary, Marys
To form the plural of common nouns ending in a consonant + *o*, generally add *es* but sometimes add *s*.	cameo, cameos studio, studios Romero, Romeros
To form the plural of common nouns ending in a consonant + *o*, generally add *es* but sometimes add *s*.	cargo, cargoes tomato, tomatoes banjo, banjos
To form the plural of most nouns ending in *f*, including all nouns ending in *ff*, add *s*. For some nouns ending in *f*, especially those ending in *lf*, change the *f* to *v* and add *es*.	chief, chiefs roof, roofs whiff, whiffs leaf, leaves elf, elves
To form the plural of some nouns ending in *fe*, change the *f* to *v* and add *s*.	knife, knives life, lives wife, wives
To form the plural of one-word compound nouns, follow the preceding rules.	blueberry, blueberries cupful, cupfuls handkerchief, handkerchiefs

To form the plural of compound nouns that are hyphenated or written as more than one word, generally make the most important word plural.	attorney general,
	  attorneys general
	brother-in-law,
	  brothers-in-law

Some nouns have irregular plural forms; that is, they do not follow any spelling rules.	basis, bases man, men ox, oxen
Some nouns are the same in the singular and the plural.	deer, deer series, series

EXERCISE 7   **Spelling Plurals.** Write the plural form of each of the following nouns. If you are uncertain of the plural form, check a dictionary. If a noun has no plural listed in the dictionary, its plural is formed in accordance with the first plural rule on page 623.

1. bookshelf
2. bruise
3. loaf
4. mother-in-law
5. Sanchez
6. soprano

7. bus	12. oasis	17. spoonful
8. dictionary	13. potato	18. staff
9. fourth grader	14. radius	19. stereo
10. journey	15. runner-up	20. witch
11. Levy	16. salmon	

Spelling *ie* or *ei*

Write *i* before *e* except after *c*,
Or when sounded like *a* as in *neighbor* and *weigh*.

> *i* before *e*: fiery, hygiene, yield
> except after *c*: ceiling, deceive, receive
> sounded like *a*: eighth, freight, reign

The exceptions to this famous rhyme include *counterfeit, efficient, either, foreign, forfeit, height, leisure, neither, protein, science, seize,* and *weird.*

EXERCISE 8 | **Spelling *ie* or *ei*.** For each of the following incomplete words, decide whether you should add *ie* or *ei*, and then write the complete word.

1. b__ge	6. for__gner
2. cash__r	7. gr__ve
3. conc__t	8. rec__pt
4. f__nd	9. sl__gh
5. f__rce	10. th__f

Spelling *sede, ceed,* or *cede*

Use **sede** in only one word: **supersede.** Use **ceed** in only three words: **exceed, proceed,** and **succeed.** Use **cede** in all other cases: **concede, recede,** and so on.

EXERCISE 9 | **Spelling *sede, ceed,* or *cede*.** Each of the following items contains an incomplete word that is missing *sede, ceed,* or *cede.* Write the full word.

1. ac_____ to his wishes	6. pro_____ with caution
2. con_____ the election	7. re_____ from view
3. ex_____ my goals	8. se_____ from the Union
4. inter_____ for her	9. suc_____ in business
5. pre_____ the verb	10. super_____ the old law

Spelling Unstressed Vowels

Many English words with more than one syllable contain an unstressed vowel sound pronounced like the *a* in *ago*, the *e* in *taken*, and the *i* in *pencil*. Dictionary pronunciations represent this unstressed vowel sound with the symbol schwa (ə).

To spell the unstressed vowel sound symbolized by schwa, think of another form of the word in which the syllable containing the vowel sound is stressed, and then use the same vowel.

For example, to spell the last vowel in *leg—l*, think of *legality*. In *legality* the *gal* syllable is stressed, and you can clearly hear the *a*. Therefore, *leg—l* also uses an *a*: The correct spelling is *legal*.

EXERCISE 10 **Spelling Unstressed Vowels.** For each of the following incomplete words, determine how to spell the missing unstressed vowel by thinking of another form of the word in which the vowel is stressed. Write the complete word and also the form of the word that you used to figure out the spelling.

1. abd__men
2. def__nite
3. edit__r
4. fant__sy
5. med__cine
6. mel__dy
7. mem__ry
8. or__gin
9. simil__r
10. sulf__r

Easily Confused Words

Some words with similar sounds are often confused. Learning the meanings and pronunciations of these words can help you avoid spelling problems. Study the following pairs of easily confused words.

accept   to agree to take; to assume; to approve
except   but; to omit

affect   to influence; to act upon
effect   a result

choose [chōōz]   to select
chose [chōz]   selected

clothes [klō*th*z, klōz]   garments
cloths [klôths]   fabrics

envelop [en vel ′əp]   to wrap or cover completely
envelope [en ′və lōp, an ′və lōp ′]   a flat wrapper for mailing a letter

formally   politely; officially; according to custom or rule
formerly   previously

lightening   making lighter in color or weight
lightning   a visible electrical discharge in the atmosphere

loose   [lōōs]   free; not confined; not tight
lose   [lōōz]   to misplace; to drop

than   in comparison with
then   at that time; next

EXERCISE 11   **Spelling Words with Similar Sounds.** In each of the following sentences, a choice of words is given in parentheses. Write the word that correctly completes the sentence.

1. Rain does not always accompany (lightening/lightning).
2. Actresses often wear expensive (clothes/cloths).
3. I gladly (accept/expect) your job offer.
4. Scientists study the (affects/effects) of volcanoes.
5. Some children watch more TV (than/then) their parents.
6. Doctors may advise you to (loose/lose) weight.
7. Each election day Americans (choose/chose) public officials.
8. Sometimes fog (envelops/envelopes) the city.
9. The sportscaster was (formally/formerly) a boxer.
10. Inflation (affects/effects) almost everyone.

Homophones

Homophones are words that have the same pronunciations but different spellings and meanings.

For example, *hole* and *whole* are homophones. Learning the meanings of homophones can help you avoid spelling problems. Study the following groups of homophones.

base   a supporting part; a designated area; not noble
bass   the lowest range in music; a bass viol or bass guitar

capital   a city that is the seat of a government; wealth
capitol   a building in which a legislature meets

dual   composed or consisting of two; twofold
duel   a prearranged, formal combat; a contest for two

holey   having holes
holy   sacred
wholly   completely; fully

flair   natural talent; perceptiveness
flare   to burn brightly and briefly; a bright, brief light

passed   moved through; elapsed; completed satisfactorily
past   the time before the present; gone by; ended; over

principal   the head of a school; greatest, first; main
principle   a basic truth; a rule of conduct

stationary   fixed; unmoving
stationery   writing paper and envelopes

straight   not curved; erect
strait   a narrow waterway connecting two larger bodies of water; a difficult position

sundae   ice cream served with one or more toppings
Sunday   the first day of the week

throes   condition of extreme pain, anguish, or struggle
throws   propels through the air; tosses; casts off

EXERCISE 12   **Spelling Homophones.** In each of the following sentences, a choice of words is given in parentheses. Write the word that correctly completes the sentence.

1. To Muslims, Mecca is a (holey/holy/wholly) city.
2. The dome of the (capital/capitol) was repainted.
3. The artist was in the (throes/throws) of creativity.
4. Some appliances have (dual/duel) voltage.
5. Fred Astaire danced with (flair/flare).
6. When enough time (passed/past), we were friends again.
7. The opera singer is a tenor, not a (base/bass).
8. The students went to the (principal's/principle's) office.
9. Ice cream (sundaes/Sundays) are very fattening.
10. He is in dire (straights/straits).

Frequently Misspelled Words

The following list contains words that are often misspelled by students in your grade. Master the words by (a) applying spelling rules where possible, (b) writing and rewriting the words, and (c) making up memory devices for problem words. For instance, if you have trouble remembering the first *o* in *laboratory*, you might remember: "A laboratory is a place in which scientists *labor.*"

abdomen	advertisement	a lot
abhor	afraid	aluminum
absence	agency	annual
accidentally	alcohol	answer
accuracy	align	antenna
accustomed	allegiance	antiseptic
ache	allot	antonym
acquit	all right	apology
address	almond	apparent

appearance
appetite
appetizer
approval
arctic
argument
asparagus
aspirin
athletics
atomic
attendant
audience
authority
autumn
awful

baggage
ballet
balloon
banana
banquet
basically
beautiful
beetle
beggar
beginning
behavior
benefited
bicycle
bookkeeper
boulder
bouquet
buffet
bureau
burglar
business

cafeteria
calendar
calorie
camera
canceled
cannibal
canoe

cantaloupe
carat
career
careless
carnival
carousel
carriage
cashier
cassette
casual
catastrophe
caterpillar
certificate
champagne
chandelier
changeable
chemistry
chlorophyll
chocolate
choir
chorus
Christmas
clarinet
cocoon
college
column
commercial
compass
competent
complexion
conscience
conscientious
conscious
consistent
contemptible
controlled
convalescent
convenient
coordinate
cougar
counterfeit
criticize
crocheted
crystal
cynical

dazzle
dealt
debris
debtor
decimal
deficit
definite
delicatessen
dependent
descend
determined
detour
develop
devise
diagram
dictionary
dinosaur
disappointed
disastrous
discipline
disease
dissatisfied
dolphin
dough
dynamite
dynasty

earring
eccentric
ecology
eighth
electricity
elementary
eligible
eliminate
eloquent
embarrass
embryo
emerald
emphasize
encyclopedia
environment
enzyme
equipped
essential

exaggerate
exceed
excellent
exercise
exhaust
expel
extraordinary

facial
facility
familiarize
fantasy
fascinating
February
fiancé
fiancée
flannel
flourish
foreign
forty
fourteen
frankfurter
fulfill
fundamental

gadget
ghoul
gourd
government
grammar
growth
gruesome
guarantee
guardian

handkerchief
hatchet
height
hippopotamus
hostile
hygiene
hypocrite
hypotenuse
hysteria

immature
immediate

incidentally
incredible
inhabitant
innocent
insistence
interruption
itinerary

janitor
jealous
jeopardy
jewelry

kangaroo
knight

label
laboratory
landlord
lavender
legitimate
leisure
leopard
library
license
licorice
lightning
lilac
llama
lullaby
lustrous
luxury

maintenance
mammal
marriage
mathematics
meteor
miniature
mischievous
misspell
molar
mosquitoes
murmur
muscle
mustache
mythology

naive
navigator
necessary
neighborhood
neither
nickel
niece
ninety
ninth
no one
nuclear
nuisance

occasion
occupant
occurrence
offered
opponent
original

pagan
pageant
pamphlet
parallel
pedestrian
peninsula
permanence
perseverance
pharmacy
phase
photosynthesis
physical
physician
physics
physique
picnic
picturesque
plaid
polar
porpoise
precede
prevalent
privilege
procedure
proceed
professor

pronunciation
pumpernickel
pursue
pyramid

radar
raspberry
receipt
recognize
recommend
reference
refrigerator
renown
resources
restaurant
rhinoceros
rhyme
rhythm
rouge

sacrifice
salmon
salve
sandal
sandwich
sapphire
sauerkraut
scallop
scandal
scene
schedule
scholar
scissors
senator
separate
several
shoulder
significance
silo

similar
sincerely
skeptical
skiing
soccer
solar
solemn
sophisticated
spaghetti
spatula
species
strategy
suburban
succeed
succumb
sufficient
sugar
sundae
supersede
swordfish
synonym
synthetic

teammate
technique
technology
temperature
temptation
tenant
theater
theory
tobacco
tolerance
tongue
tonsil
tortoise
tourist
traffic

trivial
truly
twelfth

umbrella
universal
unnatural
Uranus
usually
utensil

vaccine
vacuum
vague
variety
vessel
vicious
village
villain
vinegar
vulgar

warrant
Wednesday
whine
whirl
whisk
withhold
wizard
woolen
wrestle
wretched
writhe

yawn
yogurt
youth

zigzagged
zinc

CHAPTER 30

Business Letters, Applications, and Interviews

This chapter focuses on business writing and related skills that you will need to know when you are searching for a job, applying to a college or another school, or making other business communications. The chapter opens with a section about the format and content of business letters. It then examines job applications and other forms that you must often fill out. It concludes with valuable information about job interviews.

Business Letters

A **business letter** is a formal letter written to communicate information or request action.

A letter is often far more effective than a telephone conversation because it gives you an opportunity to organize your thoughts and to state them in specific, unmistakable terms. A letter also provides a dated written record that you can use for further reference or, occasionally, for legal proof of your communication. For these reasons, you should always keep a copy of each business letter you write, at least until the matter under consideration has been resolved or concluded.

Every business letter follows certain conventions of format and style. Generally, business letters should be neat, clear, courteous, brief, and easy to read. It is therefore advisable to *type* business letters whenever possible. Use single spacing, and leave an extra space between paragraphs and between the different parts of the letter. To make the letter visually pleasing to the reader, use wide margins and center the letter vertically on the page. In order to center the letter, you will probably have to type it once, examine its length, and then type a centered final draft. Be sure that your final draft is free of spelling, grammar, and punctuation errors as well as messy erasures or typeovers.

The standard business letter is composed of six basic parts:

    the heading
    the inside address
    the salutation
    the body
    the closing
    the signature

On the following model business letter, the six parts are labeled. The model business letter is type in **modified block style**: The inside address and the salutation align with the left-hand margin, while the heading, the closing, and the signature appear to the right of the center of the page and align on the left with each other. In modified block style each paragraph of the body may either align with the left margin or be indented. (Other examples of letters using modified block style appear on pages 638–639). In **block style** all six parts align with the left-hand margin. (An example of a letter using block style appears on page 640.)

As you examine the model letter, notice the punctuation used in its different parts, especially the heading, inside address, salutation, and closing. Correct punctuation will be covered in the next sections.

MODEL BUSINESS LETTER (MODIFIED BLOCK STYLE)

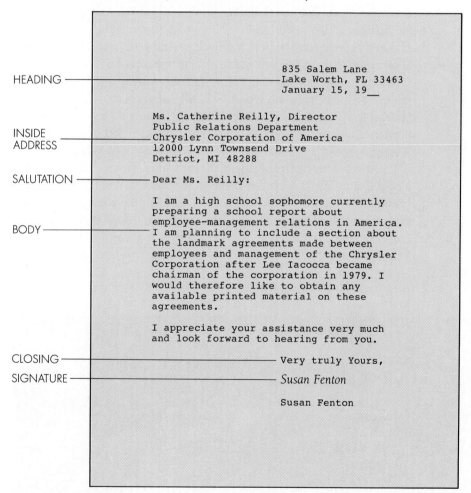

HEADING

835 Salem Lane
Lake Worth, FL 33463
January 15, 19__

INSIDE ADDRESS

Ms. Catherine Reilly, Director
Public Relations Department
Chrysler Corporation of America
12000 Lynn Townsend Drive
Detriot, MI 48288

SALUTATION

Dear Ms. Reilly:

BODY

I am a high school sophomore currently preparing a school report about employee-management relations in America. I am planning to include a section about the landmark agreements made between employees and management of the Chrysler Corporation after Lee Iacocca became chairman of the corporation in 1979. I would therefore like to obtain any available printed material on these agreements.

I appreciate your assistance very much and look forward to hearing from you.

CLOSING

Very truly Yours,

SIGNATURE

Susan Fenton

Susan Fenton

The following subsections discuss the six parts of a business letter.

THE HEADING

The **heading** contains your mailing address and the date of the letter. The name of your city, town, or village should be followed by a comma, your state, and your ZIP code. Also place a comma between the day and the year in the date. If you are using stationery with a letterhead that gives your address, your heading should consist of the date only.

In writing addresses, you should generally avoid abbreviations. However, you may use official post office abbreviations for the names of states.

THE INSIDE ADDRESS

The **inside address** contains the name and address of the party to whom you are writing. It appears two lines below the heading. If you know the name of an individual to whom you should address your letter, put it on the first line of the inside address. If you know the name of the room, a division, or a department to which you should send your letter, add this information to the name and address of the organization.

When you include the name of an individual in the inside address, use the person's full name preceded by a **title of respect** if you know this information. Four titles of respect—*Mr., Mrs., Ms.,* and *Dr.*—should be abbreviated and require periods. Most other titles, including *Professor* and *Reverend*, should be spelled out. The title *Miss* is not followed by a period.

If you know the **business title** of the individual, you should usually put it on the same line as his or her name and separate it from the name with a comma. For example, in the model business letter, the business title *Director* is included on the first line of the inside address after the name *Ms. Catherine Reilly*. If adding the business title makes the first line look too long, you may put it on a second line. In this case, no comma is used.

Mr. Carlos Ortega
Assistant Vice President

THE SALUTATION

The **salutation** is a formal greeting to the reader of your letter. It appears two lines below the inside address and is followed by a colon (:). Different kinds of salutations are used in different situations, as the following chart explains.

SITUATION	EXAMPLE
When writing to a man whose name you know, use *Mr.* unless another title (such as *Rabbi* or *Reverend*) is appropriate.	*A letter to:* Mr. Adam Stein *Salutation:* Dear Mr. Stein:
When writing to a woman whose name and title you know, use *Ms., Miss,* or *Mrs.* as she prefers unless another title (such as *Dr.* or *Professor*) is appropriate.	*A letter to:* Miss Janet Chaney *Salutation:* Dear Miss Chaney:
When writing to a woman whose name you know but whose title you do not know, generally use *Ms.* It is also possible to use the full name of the person and omit the title of respect.	*A letter to:* Rita Sinkoski, Editor *Salutation:* Dear Ms. Sinkoski: OR Dear Rita Sinkoski:
When writing to a specific person whose name you do not know, generally use *Sir or Madam.* It is also possible to use the person's business title.	*A letter to:* Personnel Manager King Record Company *Salutation:* Dear Sir or Madam: OR Dear Personnel Manager:
When writing to a company, an organization, a department, or a box number, generally use *Sir or Madam.* It is also possible to use the name of the company or organization.	*A letter to:* R & R Enterprises, Inc. *Salutation:* Dear Sir or Madam: OR Dear R & R Enterprises:

THE BODY

The **body** of a business letter communicates the information to the reader. It begins two lines below the salutation and should be single-spaced, with double spaces between paragraphs. Its contents will vary according to the kind of letter you are writing (see page 637) and the specific information that you wish to communicate. In general, however, the body should be brief, clear, and well organized. It should conclude with an expression of thanks or appreciation. If the letter follows up a previous letter or telephone conversation, this fact should be mentioned in the opening paragraph.

THE CLOSING

The **closing** of a letter is a polite word or phrase that leads into your signature. It appears two lines below the body of the letter and is followed by a comma. If the closing consists of more than one word, only the first word should begin with a capital letter. The tone of the closing may be very formal or it may be a bit more personal, depending on your relationship with the reader or the particular tone that you wish to achieve in the letter.

MORE FORMAL CLOSINGS	MORE PERSONAL CLOSINGS
Respectfully yours,	Sincerely yours
Yours respectfully,	Sincerely,
Very truly yours,	Cordially yours,

THE SIGNATURE

Your full name should be signed in ink just below the closing. Beneath your signature you should type (or print) your name. If you have a business title, you may put it below your name, as Rafael Lopez does in the example below. A woman writer may also indicate how she wishes to be addressed by including a title of respect in parentheses before her name, as Sandra Siegel does below.

Respectfully yours,   Respectfully,

Rafael Lopez   *Sandra Siegel*

Rafael Lopez   (Mrs.) Sandra Siegel
Secretary

EXERCISE 1   **Using Business-Letter Format.** Write or type the appropriate heading, inside address, salutation, closing, and signature for letters to the following parties. Use modified block style, and draw lines to indicate the placement of the body of the letter. You should use your own address and today's date for the heading, and be certain to use your own name for the signature.

1. James Kwong, Hong Kong Tourist Association, 160 Sansome Street, San Francisco, California 94109
2. Editor, *Photography Today*, 55 West 50th Street, New York, New York 10020
3. Rosalie Lavaggi, Director, Bayside Health Club, 440 Beacon Street, Boston, Massachusetts 02109
4. Consumer Information, Gulf Oil Corporation, P. O. Box 2001, Houston, Texas 77001
5. the governor of your state, a senator, a representative, your local mayor, or your town supervisor

Addressing Envelopes

On the envelope of a business letter, put your **return address**—your own name and mailing address—in the upper left-hand corner. Put the **recipient's address**—the name and address of the party to whom you are writing—just below and to the right of the center of the envelope. Be sure to include ZIP codes in all addresses. If you are unsure of a ZIP code, check a ZIP code directory at your post office or library.

```
Susan Fenton
835 Salem Lane
Lake Worth, FL 33463




          Ms. Catherine Reilly, Director
          Public Relations Department
          Chrysler Corporation of America
          12000 Lynn Townsend Drive
          Detroit, MI 48288
```

EXERCISE 2 **Addressing Envelopes.** Address the envelopes for three of the five incomplete letters that you wrote for Exercise 1. Write or type the addresses on real envelopes or in rectangular boxes drawn on paper.

Kinds of Business Letters

Business letters are written for a number of different purposes. Among them are (1) to request information or services; (2) to place an order; (3) to make a complaint or ask for an adjustment; and (4) to apply for a job, to a school, to a club, or to another organization.

THE LETTER OF REQUEST

A **letter of request** asks for information or services from an organization or an individual. An example of a letter of request is the model business letter on page 632.

Follow these steps when you write a letter of request:

1. Identify yourself.
2. Explain the reason or reasons that you need assistance.
3. State a specific request. If you are requesting the services of a guest speaker or writing about another matter that involves a date, time, and place, be sure to specify these items in your letter.
4. Conclude courteously.

THE ORDER LETTER

The **order letter** places an order for manufactured goods, magazines, or something else that requires payment. An example is the letter below, in which Louis Bolton places an order for a subscription to *Teen Life*.

Follow these steps when you write an order letter:

1. Give the necessary information about the item or items that you are ordering. If you are ordering manufactured goods, specify the quantity, size, color, and price. If you are subscribing to a magazine, specify the time length of the subscription as well as the price.
2. If you are enclosing payment, state how much you are sending. Send a check or a money order; never send cash through the mail.
3. Keep a copy of the check or money order as well as the letter until the order has been filled to your satisfaction.

AN ORDER LETTER (MODIFIED BLOCK STYLE)

```
                         1380 Peachtree Street, N.E.
                         Atlanta, Georgia 30309
                         June 3, 19___

Subscription Manager
Teen Life
Box 666
Denver, Colorado 80202

Dear Subscription Manager:

        I would like to order a one-year
subscription to Teen Life. Enclosed is a
money order for $9.00 in payment for the
subscription.

        Thank you very much for filling my
order. I look forward to receiving my
first issue of the magazine in July.

                         Yours truly,

                         Louis Bolton

                         Louis Bolton
```

THE LETTER OF ADJUSTMENT OR COMPLAINT

A **letter of adjustment or complaint** states a problem and asks that it be corrected. An example is the letter below, in which Louis Bolton complains about his failure to receive the magazine that he ordered.

Follow these steps when you write a letter of adjustment or complaint:

1. Give all the necessary details of the situation.
2. Be polite but firm. A courteous tone is more likely to get a positive response than a rude tone.
3. Ask for specific action, and indicate that you assume that this action will be taken.

A LETTER OF COMPLAINT (MODIFIED BLOCK STYLE)

```
                              1380 Peachtree Street, N.E.
                              Atlanta, Georgia 30309
                              September 15, 19--

Subscription Manager
Teen Life
Box 666
Denver, Colorado 80202

Dear Subscription Manager:

        On June 3 I sent an order for a
one-year subscription of Teen Life along
with a money order for $9.00 in payment.
It is now the middle of September, and I
have not received any copies of the
magazine.

        Please send me the July, August,
and September issues as soon as possible.
I hope I will receive all future issues
of the magazine on time.

        Thank you for your attention to
this request.

                              Yours truly,

                              Louis Bolton

                              Louis Bolton
```

THE LETTER OF APPLICATION

Though most jobs and colleges require that you fill out a preprinted application form (see pages 643-644), there are times when a letter of application may be all that is required. A **letter of application** asks that you be considered for a job, be allowed to enroll in a school or a course, or be permitted to join a club or another organization. An example is the letter below, in which Ramona Newcomb applies for an after-school job advertised in a local newspaper.

A LETTER OF APPLICATION (BLOCK STYLE)

```
83 Hudson Avenue, Apt. 8B
Albany, New York 12203
April 23, 19--

P.O. Box 221
Albany, New York 12203

Dear Sir or Madam:
I am interested in the job as a part-time florist's
assistant advertised in the classified section of
the Albany Times-Union on Sunday, April 22, 19--.

I am a high school sophomore and am available for
work on weekdays after 3 P.M. as well as on
weekends. Although I have never worked in a
florist's shop, I did have a retail job at Aldo's
Bake Shop last summer, and I also do gardening
chores for my neighbor, Mrs. Anderson.

For references, you may contact Mr. Aldo Cervini,
the owner of Aldo's Bake Shop, 430 Madison Avenue,
telephone 489-6342; Mrs. Phyllis Anderson, the
neighbor for whom I do gardening, 85 Hudson Avenue,
telephone 449-6584; and my biology teacher, Mr. Jay
Cohen, at Albany High School, telephone 449-6000.

You may reach me at 449-3124 any day after 4 P.M.

Thank you so much for considering me for the job. I
look forward to hearing from you.

Respectfully,
Ramana Newcomb
Ramana Newcomb
```

Follow these steps when you write a letter of application:

1. Identify the job, school, course, club, or organization to which you are applying.
2. Identify yourself.
3. Include relevant information involving time, hours, and so on. For instance, if you are applying for a job, state the date that you can begin and the hours that you will be available. If you are hoping to enroll in a special course, state the day, hours, and weeks or term during which the course is to be held.
4. Briefly explain your qualifications.
5. Include the names and addresses of people who may be contacted for references. If possible, give a **business reference**—a former employer or job supervisor—as well as at least one **personal reference**—a teacher, a neighbor, or another adult who knows you well. Always contact these people beforehand to make sure that they are willing to be named as references. Never list family members as references.
6. Include your telephone number and the best time at which you can be reached.
7. Be sure to conclude your letter of application in a cordial and courteous manner.

EXERCISE 3 **Writing Business Letters.** Each of the following items describes a situation and asks you to write a different kind of business letter. For each letter that you write, use your home address, today's date, and your own name.

1. Your school is having a special workshop on summer employment in your area. Write a letter of request in which you invite the head of the local Chamber of Commerce to speak at the workshop.
2. Order a model airplane kit, catalog number 1305, from the Hobby Craft Company, Box 797, Fairfield, Iowa 52556. The price is $12.00.
3. Write a letter of complaint to a made-up restaurant in your area. Complain about the quality of the food, the high prices, the cleanliness, or the poor service.
4. Write a letter applying for a summer job as a checkout clerk at your local supermarket. The job was advertised in last Sunday's classified ads in your local newspaper. Address the letter to the manager of the supermarket.
5. You wish to obtain a listing of available Audubon wildlife films, as well as information about how you can arrange to have some of these films shown at your school. Write a letter to the National Audubon Society, 950 Third Avenue, New York, New York 10022.

Job Applications and Other Forms

There are many occasions on which you will have to fill out a form of one sort or another. For instance, you may have to fill out an application for a job or a school, a government form to report your income or obtain a passport, a bank form to open a savings or checking account, or an order form to order goods from a mail-order catalog.

Follow these steps when you fill out a form:

1. Examine the entire form before writing anything down. Read the directions, and look at each item of information that the form requests. Pay careful attention to directions about how you should fill out the form: Do the directions say to print or to type the information? To use blue or black ink? To use a pencil? If the form has no specific instructions about how to fill it out, use blue or black ink and print everything except your signature.

2. Gather together the supplies and information that you will need to fill out the form. In addition to your name, address, and telephone number, forms often ask you to list your social security number, your date and place of birth, your height and weight, your parents or guardians, information about your schooling, information about jobs that you may have held in the past, and the names and addresses of people who will provide you with references. In listing *personal* references, list teachers or other school officials, neighbors, your family doctor, or other adults who know you well. Always contact these people beforehand to make sure that they are willing to be named as references. Never list family members as references.

3. Fill out the form item by item, paying careful attention to any specific instructions for the item to which you are responding. If a particular item requires a long or complicated response, write the response on a separate sheet of paper and revise it if necessary before copying it onto the form.

4. On most forms, if a particular item does not apply to you, write *N.A.* for "not applicable" or draw a line in the space provided. (The *N.A.* or line shows that you have not overlooked the item.) Only leave inapplicable items blank if the form directs you to do so.

5. In providing addresses, use commonly accepted abbreviations—like *St.* for *Street*—unless there is room to spell out all words. In providing dates, generally use a number for the month as well as the day and the year. Be careful not to confuse your birth date with the current date.

6. When you have finished filling out the form, read through it to check that you have followed all directions and left nothing out. Proofread your responses to make sure that they are free of grammar, spelling, and punctuation errors.

EXERCISE 4 **Filling Out Forms.** The following form is a typical job application. Main sections on the application have been given capital letters, and items have been numbered and sometimes further subdivided with small letters. Copy the appropriate letters and numerals for all items onto a separate sheet of paper. Next to each, write the information that you would provide if you were actually filling out the application. For items 9 and 10 under A, make up reasonable responses.

JOB APPLICATION

Please Print

A. PERSONAL DATA

1. Name _____ 2. Social Secutiry No. _____
           Last   First   Middle Initial

3. Mailing Address _____
             No.   Street   City   State   ZIP Code

4. Permanent Address _____
    (if different)   No.   Street   City   State   ZIP Code

5. Home Phone _____ 6. Business Phone _____ 7. Age _____
                          (if different)   (if 18 yrs. or under)

8. Person to Notify
    in Case of Emergency a. _____ b. _____
                        Name   Address

    c. _____ d. _____
       Phone No.   Relationship to You

9. a. Have you ever worked for us before? _____ b. If so, when? _____

    c. What was your position? _____

10. Position Desired a. _____ b. _____ c. _____

B. EDUCATION

1. Number of Years Completed _____

Type	Name	From (mo./yr.)	To (mo./yr.)	Diploma or Degree	Specialization or Major
2. High School	a. _____	b. _____	c. _____	d. _____	e. _____
3. College	a. _____	b. _____	c. _____	d. _____	e. _____
4. Technical	a. _____	b. _____	c. _____	d. _____	e. _____
5. Business	a. _____	b. _____	c. _____	d. _____	e. _____

C. SPECIAL SKILLS

1. a. Type? _____ b. Words per Minute _____

2. a. Shorthand? _____ b. Words per Minute _____

3. Explain any other special skills, experience, or training. _____

_____

D. MILITARY SERVICE
1. Branch _____ 2. Date Entered _____ 3. Date Discharged _____

4. Rank at Discharge _____ 5. Military Work Experience _____

_____

E. EMPLOYMENT HISTORY (List most recent job first.)

1. a. _____ b. _____ c. _____ d. _____
      From   To   Job Title   Pay Rate

   e. _____ f. _____
      Name of Employer   Address (include city, state, and ZIP code)

   g. _____
      Specific Duties

   h. _____
      Reason for Leaving

2. a. _____ b. _____ c. _____ d. _____
      From   To   Job Title   Pay Rate

   e. _____ f. _____
      Name of Employer   Address (include city, state, and ZIP code)

   g. _____
      Specific Duties

   h. _____
      Reason for Leaving

F. PERSONAL REFERENCES (Do not include relatives or former employers.)

Name	Address	Phone No.	Occupation	Years Known
1. a. _____	b. _____	c. _____	d. _____	e. _____
2. a. _____	b. _____	c. _____	d. _____	e. _____
3. a. _____	b. _____	c. _____	d. _____	e. _____

I hereby affirm that the information given in this application is true and complete to the best of my knowledge and belief.

G. 1. _____ 2. _____
      Signature   Date

Job Interviews

When you are hunting for a job, the last step will usually be a job interview. The person doing the hiring has examined your letter of application or job application and thinks that you have the right background for the job. Now he or she wants to meet you in order to see what you are like and how you conduct yourself. It is therefore important that you make a good impression.

Here are some guidelines for a successful job interview:

1. Investigate the job beforehand. Find out all you can about the company or business by reading any available printed material and by talking to anyone you know who works for the company or in the same field.
2. Before the interview, practice responding to questions that you are likely to be asked. You will usually be asked to explain the reasons that you are interested in the job and feel qualified for it. You will also be expected to talk about yourself in general—about your background, interests, and plans, for example.
3. Prepare in advance a few questions about the job's duties and responsibilities. Asking a few questions in the course of the interview will show that you have initiative and have thought seriously about the job.
4. Be punctual. In fact, it is best to arrive a few minutes early for the interview.
5. Dress conservatively, and give a well-groomed appearance.
6. Be polite and friendly. At the beginning of the interview, introduce yourself and shake hands before sitting down. At the end, thank the interviewer for his or her time and say that you enjoyed making his or her acquaintance.
7. Speak clearly, and listen carefully. To show that you are being attentive, maintain eye contact with the interviewer when he or she is speaking.
8. Be confident and positive. Make your skills clear, and show that you feel you are qualified for the job.
9. Answer questions honestly and straightforwardly. Do not pretend familiarity with topics about which you know little; instead, express an interest in learning about these subjects.
10. After the interview, it is appropriate to send a brief thank-you letter in which you again state that you enjoyed meeting the interviewer and express thanks for the time he or she spent with you. If you do not hear from the interviewer or company within a few weeks, you may also wish to send a follow-up letter in which you politely ask whether or not you are still being considered for the job.

CHAPTER 31

Listening and Speaking Skills

All spoken communication involves three separate elements:

the sender—the human voice
the message—the spoken words
the receiver—one or more listeners

If any of these elements is missing, the communication is incomplete. A great actor may stand on an empty stage rehearsing a playwright's lines, but if there is no one to hear them, the words do not form a communication. Word sounds may enter someone's ear, but if the mind is not active, the sounds remain only sounds. Finally, the words themselves must be clear, concise, and well chosen to communicate successfully the ideas they are meant to communicate.

In this chapter you will explore the skills necessary for good spoken—or oral—communication. To improve your listening skills, you will learn to practice responsive listening, to listen for main ideas and details, and to listen critically in order to judge the validity of what you hear. To improve your speaking skills, you will study your own voice and learn techniques for making your voice more effective. You will also discover how to enhance your speech with gestures and facial expressions, and you will examine the ways in which you should adapt your speech to different audiences.

After studying listening and speaking skills, you will apply them to two formal speaking situations—an expository speech and a meeting using parliamentary procedure—and to two informal speaking situations—informal directions or explanations and informal group discussions.

Improving Listening Skills

Listening is one of the very first ways an infant learns. You learned to talk by listening first. Then, as you grew, you learned about your world by listening to the voices of those around you. Even today, most of your learning time in school is spent in listening. Because you spend so much time listening, you tend to take it for granted and to forget that it is a skill that can be improved.

Listening involves more than just hearing what a speaker is saying. It also involves thinking along with the speaker. A responsive listener is engaged in an act of discovery to learn the speaker's purpose, to uncover the speaker's main ideas, and to determine the valdity of the speaker's ideas. The responsive listener must focus on what the speaker is saying, keep an open mind to avoid jumping to conclusions, and demonstrate attentiveness through body languages and facial expressions.

A good image to keep in mind when you are trying to focus on what someone else is saying is to think of yourself as a video receiving system that gathers and focuses the signals coming from an outside source. A poorly engineered system allows interference and results in a poor resolution of the signal. A well-designed system results in a clear, crisp, information-packed picture.

EXERCISE 1 **Responsive Listening.** Working with a partner, prepare a four- or five-sentence statement of personal information. As your partner reads his or her statement, focus only on what he or she tells you; do not try to evaluate what you hear. When your partner is finished, wait one minute, and then see if you can tell your partner what you heard. Repeat the process with your partner acting as the listener.

Listening for Main Ideas and Details

When you listen to a speaker, you are often listening for information that you want to be able to understand and remember. You have to determine which information is most important and then focus on that information. Here are some techniques for determining and focusing on the speaker's main ideas and important supporting details:

1. Be sure you understand the speaker's purpose. By understanding the purpose of the speech, you can focus on information that supports the purpose. For example, if the speaker's purpose is to inform you about how to change a typewriter ribbon, information about the typewriter's parts is an important detail. An amusing anecdote about the speaker's experience in changing a typewriter ribbon is not an important detail.
2. Listen for words that tell you where the speaker is heading and how the ideas in the speech are connected. For example, some words indicate a time sequence (*first, then, last*); some show spatial relationships (*near, far, in the middle*); some indicate additional ideas (*besides, too, moreover*); some indicate contrasting ideas (*however, nevertheless*); and some signal results (*therefore, as a result, accordingly*).
3. As you listen, ask yourself questions to help identify the main ideas and supporting details. If, for instance, you have just heard three specific examples, you might ask yourself, "What do these examples support?" By asking yourself questions, you will find that the speaker's ideas will become clearer to you and easier to remember.

4. Listen for words and phrases that signal new terms and definitions—words and phrases like *means, is called,* and *can be defined as.* Terms and their definitions are usually important details.

5. Pay attention to any visual aids that the speaker uses. For example, if a teacher writes a word or a list on the chalkboard as he or she is speaking, you can assume that the word or list is important.

6. As you listen, take notes on the important information. Taking notes will help you to organize the information and to remember it better. Do not try to write everything down; instead, focus on the information that you determine is important. Use abbreviations if you will understand them later, and use words and phrases rather than full sentences. Organize your notes, even if this means rewriting them later. Your notes should be organized to show the relationships between main ideas and supporting details. A good way to organize your notes is to use outline form (see Chapter 32).

EXERCISE 2 **Listening for Main Ideas and Details.** Listen while your teacher or a classmate reads the following passage. As you listen, take notes on the main ideas and important supporting details.

Has anyone stopped to consider the safety problems of car telephones? Advertisers of the new service, obviously trying to downplay the issue, show pictures of cool executives cruising down uncrowded highways, one hand on the wheel and one on the set. But what about the hard-driving, get-it-done-yesterday type fighting his way to work on a crowded urban highway? Will he see those distant brake lights while he's absorbed with closing a multimillion-dollar European deal?

Can drivers safely pick up a telephone, dial it, and talk at length—presumably about subjects that are too important to wait? I don't think so. The car telephone is an invitation to visual, tactile, and auditory conflict. Even if the driver has the expensive "hands-free" option, talking and listening on the phone adds a dangerous sensory complication to driving.

Too often, we accept the consequences of technology without questions about its uses and limits. What is this cellular technology? Is it a tool or a toy? If a toy, it should give the user pleasure and not subject him to unwarranted hazards. If a tool, where concentration is a necessary element, then it should be used in the repose of the back seat or a parkway rest area.

Last year, 50,000 people died in car accidents. To help combat this slaughter, many states are raising drinking ages and almost all have banned the use of stereo headphones by drivers. By allowing driving and telephoning, we are introducing an element of serious distraction, both physical and mental, that can lead to collisions.

Critical Listening

Being a good listener does not mean that you have to suspend your judgment or your ability to evaluate. Critical listeners evaluate what they hear to determine whether or not the information is valid. They are on the alert for **propaganda devices** that aim to persuade listeners through illogical or unreasonable means. Here are some common propaganda devices:

1. **Overgeneralization:** An **overgeneralization** is a statement that jumps to a broad conclusion based on too few facts. "Young people today don't know the value of a dollar" is an example of an overgeneralization. Note that the statement would not be an overgeneralization if it used a qualifying word like *some*: "Some young people . . ."

2. **Stereotyping: Stereotyping** takes the action of one member of a group as indicative of the actions of the entire group. The statement "All female gymnasts are short-legged" is a stereotype that, like all stereotypes, is based on limited observation.

3. **Testimonial:** A **testimonial** aims to persuade people to do something because a famous person does it. The testimonial appeals to emotions, not reason, by implying that if you do what the celebrity does, you will be more like the celebrity. For instance, an advertisement showing an actor or an athlete eating Zappo Cereal is meant to suggest that Zappo Cereal can give the consumer a winning smile, a great build, or another quality that the consumer admires in the actor or the athlete.

4. **Either-or error:** An **either-or error** oversimplifies by stating that only two alternatives exist—either *X* or *Y*. An example is the advertisement "Buy Smiley Toothpaste or you will get cavities." Either-or thinking is faulty because it fails to take into account that other options may be possible. The Smiley Toothpaste ad, for instance, fails to take into account that a number of other toothpastes can help prevent cavities and that toothpaste alone cannot prevent cavities.

5. **Bandwagon:** The **bandwagon** approach attempts to make you think that you should behave in a certain way because everyone else does: "Everybody's doing it; why don't you?" The logic is faulty for two reasons: (a) not everyone is doing it, and (b) even if they were, popularity is not a valid reason.

EXERCISE 3 **Listening for Propaganda Devices.** Listen to commercials on TV or radio to find at least one example of each of the five propaganda devices in the preceding list. Write a short description of each commercial, and explain how it uses the propaganda device to persuade listeners. Discuss your findings with the class.

Improving Speaking Skills

Because listeners react to voices and gestures, the way you look and sound when you speak can be as important as what you say. You have had some practice in listening while other people speak. Now you will have a chance to work on how you as a speaker affect other listeners.

The quality of the sounds you produce is not accidental. You use specific skills to control the way your voice sounds as well as to pronounce words clearly and distinctly. Improving the quality of your voice will increase the effectiveness of your speaking and make you more confident in both formal and informal speaking situations. Keep these qualities in mind:

pronunciation—the clarity and distinctness of your words
volume—the loudness and strength of your voice
tempo—the speed or rate of your speech
pitch—the level or tone of your voice

EXERCISE 4 | **Analyzing Your Voice Production.** Choose a favorite poem or a passage from a story, and read it aloud to a partner or into a tape recorder. Then use the following checklist to analyze the tape recording of your voice, or work with a partner and use the checklist to analyze each other's voices.

1. Do you pronounce words clearly and distinctly?
2. Do you speak at a suitable volume, neither too quietly nor too loudly?
3. Do you speak at a suitable tempo, neither too slowly nor too rapidly?
4. Is the pitch of your voice suitable, neither too high nor too low?
5. Do you vary the volume, tempo, and pitch of your voice to suit your meaning and to avoid sounding monotonous?

Improving Pronunciation and Speaking Expressively

Learning to control pitch, volume, and tempo is often just a matter of concentration. Learning to pronounce words clearly and distinctly calls for greater awareness. Although running words together is common in everyday speech, slurring can become a habit that is hard to break. If you slur or swallow your words, your listeners will have trouble understanding you. Try to separate your words just enough so that they can be heard.

As you become more comfortable with your voice, you will be able to control it so that it helps express the content of your speech or your feelings about what you are saying. For example, you might speak softly (but distinctly) when you read a poem about a mouse, while you might speak loudly when you read a poem about a lion.

EXERCISE 5 **Improving Pronunciation.** Read the following sentences aloud at a volume and tempo that will allow everyone in the class to hear you. Say the words as clearly and distinctly as possible without losing the natural rise-and-fall rhythm of the language.

1. What are you doing?
2. Who is that on the telephone?
3. I don't know what he means.
4. Did you call her yesterday?
5. Why don't you stay until eleven?
6. That's probably not true.
7. Isn't her birthday in February?
8. Lenore asked about the tests.
9. The seniors voted in January.
10. He's going to the library.

EXERCISE 6 **Speaking Expressively.** Choose one of the sentences in Exercise 5, and practice saying it in three different ways, each time expressing a different emotion. For example, you might read sentence 3 in an ordinary, matter-of-fact voice; in an impatient voice; and in a puzzled voice. Have a classmate identify each emotion that you tried to express.

Using Body Language

When you talk to someone, you communicate not only through your words but through your **body language**—your posture, your gestures, and your facial expressions. Body language can add to what you are saying or distract your audience from your speech. Here are some guidelines for improving body language:

1. Stand up straight, but keep your posture relaxed and natural. Since the quality and tone of your voice are affected by your ability to breathe deeply and easily, standing straight makes you sound better as well as look better.
2. Eye contact makes people feel that you are talking *to* them and not *at* them. Move your gaze around the room, and look directly at as many people as possible.
3. Keep your face expressive—that is, show the emotions appropriate to your speech. A stony expression is like a monotonous voice, and it eventually bores the listener.
4. Use gestures and shifts of posture to emphasize ideas or statements that you wish to emphasize. When you are not using your hands to gesture, let them rest quietly.

EXERCISE 7 **Using Body Language.** Working with a partner, act out a situation in pantomime. For example, you might act out a celebrity greeting fans, a police officer issuing a summons, or a circus performer walking a tightrope. Use posture, eye contact, facial expressions, and gestures, but do not use words. Have your partner guess the situation you are acting out.

Adapting Speaking Style to Audience

Without knowing it, you change what you say and how you say it to fit your audience. Good speakers make this change consciously and adapt their speaking style to suit their listeners. Here are some guidelines for adapting your speech to suit your audience:

1. Use the pitch, tempo, and volume that you feel is appropriate. For instance, if you want to excite an audience, use an enthusiastic pitch or tone; if you want to soothe an audience, use a calm tone.
2. Use words that suit your audience. The vocabulary that you use in speaking to your English class, for example, would not be the same as the vocabulary that you use in speaking to a group of small children.
3. Suit your posture and gestures to your audience. For instance, if you are talking to a group of small children, you may want to stoop or sit down.

EXERCISE 8 **Adapting Speaking Style to Audience.** Working with a partner, take turns in role-playing the following situation. Analyze each other's performances by noting how these elements change from audience to audience: (1) pitch, tempo, and volume; (2) choice of words; and (3) posture and gestures.

SITUATION   Explain to each of these audiences the reason that you were late, and apologize for your tardiness.

AUDIENCE   your best friend   one of your teachers
           a parent or a guardian   a four-year-old child
           a student you do not know   an important member of the
           well   community

Applying Listening and Speaking Skills in Formal Situations

A formal speaking–listening situation is a structured one. The structure may vary—an individual speech, a debate, a student government meeting, a panel discussion—but certain elements are always the same. The speakers know the topic of their speeches in advance and have had time to prepare. Their language may be closer to the language of writing than it is to conversation, and their style of presentation also tends to be more formal. In a formal speaking situation, only one person speaks at a time—often for a given length of time. The listeners may or may not have a chance to respond to what they hear.

Expository Speeches

An **expository speech**, like an expository essay, is informative. Its purpose is to explain something, and it is probably the kind of speech that you hear and make most often. For example, your history teacher's explanation of the causes of World War I and the football captain's analysis of last week's winning play are both expository speeches.

The most successful expository speeches are about topics that interest the listeners, and the most successful expository speakers are those who have taken the time to learn a great deal about the topics of their speeches. Follow these guidelines:

1. Make sure that the purpose of your speech—to inform—and the subject of your speech are clear to your audience.
2. Choose and focus your topic to suit the interests of your audience. For example, if you were an expert on Shakespeare and you were talking to a group of sixth graders, you might concentrate on the staging of Shakespearean action scenes. If you were talking to a group of teachers, you might focus on the best way to get students interested in reading Shakespeare.
3. Use definitions, examples, quotations, and statistics to enrich your explanation. If appropriate, use visual aids such as charts, maps, diagrams, pictures, or slides to make your explanation more clear and interesting. Visit the library to research information (see Chapter 34).
4. Prewrite your speech by preparing an outline (see Chapter 32) that shows the main points and supporting details. Also write the opening and closing statements of your speech. Work on an opening statement that captures the attention of the audience—perhaps with a startling statistic, a provocative question, or an entertaining anecdote. Your closing statement should summarize your main ideas and end on a memorable note.

5. Put your opening statement, closing statement, and outline on note cards to which you can refer as you deliver the speech. Number all the note cards so that you can keep them in order.

6. Practice delivering your speech. As you practice, keep this checklist in mind:

   Are your explanations clear? Have you used enough examples?

   Are your sentences simple enough to be understood by a listening audience?

   Have you built in some repetition of your main ideas so that your audience can understand and remember more easily?

   Are the relationships between ideas clear, or do you need more transitions?

   Are you speaking slowly, loudly, and distinctly enough for the audience to hear and understand you?

   Are you varying your voice to make your speech more interesting and to reinforce your meaning?

   Are you looking up to make eye contact with the audience rather than keeping your eyes glued to your note cards?

   Are you using gestures and facial expressions effectively?

   If you are using visual aids, are you comfortable with them? Have you worked them smoothly into your speech?

7. Try to relax when you give the speech. If you feel nervous, use this feeling to advantage by thinking of it as excitement. Excitement will give your presentation energy and interest.

8. During the speech, be aware of the audience's reactions so that you will know when an idea needs to be repeated or explained.

EXERCISE 9 **Preparing and Delivering an Expository Speech.** Prepare an expository speech that will take about eight minutes to deliver. Select a topic with which you are familiar and in which you feel your audience—the class—will be interested. You might select one of the topics below, or you might use a topic of your own choice. Follow the eight preceding guidelines for preparing and delivering an expository speech.

teaching a child to tie shoelaces
what it takes to be a computer hack
ways to make money after school
building stamina through weight training

EXERCISE 10 **Evaluating an Expository Speech.** Illustrate your own listening skills by evaluating your classmates' speeches for Exercise 9. Determine and discuss whether or not each speaker followed the eight guidelines for an effective expository speech.

Parliamentary Procedure

The meetings of organizations such as clubs or committees are often run according to a series of rules called **parliamentary procedure**, so named because the procedure was originally developed for use in the British Parliament. The rules of parliamentary procedure, which are set down in *Robert's Rules of Order*, provide a framework for making decisions or taking action within a group and enable groups to function in an orderly way.

HOW DECISIONS ARE MADE

A meeting of an organization is usually presided over by the president or another leader who does not vote on issues except in a tie vote.

1. When an issue is to be discussed by the members of a group, the president may briefly outline the main points. For instance, the president of the Health Club may begin the discussion: "The club has to decide how to raise money for the class trip. Are there any suggestions?" The president then calls on members who wish to speak.
2. A member who wishes to make a suggestion offers a formal **motion**, or proposal for specific action: "I move that our club have a health-food bake sale on election day."
3. At least one other member must **second the motion**, or express support for it: "I second the motion." If no one seconds the motion, it is automatically dropped.
4. The president announces the motion exactly as it was worded so that everyone is sure of what it says, and he or she then asks for discussion: "It has been moved and seconded that we have a health-food bake sale on election day. Is there any discussion?"
5. Members may express their views either for or against the motion. Those who speak should be sure to stick to the topic.
6. After the discussion, the president restates the motion and then calls for a **vote**: "All those in favor of the motion, say *yes*. All those opposed, say *no*." (Or the vote may be by show of hands.) For some major issues, like the election of officers, paper ballots may be used.
7. The president announces the result of the vote: "The motion is carried" or "The motion is defeated."
8. Sometimes, when a motion is introduced and discussed, a club member may feel that it is basically a good one but should be changed, or **amended**, in some way. Suppose a motion has been made and seconded that the Student Council write to a state senator to support funding for arts programs in the secondary schools. During the discussion and before the vote, a member might say: "I move to amend the motion by adding the words *and the governor* after *state senator*."

9. If the action to amend the original proposal is seconded, the president will restate the motion for amendment, *using the original wording*, and ask for discussion. Only relevant comments should be presented.

10. After discussion (if any), the president calls for a vote: "All those in favor of amending the motion by adding the words *and the governor* after *state senator*, say yes. All those opposed, say *no*." (Or the vote may be by a show of hands.) Then the president announces whether the amendment has been carried or defeated.

11. If the amendment to the action is accepted, the president calls for another vote, because now the newly worded, or amended, motion must be either accepted or defeated. If, on the other hand, the amendment to the motion is defeated, the president—after any additional discussion—would call for a vote on the original motion, as in step 6.

OTHER TYPES OF MOTIONS

A motion that calls for the organization to take some particular action or to support a particular policy is called a **main**, or **principal**, action. Other motions are **procedural**; they determine what steps the organization will take in coming to a final policy decision. Here are the most important procedural motions:

1. After a main motion has been made and seconded, members may feel that the matter should be studied more closely. If so, a motion can be made and seconded to **refer the question to a committee**. The committee may be either one in existence already or one that the president appoints specifically to examine the issue. If the group votes to send the issue to a committee, the original motion is dropped for the time being. If the motion to refer the question to a committee is not **carried**, or accepted, the original motion is considered again.

2. After a main motion has been made and seconded, members may feel that the organization should not consider the question at the present time. If so, a motion can be made and seconded to **table**, or postpone, the main motion—either for a specified time or indefinitely. If the motion to table the question is not carried, the main motion is considered again.

3. Members may decide to cut off a discussion—but only by a two-thirds vote. A motion (which itself cannot be discussed) is made and seconded to **move**, or **call**, the question. If two-thirds of the members present vote in favor of ending the discussion, the president calls for a vote on the original motion. If the motion to **call the question** is not carried, discussion on the main motion can continue.

4. A motion can be made and seconded to **adjourn**, or end, the meeting. Members must vote on the motion without any discussion.

Practicing Parliamentary Procedures. With your teacher or a classmate serving as leader, conduct a class discussion using parliamentary procedure. Include these steps: (1) making the motion, (2) seconding the motion, (3) amending the motion, (4) referring the motion to a committee, and (5) adjournment. Discuss one of the following principal motions or an issue that the class feels is particulary relevant.

Voting on motions is not the only task of an organization's meetings. There is also a prescribed procedure, called **the order of business**, for conducting the entire meeting. The president usually prepares an **agenda**, or list of tasks to be accomplished. It typically includes these tasks:

THE AGENDA FOR THE MEETING

Voting on motions is not the only task of an organization's meetings. There is also a prescribed procedure, called **the order of business**, for conducting the entire meeting. The president usually prepares an **agenda**, or list of tasks to be accomplished. It typically includes these tasks:

1. **Call to order:** The president formally opens the meeting.
2. **Minutes:** The **minutes**, or record, of the previous meeting are read by the secretary and accepted by the members after the group has made any necessary corrections.
3. **Treasurer's report:** The financial officer tells members how much money the club has.
4. **Committee reports:** Various committees may report their findings to the club as a whole.
5. **Old (or unfinished) business:** Members consider matters that were not completed at the previous meeting.
6. **New business:** New issues are brought up and may be voted on.
7. **Program:** If guest speakers or any other special events have been scheduled, the meeting is turned over to them.
8. **Adjournment:** See step 4 on page 656.

Applying Listening and Speaking Skills in Informal Situations

Informal speaking situations—the kind that you are involved in every day—include conversations, requests, and exchanges of information. Unlike formal speaking situations, informal speaking situations are unplanned, and you have no advance knowledge of what you will be talking about. There also tends to be more interaction between you and the people to whom you are talking.

For example, one type of informal speaking situation that most or all of us have experienced is talking over the telephone. A person often has a specific purpose in making a telephone call; however, like other informal speaking situations, talking over the telephone also may involve unplanned conversation about various topics. Moreover, there tends to be a fairly high level of interaction between both parties on the telephone—unless one person is impolitely monopolizing the conversation or the other person is being inattentive to what is being said.

One of the things that you are often asked to do is to tell someone how to get somewhere or how to do something. Giving directions or explanations is a little like giving an expository speech—you are adding to someone else's knowledge, and you should do it in the clearest and most efficient way possible. Unlike a formal speech, however, you have no advance knowledge of what you will need to explain and so have no time to prepare your explanation.

Here are some guidelines for giving clear directions or explanations:

1. Use precise language. Use clear numerical amounts like *two blocks* instead of vague expressions like *a little way*, and use precise nouns and verbs.

2. Tell everything in correct sequence. Use words like *first, second, next,* and *last* to make the sequence clear.

3. When appropriate, use the words and phrases that clarify spatial relationships—words and phrases like *left, right, over, under, at the top of, next to,* and *across from.*

4. Be sure to note any significant checkpoints. For example, in an explanation of how to work a photocopying machine, you would mention that the machine is ready when the red light goes on; in an explanation of how to bake a carrot cake, you would mention that the cake is ready when an inserted toothpick comes out dry.

5. In giving directions, try to include easy-to-spot landmarks, particularly if your listener will be driving to the destination. For example, in your directions you could mention stop signs, traffic lights, parks, gas stations, billboards, large or unusual-looking buildings, store signs, or

any other visual clues that would help the driver stay on course in order to reach a particular location.

6. Pay attention to your listener's reactions. If he or she seems puzzled, attempt to clarify your statements.

7. When you are finished speaking, ask the listener to repeat your directions or explanation. Make sure that everything is clear, accurate, and complete.

EXERCISE 12 **Giving Directions.** Working with a partner, explain how to get from your school to your home. Follow the seven preceding guidelines. When you are finished, your partner will explain how to get from school to his or her home.

EXERCISE 13 **Giving an Explanation.** Explain briefly how to do something—for example, how to set a watch—or how something works—for example, how to work the school photocopying machine. This time the whole class will be your audience. Follow the seven preceding guidelines for giving clear explanations.

Informal Discussions

When you hold a discussion in class, in an afterschool club, or in another group, you are usually trying to make a decision or to reach a conclusion with which most of the group will agree. For example, you may be proposing and evaluating various ideas about a particular problem, with the ultimate goal of achieving a solution to that problem—or at least a compromise.

As you may realize, for any group discussion to "work" everyone in the group needs to recognize the goal of the discussion and needs to cooperate in reaching the goal. When you use parliamentary procedure, the discussion is conducted according to set rules that move you directly toward the goal. In an informal discussion, there are no set rules, but the following guidelines can help make the discussion productive:

1. Remember that everyone taking part in the discussion is responsible for both listening and speaking. When others speak, you should listen as carefully as you would to any speaker in a more formal situation. If you feel it is helpful, take notes on what the speakers say. Try to evaluate what the other members of the group say so that you can respond intelligently. Are they presenting pertinent facts and ideas, or are they simply expressing opinions without backing them up? Are they responding to the questions of others, or are they just saying what they want to say? Are they accurately restating the ideas of other

participants, or are they distorting what the other participants have said? Learn to distinguish fact from falsehood.

2. When it is your turn to speak, you may introduce a new idea if it is appropriate or respond to an idea that has already been presented. If you are in agreement with an idea that has been presented, try to provide additional details to support the idea. If you disagree, state your reasons and back them up with supporting facts and evidence. Remember that criticism is helpful only if it is constructive: Try to offer an alternative idea if you disagree with one that has already been proposed.

3. Be courteous. Make an effort to be aware of how the other members of the group are reacting. Notice who is taking an active part and who is not, who tends to dominate the discussion, and who seems to be reluctant to participate. Try to draw out those who seem shy about speaking by asking them direct questions, inviting their responses, or referring to something they may have said earlier. Learn when to stop talking and to allow others the opportunity to speak. Though you may have several good ideas to share, you must remember that you are participating in a discussion, not giving your own lecture. A good discussion is one in which all participants can share their ideas.

4. Generally, address your remarks to the whole group. However, if you are responding to the ideas of another speaker, address your remarks directly to that person.

5. If the discussion seems to lose direction, introduce the main idea again. You might say something like, "We may be getting a little off the topic here." Taking notes, as mentioned under point 1 of these guidelines, can help you stay on track during the discussion. It can also help you to avoid unnecessarily repeating a point already mentioned.

6. If another speaker's ideas are not presented clearly, help move the discussion forward by politely restating what has been said, perhaps in the form of a question: "Annie, you said that . . . , didn't you?"

7. If someone disagrees with what you have said, defend yourself courteously and thoughtfully. A comment like "I think you may have misunderstood my position" or "Perhaps if I explain . . . , my point will be clearer" will help you avoid a confrontation and keep the discussion on track. Avoid anger and shouting about your ideas or those of another participant. Emotional exchanges will add nothing to your discussion. On the contrary, heated arguments can destroy a discussion and prevent any degree of understanding or compromise. Learning how to "count to ten" and "think before you speak" are clichés, but nonetheless they offer good advice.

EXERCISE 14 **Conducting an Informal Discussion.** Working in groups of six to eight students, conduct an informal discussion on one of the following topics. Try to observe the seven preceding suggestions for successful discussions.

The Best/Worst Shows on Television

Do People Really Learn from Their Mistakes?

Local Government Should Spend More/Less Money on X

Lyrics or Music: Which Is More Important in a Good Song?

Cars Are a Necessity/Luxury

Is Dating Out of Date?

CHAPTER 32

Study and Test-Taking Skills

This chapter will help you learn two skills that are very important to you as a student: how to study and how to take standardized tests. In the first section you will learn ways to become a better listener, reader, and note-taker. In the second section you will examine multiple-choice questions, essay questions, and strategies for answering these questions. You will also answer sample questions from the Preliminary Scholastic Aptitude Test (PSAT), a standardized test that many high school students take in October of their junior year.

Study Skills

Why do some students understand and remember more information than other students? Part of the reason may be that they have a better understanding of how to listen, to read textbooks, and to take notes.

LISTENING SKILLS

A great deal of information that you learn in school is imparted orally. Teachers speak, and you must listen and learn. To be a good listener, you must be an *active listener.* That is, you must completely fill your mind by thinking about what you hear as you hear it. The following five suggestions will help you become an active listener:

1. As you listen, think from time to time about the main points that the speaker has already made.
2. Try to think ahead of the speaker and to figure out the direction his or her speech is taking.
3. Consider what the speaker may be suggesting but not actually saying. In other words, listen "between the lines."
4. Try not to react emotionally to what the speaker is saying until you have heard all of it. If you start to think about how you feel about a particular statement, you may miss what the speaker is saying next.
5. Take notes on the important information.

Sample questions in this section (except for synonym and essay questions) are from *1979 PSAT/NMSQT Student Bulletin* and *Taking the SAT: A Guide to the Scholastic Aptitude Test and the Test of Standard Written English.* Reprinted by permission of the College Board and of Educational Testing Service, copyright owner of the sample questions.

SKILLS FOR READING TEXTBOOKS

Your textbooks are another important source of information that you are expected to learn. Many students do not learn as much as they could from their textbook reading because they do not use the help provided in the textbooks themselves. Headings, introductions, conclusions, and review questions are included in textbooks for the specific purpose of making the material more understandable. Try to follow these suggestions in your textbook reading:

1. Before you begin reading, look at the chapter titles and other headings, the introduction and conclusion, and any review questions. These aids alert you to the main points and important information.
2. As you read, concentrate on the points mentioned in the headings, the introduction and conclusion, and the review.
3. Take notes on the important information.

TAKING NOTES

Whether you are learning information by reading or by listening, taking notes will help you remember and understand the information. Notes have three important purposes. First, they help you learn the material, because the very act of writing something on paper helps to reinforce it in your mind. Second, taking notes forces you to organize the material and thus to understand it better. Third, your notes will serve as reminders when you use them later to study for tests.

In taking notes try to follow these general suggestions:

1. Take notes in your own words. Putting ideas and information into your own language helps you learn the material.
2. Concentrate on the main ideas and important facts. Do not try to write down every word or detail.
3. Be sure to write down key terms and definitions.
4. To save time, use words and phrases rather than complete sentences, and use as many abbreviations and symbols as you can. However, be sure that whatever you are writing will make sense to you when you use the notes again.
5. Organize your notes, even if you must rewrite them. Put related points together, and put subordinate details below the main ideas that they support or illustrate. The most popular method of organizing notes is outlining. Follow these steps.
    I. Use Roman numerals for main ideas.
        A. Use capital letters for ideas supporting main ideas, and list them below the main ideas.
            1. Use Arabic numbers for detailed points supporting capital-letter ideas, and list them below the capital-letter ideas.

Read the following paragraphs from a biology textbook, and think about how you would outline the information that they contain. Then examine the sample outline that follows the paragraphs.

Gnawing Mammals. The gnawers, or rodents, outnumber all of the other mammals. Of the more than 5,000 species of mammals, over 2,000 are rodents. Some, like the mouse, are tiny. Others, like the capybara of South America, may weigh more than 100 pounds. Most rodents are scattered all over the earth as small animals that make their homes in burrows. Some, however, like the squirrels, live in trees. A few, such as the muskrat and beaver, have become adapted to the water. Rats, guinea pigs, and porcupines are also members of this large order, which is called *Rodentia.*

All rodents have two pairs of large, chisellike teeth, called *incisors,* in the front of the mouth. The upper and lower pairs work together like shears to gnaw their food. Although their cutting edges are gradually worn away in the process, the incisors keep on growing throughout the life of the animal. Similarly, if the incisors are not used enough, they may actually grow in a circle and interfere with chewing, in which case the animal may starve.

—Biological Science

I. Rodents (gnawing mammals)
   A. Outnumber all other mammals—2,000 out of 5,000 species
   B. Most small and live in burrows
      1. Squirrels—trees
      2. Muskrat & beaver—water
   C. All have two pairs of incisors (large chisellike front teeth) for gnawing food
      1. Keep growing throughout animal's life
      2. If not used enough, may grow in circle & cause starvation

EXERCISE 1 **Taking Notes.** Read the following paragraph from a home economics textbook, and take notes on the important information. Be sure that your notes are organized to show main ideas, supporting ideas, and supporting details. If you like, try using outline form.

Classes of Wheat. Wheats may be classified on the basis of the time of planting or the growing season, on the color of the kernel, and on the "hardness" or "softness" of the kernel. Wheats that are planted in the spring and harvested in the fall are called *spring wheats,* whereas those that are planted in the fall and harvested the following summer are called *winter wheats.* Since these wheats remain in the ground all winter, they are grown in areas with relatively mild winters. Some wheat kernels have a reddish appearance and are called *red wheats,* whereas others are white. A hard wheat has a hard, vitreous kernel, whereas a soft wheat does not. Hard wheats are usually higher in protein than are soft wheats, and the protein has more baking strength when flour from this wheat is made into dough. Spring wheats include hard red varieties, hard white and soft white varieties, and durum wheats, which are used only for the production of macaroni products. Winter wheats may be hard, semihard, or soft. Hard winter wheats have a fairly strong quality of protein and are suitable for breadmaking purposes.

—Introductory Foods

Standardized Tests

A **standardized test** is designed to be given to large numbers of students. The participants start at a signal, are given the same tasks to complete, and are judged by the same standards. Two types of questions often occur on standardized tests: multiple-choice and essay.

Multiple-Choice Questions

Multiple-choice questions require you to choose the correct answer from two or more possibilities. They test your knowledge and ability to recall facts. Before answering multiple-choice questions, always find out if you will be penalized for a wrong answer. *If there is no penalty for a wrong answer, guess every answer and leave nothing blank. If there is a penalty for a wrong answer, do not guess unless you have eliminated most of the choices and are down to only two or three possible answers out of four or five choices.*

The following sections examine five common kinds of multiple-choice questions used on standardized reading and vocabulary tests: (1) synonym questions, (2) antonym questions, (3) analogy questions, (4) sentence-completion questions, and (5) reading-comprehension questions. The last four types of questions—antonyms, analogies, sentence completions, and reading comprehension—all occur on the verbal portion of the **Preliminary Scholastic Aptitude Test (PSAT)**, a standardized test that most students take in October of their junior year. The PSAT is essentially a shorter version of the Scholastic Aptitude Test (SAT) that many students take for college admission. It is also the qualifying test for the National Merit Scholarship competition and is sometimes called the PSAT/NMSQT. On the Preliminary Scholastic Aptitude Test, there *is* a penalty for a wrong answer. Therefore, you should not guess an answer unless you have narrowed down the choices to two or three possible answers out of the four or five choices given. Cross out the answer choices that you have eliminated so that you can concentrate on the remaining possible answers.

Synonym Questions

Synonyms are words that have the same or nearly the same meaning. For example, *increase* and *grow* are synonyms. Many standardized tests use multiple-choice synonym questions to measure your vocabulary. These questions usually ask you to choose the word or phrase that is closest in meaning to a given word. Here is a sample synonym question:

ASTONISHMENT: (A) confusion (B) interference
(C) amazement (D) resentment (E) dissension

The correct answer is (C), *amazement.*

Follow these strategies when you answer a synonym question:

1. Read *all* the choices before selecting the answer.
2. Remember that few words are exact synonyms; you must decide which word is *closest* in meaning to the given word.
3. If none of the choices seem related to the given word, think about whether the given word has another meaning or can be used as another part of speech—as a verb rather than a noun, for instance. Also consider whether the choices have other meanings or can be used as other parts of speech.
4. If you are uncertain of the answer, try using the given word in a sentence. Then replace it with each of the choices, and decide which choice best retains the meaning of the original sentence.

The preceding sample question illustrates the importance of reading all the choices given. Choice (A), *confusion,* is somewhat related to *astonishment,* but if you had chosen (A) without reading the rest of the choices, you would have chosen the wrong answer. Choice (C), *amazement,* is closest in meaning to the given word.

EXERCISE 2 **Answering Synonym Questions.** Write the letter of the word that is *most nearly the same* in meaning as the word in capital letters.

1. AMBLE: (A) leap (B) stroll (C) enjoy (D) hasten (E) complete
2. GESTURE: (A) movement (B) appearance (C) success (D) merriment (E) position

3. NEBULOUS: (A) unknown (B) calm (C) wealthy (D) dishonest (E) vague
4. STIFLE: (A) evacuate (B) distrust (C) suffocate (D) harass (E) encourage
5. FLIPPANT: (A) impertinent (B) joyful (C) indecisive (D) talkative (E) ridiculous

Antonym Questions

Antonyms are words that have opposite or nearly opposite meanings. For example, *fail* and *succeed* are antonyms. Standardized tests often use multiple-choice antonym questions to measure your vocabulary. These questions ask you to choose the word or phrase that is most nearly opposite in meaning to a given word. Here is a sample antonym question:

> TENSION: (A) dullness (B) laxness (C) balance
> (D) lack of strength (E) lack of purpose

The correct answer is (B), *laxness*.

Follow these strategies when you answer an antonym question:

1. Read *all* the choices before selecting the answer.
2. Remember that few words are exact antonyms; you must decide which word is *most nearly the opposite* of the given word.
3. Remember that many words have more than one meaning or can be used as more than one part of speech.

The preceding sample question illustrates the importance of considering alternative meanings. If you think only of the meaning "nervous strain" for *tension,* you might not realize that *laxness* is an antonym of *tension.* However, if you realize that *tension* can also mean "the tightness of a stretched rope or string," you will recognize that choice (B), *laxness,* which means "looseness," is the best answer.

EXERCISE 3 **Answering Antonym Questions.** Write the letter of the word or phrase that is *most nearly the opposite* of the word in capital letters.

1. STIFF: (A) limber (B) melted (C) succulent (D) twisted (E) silky
2. MYSTIFY: (A) praise (B) evaluate (C) rearrange (D) make clear to (E) be indifferent to
3. NEGLIGENCE: (A) ability (B) carefulness (C) importance (D) immunity (E) consistency
4. EQUILIBRIUM: (A) opposition (B) insignificance (C) lack of freedom (D) lack of contact (E) lack of balance
5. INFERNAL: (A) exquisite (B) frigid (C) ephemeral (D) mortal (E) celestial

Analogy Questions

An **analogy** makes a comparison between things that are alike in certain respects but are otherwise unlike. Analogy questions on standardized tests require you to understand the relationships between pairs of words.

SUBMISSIVE : LED ::

(A) wealthy : employed   (D) incorrigible : taught
(B) intolerant : indulged   (E) inconspicuous : overlooked
(C) humble : humiliated

You should read an analogy question in the following way: *Submissive* **is to** *led* **as** *wealthy* **is to** *employed;* **as** *intolerant* **is to** *indulged;* and so on. Your first step is to figure out the relationship between the given pair of words. Your next step is to choose the pair with the relationship most like the relationship of the given words. In the sample question, the correct answer is choice (E): *Submissive* is to *led* as *inconspicuous* is to *overlooked*.

Follow these strategies when you answer an analogy question:

1. Think about the kind or quality of relationship that exists between the given pair of words. Is the relationship one of large to small? Cause to effect? Group to individual? Part to whole? Are the two words synonyms or antonyms?

2. Pay careful attention to the order of the words in each pair. A pair of words with the relationship of large to small, for example, is not analogous to a pair of words with the relationship of small to large.

3. Make up a sentence expressing the relationship between the given pair of words. Then substitute each of the other pairs of words in your sentence to see which makes the best sense. Be sure to consider *all* the choices before selecting your answer.

In the sample analogy question, the relationship between the given pair of words is one of cause to effect. You could make up this sentence expressing the relationship: "If you are *submissive*, you will be easily *led*." If you then plug in the choices, you will find that choice (E) makes the best sense: "If you are *inconspicuous*, you will be easily *overlooked*."

EXERCISE 4 | **Answering Analogy Questions.** Write the letter of the pair of words that expresses a relationship *most like* the relationship expressed by the pair of words in capital letters.

1. CEDAR : WOOD ::
   (A) textile : silk
   (B) copper : metal
   (C) porcelain : dish
   (D) lace : dress
   (E) clay : brick

2. THIMBLE : FINGER ::
   (A) muzzle : snout
   (B) collar : neck
   (C) bracelet : wrist
   (D) helmet : head
   (E) yoke : shoulder

3. STRUT : PROUD ::
   (A) stroll : eager
   (B) saunter : humble
   (C) scurry : pompous
   (D) shuffle : graceful
   (E) slink : furtive

4. IMMENSE : LARGE ::
   (A) calm : clear
   (B) searing : quick
   (C) glaring : bright
   (D) piercing : mild
   (E) savage : cautious

5. AFFECTATION : GENUINE ::
   (A) accident : premeditated
   (B) praise : complimentary
   (C) declaration : corroborated
   (D) invention : creative
   (E) portrait : distorted

Sentence-Completion Questions

A **sentence-completion question** consists of a sentence that is missing one or two words. You are to select the word or words that best complete the sentence. Your understanding of the incomplete sentence helps you fill in the blanks. Key words within the sentence control the possible word or words that can be substituted for the blanks.

Here is a sample sentence-completion question in which two words are omitted:

> Because many people find Wagner's operas too _____, some recent productions have been _____.
> (A) old . . . outdated
> (B) long . . . abridged
> (C) loud . . . recorded
> (D) strange . . . complicated
> (E) lyrical . . . dramatized

This sentence suggests that in some recent productions the operas have been changed in some way to reduce a characteristic that many people consider excessive. The word that goes in the second blank, therefore, should suggest a reduction of the quality in the first blank. The first terms in several of the answer choices seem to fit into the first blank. However, only choice (B) has a second term that refers to a reduction of the quality in the first term. *Abridged*, which means "shortened," is the logical change that would be made to *long* operas.

Follow these strategies when you answer a sentence-completion question:

1. Be alert to the clues contained in the sentence. The given parts of the sentence will always provide clues to the correct answer.
2. If the sentence has two blanks, try to understand how the missing words are related to each other. For example, are they similar in meaning? Are they opposite? Is the second word a reduction or an increase in the quality identified by the first word?
3. Be sure to consider *all* the choices before selecting the answer.

EXERCISE 5 **Answering Sentence-Completion Questions.** Write the letter of the word or words that *best* complete the meaning of each sentence. Remember to follow the strategies listed on page 669.

Be especially sure to consider all the choices before answering.

1. Even if culture is learned rather than inherited, isn't it possible that what is learned depends upon _____ characteristics?
   (A) environmental
   (B) interrelated
   (C) social
   (D) salient
   (E) innate

2. At that time, the _____ of science was colossal; people believed that science could accomplish almost anything.
   (A) outcome
   (B) obscurity
   (C) prestige
   (D) demise
   (E) imitation

3. Although its publicity has been _____, the film itself is intelligent, well acted, handsomely produced, and altogether _____.
   (A) tasteless . . . respectable
   (B) extensive . . . moderate
   (C) sophisticated . . . amateur
   (D) risqué . . . crude
   (E) perfect . . . spectacular

4. Certain strong individuals believe that they have the right to _____ ordinary people, that they are _____ the moral responsibility that weighs upon the rest of us.
   (A) inveigh against . . . held by
   (B) trample over . . . exempt from
   (C) lead about . . . restrained by
   (D) argue with . . . confused by
   (E) infiltrate among . . . critical of

5. Prominent psychologists believe that people act violently because they have been _____ to do so, not because they were born _____.
   (A) forced . . . gregarious
   (B) forbidden . . . complacent
   (C) expected . . . innocent
   (D) taught . . . aggressive
   (E) inclined . . . belligerent

Reading-Comprehension Questions

Many standardized tests include questions based on reading passages of varying length and difficulty. These **reading-comprehension questions** are usually designed to test your understanding of the passage in several specific ways. The questions will usually ask you to do the following:

1. Understand the main idea of the passage.
2. Recall or identify facts and ideas in the passage.
3. Make inferences, or conclusions, from the facts and ideas given.
4. Evaluate the author's purpose, tone, or attitude.

Here is a sample passage followed by five reading-comprehension questions. Try to answer the questions initially on your own.

> The Mescalero Apache tribe is one of seven linguistically and culturally related peoples whose aboriginal territories stretched over large sections of present-day southwestern United States and northeastern Mexico. The Mescalero were characterized by an economic system that harmonized well with their challenging environment. In late historic times they attempted desultory farming along some watercourses, but the severe weather and short growing season of the mountains and the precarious water supply of the lowlands did not encourage cultivation of the soil. Thus the Mescalero were forced to depend on hunting and the gathering of wild harvests.
>
> Such an economy required mobility; there had to be readiness to follow the food harvests when and where they matured and to move from one hunting area to another when the supply of game dwindled. A concentration of population was inappropriate to such techniques of food procurement. As a result, the population was thinly dispersed over the immense range.
>
> Since most economic errands were carried out in small groups, there was little incentive for highly centralized leadership. It is probable that never in its history did the tribe have a single leader who was recognized and followed by all. Rather, the Mescalero leader, or "chief" (literally "he who speaks"), was, as his title suggests, a respected adviser drawn from the heads of the families who tended to camp and move together.
>
> Since he had no coercive power, he had to understand what his followers were willing to do. Serious misjudgments or unpopular counsel might cost him his position or a portion of his followers. Theoretically, the office of the leader was not hereditary; in practice, there was a tendency for sons of leaders to succeed their fathers. This was informal, however, not absolute. Typical situations which required a leader's judgment included such problems as whether to move to another site because of poor luck in hunting, repeated deaths, epidemic disease, or the proximity of enemies; whether to sanction a raid or war party; whether to sponsor an important social or ritual event to which outsiders might be invited; and what to do

about disruptive behavior such as the practice of witchcraft. The ability to lead successful raids and war parties, as well as to sanction them, was a great asset for a leader; such expeditions meant booty, and this made it possible to distribute favors widely. In a society where generosity was one of the cardinal virtues, such activity built and sustained the good will important to a leader.

1. The primary purpose of the passage is to
   (A) raise a question   (D) discuss an event
   (B) draw a comparison   (E) identify a cause
   (C) describe a group

Question 1 requires you to evaluate the author's purpose. You must decide what kind of writing the passage represents. The answer is (C), because the entire passage is a description of the Mescalero Apache tribe. It includes none of the kinds of writing mentioned in the other choices.

2. The author states that one of the personal qualities held to be of prime importance among the Mescalero Apache was
   (A) gratitude   (D) cautiousness
   (B) generosity   (E) cleverness
   (C) honesty

Question 2 requires you to recall facts from the passage. In this case the correct answer is (B), because the author says that "generosity was one of the cardinal virtues" of the tribe.

3. It can be inferred that the political organization of the Mescalero Apache tribe most resembled which of the following?
   (A) a modified democracy   (D) a form of theocracy
   (B) a fascist state   (E) a military dictatorship
   (C) an institutional monarchy

Question 3 requires you to make an inference. You must analyze factual information in the passage and reach a conclusion about the category or pattern into which the information fits. As you can see from the choices, you must have a general familiarity with the vocabulary of political organization to be able to answer the question. The passage states that the tribe probably never had a single leader who was acknowledged by everyone. The man who served as a leader when necessary was simply an adviser with no power of command. This information eliminates choices (B), (C), and (E), all of which are characterized by strong central leadership. Choice (D), *a form of theocracy*, refers to government by religious leaders, but the passage does not suggest that the leader had a religious role. Choice (A), *a modified democracy*, is the best answer.

4. It can be inferred that leading war parties reinforced a leader's power primarily by enabling him to
   (A) ensure that his power would be passed on to his son
   (B) reinforce the self-respect of his warriors
   (C) extend the boundaries of the territory over which he held authority
   (D) divert the people's attention from such problems as disease or poor luck in hunting
   (E) secure the enemies' goods for dispensation to the members of his tribe

Question 4 again requires you to make an inference. Notice that it asks you to choose the *primary* way in which leading war parties reinforced the leader's power. All of the choices are plausible answers. However, (E) is the only one mentioned by the author. Therefore, it is safe to conclude that it is the most important.

5. The author is primarily concerned with discussing
   (A) some economic and political aspects of life among the Mescalero
   (B) the dispersion of seven Apache tribes in the United States and Mexico
   (C) some tribal rituals of the Mescalero
   (D) special qualifications of a leader of the Mescalero
   (E) some effects of the Mescalero economy on the tribal hierarchy

Question 5 requires you to understand the main idea of the passage. To answer the question, you must differentiate between the main idea and secondary ideas contained in the passge. Although choices (B), (D), and (E) are discussed in the passage, choice (A) *best* describes the subject of the passage as a whole.

Follow these strategies when you answer a reading-comprehension question in order to improve your mastery of such items:

1. Before you read the passage, glance at the questions at the end to get an idea of what you should be looking for when you read.

2. As you read the passage, concentrate on *what* is being said and on *how* it is being said. Underline the main idea and key details so that you can find answers quickly.

3. In answering the questions, be sure to consider *all* the choices and to choose the *best* answer from the choices given.

Essay Questions

Essay questions require you to write answers of several paragraphs or longer. They measure your ability to think clearly, to organize facts and knowledge, and to communicate ideas in coherent language.

Here is a sample essay question from a history test:

> Analyze the factors that led to the fall of ancient Rome. In your analysis be sure to include at least three factors and to support general statements with specific facts and examples.

Follow these strategies when you answer an essay question:

1. Read the question carefully. Look for key words that tell you what you are expected to do—words like *compare, contrast, analyze, explain, describe, prove, define,* or *summarize.* Be sure to answer all parts of the question and to fulfill any requirements about the number of factors or examples you are to give.

2. Prewrite your answer by listing the information that you plan to cover. You may find that the best way to list your information is to use outline form (see pages 663–664).

3. In your opening pargraph write a thesis statement that clearly expresses the general idea of your essay. Often your thesis statement will restate portions of the essay question. For instance, an essay answering the sample question might open with this thesis statement: "The three chief factors that led to the fall of ancient Rome were *X, Y,* and *Z.*"

4. Organize the body of your essay into paragraphs, each of which has a single main idea related to the general idea in your thesis statement. For example, if you were answering the sample essay question and using the opening statement suggested in item 3, the main idea of the first paragraph of the body of your essay would be that *X* was a factor that led to the fall of ancient Rome; the main idea of the second paragraph of the body would be that *Y* was a factor that led to the fall of ancient Rome; the main idea of the third paragraph of the body would be that *Z* was a factor that led to the fall of ancient Rome. State the main idea of each paragraph of the body in a topic sentence (see Chapter 3). Then go on to support the main idea with specific facts and examples.

5. Use transitions like *therefore, in effect, however, nevertheless, next,* and *last* so that sentences and paragraphs run together smoothly.

6. Conclude with a statement or a paragraph that summarizes the main idea of your essay.

7. Reread your essay to see if it needs revision. Look especially for important points that you may have omitted.

8. Proofread your essay to make sure that grammar, usage, spelling, punctuation, and capitalization are all correct.

EXERCISE 6 **Taking a Sample Standardized Test.** The following exercise contains questions similar to those that appear on the Preliminary Scholastic Aptitude Test (PSAT). Each group of questions has its own instructions.

A. **Antonym Questions.** Write the letter of the word or phrase that is *most nearly opposite* in meaning to the word in capital letters.

1. AGILE: (A) humble (B) clumsy (C) useless (D) timid (E) ugly
2. NULLIFY: (A) examine (B) ascertain (C) slander (D) react (E) validate
3. INGENIOUS: (A) incredible (B) unintentional (C) instinctive (D) unimaginative (E) innate
4. SHIFTLESS: (A) covert (B) ubiquitous (C) industrious (D) compelling (E) opinionated
5. LOQUACITY: (A) blasphemy (B) boastfulness (C) reticence (D) servility (E) insolence

B. **Analogy Questions.** Write the letter of the pair of words that *best* expresses a relationship similar to the relationship expressed by the pair of words in capital letters.

1. WRITER : ROYALTY ::
   (A) donor : charity
   (B) shareholder : dividend
   (C) accountant : debit
   (D) banker : finance
   (E) tenant : rent
2. RIFT : UNITY ::
   (A) flaw : variety
   (B) snag : identity
   (C) blot : darkness
   (D) spark : brilliance
   (E) ripple : smoothness
3. TROWEL : BRICKLAYER ::
   (A) bark : woodsman
   (B) hinge : locksmith
   (C) porcelain : potter
   (D) ceiling : plasterer
   (E) chisel : stonecutter
4. SOLITAIRE : GAME ::
   (A) monotone : spectrum
   (B) monologue : speech
   (C) employee : corporation
   (D) airplane : travel
   (E) chapter : book
5. ASTRAL : STAR ::
   (A) universal : galaxy
   (B) celestial : comet
   (C) stellar : moon
   (D) terrestrial : earth
   (E) planetary : sun

C. **Sentence-Completion Questions.** Write the letter of the word or set of words that *best* completes each sentence.

1. If your garden plot is small, it will not pay to grow crops that require a large amount of _____ in order to develop.
   (A) moisture
   (B) rain
   (C) fertilizer
   (D) space
   (E) care

2. If we survey the development of dancing as an art in Europe, we recognize two streams of tradition that have sometimes _____ and yet remain essentially _____.
   (A) changed . . . modern
   (B) divided . . . separate
   (C) abated . . . primitive
   (D) merged . . . distinct
   (E) advanced . . . comparable

3. They argue that the author was determined to _____ his own conclusion, so he _____ any information that did not support it.
   (A) uphold . . . ignored
   (B) revise . . . destroyed
   (C) advance . . . devised
   (D) disprove . . . distorted
   (E) reverse . . . confiscated

4. Mr. Dillon is a skeptic, _____ to believe that the accepted opinion of the majority is generally _____.
   (A) prone . . . infallible
   (B) afraid . . . misleading
   (C) inclined . . . justifiable
   (D) quick . . . significant
   (E) disposed . . . erroneous

5. The excitement does not _____ but _____ her senses, giving her a keener perception of a thousand details.
   (A) slow . . . diverts
   (B) blur . . . sharpens
   (C) overrule . . . constricts
   (D) heighten . . . aggravates
   (E) forewarn . . . quickens

CHAPTERS 28–32   SKILLS

CHAPTER 28   VOCABULARY SKILLS

Using Context Clues and Greek and Latin Roots [pages 604–606 and 611–613]   Determine the meaning of the underlined work in each sentence.

1. An aqueduct linked the reservoir to smaller underground pipes.
(a) highway (b) large water pipe (c) small air vent (d) faucet
2. Chronic bronchitis is a serious health condition.
(a) clocklike (b) comic (c) recurring over time (d) related to germs
3. As she spoke, the speaker kept her notes on the lectern.
(a) long speech (b) chalkboard (c) tall reading desk (d) writing pad

Using Prefixes and Suffixes   [pages 607–611]   Identify the word that could replace the awkward underlined portion of each sentence without changing the meaning of the sentence.

4. The film's joint stars both received Academy Award nominations.
(a) costars (b) ex-stars (c) nonstars (d) superstars
5. His behavoir is cruel and lacking in pity.
(a) piteous (b) pitiable (c) pitiful (d) pitiless
6. The singer has a lyrical style tending to express things.
(a) expression (b) expressive (c) expressly (d) inexpressible

Using Foreign Expressions and synonyms   [pages 614 and 615–616] Identify the synonym for each expression in capital letters.

7. AVANT-GARDE: (a) advanced (b) bazaar (c) conventional (d) taboo
8. CARTE BLANCHE: (a) freedom (b) menu (c) purity (d) wisdom

Using Words from Proper Names and Antonyms   [pages 614–615 and 617]   Identify the antonym for each word in capital letters.

9. QUIXOTIC: (a) flexible (b) gauche (c) loathsome (d) practical
10. BRAGGADOCIO: (a) exuberance (b) fiasco (c) grandeur (d) modesty

CHAPTER 29   SPELLING SKILLS

Using Spelling Rules   [pages 620–626]   For each item identify the one word that is spelled correctly.

1. (a) changeable (b) disatisfied (c) journies (c) preferrence
2. (a) chandelier (b) refered (c) sulfer (d) supercede
3. (a) conceed (b) potatos (c) subtly (d) theif

Distinguishing Between Easily Confused Words [pages 626–628]
Identify the one underlined word that is spelled correctly in each of the
following sentences.

4. The (a) <u>stationery</u> store has been (b) <u>holy</u> remodeled and offers a
   greater selection (c) <u>then</u> it (d) <u>formally</u> did.
5. When (a) <u>lightening</u> (b) <u>envelopes</u> an airplane, it can (c) <u>affect</u> the pilot
   and cause him or her to (d) <u>loose</u> control.

CHAPTER 30   BUSINESS LETTERS, APPLICATIONS, AND INTERVIEWS

Examining Business Letters and Forms [pages 632–644]   Select the
answer that best completes each of the following.

1. A business letter written in block style uses
   (a) no space between paragraphs   (c) a colon after the closing
   (b) unindented paragraphs   (d) headings

2. The correct salutation for a letter addressed to Ms. Lee Wilson is
   (a) Dear Ms. Wilson: (c) Both *a* and *b* are correct.
   (b) Dear Lee Wilson: (d) Neither *a* nor *b* is correct.

3. A letter of application should always
   (a) be addressed to a specific person   (c) use full-block style
   (b) provide business references   (d) name the position

4. When you fill out a form, you should always
   (a) use ink   (c) leave inapplicable items blank
   (b) read it first (d) list family members as references

CHAPTER 31   LISTENING AND SPEAKING SKILLS

Examining Listening Skills and Speaking Skills [pages 646–661]
Select the answer that best completes each of the following items.

1. "Everyone is buying Achoo Tissues. Why don't you try them?" This
   advertisement uses the illogical propaganda device known as
   (a) stereotyping (b) testimonial (c) either/or thinking (d) bandwagon
2. The main purpose of an expository speech is to
   (a) inform (b) persuade (c) entertain (d) tell a story

CHAPTER 32   STUDY AND TEST-TAKING SKILLS

Answering a Synonym Question [pages 666–667]   Identify the word
that is *most nearly the same* in meaning as the word in capital letters.

1. IMPLAUSIBLE: (a) impromptu (b) influential (c) unique (d) unlikely

Answering an Antonym Question [page 667]   Identify the word that is
most nearly the opposite of the word in capital letters.

2. PRELUDE: (a) adjunct (b) aftermath (c) commentary (d) solitude

Answering an Analogy Question   [pages 668–669]   Identify the pair of words that expresses a relationship *most like* the relationship expressed by the pair of words in capital letters.

3. IMMODEST : EGOISTIC :: (a) aplomb : elite   (c) childish : infantile
                                    (b) awed : canny   (d) vengeful : angry

Answering a Sentence-Completion Question   [pages 669–670]   Identify the word or words that *best* complete the following sentences.

4. Despite her _____ claims, the gymnast performed only adequately.
    (a) anonymous (b) grandiose (c) orthodox (d) marginal

5. _____ by her _____ behavior, the teacher asked her to leave the room.
    (a) Delighted . . . forthright
    (b) Puzzled . . . ingratiating
    (c) Exasperated . . . cantankerous
    (d) Enchanted . . . charming
    (e) Encouraged . . . improving

Resources

Thinking About Thinking:
Asking Questions

The dictionary, the thesaurus, and the library are three of a writer's most valuable resources. They are tools for problem solving, and as you grow as a writer, you will need to use them in more and more sophisticated ways. As you need to answer more difficult questions, you will also need to develop your own inquiry skills—your ability to gather information from resources.

Defining the Skill

One thinking skill that is essential to gathering information is ASKING QUESTIONS. Children ask a great many questions about everything. However, a skillful thinker learns to ask the right questions in the right words and in the right order. For example, you need to ask, "What are the primary colors?" before you ask, "Which primary colors make orange?" Questions always generate more questions. The right questions open up the resource, enabling you to get the most out of it.

Applying the Skill

Look at the photograph, and list twenty questions that could be asked about it. You may want to start by asking, "Who lives here?" Then identify the questions that are most interesting to you, questions you would like to write about.

CHAPTER 33

The Dictionary and the Thesaurus

A dictionary and a thesaurus are two kinds of reference books providing important information that you will find extremely helpful when you are writing. This chapter examines dictionaries, thesauruses, and the important information that they provide.

The Dictionary

A **dictionary of the English language** is an alphabetical list of words, their meanings, and other useful information about the words.

An **unabridged dictionary** is the largest and most complete kind of dictionary. It lists over 400,000 words and gives detailed information about their histories and usage. Two of the best-known unabridged dictionaries are the *Oxford English Dictionary,* or *OED,* and *Webster's Third New International Dictionary, Unabridged.* Because most unabridged dictionaries consist of many volumes and are quite expensive, people usually consult them at a library.

A **college dictionary**, also called a **desk dictionary** or a **collegiate dictionary**, is an abridgment, or shortened form, of an unabridged dictionary. It contains from 150,000 to 200,000 words and provides less detailed histories and examples of usage than an unabridged dictionary provides. College dictionaries are convenient for everyday use and adequate for most students' purposes. Four of the most popular college dictionaries in America are *Webster's New World Dictionary of the American Language, Second College Edition; Webster's Ninth New Collegiate Dictionary;* the *Random House College Dictionary;* and the *American Heritage Dictionary.*

A **concise**, or **condensed**, **dictionary** is an abridgment of a college dictionary. Because it contains fewer words and often omits examples and word histories, a concise dictionary alone cannot meet the needs of most high school students.

While all college dictionaries contain similar information, no two dictionaries are exactly alike. For example, some dictionaries use abbreviations or symbols to indicate foreign words and expressions used in English; others put foreign words and expressions in a special section near the back of the book. To save time and get the most benefit from your dictionary, it is important to examine its contents and its explanation of its abbreviations and symbols. The **table of contents** and a **list of abbreviations and symbols** are usually near the front section of the dictionary.

The main part of a dictionary is composed of alphabetically arranged word **entries**. Although the style of these entries varies slightly from dictionary to dictionary, most entries contain the same valuable information. In the model dictionary entries that follow, the different kinds of information have been labeled. The following sections explain the labels in detail.

The Entry Word

The **entry word** is the word being examined. Entry words are listed alphabetically in the main section of a dictionary and appear in bold (dark) print. To make specific entries easier to find, some dictionaries have **thumb indexes** that show you where the entries for each new letter of the alphabet begin. Dictionaries also print two guide words at the top of each page. The **guide words** identify the first and last entry word on the page. All other entry words on the page fall alphabetically between the two guide words.

Homographs, or words that have the same spellings but different origins and meanings, are listed separately with superscript (raised) numbers after each entry word. See the model for the entry words *tell*[1] and *tell*[2].

Names of people are listed with the last name first. Sometimes a dictionary does not list people in its main section but instead lists them in a separate **biographical section** near the back of the book.

The entry word shows you two important things about the word you are looking up—its **spelling** and its **syllabification**. It may also give you information about **capitalization**.

SPELLING

Dictionaries provide correct spellings for all entry words. You can use a dictionary to check the spellings of words and to find out if compound words are spelled as solid, hyphenated, or two-word compounds.

MODEL DICTIONARY ENTRIES

ENTRY WORD ——— **tell**[1] (tel) vt. **told, tell'ing** [ME *tellen* < OE. *tellan*, lit., to
INFLECTED FORMS ——— calculate, reckon < Gmc. **taljan,* whence G. z̄ahlen, to
reckon, count: for IE. base see TALE] **1.** orig., to enumerate;
count; reckon **2.** to relate in order; narrate ; recount [to *tell* a
story] **3.** to express in spoken or written words; utter; say
EXAMPLE ——— [*tell* the facts, *tell* the truth] **4.** to report; announce; publish
DEFINITION ——— **5.** to reveal; disclose; make known [a smile that *told* her
joy] **6.** to recognize; distinguish; discriminate [unable to
tell one from the other] **7.** to decide; know [one can't *tell*
what will happen] **8.** to let know; inform; acquaint [*tell* me
about the game] **9.** to request; direct; order; command [*tell*
him to leave] **10.** to state emphatically; assure [it's there, I
PART OF SPEECH ——— *tell* you] **—vi. 1.** to give an account or description (*of*
something) **2.** to give evidence or be an indication (*of*
something) **3.** to carry tales; reveal secrets [to kiss and *tell*]
4. to produce a result; be effective; have a marked effect
IDIOMS ——— [efforts that are beginning to *tell*] ——**tell off 1.** to count
(persons, etc.) and separate from the total number **2.**
USAGE LABEL ——— [Colloq.] to rebuke severely ——**tell on 1.** to tire; wear out
2. [Colloq.] to inform against or gossip about **SYN.——tell,**
SYNONYMS ——— in this connection, is the simple, general word meaning to
convey the facts or details of some circumstances or
occurrence [*tell* me what happened]; **relate** suggests the
orderly telling of something that one has personally
experienced or witnessed [*relate* your dream to us];
recount implies the telling of events in consecutive order
and in elaborate detail and, hence, often takes a plural
object [to *recount* one's adventures]; **narrate** suggests the
SUBJECT LABEL ——— use of the techniques of fiction, such as plot development,
ETYMOLOGY ——— building up to a climax, etc. [to *narrate* the story of one's
life]; **report** suggests the recounting for others' information
PRONUNCIATION ——— of something that one has investigated or witnessed [he
will *report* the convention proceedings] See also REVEAL.[1]
ADDITIONAL ——— **tell**[2] (tel) *n.* [Ar. *tall,* a mound] *Archaeol.* an artificial mound
FORM or hill covering the successive remains of ancient
communities

—from *Webster's New World Dictionary, Second College Edition*

The current edition of *Webster's New World Dictionary* indicates that
folklore is a solid compound, *folk-rock* is hyphenated, and *folk tale* is two
words.

Dictionaries also list **variant spellings** and the preferred variant. Often
preferred spellings are first in an entry: **usable, useable.** (*Usable* is the
preferred spelling.) *Also* may indicate a less-accepted spelling: **usable** *also,*

useable. Sometimes the preferred spelling is a main entry and the less-accepted spelling has a separate entry with a cross-reference: **useable** *same as* USABLE. If a variant spelling is accepted only or mainly in Britain, an American dictionary will label it a British or chiefly British spelling.

SYLLABIFICATION

Most dictionaries break multisyllabic entry words into syllables by using spaces or midline dots. For example, the three-syllable word *tellable* would be broken into syllables as follows: **tell·a·ble**. Thus, if you have to type *tellable* on two lines, the entry word tells you to hyphenate it after the second *l* or after the *a*.

CAPITALIZATION

Dictionaries capitalize entry words that are always capitalized, as in the following entry: *Tell, William*. For words that are sometimes but not always capitalized, a dictionary clarifies the instances in which capital letters may or should be used. For instance, while the entry word *earth* is not capitalized in *Webster's New World Dictionary,* the entry says [*occas.*/**E**-], meaning "occasionally capital E," before the definition "the planet that we live on." The entry for *constitution* says [**C**-], meaning "always capital C," before defining the chief document under which America is governed.

PRONUNCIATION

Dictionaries tell you the correct **pronunciation** of each entry word. If a word has more than one acceptable pronunciation, its different pronunciations will be provided. Usually the pronunciation is given in parentheses, brackets, or slanted lines right after the entry word. Pronunciations in the model are given in parentheses.

Because there are only twenty-six letters in the alphabet but over forty sounds in spoken English, dictionaries use a special set of symbols, called **phonetic symbols**, to represent these spoken sounds. Different dictionaries use different phonetic symbols; for example, one dictionary shows the pronunciation of *youth* as (yo͞oth), while another shows it as [ūth]. To understand the sounds represented by a dictionary's phonetic symbols, consult its **pronunciation key**. The full pronunciation key appears near the front of the dictionary, while a short form usually appears at the bottom of each right-hand page.

When a word contains more than one syllable, the pronunciation indicates the syllable or syllables that are **stressed**, or emphasized. To indicate stressed syllables, dictionaries use **accent marks** (′) either before or after the stressed syllables. For example, the pronunciation for *tellable* shows that the first syllable is stressed: (tel ′ə b'l).

PART OF SPEECH

Dictionaries tell you the **part of speech** of each entry word. Usually the part of speech is abbreviated and italicized. Abbreviations include *n.* for *noun, vt.* for *transitive verb, vi.* for *intransitive verb, adj.* for *adjective,* and *adv.* for *adverb.* The abbreviation is placed before the definition or definitions to which it applies. For example, in the entry for *tell*[1] in the model, the *vt.* before the first ten definitions indicates that these definitions are for *tell* as a transitive verb; *vi.* then indicates that the next four definitions are for *tell* as an intransitive verb. Some dictionaries have separate entries for each part of speech.

INFLECTED FORMS

Inflected forms include plurals of nouns and the past tense and past participles of verbs. When these forms are irregular or confusing, a dictionary lists them in bold print near the entry word. For example, since *told,* the past tense and past participle of the verb *tell,* is irregular, the entry for *tell*[1] lists *told* after the entry word. If the past tense and past participle are different, a dictionary lists the past tense first.

Plurals of nouns that are formed by adding *s*—or *es* for nouns that end in *ch, s, sh, x, z*—are considered regular and are generally not listed in dictionaries. Irregular plural forms, however, are listed in bold print near the entry word. If there is more than one acceptable plural, the dictionary will list all acceptable forms, with the *preferred* plural listed first.

When comparative and superlative forms of two-syllable adjectives are not made by adding *more* or *most,* a dictionary lists them in bold print near the entry word. For example, in the entry for *pretty,* a dictionary will list *prettier* and *prettiest.*

ETYMOLOGY

The **etymology** is the origin and history of a word. Most dictionaries include a word's etymology in brackets or parentheses before or after its definitions. Etymologies in the model are given in brackets before the definitions. The etymology for *tell*[2] indicates that the noun comes from the Arabic (abbreviated *Ar.*) word *tall,* which means "a mound."

SUBJECT AND USAGE LABELS

If a word or a definition is restricted in its use, many dictionaries include a subject or usage label explaining the restriction. **Subject labels** like *Music* or *Chemistry* indicate that a word or a definition is restricted to a particular field or study. **Usage labels** indicate other restrictions; for example, a word may be rare, archaic, obsolete, colloquial, slang, or restricted to a particular region or dialect. Subject and usage labels immediately precede the definition or definitions to which the restriction applies. They are often abbreviated and may be italicized or put in brackets or parentheses. In the entry for *tell*[2], the subject label *Archaeol.* indicates that the noun *tell* is a term used in the field of archaeology.

DEFINITIONS AND EXAMPLES

An important function of a dictionary is to provide the **definitions**, or meanings, of words. If a word has more than one definition, each definition is numbered. Definitions for each part of speech are numbered separately. For example, in the entry for *tell*[1], the ten definitions of the transitive verb *tell* are numbered 1 to 10; new numbers are given to the four definitions of the intransitive verb *tell*.

In order to illustrate a particular definition, dictionaries sometimes include **examples** showing the word used in context. For instance, to illustrate the second definition of *tell*[1], the example "to *tell* a story" is given in brackets. Sometimes dictionaries include sketches, diagrams, or charts to illustrate or clarify definitions.

IDIOMS

Toward the end of an entry for a particular word, dictionaries may list and define common **idioms**, or expressions, in which the word is a key element. Usually these idioms appear in bold print. In the entry for *tell*[1], the dictionary lists and defines the expressions *tell off* and *tell on*.

SYNONYMS AND ANTONYMS

Dictionaries sometimes list **synonyms** or **antonyms** for an entry word. Usually they are labeled *Syn.* or *Ant.* and listed near the end of the entry. At the end of the entry for *tell*[1] in the model, a long section clarifies the different synonyms for the verb *tell*. In an entry for the adjective *telling*, you might find the following: **SYN.** See VALID. This cross-reference indicates that more synonyms for *telling* are given in the entry for *valid*.

ADDITIONAL FORMS

At the end of an entry, dictionaries sometimes list **additional forms** of the entry word. These forms usually appear in bold print without definitions. For example, at the end of the entry for the adjective *telling*, the adverb form *tellingly* is listed. From your knowledge of suffixes (see Chapter 28) and from the two definitions of *telling*, you can figure out that *tellingly* must mean "in an effective, forceful, or striking manner" or "in a manner that tells or reveals much."

EXERCISE 1 **Using a Dictionary.** Consult a college dictionary before writing your answers to each question.

1. Which of these words are spelled incorrectly? What are the correct spellings?
   (a) fieldmouse   (c) Rio de Janeiro
   (b) canteloupe   (d) wild-life
2. Is *fulfil* or *fulfill* the preferred American spelling? Where would you hyphenate the word?
3. Is *Lettish* always capitalized? What does it mean?
4. Does the word *queue* rhyme with *ski* or with *skew*?
5. Which syllable in *hexameter* is stressed? Can *hexameter* be used as an adjective? If so, with what meaning?
6. What are the past tense and past participle of *smite*?
7. What are the different origins of the two homographs spelled *fan*? What usage label, if any, does your dictionary give for either homograph?
8. What does the idiom *(to) pull (one's) punches* mean?
9. Does your dictionary list synonyms or antonyms for the word *obscure*? If so, what are they?
10. Does your dictionary list an adverb form of *suppliant* in the entry for the adjective *suppliant*? If so, identify and define the adverb.
11. What is the preferred plural of the noun *buffalo*? What other plural forms are acceptable?
12. Where would you hyphenate the word *language*? What is the etymology of the word?
13. Can *crude* be used as a noun? If so, with what meaning?
14. What are the comparative and superlative forms of the adjective *witty*? Of the adjective *beautiful*?
15. Who was *Vincent van Gogh*? When did he live? Should the *van* in his name begin with a capital *v*?

The Thesaurus

A **thesaurus** is a book or a list of words, their synonyms, and sometimes their antonyms.

The process of using a thesaurus is different from the process of using a dictionary. When you use a dictionary, you start with a word and find a meaning. When you use a thesaurus, you start with a meaning and find a word. For example, suppose you want to say that your brother annoys you but wish to use a word stronger than *annoys*. You can use a thesaurus to help you find that word.

Many thesauruses arrange entries alphabetically. In these thesauruses you would simply look up *annoy* to find a stronger synonym. Entries are subdivided according to part of speech and are followed by lists of synonyms. Antonyms may be listed as part of an entry, or a cross-reference may direct you to them.

Other thesauruses arrange entries in numbered categories based on the ideas they represent. Finding a word in this type of thesaurus is a two-step procedure. To find a stronger synonym for *annoy*, first look up *annoy* in the alphabetical index at the back of the thesaurus. In the index to *Roget's International Thesaurus*, you would find:

annoy vex 830.5
    aggravate 835.1
    provoke 900.10

Choosing *vex* as the word closest to the sense you are trying to convey, you turn to item 830.5. There you would find a list of synonyms including *torment, pester, plague, harass, bother,* and *persecute.* You can then choose the synonym that you feel is most appropriate. Before making your choice you may need to look up the precise meanings of the synonyms in a dictionary.

EXERCISE 2   **Using a Thesaurus.** Use a thesaurus to find and write two synonyms for each word below.

1. angry	5. hidden	9. sturdy
2. elegant	6. hinder	10. villain
3. flexible	7. nice	
4. generous	8. shy	

SENTENCE WRITING   **Using Synonyms.** Write an original sentence that illustrates the meaning of each synonym you found in Exercise 2. Before writing your sentences, you may wish to consult a dictionary to find the precise meaning of each synonym.

CHAPTER 34

The Library

Libraries are valuable information centers. Most **public libraries** and **school libraries** (sometimes called **learning resource centers** or **media centers**) contain a wide variety of materials that can help you with your research and writing. Libraries keep their materials in a specially organized fashion, and you should be aware of how the various items are arranged. This chapter looks at the different types of materials available at libraries and explains how to find and use the materials.

Fiction and Nonfiction Books

Libraries have a wide selection of **nonfiction** (fact-based) books as well as **fiction** (novels and stories). Most nonfiction books provide detailed information on particular topics and can be helpful tools in your research. To find out whether or not a library has the book you need, you have to look in the card catalog.

The Card Catalog

The **card catalog** is an alphabetical arrangement of individual file cards listing each of the books owned by a library.

Most fiction books in a library have two cards each, an **author card** and a **title card**. Most nonfiction books have three cards each, an **author card**, a **title card**, and a **subject card**. Usually the cards are kept in the drawers of special filing cabinets. Subject cards are usually filed in separate drawers and form the **Subject Index** of the card catalog. Author cards and title cards are usually filed together and form the **Author/Title Index**. Some libraries do not use file cards but instead maintain **on-line**, or computerized, **catalogs** or print their catalogs in paperback volumes.

The main entry on an **author card** is the author of the book, with the last name first. Author cards are filed alphabetically by the author's last name. Thus, if you wanted to find author cards for books by Jane Austen, you would look in the Author/Title Index under *A*.

The main entry on a **title card** is the title of the book. Title cards are filed alphabetically by the first word of the title, excluding *a, an,* and *the.* Thus, if you wanted to find the title card for *The Watsons*, you would look in the Author/Title Index under *W*.

The main entry on a **subject card** is the general topic of the book. Subjects cards are filed alphabetically by these general topics. Thus, if you were looking for subject cards for books about Ghana, you would look in the Subject Index under *G*. If a book deals with more than one general topic, it will usually have more than one subject card.

The examples of catalog cards on the following page show an author card, a title card, and a subject card for the same book. The three types of cards all provide basically the same information. They differ only in their main entries—the author, title, or subject. The important information on the subject card has been labeled and numbered 1 to 6. The six labels are explained below.

1. **Call number:** The **call number** is used to locate the book in the library. The number on the card corresponds to the number on the spine of the book. Library books are arranged on the shelves by call number.

2. **Main entry:** The **main entry** is the primary heading on the catalog card. On this subject card, the subject *Mountaineering* is the main entry; the author and title come below it.

3. **Publishing information:** The **publishing information** includes the location and name of the publisher and the date of publication. It may also include information about the number of the edition.

4. **Collation:** The **collation** gives the number of pages or the number of volumes. Sometimes it gives the physical dimensions of the book. Sometimes it indicates whether or not there are illustrations (abbreviated *ill.* or *illus.*).

5. **Notes entry:** The **notes entry**, when it occurs, tells whether the book has any special features, such as an introduction or a bibliography.

6. **Cross-references to the card catalog:** the **cross-references** indicate the book's other subject cards and can help you get a better idea of the topics covered in the book.

Sometimes you will find a fourth type of card in the card catalog—a **cross-reference card**. Cross-reference cards tell you to *see* or *see also* other cards in the catalog. For example, if you look up *Basketball* in the Subject Index, a card may tell you to "See *Sports—Basketball.*" This cross-reference means that subject cards for all books about basketball are filed under the subject *Sports—Basketball.* On the other hand, if you look up *Television* in the Subject Index, a cross-reference card may tell you to "See also *Broadcasting.*" This cross-reference means that while subject cards for books about television are filed under the subject *Television*, subject cards for related books are filed under the subject *Broadcasting.* Cross-reference cards are helpful when you are doing library research.

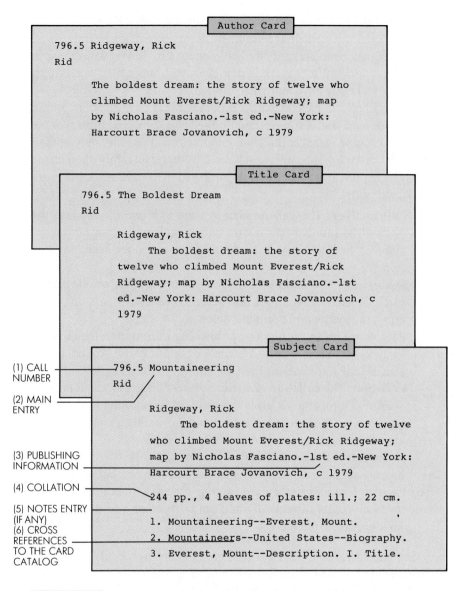

Author Card

796.5 Ridgeway, Rick
Rid

　　The boldest dream: the story of twelve who
　　climbed Mount Everest/Rick Ridgeway; map
　　by Nicholas Fasciano.-1st ed.-New York:
　　Harcourt Brace Jovanovich, c 1979

Title Card

796.5 The Boldest Dream
Rid

　　Ridgeway, Rick
　　　　The boldest dream: the story of
　　twelve who climbed Mount Everest/Rick
　　Ridgeway; map by Nicholas Fasciano.-1st
　　ed.-New York: Harcourt Brace Jovanovich, c
　　1979

Subject Card

(1) CALL NUMBER — 796.5 Mountaineering
　　　　　　　　　　Rid

(2) MAIN ENTRY

　　　　Ridgeway, Rick
　　　　　　The boldest dream: the story of twelve
　　　who climbed Mount Everest/Rick Ridgeway;
(3) PUBLISHING INFORMATION — map by Nicholas Fasciano.-1st ed.-New York:
　　　Harcourt Brace Jovanovich, c 1979

(4) COLLATION — 244 pp., 4 leaves of plates: ill.; 22 cm.

(5) NOTES ENTRY (IF ANY)
(6) CROSS REFERENCES TO THE CARD CATALOG

　　　1. Mountaineering--Everest, Mount.
　　　2. Mountaineers--United States--Biography.
　　　3. Everest, Mount--Description. I. Title.

EXERCISE 1　**Using Catalog Cards.** Refer to the sample catalog cards above in writing your answers to the following questions.

1. What is the book's call number?
2. Who wrote the book?
3. When was this edition of the book published? What company published it?
4. How long is the book?
5. Does the book contain illustrations? Does it contain any maps?

6. Under what letter of the Author/Title Index would the title card for the book be filed?
7. Under what letter of the Author/Title Index would the author card be filed?
8. Under what four subjects in the Subject Index are there subject cards for the book?

Classification and Arrangement of Library Books

The **call number**, found in the upper left corner of a book's catalog card and on the spine of the book, is based on the Dewey Decimal System, the Library of Congress System, or the library's own classification system. Library books are arranged by call number in accordance with the classification system that the library uses.

Most American libraries classify and arrange books according to either the Dewey Decimal System or the Library of Congress System.

THE DEWEY DECIMAL SYSTEM

The Dewey Decimal System was devised by Melvin Dewey, an American librarian.

In the **Dewey Decimal System**, the basic arrangement of library books is numerical.

The Dewey Decimal System organizes books by subject into ten very broad categories designated by multiples of 100:

000	General Works	**500**	Pure Sciences
100	Philosophy	**600**	Technology and Applied Sciences
200	Religion	**700**	The Arts
300	Social Sciences	**800**	Literature
400	Language	**900**	Geography and History

Each category is then further divided into another ten subdivisions designated by multiples of ten. For example, Pure Sciences, the 500's section, is further divided into 510—Mathematics, 520—Astronomy, and so on.

In the Dewey Decimal System, most libraries do not assign call numbers to novels. Instead, novels are shelved in a separate Fiction Section and alphabetized by the authors' last names. Similarly, biographies and autobiographies are usually shelved separately and alphabetized by the last names of their subjects (not authors). Biographies and autobiographies are usually classified under number 921. The spine of a biography is often stamped with the letter *B*.

THE LIBRARY OF CONGRESS SYSTEM

In the **Library of Congress System**, the basic arrangement of library books is alphabetical.

The Library of Congress System classifies books by subject into twenty broad categories designated by letters of the alphabet:

A General, Miscellaneous
B Philosophy, Religion
C History—Auxiliary Sciences
D History, Topography
E–F America (including History)
G Geography, Anthropology
H Social Sciences
J Political Science
K Law
L Education
M Music

N Fine Arts
P Language, Literature
Q Science
R Medicine
S Agriculture
T Technology
U Military Science
V Naval Science
Z Bibliography,
　　Library Science

Subdivisions of these categories are designated by using two letters; for example, *QK* indicates Botany.

EXERCISE 2　**Using Library Classification Systems.** Write the main Dewey Decimal (000, 100, etc.) and Library of Congress (A, B, etc.) category for each of the following nonfiction books.

1. *Mars, the Red Planet*, Isaac Asimov
2. The New English Bible
3. *The Complete Poems*, Elizabeth Bishop
4. *Linotype Machine Principles*, Mergenthaler Linotype Company
5. *Economics*, Paul Samuelson

Locating Library Books

Use the **call number** to locate a book in the library.

The shelf area in which most books are kept is called the **stacks. Open stacks** are those that readers can enter in order to find books for themselves. Once you have obtained a list of books and their call numbers from the card catalog, you can go to open stacks to see if the books you want are available. **Closed stacks** are restricted to library personnel. If a library uses closed stacks, you will probably have to fill out a book-request slip and present it to a member of the library staff. The slip asks for information (such as the call number, title, and author of the book) that you can copy from a book's catalog card. If a book you want is not presently available in the library, you can often **reserve** the book by filling out a special card.

Most libraries have **circulating books** that you can borrow and take home for a given period of time. To borrow books, you will probably need a library card. Libraries also have **reference books** that you must use in the library. Reference books have *Ref* or *R* above their call numbers and are usually kept in a separate section or room of the library.

EXERCISE 3 **Locating Books in Your Library.** Visit your school library or a public library to answer the following questions. Write down your answers along with the name and address of the library you visited.

1. Does the library use the Dewey Decimal System, the Library of Congress System, or a classification system of its own?
2. Does the library have a special reference section? If so, where in the library is it located?
3. Does the library assign call numbers to novels? If not, how are novels arranged?
4. What is the library's procedure for obtaining a library card and for borrowing books? For how long can most books be borrowed? Is there a fee for overdue books?
5. Use the card catalog to find out if the library has *The Oxford History of the American People* by Samuel Eliot Morison. If the book has a catalog card, list (a) its call number, (b) its length, (c) its date of publication, and (d) its publisher.

Parts of a Book

Once you have found a copy of a book for which you were looking, you may want to examine it to see if it is suitable for your purposes.

IF YOU WANT TO FIND	LOOK FOR THE
1. complete title, name of author, edition number, name of publisher, place of publication, date of publication, dates of previous editions	title page, copyright page
2. material explaining the nature, purpose, or scope of the book	preface, foreword, or introduction
3. a list of the general contents of the book and the page numbers on which the contents are found	table of contents
4. a list of the book's illustrations, charts, diagrams, maps, or tables	list of illustrations, maps, or tables

IF YOU WANT TO FIND	LOOK FOR THIS
5. additional explanations not essential to the text itself	appendix
6. an alphabetical list of technical or unfamiliar terms used in the text	glossary
7. a list of the sources used by the author or additional readings suggested by the author	bibliography, references, or suggested readings
8. an alphabetical list of the specific subjects, names, and terms used in the text, given with all of the page numbers on which they are found	index

EXERCISE 4 **Using the Parts of a Book.** Refer to the parts of this textbook in writing answers to the following questions.

1. What is the precise title of the book?
2. In what year was this edition of the book published?
3. Does the book contain a chapter on spelling? If so, how long is it?
4. Does the book teach anything about prefixes? If so, on what page or pages?

Newspapers and Periodicals

Newspapers and **periodicals** (magazines and journals) contain short articles on specific topics and provide information that is usually up to date at the time of publication. By reading a selection of articles on a particular topic, you can examine different opinions and points of view quickly.

Most libraries keep current newspapers and periodicals on shelves or racks in a reading room or area. Usually newspapers are alphabetized by the name of their city of origin. Periodicals are usually alphabetized by title.

Back issues of newspapers are normally kept on microforms (see page 702). Back issues of periodicals are sometimes kept on microforms and sometimes bound together into hardcover volumes containing six months' or a year's issues.

To find newspaper or periodical articles on a specific topic, you need to consult one or more indexes to newspapers or periodicals.

These indexes are usually found in the reference section of the library. Among the most frequently used indexes are *The New York Times Index* and the *Readers' Guide to Periodical Literature*.

THE NEW YORK TIMES INDEX

The New York Times Index lists, alphabetically by subject and author, all articles published in *The New York Times* during the period covered by the issue of the index you consult.

The *New York Times Index* is a useful source for newspaper articles on current events or history.

THE *READERS' GUIDE TO PERIODICAL LITERATURE*

The *Readers' Guide to Periodical Literature* lists, in alphabetical order by subject and author, all articles published in over 100 magazines during the period covered by the issue of the *Readers' Guide* you consult.

The *Readers' Guide* covers articles published in news magazines like *Time* and *Newsweek* and general-interest magazines like *Business Week* and *Popular Photography*. Issues are published approximately every two weeks and consolidated into bound volumes at year's end. In the sample column on page 698, important parts are labeled. To find out what the abbreviations mean, see the list at the front of the *Readers' Guide*.

EXERCISE 5 **Using the *Readers' Guide*.** Refer to the sample *Readers' Guide* on page 698 in writing your answers to the following questions.

1. When did Mary Ann Gauthier's article appear? In what magazine?
2. Under how many main headings can you find articles on gasoline and related topics?
3. How many primary subheadings are listed under the main heading for gasoline?
4. Who wrote the article on Charles de Gaulle? What is its title?
5. Give the source information (title, periodical, volume number, page numbers, and date) for the article by Milton Gendall.

GAS shipping terminals
Long, long LNG trail; two California utilities trying to bring liquefied natural gas from Indonesia and Alaska. il Forbes 124:21 + N 12 '79

GAS turbines, Automotive
Turbine with a new twist; Kronogard turbine/transmission system. J. Norbye. il Pop Sci 215:14 + O '79

GAS well drilling
Self-reliance. Buckeye style; Ohio companies producing their own gas. J. Grigsby. Forbes 124:154 O 15 '79

GASES, Rare
Atmospheric carbon tetrafluoride: a nearly inert gas. R. J. Cicerone. bibl il Science 206:59-61 O 5 '79

GASKILL, Gordon
Noble pizza prize. Read Digest 115:85-6 + O '79

GASOLINE
Catalytic production of high-grade fuel (gasoline) from biomass compounds by shape-selective catalysis. P. B. Weisz and others. bibl il Science 206:57-8 O 5 '79

Conservation
$2 a gallon for gas? Why not? M. Stone. U.S. News 87:92 N 5 '79

Prices
Cheap gas: gone and better forgotten. L. Grant. Pol Today 6:64 S '79

Rationing
Gas rationing: the latest plan. il U.S. News 87:13 O 29 '79

History
Sorry no gas. S. W. Sears. il Am Heritage 30:4-17 O '79

Taxation
$2 a gallon for gas? Why not? M. Stone. U.S. News 87:92 N 5 '79

GASOLINE consumption, Motor vehicle. See Motor vehicle engines—Fuel consumption

GASOLINE supply
Energy and the skier. A. H. Greenberg. Skiing 32:4 O '79
In the wake of crisis '79. T. Orme. Motor T 31:14 O '79
Running on empty; World Watch Institute study. L. J. Carter. Science 202:203 O 12 '79

GASTRONOMY
See also
Gluttony

GASTROPODS
See also
Snails

GAULLE, Charles de
House De Gaulle built. F. Lewis. il por N Y Times Mag p40 + N 11 '79

GAULT, Charlayne Hunter-. See Hunter-Gault, C.

GAUNAURD, Guillermo C. and Oberall, H. M.
Deciphering the scattering code contained in the resonance echoes from fluid-filled cavities in solids. il Science 206:61-4 O 5 '79 *

GAUTHIER, Mary Ann
What you can do about a phobia. Glamour 77: 198 + O '79

GAY, Larry
Woodburning furnaces. il Blair & Ketchums 6:98-110 O '79

GEIL, P. H. See Lam, R. jt auth

GELATT, Roland
Liebermann, Losey and the libertine. il Opera News 44:10-12 + N '79

GELLES, Richard J.
Myth of battered husbands and new facts about family violence. Ms 8:65-6 + O '79

GENDELL, Milton
Venice, Art News 78:156 + S '79

MAIN HEADINGS

(SUBJECT HEADING)

(AUTHOR HEADING)

SUBHEADING

TITLE OF ARTICLE

AUTHOR OF ARTICLE

SOURCE OF ARTICLE (NAME OF PERIODICAL, VOLUME NUMBER, PAGE NUMBERS, AND DATE)

SEE ALSO REFERENCE (DIRECTS YOU TO ADDITIONAL RELATED MAIN ENTRIES)

SEE REFERENCE (DIRECTS YOU TO A DIFFERENT MAIN ENTRY)

EXERCISE 6 **Using the *Readers' Guide*.** In a recent issue of the *Readers' Guide*, find the listings for two articles on each of the following topics. Write the issue or issues of the *Readers' Guide* you used and the author, title, periodical, volume number, page number or numbers, and date of each article.

1. skiing
2. bees
3. summer jobs
4. sports on television
5. singer Michael Jackson

General Reference Works

The reference section of a library contains a number of **general reference works** that can help you obtain information useful for your research. Among the most frequently consulted reference works are encyclopedias, almanacs, atlases, and dictionaries.

Encyclopedias

Encyclopedias are collections of articles on thousands of general topics. Articles are arranged alphabetically by subject. If the subject is a person, the person is listed by last name.

Encyclopedias are a good place to begin a research project. They provide a brief summary of each topic and often include a bibliography of other useful books on the topic. Some of the most frequently used encyclopedias are the *Encyclopaedia Britannica,* the *Encyclopedia Americana, Collier's Encyclopedia,* and the *World Book Encyclopedia.* Most of these encyclopedias contain from twenty to thirty volumes each, as well as a subject index to help you locate material and annually published supplements that contain up-to-date information on science, current events, and other changing fields.

EXERCISE 7 **Using Encyclopedias.** Use one or more encyclopedias to find answers to the following questions. Write down your answers along with the sources of your information.

1. Who was the first person to cross the Atlantic Ocean alone in an airplane?
2. In Greek mythology, who were the Erinyes?
3. To what island was Napoleon first exiled? To what island was he finally exiled?
4. In what war did Florence Nightingale nurse the wounded?
5. Who invented the first mercury thermometer?

Almanacs

Almanacs (also called **yearbooks**) are annual collections of facts and statistics on geography, history, current events, science, sports, entertainment, and the arts.

An almanac is a relatively up-to-date source of information. It covers material through the year preceding the year on its cover. Among the most popular almanacs are the *Official Associated Press Almanac*, the *World Almanac & Book of Facts*, and the *Information Please Almanac*. To locate information in an almanac, you will probably need to consult its index.

EXERCISE 8 **Using Almanacs.** Use one or more almanacs to find answers to the following questions. Write down your answers along with the sources of your information.

1. What two languages are spoken in Haiti?
2. What baseball team won the 1984 World Series?
3. What is the average yearly rainfall in Nashville, Tennessee?
4. What film won the 1981 Academy Award for Best Picture?
5. Who won the 1964 Nobel Peace Prize?

Atlases

Atlases are collections of maps that may provide information on topography, population, climate, rainfall, and other geographical data.

Some of the best-known atlases are the *Hammond Contemporary World Atlas*, the *National Geographic World Atlas*, the *Rand McNally Cosmopolitan World Atlas*, and the *Historical Atlas of the United States*.

EXERCISE 9 **Using Atlases.** Use one or more atlases to answer the following questions. Write your answers along with the sources of your information.

1. On what continent is Lake Titicaca?
2. Which is larger, Ghana or Nigeria?
3. What is the capital of South Korea?
4. Which is farthest north, Montreal, Canada; Edinburgh, Scotland; or Sapporo, Japan?
5. At the southern tip of what continent is Cape Horn?

Other Useful Reference Works

The following list describes other types of library reference works that you may find useful when you do research.

LANGUAGE REFERENCE WORKS

Language reference works provide information about words and usage. They include English-language and foreign-language dictionaries, thesauruses (see Chapter 33), slang dictionaries, and books on usage like *The Dictionary of American-English Usage* by Margaret Nicholson.

BIOGRAPHICAL REFERENCE WORKS

Biographical reference works give short life stories of noteworthy people. They include *Current Biography* and *Who's Who* books, which contain biographical information on *living* personalities; *Dictionary of American Biography, Dictionary of National Biography,* and *Who Was Who* books, which contain capsule biographies of noteworthy *deceased* persons; and *Webster's Biographical Dictionary*, which gives basic biographical information about contemporary and historical personalities from all over the world. Entries are arranged alphabetically by last name. To find the particular biographical reference work in which a specific person is listed, look under the person's last name in the library's *Biography Index*.

BOOKS OF QUOTATIONS

Books of quotations contain memorable quotations arranged by author, topic, or key word. Two well-known examples are *Bartlett's Familiar Quotations* and the *Oxford Dictionary of Quotations*.

LITERATURE INDEXES

Literature Indexes tell you the longer publications in which you will find shorter works of literature. For example, *Granger's Guide to Poetry* tells you where to find specific poems; the *Short Story Index* tells you where to find specific short stories.

LITERATURE HANDBOOKS

Literature handbooks include information about literary works and their authors. Examples are the *Oxford Companion to American Literature,* the *Oxford Companion to English Literature,* and the *Columbia Dictionary of Modern European Literature*.

HISTORY REFERENCE BOOKS

History reference books that you may find useful include the *Oxford Companion to American History* and the *Oxford Companion to World History*.

SCIENCE REFERENCE BOOKS

Science reference books include *A History of Technology* and *Van Nostrand's Scientific Encyclopedia*.

Using Other Reference Works. Refer to one or more of the reference works in parentheses to answer the following questions. Write down your answers and the sources of your information.

1. Where was Babe Ruth born? What was his real name? (*Webster's Biographical Dictionary, Dictionary of American Biography*)
2. Who said, "Rose is a rose is a rose is a rose"? (*Bartlett's Familiar Quotations, Oxford Dictionary of Quotations*)
3. What was the Russian writer Dostoevsky's full name? Identify two of his works. (*Columbia Dictionary of Modern European Literature, Webster's Biographical Dictionary*)
4. What other names has Leningrad had? In what years? (*Oxford Companion to World History*)
5. Who invented the hot-air balloon? (*A History of Technology, Van Nostrand's Scientific Encyclopedia*)

Other Library Resources

MICROFORMS

Microforms are tiny photographs of printed pages that are stored on filmstrips (**microfilm**) or cards (**microfiche**).

Many libraries save space by using microforms. Materials that you are likely to find on microforms include newspapers and those magazines used frequently for reference, like *Time* and *Newsweek*. Microforms must be used with special projectors at the library. Projectors are not difficult to use, but you will probably need a demonstration before you use one.

THE VERTICAL FILE

The **vertical file** is a collection of news clippings, magazine articles, photographs, pamphlets, and other brief material arranged alphabetically by subject.

The vertical file is a good source of up-to-date information on current events, science, and other changing fields. Most libraries keep a vertical file in a special cabinet in or near the reference section.

NONPRINT MATERIAL

In addition to printed material and microforms, many libraries have **nonprint material** such as filmstrips, phonograph records, computer software, videocassettes, audiocassettes, and tapes. Consult a member of the library staff for information on how to locate and use this material.

CHAPTERS 33-34 RESOURCES

CHAPTER 33   THE DICTIONARY AND THE THESAURUS

Using a Dictionary [pages 682–688]   Examine the following dictionary entry, and then answer the questions that follow it.

> **cra·ter** (krātə́r) *n.* [L., mixing bowl, mouth of a volcano < Gr. *kratēr* < *kerannynai,* to mix; for IE. base see IDIOSYNCRASY] **1.** in ancient Greece, a kind of bowl or jar **2.** a bowl-shaped cavity, as at the mouth of a volcano or on the surface of the moon **3.** a pit resembling this, as one made by an exploding bomb or fallen meteor —[C-] *Astron.* a S constellation north of Hydra
>
> —*Webster's New World Dictionary,*
> *Second College Edition*

1. What does *crater* mean here: "He carried a *crater* of water"?
   (a) lunar cavity   (b) deep pit   (c) jar   (d) constellation
2. The word *crater* should be
   (a) hyphenated after the *a*   (c) stressed in the last syllable
   (b) lowercase at all times   (d) pronounced with an *a* as in *cat*
3. The word *crater* should be used
   (a) only in the field of astronomy   (c) as a noun
   (b) only in referring to ancient Greece   (d) as a verb
4. *Crater* comes to English from
   (a) Latin and Greek (b) French and Greek (c) German (d) Hebrew

Using a Thesaurus [pages 688–689]

5. You can use a thesaurus to find
   (a) the meaning of a word   (c) synonyms for a word
   (b) the origin of a word   (d) antonyms for all words

CHAPTER 34   THE LIBRARY

Using the Library [pages 690–702]   Select the answer that best completes each of the following items.

1. To find a catalog card for the novel *A Tree Grows in Brooklyn*, look in
   (a) the Author/Title Index under A   (c) the Subject Index under B
   (b) the Author/Title Index under T   (d) Both *b* and *c* are correct.
2. Nonfiction books are arranged on library shelves
   (a) alphabetically by author's last name   (c) alphabetically by title
   (b) by the Dewey Decimal System only   (d) by call number
3. To find magazine articles about computers, consult
   (a) the *Readers' Guide*   (c) the card catalog
   (b) the *New York Times Index*   (d) the *Biography Index*
4. To find out last year's winner of the Super Bowl, consult
   (a) an encyclopedia   (c) an atlas
   (b) an almanac   (d) *Who's Who in America*

Index